Workplace Law
Handbook 2005

Edited by
Ian Faulkner

ISBN 1 900648 45 8

Published by
Workplace Law Publishing
Second Floor
Daedalus House
Station Road
Cambridge CB1 2RE
Tel. 0870 777 8881
Fax 0870 777 8882
Email info@workplacelaw.net

Text design and layout by Geoff Green/Siobhan Brown
Printed and bound in the UK by Burlington Press Ltd, Cambridge

Contents

Contents

Contents

Editor's introduction

Ian Faulkner, Workplace Law Group

Welcome to the 2005 edition of the *Workplace Law Handbook*. Over the last four years this has established itself as *the* reference work for employers and managers who want to find concise, easily accessible information on all aspects of the day-to-day running of the workplace.

In line with our policy of continually improving the Handbook's content, we have for this edition expanded the number of A–Z articles to 136 from the 92 included last time – an increase of almost 50%. Among the many new topics covered in the employment area are absence management, employment contracts, family-friendly rights and pensions, while articles on subjects such as biological hazards, environmental management systems, fire risk assessments, lighting and occupier's liability complement the wealth of information already provided on health and safety and premises-related issues.

Much of the new content has been supplied by contributors that are involved with the Handbook for the first time: these are Butler & Young, Casella Stanger, Charles Russell, Kennedys, MacRoberts, Peters & Peters, Rollits and the Society of Light and Lighting. I welcome this opportunity of acknowledging their expert and valued input together of course with that of our established contributors such as Atkins Environment, Berwin Leighton Paisner, Bird & Bird, CMS Cameron McKenna, Pinsent Masons, SafetyCO UK and Scott Wilson, to name but a few. I would also like to thank all my colleagues at Workplace Law for the support that they have lent to the project over the last few months, Ciaron Dunne and Sukina Harrison for their help with commissioning and author liaison, and Siobhan Brown for assisting with production.

The contributors have taken care to ensure that the Handbook is as up to date as possible on the day of going to press (22 November 2004) and thus takes account of developments such as the EC's proposals for modifications to the Working Time Directive, the publication of the HSE's management standards on stress, and the plans to introduce smoking bans in public places in England and Scotland. Readers can of course keep in touch on a daily basis with all the news that affects the workplace by accessing the Workplace Law Network at www.workplacelaw.net and can obtain monthly updates and comment through reading *Workplace Law Magazine*.

Returning to the policy of continual improvement mentioned above, we always welcome suggestions for new topics that could usefully be covered in future editions or indeed any observations on how we might make the content that bit better. Please email me your ideas at ian.faulkner@workplacelaw.net. Useful feedback will be rewarded with a free copy of the next edition.

Finally, please note that throughout the Handbook, in common with the style adopted in statutory instruments, and to avoid perpetual use of 'he or she', 's/he' or other variants, male pronouns should be taken as standing for the female as well. However, to cite the 'New and expectant mothers' article as an example, this does not work the other way around!

List of advertisers

Atkins Environment 237

Berwin Leighton Paisner 479

Bird & Bird 23

Butler & Young 99

Charles Russell 141

CMS Cameron McKenna 497

Kennedys 19

MacRoberts 457

Pinsent Masons 15

Rollits 269

SafetyCO UK   423

Scott Wilson 519

Workplace Law Group 12, 181, 249, 303, 355,
inside front and back covers

Employment law perspective

Michael Ryley, Partner, Pinsent Masons Employment Group

Michael Ryley is a Partner in Pinsent Masons' Employment Group and is based in the London office, advising a wide range of clients on all aspects of employment law and human resources strategy. Although his practice includes advice in contentious matters, Michael spends the bulk of his time advising on the employment law aspects of mergers and acquisitions, outsourcings, PFI schemes and facilities management contracts. He is on the Editorial Board of *Workplace Law Magazine*.

Following the DTI's pledge at the start of 2004 to limit its introduction of new legislation to just two dates each year – 6 April (being the start of the tax year) and 1 October (being the date on which the national minimum wage is revised) – it would be tempting to suggest that keeping up with new developments in employment law has become a more manageable task. However, given the quantity, diversity and complexity of the legislation that has been introduced in 2004, and which is planned for 2005, nothing could be further from the truth.

On 6 April 2004 legislation was introduced prohibiting discrimination and less favourable treatment on the grounds of sexual orientation, religion or belief. Previously it had been a simple matter for a tribunal to decide whether or not someone was of a particular sex or race (or even – but to a lesser extent – whether someone had a particular disability) before going on to decide whether discrimination, or less favourable treatment, had taken place

on the grounds of that characteristic. An employee's sexual orientation, religion or belief is generally less visible and it is therefore often more difficult for employers to ensure that all their employees' sensibilities are adequately protected. Employers may discover that, while one employee might find a level of workplace banter acceptable and amusing, another might find that it amounts to a form of discrimination about which that employee can now bring a claim. Just as employers are adjusting to this legislation, they should bear in mind that legislation prohibiting discrimination on the grounds of age is due to come into force on 1 October 2006.

Since 1 October 2004 all employers have had to comply with new statutory disciplinary, dismissal and grievance procedures. Many employers will not have noticed any great change here, because their existing policies and procedures will exceed the new minimum standards. Employers who fail to comply with the new procedures when dismissing employees will find that the dismissals are automatically unfair (in relation to those employees who have accrued the right to claim unfair dismissal) and that compensation will be increased by a minimum of 10% and could be increased by as much as 50%. At present, Parliament has not taken the additional step of implying the statutory procedures into employees' contracts of employment. This means that employers wanting to dismiss employees (while risking claims for automatic unfair dismissal) do not risk being in breach of contract if they fail to follow the procedures. However, this is a power that remains available; the indications are that this further step may be taken in 2006.

Also with effect from 1 October 2004 employers have needed to contend with new rules governing the practice and procedure of employment tribunals. There are a number of changes: for example, the time period in which an employer must respond to an employment tribunal claim will be 28 days from the date on which the tribunal sends the claim to the employer (as opposed to 21 days from when the employer receives it). There will be a fixed period of conciliation, usually 12 weeks commencing from when the tribunal sends the claim to the employer. The tribunal will not conduct a hearing before this time. However, the conciliation period can be brought to an end by either party notifying ACAS that it is unwilling to co-operate with the conciliation process. Under the new rules the tribunal may award costs up to £10,000 where a party has brought or defended a claim in a particularly objectionable way. These rules are clearly intended to encourage good behaviour by

parties. It remains to be seen how much impact this change will actually have in practice.

On 6 April 2005 the Information and Consultation of Employees Regulations will come into force: these contain mechanisms to oblige employers to consult with their employees on a number of topics, provided there is sufficient support within the workforce to initiate such discussions. Initially, these regulations will apply only to undertakings of 150 or more employees. However, implementation in respect of undertakings of 100 or more employees and then in respect of undertakings of 50 or more employees will follow in April 2007 and April 2008 respectively.

The long-awaited amendments to the Transfer of Employment (Protection of Employment) Regulations 1981 are predicted to be introduced in 2005. However, given that no draft regulations have yet been published, it is reasonable to expect that we may find ourselves waiting into 2006 before employers are able to rely on the additional certainty to business transactions that the amended regulations are intended to provide. Having waited for six years already, we should not be surprised by these further delays.

The 48-hour opt-out provision in the Working Time Directive allows employees to work more than 48 hours over a 17-week period. Currently, the UK is the only European Union member state that has an 'opt-out' facility, but the European Commission has been reviewing whether it should be withdrawn. After extensive consultation across Europe, the Commission has announced a proposal to update key aspects of the Working Time Directive. Under the proposal, if accepted by the European Parliament

and Council, the individual opt-out from the 48-hour week would remain possible, but be subject to stricter conditions to prevent abuse. If the proposal is accepted, it will be a relief to many private and public sector employers that the UK can retain the opt-out.

Hence the pace of change in employment law remains high and there is a constant stream of new legislation with which employers need to become familiar. That pattern looks set to continue for the foreseeable future.

Health and safety: criminal law developments

Daniel McShee, Partner, Kennedys Health and Safety Team

Daniel McShee is a Partner in Kennedys Health and Safety Team. He specialises in criminal law in industry, in particular gross negligence manslaughter, health and safety prosecutions and other enforcement action. He acts for individuals and corporations predominantly from the transport, health and construction sectors. He was the solicitor for the two former board members of Railtrack who were acquitted of health and safety charges arising out of the Hatfield train crash. He has extensive experience of disaster litigation and public inquiries, as well as in other aspects of regulatory defence work.

The HSE's statistics for fatal injuries show that 235 workers were killed in 2003/4, an increase of 4% on the previous year. This is the second time since 2000 that the annual statistics have shown an upward trend after a decade of continued downward trends in the 1990s.

The result of this is that the HSE and the police are taking an ever-harder line with investigations for the most serious safety breaches and there are increasing fines in the worst cases. Independent of reform, there is already a clear movement towards using the full force of the criminal law against organisations and their executives where death or injury is shown to be caused by serious negligence.

Historically, the HSE and the police have focused on the conduct of a company or organisation and only investigated individuals in exceptional cases. However, there is some evidence that this position is changing with a seemingly greater willingness to investigate individuals. The HSE produced guidance for the first time in 2003 simply called 'Prosecuting Individuals'.

Of all industries, the construction industry remains at the forefront of the HSE's priorities. Maybe that is not so surprising. The construction industry saw 70 fatal injuries to workers in 2003/4, the same as the previous year. The HSE's statistics show that 2,800 people have been killed on construction sites or as a result of construction activities in the last 25 years and the industry has a rate of five and a half times the all-industry average for workplace deaths. Construction inspectors already issue half of all prohibition notices and bring a third of all prosecutions, resulting in 500 convictions a year.

The HSE has sought to maximise its 'intervention impact' in construction in 2004 by setting up a Europe-wide initiative to address fatal and serious injuries in construction known as the FaTaL Risks Campaign.

F = Falls from height work.

T = Transport on site including mobile plant and vehicles.

L = Lifting heavy loads with cranes and other lifting machines.

In turn, the courts appear to be responding to the HSE's call for sterner penalties in both construction and other industries, particularly in the most serious cases, together with the seemingly greater willingness to investigate individuals. In particular, there appears to be a clear head of steam behind section 37 of the Health and Safety at Work etc. Act 1974 (HSWA), which makes a senior officer of a body corporate guilty of an offence where it can be shown that an offence by his organisation was committed with his consent or connivance or was attributable to his neglect.

The Hatfield train crash

The highest-profile example of this 'head of steam' over the last 18 months has been the prosecution arising out of the Hatfield train crash, a case brought by the CPS, rather than the HSE, in July 2003.

On 1 September 2004 Mr Justice Mackay dismissed various charges against three former senior Railtrack executives: a regional director and two board directors, one of whom was the former Chief Executive, Gerald Corbett. All three were represented by Kennedys.

Much has been written about the decision, sadly very little of it accurate. In fact contrary to many reports Gerald Corbett and his fellow board director were not charged with 'corporate manslaugh-

ter', that being a charge only applicable to corporate bodies. They were charged under the above-mentioned section 37 and the charges against them were dismissed not because of some defect in the law but because Mr Justice Mackay found after a detailed review of the evidence that, concerning the allegation of neglect, there was no evidence to support the prosecution case that performance or profit was placed before safety. Moreover, the judge pointed to prosecution evidence that showed that Gerald Corbett and his fellow board director had put safety first. The judge listed a series of initiatives and actions that were taken by them, all of which had been designed to ensure the safe running of the railway.

The charges of gross negligence manslaughter against the regional director were dismissed after the judge found the evidence against him to be 'vanishingly thin'.

This case is by far the clearest example of the prosecuting authorities seeking to impose individual liability for major incidents. The progress of the cases against others arising out of the same incident will have a great influence on the way the authorities approach individual liability in the future.

The Ladbroke Grove train crash

The other landmark case of the year also involved the railway industry, namely a HSWA prosecution against Thames Trains for its part in the Ladbroke Grove Rail disaster of October 1999 in which 31 people were killed and many hundreds were seriously injured.

Thames Trains admitted charges concerning the defective training of the driver involved including a specific failure to provide him with proper route

knowledge experience.

Thames was fined £2 million, the record single fine against a company to date. Events as serious as Ladbroke Grove will, it is hoped, remain rare and the fine will be a precedent only for the top end of financial penalties in the most serious cases. At the time of writing, a number of individuals from Network Rail and the company itself remain under investigation for more serious charges.

Other important cases

There have been other important cases in the last two years where either manslaughter charges have been brought emphasising the push towards individual accountability or large financial penalties have been imposed in HSWA cases.

R -v- Martin Graves & Victor Coate

On 4 April 2003, at Basildon Crown Court, a haulage company manager was imprisoned for manslaughter for four years after a man was killed in an accident caused by one of his tired drivers who had been working for 20 hours without proper rest breaks.

R -v- Ford Motor Company

On 15 June 2003, at Winchester Crown Court, Ford was fined £300,000 following the death of a contracted worker who drowned after falling into a vat of hot paint. Two directors of the service company retained by Ford were also fined for health and safety breaches, having originally faced manslaughter charges.

R -v- Paul Ellis

On 23 September 2003 a geography teacher was sentenced to 12 months' imprisonment after pleading guilty to manslaughter following the death of a 10-year-old boy under his care during a school trip.

R -v- Nishimatsu Construction Company Ltd

On 19 January 2004, at Middlesex Guild Hall Crown Court, Nishimatsu was fined £700,000 following a tunnel blow-out during the construction of the Lewisham extension to the Docklands Light Railway. Although no one was killed, the court found that the potential form of serious harm to people was significant.

R -v- Sunlight Services Group

On 8 July 2004, at Bournemouth Crown Court, Sunlight was fined £325,000 following the death of a laundry operative who had crawled into the internal workings of a large industrial washing machine to attempt to clear a blockage. He became trapped and died from heat exhaustion caused by the conditions inside the machine.

R -v- ESB Hotels

On 19 July 2004 Bolton Crown Court fined ESB £300,000 for leaving mattresses in a fire escape and £100,000 for not designating clear responsibility for moving them. The case arose from an incident when two people died and one person was overcome by fumes when a hotel was set on fire.

R -v- Nationwide Heating Systems

On 28 July 2004, at Exeter Crown Court, the Managing Director of Nationwide Heating Systems was sentenced to 12 months' imprisonment after being found guilty of the manslaughter of his apprentice heating engineer. The company was also found guilty of manslaughter.

The matter related to an incident in

February 2003 when the deceased was working at a boatyard when the highly flammable acetone solvent was used to clean a resin storage tank which ignited causing an explosion.

Summing up

All the cases mentioned in this article demonstrate the prosecuting authorities' determination to use the full force of the criminal law in cases of serious negligence in whatever industry or size of organisation they occur. In the above-mentioned 'other cases' where signifi-cant financial penalties were imposed, only Ford could be said to be a household name. This means that employers and their executives need to be aware that workplace incidents resulting in injury or death are now likely to lead to extensive HSE or police criminal investigations with all that such investigations may produce. Recent cases also suggest that the prosecuting authorities are seeking to propel the existing criminal law for health and safety further towards holding managers and directors accountable, instead of just organisations.

Contract law update

Mark Henley, Solicitor, Commercial Department, Bird & Bird

Mark Henley is a solicitor in Bird & Bird's Commercial Department where he specialises in ICT, outsourcing and public procurement law. He has worked on a wide range of ICT projects in both the public and private sectors, from PFI/PPP procurements to Internet start-up ventures.

Mark gives regular lectures on IT law and practice and acts for FM service providers and customers. He is a Microsoft Certified Professional and is always seeking to understand the technologies employed so that the legal advice he gives will work in the wider context.

In 2004 we have seen the usual crop of interesting court decisions arising from contract disputes, many of which have a direct bearing on contracts for workplace services. Unfortunately all too often workplace managers are given little or no access to legal support while they are negotiating contracts with service providers or trying to resolve disputes. The result of this is that the unfortunate manager must keep abreast of developments in contract law and practice as well as in all the other legal disciplines mentioned in this Handbook.

With that in mind, outlined below are some recent developments which should be considered when entering into new contracts for workplace services or managing existing ones.

The long-running dispute between the Co-operative Group and ICL (now Fujitsu) was settled in September 2004. Co-op's claim against ICL for breach of contract and £11 million damages arising out of a failed IT project had been rejected by the judge in the Technology and Construction Court, but the Court of Appeal subsequently ruled that those High Court proceedings had been 'unfair' and ordered a retrial. The parties settled before the retrial could go ahead.

The Co-op case indicated the risks that can arise if a contract is not put in place for a particular project. It also contained many other project management lessons such as the importance of addressing problems early, of appropriate escalation, and of documenting thoroughly inter-party review meetings and the acceptance or rejection of products and services. The case also highlighted yet again the risk that supposedly private internal emails can end up revealed in court.

It is commonplace for commercial agreements to provide that fixed sums should be paid in the event of certain breaches – for example, delay in delivery,

or early cancellation. To be enforceable as 'liquidated damages' these amounts should constitute a 'reasonable pre-estimate' of the loss which the customer would be likely to suffer as a result of the breach. If the amounts exceed the 'greatest loss' that could reasonably be foreseen, they will be regarded as penalties, and potentially unenforceable.

In 2003 the Court of Appeal restated the rule against penalties and there have been some further cases on the distinction between liquidated damages and penalties in the last 12 months. The key lesson from these cases is that the payment fixed in the contract should take account of the innocent party's duty to mitigate its difficulties, and its ability to offset the harm it suffers against the benefits which it might obtain from the same event.

The lesson is to take care when fixing sums in liquidated damages clauses. Be prepared to explain how the figures were arrived at later. And remember: they need to satisfy the legal requirements at the time the contract was entered into, so it would be sensible to keep records. The courts are more active than for many years in examining the substance of liquidated damages clauses, and in scrutinising the standard language.

In principle, the law permits a party to limit liability for the wilful default of its employees or agents in the performance of a contract, provided clear words are used. The UCTA reasonableness test will apply to such clauses in 'written standard terms of business'. In *Frans Maas -v- Samsung Electronics*, 25,700 Samsung mobile phones were stolen from a warehouse which was operated by Maas. Samsung sued for £2.6 million. In High Court proceedings which took place in February 2004, it was established that the theft had been an 'inside job' carried out by Maas employees. The standard terms of business governing the relationship contained a limit on Maas's liability of £25,000 for 'liability howsoever arising': this cap was less than 1% of the amount claimed by Samsung. Samsung argued that this cap did not cover as serious a breach as this theft; but the High Court disagreed, concluding that even the wilful default was covered by the cap and that it was legitimate for the contract to limit Maas's liability in this way. The court also held that the cap was reasonable under UCTA, bearing in mind industry practice, the bargaining power of the parties, Samsung's opportunity to insure, Samsung's opportunity to request a higher cap under the contract, and other factors. Samsung was thus only able to recover a tiny amount of its losses from Maas. Fortunately for Samsung, it appears from the judgment that the company was indeed insured.

This case illustrates how critical it is that limitation of liability clauses is given proper consideration and then set at an appropriate level. Even in the case of wilful default amounting to fraud by employees, a far-reaching limitation clause left the innocent party with only minimal rights of redress.

Cases such as the ones set out above are continually reshaping best practice in contract negotiation and management. Workplace managers would be well advised to try to find suitable sources of up-to-date information in this field. This need not be costly – many law firms, including Bird & Bird, provide legal updates for free.

Contributor profiles

ATKINS

Atkins Environment

Atkins Environment was voted one of the four best providers of environmental services by our clients for:

- best quality of work;
- best technical competence;
- best value for money;
- best at keeping to budget;
- best at keeping to deadlines; and
- best communications.

We employ around 500 environmental specialists worldwide, providing cost-effective solutions to our clients – every time. Here is a selection of our recent work, covering environmental legislation, new build and environmental improvements:

- We advised the purchaser of 420 sites in France and Spain on environmental liabilities as part of his due diligence.
- We've implemented ISO 14001 in over 200 companies across Europe – delivering real environmental improvements, not just a system.
- We're advising a global vehicle manufacturer on the application of the EU Greenhouse Gas Emissions Trading Scheme to their business.
- We've carried out numerous applications for IPPC across Europe.
- We provide a global compliance service to a major MNC – advising them on changes in legislation and how this affects them.
- We're advising a major public sector provider on improving their sustainability performance.

David Symons

david.symons@atkinsglobal.com

David Symons is an environmental expert with Atkins Environment, specialising in industrial environmental management. He holds a physical science degree and an MBA with Distinction from the University of Warwick. Over the past 15 years he has advised clients ranging from Powergen plc and HM Prison Service to the World Bank and the European Union.

Contact

Atkins Environment
Woodcote Grove
Ashley Road
Epsom KT18 5BW

Tel. 01372 756049
Fax 01372 740055
Web www.atkinsglobal.com

*berwin leighton paisner

Berwin Leighton Paisner

Berwin Leighton Paisner is a leading law firm based in the City of London. We pride ourselves on our superb client base including many leading companies and financial institutions. We strive to lead the market in the excellence of our service delivery.

We are well known for our extraordinary success in developing market leadership positions within the real estate, corporate and finance areas. We distinguish ourselves by working with our clients in creative and innovative ways to achieve commercial solutions.

Nicole Hallegua, Assistant Solicitor

nicole.hallegua@blplaw.com

Nicole Hallegua has acted on numerous contentious and non-contentious employment matters including wrongful dismissal, unfair dismissal, and race and sex discrimination cases. In particular, she has been involved in a large high-profile constructive dismissal and sex discrimination claim for a financial institution involving more than 20 witnesses and a four-week trial.

Mark Kaye, Senior Assistant

mark.kaye@blplaw.com

Mark Kaye advises on a broad range of employment matters with a particular emphasis on non-contentious corporate finance and PFI transactions, including frequently advising in relation to the application or otherwise of TUPE. Mark regularly writes articles for leading legal and personnel publications on a wide range of employment law issues.

Howard Lewis-Nunn, Barrister (Non-Practising)

howard.lewis-nunn@blplaw.com

Howard Lewis-Nunn specialises in all aspects of employment law with particular experience in advocacy in employment tribunals. He regularly advises on employment policies and staff handbooks, and also advises on data protection issues in employment.

He has worked extensively on commercial and PFI projects, advising on employment issues arising from these transactions and the application of TUPE. He is a speaker on a wide range of issues, including managing reorganisations and handling disability claims.

Mark Rose, Assistant Solicitor

mark.rose@blplaw.com

Mark Rose is an assistant at Berwin Leighton Paisner and specialises in employment law. He advises on a range of contentious and potentially contentious employment matters including unfair dismissal, discrimination, restrictive covenants and termination agreements, as well as advising on non-contentious matters such as drafting contracts and staff handbooks.

Mark also deals with the employment aspects of asset and share sales and outsourcing arrangements involving, for example, negotiation and advice in relation to warranties and indemnities and advice relating to TUPE. In addition, he assists clients in relation to business immigration issues, particularly work permits.

Hilary Ross, Partner

hilary.ross@blplaw.com

Hilary Ross specialises in EU and UK food and health and safety law. She advises key players in the catering industry on compliance strategies. Hilary has extensive experience liaising on clients' behalf with local authorities, attending interviews and appearing in court to defend proceedings.

Jackie Thomas, Assistant Solicitor

jackie.thomas@blplaw.com

Jackie Thomas specialises in all aspects of employment law, and advises on both contentious and non-contentious employment law issues, including executive service contracts, discrimination and issues arising from the termination of employment.

Contact

Berwin Leighton Paisner
Adelaide House
London Bridge
London EC4R 9HA

Tel. 020 7760 1000
Fax 020 7760 1111
Web www.blplaw.com

BIRD & BIRD

Bird & Bird

Bird & Bird is an international commercial law firm which operates on the basis of an in-depth understanding of key industry sectors. It focuses on aviation and aerospace, banking and financial services, communications, e-commerce, IT, media, life sciences and sport. Bird & Bird is proud to be working with some of the world's most innovative and technologically advanced companies, each of which depends on cutting-edge legal advice to realise its business goals.

With offices in Beijing, Brussels, Düsseldorf, The Hague, Hong Kong, London, Milan, Munich, Paris, Stockholm, and with close ties with firms in other key centres in Europe, Asia and the United States, Bird & Bird is well placed to offer its clients local expertise within a global context.

Elizabeth Brownsdon, Solicitor

elizabeth.brownsdon@twobirds.com

Elizabeth Brownsdon is a solicitor working in the Commercial Department at Bird & Bird. She advises clients on a wide range of IT matters including the licensing of software, agreements for the provision of Internet services, online terms and conditions and other legal implications of e-commerce. In addition, as a member of Bird & Bird's Information Law Group, Elizabeth regularly advises on data protection and privacy issues for all types of business and has recently been involved in a data protection audit for a large group of UK companies.

Elizabeth has particular experience of advising on the use of personal data in the online environment.

Paula Hargaden, Solicitor

paula.hargaden@twobirds.com

Paula has recently qualified into the Employment and Tax Groups at Bird & Bird, splitting her time between general employment advice and employee benefits. She has experience of various employment tribunal and High Court proceedings including discrimination, unfair dismissal, breach of confidence and failure to consult in a collective redundancy, as well as advising on share option schemes, termination payments and general employment tax queries. She also has an interest in data protection and privacy issues in relation to employees.

Mark Henley, Solicitor

mark.henley@twobirds.com

Mark Henley is a solicitor in Bird & Bird's Commercial Department where he specialises in ICT, outsourcing and public procurement law. He has worked on a wide range
of ICT projects in both the public and private sectors, from PFI/PPP procurements to
Internet start-up ventures.

Mark gives regular lectures on IT law and practice and acts for FM service providers
and customers. He is a Microsoft Certified Professional and is always seeking to understand the technologies employed so that the legal advice he gives will work in the
wider context.

Emilia Linde, Trainee Solicitor

emilia.linde@twobirds.com

Emilia Linde is a trainee in Bird & Bird's Commercial Department. She has experience
of data protection, e-commerce and Internet technology matters.

Victoria Sedgwick, Solicitor

victoria.sedgwick@twobirds.com

Victoria Sedgwick is an assistant in Bird & Bird's Commercial Department, where she
specialises in information technology and public procurement law. Since joining Bird
& Bird as a trainee she has worked on a wide range of IT projects predominantly in the
public sector.

Contact

Bird & Bird
90 Fetter Lane
London EC4A 1JP

Tel. 020 7415 6000
Fax 020 7415 6111
Web www.twobirds.com

Butler & Young Ltd
Building Control & Fire Safety Consultants
Approved Inspectors

Butler & Young

Butler & Young Ltd is a member of the BYL plc group of companies. As one of the first companies to be granted Approved Inspector status by the then Department of the Environment, Transport and the Regions in 1997, it provides independent building control throughout England and Wales as an alternative to the local authority. Butler & Young's approach to satisfying the statutory obligations of the Building Regulations and the Building Act 1984 is effective, efficient and non-bureaucratic.

Additionally the group provides services such as fire safety engineering, structural engineering, building surveying, planning supervision, party wall surveying and disability access consultancy.

Tony Dennison, Associate Director

tony.dennison@southampton.byl.co.uk

Tony Dennison, BSc, PhD, FRICS, FCIOB, MICE, is a graduate of the University of Leeds where he also undertook research into the structural behaviour of concrete shell roofs. Following civil engineering appointments with Simon-Carves of Stockport and Fermanagh County Council, he became Chief Building Control Officer to the Northern Ireland Western Group of Councils in 1973. Six years later he took up an appointment as Head of Building Control at New Forest District Council.

He edited *Building Control and Building Control Bulletin* for the Institute of Building Control for over ten years and is now an Associate Director with Butler & Young. He is also a member of the Construction Industry Council's Approved Inspector Registration Board, which accredits and monitors private sector Building Control Inspectors.

Contact

Butler and Young
Trenton House
Imperial Way
Croydon CR0 4RR

Tel. 020 8253 4900
Fax 020 8253 4901
Web www.byl.co.uk

CHARLES RUSSELL

Charles Russell

Charles Russell is one of the UK's top 40 law firms, providing a full range of services to UK and international companies and organisations, while its renowned private client and family practices continue to thrive.

We are known for our client care, high quality, expertise and friendly approach. Our strategy is simple – to help clients achieve their goals through excellent service. Fundamental to the way we work is our highly praised client management programme which is built around regular service reviews with clients. This ensures that our services are continually fine-tuned by the client and focused to meet their changing needs.

We have one of the largest and most experienced employment and pensions teams in the country. We work proactively with our clients to help prevent claims arising through initiatives such as the award-winning Manage the Risk programme. The team works closely with clients using a range of services that are vital components in any strategy to counter the risks of employment claims, from employment audits to tailored management training and a dedicated telephone and email helpline.

Experienced in carrying out cross-border corporate and commercial work, the firm can also provide clients with access to 150 recommended law firms across the world as part of the two major legal networks, ALFA International and the Association of European Lawyers.

Polly Botsford, Solicitor

polly.botsford@charlesrussell.co.uk

Polly Botsford joined Charles Russell as a trainee solicitor in 1998. She has been a qualified employment lawyer since September 2000. Polly has experience in contentious work, both in the High Court and in employment tribunals, on a wide range of issues including unfair dismissal, discrimination and breach of directors' fiduciary duties. Polly also undertakes corporate transactional work, policy reviews and employment audits. She carries out management training (and is part of the group's subcommittee on training) as well as advisory work on a broad spectrum of issues such as maternity and paternity rights and discrimination. Her clients are from a range of sectors including telecommunications, publishing and media, leisure, banking, insurance and the construction industry. Polly is part of Charles Russell's task force on age discrimination.

Carolyn King

carolyn.king@charlesrussell.co.uk

Carolyn joined Charles Russell as a trainee solicitor in September 2001 and qualified into the Employment and Pensions Group in September 2003. She specialises in all aspects of employment law, both contentious and non-contentious, and is also part of the immigration team, which advises on corporate immigration issues.

Joanne Owers, Partner

joanne.owers@charlesrussell.co.uk

Joanne Owers qualified in 1995 and joined the Employment and Pensions Group at Charles Russell in April 2001, becoming a Partner in 2003. She has a wide range of experience in all areas of contentious and non-contentious employment law, advising corporate clients on individual and collective employment law related matters. She has particular interest and expertise in discrimination claims and managing pan-European projects, including cross-border transactions and collective redundancies.

Joanne is an active member of the Employment Lawyers Association Training Committee and is a member of the ELA's Age Discrimination Working Party. She is also a member of the Law Society's Employment Law Committee and a regular speaker at ELA and CIPD events as well as client training events.

Brian Palmer, Partner

brian.palmer@charlesrussell.co.uk

Brian Palmer joined Charles Russell as a Partner in July 2000, having previously been a Partner for a number of years at another City law firm. His expertise is in both contentious and non-contentious employment matters including recruitment, service contracts, disciplinary procedures, terminations, the employment aspects of acquisitions, and unfair and wrongful dismissals. He has developed a particular specialisation in the protection of confidential information and critical teams of employees, including the use of search and freezing injunctions. Brian gives regular lectures and seminars and comments in national print and broadcast media on employment issues.

He is a recognised expert and is noted in the 2002 edition of *The Legal 500* as having 'built a reputation for delivering practical and commercial advice'.

Michael Powner, Partner

michael.powner@charlesrussell.co.uk

Michael Powner is a Partner in the Employment and Pensions Group. He qualified in 1996 and has been with Charles Russell since October 2000. Michael provides both contentious and non-contentious employment advice. He is a trained advocate with considerable experience of employment claims at every level as well as conducting mediations and advising more widely on alternative dispute resolution.

Michael has a particular interest in all aspects of business transfers and company restructuring and advises regularly on Government outsourcing contracts and the employment implications of PFI and PPP projects. He is regularly involved in negotiation of executive-level service contracts and severance terms together with the full range of employee benefits, including share option schemes, health and retirement benefits and complex bonus arrangements. Additionally he has experience of union negotiations, balloting and recognition. He has recently been asked to advise the DTI and Inland Revenue regarding substantial changes to current National Minimum Wage legislation. Michael regularly lectures at both internal and external seminars and has been appointed as a visiting lecturer to the College of Law in recognition of his expertise in the field. He is also a Trustee and Director of the worldwide charity Concern Universal.

Kris Weber, Partner

kris.weber@charlesrussell.co.uk

Kris Weber qualified in 1995 and joined Charles Russell in 2001. His area of expertise encompasses all aspects of occupational and personal pension schemes. As well as advising both employers and pension scheme trustees on a wide variety of contentious and non-contentious pensions law issues, Kris also has considerable experience of the pensions and financial services aspects of personal and stakeholder pensions. His specific interests include pension scheme funding and employment-related issues (particularly those concerning sex- or age-related discrimination). Kris is also well versed in the pensions aspects of corporate M&A activity. In *Chambers UK Legal Directory 2005* he is named as a leading individual who 'according to clients ... "demonstrates a superior knowledge of his field" and has "excellent client handling skills"'.

Kris is the author of the chapter in *Tolley's Pensions Law* entitled 'Scheme Funding and Pension Scheme Surpluses' and is a frequent contributor to the pensions trade press. He also speaks regularly at internal and external seminars and training sessions. He is Secretary to the Association of Pension Lawyers, and sits on the Legislation Committee of the Society of Pension Consultants. He has also qualified as a member of the Pensions Management Institute.

Andy Williams, Solicitor

andy.williams@charlesrussell.co.uk

Andy Williams joined Charles Russell in 2001, having qualified in 1999 with another prominent City firm. He has a broad range of experience in pension matters as well as employment issues, having regularly advised employees, employers and pension scheme trustees on a variety of contentious and non-contentious matters. He has a particular interest in advising companies on the employment and pension implications of making changes to their staff pension arrangements.

Andy is a member of the Association of Pension Lawyers and plays an active role as a member of its Education and Seminars subcommittee. He is co-author of the 'Pensions and Employment' chapter in Tolley's looseleaf publication *Trust Drafting and*

Precedents. Andy has worked on two prominent pension cases before the House of Lords, is regularly quoted in the pensions trade press and gives internal and external seminars.

Gabriella Wright, Partner

gabriella.wright@charlesrussell.co.uk

Gabriella Wright qualified in September 1996 and joined Charles Russell in 1998; she was made a Partner in May 2003. She is an employment specialist who works on both contentious and non-contentious employment matters. She is asked to advise regularly on dismissal, disciplinary and grievance situations and the employment aspects of mergers, restructurings and outsourcings. Gabriella also focuses on discrimination and equal opportunities issues, on maternity issues and on what employers must do in practice to ensure that employees' rights under the Data Protection Act are not infringed, whether dealing with access requests, job applications, third-party requests for disclosure or employee monitoring. She is a regular trainer at client training sessions and a regular speaker at Charles Russell seminars.

Gabriella is recognised in *Chambers UK Legal Directory 2005* as an expert and 'a "thoughtful, powerful and absolutely diligent" operator offering "good client handling skills and thoroughly practical advice"'.

Contact

Charles Russell
8–10 New Fetter Lane
London EC4A 1RS

Tel. 020 7203 5000
Fax 020 7203 0200
Web www.charlesrussell.co.uk

CMS Cameron McKenna

CMS Cameron McKenna's specialist construction and facilities management team is a widely recognised market leader. It has been involved in many facilities management and construction projects ranging from procuring standalone maintenance contracts to major PFI/PPP infrastructure contracts.

The team is responsible for the drafting of the two standard form contracts produced for the facilities management industry, the Chartered Institute of Building Standard Form of Facilities Management Contract and, for the Property Advisers to the Civil Estate, the PACE Government Contract/Works/10 Standard Form of Facilities Management Contract.

The team has drafted repair and maintenance contracts, together with other facilities management contracts, for a wide variety of public and private sector clients including the Department of Trade and Industry, the Royal Opera House, Pearl Assurance, Prudential Assurance (in relation to all their UK property portfolio), Brixton Estates and Taylor Woodrow Properties.

The team is also familiar with advising on claims resolution whether by litigation, adjudication or arbitration.

Jessica Burt, Solicitor

jessica.burt@cmck.com

Jessica Burt is a solicitor in the Safety, Health, Environment and Products Team of CMS Cameron McKenna dealing with contentious and non-contentious matters. She has provided articles for the Workplace Law Network, and in September 2002 was a speaker at the Commerce and Industry Group Seminar 'An Employers' Perspective' discussing stress claims.

Rupert Choat, Solicitor Advocate

rupert.choat@cmck.com

Rupert Choat is a solicitor advocate in the Facilities Management and Construction Team of CMS Cameron McKenna. He specialises in dispute resolution.

Marc Hanson, Partner

marc.hanson@cmck.com

Marc Hanson is a Partner in the Facilities Management and Construction Team of CMS Cameron McKenna. He specialises in the drafting of all forms of facilities management and construction contracts and was responsible for drafting the Chartered Institute of Building Standard Form of Facilities Management Contract and the PACE Government Contract/Works/10 Standard Form of Facilities Management Contract. Marc is also the author of *Guide to Facilities Management Contracts* (second edition, 2002) and a member of the construction committee of the British Property Federation.

Contact

CMS Cameron McKenna
Mitre House
160 Aldersgate Street
London EC1A 4DD

Tel. 020 7367 3000
Fax 020 7367 2000
Web www.cmck.com

Kennedys

Kennedys is known primarily as an insurance-driven commercial litigation practice, although the firm is also recognised for skills in the non-contentious commercial field, particularly within the insurance, construction and transport industries. Kennedys has a fast-growing reputation for its work in employment law and the healthcare and insolvency sectors. One of the leading litigation firms within the City, Kennedys has 68 Partners and over 130 other fee earners, trainees and paralegals. Kennedys' approach in all matters is recognising that the 'product' required by clients is the economic resolution of the claim, not merely the legal services necessary along the way. The firm looks at the commercial issues relevant to each case. All Kennedys' fee earners work with this philosophy in mind.

Sean Elson, Solicitor

s.elson@kennedys-law.com

Sean Elson is a solicitor at Kennedys specialising in defending individuals and corporations in regulatory prosecutions and investigations across all sectors of industry. These cases include health and safety, food safety and environmental issues as well as trading standards inquiries into trade mark and copyright offences. Sean is experienced in dealing with cases involving complex technical issues as well as large quantities of documentary evidence, having previously defended large-scale multi-million frauds at a niche *Legal 500* practice.

Daniel McShee, Partner

d.mcshee@kennedys-law.com

Daniel McShee is a Partner in Kennedys Health and Safety Team. He specialises in criminal law in industry, in particular gross negligence manslaughter (individuals and corporations), health and safety prosecutions and other enforcement action. He acts for individuals and corporations predominantly from the transport, health and construction sectors. He was the solicitor for the two former board members of Railtrack who were acquitted of health and safety charges arising out of the Hatfield train crash. He has extensive experience of disaster litigation and public inquiries. Daniel also has experience in other aspects of regulatory defence work including environmental, public health and food safety prosecutions. He has an MA with Distinction in health and safety and environmental law.

Kennedys

Contact

Kennedys
Longbow House
14–20 Chiswell Street
London EC1Y 4TW

Tel. 020 7638 3688
Fax 020 7638 2212
Web www.kennedys-law.com

maCROBERTS

MacRoberts

As one of Scotland's leading commercial law firms, MacRoberts prides itself on being highly attuned to clients' needs. Over many years, a huge range of leading British and international businesses, banks and other financial institutions have continued to trust MacRoberts' lawyers to lend a clear insight to the commercial and legal issues which face them. MacRoberts has the experience, the range of contacts and the specialist disciplines to help clients, large or small, individual or corporate, cut through extraneous matter and make the right decisions. In an increasingly frantic world there is no substitute for a commercial partner on whom you can rely. With offices in Glasgow and Edinburgh, staffed by partners who feature consistently in Scotland's legal Who's Who, MacRoberts is a firm which meets that essential client requirement.

Stephen Harte, Associate

stephen.harte@macroberts.com

Stephen Harte is an Associate in MacRoberts' Technology Media and Communications Group. He has experience of a broad scope of intellectual property matters such as software licensing, trademark management, patent disputes, passing-off claims and the control of commercial information. Stephen is particularly interested in the Internet, from both the legal and practical perspectives, and in his spare time is responsible for designing and managing the website of a small charity.

He also advises clients on the application of competition law to commercial matters, both at UK and European level, and also on commercial agency, distribution and other on-going trading arrangements.

Stephen participates in the activities of the Society for Computers and Law and the Scottish Lawyers' European Group. He trained in the Scottish Office and joined MacRoberts after two years with another major commercial law firm.

Alan J. Masson, Partner

alan.masson@macroberts.com

Alan J. Masson, WS, heads up the firm's Edinburgh Employment Law Group. He has extensive employment law experience, covering a wide rage of industrial and commercial sectors and public authorities. His work has included: advising on the restructuring of workforces in high-profile insolvencies; workforce issues in acquisitions and mergers in the UK and Europe for both UK and multinational clients; public sector employment issues; contracting-out and PFI projects; corporate immigration matters; restructuring and reorganisations at all levels; collective consultation issues; the drafting, negotiation and variation of individual contracts of employment and service agreements; a wide range of employment policies and procedures, disciplinary issues at all levels; and matters involving all forms of discrimination.

Alan is accredited by the Law Society of Scotland as a specialist in employment law.

Jill Sutherland, Senior Associate

jill.sutherland@macroberts.com

Jill Sutherland is a Senior Associate in the firm's Employment Law Group and specialises in employment law. She has been undertaking a knowledge management role for the Group since 2002 in addition to her fee-earning work.

Jill has experience of representing and advising employers and employees across a range of employment law issues. She is experienced in drafting a wide variety of employment-related documentation and has advised both employers and employees in many types of contentious and non-contentious matters. She represented trade unions and their members for several years. Jill has conducted employment tribunal hearings on behalf of both employers and employees and has experience of representation before the Employment Appeals Tribunal.

Contact details

MacRoberts Solicitors
Excel House
30 Semple Street
Edinburgh EH3 8BL

Tel. 0131 229 5046
Fax 0131 229 0849
Web www.macroberts.com

Osborne
Clarke

Osborne Clarke

Osborne Clarke is a full service commercial law firm with 700 people offering a complete range of legal services combined with a sound commercial approach and a solid understanding of the issues affecting different industries.

The firm has offices in the United Kingdom (Bristol, London and Thames Valley), Germany and the United States, and also has an alliance of offices across Europe – the Osborne Clarke Alliance. It focuses on a number of key legal disciplines, including corporate, property, tax, banking and finance, commercial, employment and litigation, drawing upon each of its service areas to provide a rounded service to its clients.

Osborne Clarke is energetic, forward thinking, conscientious, technically excellent and, above all, client-focused. So are its people. Its lawyers and support teams are high performers, carefully selected and trained to ensure clients receive a seamless service across legal disciplines and throughout its network of offices.

Kevin Bridges, Associate Solicitor

kevin.bridges@osborneclarke.com

Kevin Bridges, Dip2.OSH, MIOSH, specialises in health and safety law and related criminal and civil (public and employer's liability) litigation. He is dual qualified as a solicitor and safety practitioner. Kevin is Chairman of the Bristol and West of England Branch of IOSH. He hosts many seminars and lectures on all aspects of health and safety as well as tutoring the law modules for the NEBOSH National Diploma at the University of Bristol.

Dale Collins, Associate and Solicitor-Advocate

dale.collins@osborneclarke.com

Dale Collins is a solicitor-advocate. He is recognised in *The Legal 500* for his experience and expertise in the field of health and safety law, in addition to which he advises on the law relating to pollution control, trading standards, licensing and food safety issues. He has been an advocate in the criminal courts for more than 16 years and is one of the few solicitors in the health and safety field holding the Higher Rights Qualification for Criminal Proceedings. Dale also has an MA in Environmental Law and is an experienced lecturer.

Contact

Osborne Clarke
2 Temple Back East
Temple Quay
Bristol BS1 6EG

Tel. 0117 917 3000
Fax 0117 917 3005
Web www.osborneclarke.com

Pinsent Masons

On 6 December 2004 the two national law firms Pinsents and Masons merged to form Pinsent Masons. The new business aims to hold a distinct sectoral position in the legal market, focusing on the provision of a full range of legal services to eight Chosen Markets. Pinsent Masons has positioned the facilities management and services market at the forefront of its strategy, seeking to build upon the significant track record of the legacy firms in the industry.

Pinsent Masons has approximately 240 Partners and 900 fee-earners based in offices in London, Birmingham, Bristol, Edinburgh, Glasgow, Leeds and Manchester as well as Brussels, Hong Kong and Shanghai.

Recent facilities management work undertaken includes private sector outsourcing projects, acting for service providers and for clients commissioning services; FM work on public/private sector partnership projects; and day-to-day advice to FM service providers.

Ian Anderson, Solicitor

ian.anderson@pinsentmasons.com

Ian Anderson is a solicitor in the Employment Group at Pinsent Masons based at the firm's Glasgow Office. He previously worked in both private practice and the public sector. He has also had considerable experience as an in-house lawyer for one of Scotland's leading food manufacturers where in addition to his legal role he had board responsibility for the HR function for over two years. He therefore combines his legal knowledge with an understanding of the practical issues which arise on a day-to-day basis in the HR departments of large organisations.

He has advised on employment contract changes including annualised hours contracts, union recognition, and contentious and non-contentious employment matters. He has also experience in designing and implementing employee benefit and reward schemes.

Stuart Armstrong, Solicitor

stuart.armstrong@pinsentmasons.com

Stuart Armstrong is a specialist health and safety solicitor. He has a NEBOSH Certificate and is an affiliate member of IOSH and an associate member of IIRSM. His background prior to qualification was in local and central government where he worked for Colchester Borough Council and in the Planning and Environment Team for the Treasury Solicitor.

Stuart now provides a wide range of contentious and non-contentious health and safety services to both public and private sector clients throughout the UK. He has acted for a wide range of companies in civil and criminal matters. In addition Stuart has been asked to write articles for national newspapers and to review health and safety publications. He regularly writes on health and safety issues. He has been - invited to attend committee meetings of the Law Society and gives lectures on all aspects of health and safety law.

Hugh Bruce-Watt, Partner

hugh.bruce-watt@pinsentmasons.com

Hugh Bruce-Watt specialises in the provision of advice relating to commercial property transactions. He has significant experience of advising investors, developers, landlords and banks in retail, development, PFI and property finance work.

Hugh has been involved in all aspects of commercial property work including retail, office and industrial leasing, site assembly and development work, property finance and the property aspects of MBO/MBI transactions, business sale agreements and corporate acquisitions and sales.

Hugh leads the Property and Projects Group in Pinsent Masons' Scottish practice. He advises London-based clients on Scottish property matters but is also dual qualified and advises on property matters in England and Wales.

Siobhan Cross, Consultant

siobhan.cross@pinsentmasons.com

Siobhan Cross was a Partner in the Property Litigation Group from 1995 until 2004 when she became a Consultant. Siobhan has extensive experience of advising on all aspects of landlord and tenant law including lease renewals, rent reviews, enforcement of covenants, possession actions, site clearance and estate management issues generally. Her experience covers both commercial and residential premises. Siobhan has also advised on a wide range of other property disputes affecting development projects, such as disputes between joint venture partners and between developers and neighbouring landowners.

Siobhan is recognised as a leader in the field by all the major legal directories. She regularly contributes to the key property journals, most recently the *Estates Gazette*, in which she examined changes to the way civil procedure rules affect property litigation.

Helen Grice

helen.grice@pinsentmasons.com

Helen Grice is a solicitor in the Pinsent Masons Health and Safety Group. As a former health and safety advisor for BNFL at Sellafield, she combines legal advice with practical industry experience. She provides a full range of health and safety advice, including non-contentious (implementation of new legislation, drafting contracts and procedures, risk allocation in PFI projects and auditing against OHSAS 18001:1999) and advising after incidents (HSE and police investigations, representation at coroner's inquests and defending prosecutions).

Nationally, Helen speaks regularly at industry seminars such as those organised by IBC and the Safety and Reliability Society. She is a corporate member of the Institution of Occupational Safety and Health and the Society for Radiological Protection and wrote the construction industry chapter in the practitioner text *Corporate Liability: Work Related Deaths and Criminal Prosecutions* published by Butterworths in 2004.

Bonnie Martin, Partner

bonnie.martin@pinsentmasons.com

Bonnie Martin heads up the Property, Planning and Environment team in Pinsent Masons' Bristol office specialising in all aspects of property litigation including litigation arising out of planning and environmental law. She advises a wide range of property-owning clients and tenants including developers, contractors, retailers and the leisure industry.

She frequently advises rent review arbitrators and experts, is a trained PACT arbitrator, an ADR-accredited mediator, a member of ARBRIX, and an invited member of the RICS President's Initiative concerning the training of independent experts acting in rent review work.

Michael Ryley, Partner

michael.ryley@pinsentmasons.com

Michael Ryley is a Partner in the firm's Employment Group and is based in the London office, advising a wide range of clients on all aspects of employment law and human resources strategy. Although his practice includes advice in contentious matters, Michael spends the bulk of his time advising on the employment law aspects of mergers and acquisitions, outsourcings, PFI schemes and facilities management contracts. He is on the Editorial Board of *Workplace Law Magazine*.

Nicola Seager, Partner

nicola.seager@pinsentmasons.com

Nicola Seager is a Partner in Pinsent Masons' Property Litigation Group. She has specialised in all aspects of commercial property litigation since she qualified in 1991.

Nicola has acted for banks, plcs, insurance, property and construction companies, local authorities, an NHS Trust, a privatised port, a distribution and haulage company, landlords, tenants and developers on landlord and tenant and general property disputes, including the Landlord and Tenant Act 1954, dilapidations, rent and service charge disputes, rent reviews, specific performance, forfeiture and disclaimer of leases. She advises on disputes under development agreements, rights of light, party walls, compulsory purchase and other matters affecting development potential. She has also acted on negligence claims against property professionals.

Nick Thomas, Assistant Solicitor

nicholas.thomas@pinsentmasons.com

Nick Thomas is an assistant solicitor in the Employment Group at Pinsent Masons, where he undertakes a wide variety of contentious and non-contentious work.

Contact

Pinsent Masons
30 Aylesbury Street
London EC1R 0ER

Tel. 020 7490 4000
Fax 020 7490 2545
Web www.pinsentmasons.com

Rollits

Rollits is a leading corporate law firm with offices in Hull and York, dedicated to serving the business needs of its many commercial and institutional clients and the individuals who own and manage them. It has established an extensive reputation for corporate work, and has strong litigation, property and private capital departments. Specialist services include health and safety, employment, data protection, planning and development, commercial law, intellectual property, e-commerce and corporate finance.

Rollits is proactive and a key element of its business strategy is to provide its clients with legal services of the highest quality, which are vital to the operation of any modern business. The firm's Lexcel accreditation underlines its commitment to deliver the very best, and that, along with an ability to establish excellent client relationships, has enabled Rollits to expand and develop in what is undoubtedly a highly competitive marketplace.

Chris Platts, Partner

chris.platts@rollits.com

Chris Platts heads the Health and Safety Group at Rollits and is a health and safety specialist. He regularly represents both businesses and individuals at inquests and prosecutions for all types of accident claims. In addition he provides an across-the-board service advising on all aspects of health and safety law and practice, including advice on documentation, legislation and its implementation and how to comply, as well as health and safety due diligence on corporate acquisitions. Regular audits of health and safety systems are carried out. Chris also advises on matters of product safety and deals with any resulting claims.

David Sinclair, Trainee Solicitor

david.sinclair@rollits.com

David Sinclair, PgD FRSH, MIOSH, MaPS, trained originally as a mining engineer and worked in civil engineering and construction before taking a short-service commission with the Royal Engineers. On leaving the Army, David was the General Manager of a family-run construction firm before specialising in structural fire protection and fire certification.

Returning to university in 1994, David obtained a degree in Occupational Health and Safety and after graduation worked as a health and safety adviser in the construction, engineering and telecommunications sectors. He also lectured in health and

Rollits

safety at further and higher education level. In 1998 David became a Regional Health and Safety Adviser for ntl, before joining a national law firm as a health and safety assistant and later as a trainee solicitor.

David has developed health and safety management systems and undertaken audits, as well as successfully assisting clients to defend charges of corporate manslaughter and health and safety offences.

Contact

Rollits
Wilberforce Court
High Street
Hull HU1 1YJ

Tel. 01482 323239
Fax 01482 326239
Web www.rollits.com

SafetyCO UK

SafetyCO UK is an established group of professionals providing a fully integrated range of health and safety services to businesses throughout Europe. We have first-hand experience of:

- operating as, and working for, small companies
- the best practice standards of large organisations
- devising and delivering cost-effective training
- high-risk work activities such as construction, motor sports and marine engineering.

The working directors of SafetyCO are members of the Institution of Occupational Safety and Health, the Association for Project Safety (formerly the Association of Planning Supervisors), the British Fire Consortium, the International Institute for Risk and Safety Management, and the Working Well Together Campaign.

We operate from our offices and training centre near Maidstone – which has good motorway and main-line rail connections.

Whatever your needs, SafetyCO UK's aim – our mission statement, as some organisations might say – is to cut through the jargon, demystify health and safety, and provide practical, value-for-money solutions to enhance your business and safeguard your most valuable assets – yourself and your employees.

David Menzies, Director

David Menzies, MIOSH, RSP, is a Director of SafetyCO UK and is the lead tutor on CDM and IOSH Managing Safely courses. He is a member of the Association of Project Safety and has vast experience in the preparation of pre-tender health and safety plans and construction phase health and safety plans. David has also held senior managerial positions within a large London authority, and speaks and writes regularly for Workplace Law Network.

Phil Wright, Director

Phil Wright, FRSA, MIIRSM, TechSp, MIPD, CertEd, is a Director of SafetyCO UK and has extensive health and safety experience within the construction and maintenance industries. He is a time-served artisan tradesperson and ex-college lecturer on construction-related subjects. In 1989, he moved into the field of health and safety and has been contracted to a joint venture in Saudi Arabia surmounting language barriers.

Phil is the course administrator for Workplace Law's NEBOSH courses.

Contact

SafetyCO UK
50 Churchill Square
Kings Hill
West Malling
Kent ME19 4YU

Tel. 01732 844633
Fax 01732 844655
Email safetyco1@btopenworld.com

Scott Wilson

As a leading provider of multi-disciplinary consultancy services worldwide, Scott Wilson offers comprehensive advice and support on all building-related topics. By providing asset management advice such as strategic planning, feasibility studies, space planning, project management and health and safety advice, Scott Wilson enables the client to manage their assets in the most economical and beneficial way for their business.

Scott Wilson is familiar with all forms of building legislation and is able to assess, monitor and audit existing plant, systems and procedures to ensure they comply with current legislation.

Planned maintenance is organised and executed with forethought and control by utilising the application of recorded data. It encompasses condition-based maintenance, which is planned and progressed following information received about a system's or structure's condition.

Unplanned maintenance includes breakdown repair, corrective and emergency maintenance. Scott Wilson is able to support a client's business with the use of a simple but highly effective helpdesk system.

Scott Wilson has extensive experience of providing services under the CDM Regulations 1994 and general health and safety advice to clients, such as audits, policies, procedures, asbestos management plans and workplace inspections. Our experienced staff can provide training in most aspects of health and safety, in many cases through IOSH-accredited training programmes.

Scott Wilson's wide range of services also includes considerable experience in project management, and the company has been involved in various projects ranging from minor works to new buildings.

Andrew Richardson, Divisional Health and Safety Manager

andrew.richardson@scottwilson.com

Andrew Richardson, BSc, CEng, MICE, MaPS, is the divisional Health and Safety Manager for Scott Wilson. He is a chartered civil engineer with over 30 years' experience of designing and managing an extensive range of projects including commercial, industrial, military and historic buildings. On moving into health and safety ten years ago, he carried out the role of Planning Supervisor under the CDM Regulations. He holds a NEBOSH General Certificate in Occupational Safety and Health. At Scott Wilson, as well as providing services under the CDM Regulations, he is responsible for the health and safety of over 600 people at 20 offices throughout England, and manages and presents a programme of IOSH-accredited courses. He has also developed and presented a number of safety-related courses, including CDM and Working at Height. He provides health and safety consultancy advice to many respected companies and organisations.

Contact

Scott Wilson
Scott House
Basing View
Basingstoke
Hampshire RG21 4JG

Tel. 01256 310200
Fax 01256 310201
Web www.scottwilson.com

tarlo lyons

Tarlo Lyons

Tarlo Lyons is a leading London law firm focused on delivering commercial solutions for technology-driven business.

We have one of the largest teams of dedicated technology lawyers in England, and believe in leveraging the expertise and talent we have assembled to provide real bene-fits for our clients. We believe that success comes from contributing to our clients' objectives, and our ability to understand and work with technology is central to this.

Our intelligent document generation system DealMaker® and our leading role in euroITcounsel® demonstrate our ability to innovate in order to optimise return for our clients.

Michael Brandman, Partner

michael.brandman@tarlolyons.com

Michael Brandman joined Tarlo Lyons as a Partner in 1990. His main areas of expertise in property litigation are as follows:

- Advice and implementation of landlord's remedies for tenant default, including distress for rent, forfeiture and relief against forfeiture, statutory notices and fixed charge demands under the Landlord and Tenant (Covenant) Act and section 146 Law of Property Act 1925, statutory demands under the Insolvency Act, applications for restraining orders.
- Advice on tenant insolvency, dealing with liquidators and receivers.

Plus:

- Preparation of draft legal agreements for property transactions, including leasehold and freehold transfers, licences, property development and partnership agreements.
- Advice on legal implications of property issues associated with estates.
- Commercial property development.
- Commercial property investment.

Contact

Tarlo Lyons
Watchmaker Court
33 St John's Lane
London EC1M 4DB

Tel. 020 7405 2000
Fax 020 7814 9421
Web www.tarlolyons.com

Workplace Law Group

Workplace Law Group is now celebrating its tenth year in business and continues to provide the latest legal information, guidance and support to over 45,000 UK companies. Following an extended period of growth in recent years, Workplace Law moved to larger premises in Cambridge in 2004 to accommodate an ever-expanding workforce.

As the UK's fastest-growing and most innovative legal information specialist, we provide solutions in three core areas: building and premises law, health and safety law, and HR and employment law. There are three companies under the Workplace Law Group umbrella providing a comprehensive service to clients.

- *Workplace Law Network* – the national legal support service for business. Some of the UK's biggest employers, including the BBC, KPMG, Powergen and Tesco, turn to us for expert advice on the law of the workplace and how it affects them.
- *Workplace Law Publishing* – produces a range of books, journals and special reports on key issues for workplace managers. As well as the *Workplace Law Handbook*, major successes in 2004 included the second edition of the best-selling *Disability: Making Buildings Accessible Special Report,* and the launch of *Workplace Law Magazine.*
- *Workplace Law Training/Consultancy* – provides training, conferences and seminars on a wide range of workplace issues. Flexible bespoke in-house training can be tailored to meet the individual needs of any company.

Workplace Law Group gives you authoritative, independent, cost-effective legal advice, training and information whenever and wherever you need it. And we help you understand the issues, explaining them clearly so you can make your own decisions, based on the facts.

Over the next 12 months Workplace Law Group is committed to:

- making the law accessible through plain-English jargon-free interpretation
- giving our customers and clients a little love with personal service in everything we do.

Helen Abbott, Human Resources Consultant

helen.abbott@workplacelaw.net

Helen Abbott, BA(Hons), Chartered MCIPD, is the HR consultant for Workplace Law Group and is a member of Workplace Law's online advice panel. She has more than ten years' experience as an HR manager in the call centre, engineering, manufacturing, food and higher education sectors.

Ian Faulkner, Editor, *Workplace Law Handbook*

ian.faulkner@workplacelaw.net

Ian Faulkner is Managing Editor of Workplace Law Publishing. He has worked in the publishing industry for more than 30 years, editing and producing information on a wide variety of business-related subjects. Before joining Workplace Law, he was senior data editor for a Cambridge-based telecommunications consultancy.

David Sharp, Managing Director

david.sharp@workplacelaw.net

David Sharp is the Managing Director of Workplace Law Group Ltd. Since starting the company ten years ago David has grown the business from a single monthly facilities management publication into the UK's most dynamic legal information specialist. In this time he has established key working relationships with associations including the British Institute of Facilities Management, the Royal Institute of British Architects and the Royal Institution of Chartered Surveyors.

Contact

Workplace Law Group
Second Floor
Daedalus House
Station Road
Cambridge CB1 2RE

Tel. 0870 777 8881
Fax 0870 777 8882
Web www.workplacelaw.net

Other contributors

Casella Hazmat: Mick Dawson

Tel. 020 8551 6195. Email mickdawson@casellagroup.com

Mick Dawson is a Director with Casella Hazmat – the asbestos division of the Casella Group – and has been advising on asbestos issues for 15 years.

Mick is a Certified Competent Person in Asbestos, as determined by the British Occupational Hygiene Society (BOHS) and is an approved tutor and examiner for the BOHS asbestos proficiency modules. Along with developing technical procedures, he trains Casella staff as well as external client representatives in asbestos awareness and testing techniques.

Mick sits on the ATaC Committee promoting best industry practice, is an ARCA Governing Council member and has been involved in various roadshows given by the HSE and IOSH concerning the new asbestos regulations and their implications.

Casella Stanger: Ken Smith and Sally Goodman

Tel. 020 7902 6100
Email kensmith@casellagroup.com; sallygoodman@casellagroup.com

Ken Smith is Director of the Environmental Management, Sustainability and Risk group within Casella Stanger – the environmental consulting division of the Casella Group. He has 12 years of experience in environmental sciences and management and the wider agenda of sustainable development. Before joining Casella Stanger, he held the role of Group Sustainable Development Manager at AWG Plc.

Ken has substantial experience of sustainable development issues across the construction, government PFI, transport and utilities sectors both in the UK and internationally. He has also been responsible for undertaking many projects which have identified sustainable development-related risks, understanding how such risks impact organisations and how the risks are integrated, managed and minimised through organisational governance, audit and assurance processes. Ken has an MSc in Environmental Science, an MSc in Environmental Management and Auditing, and an MSc in Business Management and Organisational Change.

Sally Goodman is Principal Consultant in the Environmental Management, Sustainability and Risk group within Casella Stanger and is a Member of the Institute of Environmental Management and Assessment. She has extensive experience at all levels of environmental management, sustainability and CSR, from strategy development to practical implementation. Sally has developed and presented a variety of training and workshops in environmental management systems and sustainable development and has trained EMS lead auditors around the world. She was also responsible for implementing the Casella Stanger in-house EMS, which received accredited certification to ISO 14001 in October 1999.

Previously, working for DNV Certification in London and its head office in Norway, Sally was responsible for developing an accredited certification scheme for EMS, leading to DNV being one of the first certification bodies to achieve accreditation for EMAS and ISO 14001.

Sally edited Workplace Law's *Guide to Environmental Management Law and Practice 2002*.

Furniture Industry Research Association

Tel. 01438 777700. Web www.fira.co.uk

For over half a century, the Furniture Industry Research Association (FIRA) has driven the need for higher standards through testing, research and innovation for the furniture and allied industries. New and better materials, improved processes and appropriate standards have been developed to enhance the quality of furniture and assist manufacturers and retailers to become more competitive. Information on our members' products can be found on the FIRA website in the Search section.

A non-government-funded organisation, FIRA is supported by all sections of the furniture industry, ensuring ongoing research programmes that bring benefits to all and at the same time providing the Association with the influence and capability to help shape legislation and regulations.

Glass and Glazing Federation

Tel. 0870 042 4255. Web www.ggf.org.uk

The Glass and Glazing Federation (GGF) is the recognised leading authority and voice for employers and companies within the flat glass, glazing, window, home improvement, plastics and applied window film industries in the UK. It has members in more than 1,000 business locations – there is a GGF member in almost every UK town.

Members work across the industry, involved in areas such as emergency glazing, applied film, conservatories, windows, doors, fire-resistant glazing, glazing components, flat glass, curtain walling, mirrors, toughened glass, curved glass, extrusions, hardware, glass merchanting, insulated glass and laminated glass.

All GGF members have been vetted to ensure quality of service: this vetting process includes making a site visit to the company's premises, checking three years of their accounts and taking up references. Every member works to a Code of Good Practice and to the technical standards laid out in the Federation's *Glazing Manual*.

Heating and Ventilating Contractors' Association: Bob Towse

Tel. 020 7313 4900. Email btowse@hvca.org.uk

Bob Towse is Head of Technical and Safety for the Heating and Ventilating Contractors' Association (HVCA). He took on this role in July 2001 and is responsible for technical and health and safety policy for the Association. Prior to joining the HVCA, Bob was Technical Manager and Field Operations Manager for CORGI, the Council for Registered Gas Installers. As CORGI Technical Manager, Bob was instrumental in setting the CORGI technical policies and introducing much of the detailed and highly effective inspection system applied by CORGI. Bob is a member of the Council of the Institution of Gas Engineers and Managers (IGEM).

Igrox Limited

Tel. 01707 656555. Email tony.wuidart@igroxpmd.co.uk; david.cross@igroxpmd.co.uk

Igrox was established in 1976 by its present chairman, Chris Watson. The main thrust of the business at that time revolved around soil fumigation. This grew to include building, container, commodity and ship fumigations.

In the early 1990s the pest control division was created. This division has now grown to the point where Igrox is the largest independent pest control company in the UK. Following a management buyout in 2000, Mark Braithwaite became the largest shareholder.

From three key regional offices Igrox specialises in all aspects of pest management techniques. These include integrated pest management/prevention programmes designed specifically for the food industry, heritage industry, property management and domestic sites.

Igrox has the experience and expertise to deal with all species of pests including bird proofing, stored product insects, textile pests, rodents and wildlife management.

Joyce Legal: Raymond Joyce

Tel. 0121 632 2080. Email info@joycelegal.com

Raymond Joyce, the founding principal of Joyce Legal, has an established reputation as an outstanding commercial lawyer with a strong focus on the needs of the client. The range of matters on which he has successfully assisted clients is diverse and he has considerable experience in all types of dispute resolution and commercial support at board level. He is also Managing Director of Intelligent Filing Limited, which specialises in document management solutions.

Raymond's early career spanned 15 years as a chartered civil engineer where he gained wide experience in industry working with multi-disciplinary teams in the defence and power industries.

A change of career direction led him to Pinsent & Co., where he qualified as a solicitor. After a spell with Garrett & Co. (a.k.a. Andersen Legal), where he became an equity partner and built a dispute resolution team, Raymond rejoined Pinsents as an equity partner. A key member of their Dispute Resolution and Litigation department, he concentrated on the manufacturing and support services sectors.

Raymond is author of *The CDM Regulations Explained* (2nd edition) and *A Commentary on Construction Contracts: Part II of the Housing Grants Construction and Regeneration Act 1996*, both published by Thomas Telford.

Malcolm Hollis: Bartle Woolhouse

Tel. 020 7622 9555. Web www.malcomhollis.co.uk

Bartle Woolhouse, BSc(Hons), MRICS, is a Partner with the firm and is a specialist in dilapidations. He is a member of the RICS dilapidations working group and co-wrote the latest *RICS Guidance Note on Dilapidations* (4th edition).

Malcolm Hollis is renowned for expertise in building surveying and building surveying consultancy. The firm offers specialist advice on a range of issues in connection with the fabric and construction of buildings and their occupational use.

Malcolm Hollis focuses on four consultancy areas: building surveying, development, professional and construction. The firm specialises in dilapidations, party wall, rights of light and building surveys.

Paddison & Partners: David Webb

Tel. 01954 789642. Web www.paddisons.co.uk

David Webb is a Partner in Paddison & Partners, a firm of chartered surveyors with offices in Cambridge and Northampton, which he helped to form in 1992. Qualifying as a chartered surveyor in 1978, he spent some years with the Valuation Office of the Inland Revenue, the government agency responsible for assessing rateable values on property in England and Wales.

For the last 20 years, apart from a short spell assisting the Valuation Office to prepare the 1990 revaluation, he has travelled the country advising on the level of rates payable by a range of clients, from sole traders to multinational companies, local authorities and charitable organisations. The work involves advising on the lodging of appeals against rating assessments, negotiating with the Valuation Office, and liaising with councils to ensure bills are correct. There are also opportunities to exploit the various reliefs available, but little publicised, and to use the very complicated raft of legislation to best advantage.

His firm operates throughout the country and is used by the Rating Helpline of the Royal Institution of Chartered Surveyors (RICS).

Parkserve Management: David Lentz

Tel. 01903 206263. Email parkserve@aol.com

David Lentz is the Principal Consultant for Parkserve Management. His career has spanned over 30 years, including NCP management and work for local authorities. He is currently providing professional and technical support to developing countries in a consortium also designing parking for a new international airport and new nationwide traffic and parking regulation for a country in South-East Asia.

For many years in the UK, he represented local government as prosecuting officer for traffic and parking offences. In London, he was one of six managers responsible for the transition from police and traffic wardens to the new on-street, privatised and decriminalised parking system. In the private sector he has provided consultancy services to the retailer J Sainsbury's and Railtrack's station development programme, and he currently advises the Historic Royal Palaces and numerous NHS Trusts.

His principal aim is to enable organisations without in-house parking and traffic management expertise to help themselves by providing them with 'hands-on' experience so that they can master the many complex legal, technical and operational issues involved.

Peters & Peters: Elizabeth Robertson

Tel: 020 7629 7991. Email: erobertson@petersandpeters.co.uk

Elizabeth Robertson trained with Peters & Peters, qualifying in 1995. She became a Partner in 2002.

Elizabeth specialises in fraud and regulatory matters. Her particular expertise lies in acting for clients facing proceedings instituted by the Serious Fraud Office, Customs and Excise, Crown Prosecution Service and financial regulators. She has prosecuted on behalf of the Occupational Pensions Regulatory Authority. Elizabeth also advises professional clients in respect of disciplinary proceedings brought by their professional bodies.

Security Industry Authority

Tel. 08702 430 100. Web www.the-sia.org.uk

The Security Industry Authority exists to manage the licensing of the private security industry as set out in the Private Security Industry Act 2001. It also aims to raise standards of professionalism and skills within the private security industry and to promote and spread best practice.

Society of Light and Lighting: Jonathan David

Tel. 020 8675 5211. Email jdavid@cibse.org

The Society of Light and Lighting – part of the Chartered Institution of Building Services Engineers (CIBSE) – is the senior and largest professional body in the UK representing the interests of those involved in the art, science and engineering of light and lighting in their widest definition. For the last seven years, Jonathan David has been Secretary of the Society, although his other responsibilities within CIBSE have varied and currently include the CIBSE Regions. Previously he was for many years a technical editor and journalist. After working for the Institution of Electrical Engineers and the Illuminating Engineering Society, he helped to launch *Building Services Journal* and the magazine of the new Institution in 1978, and later launched and edited *Electrical Design* Magazine and the *OPUS Building Services Design File*. For some six years he worked as a freelance editor with several professional bodies in the heritage and buildings sector.

Telework Association

Tel. 0800 616008. Web www.telework.org.uk

The Telework Association, also known as the TCA, is Europe's largest organisation dedicated to the promotion of teleworking. More than 2,000 people and organisations have joined the Association since it was founded in 1993.

The Association publishes *The Teleworking Handbook* with A&C Black, *Teleworker* magazine on a bi-monthly basis and a weekly e-newsletter that includes home-based vacancies. It advises companies and individuals on homeworking issues.

Visor Consultants Limited: Peter Power

Tel. 020 7917 6026. Email info@visorconsultants.com

Peter Power is Managing Director of Visor Consultants Limited and is the author of the guide 'Preventing Chaos in a Crisis' issued by the DTI. He is a Fellow of the Business Continuity Institute, a Fellow of the Chartered Management Institute, a Fellow of the Emergency Planning Society and a Fellow of the Institute of Risk Management and is listed in the UK as an expert witness on these subjects. He is one of the most requested presenters on crisis management and business continuity and regularly runs workshops and exercises on a global basis.

Water Regulations Advisory Scheme

Tel. 01495 248454. Web www.wras.co.uk

The Water Regulations Advisory Scheme (WRAS) promotes knowledge of the Water Fittings Regulations and Water Byelaws throughout the UK and encourages their consistent interpretation and enforcement for the prevention of waste, undue consumption, misuse, erroneous measurement or contamination of water supplies. Supported by the UK water suppliers, WRAS offers a free-to-use technical enquiry service for questions of general interpretation regarding the Water Fittings Regulations, which apply to all premises that have a connection to the public water supply. It also publishes *The Water Fittings and Materials Directory,* which lists water fittings and appliances of many types that have demonstrated their compliance with the requirements of the Regulations, ensuring their acceptability to the water suppliers which enforce these Regulations.

Absence management

Helen Abbott, Workplace Law Group

Key points

- Keep accurate absence records.
- Regularly and effectively monitor absence data.
- Ensure that you have the support of senior management (vital to the success of any policy).
- Ensure that any absence policy is communicated to *all* staff.

Legislation

- Employment Act 2002.
- Disability Discrimination Act 1995.
- Access to Medical Records Act 1988.
- ACAS Code of Practice on Disciplinary and Grievance Procedures 2000.

Absence problems

High levels of absence can pose serious problems for both large and small organisations. They can:

- increase costs relating to sick pay;
- increase costs relating to overtime payments;
- increase the costs due to greater dependency on external contractors or temporary/agency staff to cover absence;
- cause lost or delayed production;
- reduce the range or standard of service to clients or customers;
- cause low morale;
- create a culture of dissatisfaction; and

- cause damage to the organisation's local reputation.

You are liable to pay employees' statutory sick pay for certain periods (see 'Sickness leave', page 478). There are no legal requirements relating directly to absence, but if you handle absence problems badly it is more likely that employees could make successful claims to employment tribunals for unfair dismissal.

High absence may be due to a particular cause but can be indicative of more fundamental organisational problems. Establishing the cause and working out a solution may call for a review of the company's policies and activities. It may be difficult to do this with the degree of rigour and objectivity required, and it may be advisable to involve someone from outside the organisation to assist with the task. However, the following advice will give you a good starting point to begin managing absence more effectively.

> ### Calculating working time lost
>
> The most common measurement of absence is working time lost. This shows the percentage of time lost over a given period and can be applied equally to full-time and part-time employees.
>
> $$\frac{\text{No. days lost due to absence}}{\begin{array}{c}\text{No. working days available}\\\text{minus holidays taken}\end{array}} \times 100 = \% \text{ working time lost}$$

Measuring and monitoring absence levels

Measure absence to find out:

- how much working time is lost (see panel above);
- where absence occurs most;
- how often individual employees are absent;
- how your organisation compares with others (e.g. public/private sector, numbers of employees, type of industry, etc.); and
- whether there are absence problems in a particular department.

Monitor absence by:

- keeping attendance records that show individual instances of absence, together with duration, reason and where in the company the employee works;
- ensuring that records can be easily analysed by section or department, month or year; and
- making sure that absence measurement figures show the scale and nature of the problem, whether there is an absence problem and which of the main categories of absence are involved. Examples are:
  - long-term sickness absence

  - short-term certified or uncertified sickness
  - unauthorised absence including lateness
  - authorised absence.

Most types of authorised absence will not be covered although they form part of the normal pattern of work. Examples of authorised absence include antenatal care, maternity or paternity leave, parental leave, jury service, trade union duties, pre-arranged hospital, doctor's or dentist's appointments, etc. In general, these types of absence can be anticipated and organised in advance.

Reducing absence levels

This can be achieved by:

- introducing an effective absence policy and communicating it to *all* employees;
- training your managers and supervisors to manage absence effectively;
- introducing return to work interviews;
- considering working conditions and job design;
- involving occupational health specialists and improving welfare measures;
- reviewing payment systems including sick pay;

- improving employment relations;
- ensuring that health and safety practices are rigorously maintained;
- considering stress risk assessments if stress is a common reason for absence;
- induction and adequate training for employees; and
- keeping in regular contact with absent employees.

Dealing with long-term sickness absence

Long-term absence can be tackled by:

- discussing the problem and all possibilities with the employee concerned;
- considering alternative work, reasonable adjustments to the job or working arrangements, whether the job can be covered by other employees or temporary replacements and how long the job can be kept open (be aware of the Disability Discrimination Act 1995, which since 1 October 2004 applies to all employers);
- considering early retirement, perhaps with enhanced pension or an ex-gratia payment;
- seeking medical opinions from a doctor appointed and paid for by the company or the employee's GP (you will need permission from the employee for this option); and
- ensuring that length of service and previous absence record are taken into consideration to guarantee fairness and consistency.

Dealing with short-term certified sickness or uncertified absence

These types of absence can be addressed by:

- interviewing employees on their return to work;
- making arrangements for medicals where necessary: you can use a doctor appointed and paid for by the company or the employee's GP (you will need permission from the employee for this option);
- ensuring that absence policies cover the provision of certificates to cover sickness absence; and
- ensuring that employees are told if their level of absence is putting their job at risk.

Dealing with unauthorised absence or lateness

Unauthorised absence or lateness can be reduced by:

- requiring absent employees to phone in by a given time on each day of absence;
- ensuring that a supervisor or manager has an informal talk with the employee on the day after absence; and
- taking disciplinary action if the unexplained absence continues or a pattern of absences occurs (e.g. Mondays, every other Friday, connected with Bank Holidays, etc.).

See also: Sickness leave (page 478).

Sources of further information

ACAS: www.acas.org.uk.

DTI: www.dti.gov.uk.

Work Foundation: 'Managing Best Practice No. 96: Maximising Attendance' (2002).

Chartered Institute of Personnel and Development: 'Employee Absence 2003: a survey of management policy and practice' (2003).

Incomes Data Services: 'IDS Study 766: Absence Management' (2004).

Accidents

Daniel McShee, Kennedys Health and Safety Team

Key points

The investigation and analysis of work-related accidents and incidents forms an essential part of managing health and safety.

Legislation

- Health and Safety at Work etc. Act 1974.
- Management of Health and Safety at Work Regulations 1999.

Overview

The HSE has recently reissued its guidance on investigating accidents and incidents. The guidance emphasises that investigation and analysis of work-related accidents and incidents forms an essential part of managing health and safety. Further, it stresses that the learning of lessons from what is uncovered by accident and incident investigation lies at the heart of preventing further events.

There are legal reasons for investigating. Sections 2 and 3 of the Health and Safety at Work etc. Act 1974 (HSWA) impose general duties on employers to ensure that their employees and those affected by the conduct of their business are, so far as is reasonably practicable, not exposed to risks to their health and safety. Following an accident, in determining whether employers have met this duty, the HSE will often look to see if there have been previous incidents and whether these have been properly investigated as part of the employer's safety management system. A failure to investigate previous incidents or learn lessons from them will be deemed by the HSE to be an aggravating feature in any further incident.

Regulation 5 of the Management of Health and Safety at Work Regulations 1999 also requires employers to plan, organise, control, monitor and review their health and safety arrangements. Health and safety investigations form an essential part of this process.

In addition to legal reasons for investigating, there are also benefits from doing so – namely the prevention of further similar adverse events which would include the prevention of business losses due to disruption, stoppage, lost orders, and the costs of criminal and civil legal actions.

Practical issues

It is the potential consequences and the likelihood of the adverse incident recurring that should determine the level of investigation, not simply the injury or ill

---

health suffered on a particular occasion. Thus for example, when investigating an incident, the HSE would look to see whether there have been any near misses in the past.

It is essential that management and the workforce are fully involved in any investigation. Depending on the level of investigation, it may be that employees, management and directors of all levels will be involved.

It is essential that an investigation is reported directly to someone with the authority to make decisions and act on recommendations.

The urgency of an investigation will depend on the magnitude and immediacy of the risk involved. The general rule is that accidents and incidents should be investigated as soon as possible in order to ensure that evidence is not lost or that memories fade.

An investigation will involve analysis of all of the information available (i.e. the incident scene, witness evidence, documentary evidence, etc.) to identify what went wrong and determine what steps must be taken to prevent it happening again.

The HSE guidance sets out a step-by-step guide to health and safety investigations.

Step 1. Gathering information

This includes finding out what happened to establish whether there were any management failings. It is important to capture information as soon as possible. If necessary, work must stop to allow this to take place. If there is any doubt about the safety of a particular type of work, piece of machinery, etc., then this should be stopped for the duration of the investigation. In the event

that this action is not taken, the HSE itself might serve a prohibition notice requiring the work activity to stop immediately where the inspector believes there to be a risk of personal injury.

Step 2. Analysing the information

Analysis involves examining all the facts to determine how the accident happened, both the direct and indirect causes. All detailed information gathered should be assembled and examined to identify what information is relevant and what information is missing.

The analysis must be carried out in a systematic way so that all possible causes (both direct and indirect) and the consequences and potential consequences of the adverse events are fully reviewed.

Step 3. Identifying suitable risk control measures

Where a proper investigation is undertaken, it should in most cases be possible to identify failings both direct and indirect – frontline and management – which led to the incident or accident taking place. This might include factors such as work pressures on performance, long hours, safety culture, etc. Once the failings have been clearly identified, this should assist in determining the remedial measures that should be implemented. All possible remedial measures should be risk assessed to ensure that making a change to a work activity, type of machinery, etc., does not in itself import greater risk than was present previously. If several risk control measures are identified, they should be carefully prioritised as a risk control action plan.

Step 4. The action plan and its implementation

At this stage, those people within the organisation who have the authority to make decisions and act on recommendations should be involved. It is good practice for those people to 'accept' the recommendations and to ensure that there is a proper action plan for implementation of the remedial measures identified. This would include a monitoring system to ensure that recommendations are indeed undertaken.

Analysis of major accidents shows that, even where previous incidents have been properly investigated in terms of identifying the failings and the appropriate remedial measures, it is the implementation of the recommendations that has failed to achieve any change and recommendations have become lost in the passage of time. Again, the HSE when investigating any incident will look to see whether any previous incidents could and should have been learned from, including the implementation of recommendations from any previous investigation.

The HSE recommends that the action plan should be based upon SMART objectives (i.e. specific, measurable, agreed and realistic) with timescales.

See also: Health and safety at work (page 295); Health and safety enforcement (page 306); Health and safety management (page 311); Risk assessments (page 469).

Sources of further information

HSG245 'Investigating accidents and incidents: a workbook for employers, unions, safety representatives and safety professionals' (HSE Books, 2004): ISBN 0 7176 2827 2.

Agency and temporary workers

Mark Rose, Berwin Leighton Paisner

Key points

- Usually, agency workers are supplied by an agency to a client business for temporary assignments. The agency and the client will enter into a contract for the supply of the named worker, and the worker will enter into a contract with the agency.

- Usually, the agency will pay and have the right to discipline the worker, but the client will give the worker day-to-day instructions.

- The main legal issues concerning an agency worker are whether he is self-employed and, if not, whether he is the employee of the agency or the client. These issues will determine the worker's entitlement to statutory employment rights and status for taxation purposes.

- Temporary employees (i.e. those people directly employed with organisations on short-term contracts) will not be entitled to claim unfair dismissal, redundancy pay or maternity rights if they do not have sufficient continuous service.

Legislation

- Employment Agencies Act 1973.

Introduction

Many employers use agency workers on short-term projects or to meet surges in demand. The most common agency arrangement is for the agency to supply temporary staff to clients, for which the agency charges a weekly fee. The worker submits his weekly timesheets to the agency, which pays the worker at an hourly rate.

In the case of more permanent positions, an employment agency may offer the client a different service, whereby the agency introduces potential candidates to the client, following which the successful candidate contracts directly with the client. Because the agency drops out of the picture, this is a standard employment relationship between the client and the worker.

Employed or self-employed?

The factors that determine an agency worker's employment status are set out in the article on 'Employment status' (page 232) and will not be repeated here. However, it should be emphasised that there are, at present, no hard and fast rules as to whether the worker is employed or self-employed. Tribunals

---

have reached different conclusions in cases with similar facts.

In general, workers find it difficult to establish that they are employees of the agency because the agency lacks sufficient day-to-day control over them. However, if the agency does exercise considerable control, a tribunal may determine that the worker is its employee for either the whole relationship (known as an 'umbrella contract') or in relation to a particular assignment.

Traditionally, agency workers have also found it difficult to show that they are employees of the client, because there is no contractual relationship between the parties. However, recent cases have suggested that an implied contractual relationship between client and worker may be established if the worker is subject to the day-to-day control of the client and there are obligations on the client to provide work and on the worker to perform that work.

Why an agency worker's employment status is important

In employment law terms, the main advantage of engaging an individual on a self-employed basis is that many employment rights do not apply. Unfair dismissal, redundancy payments and maternity rights, for example, may be claimed only by employees.

Additionally, if an individual is self-employed, he will pay income tax under Schedule D and pay National Insurance contributions at the self-employed rate. Business expenses may be set off against the individual's tax liability.

Further, the client is likely to be vicariously liable for any tortious actions committed by agency staff while at work, mainly because it will exercise day-to-day

control over the worker.

Proposed European Directive on working conditions for temporary workers

This Directive has been under consideration since 2002, but as yet no agreement has been reached. The most significant proposal is that agency workers must be given at least as favourable employment terms and conditions as a comparable worker at the hirer. Depending on the Directive's final form, this may significantly increase the cost of using agency workers.

Standards for employment agencies

The Employment Agencies Act 1973 and subsequent Regulations impose certain standards on employment agencies. These include the requirement to obtain and provide certain information to workers and clients and to agree certain terms with them before providing any services.

Temporary workers

Employers of workers on temporary contracts should be aware of the Fixed-term Employees (Prevention of Less Favourable Treatment) Regulations 2002 (which are detailed in the article on 'Fixed-term workers' (page 277). They should also be aware that temporary employees will not be able to claim certain statutory rights if they lack sufficient continuity of service. Unfair dismissal requires one year's continuous service; the right to receive a redundancy payment requires two years' continuous service; and statutory maternity pay is only payable where the woman, on the fifteenth week before her expected week of childbirth, has worked continuously for 26 weeks. However, a worker need not have acquired any length of service to make a discrimination claim.

See also: Employment status (page 232); Fixed-term workers (page 277).

Sources of further information

The DTI's page on employment agency standards can be viewed at www.dti.gov.uk/er/agency.htm.

Alcohol and drugs at work

Phil Wright, SafetyCO UK

Key points

- Ninety per cent of personnel directors from top UK organisations surveyed in 1994 stated that alcohol consumption was a problem for their organisation. While most of them regarded the problem as fairly minor, 17% described it as major. A 2003 survey reported by Alcohol Concern suggested a strong link between absenteeism and alcohol use, and estimated that alcohol was a contributory factor in around 20–25% of all workplace accidents.
- In early 2004 the HSE published a report into the scale and impact of illegal drug use by workers, which found that, overall, 13% of working respondents reported drug use in the previous year. The rate varied considerably with age, from 3% of those over 50 to 29% of those under 30.

The major concerns were:

- loss of productivity;
- lateness and absenteeism;
- safety concerns;
- effect on morale and employee relations; and
- adverse effects on company image and customer relations.

According to the HSE, alcohol is estimated to be responsible for between 3% and 5% of all absences from work in the UK, which equates to between 8 million and 14 million lost working days.

Legislation

- Health and Safety at Work etc. Act 1974.
- Management of Health and Safety at Work Regulations 1999.
- Misuse of Drugs Act 1971.
- Road Traffic Act 1988.
- Transport and Works Act 1992.

Health and safety

The Health and Safety at Work etc. Act 1974 and the Management of Health and Safety at Work Regulations 1999 place a general duty on employers to ensure, so far as is reasonably practicable, the health, safety and welfare of employees.

If you were knowingly to allow an employee under the influence of excess alcohol or drugs to continue working

---

and this were to place the employee and others at risk, you could be prosecuted.

Similarly, employees are also required to take reasonable care of themselves and others who could be affected by what they do.

Driving and transport

The Road Traffic Act 1988 and the Transport and Works Act 1992 require that drivers of road vehicles must not be under the influence of alcohol or drugs while driving, attempting to drive or when they are in charge of a vehicle.

The Transport and Works Act makes it a criminal offence for certain workers to be unfit through drink and/or drugs while working on railways, tramways and other guarded transport systems. The operators of the transport systems would also be guilty of an offence unless they had shown all due diligence in trying to prevent such an offence being committed.

What is alcohol?

Alcohol is an intoxicating drink that is brewed or distilled from cereals, fruit and even vegetables. It is often flavoured to give a distinctive smell and taste.

Alcohol is available in three forms – beer, wines and spirits – each having a different strength.

Strength of alcohol

The strength of alcohol is dependent on the amount of water added to the drink during its manufacture. The strength of an alcoholic drink is shown on a bottle or can adjacent to the ABV (alcohol by volume) and can range between 3% (normal beer) and 40% (vodka). The medical profession measures the strength of

alcoholic drinks in units and has devised the following safety guidelines for adults who drink:

- Men should drink no more than 21 units of alcohol a week (and no more than four units in any one day).
- Women should drink no more than 14 units of alcohol a week (and no more than three units in any one day).

Women as a rule become drunk faster than men because they have less water in their bodies, which means it is more difficult for the alcohol to dissolve.

Here is a basic guide to the number of units of alcohol contained in various drinks:

- Small glass of wine: 1 unit.
- Large glass of wine: 2 units.
- Half pint of normal-strength (3%) beer or lager: 1 unit.
- Half pint of strong beer or lager: 2 to 2.5 units.
- Single whisky: 1 unit.

Effects of alcohol

Alcohol enters the bloodstream and reaches the brain in a matter of minutes. However, once it reaches the body's filter system – the liver – it will take an hour to break down just one unit of alcohol.

The way alcohol affects us as individuals depends on how much we have drunk. The more alcohol you have had, the more you will be affected. An individual may be affected in a number of ways. For example:

- vision may become blurred;
- speech may become slurred;
- balance may be lost;
- judgement may be impaired; and

- behaviour may become aggressive.

The following are examples of specific situations when the best advice is not to drink at all:

- before or during driving;
- before using machinery, electrical equipment or ladders; and
- before working or in the workplace when appropriate functioning would be adversely affected by alcohol.

Drugs at work: the legal position

The Misuse of Drugs Act 1971 makes it illegal for any person knowingly to permit drug use on their premises except in specified circumstances (e.g. when they have been prescribed by a doctor).

As we have already seen, provisions of the Health and Safety at Work etc. Act 1974, the Management of Health and Safety at Work Regulations 1999, the Road Traffic Act 1988 and the Transport and Works Act 1992 also apply (see 'Health and safety' and 'Driving and transport' above).

Drugs at work policy

The HSE advises implementing a written policy on drugs – including alcohol – at work. This should consider the following issues:

- Is there a problem? Have procedures in place to find out if there could be an existing problem, e.g. by examining sickness records and consulting with staff.
- Screening. A recent survey found that four out of five employers would be prepared to drug-test their employees if they thought productivity was at stake, but that very few

firms at present actually do test their workers for banned substances.

- Procedures if a problem is discovered. What will you actually do if you find that an employee is under the influence of drugs at work? The HSE advises that the policy should seek to help employees rather than lead simply to dismissing them, but the policy must say that possession or dealing in drugs at work will be reported immediately to the police.

Random drug testing

Gabriella Wright, partner at leading law firm Charles Russell and employment law expert, suggests: 'To test in the first place you should make express provision for this in the employment contract, so employees know what the score is when they take the job on. Make sure there is a good reason for testing, for example health and safety, where the employer could be liable to prosecution if it didn't take steps to ensure the safety of its workforce.

'When testing will be carried out should also be made clear: if you're going to test only if you have concerns about an individual's fitness for work, say so; if you're going to random test, say so. Make clear what the consequences of a positive result will be (the reasonableness of any penalty will depend upon the nature of the business and the employee's role in it). Wherever possible, obtain consent for each test undertaken. Make clear what the consequences of refusing a test will be – if it is a disciplinary offence, say so.

'If the contract does not address these issues, employees pressurised to submit to a test may resign and claim constructive dismissal and any dismissal by the employer might well be unfair. Conversely, if the rules are clearly spelt out and communicated, this will assist an employer in persuading a tribunal that any subsequent dismissal was fair.'

Employers have no explicit legal right to force employees to undertake drug tests. Drug testing at work would need to be justified on health and safety grounds. For example, you may be able to argue that if dangerous machinery or driving is involved then drug tests are justified. Employers should also make sure that the results of drug tests are handled in such a way to comply with the Data Protection Act 1998.

According to Gabriella Wright: 'Data protection rules mean that testing is only likely to be justifiable if as part of a voluntary health and safety programme or to prevent a significant risk to health and safety in the workplace, or to determine an individual's fitness for work. Wherever possible, less intrusive means should be used. In all cases the employer must carry out an impact assessment, weighing up the business risk to be addressed against the disadvantage caused to the individual in being asked to submit to a test.

'Any negative impact on an individual's human rights does not necessarily preclude drug testing, even random testing, where the risk being addressed justifies the intrusion, for example where public safety is at stake. Above all it is a question of proportionality and balancing the employer's and employee's differing interests and needs.'

> *See also*: Data protection (page 163); Dismissal (page 197); Driving at work (page 208); Monitoring employees (page 392).

Sources of further information

HSE web page on alcohol and drugs: www.hse.gov.uk/alcoholdrugs.

Institute of Alcohol Studies: www.ias.org.uk.

Alcohol Concern: www.alcoholconcern.org.uk.

Asbestos

Mick Dawson, Casella Hazmat

Key points

The use of asbestos in buildings and construction materials is now completely prohibited and only a few specialised engineering uses are permitted. In May 2004 a new regulation within the Control of Asbestos at Work Regulations 2002 placed a duty on building owners and those in control of workplaces to manage the asbestos-containing materials (ACM) within their buildings by formulating an asbestos management plan.

This will involve assessing whether buildings have ACM, generating risk assessments for each occurrence and having a process to manage the ACM to reduce the risk of exposure to that material.

Legislation

- Control of Asbestos at Work (CAW) Regulations 2002.
- Asbestos (Licensing) Regulations 1983, last amended 1998 (ASLIC).
- Asbestos (Prohibition) Regulations 1992, amended 1999 and 2003.
- Special Waste Regulations 1996.

The CAW Regulations 2002 superseded the CAW Regulations 1987 and all amendments. They came into force in November 2002 with some parts having a lead-in period of up to two years.

The Regulations

Exposure to asbestos is hazardous to health. The three main conditions – asbestosis, lung cancer and mesothelioma – can all be fatal. Current HSE estimates put the death rate in the UK from asbestos-induced diseases at around 4,000 a year, and likely to increase until 2015 or later. Workers in the maintenance and construction trades comprise the largest group of people contracting the diseases, rather than those who worked in the old asbestos-manufacturing and installation industry.

The provisions fall under the umbrella of the Health and Safety at Work etc. Act 1974. The CAW Regulations are supported by three Approved Codes of Practice (ACoPs) and a number of guidance documents.

The ACoPs give advice on the preferred means of compliance with the CAW Regulations. This advice has special legal status as outlined by each document which states that 'if you are prosecuted for a breach of health and safety law and it is proved that you did not follow the relevant provisions of an ACoP you will need to show that you have complied with the law in some other way or the court will find you at fault'.

ACoP L127: The Management of Asbestos in Non-domestic Premises

Regulation 4 of the CAW Regulations imposes a more practical duty on those in control of buildings. The duty holder will have to:

- take reasonable steps to find ACM and check their condition;
- presume materials contain asbestos unless there is strong evidence they do not;
- make a written record of the location and condition and keep it up to date;
- assess the risk of exposure; and
- prepare a plan to manage that risk.

Regulation 4 is also known as 'the duty to manage' and introduced the concept of a management plan. After an 18-month lead-in period, the regulation came into effect in May 2004 and applies to managing ACM in non-domestic premises, although the common parts of domestic premises are included. It is likely to be extended at a later date to include rented domestic premises.

However, landlords have a duty to fulfil the same obligations under the Defective Premises Act 1974 (and also the Management of Health and Safety at Work Regulations 1999), and by taking actions in line with this ACoP they would be demonstrating a satisfactory level of compliance.

The duty holder is defined as being anyone with a contractual, or tenancy, obligation in relation to the maintenance and repair of buildings, or, where there is no contract, anyone in control of the buildings.

The duty holder will need to have in place a management plan for how the issues of asbestos within his buildings will be addressed. The management plan should consist of:

- details of each ACM and an explanation of the risk assessment (the algorithm);
- table of priorities and timescales;
- personnel and responsibilities;
- training for employees and contractors;
- procedures for preventing uncontrolled maintenance and building work;
- procedures for ensuring information on ACM is made available to those that need it;
- arrangements for monitoring ACM; and
- arrangements for updating and reviewing the management plan.

A guidance booklet supports the ACoP: HSG227 'A comprehensive guide to managing asbestos in premises'. A summary of this guidance is reproduced in the free leaflet INDG223 (rev. 3) 'A short guide to managing asbestos in premises'.

Management options

There are a number of options available to building managers to fulfil their duties under ACoP L127.

Option A

A comprehensive survey and removal programme is an option that would be thorough and would ensure compliance. This, however, would be disruptive and extremely costly, and the HSE does not advise this as the preferred approach.

Option B

Do nothing in the short term and assume that all unidentified material contains asbestos and survey before work is carried out. This would protect those coming into contact with asbestos but may lead to greater cost in the long run and would be difficult to manage, thus making it difficult to prove that the ACoP is being complied with.

Option C

Introduce a planned survey programme based on a management system that reviews the property stock and identifies where asbestos is likely to be present, e.g. in buildings constructed between 1960 and 1980, boiler rooms, ducts, service risers, etc. Surveys would then be carried out in those buildings or areas where ACM are most likely to be present and risk would be assessed on a case-by-case basis. If the material is in good condition and unlikely to be disturbed, then it can be left in place. An asbestos management system should be maintained and updated when action is taken as well as ensuring that all information is made available to those who could come into contact with asbestos.

Asbestos surveys

The document MDHS 100 'Surveying, sampling and assessment of asbestos-containing materials' was published by the HSE in July 2001. It contains the recommended procedures for assessing asbestos risk and describes the three types of asbestos survey:

- *Type 1*. Presumptive location and assessment – an invasive inspection but without sampling.
- *Type 2*. Standard sampling and assess-

ment – the same detail as a Type 1 survey but with sampling.
- *Type 3*. Full access pre-demolition/ refurbishment – as Type 2 but extended to embrace a more rigorous inspection for ACM used within the building fabric.

The HSE generally recommends that a Type 2 is the level of survey required to adequately manage ACM in buildings unless they have been constructed fairly recently or are small and of simple construction.

ACoP L28 (4th edition): Work with Asbestos Insulation, Asbestos Coating and Asbestos Insulating Board

This document applies to work with those ACM that are more generally known as 'licensable' materials, whereby only those companies and organisations that have an HSE licence can work on or with the materials. It is generally regarded as the 'bible' for asbestos removal contractors.

This ACoP does not apply to:

- asbestos cement;
- materials made of bitumen, plastic, resin, etc.;
- contaminated land;
- work of brief duration as described in Regulation 3(2)(a) of ASLIC; and
- manufacturing processes.

This ACoP sets out the requirements for risk assessments, plans of work, training and HSE notification while working with the more hazardous types of ACM. It also provides more detail on the use of control measures and decontamination facilities, provisions to prevent the spread of asbestos fibre using enclosures, and standards for air monitoring and analysis.

ACoP L27 (4th edition): Work with Asbestos Which Does Not Normally Require a Licence

This document applies to non-licensable work on, or which disturbs, building materials containing asbestos and also the sampling and analysis of ACM. Its coverage thus includes:

- asbestos cement (such as cleaning, repairing or removing);
- materials of bitumen, plastics, resins or rubber which contain asbestos where the thermal and acoustic properties are incidental to its main purpose; and
- minor work (an activity of less than two hours' duration) with asbestos insulation, asbestos coating and asbestos insulating board.

Two guidance booklets support the ACoP and are aimed at the building maintenance and allied trades: HSG213 'Introduction to asbestos essentials' and HSG210 'Asbestos essentials task manual'.

Asbestos (Licensing) Regulations 1983, amended 1998

Work on ACM has been a licensable activity since 1983. This means that anyone who removes, repairs or seals asbestos coatings (including textured coatings or 'Artex'-type finishes), asbestos insulation (lagging) or asbestos insulating board (including ceiling tiles) must hold a current licence issued by the HSE.

The Regulations do not apply to asbestos cement or other bonded products. Further information on these exemptions may be found in L11 'A Guide to Asbestos (Licensing) Regulations' (2nd edition).

Asbestos (Prohibition) Regulations 1992, amended 1999 and 2003

The Asbestos (Prohibition) Regulations ban the supply, use and importation of asbestos products. In 1999 the use of asbestos cement products was banned, meaning that all ACM building products were finally outlawed, with the only derogations being for certain specialised engineering uses.

By implication, asbestos cement products may be present in any building constructed up to 1999. However, throughout the 1990s, the use of asbestos building products was being specified less and less by architects and designers as the development and production of non-asbestos alternatives increased.

In August 2003 the Regulations were further updated to clarify the standing on the importation and supply of products such as minerals and aggregates. Because asbestos is a naturally occurring mineral, there are certain forms of rock such as marble and quartz which may contain low levels of asbestos as an impurity. Because these do not pose a health risk, and because the UK Government cannot ban them under EU trade laws, the Regulations have been amended to include only those mineral and aggregates to which asbestos fibre has been intentionally added.

Special Waste Regulations 1996

The disposal of ACM as a waste product is controlled by the Special Waste Regulations. These state that waste must be disposed of as 'hazardous' if the asbestos fibre is more than 0.1% of the product by weight.

Essentially this means that all asbestos products and waste have to be disposed of in accordance with the Regulations by means of a registered carrier (which can be the licensed asbestos removal contractor) under a consignment note procedure.

Checklist of key action points

- Assess the likelihood of ACM in your premises.
- Decide whether a survey is needed.
- Decide whether an outside company needs to conduct the survey.

- Incorporate the survey information into an asbestos management plan.
- Make this information available to anyone on site who may need it, e.g. contractors.
- Keep the information up to date.

See also: Hazardous/special waste (page 524).

Sources of further information

HSE publications: www.hsebooks.com.

HSE asbestos information: www.hse.gov.uk/pubns/asbindex.htm.

HMSO bookshops: www.the-stationery-office.co.uk.

Accredited asbestos testing and inspection companies: www.ukas.com.

Asbestos Removal Contractors Association (ARCA): www.arca.org.uk.

Asbestos Testing and Consulting Division of ARCA (ATaC): www.atac.org.uk.

British Occupational Hygiene Society: www.bohs.org.

Asbestos: Duty to Manage – Special Report, edited by Kathryn Gilbertson and John Richards (ISBN 1 900648 71 7, £99.00) is available from Workplace Law Publishing. Call 0870 777 8881, or visit www.workplace.law.net.

Biological hazards

David Sharp, Workplace Law Group

Key points

- Biological hazards include fungi, moulds, bacteria and viruses. The effects of biological contamination in humans can lead to mild conditions such as nausea through to potentially lethal conditions such as hepatitis.
- Biological agents are covered by the Control of Substances Hazardous to Health Regulations 2002, which impose a responsibility on employers to carry out a risk assessment for all hazardous substances. Thorough testing and good hygiene practice can help to control the risks of contamination.

Legislation

- Control of Substances Hazardous to Health Regulations 2002.
- Notification of Cooling Towers and Evaporative Condensers Regulations 1992.

Types of hazard

Many workplaces will find themselves exposed to biological risks, which must be properly controlled in order to avoid contamination. There are four principal types of biological agent:

- *Fungi*. These produce spores which can cause allergic reactions when inhaled.
- *Moulds*. These are a group of small fungi that thrive in damp conditions. They can bring on allergic reactions including athlete's foot and asthma.
- *Bacteria*. These are very small single-celled organisms, which are gradu-

ally becoming immune to treatment. The effects of contamination in humans range from mild nausea to potentially lethal conditions such as legionnaire's disease and tuberculosis.

- *Viruses*. These are minute non-cellular organisms, smaller than bacteria. As with the common cold, there is no way of controlling viruses other than the body's own natural defences. Extremely dangerous forms of virus include AIDS and hepatitis.

The risks from biological hazards are increased where a thorough cleaning and maintenance regime is not put in place. The presence of the legionella bacteria in water systems and air-conditioning units can result in an outbreak of legionnaire's disease: the UK's most high-profile case occurred in Barrow-in-Furness in 2002.

Similarly, poor hygiene in the use and handling of food can increase the spread of biological hazards. Employers should put in place a policy for managing food in fridges in order to separate meats, cooked food, raw food and liquids so that the effect of minor spillages is minimised. Many employers also enforce a policy preventing workers from eating at their desks or on the shop floor, and ensure that food waste goes into special bins. The advantage here is that food waste can be dealt with specially (both inside and outside the building) to avoid attracting rodents – a further cause of the spread of disease.

Risk assessments

A COSHH risk assessment should be undertaken to consider the risks arising from biological hazards. As with other risk assessments, the process should first identify the presence of biological agents in the workplace, and the people who might be affected by them. The assessment should take into account the features of a particular hazard (such as the legionella bacteria) and should evaluate the risk.

In order to conduct a robust risk assessment it is important to carry out accurate monitoring in the form of environmental testing (such as air and water quality monitoring). The risks from biological hazards will be reduced through regular maintenance and cleaning, and through the exercise of good hygiene practice, reinforced through information, instruction, training and supervision

---

See also: COSHH/hazardous substances (page 153); Legionella (page 358).

Sources of further information

Department of Health: www.doh.gov.uk. Telephone: *England* 020 7210 4850; *Scotland* 0131 7210 4850; *Wales* 029 2082 5111.

Food Standards Agency: www.food.gov.uk. Telephone: *England* 020 7276 8000; *Northern Ireland* 028 9041 7711; *Scotland* 01224 285100; *Wales* 029 2067 8999.

L5 'Control of substances hazardous to health. The Control of Substances Hazardous to Health Regulations 2002. Approved Code of Practice and guidance', 4th edition (HSE Books, 2002): ISBN 0 7176 2534 6.

'Infection risks to new and expectant mothers: a guide for employers' (HSE Books, 1997): ISBN 0 7176 1360 7.

ING342 'Blood-borne viruses in the workplace: guidance for employers and employees' (HSE Books, 2001): ISBN 0 7176 2062 X.

IAC27REV2 'Legionnaires' disease: a guide for employers' (HSE Books, 2001): ISBN 0 7176 1773 4.

INDG253 'Controlling legionella in nursing and residential care homes' (HSE Books, 1997).

Bomb alerts

Andrew Richardson, Scott Wilson

Key points

The legislation which requires an employer to deal with bomb alerts is Regulation 8 of the Management of Health and Safety at Work Regulations 1999, which requires employers to put into place procedures for serious and imminent danger and for danger areas.

Legislation

- Health and Safety at Work etc. Act 1974.
- Management of Health and Safety at Work Regulations 1999.

Required procedures

The Regulations require employers to:

- establish and where necessary action appropriate procedures to be followed in the event of serious and imminent danger to persons at work;
- nominate sufficient numbers of competent persons to implement those procedures in so far as they relate to evacuation from the premises;
- inform any person at work of the nature of the hazard and of the steps taken or the steps to be taken to protect them from it;
- enable the persons concerned to stop work and proceed to a place of safety in the event of their being exposed to serious, imminent and unavoidable danger; and
- except in exceptional circumstances, require the persons concerned to be prevented from resuming work in any situation where there is still serious and imminent danger.

All emergency procedures have to be written down and have to be effectively communicated to all personnel on the premises including all visitors, contractors, etc. Details of the possible different types of bomb and the different steps required for each will need communicating to all employees.

The procedures must identify the nature of the risk and should take into account the seriousness and danger that the risk poses.

Responsibilities for specific employees – e.g. receptionists who may take the bomb threat call, maintenance staff who may need to shut down ventilation systems and wardens who may have a duty to ensure the work areas are rapidly evacuated and clear – should all be clearly identified.

The person who has been designated

as the competent person responsible for these procedures should be clearly identified and his role, responsibilities and authority detailed.

Any other emergency procedures required under any other health and safety legislation in respect of dangerous substances, explosives, etc., should be included in the procedural document.

The procedural document must detail how and when the procedures should be implemented to allow people sufficient time to get to a place of safety and should allow for other emergencies which may occur at the same time.

Work should not resume while a serious danger remains. Expert advice from authorities such as the police and fire brigade should be obtained if in doubt.

> *See also*: Crisis management and business continuity (page 158; Emergency procedures (page 218); Risk assessments (page 469).

Sources of further information

The Home Office document 'Bombs: Protecting People and Property' (1994) has now been superseded by the Security Advice pages available on the Security Service (MI5) website, which has good basic information and useful links. Specific advice on bomb-threat procedures can be found at www.mi5.gov.uk/output/Page41.html.

The Government has a new website 'Preparing for Emergencies – what you need to know' at www.pfe.gov.uk/index.htm.

A booklet 'Expecting the unexpected – business continuity in an uncertain world' (2003) is also available as a download at www.londonprepared.gov.uk/business/london_first.pdf. Although aimed at the business community in London, it contains much relevant information.

Boundaries and party walls

Edited by Nicola Seager, Pinsent Masons

Key points

- The position of a boundary on a plan is normally only indicative, and its exact position normally has to be plotted on the ground.
- Works to a party wall need to conform to the procedures in the Party Wall etc. Act 1996.
- The erection of a wall or fence may require planning permission if it exceeds certain heights.
- Boundary disputes should be resolved as soon as possible without recourse to litigation, which will sour relations between neighbours still further.

Boundary lines

A boundary line is an invisible line between adjoining properties. Its position is ascertained from title deeds and documents, from plans and measurements referred to in these, and from inspection of the site. Frequently precise positioning is not possible: plans, measurements and descriptions are not necessarily accurate when compared to what appears to be obviously long established on the ground.

There may be a structure along a boundary. This could be a wall or fence on one side of the boundary or a party wall with the boundary along its centre line. The external or (in the case of a terraced house) internal wall of a building may also be a boundary wall or a party wall.

Position of boundary lines

In relation to registered land, the general boundaries rule is that boundary lines on the Land Register are only to be taken as general indications as to their precise position (Land Registration Act 2002, section 60). This is the starting point for ascertaining the position of a boundary line but is no guarantee on a sale of premises. The commonly used standard conditions of sale reflect this by stating that a seller does not guarantee his property boundaries. An application may be made to the Chief Land Registrar to determine the exact line of the boundary (Land Registration Rules 2003, Part 10).

If an established boundary structure is reasonably close to this line, it is likely that structure will be immediately adjacent to or, in the case of a party wall, on the true boundary line. In the case of ancient field boundaries, which can exist in developed areas, where there is or was a hedge and a ditch, the presumption is that the boundary is on the far side of the ditch from the hedge.

Ownership of a boundary

A boundary, as such, does not belong to anyone – it is simply the point at which two properties meet. However, the wall which marks the edge of a building will generally belong to that building and be the responsibility of the owner of the property on that side of the boundary line.

Covenants in title deeds to maintain walls or fences, and 'T' marks on the inside of a boundary line on a deeds plan in the title, are all indicators as to which owner is responsible for or owns the boundary structure. But this may not be conclusive. Where a wall divides two buildings, it will normally be a party wall.

Party walls

A party wall is a wall owned or used by two adjoining owners. Commonly, the boundary runs down the centre line and each owner is deemed to own the wall up to the centre line and to have rights over the other half. Special rules apply under the Party Wall etc. Act 1996. The provisions of this Act are very detailed and before taking any steps under it an owner should consult a surveyor or solicitor with specialist knowledge. The Act also details the different types of party wall. In buildings on several floors in multi-occupation, a floor/ceiling may also be a party structure within the Act.

New walls or fences along the boundary

There are limits on the height of man-made boundary structures which can be erected without obtaining planning legislation (Town and Country Planning (General Permitted Development) Order 1995). There is a maximum height of one metre above ground next to a highway and of two metres on all other boundaries. Anything higher will require planning permission.

The owner of land can put up a wall or fence on his land up to the boundary. It may also be possible to construct a wall or fence across a boundary.

Under the Party Wall etc. Act, an owner may put up a new party wall, after appropriate statutory notices, if his neighbour agrees. If the neighbour does not agree, the new wall must be on the building owner's side, but footings may be placed on the adjoining owner's land. A new wall must not interfere with established rights such as rights of light to windows or rights of way.

Boundary structures next to highways may be subject to restrictions or controls, particularly next to access points and on corners where there are vision splays. While security fencing will be permitted in general, anything that is likely to cause harm to children and deterrents designed to injure trespassers, such as broken glass on top of walls, should be avoided as it is likely to result in civil or criminal liability if someone is in fact injured.

Maintaining the boundary structure

If you own the boundary structure, you will be responsible for maintaining it in a safe condition unless the deeds require the adjoining owner to do so. If it causes damage to the neighbouring property by collapse or by parts of it falling onto that property, you may be liable. You can and should insure against this risk.

Check your policy to see that this risk is covered. The cost of rebuilding in case of damage can also be included in your policy.

Existing structures on boundaries may have rights of support. Any activity on the adjoining property that lessens or removes that support will not generally be permissible. However, if the scheme of work is carried out to a party wall under the Party Wall etc. Act, both building owners should have the comfort of having a scheme approved by independent surveyors.

Entry onto neighbouring land to carry out work

If you need access to the neighbouring property to repair or rebuild the boundary structure (which may actually be the wall of your building), your deeds may give you rights.

You also have limited rights for this under the Access to Neighbouring Land Act 1992 (but this does not allow new development). You need to give notice of your intentions to the owner and occupier of the adjoining property.

If he is not willing to give you access, you can apply to the court for an order that he must give necessary access. You will be responsible for any damage caused to his property in the course of exercising the right.

The Party Wall etc. Act contains alternative arrangements for allowing entry onto adjoining land for carrying out work to party walls. The Act has a strict regime of notices and counter-notices with detailed timescales, and provisions for resolution by independent surveyors if the owners cannot agree.

The Act assumes the involvement of specialist surveyors, whose advice should be sought from the outset.

Hedges and trees

Overgrown hedges, particularly leylandii, can be a particular problem.

The Anti-social Behaviour Act 2003 contains provisions (which are expected to come into force in 2005) to enable a local authority, on receiving a complaint, to force remedial action in respect of evergreen hedges which are more than two metres high and adversely affect the reasonable enjoyment of another person's land. In such a case the owner can be required to ensure that the hedge is kept to a height of no more than two metres.

If there are trees or hedges belonging to a neighbouring property that actually overhang your boundary, you can trim the offending overhanging branches. However, you must return the trimmings to the owner of the tree or hedge. Before exercising this right, it is advisable to warn the neighbouring owner that you intend to do so.

Hedges in rural areas are increasingly subject to conservation controls, particularly where they are next to open or agricultural land. For example, hedges more than 20 metres long with open or agricultural land on at least one side may not be removed without the consent of the Countryside Agency.

Boundary disputes

The costs of taking legal action are usually out of all proportion to the value of the property concerned and only lead to soured relations between adjoining owners. Therefore try to reach an amicable agreement – a reasonable compromise is much quicker and less painful in terms of cost, time and confrontation.

If you agree terms, have them put in

writing and place a copy with each owner's deeds.

If you have to take legal action, it is principally an action for trespass.

Where the boundary is not clear, you can apply to the court for a declaration to determine this. However, the court has a discretion as to whether or not it will make a declaration.

If the dispute is urgent, as where the neighbour is carrying out works on the disputed land, you can apply for an injunction to stop the work while the dispute is decided. However, courts are reluctant to take such a drastic step, and, if you ultimately lose the argument, damages and costs may be awarded against you.

Damages are the general remedy, but damages for loss in boundary dispute cases, as in any other case, can only reflect the actual value of the loss. In boundary disputes this is usually nominal.

If the Land Registry makes an error on the title plan as to the location of a boundary line, you may have a claim for rectification or compensation.

Compensation will again only reflect the value of what has been lost by the Registry's mistake. Rectification can be a long and costly remedy unless both parties agree.

Mediation to settle a dispute may be required. Under the Civil Procedure Rules introduced in 1999, there is a duty on both parties to act reasonably in exchanging information and to try to avoid the need for proceedings in court.

See also: Nuisance (page 406).

Building Regulations

Tony Dennison, Butler & Young Ltd

Key points

The Building Regulations are made under powers in the Building Act 1984. They apply in England and Wales, and the majority of building projects have to comply with them. They exist to ensure the health and safety of people in and around all types of building (i.e. domestic, commercial and industrial). They also provide for energy conservation and for access into and around buildings.

The Building Regulations contain various sections dealing with definitions, procedures, and what is expected in terms of the technical performance of building work. For example, they:

- define what types of building, plumbing and heating projects amount to 'building work' and make these subject to control under the Building Regulations;
- specify what types of building are exempt from control under the Building Regulations;
- set out the notification procedures to follow when starting, carrying out and completing building work; and
- set out the 'requirements' with which the individual aspects of building design and construction must comply in the interests of the health and safety of building users, energy conservation, and access into and around buildings.

What is 'building work'?

'Building work' is defined in Regulation 3 of the Building Regulations. The definition means that the following types of project amount to 'building work':

- the erection or extension of a building;
- the installation or extension of certain building services or fittings;
- an alteration project involving work that will temporarily or permanently affect the ongoing compliance of the building, service or fitting with the requirements relating to structure, fire or access to and use of buildings;
- the insertion of insulation into a cavity wall; and
- the underpinning of the foundations of a building.

Whenever a project involves 'building work', then it must comply with the

Building Regulations. This means that the works themselves must meet the relevant technical requirements and they must not make other fabric, services and fittings worse than they previously were.

The Building Regulations may also apply to certain changes of use of an existing building even though the work involved might not seem like 'building work'. This is because the change of use may result in the building as a whole no longer complying with the requirements that will apply to its new type of use, and so having to be upgraded to meet additional requirements. It must always be remembered that a change of use under Building Regulations is usually different to a change of use under planning.

Two systems of building control

If the work amounts to 'building work' it will be subject to, and must comply with, the Building Regulations. To help achieve compliance with the Regulations, developers are required to use one of two types of building control service:

- Local authority building control service. This can be contacted at the district, borough or city council.
- An approved inspector's building control service. Approved inspectors are private sector companies or practitioners and are approved to carry out the building control service as an alternative to the local authority. Approved inspectors can provide the service in connection with most sorts of building project involving new buildings or work to existing buildings, including extensions or alterations to homes. For insurance reasons most approved inspectors

cannot currently deal with projects involving building new houses, or flats for sale or private renting. Most approved inspectors belong to the Association of Consultant Approved Inspectors.

Contravening the Building Regulations

The Building Regulations can be contravened in two ways:

- by not following the correct procedures; and
- by carrying out building work that does not comply with the requirements contained in the Building Regulations.

The local authority has a general duty to enforce the Building Regulations in its area and will seek to do so by informal means wherever possible.

Where an approved inspector is providing the building control service, the responsibility for checking that the Building Regulations are complied with during the course of building work will lie with that inspector. However, approved inspectors do not have enforcement powers. Instead, in a situation where they consider that building work does not comply with the Building Regulations, they will not provide a final certificate and additionally will notify the local authority that they are unable to continue. If no other approved inspector takes on the work, the local authority will take on the building control role. From this point the local authority will also have enforcement powers to require the work to be altered if it considers this necessary.

If a person carrying out building work contravenes the Building Regulations, the local authority may decide to take him to the magistrates' court, where he could be fined up to £5,000 for the contravention and £50 for each day the contravention continues (Building Act 1984, section 35).

This action will usually be taken against the builder or main contractor, although proceedings must be taken within six months of the offence (Magistrates' Courts Act 1980, section 127).

Alternatively, or in addition, the local authority may serve an enforcement notice on the owner requiring alteration or removal of work that contravenes the Regulations (Building Act 1984, section 36). If the owner does not comply with the notice, the local authority has the power to undertake the work itself and recover the costs of doing so from the owner.

Current Regulations

- Building Regulations 2000 (SI 2000 No. 2531).
- Building (Amendment) Regulations 2001 (SI 2001 No. 3335).
- Building (Amendment) Regulations 2002 (SI 2002 No. 440).
- Building (Amendment) (No. 2) Regulations 2002 (SI 2002 No. 2871).
- Building (Amendment) Regulations 2003 (SI 2003 No. 2692).
- Building (Amendment) Regulations 2004 (SI 2004 No. 1465).
- Building (Amendment) (No. 2) Regulations 2004 (SI 2004 No. 1808).
- Building (Approved Inspectors etc.) Regulations 2000 (SI 2000 No. 2532).
- Building (Approved Inspectors etc.) (Amendment) Regulations 2001 (SI 2001 No. 3336).
- Building (Approved Inspectors etc.) (Amendment) Regulations 2002 (SI 2002 No. 2872).
- Building (Approved Inspectors etc.) (Amendment) Regulations 2003 (SI 2003 No. 3133).
- Building (Approved Inspectors etc.) (Amendment) Regulations 2004 (SI 2004 No. 1466).

Approved Documents

Practical guidance on ways to comply with the functional requirements in the Building Regulations is provided in a series of 14 Approved Documents. Each document contains:

- general guidance on the performance expected of materials and building work in order to comply with each of the requirements of the Building Regulations; and
- practical examples and solutions on how to achieve compliance for some of the more common building situations.

Part A – Structural Stability (2004 edition)

Part A of the Building Regulations is concerned with the strength and stability of a building. It remained almost unchanged between 1992 and 1 December 2004, when a new edition of the Approved Document came into force.

Part A1 seeks to ensure that a building is constructed in a manner and from materials that ensure all loads are transmitted to the ground:

- safely; and
- without causing deflection or deformation of any part of the building, or movement of the ground, that will impair the stability of any part of another building.

Part A2 deals with ground movement

and requires a building to be constructed in such a way that ground movement caused by swelling, shrinkage or freezing of the subsoil, or land-slip or subsidence, will not impair the stability of any part of the building.

Structural safety depends on a successful combination of design and construction, particularly:

- loading;
- properties of materials;
- detailed design;
- safety factors; and
* workmanship

The Approved Document gives detailed guidance on the construction of certain residential buildings no greater than three storeys in height and other small buildings of traditional construction. All other buildings should be designed to the relevant Code of Practice.

Structural design is heavily dependent on the guidance contained in British Standards and Codes of Practice. These give information on:

- loadings;
- structural work in timber;
- structural work in masonry;
- structural work in reinforced, pre-stressed and plain concrete;
- structural work in steel;
- structural work in aluminium; and
- foundations.

Part A3 requires that a building does not suffer from disproportionate collapse as a result of an accident in a part of the building. It seeks to ensure that should an accident occur in or around a building, such as a gas explosion or vehicle impact, the building is sufficiently tied together to avoid a catastrophic collapse.

Part B – Fire Safety (2000 edition, amended 2000 and 2002)

Part B aims to ensure the safety of the occupants and of others who may be affected by a fire in a building, and to provide assistance for firefighters in the saving of lives.

Therefore, buildings must be constructed so that if a fire occurs:

- the occupants are given suitable warning and are able to escape to a safe place away from the effects of the fire;
- fire spread over the internal linings of the walls and ceilings is inhibited;
- the stability is maintained for a sufficient period of time to allow evacuation of the occupants and access for firefighting; and
- fire spread within the building and from one building to another is kept to a minimum; and
- satisfactory access and facilities are provided for firefighters.

It is not a function of the Regulations to minimise property damage or insurance losses in the event of fire.

Part B1 applies to all building types (except prisons). In some parts of the country there may be other legislation that imposes additional requirements on the means of escape from a building. In inner London reference needs to be made to the Building (Inner London) Regulations 1987 and elsewhere Local Acts of Parliament (e.g. the Hampshire Act 1983) may apply.

The Approved Document gives specific guidance on the design of means of warning and escape for dwellings (houses, flats and maisonettes). Other building types are dealt with by reference to general principles that address means of giving warning, and horizontal and vertical escape. Guidance is also given on:

- lighting of escape routes;
- provision of exit signs;
- fire protection of lift installations;
- performance of mechanical ventilation and air-conditioning systems in the event of fire; and
- construction and siting of refuse chutes.

Part B2 gives guidance on the choice of lining materials for walls and ceilings. It concentrates on two properties of linings that influence fire spread:

- the rate of fire spread over the surface of a material when it is subject to intense radiant heating; and
- the rate at which the lining material gives off heat when burning.

It also gives guidance on how these properties can be controlled, mainly by restricting the use of certain materials.

Part B3 deals with measures to ensure:

- stability of the load-bearing elements of the structure of a building for an appropriate time in the event of fire;
- subdivision of the building into compartments by fire-resisting construction such as walls and floors;
- sealing and subdivision of concealed spaces in the construction to inhibit the unseen spread of fire and smoke;
- protection of openings and fire-stopping in compartment walls and floors; and
- provision of special measures to car parks and shopping complexes.

Part B4 seeks to limit the possible spread of fire between buildings. It does this by:

- making provisions for the fire resistance of external walls and by limiting the susceptibility of their external surfaces to ignition and fire spread;
- limiting the extent of openings and other unprotected areas in external walls in relation to the space separation from the boundary of the site; and
- making provisions for reducing the risk of fire spread between roofs and over roof surfaces.

Part B5 gives guidance on:

- installation of fire mains within the building;
- provision of vehicle access for high reach and pumping appliances;
- access for fire service personnel into and within the building; and
- venting of heat and smoke from basements.

There is interaction between the Building Regulations and other fire safety requirements in England and Wales. It is therefore important for developers and designers to adhere to set procedures to ensure that owners and occupiers do not need to carry out extra building work at the end of a project. The Building Regulations cover means of escape, fire alarms, fire spread, and access and facilities for the fire service, but, for certain buildings, additional requirements are imposed by the Fire Precautions Act 1971 and the Workplace Fire Regulations. Because of this, there are statutory requirements on the building control body to consult with the fire authority in these cases. Details of the consultation procedure can be found in *Building Regulations and Fire Safety Procedural Guidance* published by the ODPM (February 2001).

Part C – Site Preparation and Resistance to Contaminants and Moisture (2004 edition)

Part C of the Building Regulations is concerned with site preparation and resistance to contaminants and moisture. It remained almost unchanged between 1992 and 1 December 2004, when a new edition of the Approved Document came into force.

Part C1 deals with site preparation and the possibility of contaminants.

- Attention needs to be given to the removal of vegetable matter, topsoil and pre-existing foundations.
- Site investigation is recommended as the method for determining how much unsuitable material should be removed.
- Remedial measures are required to deal with land affected by contaminants. These include materials in or on the ground (including faecal or animal matter) and any substance that is, or could become, toxic, corrosive, explosive, flammable or radioactive. Therefore it includes the naturally occurring radioactive gas radon and gases produced by landfill sites, such as carbon dioxide and methane.
- The area of land that is subject to measures to deal with contaminants includes the land around the building.
- Protection from radon includes buildings other than dwellings.
- Guidance is included relating to

subsoil drainage and the risk of transportation of water-borne contaminants.

Part C2 deals with resistance to moisture and seeks to ensure that the floors, walls and roof of a building are constructed in such a way that moisture cannot penetrate the building nor will condensation occur.

- Guidance recommends that in order to reduce the condensation risk to floors, walls and roofs reference should be made to BS 5250 and to 'Limiting thermal bridging and air leakage: robust details' and BR 262 'Thermal insulation: avoiding risks'.
- Guidance is now provided on the use of moisture-resistant boards for the flooring in bathrooms, kitchens and other places where water may be spilled from sanitary fittings or fixed appliances.
- Reference is made to BS 8208 for assessing the suitability of cavity walls for filling.
- Where walls interface with doors and windows, checked rebates are now recommended in the most exposed parts of the country.
- Where Part M requires level access, there is a need to pay particular attention to detail in exposed areas to ensure adequate provision is made for resistance to moisture.

Former requirement F2 'Condensation in roofs' has been transferred to Part C as it deals with effects on the building fabric rather than ventilation for the health of occupants.

Part D – Toxic Substances (1985 edition, amended 1992 and 2000)

Part D is probably the least used of the Approved Documents. It was introduced when urea formaldehyde foam was a popular method of providing cavity insulation in buildings. The foam can give off formaldehyde fumes which can be an irritant to occupants. The Approved Document gives guidance on:

- the type of materials used for the inner leaf of the cavity together with the suitability of walls for filling;
- details of the foam itself; and
- the credentials of the installer.

In recent years the popularity of urea formaldehyde foam has declined.

Part E – Resistance to the Passage of Sound (2003 edition, amended 2004)

Part E1 deals with the protection against sound from other parts of the building and adjoining buildings. It aims to achieve adequate sound insulation to walls and floors between dwelling houses, flats and rooms for residential purposes.

A room for residential purposes means a room, or suite of rooms, which is not a dwelling house or flat and which is used by one or more persons to live and sleep in, including rooms in hotels, hostels, boarding houses, halls of residence and residential homes, but not including rooms in hospitals, or other similar establishments, used for patient accommodation. The requirements for resistance to airborne and impact sound for floors also include stairs where they form part of the separating element between dwellings.

Site testing of sound insulation is intended on a sampling basis. However, as an alternative, robust details have been available to the industry since 1 July 2004. Robust Details Ltd is a non-profit-distributing company, limited by guarantee, set up by the house-building industry. Its objectives are broadly to identify, arrange testing and, if satisfied, approve and publish design details that, if correctly implemented in separating structures, should achieve compliance with requirement E1. It also carries out checks on the performance achieved in practice.

The robust design details are available in a handbook that may be purchased from Robust Details Ltd. The company can be contacted at: PO Box 7289, Milton Keynes MK14 6ZQ; tel. 0870 240 8210; fax 0870 240 8203; email administration@robustdetails.com. More information can be found at www.robustdetails.com.

Although the design details are in the public domain, their use in building work is not authorised unless the builder has registered the particular use of the relevant design detail or details with Robust Details Ltd to identify a house or flat in which one or more of the design details are being used.

The requirement for appropriate sound insulation testing imposed by the Regulations does not apply to building work consisting of the erection of a new dwelling house (i.e. a semi-detached or terraced house) or a building containing flats where robust details are registered and adhered to.

Part E2 sets standards for the sound insulation of internal walls and floors in dwelling houses, flats and rooms for residential purposes. Site testing is not intended.

Part E3 controls reverberation in the

We are here to help

with our extensive range of consultancy services.

Providing professional, practical expertise and support to the building and construction industry for over 30 years.

BYL plc Group of Companies operate nationwide and provide their services over the numerous disciplines listed here.

www.byl.co.uk

 Butler & Young Ltd
Building Control & Fire Safety Consultants
Approved Inspectors

 Butler & Young (Scotland) Ltd
Construction & Property Consultants

 **BYL (Construction Consultants) Ltd**
Structural Engineers, Chartered Building Surveyors
Planning Supervisors, Party Wall Surveyors,
Disability Access Consultants

 **Trenton Fire Ltd**
Fire Safety Engineering Consultants

 **Butler & Young (Training) Ltd**
CPD Training

 **BYL plc**
Consultancy Services

Trenton House, Imperial Way, Croydon, Surrey CR0 4RR
Tel: 020 8253 4900 Fax: 020 8253 4901 **FREEPHONE 0800 652 7172**

common parts of buildings containing flats or rooms for residential purposes. Site testing is not intended.

All new school buildings are now controlled under the Building Regulations, and Part E4 covers the sound insulation, reverberation time and indoor ambient noise levels. Guidance on meeting the requirement is given in *Building Bulletin 93* published by the Department for Education and Skills (DfES).

Part F – Means of Ventilation (1995 edition, amended 2000)

On 21 July 2004 the ODPM issued a consultation document containing proposals substantially to amend Part F. The consultation period closed on 22 October 2004 and it is envisaged that a new edition of Part F will be introduced on 1 January 2006. Until then the current edition remains in force.

Part F1 gives guidance on the dispersal of water vapour and its extraction where it is produced in significant quantities (e.g. in kitchens, bathrooms and utility rooms). It also covers extraction of pollutants that are a danger to health from areas where they are produced in significant quantities (e.g. restrooms where smoking is permitted). The main approach is rapid dilution of water vapour and pollutants (usually by providing openable windows), background ventilation to provide a minimum supply of fresh air over long periods, and air supply through mechanical ventilation and air-conditioning systems for nondomestic buildings where these are proposed.

The provisions in the Approved Document for requirement F1 would, if followed, prevent the service of an improvement notice with regard to the requirements for ventilation in Regulation 6(1) of the Workplace (Health, Safety and Welfare) Regulations 1992.

Part F2 acknowledges that in a roof space and in the spaces above insulated ceilings there is a risk that condensation will form in the space above the insulation. This Part is aimed at limiting condensation so that the thermal performance of the insulating material, and the structural performance of the roof construction, will not be substantially and permanently reduced. However, the guidance in Part F2 transfers to the new Part C Approved Document published on 1 December 2004.

Reference should also be made to Approved Document B for guidance on the design of mechanical ventilation and air-conditioning systems for the purpose of fire safety and to Approved Document J in relation to the provision of combustion air to appliances.

Further detailed guidance is given in the BRE report BR 262 'Thermal insulation: avoiding risks'.

Part G – Hygiene (1992 edition, second impression (with amendments) 1992, further amended 2000)

Part G1 gives guidance on the scale of provision of sanitary conveniences and washing facilities in dwellings (houses, flats and maisonettes) and houses in multiple occupation. For other building types reference is made to other relevant legislation. The reference to Regulations made under the Offices, Shops and Railway Premises Act 1963 and the Factories Act 1961 can be ignored since both have been replaced by recommendations contained in the Workplace (Health, Safety and Welfare) Regulations 1992. Reference should also be made, as appropriate, to the Food Hygiene (General) Regulations 1970 (amended by the Food Hygiene (Amendment) Regulations 1990), which apply to premises used for the purposes of a food business.

Reference can also be made to BS 6465:1994 Part 1 'Sanitary installations. Code of practice for scale of provision, selection and installation of sanitary appliances'.

Part G2 gives guidance on the provision of bathrooms and recommends that the same provision applies also to a house in multiple occupation.

Part G3 provides guidance on the installation of unvented hot-water storage systems. The Approved Document recommends that such a system should be the subject of an agreed method of approval or assessment and should be installed by a competent person. It must also comply with the Water Supply (Water Fittings) Regulations 1999.

Part H – Drainage and Waste Disposal
(2002 edition)

Part H1 gives guidance on the design of above-ground sanitary pipework and below-ground foul drainage. It stresses the need for the drainage system to be designed and constructed to:

- convey foul water to a suitable outfall (a foul or combined sewer, cesspool, septic tank or holding tank);
- minimise the risk of blockage or leakage;
- prevent the entry of foul air into the building under normal working conditions;
- be ventilated;
- be accessible for clearing blockages; and

- not increase the vulnerability of the building to flooding.

Sewers (i.e. a drain serving more than one property) should normally have a minimum diameter of 100mm when serving no more than ten dwellings. Sewers serving more than ten dwellings should normally have a minimum diameter of 150mm. Access points to sewers should be in places where they are accessible and apparent for use in an emergency.

Part H2 deals with the siting, construction and capacity of wastewater treatment systems and cesspools so that they:

- are not prejudicial to health or a nuisance;
- do not adversely affect water sources or resources;
- do not pollute controlled waters; or
- are not sited in an area where there is a risk of flooding.

They should be adequately ventilated and should be constructed so that the leakage of the contents and the ingress of subsoil water is prevented.

Wastewater treatment systems should be considered only where the nature of the subsoil indicates that the operation of the system and the quality and method of disposal of the effluent will be satisfactory and where connection to mains drainage is not practicable.

The quality of the discharged effluent is not covered by the Building Regulations, but some installations may require consent for discharge from the Environment Agency.

Additionally, the Environment Agency may take action against any person who knowingly permits pollution of a stream, river, lake, etc., or groundwater, by requiring him to carry out works to prevent the pollution (Water Resources Act 1991 (as amended), section 161A).

Part H2 also contains guidance on:

- the siting and construction of drainage fields; and
- the provision of information regarding the nature and frequency of the maintenance needs of wastewater systems and cesspools.

Part H3 gives guidance on the need for rainwater from roofs and paved areas to be carried away either by a drainage system or by some other means.

Where provided, a rainwater drainage system should:

- carry the flow of rainwater from the roof to a suitable outfall (a surface water or combined sewer, soakaway or watercourse);
- minimise the risk of blockage or leakage; and
- be accessible for clearing blockages.

The Approved Document contains guidance on:

- precautions to be taken where rainwater is permitted to soak into the ground;
- siphonic roof drainage systems;
- eaves drop systems;
- rainwater recovery systems;
- drainage of paved areas;
- the design of soakaways and other infiltration drainage systems; and
- the use of oil separators.

Part H4 gives guidance on the construction, extension or underpinning of a building over or within 3m of the centreline of an existing drain, sewer or disposal main shown on the sewerage

undertaker's sewer records.

Building work should be carried out so that it will not:

- cause overloading or damage to the drain, sewer or disposal main; or
- obstruct reasonable access to any manhole or inspection chamber.

Future maintenance works to the drain, sewer or disposal main must be possible without undue obstruction, and the risk of damage to the building must not be excessive due to failure of the drain, sewer or disposal main.

The guidance also explains that precautions should be taken if piles are to be placed close to drains.

Part H5 is designed to ensure that:

- rainwater does not enter the public foul sewer system where it may cause overloading and flooding;
- rainwater does not enter a wastewater treatment system or cesspool not designed to take rainwater where it might cause pollution by overloading the capacity of the system or cesspool; and
- foul water, including run-off from soiled or contaminated paved areas, does not enter the rainwater sewer system or an infiltration drainage system intended only for rainwater.

Part H6 gives guidance on the design, siting and capacity of refuse containers and chutes for domestic developments.

For non-domestic developments it is recommended that the collecting authority is consulted regarding:

- the volume and nature of the waste, and the storage capacity required;
- any requirements for segregation of waste for recycling;

- the method of storage, including any proposals for on-site treatment;
- the location of storage areas, treatment areas and waste collection points; and
- the means of access to these, hygiene arrangements, hazards and protection measures.

Part J – Combustion Appliances and Fuel Storage Systems (2002 edition)

Parts J1 to J3 apply only to fixed fuel-burning appliances and incinerators. The Approved Document gives advice on:

- the amount of air supply needed for safe combustion of the fuel;
- the construction of hearths, fireplaces, flues and chimneys;
- the location of boilers; and
- separation of flues and chimneys from structural timbers and thatch.

The guidance also includes ways of demonstrating that the safe performance of combustion installations is not undermined by mechanical extract ventilation systems.

Part J4 calls for a notice providing the performance characteristics of the hearth, fireplace, flue or chimney to be fixed in an appropriate place in the building. The Approved Document gives guidance on the form, content and location of such notices.

Part J5 gives guidance on the protection of oil and LPG fuel storage systems from fire. This includes the positioning and/or shielding so as to protect these systems from fires that might occur in adjacent buildings or on adjacent property.

Part J6 makes provision for protection against leakage from oil storage tanks polluting boreholes and water and drainage courses and for permanent labels containing information on how to respond to oil escapes to be positioned in a prominent position.

Part K – Protection from Falling, Collision and Impact (1998 edition, amended 2000)

Part K1 deals with the design, construction and installation of stairs, ladders and ramps. In a public building the standard of provision may be higher than in a dwelling to reflect the lesser familiarity and number of users.

It deals with:

- the rise and going of stairs (i.e. their steepness);
- provision of handrails; and
- allowing sufficient headroom over a stair.

Parts K2 and K3 cover:

- provision of guards designed to prevent pedestrians from falling;
- provision of vehicle barriers capable of resisting or deflecting the impact of vehicles; and
- measures to protect people in loading bays from being struck or crushed by vehicles by providing adequate numbers of exits or refuges.

Part K4 gives guidance on the installation of windows so that parts that project when the window is open are kept away from people in and around the building and on the provision of features that guide people away from open windows, skylights and ventilators. The Approved Document also describes measures designed to prevent the opening and closing of doors and gates from presenting a safety hazard. These include vision panels in doors and safety features to prevent people being trapped by doors and gates.

Recommendations for the design of stairs for means of escape included in Approved Document B (Fire Safety) and for the design of stairs and ramps for use by disabled people in Approved Document M (Access to and Use of Buildings) should also be considered.

Compliance with Part K (and where appropriate Part M as it relates to stairs and ramps) would prevent the service of an improvement notice with regard to the relevant requirements of the Workplace (Health, Safety and Welfare) Regulations 1992.

Part L – Conservation of Fuel and Power (2002 edition)

This Part has been subdivided into two distinct Approved Documents: Part L1 covering dwellings and Part L2 covering all other types of building.

Part L1 gives three methods for demonstrating reasonable provision for limiting heat loss through the fabric of the building. These are:

- the elemental method;
- the target U-value method; and
- the carbon index method.

Other features of the Approved Document include:

- work on existing dwellings;
- guidance on reasonable provision for replacement windows and boilers;
- work in historic buildings;
- heating and hot water systems;
- internal lighting;
- external lighting; and
- conservatories.

The Standard Assessment Procedure (SAP) rating for each new dwelling must still be calculated and given to the local authority in accordance with requirement 16 of the Regulations or to the approved inspector in accordance with Regulation 12 of the Approved Inspectors Regulations. However, the rating cannot be used as a means of showing compliance with Part L1.

Guidance on ways of limiting heat losses due to thermal bridging at junctions and around openings, and through unwanted air leakage, is given in the Approved Document by reference to the following publications: *Limiting thermal bridging and air leakage: Robust construction details for dwellings and similar buildings* (TSO, 2001) and BRE IP 17/01 'Assessing the effects of thermal bridging at junctions and around openings in the external elements of buildings'.

Heating and hot water systems need to be commissioned and provided with user manuals. The Approved Document indicates that building control bodies can accept a commissioning plan recommended by the Chartered Institution of Building Services Engineers (CIBSE) or the Building Services Research and Information Association (BSRIA).

Part L2 gives three methods for demonstrating reasonable provision for limiting heat loss through the fabric of the building. These are:

- the elemental method;
- the whole building method; and
- the carbon emission calculation method.

Other areas covered by the Approved Document include:

- work on existing buildings;

- guidance on reasonable provision for replacement windows, heating and hot water systems, lighting systems, and air-conditioning or mechanical ventilation systems;
- air leakage standards, thermography and air pressure testing;
- how solar overheating may be avoided;
- providing building logbooks;
- installation of energy meters;
- how to carry out trade-off calculations between construction elements, and between construction elements and heating system efficiency; and
- luminaire efficacy requirement for lighting installations

Guidance on avoiding technical risks (such as rain penetration, condensation, etc.) that might arise from the application of energy conservation measures is given in BRE Report 262 'Thermal insulation: avoiding risks' (updated November 2001 edition published by BRE and TSO).

Part M – Access to and Use of Buildings (2004 edition)

Part M covers access to and use of buildings. It used to deal solely with access and facilities for disabled people but is now universally inclusive to encourage the provision of an accessible environment for all.

Parts M1 to M3 cover:

- the use of access statements;
- access to the main entrances to the building from the edge of the site and from car parking within the curtilage;
- access into and within the building and from one building to another on a site;

- the provision of lifts;
- access to and use of the building's facilities;
- design of the building's elements so that they are not a hazard;
- the provision and design of sanitary accommodation and changing and showering facilities;
- the provision and design of accommodation for disabled people in audience or spectator seating;
- aids for communication for people with impaired hearing or sight;
- accessibility of switches and controls; and
- visually contrasting surfaces and fittings.

Part M4 covers the provision of reasonably accessible sanitary conveniences in dwellings.

There is interaction between the Building Regulations, the Disability Discrimination Act 1995 and the Disability Discrimination (Employment) Regulations 1996. It is therefore important for developers and designers to appreciate how all these pieces of legislation might apply to a particular scheme. This should ensure that owners and occupiers do not need to carry out extra building work at the end of a project.

Part N – Glazing: Safety in Relation to Impact, Opening and Cleaning (1998 edition, amended 2000)

People using buildings may come into contact with glazing in critical locations, such as doors, door side panels and at low level in walls and partitions. Part N1 describes measures to be adopted to reduce the likelihood of cutting and piercing injuries occurring from contact with such glazing by making sure that it will break safely, be robust or be permanently protected.

Part N2 gives guidance on the measures that might be adopted to indicate the presence of large uninterrupted areas of transparent glazing with which people might collide. It does not apply to dwellings.

Part N3 provides guidance on the safe operation of openable windows, skylights and ventilators relating to the location of controls and the prevention of falling. It does not apply to dwellings.

Part N4 gives guidance for the safe means of access for cleaning glazed surfaces where there is danger of falling. Guidance is also given for safe cleaning where the glazed surfaces cannot be reached from the ground, a floor or some other permanent stable surface. Again it does not apply to dwellings.

Parts N3 and N4 contain similar provisions to those in Regulations 15(1) and 16 of the Workplace (Health, Safety and Welfare) Regulations 1992.

Part P – Electrical Safety (2004 edition)

A new section of the Regulations will be introduced on 1 January 2005. The intention is to control electrical safety in dwellings and the requirements are that:

- reasonable provision shall be made in the design, installation, inspection and testing of electrical installations to protect persons against fire and injury; and
- where an electrical installation is provided, extended or altered, sufficient information shall be provided so that persons wishing to operate, maintain or alter the installation in the future can do so reasonably safely.

Part P will apply in England and Wales to fixed electrical installations in dwellings and in:

- dwellings and business premises that have a common supply;
- common access areas in blocks of flats;
- shared amenities in blocks of flats such as laundries and gymnasiums; and
- outbuildings, including sheds, garages and greenhouses, supplied from a consumer unit located in any of the above.

The main way of complying will be to follow the technical rules in BS 7671:2001 and the guidance given in installation manuals that are consistent with this standard, e.g. IEE On-Site Guide and Guidance Notes Nos 1 to 7.

With certain exceptions, notification of proposals to carry out electrical installation work must be given to a building control body before work begins.

This prior notification is not necessary if:

(a) the proposed work is to be undertaken by a competent person, i.e. a firm that has been approved by and certificated by an approved competent person scheme. These are currently operated by:

- BRE Certification Ltd (ECA & IEE);
- British Standards Institution;
- ELECSA Ltd (BBA & FENSA);
- NICEIC Certification Services Ltd; and
- Zurich Certification Ltd.

(b) the proposed work is minor work. This comprises:

- work that is not in a kitchen or special location:

– adding lighting points to an existing circuit;

– adding socket outlets and fused spurs to an existing circuit;

– installation/upgrading of main and supplementary equipotential bonding;

• work in all locations:

– replacing accessories such as socket outlets, control switches and ceiling roses;

– replacement of the cable for a single circuit only;

– re-fixing or replacing the enclosures of existing components; and

– providing mechanical protection to existing fixed installations.

See also: Biological hazards (page 84); COSHH/hazardous substances (page 153); Disability access (page 179); Energy management (page 236); Fire: means of escape (page 263); Glass and glazing (page 290); Safety signage (page 483); Ventilation and temperature (page 513); Waste management (page 526).

Sources of further information

Building Regulations: Explanatory Booklet (ODPM, 2003).

Billington, M. J.: *Manual to the Building Regulations* (TSO, 2001): ISBN 0 11 753623 7.

Bullying and harassment

Helen Abbott, Workplace Law Group

Key points

- Ensure that a formal statement or policy exists and is supported by senior management.
- Issue a clear statement that bullying and harassment are totally unacceptable.
- Investigate alleged incidents thoroughly and immediately.
- Provide access to counselling and advice for recipients, where practicable, or consider giving time off for these activities.
- Make appropriate use of grievance and disciplinary procedures.
- Train your managers to increase knowledge and awareness.

Legislation

- Sex Discrimination Act 1975.
- Race Relations Act 1976.
- Disability Discrimination Act 1995.
- Employment Equality (Sexual Orientation) Regulations 2003.
- Employment Equality (Religion or Belief) Regulations 2003.

What are bullying and harassment?

Bullying is an abuse or misuse of power that may be characterised as offensive, intimidating, malicious or insulting behaviour intended to undermine, humiliate, denigrate or injure the recipient.

Harassment, in general terms, is unwanted conduct affecting the dignity of men and women in the workplace. It may be related to age, sex, disability, religion, nationality or any personal characteristic of the individual and may be persistent or a single incident.

The key is that the actions or comments are viewed as demeaning and unacceptable by the recipient.

How can bullying and harassment be recognised?

It is good practice for employers to give examples of what is unacceptable behaviour in their workplace. These may include:

- spreading malicious rumours or insulting someone (particularly on the grounds of race, sex, disability, sexual orientation, religion or belief);
- ridiculing or demeaning someone – setting them up to fail;
- copying memos that are critical about someone to others that do not need to know;
- exclusion or victimisation;
- unfair treatment;
- unwelcome sexual advances – touch-

ing, standing too close, displaying offensive materials;

- making threats or comments about job security without foundation;
- deliberately undermining a competent employee by overloading and constant criticism; and
- blocking or refusing promotion or training opportunities.

Why do employers need to take action?

Not only are bullying and harassment unacceptable on moral grounds, but they could cause serious problems for an organisation, including:

- poor morale and poor employee relations;
- loss of respect for managers and supervisors;
- poor performance;
- lost productivity;
- absence;
- resignations;
- damage to company reputation; and
- tribunal and other court cases and payment of unlimited compensation.

The legal position

It is not possible to make a direct complaint to an employment tribunal about bullying. However, employees can bring complaints under laws covering discrimination and harassment. These can include discriminating on the grounds of sex, race, disability, sexual orientation, religion or belief and, from December 2006, age. Employers are usually responsible in law for the acts of their employees and must show a duty of care to ensure that a breach of contract does not take place.

What should employers do?

- Consider a formal policy and gain a statement of commitment from senior management.
- Set a good example.
- Maintain fair procedures.
- Set standards of behaviour.
- Ensure complaints are handled confidentially, fairly and sensitively.

Formulating a policy

- Issue a clear statement that bullying and harassment will not be tolerated.
- Give examples of unacceptable behaviour.
- State that bullying and harassment may be treated as disciplinary offences.
- Outline the steps you will take to prevent bullying and harassment.
- Outline the responsibilities of supervisors and managers.
- Give reassurance of confidentiality for any complaint.
- Ensure protection from victimisation.
- Refer to grievance procedure (informal and formal), including timescale for action.
- Refer to disciplinary procedure, including timescale for action.
- Begin investigation procedures, including timescale for action.
- Include provisions for counselling and support.
- Arrange training for managers.
- Decide how to implement, review and monitor the policy.

How should employers respond to a complaint?

There are three basic options:

- *Informal approach.* In some cases people are unaware that their behaviour is unwelcome. Sometimes a 'quiet word' can lead to greater understanding and an agreement that the unwelcome behaviour will stop.
- *Counselling.* This can provide a vital and confidential path for an informal approach and sometimes the opportunity to resolve the complaint without the need for formal action. Other options include employee assistance programmes funded by the employer.
- *Disciplinary procedures.* Where an informal approach is not suitable or has failed, the employer may resort to the disciplinary procedure. It is important to follow a fair procedure with regard to both the complainant and the person accused. For more details of the disciplinary procedure, see page 184.

What should be considered when imposing a penalty?

Action taken must be reasonable in the circumstances. In some cases, counselling or training may be more appropriate than disciplinary action. When a penalty is imposed, consider the employee's general disciplinary record, action in previous cases, any explanations or mitigating circumstances, and whether the penalty is reasonable.

Written warnings, suspension or transferring the bully or harasser are examples of disciplinary penalties in a proven case. Suspension or transfer could breach the employee's contract if he suffers a detriment and lead to a constructive dismissal claim, so check the contract of employment carefully before imposing this.

When gross misconduct has taken place, dismissal without notice may be appropriate. Since October 2004, all employers contemplating dismissal or action short of dismissal such as loss of seniority have had, as a minimum, to follow a three-step statutory procedure.

Finally, review your harassment and bullying policy on a regular basis to ensure that it remains effective.

See also: Disciplinary and grievance procedures (page 184); Discrimination (page 189); Dismissal (page 197).

Sources of further information

Disability Rights Commission: www.drc-gb.org.

Equal Opportunities Commission: www.eoc.org.uk.

Employee Assistance Professionals Association (EAPA): www.eapa.org.uk.

Race Relations Employment Advisory Service (RREAS): 0121 452 5448.

Morris, Sue: *Sensitive Issues in the Workplace: A Practical Handbook* (The Industrial Society, 1993): ISBN 1 85835 023 9.

Ishmael, Angela with Alemoru, Bunmi: *Bullying and Violence at Work* (The Industrial Society, 1999): ISBN 1 85835 104 9.

Buying and selling property

Edited by Hugh Bruce-Watt, Pinsent Masons

Key points

- A buyer will want to ensure it acquires a property with good and marketable title through due diligence.
- A survey and an environmental audit are recommended.
- Until contracts are exchanged, either party can withdraw without penalty. After contracts are exchanged, both parties are legally bound.
- A buyer is generally responsible for insurance as soon as contracts are exchanged.

Overview

This article discusses the acquisition and disposal of freehold land and buildings.

A purchase or sale is best described by outlining the various stages involved. This procedure applies in England and Wales. The law and procedure are different in Scotland and outside the ambit of this publication.

Legislation

The principal piece of legislation is the Law of Property Act 1925 although there is a significant volume of succeeding legislation.

The pre-contract stage

Firms of chartered surveyors usually deal with the disposal of commercial property. It is not essential to buy or sell through a commercial surveyor, but such firms have knowledge of market conditions.

Surveyors will often agree 'heads of terms' setting out what has been agreed between the seller and the buyer and covering such things as the parties, property, price, timetable and any particular conditions.

A buyer will want to acquire a property which has good and marketable title, as otherwise the buyer might be concerned about its value and the ability to dispose of the property in the future. Without good and marketable title it might also be difficult to raise finance on the strength of the security of the property. This involves the process of due diligence, i.e. the investigation of the property by the buyer before entering into the contract. There are three possible approaches:

- A full title investigation is carried out by the buyer's solicitors.
- A certificate of title is given by the seller's solicitors.
- Warranties are given by the seller in the contract.

Additionally, there might be a combination of any of these.

Title investigation

This involves the buyer's solicitor investigating the seller's legal title to the property and checking whether there are any restrictive covenants or other matters affecting the property. In addition, pre–contract enquiries will be raised with the seller's solicitors and various searches carried out against the property.

The buyer should also arrange for a survey to be carried out to make sure that the property is sound and that the sale price is not excessive. The buyer will need to consider investigating for contamination, particularly if the property has a history of industrial use.

Certificate of title

Instead of the buyer making a full investigation of the property, the seller's solicitor could produce a certificate of title confirming that the property has good and marketable title and disclosing all information it has in respect of the property.

Unless the seller gives a warranty as to the accuracy of the certificate, the buyer will in essence be relying on the seller's solicitor's professional indemnity policy.

A certificate is useful if there is insufficient time for the buyer to carry out its investigation, if a large number of properties are involved, and where the seller's solicitor acted on the original purchase and so is already in possession of much of the information needed to complete the certificate.

The terms of the certificate will still need to be negotiated and the statements given may be qualified or disclaimers imposed.

Warranties

The seller can give warranties about the property to the buyer which provide the latter with a form of insurance. Ideally they should protect the buyer in respect of the presence of factors relating to the property of which it is unaware and which detrimentally affect the property.

Warranties are vital if the property is acquired as part of a share acquisition (see page 114 below) to cover the unknown liabilities, actual or contingent, and therefore go beyond matters of pure title.

However, the buyer will need to consider whether the warranties are worth the paper they are written on as it is obviously essential that the seller is financially able to satisfy any claim under the warranties.

The warranties are usually qualified by a separate disclosure letter which will be annexed to the contract. If an item is excluded from the warranties, the risk passes to the buyer. It is therefore essential that there is also an express warranty in the contract that the disclosure letter is accurate.

There may also be some general disclaimers, e.g. that the buyer is aware of all matters apparent from a physical inspection of the property (which means that a survey should be commissioned).

The contract

Most disposals or acquisitions are preceded by exchange of contracts. Until contracts are exchanged, neither party is committed to the transaction and either may withdraw at any time.

A contract is a binding agreement between the buyer and the seller which sets out all the relevant details and the agreed terms. Sometimes completion is conditional, e.g. on planning permission being granted.

Once contracts are exchanged, neither party may withdraw from the transaction without being in breach of contract and facing a possible claim for damages or specific performance. Specific performance is an order by the court requiring the party in default to complete the transaction. It is a discretionary remedy and will normally be awarded only where damages alone are not regarded as being an adequate remedy.

Contracts should not be exchanged until any pre-contract investigations and surveys have been made and the buyer's funding is in place.

If there is a chain of related sales and purchases (common in residential transactions), then all the parties in the chain need to be ready to exchange at the same time. This can lead to delay.

On an exchange of contracts a deposit is usually paid by the buyer, normally 10% of the purchase price. It is usual for the deposit to be held by the solicitor for the seller pending completion, although in certain circumstances the deposit may be used for an onward purchase by the seller. The buyer may lose its deposit if it does not complete the purchase in accordance with the terms of the contract.

Unless the contract says otherwise, the buyer is responsible for insuring the property as soon as contracts are exchanged.

Completion

Completion is when legal ownership is transferred. It is at this stage that the balance of the purchase price is paid over and possession of the property is given to the buyer. The completion date is fixed in the contract and traditionally is four weeks after the exchange, although it can be much earlier or later (depending on what the parties agree).

The transfer

The transfer is the document which formally transfers the property from the seller to the buyer. The transfer describes the property and any rights, restrictive covenants, shared facilities, rights of way and other matters which affect the property and subject to which the buyer will take the property.

Where the property is sold subject to covenants (such as restrictions on the use of the property), the buyer will usually agree in the transfer to observe and perform these covenants and to indemnify the seller for any loss caused to the seller if the buyer fails to comply with them.

Stamp duty land tax

Stamp duty land tax is payable by the buyer on the transaction. A wide range of transactions is subject to SDLT – essentially any dealing with an interest in land. The rate of SDLT varies according to the price paid. Transactions not exceeding a value of £60,000 (for residential property) or £150,000 (for commercial property) are exempt from SDLT. The maximum rate is 4% where the price is more than £500,000.

On commercial property sales, value added tax at 17.5% may be chargeable on the purchase price, and the stamp duty in such cases is charged on the VAT-inclusive figure.

After completion

The transfer must be sent to the Land

Registry so that the buyer can be registered as the new owner of the property. A registration fee is payable which is calculated according to the price paid. The maximum fee is currently £700. Once registration is complete, the Land Registry will issue a title information document which provides that the buyer is the owner of the property and also includes a plan of the property and details of any matters affecting the property such as rights of way and restrictive covenants. It is recommended that older title deeds are retained to assist in resolution of disputes involving rights of way, boundaries or covenants.

Acquisition of a property as part of a business purchase

Sometimes a property is acquired as part of the purchase of a business. This can happen when a buyer acquires all the shares in a company. The buyer steps into the shoes of the seller so that there is simply a change in control rather than a change in the owner of the business (and as a consequence of any property owned by the company). As there is no change in ownership, the buyer will take on all existing liabilities of the company in respect of the property.

Although searches will be carried out, enquiries raised and a contract entered into, there is no need for a transfer to be completed (because there is no change in the name of the owner) and consequently no need for a Land Registry application to be made. There are various tax and other considerations on a share purchase including possible stamp duty savings, as stamp duty on a share purchase is currently fixed at 0.5% of the price. Specialist advice on how to structure the acquisition or disposal of the property is recommended.

Catering: food safety

Hilary Ross, Berwin Leighton Paisner

Key points

Before starting a catering business, one must ensure that the premises are registered with the local authority at least 28 days before opening.

Food should be prepared in accordance with the Food Safety Act 1990 and underlying legislation. The Act is the principal food-control measure in the UK. It sets out general duties of caterers in respect of food safety and quality together with general consumer protection measures. Subordinate legislation made under the Act fleshes out requirements to be followed by caterers and other food operators and businesses in relation to matters such as claims, advertising, hygiene and temperature control.

Legislation

- Food Safety Act 1990.
- Food Premises (Registration) Regulations 1991.
- Food Labelling Regulations 1996.
- Food Labelling (Amendment) Regulations 1999 and 2003.
- Food Safety (General Food Hygiene) Regulations 1995.
- Food Safety (Temperature Control) Regulations 1995.

Food Safety Act 1990

General duties in relation to safety and quality

It is a criminal offence to adulterate food in any way that would make it harmful to health. For these purposes, 'adulteration' includes:

- adding any article or substance to food;
- using any article or substance as an ingredient in the preparation of food – e.g. adding caustic soda instead of baking powder to a product;
- taking out any constituent from a food; and
- subjecting the food to any other process or treatment.

Unless there has been a deliberate act of sabotage, it is rare for proceedings to be brought under this provision of the Act.

Proceedings in relation to food safety are more likely to be brought for selling food that fails to comply with food safety requirements. This includes food that:

- has been rendered injurious to health. In such cases, the food must cause ill health or be dangerous to consumers;

- is unfit for human consumption. Again, the food must be injurious or dangerous to health;
- is so contaminated (by extraneous matter or otherwise) that it would not be reasonable to expect it to be used for human consumption. This includes mouldy or stale food. In relation to this provision, there is no need to show it is harmful to the consumer.

Consumer protection provisions

The Act also protects consumers from food that is safe but of unsatisfactory quality. It is an offence under the Act if the food sold to the consumer is not:

- of the *nature* demanded (e.g. the food sold is different to that requested such as re-formed fish being sold as scampi);
- of the *substance* demanded (this applies where the composition differs from that requested, e.g. glass in a pizza); or
- of the *quality* demanded (this includes mouldy, bad and decomposed food as well as food that fails to meet commercial quality standards – e.g. excess sugar in diet cola).

The Act also protects the consumer from false claims in relation to foods by making it an offence to label, present, display or advertise food in such a way that it is falsely described or is likely to mislead as to the nature, substance or quality of the food. For example, a menu describing a cocktail as Red Bull and Vodka would be misleading if the cocktail did not contain Red Bull but a substitute product.

There are similar provisions in the Trade Descriptions Act 1968 that apply to products generally and not just food products.

Food Labelling Regulations 1996

The Food Labelling Regulations set out requirements for the labelling of food products. Usually food sold by caterers does not need to be labelled. However, there are certain exceptions. Foods that contain irradiated ingredients or ingredients that have been genetically modified must be labelled as such.

Any intentional use of GM ingredients at any level must be labelled. This is regardless of whether GM material is detectable in the final product. But it is not necessary to label small amounts (e.g. below 0.9% for approved GM ingredients and 0.5% for unapproved varieties that have received a favourable assessment).

Food that is pre-packed to sell directly to customers must also be labelled as set out above. This would apply to sandwiches, etc., that are prepared in advance.

All this information must be on a label attached to the food, the menu or a notice. Part III of the Regulations requires attention in this context as it applies to claims and descriptions in the labelling and advertising of food products, meaning that it will apply to adverts for food products sold by caterers. It identifies the following:

- *Prohibited claims.* These are claims that a food has a tonic property or that it has the property of treating, preventing or curing disease. This prohibition prevents caterers from making medicinal claims for products on their menus. For example, although it would be permissible to mention the health maintenance properties of calcium, it would not be permissible to say that calcium could help prevent osteoporosis.

- *Restricted claims.* These include claims for reduced or low energy, protein, vitamins and minerals.

- *Misleading descriptions.* Part III sets out when certain wording such as 'ice-cream' and 'starch reduced' can be used.

These prohibitions and restrictions need to be taken into account by caterers when drafting menus.

Hygiene

The Food Safety (General Food Hygiene) Regulations 1995 identify the general obligations on proprietors of food businesses in relation to hygiene. Of particular importance is Schedule 1, which sets out the rules of hygiene. The Schedule is divided into ten chapters that lay down both general and specific legal requirements relating to the hygienic operation of a food business:

- Chapter I lays down general requirements for ensuring hygiene of premises including cleaning, maintenance, layout, design, construction and size. It also covers welfare amenity provisions (such as sanitary accommodation, washing and clothing), storage facilities and environmental provisions (including temperature, lighting and ventilation).

- Chapter II lays down more specific requirements for food preparation, treatment areas and rooms. These requirements apply to all rooms where food is prepared, treated or processed except for dining rooms. It covers matters such as floors, walls, ceilings, overhead fixtures, windows, doors and washing facilities for foods.

- Chapter III covers requirements for moveable or temporary premises such as stalls and delivery vehicles.

- Chapter IV sets out the standards that must be maintained in relation to hygiene when transporting food. This would include caterers that make home deliveries.

- Chapter V requires food businesses to keep clean all articles, fittings and equipment with which food comes into contact and is intended to prevent cross-contamination from one foodstuff to another.

- Chapter VI (food waste) lays down requirements to minimise any food safety risk that inevitably arises from working debris and food waste generally.

- Chapter VII prescribes the quality of water to be used in a food business. In particular, it requires an adequate supply of 'potable water' which must be used whenever necessary to ensure foodstuffs are not contaminated.

- Chapter VIII (personal hygiene) sets out the legal requirements designed to achieve 'clean person' strategies. Personnel have two general legal obligations. First, every person working in the food-handling area must maintain a high degree of personal cleanliness and must wear suitable, clean and where appropriate protective clothing. Second, people working in food-handling areas who either know or suspect that they are suffering from or carrying a disease likely to be transmitted through food must report the condition to the proprietor of the catering business.

- Chapter IX sets out provisions applicable to foodstuffs. It requires that food businesses must not accept any raw material or ingredients if they are known to be or suspected to be contaminated. Once accepted, raw materials must be stored in appropriate conditions designed to prevent harmful deterioration and protect them from contamination.

- Chapter X (training) stipulates that caterers must ensure that their food handlers are supervised and trained in relation to food hygiene matters. The training must be commensurate with their work activities.

Although the Regulations are fairly complex, the *Industry Guide to Good Hygiene Practice: Catering Guide* (see 'Sources of further information' below) provides detailed guidance on how to comply with them and should be consulted when implementing a hygiene strategy.

Food safety management

The Food Safety (General Food Hygiene) Regulations 1995 also require proprietors of food businesses to identify steps in their activities that are critical to ensuring food safety and take measures to ensure that adequate safety procedures are identified, implemented, maintained and reviewed. This is commonly referred to as a Hazard Analysis of Critical Control Points (HACCP) system, or, if it is applied to the catering industry, it is referred to as Self-Assured Catering.

An HACCP system requires that a catering operation is analysed step by step. In particular, it requires that stages in preparation at which hazards exist are identified, together with the means by which they can be controlled. These may be as simple as introducing temperature controls, e.g. cooking chicken to a minimum temperature of 75°C or ensuring that it is chilled before cooking. An HACCP system is the key to successfully defending any proceedings brought under the Regulations or the Food Safety Act. The defences available under the Food Safety Act are looked at in more detail below.

Temperature controls

Controlling temperatures is one of the most significant ways of ensuring food safety. The Food Safety (Temperature Control) Regulations 1995 set out requirements for foods that are likely to support the growth of pathenogenic microorganisms or the formation of toxins at temperatures that would result in a risk to health. In particular, they stipulate when foods must be kept chilled, e.g. salads, dressings, cheese, smoked or cured products, sandwiches, raw meat or poultry. They also detail temperatures that should be reached during cooking, those that should apply to hot food and cold food displays, and when reheating of food products is acceptable.

Menus

It is essential that the prices of food and drink sold at the premises are clearly displayed. The easiest way to do this is on a menu. Generally, prices should include VAT when appropriate. There are few rules setting out the composition of food; the exceptions are sausages and burgers, which must contain a prescribed amount of meat.

Care has to be taken when drafting menus to ensure that they are not mis-

---

Food safety checklist

- Are the premises registered with the local authority?
- Has a liquor licence been obtained where alcohol is to be sold?
- Does the construction and layout of the premises comply with the hygiene regulations?
- Are suppliers reputable and reliable?
- Have the critical control points been identified and controls put in place?
- Have the staff been properly trained in all aspects of food safety, hygiene and temperature control?
- Is there a detailed cleaning schedule in place?
- Is waste picked up on a regular basis?
- Are there adequate pest control measures in place?
- Is equipment regularly cleaned and inspected? (This is particularly important for oil filtration systems).
- Are proper temperature controls in place?
- Are all of the above steps documented?

---

leading and that they do not falsely describe the foods in the menus. For example, it would not be acceptable to describe an omelette as freshly cooked if the caterer buys it from frozen and then reheats it. Guidance can be found in the report *Criteria for the Use of the Terms Fresh, Pure Natural etc. in Food Labelling* published by the Food Standards Agency that sets out terms which should be avoided or used only sparingly. These include the terms 'country-style', 'home-made', 'authentic', 'original' and 'traditional'. It also explains when the words 'fresh', 'natural' and 'pure' should be used.

Defences

If a breach of the Food Safety Act occurs, it is likely that a prosecution will result. In order to defend proceedings, it is necessary to prove to the court that all reasonable steps had been taken to avoid the offence occurring. This is known as a due diligence defence. What is reasonable will depend on the size of the business and its resources as well as the seriousness of the breach. If steps have been taken to comply with the legislation and controls have been put in place in relation to hygiene, food safety and management, even if an employee has made a mistake that has caused the system to break down, it is likely that the proceedings can be defended.

Penalties

For a conviction under the Food Safety Act in the lower courts, the fine can be up to £20,000 and/or six months' imprisonment. In the higher courts, the fine is unlimited and up to two years' imprisonment can be imposed. In relation to subordinate legislation, in the lower courts a maximum fine of £5,000 can be imposed or an unlimited fine in the higher courts.

See also: Catering: health and safety issues (page 121).

Sources of further information

Food Standards Agency: www.food.gov.uk.

Chartered Institute of Environmental Health: www.cieh.org.uk.

Industry Guide to Good Hygiene Practice: Catering Guide (Chadwick House Group, 1997): ISBN 0 900103 00 0.

Catering: health and safety issues

Hilary Ross, Berwin Leighton Paisner

Key points

Caterers must work in a way that protects the health and safety of employees and those people who could be affected by their activities. The law imposes general duties on caterers as employers to ensure their businesses are run safely and sets out ways in which this can be achieved.

Legislation

- Health and Safety at Work etc. Act 1974.
- Management of Health and Safety at Work Regulations 1999.
- Health and Safety (First Aid) Regulations 1981.
- Health and Safety (Miscellaneous Amendments) Regulations 2002.
- Reporting of Injuries, Diseases and Dangerous Occurrences Regulations 1995 (RIDDOR).
- Workplace (Health, Safety and Welfare) Regulations 1992.
- Fire Precautions Act 1971.
- Fire Precautions (Workplace) Regulations 1997.
- Fire Precautions (Workplace) (Amendment) Regulations 1999.
- Management of Health and Safety at Work and Fire Precautions (Workplace) (Amendment) Regulations 2003.

- Provisions for Use of Work Equipment Regulations 1998.
- Manual Handling Operations Regulations 1992.
- Control of Substances Hazardous to Health Regulations 2002.
- Health and Safety (Safety Signs and Signals) Regulations 1996.
- Electricity at Work Regulations 1989.
- Gas Safety (Installation and Use) Regulations 1998.
- Lift Operations and Lifting Equipment Regulations 1998.

Health and Safety at Work etc. Act 1974

The Health and Safety at Work etc. Act 1974 imposes a number of general duties on all employers to ensure their business is conducted in a manner that minimises health and safety risks to its employees, customers and third parties such as contractors.

Employers' general duties to em-

---

ployees include:
- devising and maintaining a safe system of work;
- providing and maintaining equipment;
- ensuring that the use, handling, storage and transport of articles and substances are done safely;
- providing training and supervision;
- maintaining the workplace (including entrances and exits) in safe condition; and
- providing a safe working environment which includes adequate facilities.

It is important to note that the general duty to provide safe conditions extends not only to employers but also to people such as landlords who exercise some control over premises or plant and equipment. The way in which an employer fulfils its duties to employees, visitors and third parties is set out in more detail in subordinate legislation.

Risk assessments

The Management of Health and Safety at Work Regulations 1999 set out in broad terms how health and safety should be managed. They provide detailed guidance, and one of the most important issues they address is the requirement to carry out risk assessments. In particular, they require that a suitable and sufficient risk assessment for the activities undertaken by the employer must be carried out.

The purpose of the risk assessment is to identify:

- hazards caused by the procedures in relation to the business's activities;
- risks that arise from those hazards; and

- procedures to eliminate or control those risks.

Where there are more than five employees, the risk assessments must be recorded in writing. Guidance issued by the HSE makes it clear that risk assessments should not be over-complicated and should highlight significant hazards that could result in serious harm or affect several people. The assessments should be reviewed from time to time to ensure that the precautions are working effectively. It should be noted that the risk assessment needs only to be suitable and sufficient. This does not mean perfect.

When carrying out the risk assessments, specific considerations should be given to vulnerable employees or third parties such as people under the age of 18 or new and expectant mothers. In relation to people under the age of 18, the risk assessment will need to take into account the young person's inexperience and immaturity and lack of awareness of risks within a workplace.

When employing contractors, etc., a copy of a risk assessment for the work they undertake should be provided by their employer. The contractors' employer should also be provided with copies of the risk assessments relating to the premises at which the work will be undertaken.

Once hazards and risks have been identified, safe systems of work should be devised to ensure that employees do not come to harm and procedures should be put in place to ensure the safety of third parties. In this respect, it is particularly important that training and information are provided to employees and appropriate third parties to ensure that they are aware of the risks and the necessary procedure to be taken to avoid them. These procedures should be encapsulated in a company health and safety manual. The manual should also set out an organisation chart detailing the health and safety responsibilities of individuals within the company.

It is also necessary to carry out a risk assessment that deals specifically with the risks arising from fire. This risk assessment must identify the steps that need to be taken to meet fire safety requirements and in particular what procedures must be followed in the event of an emergency. It is important that the risk assessment takes into account the needs of disabled people in the event of a fire. A fire certificate is not enough to meet fire safety requirements: a detailed assessment is necessary.

Safety signs

The Health and Safety (Safety Signs and Signals) Regulations 1996 provide details of signage that can be used to help control risks that have been identified in risk assessments. This includes signage to identify corrosive, flammable or explosive substances. The Regulations set out the format that signage should take, including details of the shape, colour and pattern of safety signs. It is necessary to ensure that safety signs are maintained in good condition.

Workplaces

The Workplace (Health, Safety and Welfare) Regulations 1992 aim to ensure adequate welfare facilities are provided for employees. In summary, they cover the following areas:

• The maintenance of the workplace

including equipment. In this regard steps should be taken to ensure that equipment and the workplace in general are maintained in good repair and that any problems that may arise are rectified.

• The provision of ventilation, lighting and temperature control.

• The maintenance of cleanliness in the workplace including equipment and furniture.

• Protection from falls and falling objects. This is particularly important for the catering industry as one of the greatest causes of accidents is slips, trips and falls. Employers must ensure that floors and traffic routes are of sound construction and do not present tripping or slipping hazards. These traffic routes and floors should be maintained and kept free from waste, clutter and other objects. Where floors are likely to get wet (e.g. around dishwasher areas), procedures should be put in place to minimise the risks arising from this. These could include the use of matting, a wipe-as-you-go procedure and the provision of non-slip shoes. Physical safeguards should be provided where there is a risk of somebody falling a distance likely to cause personal injury. This calls for the specific consideration of the maintenance and cleaning of windows and roofs. Windows and doors that are made of glass should contain safety glass and should be marked so they are easily visible.

• The provision of sanitary conveniences and washing facilities. When up to five people are at work at the same time, there should be at least one WC and one wash station, two of each for up to 25 workers, three for up to 50 and so on for every 25 extra workers.

- Changing and rest facilities. A rest-room (a rest area) should be provided with adequate seating for employees. There should be the provision of a warm, dry, well-ventilated area to hang personal clothing, and drinking water must be available. Where employees eat meals at work, then the means of preparing a hot drink must also be provided.

Equipment

The Provision and Use of Work Equipment Regulations 1998 set out the safety requirements for the provision and use of equipment at work. In particular, they require that equipment should be of suitable construction and design for the purpose for which it is intended. Work equipment must be used only in relation to work activities for which it is meant and it should be regularly maintained and inspected. Where appropriate, written instructions and training should be provided to enable employees to use the equipment.

Manual handling

The Manual Handling Operations Regulations 1992 prescribe measures that employers must follow to reduce the risk of injury to their employees that can arise from manual handling activities. First, employers are required to establish if the manual handling operation that gives rise to risk can be avoided altogether. This could be done by reorganisation or the introduction of mechanical aids. If the operation cannot be avoided, then it is necessary to assess the risk and try to implement controls to

reduce the risk as far as reasonably practicable.

Once a safe system of work has been devised in relation to manual handling, it is important that it is maintained and that there is adequate monitoring to ensure that there are no deviations from these procedures.

Where automated systems are introduced in place of manual handling, then regard has to be given to the Lifting Operations and Lifting Equipment Regulations 1998. Such equipment must be regularly inspected, and, where an employer does not have the requisite competence to do this, he must retain someone who does. For so long as the equipment is in use, it is necessary to keep a copy of the inspection report for two years or until the next report is made.

Control of hazardous substances

It is a necessary part of every caterer's business to deal with hazardous substances. Hazardous substances can come in many shapes and sizes such as liquids, gas, dust and micro-organisms and may occur naturally or be artificially produced. If they create a hazard to health, then it is necessary either to prevent exposure to that substance or, if this is not reasonably practicable, to control employees' and third parties' exposure to the substance. It is particularly important to assess the level, type and duration of exposure. Once this has been done, preventive or control measures can then be introduced.

The most common type of hazardous substance found in the catering industry is cleaning materials. In such cases, because the use of such hazardous substances cannot be avoided, information should be provided to employees stating what action should be taken in the event of an accident or emergency and employees should be trained on how to use the products safely.

Use of electricity

The design, installation and operation of electrical and gas systems are highly regulated. The Electricity at Work Regulations 1989 and the Gas Safety (Installation and Use) Regulations 1998 set out detailed requirements for the health and safety precautions that must be taken when dealing with gas or electricity.

Accident reporting

Employers are under an obligation to report serious work-related health and safety incidents, diseases or deaths.

The Reporting of Injuries, Diseases and Dangerous Occurrences Regulations 1995 (RIDDOR) set out which types of accidents are reportable and how quickly they should be reported. There is now a central reporting system, the Incident Contact Centre at Caerphilly.

There is a distinction between a reportable accident, which is an accident associated with work activities, and reportable diseases which require to be diagnosed by a doctor. The list of major injuries, dangerous occurrences and diseases that require to be reported are extensive. However, in summary, injuries that should be reported are:

- fractures (except of fingers or toes);
- amputations;
- dislocation of knees, hips, shoulders or spine;
- temporary or permanent loss of sight (including any penetrating injury to the eye);
- injury leading to hypothermia or heat-induced illness;

- unconsciousness;
- admittance to hospital for more than 24 hours; and
- exposure to a harmful substance(s).

Dangerous occurrences which would need to be reported include:

- the collapse, failure or overturning of load-bearing lifting machinery;
- electrical short-circuits leading to a fire explosion;
- the collapse of scaffolding; and
- the escape of any substance that could lead to death or major injury.

Reportable diseases include:

- occupational dermatitis or asthma; and
- repetitive-strain-type injuries.

Incidents that must be reported without delay are:

- a dangerous occurrence;
- death of any person due to an employer's activities;
- a major injury suffered by any person at work; and
- injury to any third party (e.g. contractors, visitors, etc.) that requires their admission to a hospital.

Although it is not specified how incidents should be reported, this must be done by the fastest means practicable, which would normally be by telephone.

Other injuries must be notified within ten days. These include a three-day injury suffered by an employee due to a work-related incident. This means that, where a person is unable to carry out work because of an injury for more than three consecutive days, then the incident must be notified. The day of the accident does not count towards this time period, but non-work days are included. There is a specific form, a form F2508, that must be completed to send to the Incident Contact Centre.

Offences

Offences under health and safety legislation can be subject to a fine of £20,000 in the lower courts and an unlimited fine in the higher courts.

Defences

There is no true defence to proceedings brought under health and safety legislation. Where a defendant can show that it did everything that was reasonably practicable (i.e. it did all that it could to prevent an accident), then proceedings may be successfully defended. However, it is notoriously difficult to mount such defences.

See also: Accidents (page 69); Catering: food safety (page 115); COSHH/ hazardous substances (page 153); Electricity and electrical equipment (page 214); Health and safety at work (page 295); Health and safety management (page 311); Manual handling (page 380); RIDDOR (page 466); Risk assessments (page 469); Safety signage (page 483).

Sources of further information

HSE: www.hse.gov.uk.

Incident Contact Centre Website: www.riddor.gov.uk.

CCTV monitoring

Victoria Sedgwick and Emilia Linde, Bird & Bird

Introduction

Increasingly CCTV has become the principal method of carrying out surveillance of areas of public access, although most members of the public remain unaware and largely unconcerned over the presence of cameras. Primarily, it is claimed, CCTV is a benefit as it can protect both the public and property, but there is no escaping the fact that CCTV can also be misused as a means of covert observation.

Few of us actively object to the use of CCTV, recognising that there are benefits to the community that may override any concerns of a 'Big Brother' approach to policing. However, this attitude does not naturally extend to the use of CCTV cameras in the workplace: employees remain suspicious of any form of surveillance by their employers at work and the Information Commissioner has recognised that special considerations apply in that particular context.

Data Protection Act 1998

The introduction of the Data Protection Act 1998 may have given reassurance to users and subjects of video recording alike as it brought in systematic legal controls over CCTV surveillance. However, since the Court of Appeal case of *Durant -v- Financial Services Authority* (2003), it has become clear that not all

CCTV usage is covered by the Data Protection Act. Thus, in order for the Act to apply, the information in question has to affect the subject's privacy. The subject's privacy is deemed to be affected if he is the focus of the information, and if the information reveals something significant about him. If these two criteria have not been met, the Data Protection Act may not apply to the information captured. Thus, if only a general scene is recorded without any incident taking place, and with no focus on any specific individual's activities, these images will fall outside the Data Protection Act. More information about the Durant case is available from the Office of the Information Commissioner or from his website. Contact details can be found in 'Sources of further information' on page 130.

However, if images of individuals are processed and an individual can be identified either from those images on their own, or in conjunction with any other information that a controller of the system has, or is likely to have, in its possession, then these images will amount to personal data.

It is also worth noting that 'sensitive personal data' (for which the Act applies more stringent processing guidelines) includes information about the commission or alleged commission of any offence and about any proceedings for an offence committed or alleged to have been committed.

Human Rights Act 1998

Indiscriminate and unjustified use of CCTV surveillance and monitoring could also potentially be a breach of the Human Rights Act in relation to the right to respect for privacy.

Code of Practice for Users of CCTV

The Information Commissioner finalised and published a CCTV Code of Practice in July 2000. It sets out the measures that must be adopted in order to ensure that the CCTV scheme complies with the Data Protection Act and goes on to offer guidance for good practice.

The Code of Practice does not apply to:

- targeted and intrusive surveillance activities (covered by the Regulation of Investigatory Powers Act 2000);
- use of surveillance techniques by employers to monitor their employees (to be covered by a Code of Practice on the Use of Personal Data in Employer/Employee Relationships);
- security equipment (including cameras) installed in homes by individuals for home security purposes (likely to be exempt from the Act); or
- use of cameras by the media for journalism or artistic or literary purposes.

The Code is available from the Office of the Information Commissioner or from his website. The full text should be consulted, but the main practical requirements are summarised in the following paragraphs.

Users must conduct an initial assessment before installing and using CCTV.

They must establish the purposes for which they need CCTV and ensure that a notification has been lodged with the Office of the Information Commissioner which covers those purposes.

Cameras should be positioned in such a way as they can only monitor areas intended to be covered by the CCTV scheme. The operators of the equipment must be aware that they may only use the equipment in order to achieve the purpose notified to the Information Commissioner. If possible, movement of the cameras should be restricted so that the operators cannot monitor areas not intended to be covered.

Clearly visible and legible signs should be used to inform the public that they are entering a zone which is monitored. The signs should contain the following information:

- the identity of the person or organisation responsible for the scheme;
- the purpose of the scheme; and
- details of whom to contact regarding the scheme.

The contact point should be available to members of the public during office hours, and employees staffing the contact point should be aware of the relevant policies and procedures.

Signs may be inappropriate where CCTV is used to obtain evidence of criminal activity. However, the Code sets out tight controls over the use of CCTV in these circumstances.

The images captured by CCTV equipment should be as clear as possible, to ensure that they are effective for the purposes intended. Cameras should be properly maintained and serviced and good-quality tapes used. If they record dates and times, these should be accurate. Consideration must also be given to the physical conditions in the camera locations (e.g. infrared equipment may need to be used in poorly lit areas).

Images should not be retained for longer than necessary. While they are retained, access to, and security of, the images must be controlled in accordance with the Seventh Data Protection Principle of the Act, which sets out security requirements. If images are disclosed, the reasons for disclosure must be compatible with the purposes notified to the Information Commissioner. All access to or disclosure of the images should be documented.

The Information Commissioner has also issued some guidance on the use of CCTV systems following the Durant case.

Employment Practices Code

The Information Commissioner published Part 3 of the Employment Practices Code on Monitoring at Work in June 2003. This publication spells out the basic 'dos and don'ts' for employers who monitor the activities of their employees. In doing so, the Information Commissioner has attempted to strike a balance between the needs of employers and the needs of employees.

The Code stresses the need for proportionality: any adverse impact of monitoring must be justified by the benefits to the employer and others. In order to assess whether monitoring is justified, the Code envisages that organisations will carry out impact assessments to determine the purpose and likely impact of monitoring, whether there are any alternatives and what obligations will arise. Continuous monitoring of employees is only likely to be justified where there are particular safety or security concerns that cannot be adequately met in other, less intrusive ways.

All employees and visitors should be aware that CCTV is in operation and of the purposes for which the information will be used. Covert monitoring of performance cannot be justified except in very limited circumstances: specifically, where openness would prejudice the prevention or detection of crime or the apprehension of offenders. However, before covert monitoring is used, among other things, employers must identify specific criminal activity and establish that there is a need to use covert monitoring to obtain evidence. Employers should ensure that covert monitoring is not used in areas employees could reasonably expect to be private.

Employees and trade unions have resisted the placing of CCTV cameras in the workplace. At Guy's and St Thomas' Hospitals the public sector union UNISON threatened industrial action over the placing of surveillance cameras in locker rooms.

However, where employees or their trade unions perceive a benefit in such surveillance techniques, acceptance of the cameras is likely to follow – e.g. where CCTV surveillance at work is for security purposes or is intended solely to detect, and so protect employees from, intruders. The monitoring of construction sites is now commonplace and in a recent industrial dispute involving workers on the Jubilee line, security data was used in reverse of its usual application to prove that union members could not have been in the vicinity of a suspected act of vandalism.

British Standard

The British Standards Institution has

issued the Code of Practice BS 7958:1999 'Closed-circuit television (CCTV): management and operation', which covers the handling of CCTV video materials. It requires that appropriate security measures are taken to prevent unauthorised access to or alteration, disclosure, accidental loss or destruction of recorded material so that an audit security trail can be established. This addresses the concerns of organisations such as the British Securities Industry Association that modern digital imaging systems have the capability to fabricate a video and wrongly implicate an individual in a crime. The BSIA has pointed out that it is essential for maintaining the integrity of actual CCTV images to adopt procedures which can be readily subjected to an audit trail.

Conclusion

Workplace managers responsible for CCTV use should familiarise themselves with the Information Commissioner's Code of Practice on CCTV and Employment Practices Data Protection Code. Clear guidelines for use should be given to the camera operators and care should be taken in relation to the placing of warning signs, to ensure that inadvertent breaches of the Data Protection Act and the Human Rights Act do not occur.

> *See also*: Data protection (page 163); Monitoring employees (page 392).

Sources of further information

More information can be obtained from the Information Commissioner's website (www.informationcommissioner.gov.uk) or from the enquiry line on 01625 545745.

CCTV User Group: PeterCCTV@aol.com.

'Data Protection Policy and Management Guide, version 1.0' (ISBN 1 900648 33 4, £34.99) is available as an electronic download from the Workplace Law Network. Call 0870 777 8881 for details, or visit www.workplacelaw.net.

CDM

Raymond Joyce, Joyce Legal

Introduction

One of the remarkable characteristics of the Construction (Design and Management) Regulations 1994 (CDM Regulations) has been the continuing debate and commensurate professional press coverage as to whether the intended benefits of the Regulations have been realised. The HSE has said that there will be a review of the Regulations, and there is a genuine prospect that the role of the planning supervisor will change radically or disappear altogether. For the time being, however, the Regulations continue to be enforced and there are many professionals who believe that they have had a beneficial impact on the construction industry. Recently there has been more attention given to the role of designers in promoting safer construction, and consequently designers can expect to attract more interest from the HSE now and as part of the intended review.

Do the CDM Regulations apply?

Many building and construction operations are small enough to be excluded from the CDM Regulations. In all cases demolition comes within the full ambit of the Regulations.

Apply the CDM Regulations if there is any doubt. The flow chart on page 132 is a quick reference to indicate whether the work is subject to the Regulations.

The procurement process

Who is the client? In the case of facilities management, the identity of the client, for the purposes of the CDM Regulations, is a crucial decision (Regulation 4). The owner of the facility can be the client and that is the obvious choice. However, because the management of real estate is increasingly being outsourced, the client can be the contractor.

The most important role for the client is the appointment of the planning supervisor and the principal contractor. The client must also ensure that a health and safety plan is completed before construction starts (see below).

The role of the planning supervisor

Some training for this role is certainly required, but the idea behind the scheme is that practising construction professionals can assume the role of planning supervisor, although not necessarily to the exclusion of other contributions to a project.

The main responsibilities of the planning supervisor are as follows:

- Completion of notice to the HSE (Regulation 7).
- Ensuring, so far as is reasonably practicable, that the design of any structure includes adequate regard to:
  – the avoidance of foreseeable risks;

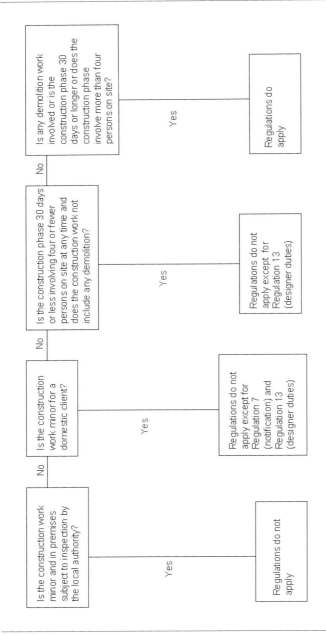

CDM flowchart. Do the CDM Regulations apply?

Is the construction work minor and in premises subject to inspection by the local authority?

No → Is the construction work minor for a domestic client?

No → Is the construction phase 30 days or less involving four or fewer persons on site at any time and does the construction work not include any demolition?

No → Is any demolition work involved or is the construction phase 30 days or longer or does the construction phase involve more than four persons on site?

Yes → Regulations do not apply

Yes → Regulations do not apply except for Regulation 7 (notification) and Regulation 13 (designer duties)

Yes → Regulations do not apply except for Regulation 13 (designer duties)

Yes → Regulations do apply

– combating risks at source; and

– giving priority to measures which will protect all persons at work (Regulation 14(a)).

- Provision of adequate information by the designer (Regulation 13(2)(b)).
- Communication between designers (Regulation 13(2)(c)).
- Arranging preparation of the health and safety plan (Regulation 15(1)).
- Creation or updating of the health and safety file (Regulation 14(d) and (e)).

In facilities management the obligation to maintain a health and safety file should not be underestimated. This document should always be included in the information provided to designers and made available to all interested parties. It would not be unreasonable to overstate the serious commercial and technical consequences of omitting to pay due regard to the health and safety file.

The designer

The Construction (Design and Management) (Amendment) Regulations 2000 changed the definition of a designer. The definition of a designer introduced by Regulation 2(1) is limited to a person who 'prepares a design' in the course of his work. Additionally, Regulation 2(3A) provides that any reference in the Regulations to a person preparing a design shall include a reference to his employee or other person at work under his control preparing it for him. The change ensures that the duty in Regulation 13(2) (Requirements on designer) applies to a person where his employee or other such person prepares a design for him. This position closes the loophole created by the Court of Appeal case of *R -v- Paul Wurth SA*.

The duties of the designer are:

- to make the client aware of its duties (Regulation 13(1));
- to give adequate regard to health and safety in the design (Regulation 13(2)(a));
- to provide adequate information about the health and safety risks of the design to those who need it (Regulation 13(2)(b)); and
- to co-operate with the planning supervisor and, if appropriate, other designers (Regulation 13(2)(c)).

Principal contractor

The appointment of the principal contractor is mandatory on all construction work covered by the CDM Regulations. Contracting includes the management of construction.

Doing the work brings the risk assessments to the fore. Up to and until work starts, the work of the designer and planning supervisor has been an intellectual effort. It is not surprising therefore that the principal contractor has a long list of obligations and requirements:

- Completion of the health and safety plan (Regulation 16).
- Introduction of procedures to ensure co-operation between all contractors (Regulation 16(1)(a)).
- Ensuring compliance with rules in the health and safety plan (Regulation 16(1)(b)).
- Controlling access to site of authorised persons (Regulation 16(1)(c)).
- Displaying a notice including the particulars of the work as provided to the HSE (Regulation 16(1)(d)).
- Provision of further information to the planning supervisor for inclusion in the health and safety file

(Regulation 16(1)(e)).

- Management of the site including directions to other contractors and making of rules (Regulations 16(2) and 17(1)).
- Bringing the rules in the health and safety plan to the attention of persons who may be affected by them (Regulation 16(3)).
- Training in health and safety (Regulation 17(2)).
- Making arrangements for feedback from employees and self-employed persons (Regulation 18).

Competence (Regulation 8) and adequate resources (Regulation 9)

The CDM Regulations require that all of the parties to a construction project should be competent and have adequate resources to perform the functions and obligations created by the Regulations.

It has been difficult to convey to those involved in construction that there is no prescriptive formula as to whether a person is, or is not, competent and has adequate resources.

The CDM Regulations compel the parties to address the issues of competence and adequate resources and therefore there must be evidence of some attempt to find the answers.

Sources of further information

Joyce, R. E.: *The CDM Regulations Explained*, 2nd edition (Thomas Telford, 2001): ISBN 0 7277 3036 3.

McLennan, Peter, Nutt, Bev and Walters, Roger: *Refurbishing Occupied Buildings: Management of risk under the CDM Regulations* (Thomas Telford, 1998): ISBN 0 7277 2732 X.

HSC, Construction Advisory Committee: 'A guide to managing health and safety in construction' (HSE Books, 1995): ISBN 0 7176 0755 0.
HSC, Construction Advisory Committee: 'Designing for health and safety in construction: a guide for designers on the Construction (Design and Management) Regulations 1994' (HSE Books, 1995): ISBN 0 7176 0807 7.

The following HSE information sheets may be downloaded from www.hse.gov.uk:

Construction Sheet No. 39: The role of the client.
Construction Sheet No. 41: The role of the designer.
Construction Sheet No. 43: The health and safety plan during the construction phase.
Construction Sheet No. 44: The health and safety file.

Association for Project Safety (formerly the Association of Planning Supervisors): www.aps.org.uk.

Obviously a knowledge of health and safety practice gained by attendance on courses and experience and an understanding of the CDM Regulations are a good starting point.

Health and safety plan

Regulation 15 sets out the requirements of the health and safety plan which covers the pre-tender and pre-construction stages. The health and safety plan has been the cause of an enormous proliferation of paperwork associated with construction works, much of which has been totally unnecessary. The health and safety plan should contain detail in proportion to the nature, size and level of health and safety risks involved. The value of a health and safety plan is all the greater if it is read. The skills required in writing an adequate health and safety plan draw upon a genuine understanding and expertise in identifying hazards and associated risks.

The health and safety plan is often overlooked as being a linchpin of the entire health and safety management scheme. Regulation 10 states: 'Every client shall ensure, so far as is reasonably practicable, that the construction phase of any project does not start unless a health and safety plan complying with regulation 15(4) has been prepared in respect of that project.'

Health and safety file

In the project management of maintaining fixed assets, the health and safety file is a very important document. The health and safety file should be reviewed and updated to accommodate changes to the fixed asset which in turn may affect the hazards and risks for future maintenance, including ultimately demolition. A failure to maintain this document so that it is available to all interested parties and in particular to planning supervisors is at worst a criminal offence and at best professionally negligent.

The commercial consequences of failing to have an adequate health and safety plan can affect the future sale of the fixed asset and/or the ability to raise finance.

See also: Construction site health and safety (page 145).

Childcare provisions

Carolyn King, Charles Russell Employment and Pensions Service Group

Key points

- The workforce of employers throughout the UK is largely made up of individuals, both male and female, who have responsibility for the care of children and who have childcare needs.
- A number of family-friendly rights are granted to such individuals of which employers must be aware.
- As well as having to comply with the legal and statutory obligations, employers are now increasingly being encouraged, through campaigns such as the Work-Life Balance Campaign, to support Government-driven initiatives which assist employees and workers to meet their childcare needs.

Legislation

- Workplace (Health, Safety and Welfare) Regulations 1992.
- Family-friendly legislation (see 'Family-friendly rights', page 251). The so-called family-friendly legislation now encompasses a wide variety of rights (granted to employees but not workers) which employees may exercise in order to assist them with their childcare needs. By way of summary, these rights include:
  – maternity leave and adoption leave of up to 52 weeks;
  – paternity leave of either one or two consecutive weeks, for which statutory paternity pay is payable;
  – unpaid parental leave of up to 13 weeks for each child up to the child's fifth birthday (or 18 weeks' leave in the case of a disabled child up to the child's eighteenth birthday);
  – for parents of children under 6 (or 18 if disabled) who have responsibility for the child's upbringing, the right to request a flexible working arrangement. This is the most recent of the family-friendly provisions, and arguably the most significant.

Workplace nurseries and employer-supported childcare

According to Daycare Trust, the national childcare charity, only one in ten employers offer assistance to their staff with childcare, 5% of workplaces offer nursery places and 5% of employers offer financial assistance towards childcare costs. Government-driven and trade-union-backed initiatives such as the SureStart Strategy seek to encourage greater employer-supported childcare through various schemes. Under these schemes, employees sacrifice a portion of their salary to be paid towards childcare costs. There are tax incentives available to both employer and employee in respect of that portion of the salary sacrificed. The schemes include the following:

- *Workplace nurseries*. This is where the employer is wholly or partly responsible for funding and managing the provision of childcare facilities (either a workplace nursery or an in-house/on-site holiday playscheme) on work premises. For small employers, this can be done jointly with other companies. In respect of this cost, the employer is exempt from employer's National Insurance contributions (NICs) and the employee is exempt from employee's Class 1 NICs and income tax.

- *Childcare vouchers*. These can be issued to childcare providers to pay for all forms of childcare, both registered and unregistered. There are tax incentives and savings available to both employer and employee who are exempt from making NICs. Changes to the childcare voucher scheme are due to come into effect in April 2005 which will exempt the payment of income tax by the employee and will require the employer to offer the vouchers to all staff in order to benefit from the tax/NIC exemptions (at present, employers can choose which staff are entitled to receive the voucher). The April 2005 changes will also mean that the vouchers can only be used to pay for registered or approved childcare.

- *Childcare subsidies*. An example would include a £5-a-day subsidy for a holiday playscheme. Employers are exempt from employer's NICs and, as a result of the changes in April 2005, employees will also benefit from both income tax and NIC exemptions. The April 2005 changes will also require employers to offer the subsidy to all staff in order to benefit from the tax/NIC exemptions (at present, employers can choose which staff are entitled to the subsidy).

- *Enhanced employee rights*. An increasing number of employers are opting to provide enhanced maternity, paternity and parental leave rights over and above the statutory minimum levels, extra statutory emergency leave to deal with a sick child or problems with childcare, and career breaks or sabbaticals.

Health and safety considerations

In the case of workers who bring their children to work, a number of health and safety considerations must be borne in mind.

In addition to the common law duty of care that an employer owes to provide its workers with a safe place of work, the employer also owes a common law duty of care to visitors while they are on its premises under the concept of occupier's liability. This will extend to children while they are in the workplace. The legislation states that employers must be 'prepared for children to be less careful than adults'. It is therefore essential, in any situation where children are present in the workplace, either in the provision of a workplace nursery or otherwise, that a full risk assessment is carried out and that health and safety risks are regularly monitored. Employers should also ensure that sufficient insurance arrangements are in place to safeguard against any incidents involving children in the workplace.

Under the Workplace (Health, Safety and Welfare) Regulations 1992, employers must comply with specific obligations with regard to employees who are pregnant or breast-feeding. An employer must provide suitable rest facilities for such workers which are suitably located (e.g. close to toilet facilities). Where necessary, the employer should provide appropriate facilities for new or expectant mothers to lie down. In this regard, employers are best advised to speak to the individual concerned to discuss what adjustments or alterations, if any, are necessary. A breach of the health and safety legislation in relation to new and expectant mothers can have serious consequences for an employer, rendering it liable to a claim for sex discrimination or even criminal prosecution following a complaint to the HSE.

See also: Family-friendly rights (page 251); Flexible working (page 280); New and expectant mothers (page 398); Occupier's liability (page 409).

Sources of further information

Inland Revenue: www.inlandrevenue.gov.uk.

Sure Start is a Government programme aiming to increase the availability of childcare: www.surestart.gov.uk.

Working Families: www.workingfamilies.org.uk.

Daycare Trust, the national childcare charity campaign, has useful information for employers on how they can become involved in childcare initiatives: www.daycaretrust.org.uk.

Children at work

Carolyn King, Charles Russell Employment and Pensions
Service Group

Key points

- A child is a person not over compulsory school age (i.e. up to the last Friday in June in the academic year of his sixteenth birthday). Note that a young person (see page 139) is a person who has ceased to be a child but is under 18.
- The employment of children in the UK is subject to limitations regarding the number of hours that they can work.
- Children also have a number of special rights and protections in the workplace justified on health and safety grounds. It is important for all employers of children to be aware of the legal framework.
- Any organisation employing a child of compulsory school age must inform the local education authority in order to obtain an employment permit for that child. Without one, the child may not be covered under the terms of the employer's insurance policy. (This does not apply, however, in respect of children who are carrying out work experience arranged by their school.)

Legislation

- Children and Young Persons Act 1933 (as amended).
- Employment Rights Act 1996 (as amended).
- Education Act 1996 (as amended).
- Management of Health and Safety at Work Regulations 1999.
- Children (Protection at Work) Regulations 1998 (implementing the provisions of the EC Directive on the Protection of Young People at Work (94/33/EC)).
- Working Time Regulations 1998.
- Working Time (Amendment) Regulations 2002.

In addition, the United Nations Convention on the Rights of the Child (for these purposes, all persons under 18) provides that Member States have an obligation to protect children at work, set minimum ages for employment and regulate conditions of employment

Key restrictions on the employment of children

No child may be employed to carry out any work whatsoever (whether paid or unpaid) if he is under the age of 14. This is subject to some specific exceptions, e.g. in relation to children working in television, the theatre or modelling.

A child may not:

- do any work other than light work;

- work in any industrial setting such as a factory or industrial site;
- work during school hours on a school day;
- work before 7 a.m. or after 7 p.m.;
- work for more than two hours on any school day;
- work for more than 12 hours in any week during term time;
- work more than two hours on a Sunday;
- work for more than eight hours on any day he is not required to attend school (other than a Sunday) (or five hours in the case of children under 15);
- work for more than 35 hours in any week during school holidays (or 25 hours in the case of children under the age of 15); or
- work for more than four hours in any day without a rest break of at least one hour; or
- work without having a two-week break from any work during the school holidays in each calendar year.

Entitlement to holidays and time off

Under the Working Time Regulations 1998, all adult employees are entitled to at least four weeks' paid annual leave. In the case of *Addison -v- Ashby* [2003] IRLR 211, however, the Employment Appeal Tribunal ruled that this entitlement does not apply to a child. The Children and Young Persons Act 1933 provides that a child is entitled to two consecutive weeks without employment during a school holiday; however, this period of time is unpaid.

Health and safety considerations

The main source of health and safety legislation in relation to the employment of a child or young person is the Management of Health and Safety at Work Regulations 1999. Under these Regulations, the term 'young person' means any person under 18.

- Before a young person starts work, the employer must carry out a risk assessment taking into account various issues such as the inexperience and immaturity of the young person, the nature of the workstation, the risks in the workplace including the equipment which the young person will use, and the extent of health and safety training provided.
- Young persons cannot be employed to carry out any work:
  – beyond their physical or psychological capacity (such as heavy manual labour);
  – involving harmful exposure to toxic or carcinogenic agents or radiation;
  – involving the risk of an accident which a young person is more likely to suffer owing to his insufficient attention to safety or lack of experience; or
  – in which there is a risk to health from extreme cold, heat, noise or vibration.

A breach of the Regulations, if sufficiently serious, could lead to criminal prosecution following a complaint to the HSE.

See also: Risk assessments (page 469); Working time (page 552); Young persons (page 561).

Sources of further information

Department of Trade and Industry: www.dti.gov.uk.

Confined spaces

David Sharp, Workplace Law Group

Key points

- Each year around 15 people are killed as a result of accidents from work in confined spaces, and dozens more are injured. The most common causes are asphyxiation through lack of oxygen and poisoning through exposure to dangerous substances.
- The Confined Spaces Regulations 1997 were introduced to put stricter controls on work in confined spaces. They include a definition of confined spaces and the risks associated with working in them.

Legislation

- Confined Spaces Regulations 1997.
- Electricity at Work Regulations 1989.
- Health and Safety at Work etc. Act 1974.
- Management of Health and Safety at Work Regulations 1999.
- Control of Substances Hazardous to Health Regulations 1999.
- Personal Protective Equipment at Work Regulations 1992.
- Provision and Use of Work Equipment Regulations 1998.
- Workplace (Health, Safety and Welfare) Regulations 1992.

Work in confined spaces

Work in confined spaces is especially hazardous and should be eliminated wherever possible – there has to be a very good reason why such work is required. The risks from work in confined spaces relate to access to and egress from the confined space, as well as work undertaken in the confined space itself.

The definition of a 'confined space' is set out in the Confined Spaces Regulations 1997. It means 'any place, including chamber, tank, vat, silo, pit, trench, pipe, sewer, flue, well or similar space in which, by virtue of its enclosed nature, there arises a reasonably foreseeable specified risk'.

'Specified risk' is defined as 'a risk arising to any person at work of: serious injury arising from fire or explosion; loss of consciousness arising from an increase in body temperature; loss of consciousness or asphyxiation arising from gas, fume, vapour or the lack of oxygen; drowning arising from the increase in the level of liquid; and asphyxiation arising from a free flowing solid or because of entrapment by it'.

The two principal risks of work in confined spaces come from the potential presence or build-up of dangerous substances (such as toxic gases, vapours or

fumes) and from the potential deprivation of oxygen. The danger of asphyxiation from entering confined spaces is
well known. A lack of oxygen, and in
some instances the build-up of hazardous gases such as carbon dioxide and
hydrogen sulphide, can result in people
being quickly overcome with little or no
warning before they become unconscious.

The nature of the task can make the
work especially hazardous, particularly if
it requires the use of welding equipment,
solvents or spark-emitting machinery.

Other risk factors include: mechanical
hazards, such as entanglement with
machinery such as drilling equipment;
lone working, which is sometimes
required in confined spaces; and the
potential instability of the space, e.g.
where there is a risk of collapse when
working in trenches.

A risk assessment should be undertaken by a competent person who has
experience of the type of work to be
undertaken. It is likely that the findings
of the risk assessment will be documented in a permit to work. A permit to
work will normally be required for any
work undertaken in confined spaces to
ensure that strict controls are in place
before work can begin. Control measures
will include: stringent monitoring of air
and ventilation; provision of respiratory
equipment; training and supervision of
competent workers; and proper consideration of emergency procedures.

Case summary

There have been dozens of cases where
workers have died or suffered injuries
from work in confined spaces. In July
2004 the HSE issued a further warning to
the manufacturing industry following
the deaths of three employees in a slurry
tank. The employees, working on a farm
near Thetford, Norfolk, were asphyxiated
in the tank after being overcome by
carbon dioxide. A fourth worker, who
also entered the tank, was fortunate to
escape with his life.

The HSE was keen to emphasise the
importance not only of assessing the
risks, but also of ensuring that safe systems of work are implemented. 'This incident highlights the risks common to all
industries and everyone ... It's no good
managers implementing a safe system of
work and assuming employees will
follow it. Workers need to be carefully
trained and supervised by a competent
manager. Senior management must
carry out regular checks to be sure the
correct procedures are always followed.'

In 2002 the Workplace Law Network
reported on A & P Falmouth Ltd, a ship
repair company based in Cornwall,
which was fined £10,000 plus £6,627
costs after pleading guilty of failure to
ensure the health and safety of two
employees.

During February 2001 John Webb and
Desmond Martin were carrying out
repair work for the company on a split
hopper barge. A little after midnight
when they had finished work on the hull
of the vessel, the two men climbed into a
port void 12.5m × 6m × 4.5m through a
small manhole to start painting, using a
paint containing xylene and butanone
solvents. Although he was in a 'dazed
and drunken-like condition', Mr Webb
managed to climb out of the tank to get
medical help, while Mr Martin lay
unconscious. Both men were taken
straight to hospital, but fortunately neither suffered from long-term injury.

The HSE prosecuting inspector, David

Corey, said: 'The risks of working in confined spaces like this tank, with solvent-based paints, are well known, as are the precautions that need to be taken. The men should have been trained, informed and supervised to a higher standard than was the case on this occasion. The systems of work and entry procedures should have ensured the full and correct use of the necessary personal protective equipment, there should have been some form of forced ventilation provided, and the provision for raising the alarm should have been made.'

See also: COSHH/hazardous substances (page 153); Lone working (page 374); Permits to work (page 422).

Sources of further information

INDG258 'Safe work in confined spaces' (HSE Books, 1997): ISBN 0 7176 1442 5.

L101 'Safe work in confined spaces. Approved Code of Practice, Regulations and guidance' (HSE Books, 1997): ISBN 0 7176 1405 0.

Construction site health and safety

David Menzies, SafetyCO UK

Legislation

* Construction (Health, Safety and Welfare) Regulations 1996.

Purpose of the Regulations

The Construction (Health, Safety and Welfare) Regulations came into force on 2 September 1996 and replaced various Regulations from the 1960s. However, the Construction (Head Protection) Regulations 1989 remain in place. The 1996 Regulations are designed to preserve the health, safety and welfare of everyone who carries out 'construction work' as well as protecting others affected by this work. They lay down detailed requirements for ways of working when carrying out construction work.

It should be noted that the present Regulations dealing specifically with working at height are likely to be changed, or replaced altogether, when the Work at Height Regulations come into force some time in 2005.

When do the Regulations apply?

The Regulations apply to 'construction work' carried out by a person at work. Construction work is broadly defined as 'the carrying out of any building, civil engineering or engineering construction work'.

The Regulations do not apply to a workplace on a construction site which is set aside for non-construction work. The Workplace (Health, Safety and Welfare) Regulations 1992 apply to such workplaces (e.g. on-site catering rooms, office facilities).

The Regulations cover a wide range of activities such as taking precautions against falls and work on structures together with matters such as traffic routes, emergency procedures and weather protection. The full list of all items covered by the Regulations can be found in the table on page 146. Some of the Regulations (those marked with an asterisk in the table) only apply to construction work at a construction site. 'Construction site' is defined as 'a workplace where the principal activity being carried out is construction work'.

The remaining Regulations have a wider application, as they apply to construction work carried out by a person at work, irrespective of whether this work is carried out at a construction site.

Who has duties under the Regulations?

* Employers whose employees carry out construction work.
* Every self-employed person carrying out construction work.
* Every person who controls the way in

Summary of Construction (Health, Safety and Welfare) Regulations 1996

Duty	Regulations
Safe place of work	5
Precautions against falls	6 and 7
Falling objects	8
Work on structures, demolition or dismantling and explosives	9, 10 and 11
Excavations, cofferdams and caissons	12 and 13
Prevention of drowning	14
Traffic routes*	15
Doors and gates	16
Vehicles	17
Prevention of risk from fire	18
Emergency routes and exits*	19
Emergency procedures*	20
Fire detection and firefighting*	21
Welfare facilities (including the provision of sanitary and washing facilities, supply of drinking water, and provision of rest facilities and facilities to change and store clothing)*	22
Provision of fresh air	23
Temperature and weather protection	24
Lighting	25
Good order on the construction site*	26
Training	28
Inspection	29
Reports	30

*denotes Regulations which apply to construction work carried out on a construction site only.

which construction work is carried out.

- Every employee who carries out construction work.
- Every person at work has a duty to co-operate and report defects to ensure compliance.

Duties under the Regulations

The general duty: Regulation 5

Regulation 5 imposes a general duty, so far as is reasonably practicable, to ensure a safe place of work and safe means of access to and from that place of work without risk to the health and safety of any person at work there. In particular, management or supervisory duties include those outlined below.

Training: Regulation 28

Where necessary to reduce the risk of injury to any person, every person carrying out construction work shall possess the necessary training, technical knowledge or experience.

Alternatively, they should be under such degree of supervision by a person having such training, knowledge or experience as may be appropriate, having regard to the nature of the activity.

Inspection: Regulation 29

Regulation 29 provides that the following places of work shall only be used to carry out construction work if that place of work has been inspected by a competent person:

- Any working platform or part thereof or any personal suspension equipment provided pursuant to paragraph 3(b) or (c) of Regulation 6 (Precautions against falls).
- Any excavation support pursuant to Regulation 12.
- Cofferdams (watertight enclosures

pumped dry for work in building bridges) and caissons (watertight chambers inside which work can be carried out on underwater structures).

Further, where a place of work includes any of the above three, any employer (or other person in control of the way construction is carried out) shall ensure the scaffold, excavation, cofferdam or caisson is stable and of sound construction and the safeguards required by the Regulations are in place *before* their employees first use that place of work.

The further requirements in respect of the timing of inspections can be found in the Regulations at Schedule 7.

Reports: Regulation 30

Where an inspection is required under Regulation 29, the person who carries out the inspection shall prepare a report, which includes particulars specified by the Regulations.

See also: Emergency procedures (page 218); Means of fighting fire (page 267); Fire risk assessments (page 271); Head protection (page 293); Health and safety at work (page 295); Risk assessments (page 469); Working at height (page 321).

Sources of further information

HSG150 'Health and safety in construction' (HSE Books, 1996): ISBN 0 7176 2106 5.

HSG224 'Managing health and safety in construction' (HSE Books, 2001): ISBN 0 7176 2139 1.

'Designing for health and safety in construction' (HSE Books, 1995): ISBN 0 7176 0807 7.

Contract disputes

Rupert Choat, CMS Cameron McKenna

Key points

As disputes are expensive and time-consuming, it is advisable to manage them by:

- including appropriate dispute resolution provisions in contracts;
- anticipating disputes in record-keeping practices; and
- handling disputes effectively.

Legislation

- Arbitration Act 1996.
- Housing Grants, Construction and Regeneration Act 1996.

Dispute resolution provisions in contracts

Wherever possible, when drafting any pro-forma contracts and when negotiating contracts, it is advisable to consider the various available dispute resolution methods and to include clauses providing for the chosen method(s). Some 'picking and mixing' of methods is possible.

Negotiation

Discussions invariably occur before any dispute goes to formal proceedings. Even if formal proceedings are commenced, negotiation remains one of the most effective ways of resolving disputes.

It may help to discuss disputes on a 'without prejudice' basis, so that what is said cannot be referred to later in any formal proceedings. This can promote a frank exchange of views.

Some contracts provide for a structured approach to discussions. For instance, a dispute may be required to be considered initially by those at project level. If this is unsuccessful within a specified time, the dispute may go to board or principal level. The contract might make compliance with this procedure a precondition to the commencement of any formal proceedings.

Court proceedings

Generally, unless the contract otherwise provides (e.g. by providing for arbitration), the courts can decide the parties' disputes.

Proceedings are started by issuing a claim form.

The Civil Procedure Rules govern court proceedings.

The courts deal with disputes according to their value and complexity. Directions are given to the parties to prepare their dispute for trial. Directions usually provide for the production of statements of case, disclosure of documents, exchange of witness statements and expert reports (if necessary).

Court proceedings are public.

Arbitration

Parties to a contract can agree that their disputes will be resolved by arbitration rather than by the courts. This can be done either in the contract or 'ad hoc' once a dispute arises.

The Arbitration Act 1996 governs arbitration.

Generally the parties decide who the arbitrator(s) will be, or, failing that, a nominating body decides. The parties can agree the procedure for the arbitration by which the dispute will be decided. They might agree on a procedure similar to court proceedings or they might opt for the dispute being decided on paper without a hearing.

Arbitration is a confidential process.

One disadvantage of arbitration is that third parties cannot be joined in the arbitration without the consent of all concerned. This is not the case with court proceedings.

Adjudication

The Housing Grants, Construction and Regeneration Act 1996 empowers a party to a written 'construction contract' to refer any dispute arising under the contract to adjudication. The option to go to adjudication exists in addition to the right to go to court or arbitration (whichever is applicable).

Adjudication is rough and ready but usually cheaper than court proceedings or arbitration. The appointed adjudicator is required to reach a decision within 28 days of the dispute being referred to him (subject to extensions). The adjudicator's decision is temporarily binding pending the outcome of any subsequent court proceedings or arbitration.

There is some uncertainty as to the extent to which facilities management contracts are construction contracts. To avoid confusion it is usually sensible to provide expressly for adjudication in such contracts.

Alternative dispute resolution (ADR)

Parties to a contract can agree that their disputes will be resolved by any of a number of forms of ADR. This can be done either in the contract or 'ad hoc' once the dispute arises. The parties may agree that ADR is a precondition to court proceedings or arbitration.

- One method of ADR is mediation. The parties or an appointing body of the parties' choice appoint the mediator, whose role is facilitating the resolution of the dispute. The mediation is held 'without prejudice'. The process is non-binding. Any party can withdraw at any time, and there is no guarantee of a resolution at the end of the mediation.

- Another method of ADR is expert determination. It is particularly suited to disputes that turn on technical rather than legal issues. A third-party expert is appointed to reach a decision on the dispute. The parties agree a (usually short) timetable that may allow them to make submissions to the expert. The parties may agree that the expert's decision will be final and binding or that it will be subject to review by the courts or arbitration.

Record keeping

Good documentary records tend to help in resolving disputes and may reduce any legal costs you incur.

Bear in mind that in court and arbitration proceedings you will invariably be directed to disclose to the other party relevant documents under your control (including documents that are prejudicial to your case). Disclosable documents will include emails and other electronic documents. Documents are generally disclosable even if they contain confidential information.

It is advisable to retain documents for between six and 15 years after the matter to which they relate ends (depending upon the nature of the contract).

Handling disputes

When a dispute arises, try to address it early rather than allowing it to escalate. If it is not possible to resolve the dispute by discussion, check the contract to see which dispute resolution method(s) apply. Consider also whether you want to suggest another method not provided for by the contract (e.g. mediation). In some cases statute may dictate that a certain dispute resolution method applies even if it is not specified in the contract (e.g. adjudication in construction contracts).

It invariably favours a party during any formal proceedings if they have behaved reasonably in conducting the dispute (especially if the other party has not). For instance, if a party unreasonably refuses a proposal to mediate a dispute, that party may later incur a costs penalty.

Remember that even if you win the dispute, you will not recover all of your legal costs and will find it difficult to recover compensation for management time spent in handling the dispute.

Sources of further information

Civil Procedure Rules: www.dca.gov.uk/civil/procrules_fin/index.htm.

Arbitration Act 1996: www.hmso.gov.uk/acts/acts 1996/1996023.htm.

Housing Grants, Construction and Regeneration Act 1996: www.hmso.gov.uk/acts/acts 1996/1996053.htm

---

Contractors

Daniel McShee, Kennedys Health and Safety Team

Key points

An employer's undertaking for the purposes of section 3 of the Health and Safety at Work etc. Act 1974 may include the work undertaken by an independent contractor for him.

Legislation

- Health and Safety at Work etc. Act 1974.
- Management of Health and Safety at Work Regulations 1999.
- Construction (Design and Management) Regulations 1994.

Overview

Section 3 of the Health and Safety at Work etc. Act 1974 (HSWA) imposes a duty on employers to non-employees to conduct their business, so far as is reasonably practicable, to ensure that those persons are not exposed to risks to their health and safety. This duty may extend to contractors and those employed by them.

Whether or not this is so will depend on whether the risk forms part of the conduct by the employer of his 'undertaking'.

In the leading case of *R -v- Associated Octel* (1996), an employee of a specialist cleaning contractor was badly burned while working at the defendant's (Octel's) plant. Like all other contractors on the site, the contractor worked subject to the defendant's 'permit to work system'.

Octel was prosecuted for a breach of section 3(1). It claimed there was no case as the employee was from an independent contractor and not part of its undertaking. The case went to the House of Lords, which held that the key issue of the extent to which an independent contractor can be left to its own devises will depend on whether the work forms part of the employer's undertaking. If it does form part of the undertaking, then the employer's duty under section 3 extends to ensuring that, so far as is reasonably practicable, the contractor's work is undertaken without risk.

Where a prosecution is brought and there is a dispute on the facts, it will be for the HSE to prove that a contractor's work formed part of an employer's undertaking.

Practical effect

Work undertaken by a contractor is usually covered in a contract. It is good practice for health and safety responsibilities to be written into such a contract. However, the duties under HSWA cannot be passed from one party to another by a contract.

Thereafter the effect of HSG65 'Successful health and safety management' (see 'Sources of further information' below) will apply to the work of independent contractors as it does to the employer if the work forms part of the employer's undertaking. It is important to remember that both parties will have duties under health and safety law.

Thus the arrangements for ensuring proper health and safety management envisaged by HSG65 will apply in these circumstances to a contractor's work. This means that where an employer uses contractors it will be expected to have a health and safety policy in place together with an organisation to measure and audit the contractor's performance and to review it regularly.

The first step for the employer will be to identify the job it wants the contractor to do. An employer should undertake a risk assessment before using contractors to ensure that the use of contractors generally will not import risk that is not as low as reasonably practicable. This would include specific checks of the contractor involved to ensure that it is properly licensed, competent and qualified to undertake the role on behalf of the employer. HSE guidance suggests that this would entail looking at the proposed

contractor and determining matters such as:

• experience in the type of work concerned;
• qualifications and skills;
• recent health and safety performance; and
• what its recent health and safety policies are.

Where employers use contractors, they should have systems to ensure that there is proper supply of information, instruction and training to the contractor. There must be proper management and supervision and the employer should undertake monitoring, auditing and sample checking to ensure that the contractor's work, which forms part of its own undertaking, is being conducted in a legally compliant way.

The Management of Health and Safety at Work Regulations 1999 are of particular importance in any employer–contractor relationship. These set out the requirements for a health and safety management system in all workplaces.

See also: Health and safety at work (page 295); Health and safety management (page 311); Health and safety policies (page 316); Risk assessments (page 469).

Sources of further information

HSE website (www.hse.gov.uk) and information line (08701 545 500).

L21 'Management of health and safety at work. Management of Health and Safety at Work Regulations 1999. Approved Code of Practice and guidance' (HSE Books, 2000): 0 7176 2488 9.

HSG65 'Successful health and safety management' (HSE Books, 1997): 0 7176 1276 7

COSHH/hazardous substances

Phil Wright, SafetyCO UK

Key points

The Control of Substances Hazardous to Health Regulations (COSHH Regulations) were first introduced in 1988, with the latest revision coming into effect in 2003. The employer's responsibilities under the Regulations are:

- to assess health and safety risks;
- to decide upon precautions to prevent ill health;
- to prevent or control exposure;
- to ensure the controls are used and maintained;
- to monitor exposure and carry out health surveillance if necessary; and
- to provide information, training and supervision for employees.

The employee's responsibilities are:

- to follow the rules and safe system of work; and
- to co-operate with any monitoring and health surveillance.

Legislation

- Control of Substances Hazardous to Health Regulations 2002.
- Chemicals (Hazard Information and Packaging for Supply) (Amendment) Regulations 2002.

Compliance advice

The COSHH Regulations should not be considered in isolation but looked at together with other relevant legislation – notably the Management of Health and Safety at Work Regulations 1999 with their requirement for an assessment of risk.

What is a hazardous substance at work?

A hazardous substance at work is any material or substance (product) with the potential to cause illness or injury (ill health) to persons who come into contact with them. Biological agents capable of causing any ill-health effect are also covered by the COSHH Regulations. Asbestos and lead are not covered because they have their own specific regulations.

How are hazardous substances defined?

Hazardous substances can be specified by law or recognised by experience or

---

with common sense. The product should be regarded as hazardous to health if it is hazardous in the form in which it occurs, or is used, in the workplace. A length of hardwood is not a health hazard until it is machined or sanded creating fine dust which may cause irritation of nasal passages, and possible nasal cancer.

The first line of defence for the user of a hazardous substance is often the hazard warning symbol (black with orange background) on the product, meaning one of the following:

- toxic or very toxic;
- irritant or harmful;
- highly or extremely flammable;
- corrosive;
- oxidising;
- explosive; or
- dangerous for the environment.

Many items such as timber, bricks and blocks are not supplied with hazard warning symbols but present a hazard when dust is generated.

Types of ill health caused by hazardous products include:

- skin irritation;
- asthma;
- poisoning;
- infection; and
- cancer.

The effects on health resulting from contact with hazardous substances can be short term (headaches, dizziness, nausea) or long term (lung disease, liver or kidney dysfunction).

Routes of entry into the body are:

- inhalation;
- ingestion;
- skin absorption;

- penetration or open wounds; and
- eyes.

An important precaution for the user of the hazardous product is therefore to maintain good standards of personal hygiene – washing before eating, drinking, smoking or using toilet facilities.

Three steps to ensure safe use of hazardous products

Step 1

The employer or controller of premises must compile a complete register of all products in use in the workplace.

Step 2

The safety data sheet of the specific product must be obtained from the manufacturer or supplier (they are required to provide this information by law). All safety data sheets incorporate 16 standard categories of information including first-aid measures and the personal protective equipment (PPE) required.

They will also confirm if a maximum exposure limit (MEL) or occupational exposure standard (OES) applies to that product. If they are relevant to that product, then the precautions required to ensure safe use will be even more stringent.

Step 3

The employer must carry out a COSHH assessment, using the information contained within the safety data sheet, to cover the actual use of that product in that specific workplace.

The competent person preparing the assessment must decide upon the actual control measures that need to be followed when the product is stored, used and disposed of.

The COSHH assessment must be brought to the attention of any employees who use that product to ensure that they:

- are aware of the health risks; and
- know the precautions to be taken

As with other types of assessment, consideration should be given by the competent person to the hierarchy of risk control. For example:

- must that product be used?
- could a safer product be used (e.g. water-based gloss paint rather than solvent based)?
- can the work process be enclosed, or local exhaust ventilation be provided?
- what type of PPE is necessary?

Personal protective equipment

The use of PPE should be considered as the last resort in a safe system of work. To be effective it must be:

- suitable for the hazard;
- suitable for the user;
- looked after and maintained; and
- used by a trained person.

Whatever control measures are specified in the COSHH assessment, they will be effective only if applied correctly. Proper supervision of the work activity is therefore vital.

See also: Biological hazards (page 84); Personal protective equipment (page 425).

Sources of further information

L5 'Control of substances hazardous to health' (HSE Books, 2002): ISBN 0 7176 2534 6.

EH40 'Occupational exposure limits' (HSE Books, 2003): 0 7176 2194 4.

HSG97 'A step-by-step guide to COSHH assessment' (HSE Books, 2004): ISBN 0 7176 2785 3.

Criminal records

Howard Lewis-Nunn, Berwin Leighton Paisner

Key points

- Other than in some excepted situations, employees or applicants are not obliged to disclose their past or 'spent' convictions once the appropriate period of time for their conviction has elapsed. The appropriate length of time before the conviction is spent depends on the nature of the sentence.
- Sentences of imprisonment for more than 30 months are never spent.
- Individuals can be required to disclose spent convictions when applying for jobs in certain sectors, where trust is a particular concern.

Legislation

The principal legislation dealing with the disclosure of spent convictions is the Rehabilitation of Offenders Act 1974. Various amendments have been made by Orders in Council, chiefly to identify sectors of work where employers are entitled to know about spent convictions.

Criminal records are also classed as 'sensitive personal data' under the Data Protection Act 1998 and so employers will be required to obtain the individual's explicit consent before making use of such information.

Rehabilitation of Offenders Act 1974

The Act provides that, unless there is an express exception, once a conviction has been spent an individual is a 'rehabilitated person'. The Act sets out a tariff for the timescales before various sentences are classed as spent. Sentences exceeding 30 months or for life or at Her Majesty's pleasure are never spent.

Once a conviction is spent an individual is not required to give any details and is treated as if he had not been convicted. Any requirement that imposes an obligation (whether legal or contractual) on an individual to disclose information is deemed not to require disclosure of spent convictions or any related matters and he is not required to answer any questions in a way that will reveal his spent convictions. He shall not be prejudiced in law for any failure to disclose his spent convictions. An employer may still ask for disclosure of current (i.e. unspent) convictions.

Consequently, unless an exception applies, an employer has no valid grounds for refusing to employ someone or dismissing him for possessing or failing to disclose a spent conviction. A dismissal on these grounds is likely to be unfair. However, it is not clear what remedy could be pursued for a refusal to employ someone.

Exceptions

A number of occupations have been identified where spent convictions must be disclosed and an individual may therefore be dismissed or excluded from employment because of a spent conviction.

The professions include barristers, solicitors, accountants, teachers, police officers, healthcare professionals, officers of building societies, chartered psychologists, actuaries, registered foreign lawyers, legal executives, and receivers appointed by the Court of Protection. More recently, the exempted occupations have been widened to include anyone who would have access to persons under the age of 18 or vulnerable adults (this includes the elderly and mentally impaired). Organisations employing individuals in any of these occupations are entitled to ask about spent convictions and the potential employee is required to give details.

Criminal Records Bureau

The Government has established the Criminal Records Bureau as a central point for employers to obtain details of potential employees' criminal convictions. Currently, this system is only available to organisations within the exempt categories for employment, in particular those working with persons under 18 or vulnerable adults. Two types of disclosure certificates can be obtained at present: standard and enhanced disclosure. Both provide details of all convictions including spent convictions. Enhanced disclosure is intended to provide a more thorough check when extensive and unsupervised contact with persons under 18 and vulnerable adults is likely.

Future changes

The CRB will be introducing a basic disclosure certificate which is intended for all types of employment. This will be issued solely to individuals and cover only unspent convictions. Employers may therefore require this as a matter of course from individuals before offering them employment.

> *See also*: Data protection (page 163); Dismissal (page 197).

Sources of further information

Information Commissioner: www.informationcommissioner.gov.uk.

Criminal Records Bureau: www.crb.gov.uk.

Chartered Institute of Personnel and Development: www.cipd.co.uk.

National Association for the Care and Resettlement of Offenders (Nacro): www.nacro.org.uk.

Crisis management and business continuity

Peter Power, Visor Consultants Limited

Key points

- Crisis management (CM) is recognised as a key component of business continuity management (BCM) set out in the BSI's Publicly Available Specification (PAS) 56: see 'Sources of further information' on page 161.

- BCM is a holistic management process that identifies potential impacts threatening any organisation. It provides a framework for building resilience with the capability for an effective response that safeguards all stakeholder interests.

- The primary objective is to allow the executive of any organisation to continue to manage under any adverse conditions through the introduction and practice of effective resilience strategies, recovery objectives, and CM and BC structures.

- CM and BC require prior preparation and training to enable teams and individuals better to understand how they should work in likely crisis situations by first simulating some likely test scenarios and learning from the results.

- The UK Government is actively encouraging all organisations (public and private) to increase their resilience by having BC plans to fall back on should any crisis occur.

- Several leading insurers are lobbying the Government to make BC plans a legal requirement so that all companies must have business-interruption arrangements (BC plans) in place before they can secure insurance cover.

- Despite several high-profile terrorist events, research suggests that many companies are still failing to take serious risk-prevention measures. The Government is concerned because it will often have to act as insurer of last resort when a major event occurs.

- CM and BC should not be considered a 'grudge purchase' but as a process that enables an employer to fulfil its duty of care, corporate social responsibilities and any insurance pre-conditions.

Legislation

- Under the Management of Health and Safety at Work Regulations 1999

employers are required to develop procedures to deal appropriately with serious and imminent danger, and to appoint competent persons to activate those procedures. Employers must consider all potential dangers (e.g. fire, bomb threats and public disorder).

- Any private sector organisation that provides a defined service to the UK critical infrastructure (Category 2 responder as defined in the Civil Contingencies Act, which received Royal Assent in November 2004) will be required by law to have a tested BC plan.

Importance of business continuity management

Some years ago one talked only about disaster recovery plans, which, as the term implies, dealt specifically with trying to recover operations post-event, rather than increasing resilience and planning to continue key activities irrespective of the crisis scenario. Quite often in any case disaster recovery plans dealt only with IT restoration so that the rest of the organisation was more or less ignored.

Nowadays the situation has changed considerably as it becomes clear that all critical business or operating needs should be capable of sustainable existence, albeit on a reduced scale, if any organisation is going to continue operating when a crisis occurs, especially in a world of increasing threats and risks as well as rising insurance premiums. There are three basic reasons why all organisations should get to grips with this now:

- *Moral.* They have a duty of care towards staff and other stakeholders. They also have a duty to run their operations efficiently, to exercise best practice and to comply with regulations.

- *Physical.* They need to demonstrate robustness by employing intelligent security measures to deter incidents and to have suitable contingency plans in place in case an incident occurs.
- *Conceptual.* They must view risks and threats as an end-to-end process and examine exposures caused by anything from supply chain failure to terrorist bombs.

If it is going to be successful, the corporate response also has to embody three features to ensure success. It has to be:

- feasible;
- relevant; and
- attractive.

Additionally, there is the issue of 'foreseeability'. For example, we have all been warned about the inevitability of terrorist attacks by members of the Government and the directors of our security services. But terrorism is by no means the only threat to worry about. The majority of disasters in the UK are due to such factors as fires, floods, corrupt data and supplier failure.

Responding to disaster: how to prepare

It is vital that any response to a disaster comes from the top. Nowadays the directors of any company have a responsibility to avoid being crisis-prone and to demonstrate more than just routine boardroom know-how.

The danger is that, when a drama does start to unfold, the situation can immediately turn into a crisis. For example, you may call for the executive crisis team only to discover they have no idea about their role in the BC plan and have never been coached to work as crisis managers in any case.

Prior preparation and training in CM and BC are essential as experience suggests that, when suddenly faced with any untoward occurrence, directors and managers have a tendency from the outset to try to follow routine or familiar references. Indeed, the more disturbing the situation, the stronger is the urge to take refuge in familiar procedures. Yet such procedures are going to be the most inappropriate ones to follow since they do not work in unfamiliar situations.

Taking the following steps will help ensure that your preparation is successful:

- Involve everyone in the organisation.
- Ensure that your BCM process mirrors the changing and developing organisational needs.
- Build on existing management procedures, particularly risk management and any past contingency activities.
- Audit and maintain the BCM process continuously to ensure that it becomes an integral part of your company's culture.

Objectives of business continuity management

If BCM is applied properly, it should achieve the following:

- Identify and list key performance indicators (KPIs).
- Enable the identification of:
  - mission-critical activities (MCAs), which should be restored as soon as possible;
  - recovery time objectives (RTOs), which show the timescale to recover MCAs;
  - recovery point objectives (RPOs),

which show the time when work should be restored following an incident; and
  - levels of business continuity (LBCs) to show the minimum level of continued output of services acceptable to the organisation to achieve its business objectives, notwithstanding any existing IT disaster recovery plans.
- Suggest the necessary levels of work area recovery (WAR) where pre-designated workspace might be allocated for use in a crisis (e.g. denial of access to a building) to provide minimum necessary equipment and services at short notice.
- Validate any business impact analysis (BIA), which determines what the impact on the organisation would be if MCAs were disrupted.
- Identify and correct any gaps in your own operations in terms of competence and capability when responding to a crisis situation.
- Demonstrate and provide evidence that your organisation is discharging its legal, regulatory and corporate governance accountability and responsibilities.

Putting the process in place

BCM is a process that is best driven from the top of the organisation. The ideal first stage should be an acceptance by the board or the executive committee of the organisation that BCM is a valid approach to take. A member of the board or executive should be given overall responsibility for the process and appointed as sponsor or champion. This ensures that the process is given the correct level of importance within the organisation and a greater chance of effective implementation.

An overall BCM co-ordinator should then be appointed to report directly to the board or executive member responsible for BCM. This person is ideally someone who understands the business's structure and people. He needs good programme management, communication and interpersonal skills and should be an effective team leader. In addition a budget must be allocated for the initial stages of the process.

According to the scale of the organisation or workload, the BCM co-ordinator may need the support of BCM analysts, lower-level or regional teams and appropriate administrative staff.

For larger operations, the best way to approach BCM is by matrix team management, whereby the team includes managers from key divisions and/or locations. They will not be full-time members of the team, but they will need to dedicate appropriate time to the BCM process.

The aim is to ensure that BCM is part of every manager's normal responsibilities. Therefore the BCM co-ordinator must make certain that all senior management in the organisation understand the importance of BCM and why it is being established: the programme's objectives and critical success factors must be clearly defined. Unless this is successfully achieved, the CM and BC programme cannot properly move forward.

Conclusion

If all the above procedures sound too complicated or expensive, this is nothing compared to the likely costs, penalties and damage to reputation that would be suffered by an organisation that did not prepare its own CM and BC structures before disaster struck, directly or indirectly.

Lord Levene, Chairman of Lloyd's, hit the nail on the head when he recently talked about new global risks that threaten corporations including, but not limited to, business interruption costs, corporate fraud and increased liability claims: 'Looking ahead ten years, I firmly

---

Sources of further information

Business Continuity Institute (BCI): www.thebci.org.

Civil Contingencies Secretariat (Cabinet Office): www.ukresilience.info. The site provides links to government and non-government sources on a wide variety of emergencies and crises that can affect the UK, plus emergency planning guidance and government information. It contains full details of the Civil Contingencies Act.

PAS 56:2003 'Guide to Business Continuity Management' (ISBN 0 58 041370 5) is published by the BSI in association with the Business Continuity Institute.

'Understanding and Developing Business Continuity Management' (ISBN 1 900648 15 6, £34.99) is available as an electronic download from the Workplace Law Network. Call 0870 777 8881 for details, or visit www.workplacelaw.net.

believe that the most successful, least crisis-prone businesses will be those whose boards have shown firm resolve and taken decisive action. Effective, integrated strategies for dealing with tomor-row's risks require a change in culture at board level now.' Would anyone disagree?

See also: Bomb alerts (page 86);
Emergency procedures (page 218); IT
security (page 338

Data protection

Elizabeth Brownsdon, Bird & Bird

The Data Protection Act 1998 came into force on 1 March 2000, replacing the Data Protection Act 1984. The Act offers more protection to individuals than the 1984 Act and imposes more onerous obligations on organisations which process personal data. The Act also gives individuals certain rights in respect of their personal information.

It is important for companies to know about the Act and whether it applies to them, particularly because of certain criminal offences that may be committed as a result of handling personal data incorrectly.

Does the Act apply to your company?

In short, the Act regulates the processing of personal data which is either held on a computer or intended to be held on a computer or held in paper form in what the Act describes as a relevant filing system. In order to work out if the Act applies to the activities carried out by your company, it is necessary to look at these and other definitions in the Act in further detail.

Personal data

This is defined as information which relates to living individuals who can be identified from it (whether from the data on its own or when used in conjunction with other information in the possession of, or likely to come into the possession of, the data controller). This may therefore include details such as postal address or email address as well as facts and opinions held about an individual. Recent case law has suggested that, in order to be personal data, the information must (a) be biographical in a significant sense and (b) have the individual as its focus. In other words, the information must affect a person's privacy, whether in his personal or family life, business or professional capacity. However, truly anonymous data such as aggregated statistics will not be regulated by the Act. The Act also recognises that some data is to be regarded as sensitive personal data and can be processed only under strict conditions. Such data is information on racial or ethnic origin, political opinions, religious or other beliefs, trade union membership, health, sex life, and criminal proceedings or convictions.

Processing

Under the Act this means 'obtaining, recording or holding information or data or carrying out any operation or set of operations on the information or data'. This is a very wide definition, and if your company holds personal data then it is likely that any activities carried out by the company in relation to such data will fall within its scope. Processing may only be carried out in accordance with the data protection principles which are outlined below.

Data controller

This is defined as someone who determines how and for what purpose personal data is processed. Obligations in the Act fall mainly on data controllers. This is likely to be the company rather than the individual workplace manager. Lesser obligations fall on data processors who are those people (other than employees of a data controller) who process personal data on behalf of a data controller.

Relevant filing system

The key elements of this definition are that there must be a set of information, e.g. a grouping together of things with a common theme or element. It follows that a mere list of names is unlikely to amount to a set of information about individuals. The set must be structured, by reference either to individuals or to criteria relating to individuals, and specific information relating to an individual must be readily accessible. Again, recent case law has suggested that this definition is to be interpreted narrowly and that (a) files need to indicate clearly at the outset of the search whether personal data is held within the system and (b) there is a sufficiently sophisticated and detailed means of readily indicating whether and where in an individual file or files specific criteria or information can be readily located.

Data controllers and their responsibilities

Having worked out if the Act applies to the information held by your company, you should then consider what responsibilities lie with the data controller.

Anyone processing personal data as a data controller must comply with the eight enforceable principles of good practice. These say that data must:

(1) be fairly and lawfully obtained and processed;
(2) be processed for limited purposes and not in any manner incompatible with those purposes;
(3) be adequate, relevant and not excessive;
(4) be accurate and where necessary kept up to date;
(5) not be kept for longer than necessary;
(6) be processed in line with the data subject's rights;
(7) be secure; and
(8) not be transferred to countries outside the EEA without adequate protection.

Most of these points are self-explanatory, but it is worth mentioning the first principle in further detail.

This principle requires that the processing of data must be fair and lawful. The Act states that, in order to ensure fairness, data controllers have to ensure - that:

- data is obtained in accordance with the fair processing code. This requires data controllers to make certain information readily available to individuals (e.g. the name of the data controller and the purposes for which the data will be processed);
- certain pre-conditions are met to justify the processing of personal data. At least one condition in Schedule 2 of the Act must be met for any processing of personal data and at least one condition in Schedule 3 must be met if sensitive personal data is

being processed; and

• the individuals must not be misled or deceived as to the purposes for which their data will be processed.

The data controller also needs to be aware of the data subjects' rights when processing personal data. Under the Act, data subjects are granted four key rights:

(1) a right of access to personal data held;

(2) a right to prevent processing that might cause substantial damage and distress;

(3) a right to prevent automated decision-taking; and.

(4) a right to prevent processing for direct marketing purposes.

In relation to subject access, data controllers should be aware that generally an individual has a right to be provided with copies of all information held about that individual within 40 days of a request being made. Although there are limited grounds for withholding certain information, systems should be structured so that requests can be satisfied as easily as possible.

Notification

Most data controllers will need to notify the Information Commissioner, in broad terms, of the purposes of their processing, the personal data processed, the recipients of the personal data processed and if relevant any transfers of data overseas. This information is made publicly available on a register. Under the Act, data controllers must comply with the data protection principles even if they are exempt from the requirement to notify.

Criminal offences

Data controllers can commit criminal offences under the Act. These offences include:

• failing to notify the Information Commissioner either of the processing being undertaken or of any of the changes that have been made to that processing; and

• failing to respond to an information notice or breaching an enforcement notice issued by the Information Commissioner.

Individuals can also commit criminal offences if they obtain, disclose or sell personal data without the consent of the

---

Sources of further information

If your company processes personal data and is concerned about the Act, more information can be obtained from the Information Commissioner's website (www.informationcommissioner.gov.uk) or from the enquiry line on 01625 545745. You should also be aware of the various Codes of Practice which have been issued by the Commissioner and are available on the website, e.g. 'CCTV Guidance and Employment Practices Code'.

'Data Protection Policy and Management Guide, version 1.0' (ISBN 1 900648 33 4, £34.99) is available as an electronic download from the Workplace Law Network. Call 0870 777 8881 for details, or visit www.workplacelaw.net.

---

data controller. The Information Commissioner regards this as the most serious of offences which can be committed under the Act.

See also: CCTV monitoring (page 127); Monitoring employees (page 392); Private life (page 439).

Workplace deaths

Stuart Armstrong, Pinsent Masons

Key points

- The police and the HSE have a protocol for investigating workplace deaths, and the HSE has a policy which requires it to investigate individuals.
- Prosecution (and conviction) rates are increasing under existing laws.
- To convict a company of manslaughter, the courts must first convict an individual who is a 'directing mind' of the organisation.
- Proposals for new offences of corporate killing (relating to individuals and organisations) are intended to make it easier to secure convictions.
- Although a new offence of corporate killing is likely, the wait for legislation goes on.

Legislation

- Interpretation Act 1978, section 5 and Schedule 1.

Cases

- *R -v- Adomako* [1995] 1 AC 171.
- Attorney General's Reference No. 2 of 1999.

Overview

The police and the HSE jointly investigate workplace deaths, including work-related road traffic accidents. The police will take charge of the initial investigation and they are often advised in a technical capacity by HSE inspectors. Where either find evidence of culpability, those responsible may currently face charges:

- of manslaughter, which carries penalties of up to life imprisonment for individuals and an unlimited fine for organisations; or
- under health and safety legislation, which can carry penalties of up to two years' imprisonment (rare) or an unlimited fine.

Prosecution and conviction rates are increasing. Although there have only been six convictions of organisations for manslaughter, increasing numbers of cases are being considered by the Crown Prosecution Service (CPS) as suitable for prosecution. Nine company directors and four owners of businesses have so far been convicted under existing laws (at the time of writing).

To convict an organisation of manslaughter, the first step is for the prosecution to convict one or more persons in a senior capacity in the organisation of manslaughter by gross negligence. Only if that person is considered to be a directing mind of the organisation and acting in that capacity can the organisation itself be convicted of manslaughter.

Manslaughter investigations

Currently, workplace deaths are investigated in accordance with a protocol between the Association of Chief Police Officers (ACPO), the HSE and the CPS. This also covers work-related road traffic accidents (e.g. involving lorry drivers or managers travelling to meetings).

The protocol gives the police primacy in conducting the investigation and allows them to seek assistance from the HSE, thus utilising the HSE's specialist knowledge and effectively allowing the HSE to conduct its own preliminary investigations. In most cases, the HSE investigates with the police, using its greater knowledge of health and safety management systems, and frequently joint interviews take place. A senior police officer then reviews the evidence to decide whether manslaughter charges are possible. The final decision to bring a manslaughter prosecution and a subsequent 'corporate manslaughter' prosecution rests with the CPS.

Coroner's inquest

The coroner investigates all cases of sudden death to determine the identity of the deceased, and when, where and how he came to his death. Workplace fatalities are normally subject to an early inquest which convenes in order to allow the deceased to be buried.

The coroner will then adjourn the inquest until any consideration of prosecution for manslaughter (or, in the case of a road-related workplace fatality, possible driving offences) is concluded. This may mean that the inquest does not resume until several years after the accident. If the CPS decides that there is insufficient evidence to bring a manslaughter or driving prosecution, then the coroner's inquest will resume. If a criminal trial takes place which examines the facts and considers the cause of death, then in these circumstances only an administrative (paper-based) inquest will be held.

Where an inquest takes place into a workplace fatality, it will do so before a jury. Several verdicts are available to the jury, including misadventure, unlawful killing, accidental death or an 'open' verdict.

The HSE will prepare a report on the workplace fatality for the coroner at the resumed inquest. After the inquest, if an unlawful killing verdict is returned, then this may lead to reconsideration of the evidence by the CPS, prior to any decision being taken by the HSE as to whether it will prosecute for a breach of health and safety law.

Manslaughter: individuals

An individual may be found guilty of gross negligence manslaughter if a jury is satisfied that:

- the individual owed a duty of care to the deceased;
- the individual breached that duty of care; and
- the breach was so grossly negligent in all circumstances that the individual deserves criminal sanctions (i.e. imprisonment).

The convicted individual will then face a sentence of up to life imprisonment. However, to date, there have been few convictions, with most sentences being suspended.

Prosecutions are on the increase. In part this may be because in early 2000 the courts found that the CPS had been using the wrong test when deciding whether to prosecute. Also the police are now investigating more instances of work-related deaths.

Those individuals most vulnerable to manslaughter charges are those with day-to-day management of work activities, i.e. directors of small companies, contracts managers, site managers and supervisors.

Manslaughter: organisations

Some organisations (such as companies and some partnerships) are classed as 'legal persons'. As such, these organisations may face criminal charges. To convict an organisation of manslaughter by gross negligence (sometimes referred to as corporate manslaughter), the CPS must:

- first convict a director or senior manager of manslaughter by gross negligence; and then also
- show that the convicted director or senior manager represented the 'directing mind' of the company in relation to the death.

It is frequently easier to identify the convicted director or manager of a small company as the directing mind. For large companies, it is often difficult to find a director or senior manager representing the company's directing mind who also has sufficient involvement in day-to-day activities to be charged with manslaughter.

For this reason, the only successful prosecutions to date have been against small companies.

Other charges

If manslaughter charges are not brought, the HSE is still likely to prosecute culpable individuals and organisations under separate health and safety legislation for health and safety offences.

Corporate killing

Proposed offences of corporate killing (by either an individual or organisation) were put forward by the Law Commission as early as 1996 and provisional proposals were even suggested in 1994. However, to date, the Government has failed to implement its manifesto commitment, announced in May 2000, that it would introduce the measures proposed by the Law Commission. In May 2003 the Government reaffirmed its commitment to bringing these proposals into force and the Home Secretary predicted that detailed proposals would be ready early in 2004. However, no such proposals have been released. It has been suggested that difficulties with implementing new legislation in this area relate to the applicability of the new laws to Crown bodies such as the Army and the Prison Service, and to difficulties in drafting legislation to incorporate human rights issues.

Previous draft proposals for new offences of corporate killing were intended to make it easier to convict large companies as well as individuals following workplace deaths. These offences were drafted so as only to require proof:

- of a management failure within the organisation, which was the cause of death, or one of several of the causes of death; and
- that this failure represented conduct falling far below that which could be

expected of the individual or the organisation in the circumstances.

It has also been proposed that the HSE should be able to investigate and prosecute these new offences. Convicted organisations would face a potentially unlimited fine, possibly linked to turnover whereas convicted individuals would face a fine or imprisonment.

Other suggested changes have previously included a new offence of killing by gross carelessness. However, this offence has not received the Government's support.

Minimising liability

The one certain way of avoiding manslaughter charges is to ensure that no one dies as a result of their work activities. Although this may seem obvious, nearly two-thirds of work-related deaths result from just three causes:

- falls from height;
- being struck by a moving vehicle; and
- being struck by a moving or falling object.

In the construction industry alone between 1996 and 2004 there have been 332 deaths from falls, 89 deaths as a result of falling objects and 71 deaths caused by moving vehicles.

By focusing their attention on these hazardous areas, employers can minimise the risks and disruption of both deaths and prosecution.

Other simple measures include:

- promptly informing senior managers of any dangerous circumstances or near miss;
- obtaining specialist legal advice, in particular before any incidents arise, and certainly before any police or HSE interviews; and
- dealing sensitively and appropriately with those involved in the accident and relatives of those killed or injured.

See also: Accidents (page 69); Construction site health and safety (page 145); Health and safety at work (page 295); Health and safety management (page 311); Health and safety policies (page 316); RIDDOR (page 466).

Sources of further information

Home Office proposals for new manslaughter legislation: www.homeoffice.gov.uk/consult/invmans.htm.

MISC491 'Work-related deaths: A protocol for liaison' (HSE Books, 2003).

'Health and Safety Policy and Management Guide, version 1.0' (ISBN 1 900648 35 0, £59.99) is available as an electronic download from the Workplace Law Network. Call 0870 777 8881 for details, or visit www.workplacelaw.net.

Accredited health and safety training is also available from the Workplace Law Network, including the NEBOSH National General Certificate and IOSH Managing Safely.

Dilapidations

Bartle Woolhouse, Malcolm Hollis

Key points

'Dilapidations' is a term used to describe the obligations of a lease that relate to a requirement to undertake building works to the property to which it refers.

If a building has been damaged, and assuming that action is required, then the first task will be to seek to determine what the breaches are, generally by recording them in a schedule of dilapidations.

The remedies that are available will be influenced principally by the length of the term of the lease that is remaining. However, when these remedies are to be imposed on the other side, especially where this takes the form of financial compensation, the actual losses that these breaches cause need to be taken into account.

This text is only applicable to the practice of dilapidations in England and Wales; dilapidations claims in Scotland and Northern Ireland have a number of significant differences, although many aspects of the procedures and processes described may be relevant to claims in these and other countries.

It is advisable for landlords or tenants to appoint a suitably qualified surveyor to act for them in identifying dilapidations claims and resolving disputes that invariably arise concerning such obligations.

Legal framework

The introduction of the Civil Procedure Rules 1998 (CPR) – more commonly referred to as the Woolf Reforms – has had a significant impact on how dilapidations claims are processed.

The CPR encourage parties to exchange full information before proceedings are issued, to enable the parties to avoid litigation where possible and support the efficient management of proceedings where litigation cannot be avoided.

These objectives are addressed by way of pre-action protocols that require parties to a dispute not to exaggerate claims or be unnecessarily obstructive in defending them.

Both landlords and tenants must now understand that compliance with such protocols means the early production of all documentation that is relevant to a claim and giving assistance to the surveyor instructed in progressing an 'open' dialogue. The consequences of not doing so may result in substantial financial penalties imposed by the courts should litigation prove necessary.

Schedule of dilapidations

This will normally deal with certain or all of the following:

- *Repair* – determining in any one case whether actual disrepair has occurred is the most complex area in dilapidations and beyond the scope of this text. See 'Sources of further information' below.
- *Improvements and alterations* – normally formalised by means of licences appended to the lease.
- *Tenant's fixtures* – generally affixed to the premises in a permanent manner and becoming part of it.
- *Compliance with statutes* – ensuring works conform and are carried out in accordance with the provisions of any statute or regulation.
- *Implied obligations* – terms concerning the condition of the premises may be implied into the tenancy.
- *Decoration* – usually required on a cyclical basis during the course of the lease and in the final year of the term.
- *Other heads of claim* – including professional fees, VAT and other consequential losses that flow from the breaches identified.

Landlord's remedies

These are dependent on the time during the lease term when the breach arises. The remedy chosen will depend on the landlord's objective. Those usually available are as follows:

- *Damages* – this is the amount by which the landlord's reversion has been diminished by the breaches and is normally based on the cost of the works. After the lease has expired this is the only remedy. There may be statutory restrictions on the claim arising from the provisions of section 18(1) of the Landlord and Tenant Act 1927. This limits any claim for disrepair to the damage suffered to the value of the reversion. This general principle also applies in common law.
- *Landlord's entry* – notification is given to the tenant of the relevant breaches, requiring that he undertake the work within a specified period of time. In default, the landlord may enter the building, carry out the work and recover the cost as a debt. More commonly referred to as the '*Jervis -v- Harris* remedy', these situations merit very careful consideration on both sides before actions are taken.
- *Forfeiture* – a process by which a landlord can seek to recover possession of a building. Breach by a tenant may enable the landlord to assert that the tenancy is at an end. This right is governed by section 146 of the Law of Property Act 1925 and the Leasehold Property (Repairs) Act 1938.
- *Break and renewal notices* – some leases allow their term to be reduced, by either the landlord or tenant, by way of the service of 'break notices'. In some instances these break notices are valid only if certain conditions are met. These conditions, termed 'conditions precedent', can include obligations of the tenant under dilapidations. In practical terms it is extremely difficult to satisfactorily achieve compliance in such cases. They may need to be negotiated away, if possible, but often at a significant extra cost.

Tenant's remedies

The tenant may need to serve notice on the landlord to remedy a breach before a liability can arise. The main options available are as follows:

- *Damages* – unless the landlord was in breach of covenant at the time the disrepair occurred, he will not be liable for damages. Assuming that there has been a breach, there are no statutory restrictions on the tenant's claim for damages against the landlord.
- *Tenant carries out work* – the tenant may have an express or implied right to carry out work in default of the landlord so doing, particularly if he is suffering damage from the breach. In such cases he should notify the landlord first.
- *Set-off* – it can be convenient for a tenant to seek to 'recover' any damages by setting them off against monies due to the landlord. This remedy is, however, sometimes prohibited.
- *Repudiation* – in contract law, where a party to a contract is in serious breach, it is generally open to the other party to accept that breach as repudiating the contract – i.e. bringing it to an end. The current prevailing view is that this principle applies to leases.

Considerations for tenants in deciding whether or not to carry out works

If the tenant is not compelled to do the work he has to weigh up the advantages

and disadvantages of doing so:

- *Advantages*
  - occupying a repaired property
  - potential to save money, e.g. VAT
  - control of work (contractor and programme)
- *Disadvantages*
  - disruption in operations or trade
  - risk associated with project, e.g. costs
  - risk of not correctly interpreting obligations
  - loss of statutory defences

Considerations for landlords in deciding whether or not to carry out works

The landlord may have no compulsion to carry out works, but he must equally weigh up his options:

- *Advantages*
  - proof of claim: evidence of expenditure and loss
  - may aid reletting
  - preserves property value
- *Disadvantages*
  - forward funding
  - exposure to claims of excessive disruption (where the lease remains in force).

See also: Landlord and tenant: lease issues (page 345); Landlord and tenant: possession issues (page 354).

Sources of further information

Dowding, N. and Reynolds, K.: *Dilapidations: The Modern Law and Practice*, 2nd edition (Sweet & Maxwell, London, 2002): ISBN 0 42179 640 5.

Fleming, M.F., McKinlay, J. and McMillan, A.: *Dilapidations in Scotland*, 2nd edition (Sweet & Maxwell, London, 2003): ISBN 0 41401 513 4.

Hollis, M.: *Dilapidations*, 3rd edition (College of Estate Management, Reading, 2002): ISBN 1 89976 954 4.

King, V. and Williams, P.J.G.: 'What effect will the Disability Discrimination Act have on landlord and tenant relationships?', *Estates Gazette* (2002).

Smith, P.F.: *West and Smith's Law of Dilapidations*, 11th edition (Estates Gazette, London, 2001): ISBN 0 72820 352 9.

Woodfall's Landlord and Tenant (loose-leaf), 28th edition (Sweet & Maxwell, London, 1978): ISBN 0 42122 820 2.

Williams, D. (ed.), *Handbook of Dilapidations* (loose-leaf) (Sweet & Maxwell, London, 1992 (plus updates): ISBN 0 42144 500 9.

Shapiro, E. and Majors, I.: 'Dilapidations claims – the VAT options', *Chartered Surveyor Monthly* (May 1997).

Directors' responsibilities: employment, health and safety, and financial management

Brian Palmer, Charles Russell Employment and Pensions Service Group

Key points

- Company directors are responsible for the management of their companies. However, they act on behalf of the owners and must consider their interests in everything they do. They also have responsibilities to the company's employees and its trading partners, and under statute these duties may be supplemented or modified by a company's memorandum and articles of association.
- Directors are responsible for ensuring that the company complies with the various requirements imposed upon it by law.
- Although generally the company is liable for any failure to comply with legal requirements, in certain circumstances the directors can be held personally liable where the default was due to their neglect or connivance.

Legislation

- Companies Acts 1985 and 1989.
- Insolvency Act 1986.
- Company Directors Disqualification Act 1986.
- Value Added Tax Act 1994.
- Health and Safety at Work etc. Act 1974.
- Management of Health and Safety at Work Regulations 1999.

Directors' duties

Fiduciary duties

A director must act honestly and in good faith in the interests of the company as a whole. He must not use information gained as a director to further his own interests, nor must he seek to apply company assets for his own gain. For example, a director must not receive commission on a transaction between the company and a third party or offer to take up, on a private basis, work offered to the company.

A director must disclose any direct or

indirect personal interests in a contract and will have to account for any profit made unless he complies with this requirement before the contract was entered into.

When considering if a director has breached his duty of good faith, the courts will assess whether or not the director reasonably believed the act in question was in the best interests of the company.

Duty of skill and care

A director must exercise reasonable skill and care. The standard expected of him is 'not merely by [what] he knows, but also that which he ought to know as a reasonable diligent person having the knowledge, skill and experience of a person carrying out his tasks' (*Bairstow -v- Queens Moat Houses Plc*). Broadly speaking, he should act with the same care with regard to the company's assets as he would if he were dealing with his own property.

Directors are generally not liable for the actions of their fellow directors, if they knew nothing about them and took no part in them, though it is dangerous to turn a blind eye.

Duties to employees

While a director owes no common law duty to consider the interests of the workforce, the Companies Act 1985 (CA 1985) recognises the principle that the interests of the workforce fall within the wider picture of the interests of the company.

Directors must comply with employment law in dealings with employees. Directors personally can be sued for unfair work practices such as unfair dismissal and racial, sexual, disability and other discrimination. Directors must act quickly to ensure the company complies with any new employment laws.

Health and safety issues

A company has various obligations to fulfil under the Health and Safety at Work etc. Act 1974 (HSWA) and the Management of Health and Safety at Work Regulations 1992 (MHSWR). The most important of these are as follows:

• A duty to ensure, so far as is reasonably practicable, the health, safety and welfare of its employees. The size of the company and the activities that are carried on by it will be taken into account when assessing what is reasonably practicable.

• A duty to carry out a risk assessment and implement procedures to minimise any risks that are highlighted.

• A duty to provide (and periodically revise) a written health and safety policy, to implement it and to bring it to the attention of employees.

These are the company's responsibility, but the directors would be breaching their duties to the company by failing to take the appropriate measures. Furthermore, directors can be prosecuted under section 37 of HSWA where the offence committed by the company occurred with their consent or connivance or through neglect on their part.

It would be wise for directors to ensure they have health and safety systems in place. The HSE provides comprehensive guidance on this issue.

Financial responsibilities
Accounts

CA 1985 requires directors to maintain accounting records that:

- show the company's transactions and its financial position;
- contain entries of all receipts and payments, including details of sales and purchases of goods, and a record of assets and liabilities; and
- show stock held at the end of each year.

Records must be kept at the company's registered office and retained for a period of six years.

Annual audited accounts, consisting of a profit and loss account, must be approved by the members of the company at a general meeting (usually the AGM) and then filed with the Registrar of Companies within ten months of the end of the company's financial year (seven months for a public company).

Statutory returns, including the annual report and accounts, the annual return and notice of changes to directors and secretaries, must be filed with the Registrar of Companies on time.

Failure to comply with these requirements renders the company liable to a penalty and directors liable to a fine.

Directors are also responsible for filing tax returns.

Financial management

Directors must exercise prudence in the financial management of the company. In the event of insolvency, directors can find themselves personally liable to creditors where it can be shown that they acted outside of their powers or in breach of their duties or were engaged in wrongful or fraudulent trading. The latter offences will be committed where a director continues to incur liabilities on behalf of the company where he knows or ought to have known that the company was, or inevitably would become, insolvent or there was no reasonable prospect of repaying debts.

Other duties

Directors must maintain various statutory books at the company's registered office including:

- a register of members;
- a register of mortgages and charges;
- a register of debenture holders; and
- a register of directors' interests.

An annual return must be filed with the Registrar of Companies within 28 days of either the anniversary of its incorporation or made-up date of the company's previous annual return.

Directors must ensure that minutes are taken at board meetings, giving a record of all decisions taken.

Checklist: practical steps for directors

All directors should:

- check the company's memorandum

Sources of further information

For guidance on health and safety see the HSE's website: www.hse.gov.uk.

'Health and Safety Policy and Management Guide, version 1.0' (ISBN 1 900648 35 0, £59.99) is available as an electronic download from the Workplace Law Network. Call 0870 777 8881 for details, or visit www.workplacelaw.net.

and articles of association to establish the scope of their powers;

- ensure that minutes are maintained;
- be alert to conflicts of interest between the company and themselves as individuals;
- always comply with employment law;
- ensure that the company operates a comprehensive system for assessing and minimising health and safety risks;
- keep informed about the company's financial position – ignorance will not save them from facing personal liability in certain circumstances; and

- make sure that the company obtains insurance to protect them in the event of their facing personal liability.

See also: Bullying and harassment (page 108); Discrimination (page 189); Health and safety at work (page 295); Health and safety management (page 311); Health and safety policies (page 316); Risk assessments (page 469).

Disability access

Edited by Michael Brandman, Tarlo Lyons

Key points

The governing statute is the Disability Discrimination Act 1995.

The Act imposes separate (but similar) duties on employers and organisations that provide services to the public. The overriding duty is not to discriminate against a disabled person.

'Disability' includes any impairment that makes it substantially difficult for a person to carry out normal day-to-day activities. The disability must have lasted for at least 12 months or be likely to last for that period. Examples are given in leaflet DL60 available from the Disability Rights Commission (DRC).

The Act may require changes to be made to an organisation's policies, practices and procedures.

Employers and service providers may in addition be required to make physical adjustments to buildings to improve accessibility by their employees.

Duties and claims

The governing statute is the Disability Discrimination Act 1995, together with its Regulations and Codes of Practice.

The two duties imposed on employers and service providers by the Act are:

- not treating disabled persons less favourably than persons who are not disabled, for a reason which relates to the disability, without justification (there are only limited grounds which constitute justification and they are set out in the Act); and
- not breaching certain duties contained in the Act.

Breach of the Act is not a criminal offence. Claims for breach of duty are brought by individual disabled people.

Claims are heard in either the employment tribunal (employment duties) or the county court (service provision duties). Remedies available include unlimited compensation.

Duties on employers

These duties are contained in Part II of the Act. Duties are owed only to employees or job applicants, not to the public at large.

The number of people employed at the premises is not relevant. The normal definition of employee is widened. The duty can extend to self-employed people who provide personal services or contract workers employed by someone else (e.g. an employment business).

The employer's main duty (other than not to discriminate) is to take reasonable steps to ensure that no arrangements or physical features of the employer's premises place a disabled person at a substantial disadvantage compared to a person who is not disabled. This may involve making one or more adjustments, such as:

- making reasonable adjustments to premises (see 'Physical adjustments' below);
- acquiring or modifying equipment; and
- modifying instructions or reference manuals

but only where it is reasonable to do so.

Examples of good practice are contained in a Code of Practice. This is not legally binding, although in the case of a dispute the tribunal may consider whether the employer has complied with its recommendations.

Many of these possible changes involve management responsibilities, but will have knock-on effects on workplace managers. Compliance with these duties will involve a discussion with the disabled 'employee' to ascertain his requirements and priorities. This is important because it is not a defence for the employer to simply show that the discrimination took place without its knowledge or approval.

It should be recognised that, in the context of disability discrimination, discrimination against an employee who is disabled and who is dismissed on grounds that have no connection with the disability is not unlawful. However, this demands meticulous record keeping to minimise exposure to discrimination claims.

In a recent landmark ruling, the House of Lords has decided that the duty to disabled employees can involve positive discrimination. This can entail transferring, without competitive interviews, a disabled employee from a post the duties of which he can no longer undertake to a post within his capabilities.

Duties on service providers

These duties are contained in Part III of the Act. They apply to all organisations, of whatever size, that provide services, goods or facilities to the general public or a section of it, with or without payment. They are described as 'service providers' in this article.

The only exceptions are:

- clubs which are genuinely private; and
- public transport (but infrastructure such as bus stations is subject to the Act).

The main duties owed to disabled visitors are:

- not to discriminate against disabled people (unjustified less favourable treatment);
- to take reasonable steps to change practices, policies and procedures which make it impossible or unreasonably difficult for disabled people to use the service (this is principally a management issue); and
- to provide auxiliary aids where this is reasonable.

Physical adjustments

Service providers are required to take reasonable steps to modify physical features of premises which make it impossible or unreasonably difficult for disabled people to use the service. 'Physical fea-

Disability: Making Buildings Accessible Special Report

The UK's No.1 guide for architects, designers, building managers and surveyors

The **Disability: Making Buildings Accessible Special Report** is now in its third year of publication and continues to provide readers with the highest quality information and practical guidance on the Disability Discrimination Act (DDA).

This second edition, edited by Keith Bright, FRICS NRAC Consultant, will give you all the information you need on changes to the legislation, including the provisions of the Building Regulations Part M (accessibility).

The authoritative special report will help you to:

- understand the legal requirements of the DDA and Building Regulations Part M

- establish what changes need to be made to buildings and how much they will cost

- avoid the risk of legal action

- manage difficulties with historic buildings, site security and fire safety

Practical advice from legal experts

There are highly practical sections on frequently overlooked issues, such as the use of colour and contrast, wayfinding and signage, and issues related to the design and management of transport environments.

 Essential reading for all property professionals and owners
George Ferguson, RIBA President

The report also examines issues of fire safety that apply to the needs of disabled people, including the compromises which may have to be made when considering safe access, egress and security requirements. The report includes the full text of the DDA.

There is practical advice relating to historic buildings and premises protected by planning conditions where there are differing demands between aesthetics, practicality and the obligations imposed under accessibility legislation.

Our team of expert authors have produced an essential reference text designed to help you comply with or advise on the requirements of Part III of the DDA as cost-effectively as possible.

- The **Disability: Making Buildings Accessible Special Report 2nd edition** is priced at £99.00 incl VAT

- Free delivery, packaging and postage

- Over 200 A4 pages of information

- ISBN 1-900648-84-9

workplace law publishing

Call to order your copy now on:
0870 777 8881 quoting ref. 1860

BIFM, RIBA, RICS and Workplace Law Network members save 10% on all publications tures' includes furnishings. Employers have a similar duty in respect of their employees.

This duty does not override any requirement to obtain any consents which may be necessary such as planning consent, listed building consent or landlord's consent. Landlords are not able to refuse consent unreasonably to physical adjustments, regardless of what is stated in the lease.

Not all service providers have to make adjustments or at least on the same scale. The Act only requires them to do what is reasonable in the circumstances. This takes into account the size of the business or organisation and the financial resources available to it.

Where a building met the requirements of Part M of the Building Regulations at the time of its construction, and continues to meet them, no further adjustments will be necessary. But this will not cover every provision of a building – for example, Part M does not apply to door handles.

Where this has not been previously undertaken, commissioning of a disability access audit should be undertaken without delay. Practical examples of adjustments, some of which are relatively cheap, include:

- lifts;
- temporary or permanent ramps;
- handrails;
- locations of switches and sockets;
- alteration of door handles and taps;
- contrasting colours on walls, floors and staircases;
- accessible toilets;

- improved lighting; and
- improved signage.

Examples of reasonable steps to take are contained in a Code of Practice which will be admissible evidence in a civil claim for compensation.

Possible reasons for treating a disabled visitor less favourably

These include:

- avoiding damage to the health and safety of the disabled person or any other person;
- where the disabled person is incapable of giving informed consent or entering into a legally binding agreement;
- if otherwise the service provider would be unable to provide the service;
- when an adjustment would fundamentally alter the nature of a business or service; and
- if, where a disabled customer is charged more for a service, it would cost more in materials or labour to meet his particular needs.

Note that in the event of a claim, provided that the service provider has properly addressed the issues before the event giving rise to the claim, if its reasons are genuine and it is reasonable for the service provider to hold them, it may escape liability. The reasons will, however, be tested against the Code of Practice.

See also: Building Regulations (page 92); Discrimination (page 189).

Sources of further information

For more information on the duties under the Disability Discrimination Act 1995, and to obtain the Codes of Practice, contact the Disability Rights Commission (DRC) (tel. 08457 622 633; www.drc-gb.org). It supplies information cards on specific topics, as well as leaflets – e.g. DL60 'Definition of disability' and DLE7 'Employing disabled people: a good practice guide for managers and employers'.

For advice on access audits and accessibility generally, contact the Centre for Accessible Environments (tel. 020 7840 0125; www.cae.org.uk).

For advice on access audits, contact the National Register of Access Consultants (tel. 020 7735 7845; www.nrac.org.uk).

Disability: Making Buildings Accessible – Special Report, 2nd edition, edited by Keith Bright (ISBN 1 900648 84 9, £99.00) is available from Workplace Law Publishing. Call 0870 777 8881, or visit www.workplace.law.net.

Disciplinary and grievance procedures

Pinsent Masons Employment Group

Key points

- Contracts and statements of terms must incorporate disciplinary and grievance procedures.
- Written procedures are helpful in this respect. If there are none, then there are certain minimum steps which employers must undertake, as otherwise any decision to dismiss will be automatically unfair. The Advisory, Conciliation and Arbitration Service (ACAS) guidelines form the accepted basis for such procedures. In June 2004 ACAS produced draft guidance on the new legal procedures.
- Employees should be accompanied at disciplinary and grievance hearings.
- In unfair dismissal cases, an important consideration will be whether at least the statutory minimum procedure was followed.

Legislation

- Employment Rights Act 1996.
- Employment Act 2002.
- Employment Act 2002 (Dispute Resolution) Regulations 2004.

Written procedures

Procedural fairness in the workplace is essential if employers are to avoid falling foul of employment protection laws.

Best practice therefore demands the introduction of fair written procedures to deal with disciplinary issues and to resolve grievances.

Statement of terms and conditions

Every employer is obliged to provide to each employee within two months after the beginning of the employee's employment a written statement of terms and conditions of his employment which specifies (among other things):

- any disciplinary rules applicable to the employee;
- a person to whom the employee can apply if dissatisfied with any disciplinary decision;
- a person to whom the employee can apply to seek redress of any grievance; and
- the manner in which any application should be made.

Disciplinary and grievance procedures are generally structured in a tiered system whereby if the grievance is not resolved or there is a recurrence of misconduct the next step of the procedure is taken.

Grievance procedure

In a grievance procedure, there will ordinarily be provisions for making several attempts to resolve a grievance. These will start with an informal approach and lead to a requirement for the grievance to be put in writing.

Each attempt to resolve the grievance typically involves a higher level of management for the employee to approach, usually working directly up the line of management responsibilities. On a practical note, when preparing such a procedure, care should be taken to avoid an open-ended series of hearings coming from the one grievance which could lead to very senior managers becoming involved. On the other hand, the procedure should make provision for employees to be sure that their grievance is being considered by the employer and not dismissed at a junior manager level. Employees should also be able to bypass a particular manager if that manager is personally involved in the grievance (e.g. where he is alleged to have harassed an employee).

If an employee raises a grievance and does not follow the minimum statutory procedure, he will not be entitled to make an application to an employment tribunal on that grievance. The minimum procedure is as follows:

- *Step 1*. The employee must inform the employer of the grievance in writing.
- *Step 2*. The employee will be invited by the employer to a meeting to discuss the grievance where the right to be accompanied will apply. The employee must take all reasonable steps to attend this meeting. After the meeting, the employer will notify the employee of its decision in writing.
- *Step 3*. The employee will be given the right to an appeal meeting if he feels the grievance has not been satisfactorily resolved and will be notified of the final decision.

An employee cannot make an application to an employment tribunal within 28 days of having lodged the grievance with his employer.

Right to be accompanied

It is perhaps worth looking in more detail at the right of an employee to have a companion attend with him at both grievance and disciplinary hearings. Employees can have a work colleague or trade union official (salaried or voluntary) attend, but this does not extend to include family members or legal representatives unless they have a contractual right to do so: sometimes procedures have been written to include a wide right to be accompanied going beyond the legal requirements.

The companion may have quite an extensive role, including helping the employee put his case, but, while ACAS suggests it is best practice to allow the companion to question witnesses, the employer does not have to agree to this.

An employee does not have a right to request a companion at an investigatory meeting which sometimes comes before a grievance or disciplinary hearing. However, it is important that the employer recognises that such meetings can turn into hearings and that it may be prudent to allow a companion to be present if the employee wants one to attend.

The remainder of this article deals with disciplinary procedures.

ACAS Code of Practice on Disciplinary and Grievance Procedures

The ACAS Code of Practice on Disciplinary and Grievance Procedures provides guidelines for employers on whether an employee has been treated fairly in disciplinary procedures.

The steps taken by an employer to deal with a disciplinary issue will inevitably be compared by an employment tribunal with the ACAS Code when determining whether a fair procedure was followed. If the statutory minimum procedure is not followed, the dismissal will be automatically unfair and the compensation increased by between 10% and 50%.

- *Step 1*. Write to the employee notifying him of the allegations against him and the basis of the allegations and invite him to a meeting to discuss the matter.
- *Step 2*. Hold a meeting to discuss the allegations – at which the employee has the right to be accompanied – and notify the employee of the decision.
- *Step 3*. If the employee wishes to appeal, hold an appeal meeting at which he has the right to be accompanied – and inform him of the final decision.

Best practice suggests that an employer should have a written procedure, carefully drafted to take into account the advice set out in the ACAS Code, and the employer should seek to follow the proce-dure in each case. Each employer is required to have in place a written procedure which if not provided to the employee individually is reasonably accessible.

The written procedure should be incorporated in such a way so as not to be a part of the employment contract, so that it can more easily be changed from time to time. This can be done by making express provision for the employer to amend it. In the case of a contractual policy, the employee may sue the employer or seek to obtain an injunction or interdict for failure to follow it. Remember that, if the procedure does not as a minimum meet the statutory test, following such a procedure will be automatically unfair.

Avoiding unfair dismissal

Section 98(1) of ERA sets out the potentially fair reasons for which an employee may be dismissed (see 'Dismissal', page 197).

However, even if a fair reason exists, the employer must act reasonably to avoid an unfair dismissal.

An important aspect of this is whether a proper procedure was followed by the employer in arriving at its decision to dismiss the employee.

Employment tribunals have developed key practical points for employers to follow to avoid unfair dismissals, and guidance is taken from the ACAS Code and from the ACAS handbook *Discipline at Work*.

Disciplinary procedures should be capable of covering a variety of circumstances with implications for the employee ranging from an informal warning to dismissal.

For issues of capability or performance, employers should follow a series of warnings in stages. Typically an employer should issue:

- a verbal warning;
- followed by a written warning;
- followed by a final written warning; and
- finally dismissal.

Very serious matters may merit leapfrogging some of those stages. At each stage of the disciplinary proceedings, the following should take place:

- prior written notice of a meeting or hearing;
- details of how the employee has fallen short of expected performance;
- clarification of how the employee is to improve and the timescale required; and
- warning that, if the employee fails to improve, the next disciplinary stage will follow, ultimately up to dismissal.

In cases of misconduct, the key is to follow a procedure where the allegations are put to the employee. The employee must know the allegations against him, but he is not entitled to know the iden-

tity of a fellow employee who may have supplied the employer with the information required to make the allegation.

It is essential that the employer investigates the matter fully, that the employee is given full opportunity to explain his actions and given the opportunity to comment on the evidence against him, and that decisions are taken based only on evidence which has been put to the employee.

Principles of natural justice always go hand in hand with disciplinary procedures. Accordingly:

- employees should know the allegations made against them;
- employees should have an opportunity to state their case; and
- the employer's decision makers should act in good faith and not be biased.

Disciplinary procedures should also list conduct which will be classed as 'gross misconduct' potentially meriting jumping straight to a dismissal hearing stage.

Procedures should also include an express right to suspend the employee pending further investigation.

Suspension should be on full pay. This allows the employee to be removed from

---

Sources of further information

ACAS Code of Practice on Disciplinary and Grievance Procedures: www.acas.org.uk.

Department of Trade and Industry: www.dti.gov.uk.

'Non-Contractual Disciplinary and Dismissal Policy and Management Guide, version 1.0' (ISBN 1 900648 31 8, £34.99) is available as an electronic download from the Workplace Law Network. Call 0870 777 8881 for details, or visit www.workplacelaw.net.

---

the workplace while an investigation is carried out, but it should be made clear that this is not a sanction or an indication that the employer has made any decision on the matter.

The procedure should provide for a right to appeal at each stage. Whenever possible this should be to someone not previously involved and preferably should be to a more senior level than the decision taker. If a decision to dismiss is taken, the employer should be careful with regard to the date of the dismissal as if the dismissal is without notice or is summary dismissal the appeal will be for reinstatement. If the employee is dismissed with notice and the appeal is rejected, the notice period will run from the original decision to dismiss, not the date of the appeal, provided this is clearly stated in the dismissal letter.

See also: Dismissal (page 197); Employment disputes (page 228).

Discrimination

Pinsent Masons Employment Group

Key points

- Presently employment legislation makes unlawful discrimination on the grounds of sex, marital status, race, disability, sexual orientation, and religion or belief. In the future it will include discrimination on the grounds of age.
- Discrimination will usually be direct or indirect, but can also arise due to victimisation.
- Workplace managers need to act to avoid discrimination at all stages of employment – recruitment, the provision of benefits, promotion and dismissal – to avoid claims for unlimited compensation being made.

Legislation

- Sex Discrimination Act 1975.
- Race Relations Act 1976.
- Disability Discrimination Act 1995.
- Age Diversity in Employment: A Code of Practice (June 1999).
- Race Relations Act 1976 (Amendment) Regulations 2003.
- Disability Discrimination Act 1995 (Amendment) Regulations 2003.
- Sex Discrimination Act 1975 (Amendment) Regulations 2003.
- Employment Equality (Sexual Orientation) Regulations 2003.
- Employment Equality (Religion or Belief) Regulations 2003.

What is discrimination?

Discrimination laws preclude employers from treating workers differently for reasons that are based on their sex, marital status, race, disabilities, sexual orientation, and religion or belief.

The law on racial and sexual discrimination is now quite long established and the most recent legislation on discrimination on grounds of sexual orientation follows a similar approach while that on disability discrimination differs in certain respects. Each area of discrimination will be covered in a separate section in this article.

Discrimination can be split into three categories – direct, indirect and victimisation:

- *Direct*. This is where a decision or action is taken on the sole grounds of the individual's distinctive characteristics – e.g. preferring a male applicant to a female applicant when the female has the better qualifications.
- *Indirect*. When employers stipulate what they consider essential requirements for a position, this will sometimes be regarded as a means of

discrimination. For example, where an employer insists on a wide mobility clause in its contract of employment, this could be interpreted as discriminating against women as they are more likely to be the 'second earner' and therefore less able to relocate. Another example is a requirement for a GCSE in English for a position that does not require any degree of literacy as this can discriminate against ethnic minorities. Indirect discrimination is often less easy to spot than direct discrimination.

• *Victimisation*. This is where an individual is treated less favourably because he has threatened to bring proceedings, give evidence or information, or make some genuinely held allegation of discrimination

Discrimination laws are couched in terms where those protected are not only employees but also contractors who are engaged personally to carry out work.

An employer is responsible for the discriminatory acts carried out by its employees 'in the course of their employment' (a fairly wide definition) unless the employer has taken reasonable steps to prevent the discriminatory conduct. It is therefore important not only that employers have in place policies to prevent discrimination but also that they take active steps to ensure that staff are aware of their content.

Impact of the Human Rights Act 1998

The Human Rights Act 1998 came into force on 2 October 2000 and requires the courts and tribunals to interpret UK law in a way that is compatible with the European Convention on Human Rights.

It includes a right to freedom of conscience, thought or religion, which could widen the scope of the current laws on discrimination on grounds of racial group/origin or religious group.

Further, other relevant provisions allow the right not to be subjected to inhuman or degrading treatment and the right to respect for private life and freedom of expression (which could include the right to wear certain clothes at work, linked to religion or otherwise).

Moreover, Article 14 of the Convention provides that all of the rights contained within the Convention shall be secured without discrimination on any ground such as sex, race, colour, language, religion, political or other opinion, national or social origin, association with a national minority, property, birth or status. This could potentially widen the concept of discrimination beyond the scope of the discrimination legislation currently in force in the UK. However, the impact of this in the workplace has been fairly limited to date.

One area which may become increasingly contentious is religious observance at work. Article 9 protects freedom of thought, conscience and religion.

Sex discrimination

The Sexual Discrimination Act 1975 prevents direct discrimination, indirect discrimination and victimisation.

Direct sex discrimination, as explained above, is treating a woman less favourably than a man (or vice versa) or a married person less favourably than a non-married person – cases of the latter normally occurring where an employer fears that a woman will want to take time out for a family. The comparison that is used is between the person claiming discrimination and another person with similar skills and qualifications and the test is whether the person would have been treated the same but for his or her sex.

It is also unlawful to discriminate against transsexuals.

Invariably if a woman is disadvantaged because she is pregnant this will be discriminatory. Care should be taken to ensure that during the woman's absence she is kept informed of any new vacancies or promoted positions that become available to avoid any claims that she is being discriminated against.

Indirect sex discrimination occurs where there is a provision, criterion or practice which, even though it is applied equally to a man and a woman, is still discriminatory because the proportion of women in percentage terms able to comply with it is considerably smaller than men, it is not justified (an employer needs to justify with good economic business reasons) and it is to the person's detriment (i.e. she has lost out).

The concept of a 'provision, criterion or practice' was introduced in 2001. This has had the effect of widening the scope of activities that may be regarded as discriminatory. For example, it may be broad enough to include informal work practices such as a long-hours culture which would be seen as having greater impact on women as they tend to have primary childcare responsibilities.

Indirect discrimination has often arisen when fewer or lesser benefits are given to part-time workers than are given to full-time workers, because more women work on a part-time basis. Making decisions on the assumption that women will stay at home and men will go out to work is also liable to lead to claims of discrimination.

Workplace managers should also note that good justification will be required to prevent charges of discrimination where female employees are refused requests to return part-time or to job share after a pregnancy (see also 'Family-friendly rights', page 251).

Particular danger arises through discriminatory advertisements and descriptions of jobs suggesting that only men or women should apply or introducing qualifications or experience that is weighted towards one sex rather than the other.

Sexual harassment (unwanted or offensive behaviour) is not sex discrimination as such and of itself is not a breach of the Sex Discrimination Act. However, the courts have held that the effect of the harassment may constitute discrimination, particularly where the woman's day-to-day working conditions are affected.

Employers are able to make a defence where a 'genuine occupational qualification' necessitates the employment of one sex. Examples are where a man or woman is needed for decency or privacy and where there is a need to live at the premises in provided accommodation and the facilities are only for one sex. Further exceptions exist for institutions such as all-male hospitals and prisons or care services. Also, employers will not discriminate if they are simply complying with statutory obligations such as health and safety requirements.

Employers should also be aware that, after the employee leaves, any discrimination of that individual will be unlawful if the act of discrimination arises out of and is closely connected to the employment relationship.

Employment tribunals have unlimited scope to compensate affected individuals not only for pure financial loss but also for injury to feelings.

Race discrimination

The Race Relations Act 1976 prohibits direct discrimination, indirect discrimination and victimisation.

As explained at the beginning of this article, direct discrimination is to treat one person less favourably than another. Examples in the context of race discrimination would be not to promote someone because he is Indian and not to employ a Sikh because he might not 'fit in' with white workers.

Indirect discrimination will occur when the employer applies a requirement or condition with which a considerably smaller proportion in a racial group can comply compared to those who are not in the racial group (e.g. requiring a Sikh who wears a turban to wear a construction-site helmet). Also the person must have been disadvantaged by the actions. If the employer can justify the requirement for a reason other than the race of the person, this is a defence to a claim for indirect discrimination. If an individual proves a case of indirect discrimination, the burden of proof shifts to the employer to prove that it was not racially discriminatory.

A wide definition of race is provided in the legislation under the term 'racial grounds', i.e. colour, race, nationality, ethnic or national origins. A 'racial group' is a group defined by reference to those characteristics.

Workplace managers should note that employers can discriminate if they segregate racial groups, even if the facilities given to them are of equal quality.

One unusual aspect of this form of discrimination that has arisen is the finding that organisers of events have been held liable for racial abuse of guests by a 'comedian' who was not an employee, purely because they were in control of that person and could have taken steps to prevent the racially abusive remarks.

A decision to discriminate on racial grounds may be justified in a few cases. The most important exception is where a 'genuine occupational qualification' exists. There are now two separate situations and different rules apply. The new defence is where the discrimination was on the grounds of race or ethnic or national origins (which is only one part of the wider definition of 'racial grounds') and being of a particular race is a genuine requirement. Such a requirement must be proportionate in the particular case and the individual who was subject to the discrimination must not be of the race in question. The old rules continue to apply where the new rules do not, such as where:

- being a member of a racial group is a requirement for authenticity in a dramatic performance or other entertainment, or for authenticity purposes as an artist's or photographic model;
- the work is in a place where food or drink is consumed by the public and a particular race of person is required for authenticity (e.g. Chinese or Indian restaurants); or
- the job holder provides his or her racial group with personal services promoting their welfare (e.g. an Afro-Caribbean nursery nurse in an Afro-Caribbean area) where those services can be more effectively provided by a person of that racial group.

Instructions to or pressure of staff to discriminate is also unlawful (e.g. the owners of a truck rental company instructing staff to tell Asian customers that no trucks are available for hire).

Harassment is now a separate form of discrimination where a person's unwanted conduct violates another's dignity or creates an intimidating, hostile, degrading, humiliating or offensive environment. The test is an objective one and it is not enough that a particular individual actually believed his environment fell into that category and all the circumstances must be taken into account.

Employment tribunals have unlimited scope to compensate affected individuals not only for pure financial loss but also for injury to feelings.

Disability discrimination

The Disability Discrimination Act 1995 prohibits direct discrimination, indirect discrimination and victimisation. Since 1 October 2004 harassment has been a separate act which is regarded as unlawful in its own right.

This includes discrimination against people with disabilities in terms of services provided to them as members of the public as well as in the field of employment rights. Since 1 October all employers regardless of size can be found guilty of discrimination.

There are two aspects to disability discrimination. The first is where an employer treats a disabled person less favourably because of a disability than he would treat another person who is not disabled. There is a defence where the actions are justified, but there must be substantial reasons. The second is where an employer fails to make 'reasonable adjustments' to the physical nature of its

premises to ensure that disabled people are not placed at a disadvantage. Failure to make such adjustments will be discrimination unless it can be justified. This can include taking into account the cost relative to the size of the employer and the practicality of the adjustment.

Examples of what may be regarded as reasonable adjustments are as follows:

- changing building structure (e.g. by introducing ramps, lowering switches or panels, moving doors and widening entrances) – but remember most people affected by the Act are *not* in a wheelchair;
- permitting different working hours (e.g. to deal with tiredness or medical treatments);
- providing specialist or modified equipment (e.g. computer screens or adapted/different chairs); and
- providing training (e.g. for use of specialist equipment or extra training for someone whose disability may make him slow).

Meaning of 'disability'

There are no duties or liabilities to an individual if there is no 'disability' as defined in the legislation. It is therefore important that there is an understanding that not all medical conditions constitute disability.

For a disability to exist, there needs to be a physical or mental impairment (if mental, it needs to be medically recognised) which has a substantial and long-term adverse effect (i.e. lasts or is likely to last 12 months or is likely to recur). There also needs to be a resulting effect on the person's ability to carry out 'normal day-to-day activities'.

The DTI has issued a Code of Conduct

to which workplace managers should refer by way of guidance. The following examples show the type of physical activities that are regarded as being normal or day to day:

- mobility (moving, changing position);
- manual dexterity (use of hands and fingers with precision – e.g. the inability to use a knife and fork may be disability, but the inability to pick up a tiny item such as a pin may not);
- physical co-ordination, where again it may be a matter of degree;
- continence;
- ability to lift or move everyday objects;
- speech, hearing and eyesight;
- memory and ability to learn, concentrate or understand; and
- perception of risk or physical danger.

Care must be taken that the standard that is regarded as 'normal' must be that of an average individual and not someone within a group of people who are particularly skilled. For example a seamstress who cannot sew because of problems handling a needle and therefore unable to do her job may not be suffering a 'disability' when her problem is measured against 'normal' individuals rather than other seamstresses.

Schizophrenia, claustrophobia, epilepsy, back injuries, depression, blindness, arm pains and dyslexia have all been found to constitute 'disabilities'. However, each of these cases has been decided on the level of disability of an individual, and it cannot be taken to be a rule that because someone suffers from arm pains he is disabled in terms of the law. Further guidance is given by the Dis-

ability Discrimination (Meaning of Disability) Regulations 1996.

The legislation is very specific on the subject of substance abuse and excludes alcohol, nicotine or substance dependency as a disability. Again, however, caution is warranted as the effects of the abuse could result in physical disabilities (e.g. liver damage) which would be covered by the law.

Workplace managers should take care in avoiding disability discrimination in terms of advertisements, terms and conditions of employment, benefits provided to staff, dismissals and victimisation.

If an employee is ill, particularly where that illness is long term and a dismissal is contemplated, the disability discrimination legislation needs to be considered carefully and specialist advice taken as this area is fraught with potential issues.

Discrimination on the grounds of sexual orientation

The Employment Directive sets out an anti-discrimination 'principle of equal treatment' in the context of sexual orientation and this has now been implemented through the Employment Equality (Sexual Orientation) Regulations 2003.

The Regulations contain sections dealing with discrimination in employment and vocational training, the vicarious liability of employers, exceptions and enforcement.

The law applies to recruitment, terms and conditions, pay, promotion, transfers and dismissals. It applies to all employers regardless of their size.

The Regulations cover:

- direct discrimination (i.e. less

favourable treatment on the grounds of sexual orientation);
- indirect discrimination whereby a provision or practice is applied which disadvantages people of particular sexual orientation and which is not objectively justified as a proportionate means of achieving a legitimate aim;
- harassment or conduct which violates dignity or creates an intimidating, hostile, degrading, humiliating or offensive environment; and
- victimisation (i.e. less favourable treatment because of something done in connection with the legislation).

'Sexual orientation' covers orientation towards persons of the same sex (gays and lesbians), the opposite sex (heterosexuals), and the same and opposite sex (bisexuals). The law applies to discrimination on the grounds of perceived as well as actual sexual orientation.

To date there has been little case law concerning such discrimination.

Discrimination on the grounds of religion or belief

The Employment Directive sets out an anti-discrimination 'principle of equal treatment' in the context of religion or belief. The Employment Equality (Religion or Belief) Regulations 2003 came into force in December 2003.

The Regulations contain sections dealing with discrimination in employment and vocational training, the vicarious liability of employers, exceptions and enforcement.

The law applies to recruitment, terms and conditions, pay, promotion, transfers and dismissals. It applies to all employers

regardless of their size.

The Regulations prohibit:

- direct discrimination (i.e. less favourable treatment on the grounds of religion or belief);
- indirect discrimination whereby a provision or practice is applied which disadvantages people of a particular religion or belief and which is not objectively justified as a proportionate means of achieving a legitimate aim;
- harassment or conduct which violates dignity or creates an intimidating, hostile, degrading, humiliating or offensive environment; and
- victimisation (i.e. less favourable treatment because of something done in connection with the legislation).

The Regulations relating to religion or belief define religion or belief as meaning 'any religion, religious belief or similar philosophical belief'. It remains to be seen how employment tribunals will interpret the Regulations.

Age discrimination

Age legislation is required to comply with the Equal Treatment Directive and has to be implemented by 2006. The period of consultation ended on 20 October 2003, but the consultation on the actual wording of the Regulations which should have commenced early in 2004 has yet to start. Currently employers commonly discriminate against employees or prospective employees because they are perceived to be either too young or too old for a role. This approach will be made unlawful unless employers can objectively justify any such decisions. Both older and younger workers will be free to bring claims before an employment tribunal if they have been discriminated against. The key points are as follows:

- Direct discrimination on grounds of age will be outlawed. It will become unlawful to reject job applicants because of their age unless justification is given.
- Indirect discrimination based on age will be unlawful. A requirement therefore which people of a certain age are less likely to comply with will be unlawful unless it can be justified.
- Employees aged 65 and over will be able to bring claims for unfair dis-

missal and for redundancy payments.
- Employers will therefore need to review current recruitment, promotion and reward practices in terms of potential direct and indirect age discrimination claims.
- Employers will also need to review recruitment, selection and promotion procedures and prepare draft age discrimination policies.

See also: Disability access (page 179); Family-friendly rights (page 251); Human rights (page 329); Private life (page 439).

Sources of further information

'Code of practice for the elimination of discrimination in the field of employment against disabled persons or persons who have had a disability' (DfEE, 1996): ISBN 0 11 703419 3. Available from The Stationery Office: www.tso.co.uk.

ACAS (www.acas.org.uk) has published guidance to the legislation prohibiting discrimination on grounds of sex, race, sexual orientation, and religion or belief.

'Equal Opportunities Policy and Management Guide, version 1.0' (ISBN 1 900648 64 4, £34.99) is available as an electronic download from the Workplace Law Network. Call 0870 777 8881 for details, or visit www.workplacelaw.net.

Dismissal

Pinsent Masons Employment Group

Key points

Employers must dismiss employees in accordance with contract terms in order not to breach the contract and become liable for wrongful dismissal. Regardless of whether there is a breach of contract, dismissals will be unfair unless:

- the dismissal is for one of a list of potentially fair reasons;
- the employer acts reasonably in dismissing the employee; and
- the employer has followed a fair procedure.

Legislation

- Employment Rights Act 1996.
- Employment Act 2002.

What is dismissal?

A number of key employment law rights arise when a 'dismissal' takes place. Dismissal is an act of the employer which occasions a termination of the employment relationship. A resignation – although an act of the employee, not the employer – can also constitute a 'constructive dismissal' where it is in response to a breach of contract by the employer.

Dismissal can also include the expiry and non-renewal of a fixed-term contract.

Notice

Dismissal by an employer can be with or without notice. The amount of notice required will usually be set out in the employment contract. If that is silent, 'reasonable' notice must be given, the length of which will vary depending on the employee's circumstances.

In any event, the following statutory minimum notice must be given by an employer:

- An employee who has been continuously employed for one month or more but less than two years is entitled to not less than one week's notice.
- An employee who has been continuously employed for two years or more but less than 12 years is entitled to one week's notice for each year of continuous employment.
- An employee who has been employed for 12 years or more is entitled to not less than 12 weeks' notice.

Generally, once notice has been given it cannot be withdrawn, save by mutual consent.

Failure by an employer to give notice in accordance with the terms of the con-

---

tract will leave the employer liable to pay damages to the employee in respect of salary and other benefits which would have fallen due in the notice period. If there is a 'pay in lieu of notice' (PILON) clause in the employee's contract, there will be no breach of contract if notice money is paid instead of the employee working out his notice.

The tax treatments of these two types of payment are different. As the latter payment is contractual, the employee will be liable for income tax, whereas the former is treated as damages and may be free of tax up to £30,000.

An act of gross misconduct or gross negligence on the part of an employee may be expected to justify dismissal without notice, sometimes referred to as 'summary dismissal'.

Unfair dismissal

Save for certain special cases (see below), employees must have one year's continuous service (at the date the dismissal takes effect) in order to have the right to claim that they have been unfairly dismissed. A fair dismissal has two elements:

- The employer's reason to dismiss must be one of a list of potentially fair reasons (section 98(1), Employment Rights Act 1996 (ERA)).
- Even if a fair reason exists, it must have been reasonable in all the circumstances for the employer to dismiss the employee (section 94(4), ERA). In other words, the employer must follow a fair procedure (see 'Disciplinary and grievance procedures', page 184).

Potentially fair reasons for dismissal

1. Lack of capability or qualifications

Capability is skill and ability to do the job. This is most often relevant for poor performance or physical incapability such as injury or sickness. Lack of qualifications could involve a practical qualification necessary to do the job which may be lost during employment (e.g. a driver losing a driving licence).

2. Conduct

In other words, misconduct on the part of the employee.

3. Redundancy

For the purposes of the ERA an employee who is dismissed shall be taken to be dismissed by reason of redundancy if the dismissal is wholly or mainly attributable to the fact that his employer has ceased or intends to cease to carry on the business for the purposes of which the employee was employed by him, or to carry on that business in the place where the employee was so employed, or where the requirements of that business for employees to carry out work of a particular kind, or for employees to carry out work of a particular kind in the place where the employee was employed by the employer, have ceased or diminished or are expected to cease or diminish.

4. Continued employment would breach legislation

For example where, if the employment continued, either the employer or the employee would be in breach of health and safety laws.

5. 'Some other substantial reason'

In some ways this is a catch-all to allow

tribunals to respond to the circumstances of individual cases. It can cover a multitude of cases including dismissals by reason of a reorganisation and dismissals in order to achieve necessary economies.

Fairness of the dismissal

Having determined that a potentially fair reason exists, one must then ask the question whether the employer has acted reasonably in all the circumstances in dismissing the employee as a consequence of the reason. Has the employer followed a fair and proper procedure?

Tribunals will take account of the size and administrative resources of the employer. The question of fairness is closely linked to disciplinary procedures and the need to follow a fair procedure in disciplining and dismissing the employee and meeting the minimum statutory standards (see 'Disciplinary and grievance procedures', page 184).

What is appropriate in terms of procedure will vary depending on the reason for the dismissal. The employer must follow a fair and reasonable procedure and the tribunal will look at whether the decision to dismiss the employee and the procedures followed measure up to the standards expected of employers.

Some key procedural points which workplace managers should follow for the most common dismissals are as follows:

1. Capability

- Tell the employee precisely why his performance is poor and what is needed to improve it.
- Explain the next stage of disciplinary action if there is still no improvement (leading up to eventual dismissal).
- Give the employee an opportunity to explain his case at each stage.
- Consider whether training is needed or if an alternative job can be offered.

2. Sickness

- Investigate the true medical position and prognosis for recovery (usually through a medical report).
- Consult with the employee.
- Can the employer be expected to wait any longer for recovery?
- The employer should also consider the Disability Discrimination Act 1995 before taking further action.

3. Conduct

- The question is whether the employer has reasonable grounds to believe the employee is guilty of misconduct.
- Carry out a full investigation.
- Inform the employee of all the allegations in advance of disciplinary meetings.
- Put all the evidence of misconduct to the employee.
- The employee must have an opportunity to put his case on the evidence.
- Dismiss only on the evidence put to the employee.

4. Redundancy

Although a potentially fair reason for dismissal, redundancy can give rise to unfair dismissals where there is a failure to follow a fair procedure. Fair and proper procedures are based on:

- giving the employee advance warning of the potential redundancy situation;
- consulting with the employee as to the selection criteria to be used;

- considering alternative employment;
- the employer taking a decision to dismiss for reasons of redundancy only after proper consultation has taken place;
- allowing the employee time off to look for alternative jobs; and
- continuing to look for alternative jobs for the employee within the organisation.

Unfair dismissal remedies

Employees have three months after the date of dismissal in which to bring a claim before an employment tribunal or, alternatively, employers and employees can decide to place the dispute before an ACAS-appointed arbitrator under the ACAS Arbitration Scheme. The scheme is devised to provide a quicker, cheaper and, where possible, more amicable resolution to this type of dispute. However, very few people have elected to follow this route to date. Remedies available to both the tribunal and an ACAS arbitrator include re-engagement or reinstatement, both of which are imposed only rarely. More usually, compensation is awarded.

This falls under two heads:

- The first is the basic award, calculated by reference to salary, age and length of service, subject to a maximum which was increased on 1 February 2004 to £8,100.
- The second is the compensatory award which is designed to reimburse the employee for actual losses and is at the discretion of the tribunal subject to a maximum, also increased on 1 February 2003 and now set at £55,000. The overall cap has been increased significantly in recent years and is likely to keep rising in the future.

Automatically unfair reasons

Detailed provisions exist for claims which do not require one year's continuous service and where dismissal for that reason may be automatically unfair.

The most important of these are dismissals for:

- membership of a trade union or for participating in trade union activities;

Sources of further information

DTI publication PL 714 Rev. 11: 'Dismissal – fair and unfair: a guide for employers': www.dti.gov.uk/er/individual/fair-pl714.htm.

ACAS Code of Practice on Disciplinary and Grievance Procedures. This can be ordered via the ACAS website: www.acas.org.uk.

Employment Tribunals Online: www.employmenttribunals.gov.uk.

'Non-Contractual Grievance Policy and Management Guide, version 1.0' (ISBN 1 900648 30 X, £49.99) is available as an electronic download from the Workplace Law Network. Call 0870 777 8881 for details, or visit www.workplacelaw.net.

- taking action on specified health and safety grounds (including leaving premises due to danger);
- bringing statutory rights to the attention of the employer;
- pregnancy or related reasons;
- holding the status of a part-time worker;
- detrimental treatment under the Working Time Regulations 1998 or Minimum Wage Act 1998;
- exercising a right to be accompanied by a union representative or fellow worker at a disciplinary or grievance hearing (see 'Disciplinary and grievance procedures', page 184);
- asserting rights under the 'whistle-blowers' legislation (see 'Whistle-blowers', page 542);
- taking leave for family reasons;
- refusal of Sunday working by shop and betting employees;
- performing certain functions as a trustee of an occupational pension scheme; and
- performing certain functions as an employee representative under TUPE or collective redundancy legislation.

See also: Disciplinary and grievance procedures (page 184); Employment disputes (page 228); Redundancy (page 455); Whistleblowers (page 542).

Display screen equipment

Andrew Richardson, Scott Wilson

Key points

- Use of display screen equipment (DSE) constitutes an adverse health hazard.
- Workers using or operating DSE can suffer postural problems, visual problems, and fatigue and stress.
- Employers must identify users or operators – those whose normal work is to habitually use VDUs. Laptops and homeworkers are included.
- Employers must carry out a risk assessment of these people's work, using trained personnel.
- Employers must analyse workstations and ensure they meet minimum standards.
- Employers must provide breaks and variety in the DSE users' or operators' work.
- Employers must provide and pay for eye and eyesight tests, and provide spectacles (where needed for screen-viewing distance), if employees request.
- Employers must provide training and information.

Legislation

- Health and Safety at Work etc. Act 1974.
- Management of Health and Safety at Work Regulations 1999.
- Workplace (Health, Safety and Welfare) Regulations 1992.
- Provision and Use of Work Equipment Regulations 1998.
- Health and Safety (Display Screen Equipment) Regulations 1992 (as amended by the Health and Safety (Miscellaneous Amendments) Regulations 2002)

Display Screen Equipment Regulations

The Regulations define what is deemed to be DSE, who is deemed to be a 'user' or 'operator' and what a workstation comprises. The criteria for determining who can be designated as a user or operator, as updated in 2003, state that it will be generally appropriate to classify people as a user or operator if they:

- normally use DSE for continuous or near-continuous spells of an hour or more at a time; and
- use DSE in this way more or less daily; and
- have to transfer information quickly to or from the DSE; and

---

- need to apply high levels of attention and concentration; or
- are highly dependent on DSE or have little choice about using it; or
- need special training or skills to use DSE.

The Regulations require that all employers carry out a suitable and sufficient risk assessment on the workstations and it is suggested that a suitable way is to use an ergonomic checklist. Within the appendices of the new Regulations is an example of a checklist that can be used. The checklist aids the employer in assessing the following:

- *Display screen*. Are the characters clear and readable, is the text size adequate, is the image stable, is the screen size suitable, can you adjust the screen brightness and contrast, can the screen swivel and tilt, is it free of glare and reflections, and are there window coverings in an adequate condition?
- *Keyboard*. Is it separate from the screen, does it tilt, is there a comfortable keying position, does the user have a good keyboard technique and are the keys easily readable?
- *Mouse/trackball*. Is it suitable for the task, is it close to the user, is there wrist/forearm support, does it work smoothly, can the software adjust the pointer speed and accuracy?
- *Software*. Is the software suitable for the task?
- *Furniture*. Is the work surface large enough, can the user reach all of the equipment, are the surfaces free from glare, is the chair suitable, is the chair stable, does the chair adjust in terms of back height and tilt, seat height, swivel mechanism

and castors, etc., is the back supported, are the arms horizontal and eyes the same height as the top of the VDU, are the feet flat on the floor?

- *Environment*. Is there room to change the position, is the lighting suitable, is the air comfortable, is the heating level comfortable, are the levels of noise comfortable?
- *The user/operator*. Have they any other problems, have they experienced discomfort, do they know of their entitlement to eye and eyesight testing, do they take regular breaks?

Trained personnel, generally meeting the following criteria, must carry out these assessments. They must be familiar with the main requirements of the DSE Regulations and should have the ability to:

- identify hazards and assess risks;
- draw upon additional sources of information on risk as appropriate;
- draw valid and reliable conclusions from assessments and identify steps to reduce risk;
- make a clear record of the assessment and communicate findings to those who need to take action and to the worker concerned; and
- recognise their own limitations as to the assessment so that further expertise can be called upon if necessary.

These assessments must be reviewed whenever:

- a major change occurs to the software, equipment or workstation;
- the workstation is relocated;
- the environment is changed; or
- there is a substantial change to the tasks or amount of time using DSE.

The purpose of the risk assessment is to reduce the risk of the workforce suffering postural problems, visual problems, and fatigue and stress.

Regulation 3 clarifies that the Regulations apply to all workstations, not just those used by users or operators. The Regulations require all employers to ensure their workstations meet the requirements set out in the schedule encompassed within the Regulations. This includes the use of laptop computers and homeworking.

The Regulations set out the criteria for ensuring that the daily work routine of users will not contribute towards any of the risks identified earlier and advises on the nature and timing of breaks. If you are a user or operator, then Regulation 5 places a duty upon the employer to provide eyesight tests and special corrective appliances (normally spectacles) for DSE use.

The Regulations require that all users or operators be provided with information on a number of relevant points including:

- the DSE Regulations themselves;
- risk assessment and means of reducing risk;
- breaks and activity changes; and
- eye and eyesight tests

  and to have initial training and training when the workstation is modified (Regulation 6).

Appendices within the Regulations give guidance on the use of laptop computers and compliance with the Regulations and the use of mouse, trackball or other pointing devices.

See also: Eye and eyesight tests (page 246); Furniture (page 284).

Sources of further information

The main source of information in relation to the use of DSE is L26 'Work with Display Screen Equipment – Health and Safety (Display Screen Equipment) Regulations 1992 as amended by the Health and Safety (Miscellaneous Amendments) Regulations 2002 – Guidance on Regulations' (HSE Books, 2003): ISBN 0 7176 2582 6. The document provides all the guidance needed by employers and identifies any further documentation that is relevant.

A shorter basic guide 'Working with VDUs' (revised 2003) can be downloaded at www.hse.gov.uk/pubns/indg36.pdf.

The Workplace Law Network provides training in working with display screen equipment, including a one-day course on workstation risk assessments. Call 0870 777 8881 for details, or visit www.workplacelaw.net.

Dress codes

Jackie Thomas, Berwin Leighton Paisner

Key points

Employers seek to apply dress codes to their employees for many reasons. In doing so, however, it is important that employers consider any potentially discriminatory implications as dress codes have historically been challenged under both the Sex Discrimination Act and the Race Relations Act.

Furthermore, since the European Convention on Human Rights has been incorporated into UK law by way of the Human Rights Act, it may also be possible to challenge the application of a dress code on the basis that it infringes the employee's human rights.

To avoid potential liability, employers should ensure that the policy applies evenly to both men and women and that any requirements imposed are reasonable when balancing the rights of the employee and the requirements of the employer's business. Factors which may be relevant include:

- whether the employee has contact with the public;
- whether the dress code is necessary for performance;
- health and safety; and
- illegality.

Legislation

- Sex Discrimination Act 1975.
- Race Relations Act 1976.
- Human Rights Act 1998.
- Employment Equality (Religion or Belief) Regulations 2003.

In what situations will an employer seek to enforce a dress code?

Dress codes are used in the workplace for a number of reasons. First, they may be applied for reasons of food hygiene. Second, employers may require em-ployees to wear a uniform in order to signify their status (e.g. a ticket inspector). Finally, they are also used by many employers merely as a way of ensuring that their employees are dressed appropriately (whether or not the employees concerned come into contact with the employer's clients or customers).

Impact of the Sex Discrimination Act on dress codes

The Sex Discrimination Act provides that it is discriminatory for an employer to treat an employee less favourably than it would treat an employee of the opposite sex. This amounts to direct discrimination and the employer cannot defend such a claim on the grounds that the treatment is justified.

There are numerous cases of employees claiming that their employer's dress code is directly discriminatory. Examples include provisions of policies which prevented female employees from wearing trousers or which prevented male employees from having long hair. In 2003 two tribunals simultaneously considered whether it was discriminatory for a policy to require a male employee to wear a tie. The tribunals in these claims reached conflicting conclusions, in one case finding that such a policy was discriminatory and in the other concluding that the employer's policy was acceptable.

The reasoning for this conflict is that tribunals will not directly compare the treatment of men and women in respect of each requirement of the dress code. The crucial issue will be whether, when viewed as a whole, the policy treats men and women in a generally equivalent manner in order to enforce a 'common principle of smartness'. In fact, this principle was expressly reaffirmed by the Employment Appeals Tribunal (EAT) in relation to the appeal of the case in which the tribunal had found the dress code to be discriminatory.

The EAT held that the policy did require women to dress to an equivalent level of smartness (despite the fact that they did not do so in practice) and so the tribunal should properly have considered whether the requirement for a man to wear a collar and tie with no specific requirements for what a woman should wear was in itself discriminatory. The tri-

bunal had not considered this point and so the matter was remitted to a fresh tribunal.

Potential claims under the Race Relations Act

It is also possible for claims to arise under the Race Relations Act if an employer's dress code policy has a disparate impact on a particular racial group. An example which resulted in a claim was a policy which required a Sikh to shave his beard for health and safety reasons. The employee claimed that this amounted to indirect discrimination (in that it was more difficult for Sikhs as a racial group to comply), but the tribunals held that the employer's actions were justifiable as the policy was in place for reasons of food hygiene. To the extent that such a requirement could not be justified it would be discriminatory.

Historically, such claims were limited by the fact that the Race Relations Act did not prevent discrimination on the grounds of religious belief unless the individual could also be said to fall within a particular racial group. However, this loophole has now been closed by the introduction of the Employment Equality (Religion or Belief) Regulations 2003.

Human rights issues

As well as being potentially discriminatory, it is also possible for a dress code to infringe an employee's human rights. The European Convention on Human Rights has now been incorporated into UK law by the Human Rights Act. Of the rights it enshrines, Article 10 (the right to freedom of expression), Article 9 (freedom of thought, conscience and religion) and Article 14 (prohibition on discrimination) are all relevant when considering dress codes.

In the case of most private sector employers, employees will not be able to bring a claim directly under the Human Rights Act, but the employees of public authorities may be able to do so. Further, since the tribunals are required to construe existing laws in a way which is compatible with these rights, future claims based on discrimination legislation may also need to take into account these rights when balancing the needs of the employer with the rights of the employee.

See also: Discrimination (page 189); Human rights (page 329).

Sources of further information

Equal Opportunities Commission: www.eoc.org.uk.

Commission for Racial Equality: www.cre.gov.uk.

Driving at work

Jessica Burt, CMS Cameron McKenna

There are twin areas of concern for employers in relation to workplace driving which overlap to a greater or lesser degree depending on the employer organisation:

- Road traffic law and the Highway Code.
- Health and safety legislation.

Legislation

- Health and Safety at Work etc. Act 1974.
- Management of Health and Safety at Work Regulations 1999.
- Provision and Use of Work Equipment Regulations 1992.
- Road Traffic Act 1988.
- Road Vehicles (Construction and Use) Regulations 1986 (as amended).
- Road Vehicles (Construction and Use) (Amendment) (No. 4) Regulations 2003.
- Road Transport Directive (2002/15/EC).
- Council Regulation 3821/85 on recording equipment in road transport.

Cases

- *R -v- Martin Graves and Victor Coates* April 2003: re corporate manslaughter.
- *Skills Motor Coaches Ltd and others*: C-297/99 – European Court of Justice – 18.01.01: re tachograph recording.

Road traffic law and the Highway Code

These lay down certain rules and restrictions (e.g. speed limits) and are normally enforced by the police and the courts. While the driver of the vehicle will primarily be held responsible for any offence, employers may also be liable, for instance in setting timetables or schedules so tight that the driver would be breaking speed limits if he attempted to meet them. The Magistrates Act 1980 may also be relevant to employers in England and Wales who aid, abet, counsel or procure an offence. Employers are also responsible for ensuring their company vehicles are properly taxed and insured.

Health and safety legislation

Employers should manage the risks associated with at-work road journeys and other on-the-road work activities within the framework they should have in place for managing health and safety within their organisations. Occupational drivers or people employed to work on or by roads should be offered the same protection as those working within fixed workplaces. Employers also have a responsibility to ensure that others are not put at risk by the work activities of their employees.

Any breach of an employer's statutory or regulatory duties towards its employees giving rise to criminal liability may also be relied upon by a civil claimant as evidence of an employer's breach of duty in a negligence action and indeed in support of a claim for constructive dismissal.

There has been a growing emphasis since the publication of the Work-related Road Safety Task Group's Report recommendations in 2001 (see 'Sources of further information' below) towards health and safety legislation and the responsibility of employers to take precedence in any work-related vehicle accident.

In light of this it is important that employers implement a health and safety policy for driving at work and keep abreast of the developments affecting workplace driving. The main areas are currently:

- working time;
- mobile phones; and
- regulatory compliance/Motor Insurance Database.

These are discussed in the sections that follow.

Working time

Although the Working Time Directive has been law in the UK since 1998, it previously excluded key areas of air, rail and road. New EU legislation by way of the Road Transport Directive 2002/15/EC (vehicles over 3.5 tonnes) is to be implemented by 23 March 2005, and the Horizontal Amending Directive, which amends the Working Time Regulations with effect from 1 August 2003 for drivers of smaller vehicles, implements an average of 48 hours per week with adequate rest periods alongside other requirements.

Fleet managers should have procedures in place to ensure that no workers are operating vehicles for longer than the permitted periods and are fit to drive with adequate rest periods allocated. The Road Transport Directive states a break of 30 minutes to be mandatory after six hours and a break of 45 minutes between six and nine hours. Specific guidance from the HSE on what constitutes 'adequate rest' is, however, still awaited.

Mobile phones

Under previous laws motorists could only be prosecuted for using mobiles if they failed to keep proper control of their vehicle. In addition to this there is now a new offence under the Road Vehicles (Construction and Use) Regulations of driving while using a hand-held mobile phone which took effect from 1 December 2003. Drivers committing this offence will be liable to pay a £30 fixed penalty or a maximum fine on conviction in court of £1,000. (Lorry, bus and coach drivers face a fine of £2,500.) The Department for Transport (DfT) intends that in future the offence should also attract three penalty points and the fixed penalty fine be increased to £60.

The 2003 Regulations apply in all circumstances other than when the vehicle is parked, with the engine off. This means that the prohibition applies even if a vehicle has paused at traffic lights, stopped in a temporary traffic jam, or is in very slow-moving traffic.

Under the 2003 Regulations the definition of 'hand held' means that a mobile phone or other device will fall into the 'hand-held' category if it is held at some point during the course of making or receiving a call or fulfilling some other interactive communication function. An interactive communication function includes sending or receiving oral or written messages, facsimile documents, or still or moving images, or accessing the Internet. The definition of 'hands free' is such that some products which are marketed as 'hands free' may still lead to an offence under the new Regulations as they require the user to hold the phone in order to press buttons or to read a message on the phone's screen.

The DfT has devised that the pushing of buttons on a phone while, for example, it is in a cradle, on the steering wheel or on the handlebars of a motorbike is allowed, provided that the phone is not held. Hands-free products which do not require drivers to significantly alter their position in relation to the steering wheel in order to use them have not fallen foul of the change in the law.

Employers' liability

The 2003 Regulations also created an offence of 'causing or permitting' another person to drive while using a hand-held phone or other similar device. Employers may, therefore, be prosecuted if they require their employees to use their phones when driving.

The DfT has stated that employers cannot expect their employees to make or receive mobile phone calls while driving. This must be reflected in the company's health and safety policy and risk management policy. Information from the DfT indicates that employers will not be liable simply for supplying a telephone or for telephoning an employee who was driving. However, employers must send a clear message to employees that they are forbidden to use their hand-held mobile phones while driving and their employer will not require them to make or receive calls when driving.

Employers should inform their staff

that, when driving, hand-held mobile phones should be switched off, or, if switched on, the calls should be left to go through to voicemail, and that a safe place to stop should be found to check messages and return calls. Company policy should specify that using a hand-held phone or similar device while driving is a criminal offence and will be treated as a disciplinary matter.

If no policy is implemented and employers are shown to have permitted the use of a hand-held mobile phone while driving, they may be:

• liable under the Road Vehicles (Construction and Use) Regulations 2003;
• vicariously liable if an employee causes an accident while driving on business;
• liable under the Health and Safety at Work etc. Act 1974 as employers are obliged to provide a safe system of work and to do what they reasonably can to ensure the safety of staff and others; and
• liable if there is a fatal accident involving the use of a hand-held mobile phone while driving. Where this practice was well known and encouraged throughout the company, there could be the possibility of a criminal corporate manslaughter prosecution against directors, as has been the case with reference to the Working Time Regulations.

Hands-free mobile phones

The DfT regulatory impact assessment on the subject has stated that, while the use of any mobile phone by drivers is not recommended, hands-free kits are widely available and the use of these kits is still legal.

However, employers should be aware that this does not mean that drivers will be exempt from prosecution altogether if they use hands-free kits. Dangerous and careless driving can still be committed as separate offences under the Road Traffic Act 1988.

Extensive research shows evidence that using a hands-free phone while driving distracts the driver and increases the risk of an accident. Therefore, although it is thought that a hands-free ban would be unenforceable, nevertheless employers should seriously consider if it is safest for them to ban employees using hands-free equipment too. Many businesses have used 'best practice' and employed an outright ban.

Employers who install hands-free kits should balance the commercial advantage of this with the potential risk of future liability were an employee to cause an accident while speaking on the phone and driving.

If employers provide employees with hands-free kits, a risk assessment should be carried out and very clear guidance on the use of such kits should also be provided (i.e. to limit outgoing calls to emergency use and when it is safe to do so, to use voice activation technology when making outgoing calls, to tell all incoming callers that one is driving and to keep calls short). Appropriate hands-free sets should be provided (see above) and, if employees use their own, their standard should be checked.

Practical tips for employers

The main points on which employers should consider giving guidance to their employees should include the following:

General guidance:

- Switch off the phone while driving and let it take messages.
- Or leave the phone switched on and let the call go into voicemail.
- Alternatively, ask a passenger to deal with the call.
- Find a safe place to stop before turning off the engine and picking up the messages and returning calls.

Minimum guidance if hands-free phones permitted:

- Limit outgoing calls to emergency use and when it is safe to do so.
- Use voice activation technology when making outgoing calls.
- Tell all incoming callers that one is driving and ask them to keep the call short.
- A clear section should be inserted into the company health and safety policy on company procedure on the use of mobile phones and driving. This should be brought to the attention of all employees: breach of the policy should be a disciplinary offence and compliance with the policy monitored.

Regulatory compliance/Motor Insurance Database

It is a given that all vehicles should be taxed and insured (and have up-to-date MOT where necessary), but some half a million vehicles have also yet to be entered on to the Motor Insurance Database. As part of the 4th EU Motor Insurance Directive it was a requirement that companies ensure that details of every vehicle in their fleet was on the Motor Insurance Database (MID) by 20 January 2003. Fleets could be subject to fines of up to £5,000 for not registering vehicles on the database, which was created as part of a major anti-crime initiative to reduce the problem of uninsured driving.

Employers should check that privately owned vehicles are not used for work purposes unless they are insured for business use and, where the vehicle is over three years old, they have a valid MOT certificate.

Occupational road risk policy

In order to comply with the above legislative requirements, it is recommended to employers that they implement a formal policy covering 'occupational road risk' as part of their overall safety inspections.

The main implementation of this policy should be to provide for regular risk assessments. It is a requirement under the Management of Health and Safety at Work Regulations 1999 that all employers carry out an assessment of the risks to the health and safety of their employees, or themselves, while they are at work, and to other people who may be affected by their work activities. This includes any driving activity on the road. The Regulations require the risk assessment to be reviewed periodically to ensure that it remains valid.

Employers should consider the risks to employees on the road in the same way as for those in a workplace.

Such risk assessments should include steps to ensure that employees are competent to drive, or work, safely on the road, such as document checks, health checks and testing for drugs or alcohol as part of a confidential health procedure.

As stated above, the use of hand-held mobile phones should be prohibited while driving and this should extend to office employees telephoning colleagues

on the road. Hands-free devices should have guidelines as to when and how they may be utilised.

The number of working/driving hours should be monitored and rest breaks prescribed.

Full insurance and vehicle safety checks should be carried out on a regular basis. There should be a clear procedure for defect reporting.

As well as checking the competency, training and fitness of drivers, the suitability of vehicles should also be monitored. If vehicles are provided by employers to drivers, they may be covered under the Provision and Use of Work Equipment Regulations 1992 and employers should ensure all safety equipment is in good working order and updated.

Workplace transport cases

A case which illustrates the combination of working time and dangerous driving is that of *R -v- Martin Graves and Victor Coates*, which was heard at Basildon Crown Court on 4 April 2003. A haulage company owner and one of his lorry drivers were each jailed for four years following a road accident in which an articulated lorry crashed into the back of a vehicle, killing the driver. The lorry driver had been working continuously for 20 hours without proper rest breaks and was suffering from sleep deprivation. The company owner was found guilty of manslaughter and the lorry driver was convicted of causing death by dangerous driving. Both men were also convicted of tachograph offences relating to falsifying records.

In *Criminal Proceedings against Skills Motor Coaches Ltd and others C-297/99 – European Court of Justice – 18.01.01* it was held that a driver who went to a specific place, other than the undertaking's operating centre, indicated to him by his employer in order to take over and drive a vehicle was satisfying an obligation towards his employer. During that journey, therefore, he did not freely dispose of his time. The court had already held that 'period of work' for the purposes of the Regulation included times at which the driver was actually engaged in activities having a bearing on driving, including driving time (*Michielsen* C-394/92 [1994] ECR I-2497). Time spent by a driver to reach the place where he took over a tachograph vehicle was liable to have a bearing on his driving, in that it would affect his state of tiredness. In the light of the aim of improving road safety, such time had to be regarded as forming part of all other periods of work within the meaning of Article 15 of Council Regulation 3821/85 on recording equipment in road transport. The question whether the driver had received precise instructions as to how he should travel was not decisive. By going to a specific place at some distance from his employer's operating centre, the driver was performing a task required of him by virtue of his employment relationship. Therefore, the obligation to record such a period applied regardless of whether it preceded the taking over of a tachograph vehicle.

Summary

The emphasis has shifted to an investigation of the employer in any workplace accident. It is essential that there is a policy and safety procedure in place so that compliance with health and safety legislation can be seen to be actively implemented and ongoing. This will not only protect against any HSE investigations but will also help to protect against any civil claims.

See also: Vehicles at work (page 510); Working time (page 552).

Sources of further information

The HSE web pages on work-related road safety may be found at www.hse.gov.uk/roadsafety/index.htm.

INDG382 'Driving at work: managing work-related road safety' can be downloaded from www.hse.gov.uk/pubns/indg382.pdf.

'Managing Occupational Road Risk: The RoSPA Guide' is available from RoSPA. Call 0870 777 2090, or visit www.rospa.org.uk.

The Work-related Road Safety Task Group's Report is accessible at www.hse.gov.uk/roadsafety/traffic1.pdf.

Think! Road Safety website: www.thinkroadsafety.gov.uk.

'Driving at Work Policy and Management Guide, version 2.0' (ISBN 1 900648 41 5, £74.99) is available as an electronic download from the Workplace Law Network. Call 0870 777 8881 for details, or visit www.workplacelaw.net.

Electricity and electrical equipment

Phil Wright, SafetyCO UK

Key points

- The ratio of fatalities to injuries is higher for electrical accidents than for most other categories of injury. If an electrical accident occurs, the chances of a fatality are about 1:30 compared with a ratio of 1:800 for other types of accident. The consequences of contact with electricity are burns, electrocution, explosion and fire.
- Almost a quarter of all reportable electrical accidents involve portable electrical equipment. It is a requirement of the Electricity at Work Regulations 1989 that portable electrical equipment (or portable appliances) are tested at regular intervals, though the legislation does *not* specify a 'correct' or minimum interval between tests.

Legislation

- Electricity at Work Regulations 1989.
- Management of Health and Safety at Work Regulations 1999.

Cause of electrical failure

Failure and interruption of electrical supply are most commonly caused by:

- damaged insulation;
- inadequate systems of work;
- inadequate over-current protection fuses (circuit breakers);
- inadequate earthing;
- carelessness and complacency;
- overheated equipment; and
- poor maintenance and testing.

Prevention of electrical accidents

Regulation 4(3) of the Electricity at Work Regulations 1989 states that 'work on or near to an electrical system shall be carried out in such a manner as not to give risk, so far as is reasonably practicable, to danger'. The golden rule of electrical safety is that equipment to be worked on should always be made dead.

Almost a quarter of all electrical accidents involve portable equipment; and the risks are greater because the hands are usually already tightly gripping the equipment, making it almost impossible for the victim to let go. The following points should carefully be considered to minimise the risks of using electrical equipment:

- Correct selection of equipment.
- Selection of lowest practicable voltage, i.e. use of transformers.
- Correct use of equipment.
- Use of residual current devices, circuit breakers.
- Training.
- Issue of personal protective equipment (PPE).
- Safe storage.
- Reporting defects immediately.
- Insulating and double-insulating equipment.
- Checking plugs, couplers and fuses.
- Routine inspection and maintenance by a competent person

Electrical installations and appliances

The flow of electric current through anything that will conduct it will cause heating. This effect is used deliberately in many types of electrical appliances, but the design will ensure that overheating does not occur. In appliances where the heating effect is not wanted but unavoidable, provision for cooling will be incorporated.

If an appliance is faulty (there are a number of possible ways in which it could be) or the flow of heat away from the device is restricted, overheating and the ignition of surrounding combustible material can result. This is equally true with regard to the wiring installation that carries electricity to an appliance or other device that uses it.

To reduce the possibility of fire it is essential that all electrical work is done competently, that electrical appliances are used correctly, and that all electrical installations and devices are either maintained in good condition or taken out of use.

Portable appliance testing (PAT)

Portable electrical equipment needs testing at regular intervals, but it is important to note that there is no statutory inspection period for such equipment. The HSE definition of portable equipment is equipment that is 'not part of a fixed installation but may be connected to a fixed installation by means of a flexible cable and either a socket and plug or a spur box or similar means. It may be hand held or hand operated while connected to the supply, or is intended or likely to be moved while connected to the supply.' Auxiliary equipment such as plugs and extension leads is included in the definition.

The frequency of testing portable appliances will depend on a number of factors, including the nature of the work task, frequency of use and environmental conditions (e.g. indoor/outdoor use).

Electrical shock and treatment

Most electrical shocks occur because of earth faults. This is because the earth connector on an appliance is either broken or not connected. In the event of direct contact between the live conductor and the casing, the casing becomes live. Anyone touching the casing would become the earth conductor and suffer an electrical shock.

Your body is an electrical conductor. A current will flow through it when you touch a live conductor and make a connection to earth.

The strength of the current depends on the state of health, age, dampness of the skin and other factors.

It is absolutely essential that when people are at risk from electricity adequate first-aid facilities are available. The

Action to be taken when faced with an electrocution

1   Act at once – any delay may be fatal!
2. Assess the situation – make sure that it is safe to approach the casualty.
3. Isolate the casualty from the electrical supply:
    (a) Turn off the electricity.
    (b) If that is not possible pull casualty clear with a dry insulator, e.g. rubber gloves, rope, newspaper, wooden pole
    Stand on a dry non-conducting surface, e.g. rubber mat, wooden board.
    Do not touch casualty's bare skin.
4. Check that the airway is clear.
5. Check for signs of breathing.
    (a) If breathing – place in recovery position and call for medical aid.
    (b) If *not* breathing – call for someone to get medical aid, begin mouth-to-mouth. When calling for medical or emergency aid, ensure that clear information is given to the emergency services. Do not use local or slang terms for addresses.
6. Start mouth-to-mouth ventilation – speed in starting mouth-to-mouth is essential!
    (a) Recheck airway is clear.
    (b) Remove obstruction around face and neck.
    (c) Open airway, seal the nose.
    (d) Begin mouth-to-mouth – give two inflations as quickly as possible.
    (e) Check breathing and circulation.
7. If after two ventilations there is no response – start external chest compressions.
    (a) Locate centre lower half of breastbone.
    (b) With arms straight, press vertically down 4cm – repeat 15 times.
8. If necessary repeat mouth-to-mouth and external chest compressions cycle.
9. Do not leave the casualty.
10. Continue to monitor the casualty until medical aid arrives.

first-aider(s) must be trained to protect themselves and others, and to give first-aid treatment for electrocution.

The passage of the electric current through the body affects the central nervous system, the muscles and the heart. It may produce:

- muscular spasm (frozen grip);
- burns where it enters and leaves the body; or
- restriction of breathing.

Appropriate notices explaining electrical-shock procedures should be posted in prominent positions wherever they may be needed.

See also: First aid (page 275); Personal protective equipment (page 425).

Sources of further information

HSE web page on electrical safety: www.hse.gov.uk/electricity/index.htm.

INDG354 'Safety in electrical testing at work: general guidance' (HSE Books, 2002): ISBN 0 7176 2296 7.

HSR25 'Memorandum of guidance on the Electricity at Work Regulations 1989. Guidance on Regulations' (HSE Books, 1998): ISBN 0 7176 1602 9.

Emergency procedures

Phil Wright, SafetyCO UK

Key points

- Regulation 8 of the Management of Health and Safety at Work Regulations 1999 requires every employer to establish appropriate procedures to be followed in the event of serious and imminent danger to persons at work.
- Regulation 9 of the same Regulations requires an employer – or controller of premises – to ensure that any necessary contacts are arranged with external services, particularly with regard to first aid, emergency medical care and rescue work.
- The Fire Precautions (Workplace) (Amendment) Regulations 1999 require an employer – or controller of premises – to carry out a fire risk assessment of their premises.

Legislation

- Fire Precautions Act 1971.
- Fire Precautions (Workplace) (Amendment) Regulations 1999.
- Fire Safety Regulatory Reform Order (proposed).
- Management of Health and Safety at Work Regulations 1999 and associated Regulations.

It should be noted that the Government has consulted widely on the introduction of a new piece of overarching legislation intended to bring the management of fire safety in occupied buildings under one roof. The proposed Fire Safety Regulatory Reform Order was intended to be introduced in spring 2004, but no revised introduction date has yet been set.

Fire risk assessment

The key points of a fire risk assessment are:

- Identification of any fire hazards – such as readily combustible materials, highly flammable substances and sources of heat.
- Identification of any persons who are specially at risk, and making special provisions for persons with disabilities.
- Identification of where fire hazards can be reduced or removed.
- Recording the findings.

The competent person undertaking the assessment needs to address the following issues:

- Legal/general.
- Means of escape.

- Fire alarms/fire detection
- Special risks.
- Firefighting equipment.
- Emergency lighting.
- Maintenance.
- Housekeeping.
- Notices.

Emergency evacuation plan

The information gained from a fire risk assessment would enable the employer, or controller of premises where more than one business is based, to formulate an emergency evacuation plan to cover not only fire but other emergencies relating to a bomb threat or major incidents or accidents.

The plan could be based on four distinct stages:

- Recognition of the emergency.
- Communication of the emergency.
- Preparation for the evacuation.
- Action in the emergency evacuation.

The plan should also cover the following issues:

- Action to be taken by person discovering the emergency.
- How the emergency services are to be called and who is responsible.
- Type of warning system (bells/klaxon) and location of call points.
- Escape routes.
- Duties and identities of persons with special responsibilities.
- Safe assembly points.
- Procedures for dealing with the emergency services on arrival.
- Training required for all employees or occupiers.

Information for and training of employees

As with other assessments and safety plans it is essential that all employees or occupiers of premises are given adequate instructions and information on the action to be taken in the event of an emergency evacuation.

Each individual should have the information in written form, reinforced with practical demonstrations in the form of regular drills. They should know the basics:

- How to raise the alarm, and call for assistance if necessary.
- What to do when hearing the alarm – leaving the building without delay using the nearest safe exit route.
- To report to the designated assembly point.
- Not to re-enter buildings until instructed by the competent person in charge along with general information such as not to use the lifts.

Facilities managers need to be aware of the implications if fire action notices (which should be positioned at every fire alarm call point) state that persons should tackle the fire with the equipment if they feel able to do so.

This would require suitable practical training in the choice of, and correct way to use, the proper extinguishers – bearing in mind the importance of the right type of extinguisher for the type of fire, and the weight of some extinguishers.

Practise the emergency evacuation

Emergency evacuation practices (or drills) should be carried out every six months (every three months if night-time working at the premises is involved).

It is the responsibility of the appointed manager or management team for the premises to organise and document the manner in which the drill is carried out.

Records of such drills should be kept containing:

- exact location of the drill;
- date and time;
- total number of participants;
- the evacuation time;
- any problems identified;
- actions required to be taken; and
- date of next drill.

Equipment testing

All equipment that could be involved in an emergency evacuation should be tested at the required intervals (which will vary from weekly to annually). This will include:

- detection and alarm system;
- firefighting equipment;
- automatic door release units; and
- emergency lighting.

Contact with external services

A register should be maintained by the facilities manager, and be readily available, detailing the addresses, telephone numbers and contact names of all the emergency services – i.e. ambulance, fire and police.

Relevant information of each employer's undertaking and premises should be provided to the emergency services.

In July 2004 the Government issued a consultation paper entitled 'Emergencies for Fire and Rescue Authorities', in which it was proposed that a more coherent strategy should be applied to establish the responsibilities of fire and rescue authorities and the way they co-operate with other authorities in an emergency situation. Following completion of the consultation in December 2004, the Government intends to issue a new Order in 2005.

See also: Fire extinguishers (page 255); Fire: means of escape (page 263); Fire risk assessments (page 271); Lighting (page 367); Means of fighting fire (page 267).

Sources of further information

'Emergencies for Fire and Rescue Authorities: A consultation document' (Office of the Deputy Prime Minister, 2004): www.odpm.gov.uk.

INDG246 'Prepared for ... emergency' (HSE Books, 1997): ISBN 0 7176 1330 5. Provides guidance for SMEs in the chemical industry.

Employee consultation

Joanne Owers, Charles Russell Employment and Pensions
Service Group

Key points

- The Information and Consultation of Employees Regulations 2004 (ICER) come into force in April 2005 and will affect undertakings with 150 or more employees.
- The Regulations provide a statutory basis for reaching agreement on keeping employees informed and consulted about matters affecting their employment.
- The Regulations will affect all undertakings with 50 or more employees from April 2008.
- The request to negotiate an agreement is triggered where either the employer starts the process or there is a valid employee request.
- Where there is a valid pre-existing agreement in place, the employer may ballot the workforce to determine whether they endorse the employee request.
- If the workforce do not endorse the request, the pre-existing arrangement continues.
- If negotiations fail to lead to agreement, the 'default provisions' will apply.
- If there is no employee request or the employer does not commence negotiations, there is no obligation to establish an information and consultation (I&C) agreement.

Legislation

- Information and Consultation Directive (2002/14/EC).
- Draft Information and Consultation of Employees Regulations 2004.

Introduction

ICER comes into force in April 2005 and implements the EU Information and Consultation Directive. These Regulations are aimed at providing a statutory basis for keeping employees informed and consulted about employment issues which affect them in the workplace. This is a significant piece of legislation which will have a dramatic effect on managing industrial relations in the UK, particularly for employers who are not used to dealing with issues on a collective basis.

The Regulations will come into force in stages depending on the number of employees in the particular undertaking:

- 150 or more employees: 6 April 2005.
- 100 or more employees: 6 April 2007.
- 50 or more employees: 6 April 2008.

ICER applies to both public and private undertakings carrying out an economic activity, whether or not operating for gain. It is the number of employees employed by an individual undertaking that is relevant, not those employed by a subsidiary or parent company.

Pre-existing agreements

If there is a valid pre-existing agreement and fewer than 40% of employees in an undertaking make a request for an I&C body, an employer may ballot its workforce to see whether it endorses the request for a new body.

Where a ballot is held, and 40% of the workforce and a majority of those who vote endorse the employee request for a new I&C body, the employer is obliged to negotiate a new agreement.

Where fewer than 40% of the workforce or a minority of those voting endorse the employee request for a new agreement, the employer will not be under an obligation to negotiate a new I&C agreement.

ICER sets out the conditions which need to be satisfied to be a valid pre-existing agreement. These include that it must be in writing, cover all the employees, have been approved by them, set out how information is given and seek their views on this information.

The agreement must have been in place before an employee request under ICER was made.

Negotiating an I&C agreement under ICER

There are two ways to trigger negotia-

tions for an I&C agreement:

- if a valid request under ICER has been made by at least 10% of the employees in an undertaking (subject to a minimum of 15 and a maximum of 2,500 employees); or
- if the employer initiates the process itself.

Any disputes about the validity of employee requests will be dealt with by the Central Arbitration Committee (CAC).

An employer must initiate negotiations for an agreement as soon as reasonably practicable and within three months at the latest. During this three-month period, the employer must:

- make arrangements for its employees to appoint or elect negotiating representatives; and
- inform employees in writing of the identity of the representatives who have been elected and then invite those representatives to enter into negotiations to reach an ICER agreement.

Negotiations for reaching an agreement may last for up to six months, which is extendable by agreement. If a negotiated agreement is not reached, the 'default model' will apply (see below). There is a further six-month period for an employer to set up the necessary consultation body or reach a negotiated agreement.

Criteria for a negotiated ICER agreement

A negotiated agreement must comply with certain criteria. It must:

- be in writing and dated;

- cover all employees in the undertaking or group of undertakings;
- be signed by or on behalf of the employer;
- set out the circumstances in which employers will inform and consult – ICER gives employers and employees the freedom to agree on the subject matter, method, frequency and timing of information and consultation best suited to the employer's particular circumstances;
- provide *either* for the appointment or election of I&C representatives *or* for information and consultation directly with employees; and
- be approved by the employees.

Duration of agreement

Once a negotiated agreement is in place, there is a three-year moratorium on making further requests.

The 'default model'

If negotiations to reach an agreement fail, the 'default model' will apply. Employers have a further six months to facilitate the election of representatives. This must be via a ballot with one employee representative per 50 employees subject to a minimum of two and a maximum of 25. If an employer fails to arrange this, it may be subject to a penalty fine of up to £75,000.

Information must be provided to I&C representatives on:

- the recent and probable development of the undertaking's activities and economic situation;
- the situation, structure and probable development of employment within the undertaking and on any anticipatory measures envisaged, in particular where there is a threat to employment; and
- decisions likely to lead to *substantial* changes in work organisation or in contractual relations (including those covered by existing legislation in the area of collective consultation on collective redundancies and business transfers).

In respect of the second and third issues, the representatives must be consulted as well as informed.

Other factors

Protection of confidential information

There is a statutory duty of confidentiality on all I&C representatives in respect of information the employer discloses to them. However, they can challenge this duty before the CAC. Employers need not disclose information where to do so would 'seriously harm the functioning of the undertaking or be prejudicial to it'.

Compliance and enforcement

A complaint may be made to the CAC that an employer has failed to establish a negotiated agreement or has failed to inform and consult with employees in accordance with a negotiated agreement or the default model. This must be done within three months of the failure.

These compliance mechanisms do *not* apply to pre-existing agreements.

The CAC may make a declaration and an order requiring the defaulting party to take such specified steps as are necessary to comply with the I&C agreement within a specific period of time.

There is a maximum penalty of £75,000 for the employer's failure.

Overlapping issues

Where an employer is under information and consultation obligations arising from TUPE or collective redundancy legislation, it is excused from the obligations to consult under ICER, provided it notifies I&C representatives of this.

Protection for I&C representatives

I&C representatives are entitled to reasonable paid time off work during normal working hours and have the right not to be dismissed or suffer any detriment.

Practical steps for employers

In the run-up to April 2005, employers essentially have three options. These are:

- negotiate a voluntary I&C agreement;
- negotiate an I&C agreement with employee representatives *after* April 2005; or
- do nothing and allow the default provisions in ICER to apply.

The advantages to an employer of negotiating a voluntary agreement are that it is seen to be proactive, it can seize control of the process and a more flexible agreement may result. The default model is much less flexible with set categories of information and consultation and a predetermined number of representatives.

In preparation and in order to determine which option to follow, employers should:

- carry out an audit of any existing information and consultation processes;
- assess the likelihood of employees making an ICER request or other improvements to existing information and consultation structures;
- develop a strategy for dealing with any request – e.g. how to run internal elections, what the organisation is willing to 'consult' with employee representatives about;
- educate and train management in dealing with employees collectively, particularly where trade unions are likely to be represented on the consultation body;
- consider improving on existing consultation bodies/procedures; and
- consider what competitors are doing.

Sources of further information

A copy of the draft regulations and DTI guidance which includes suggested contents for I&C agreements may be found at www.dti.gov.uk/er/consultation/proposal.htm.

Employment contracts

Alan Masson and Jill Sutherland, MacRoberts

Key points

A contract of employment can be created very simply. It does not require to be in writing. Statutory requirements impose minimum obligations on employers to issue a written statement confirming the main particulars of employment. Employers can seek to regulate the employment relationship and comply with legal obligations by providing a more extensive written contract. Once contractual terms have been created, they should not be changed unilaterally. Whether they are in writing or not, a particular process requires to be applied to avoid claims of breach of contract and, in serious cases, constructive unfair dismissal.

Legislation

- Equal Pay Act 1970.
- Copyright, Designs and Patents Act 1988.
- Data Protection Act 1988.
- Employment Rights Act 1996.
- Employment Act 2002.
- Employment Act 2002 (Dispute Resolution) Regulations 2004.

Introduction

A contract of employment is created when one party accepts an offer of employment from another. Although a written contract is not required to create the employer–employee relationship, it is good practice to put the terms of the employment beyond doubt by recording them in written form. This can often be done by issuing the proposed contract or a note of the main contractual terms that will apply with the letter of offer of employment. It is good practice to ask the employee to sign the written contract to clearly signify acceptance of the terms contained within it.

Certain terms are implied into every contract by law, such as the implied duty of trust and confidence, the duty to take care of health and safety, and the obligation of equal pay.

Providing written terms: the compulsory elements

Section 1 of the Employment Rights Act 1996 (ERA) places a statutory duty on employers to provide employees with particulars in writing of certain fundamental contractual terms. Since 1 October 2004 employers have been able to provide these in the form of a written contract, although they can still be provided in a simple statement of employment particulars.

The main requirements are as follows:

- Where an employee begins employment, the employer must give the employee a written statement of particulars of employment (section 1(1), ERA).

- The written statement may be given in instalments but shall not be given later than two months after commencement of employment (section 1(2), ERA).

- The written statement shall contain names of the employer and employee, the date when the employment commenced and the date when the period of continuous employment commenced (section 1(3), ERA).

- The written statement requires to contain details of all of the following particulars as at a date not more than seven days before the date of the statement (section 1(4), ERA):

  (a) scale or rate of remuneration, or method of calculating remuneration;

  (b) the intervals at which remuneration is paid;

  (c) any terms and conditions relating to normal hours of work;

  (d) any terms and conditions relating to entitlement to holidays, including public holidays and holiday pay (the latter sufficient to calculate the precise amount payable), incapacity for work due to sickness or injury, and the provision of sick pay;

  (e) length of notice required to terminate employment;

  (f) title of the job the employee is employed to do or a brief description of it;

  (g) the duration of the employment if it is not permanent;

  (h) the place or places the employee is required to work at;

  (i) any collective agreements that affect the terms of employment;

  (j) where the employee is required to work outside the UK, the length of that period and the currency he will be paid in and any additional remuneration or benefits payable to him as a result; and

  (k) whether there is a contracting-out certificate in force for the purposes of the Pensions Schemes Act 1993, stating that the employment is contracted out.

The written statement should also contain a note specifying any disciplinary rules applicable to the employee or referring the employee to an easily accessible document containing that information (section 3, ERA). The note must contain details of to whom the employee can apply if dissatisfied with a disciplinary decision or for the purposes of seeking redress of any grievance. Since 1 October 2004 there has no longer been any exemption from these requirements, in relation to disciplinary and grievance issues, for those employers who employ 20 or fewer employees. Employers who fail to comply with these requirements now risk additional financial penalties of between two and four weeks' pay if relevant employment tribunal claims are made.

Any changes to the compulsory elements should be notified in writing within one month of the change.

Providing written terms: other important issues

Many employers will provide written contractual terms to exercise control over other important issues. Which issues will be appropriate will always depend on the individual circumstances of the particular contract. Some examples of these additional terms are as follows:

- Data protection terms, designed to give fair notice of the purposes for which data processing will be carried out, for compliance with the Data Protection Act 1988.
- Restrictions on acceptance of other work during employment.
- Flexibility clause (e.g. requirements to work overtime, undertake other duties, mobility clauses).
- The ability to put employees on lay-off or short-term working.
- Confidentiality terms, which give the employee notice of the types of information to be regarded as confidential during and after employment.
- Authority for deductions from wages (e.g. overpayments of holiday pay or expenses).
- Garden leave terms, designed to allow the employer to require the employee to stay away from work, often used to protect business interests during notice periods.
- Intellectual property terms, which set out ownership of copyright of work created during employment and assign rights to it.
- Restrictive covenants, which impose restraints post-employment on competition, solicitation of customers and significant employees and the use of trade secrets of the employer.

Many of these clauses will be subject to legal restrictions in relation to enforceability and it is essential that they are drafted in a manner that will be legally compliant.

Altering terms and conditions of employment

Once established, contractual terms can be varied but only if the consent of both parties to the proposed variation is achieved. One option to encourage the acceptance of new terms is to 'buy out' existing terms with a financial payment.

If consent is not forthcoming, then the other route is to serve notice that the contract is being brought to an end and issue a new contract, containing the new terms, simultaneously. It is possible that such actions can give rise to claims of unfair dismissal, so a careful analysis before taking this action is advised. If the original contract is not brought to an end, breach of contract claims are possible if the original contractual terms are not met. If the breach is fundamental, this can lead to claims that the employee has been constructively dismissed.

See also: Data protection (page 163); Dismissal (page 197); Intellectual property (page 335); Pensions (page 418); Sickness leave (page 478); Working time (page 552).

Sources of further information

Advisory, Conciliation and Arbitration Service (ACAS): www.acas.org.uk.

Department of Trade and Industry (DTI): www.dti.gov.uk.

Employment disputes

Polly Botsford, Charles Russell Employment and Pensions
Service Group

Key points

- Most claims brought against a company by job applicants, employees, workers and ex-employees (and also contractors and agency workers) are brought in an employment tribunal. Sometimes claims may be brought in the County Court or High Court.
- The employment tribunal has jurisdiction to hear most of employment-related litigation (dismissal, discrimination, working time, TUPE). It is a relatively less expensive forum and is less formal. Historically, each party has met its own legal costs although tribunals are beginning to make costs awards in particular circumstances.
- Breach-of-contract claims can be brought in the employment tribunal if they are for £25,000 or less. Breach of contract claims where the possible damages are above £50,000 are heard in the County or High Courts.
- The County and High Courts are more formal and expensive. It is possible to get costs awards against the losing party.
- Mediation is an increasingly popular option for employers and employees as a means of avoiding having to go to court or to an employment tribunal.
- ACAS is the Government's conciliation service and is responsible for conciliating between the parties in cases brought in the employment tribunal.
- It is now also possible to use ACAS as an arbitrator in a dispute if it is an unfair dismissal case.

Legislation

- *Employment tribunal*: Employment Tribunal (Constitution and Rules of Procedure) Regulations 2004.
- *County/High Court*: Civil Procedural Rules.

Proceedings brought in the employment tribunal

The tribunal's procedural regulations are governed by the 'overriding objective' which is to enable tribunals to deal with cases justly such as ensuring the parties are on an equal footing, saving expense, dealing with the case in ways which are proportionate to the complexity of the issues, and ensuring the case is

---

dealt with expeditiously and fairly.

A case is started when the employee (since October 2004 known as 'the claimant') presents the Secretary of the Tribunals with a written application in the appropriate form. From 6 April 2005, this is the claim form (or ET1).

There are distinctive time limits for lodging claims in the employment tribunal: these are normally three months from the date of the act being complained of. The time limits are strictly enforced. However, with the new disciplinary and grievance procedures, an extension will be granted in circumstances arising out of those procedures.

The employer is 'the respondent' and submits a defence known as 'a Response Form' (or ET3).

After the response form is in, the case will be prepared for a hearing. To do so, a number of tasks must be undertaken by both parties: disclosure of documents, requests for additional information, exchanging witness statements. Sometimes these matters will be ordered by the employment tribunal in correspondence or (since 1 October 2004) following a case management discussion.

Sometimes there may be issues which would be dealt with at a pre-hearing review (e.g. in complex discrimination cases). After the hearing, judgment is made either orally or in writing or both. Either party may appeal the decision to the Employment Appeals Tribunal. Again, strict time limits apply.

The employment tribunal does not normally order that the unsuccessful party pay the costs of the winner. However, the tribunal can order costs now in certain circumstances such as where:

- a party or his representative has acted vexatiously, abusively, disruptively, or otherwise unreasonably in bringing or conducting the proceedings or the bringing or conducting of proceedings has been misconceived;
- the hearing was adjourned at the request of one party; or
- a party has not complied with a tribunal's directions order (e.g. to supply documents or particulars).

The maximum amount of costs that can be ordered is £10,000.

The employment tribunal can also make wasted costs orders and preparation time orders.

Settlement via the Advisory, Conciliation and Arbitration Service (ACAS)

An ACAS officer is attached to every claim for unfair dismissal or unlawful discrimination and has a *duty* to conciliate during certain 'conciliation periods' (which vary in length depending on the type of claim) and the power to conciliate at all times. The ACAS officer has no duty to advise on the merits of the claim and will not enter into lengthy discussion on legal points.

The ACAS officer will contact each party (by letter or telephone) at the start of proceedings in the employment tribunal. He can negotiate between the parties towards a settlement. A settlement agreement reached through ACAS is binding and effective. It is normally recorded on a 'COT3 form'.

ACAS has also set up an arbitration scheme for unfair dismissal cases as a form of alternative dispute resolution (see below). This is different from conciliation in that ACAS provides an independent arbitrator who hears the evidence and decides the case for the employer and employee. As an arbitrator, ACAS can award the same level of payments as a tribunal against employers.

County Court and High Court

Employment disputes can also give rise to a civil action which is heard in either a County Court (if it is a small claim or if it is not a complex matter) or the High Court. The High Court will not hear a claim whose value is less than £15,000 (or less than £50,000 where personal injury damages are involved). There are three tracks: small claims (under £5,000); fast track, which is for claims between £5,000 and £15,000; and multi-track for claims above £15,000. The main types of civil actions relating to employment are wrongful dismissal/breach of contract or injunctions to stop employees joining a competitor, setting up in competition or disclosing confidential information.

The High Court sits at the Royal Courts of Justice in London as well as at some major court centres around the country. Most employment-related civil actions are heard in the Queen's Bench Division of the High Court.

The parties can appeal a decision of the High Court to the Court of Appeal and in certain rare circumstances on to the House of Lords or European Court of Justice.

Alternative dispute resolution

Alternative dispute resolution encompasses many methods for parties avoiding going to court and settling legal disputes through other means. Mediation is one of those means; arbitration is another.

Mediation is used in employment-related claims very successfully because:

- it can be a cost saving for both parties;
- it is less intimidating than a court or tribunal;
- it does not involve lengthy trials or hearings; and
- it focuses less on the legal issues and so can be a lot less complex.

Arbitration is used in more complex commercial cases and international cases and is not generally used in domestic employment disputes apart from the new ACAS arbitration scheme mentioned above.

There are a number of bodies which provide alternative dispute resolution such as the Centre for Effective Dispute

---

Sources of further information

Civil Procedural Rules: www.dca.gov.uk/civil/procrules_fin/index.htm.

Employment Tribunals Online: www.employmenttribunals.gov.uk.

ACAS: www.acas.org.uk.

Employment Appeals Tribunal: www.employmentappeals.gov.uk.

Centre for Effective Dispute Resolution: www.cedr.co.uk.

Resolution (CEDR), the ADR Group and In Place of Strife. Also many barristers' chambers provide mediation services.

See also: Disciplinary and grievance procedures (page 184).

Employment status

Alan Masson and Jill Sutherland, MacRoberts

Key points

Status is a fundamental concept in relation to employment law. It is the nature of the relationship that determines status. The status chosen by the parties themselves will normally be conclusive, unless it is incorrect given the other facts that are relevant.

The type of status an individual has (e.g. whether he is an employee, a worker or a truly independent contractor) will determine the employment rights, if any, that he has. For most individuals the test for determining status for employment law purposes is primarily factual in that particular factual issues will be considered and the legal test will then be applied to those facts. Some individuals carry out work that is itself determinative of a certain status (e.g. Crown employees, ministers of religion and apprentices).

Status is also important for the purposes of taxation. A distinct but not dissimilar test applies for making a decision on status for taxation purposes.

Legislation

- Sex Discrimination Act 1975.
- Race Relations Act 1976.
- Transfer of Employment (Protection of Employment) Regulations 1981.
- Social Security Contributions and Benefits Act 1992.
- Disability Discrimination Act 1995.
- Employment Rights Act 1996.
- Public Interest Disclosure Act 1998.
- National Minimum Wage Act 1998.
- Working Time Regulations 1998.
- Employment Relations Act 1999.
- Part-time Workers (Prevention of Less Favourable Treatment) Regulations 2000.
- Employment Act 2002.
- Fixed-term Employees (Prevention of Less Favourable Treatment) Regulations 2002.
- Employment Equality (Religion or Belief) Regulations 2003.
- Employment Equality (Sexual Orientation) Regulations 2003.
- Conduct of Employment Agencies and Employment Businesses Regulations 2003.

Basic categories

The most basic types of status in employment law are:

- employee;

- worker; and
- independent contractor/true self-employment.

All employees are workers, but not all workers are employees.

Note that for the purposes of assessing whether an individual is entitled to paid leave in terms of the Working Time Regulations 1998 (a recent frequent area of dispute) there will be a hybrid category of individuals who display some of the categories of a worker and some of those of the truly independent contractor. Those individuals will be entitled to paid leave in terms of those Regulations.

Employees

A person with employee status is likely to have an extensive framework of rights and obligations that flow from that status. He is likely to be taxed under Schedule E.

For employment status to exist, the irreducible minimum is that there is mutuality of obligation and sufficient control of one party by the other. The test set out in the case of *Ready Mixed Concrete -v- Minister of Pensions* [1968] 2QB 497 515C still represents the fundamental test for determining whether an individual is an employee or not for employment law purposes. An individual is an employee if:

- he agrees that, in consideration of a wage or other remuneration, he will provide his personal work and skill in the performance of some service for the employer;
- he agrees that he will be subject to the employer's control to a sufficient degree in supplying that service; and
- the other provisions of the contract

are consistent with it being one of employment.

In practice courts and employment tribunals will look at a number of issues when deciding whether or not someone is an employee for employment law purposes. The first issue is likely to be whether there is a written contract, written statement of employment particulars or other relevant written documentation. Other issues such as recruitment material (e.g. advertisements and job descriptions) may be relevant. Likewise, how the working relationship operates in practice may be relevant.

The following factors are indicative of employment status:

- obligation to provide personal service;
- employer dictates how and when the work will be carried out;
- no obligation to provide a replacement;
- the payment of sick pay; and
- no obligation to provide equipment to undertake the work.

None of the factors set out above is conclusive in itself and all relevant factors should be considered before a view is reached. However, the written documentation is likely to be persuasive unless it is clearly wrong or a sham.

Workers

A person who is a worker but not an employee is likely to enjoy a less extensive framework of employment rights than employees. He is likely to be taxed under Schedule D but may in certain circumstances be taxed under Schedule E.

In determining whether an individual has the status of a worker, a statutory

Checklist of employment rights

This checklist shows whether employees and workers possess the employment rights listed.

Employment rights	Employee	Worker
Protection against unfair dismissal	Yes, subject to one year's continuous employment except in those cases where that is not necessary	No
Statutory redundancy payments	Yes, subject to two years' continuous employment and not being older than 65	No
Protection against discrimination	Yes on grounds of sex, race, disability, religion or belief, or sexual orientation	Yes, if a contract worker. Otherwise no
Protection and rights under Working Time Regulations, e.g. paid holiday leave and restrictions relating to the number of hours individuals can work, and the right to time away from work	Yes	Yes
Statutory right to be accompanied at disciplinary and grievance hearings	Yes	Yes
Protection against discrimination on basis of fixed-term status	Yes	No
Protection against discrimination on basis of part-time status	Yes	Yes
Right to the national minimum wage	Yes, subject to age restrictions	Yes, subject to age restrictions
Protection under TUPE Regulations	Yes	No
Right to statutory maternity pay and statutory sick pay	Yes, subject to qualifying conditions being met	No

test applies. An individual is a worker if:

- he works under a contract; and
- he undertakes as an individual to do or perform personally any work or services for another party and the other party is not a client or a customer of any profession or business undertaking carried on by him.

Agency workers

An area where disputes about whether an individual is an employee or a worker frequently arise is in relation to agency workers. Typically these arise where there is a tripartite relationship involving an individual, an end user and another party who introduces or supplies the individual to the hirer (e.g. an employment agency or business). It is possible that such individuals do not have employment status with either the agency or the end user, but recently the courts appear to be moving towards making purposive decisions that aim to find employment status with one or the other.

The most recent case law (*Dacas -v- Brook Street Bureau (UK) Ltd* [2004] IRLR 358) indicates that in determining the issue of whether or not an individual has employee status a pragmatic overview of

the facts may be taken. For example, if the employment agency dismisses the individual because it was instructed to do so by the hirer, the courts may decide that ultimately the decision to dismiss was taken by the end user. Having the authority to dismiss is a factor consistent with being the employer. The traditional mechanism of using the agency to implement the decisions and make payments may not be enough to avoid the conclusion that the end user is the employer. Increased care should be taken in relation to agency workers.

The Conduct of Employment Agencies and Employment Businesses Regulations 2003, most of which have been in force since April 2004, regulate the manner in which these organisations do business. These require an employment business (i.e. an organisation which supplies individuals to work for another business) to agree with the work-seeker the basis on which he is employed (e.g. what his employment status is) and set this out in a written document.

See also: Agency/temporary workers (page 72); Employment contracts (page 225).

Sources of further information

For guidance about the determining status for tax purposes: www.inlandrevenue.gov.uk.

For general guidance: www.acas.org.uk.

Energy management

David Symons, Atkins Environment

Energy is often driven by cost. But every use of gas and electricity you have also has an environmental impact from the carbon dioxide emitted. Carbon emissions are most companies' largest environmental impact and biggest contribution to global warming. So reducing energy consumption makes sense – both to reduce costs and also to reduce your environmental impact.

What controls exist on energy use?

The Building Regulations 2000 have set new standards for energy efficiency in new buildings since April 2002 and further amendments have recently been proposed by the Office of the Deputy Prime Minister. Key requirements include minimum standards for lighting, air conditioning, refrigeration, heat loss of buildings and hot water systems. The Building Regulations cover construction of new buildings, extensions and refurbishment work and apply to both domestic and commercial properties in England and Wales.

Full details are contained in the revised Approved Document L 'Conservation of fuel and power'. This is split into two parts:

- L1 'Conservation of fuel and power in dwellings'.
- L2 'Conservation of fuel and power in buildings other than dwellings'.

There is no obligation to use the techni-cal guidance contained in Part L if other methods used can be proved to meet the technical requirements of the Regulations.

Carrying out a survey

In order to manage energy, you first need to know where the energy is used. An energy survey is a good start and will provide you with an overview of your use and the opportunities. Specialist consultants can help with this, and, if you are an SME, the Carbon Trust will carry out the survey for free.

Managing your energy

After the survey, make sure that the following points are well covered on your site:

- Monitor energy consumption regularly. Energy consumption for particular applications can be compared with benchmark figures to give an idea of how they compare with nationally recognised performance indicators. This provides the basis for setting realistic targets for reduction.
- Pass information on energy consumption to staff to encourage participation in energy-saving initiatives.
- Ensure that energy efficiency is a key issue when selecting new equipment or replacing existing equipment.
- It is essential that planned programmes of maintenance are imple-

mented to ensure that equipment is running efficiently. Maintenance records must be kept to ensure that the maintenance programme is being carried out.

- Maintain full records of energy consumption and plant capacities.

Reducing energy demand

Reducing the amount of energy you use reduces costs and your environmental impacts. Much work can be done at little or no cost and includes the following:

- Encouraging staff to turn off equipment when it is not required. This can be achieved through awareness campaigns and promotional literature.
- Using automatic control systems. The level of complexity of any control system must be appropriate for the application. For example, if an office has an over-complex lighting control system, it may be disabled if the requirements of the building occupants are not being met. Simple, robust systems are often the most effective.
- Replacing old inefficient plant or equipment with more efficient alternatives may be the most effective way of achieving energy savings when the capital is available. Innovative energy-saving measures, such as combined heat and power (CHP) systems or generating energy from waste, should also be considered.

Enhanced capital allowances

Profit-making businesses can also claim enhanced capital allowances (ECAs) on qualifying investments in energy-efficient equipment. These range from

technical equipment, such as variable speed drives, through to low-energy light bulbs. The ECAs effectively mean that the Government pays 8% of the cost of the investment in energy-efficient equipment.

To take an example:

- Corporation tax on profits is 30%.
- If your company makes £10m in profit, it pays £3m corporation tax.
- If you invest (for example) in £1m of energy efficiency measures, you can offset this investment against your profits and so reduce the amount of tax which you pay.
- Thus, although you make £10m profit, you only need to pay tax on £9m, recouping 30% of the investment cost immediately.

Businesses may obtain tax relief, in the form of capital allowances, for their investment in machinery and plant. This relief is normally given at a rate of 25% a year on the reducing balance basis, which spreads the benefit over a number of years (about 95% of the cost is relieved in eight years).

ECAs enable businesses to take relief on the full cost in the first year. The scheme will bring forward relief, so the capital allowances can be set against profits of a period earlier than would otherwise be the case. The benefit to a business of ECAs is thus a cash-flow boost resulting from the reduction of the business's tax bill for the year in which the investment is made.

Negotiating energy contracts

Energy costs vary considerably between suppliers, and costs can be minimised by looking for a supplier who can best match your requirements.

Buying 'green' electricity – power produced from renewable resources – is also a simple way of improving your environmental performance at low cost.

Generating it yourself

Maybe this is not the cheapest option available at present, but it is excellent in terms of public relations and for providing a clear message of your environmental intentions. Solar panels can produce either electricity or hot water for your building while wind turbines can now be mounted on the roof of even small buildings. Grants are available from the Energy Saving Trust to support schemes.

See also: Building Regulations (page 92).

Sources of further information

The Carbon Trust is an excellent source of advice on energy efficiency, publications and free support: www.thecarbontrust.co.uk.

Information on the enhanced capital allowances programme: www.eca.gov.uk.

Information on solar grants and renewable energy: www.est.org.uk.

Practical advice on domestic energy management: www.saveenergy.co.uk.

Environmental management systems

Ken Smith and Sally Goodman, Casella Stanger

Introduction

'Environmental responsibility' is a term commonly used in boardrooms throughout the UK. This highlights that effective management of environmental issues is an area of concern for many businesses, from large FTSE 100 companies to smaller organisations.

This interest in environmental responsibility is generated for different reasons within each company. However, they all aim to achieve the same goal – to minimise and control potential negative environmental impacts and risks.

Many organisations in the UK are achieving this goal by the implementation of an environmental management system (EMS).

What is an environmental management system?

An EMS is a powerful tool for the identification and management of environmental risks. It also provides a mechanism for delivering performance improvements, effecting resource savings and promoting environmental best practice.

There are two EMS standards to which an organisation can receive external certification: the EU-based Eco-Management and Audit Scheme (EMAS) and the international standard ISO 14001:1996. Both standards represent best practice in environmental management and have been widely accepted by UK businesses with (at the time of writing) more than 2,900 ISO 14001 certificates and almost 90 EMAS registrations currently issued within the UK. More than 60,000 ISO 14001 certificates have been issued worldwide.

ISO 14001 is applicable to any type and size of organisation, anywhere in the world. It can be applied to individual sites, or to entire organisations. Some organisations choose to implement ISO 14001 in a phased manner, site by site, or plant by plant, or subsidiary by subsidiary. Others design the EMS at corporate level and require each site or plant to interpret and implement the EMS accordingly. Which approach is chosen depends very much on resources and the existing company culture.

EMAS is based on an EU regulation. The main difference between EMAS and ISO 14001 is that EMAS requires the additional production of a periodic public environmental 'statement' (in reality, a detailed report) which describes an organisation's environmental impacts and data, its environmental programme, the involvement of stakeholders and progress in achieving improvement in performance.

Whichever standard is used as the

basis for an EMS, there are three underlying principles that form the backbone of the system:

- Compliance with applicable environmental legislation.
- Prevention of pollution.
- Continual improvement.

Both EMAS and ISO 14001 specify that an effective EMS should be based around the following stages:

- *Planning* – including development of an environmental policy, the identification and evaluation of environmental aspects and impacts, the development of objectives and targets, and the preparation of an 'environmental management programme' (action plan).
- *Implementation* – including defining roles and responsibilities, assessing competence and delivering training, communications, documentation and document control, operational control and emergency preparedness.
- *Checking and corrective action* – including monitoring of performance, specifying corrective action, record keeping and auditing.
- *Review* – strategic level review ('management review').

Why implement an EMS?

The use of EMSs to control environmental risks is not a new concept. EMSs have been externally reviewed since 1992, with the number being externally certified within the UK growing all the time. This demonstrates that there are recognised and continued benefits from implementing an EMS, some of which are as follows:

- A more systematic approach to business management.
- Reduced risk of prosecution and improved relationships with regulatory authorities.
- The confidence to do business in what before may have been viewed as high-risk areas or processes.
- Financial benefits in terms of, for example, reduced waste and energy bills.
- Competitive advantage over organisations with less developed risk management procedures.
- Improved public profile and better relationship with stakeholders.
- Improved staff motivation, retention and attraction.

Types of EMS

An EMS can take many forms, from detailed and prescriptive procedures, to simple flowcharts. It can also be delivered and communicated in many different ways, from paper copies of procedures to electronic systems held on company intranets.

The type of EMS that an organisation chooses depends on the size and culture of the organisation and the existing communications process. One example that a large multi-site organisation may opt to use is an Internet-based software package such as Oxegen. This is a software package that can assist an organisation in rapidly establishing its EMS or to maintain and keep live its existing system. Oxegen is currently used in a variety of sectors including automotive, retail, forestry and local government.

Alternatively an SME may opt to install a simple flowchart-based system to provide clear instructions which all levels of staff can understand.

Integration

Although an EMS can be designed as a stand-alone system, it is now best practice to integrate the environmental management requirements with health and safety and quality management systems. It is also increasingly common to find EMS being integrated with systems for improving corporate social responsibility or corporate governance.

Certification

Certification is a process by which an independent third party audits a management system against a recognised standard.

In the UK, certification bodies are accredited (given a licence to operate) by the United Kingdom Accreditation Service (UKAS). UKAS is the sole national body recognised by government for the accreditation of testing and calibration laboratories and certification and inspection bodies.

There are many certification bodies operating in the UK, among which are the British Standards Institution (BSI), BVQI, DNV, Lloyd's Register Quality Assurance (LRQA) and SGS.

Sources of further information

EMAS Helpdesk: europa.eu.int/comm/environment/emas/index.htm.

ISO 14000 Information Center: www.iso14000.com.

International Organisation for Standardisation (ISO): www.iso.ch/iso.

UKAS: www.ukas.com.

Oxegen: www.oxegen.com.

Certification bodies:
British Standards Institution (BSI): www.bsi-global.com.
BVQI: www.bvqi.com.
DNV: www.dnv.com.
Lloyd's Register Quality Assurance (LRQA): www.lrqa.com.
SGS: www.uk.sgs.com.

Equal pay

Michael Powner, Charles Russell Employment and Pensions Service Group

Key points

- The principle of equal pay originates from Article 141 of the Treaty of Rome. Article 141 and, later, the Equal Pay Directive underpinned the rights in Europe to equal pay between men and women. The UK implemented these EU provisions by the Equal Pay Act 1970 (EPA).
- The EPA gives the right to equal pay for both men and women employed in an establishment in the UK, although for ease of reference the presumption in this article is that a woman is the affected employee.
- The EPA implies an equality provision into any employment contract that does not already include one. This provision applies to all terms and conditions of employment and not only to pay but, for example, sick pay provisions. Any term in a contract which purports to limit or exclude any provision of the EPA is unenforceable.
- The implied equality provision modifies the contract of employment in any situation where a woman is engaged in *like work* to a man, on *work rated as equivalent* to work done by a man, or on *work of equal value* to that done by a man unless her employer can justify the difference in pay due to a material factor which is not sex. If in breach, the employee's remedy is a claim for breach of contract.
- Equal pay questionnaires can be served before a claim is issued at the employment tribunal to establish facts which are material to a potential claim.
- A claim for sex discrimination under the Sex Discrimination Act 1975 (SDA) is commonly brought together with a claim under the EPA with the potential prospect of unlimited damages. A Code of Practice issued by the Equal Opportunities Commission in 1997 that deals with the steps to be taken by an employer to ensure equality of pay is admissible in evidence in both EPA and SDA claims.

Legislation

- Treaty of Rome, Article 141.
- Equal Pay Directive (75/117/EEC).
- Equal Pay Act 1970.
- Equal Pay Act 1970 (Amendment) Regulations 2003.
- Equal Pay (Questions and Replies) Order 2003.

Like work, work rated as equivalent and work of equal value

Like work

A woman is employed on like work with a man if the woman's and man's work is of the same or a broadly similar nature. Employers need to consider the nature and extent of the differences between the work and the frequency with which such differences occur. For example, a cook in a director's dining room was held to be engaged on like work with the assistant chefs of the company's factory canteen.

Work rated as equivalent

An objective job-evaluation study can be carried out in respect of a woman's and man's work, and the woman's job is rated for equivalence on the basis of the demand made in terms of matters such as skill or effort required, or level of responsibility.

Work of equal value

A woman's work may be of equal value to a man's in terms of the demands made on her, even if it is not like work or rated as equivalent. A woman may therefore potentially still claim equal pay with a man even if he is doing a different job. For example, a female cook employed as a canteen assistant succeeded in a claim for equal pay with a male skilled tradesman. Where work is claimed to be of equal value, an independent expert is often appointed to determine the issue.

Material factor defence

If a woman can establish that she is engaged on like work, work rated as equivalent or work of equal value, she will not have any redress if the employer can show that the variation between the woman's contract and the man's contract is genuinely due to a material factor which is not the difference of sex.

Implied equality provision

If the employer cannot justify the difference in pay, the implied equality provision operates so that:

- any contractual term which is less favourable to a woman is modified to become as favourable as the corresponding term in the man's contract; and
- any beneficial term in a man's contract which is not included in the woman's contract is included into the woman's contract.

To give a simple example, if a man is paid £500 more per month than a woman for like work, the equality provision will entitle the woman to that extra £500 per month.

Remedies

These are:

- back pay (limited to six years) representing the difference in pay between the woman and the 'equal' or 'equivalent' employee with interest; and
- the same level of pay or benefits as her comparator for the future (if the complainant remains in the same job).

Procedure

As with discrimination claims, cases can be brought while the employee is still employed. In the standard case, claims must be brought at any time during employment or within six months of leaving employment.

An individual may submit equal pay questionnaires to the employer, either before a claim is made to the tribunal or within 21 days of such a claim being lodged. Employers are not obliged to answer these questionnaires, but the tribunal may draw an adverse inference if a questionnaire is not answered deliberately and without reasonable cause in an eight-week window from it being served, or where the reply is evasive or equivocal. This includes an inference that the equality provision has been breached.

New legislation

The Equal Pay Act 1970 (Amendment) Regulations 2003 came into force on 1 October 2004, amending the EPA and the tribunal procedural rules. Under the amended EPA, a tribunal can choose to determine the question of equal value itself rather than appoint an independent expert. Where a job evaluation study ascribes different values to the work of the claimant and the comparator, the tribunal will be bound to conclude that the work is not of equal value unless it has reasonable grounds for suspecting that the study discriminated on the ground of sex, or that there are other reasons why it cannot be relied upon.

New tribunal procedural rules will apply to all equal pay claims and new case management powers have been conferred on tribunals.

See also: Discrimination (page 189).

Sources of further information

Equal Opportunities Commission (EOC): www.eoc.org.uk. The EOC Code of Practice on Equal Pay gives useful practical guidance.

Advisory, Conciliation and Arbitration Service (ACAS): www.acas.org.uk.

Eye and eyesight tests

Andrew Richardson, Scott Wilson

Key points

- Use of display screen equipment (DSE) constitutes an adverse health hazard.
- Users or operators of DSE can suffer visual fatigue or headaches.
- DSE does not cause permanent damage to eyesight, but pre-existing eye conditions may be accentuated.
- Employers must provide and pay for eye and eyesight tests if employees request.
- Tests must be carried out by a registered ophthalmic optician or medical practitioner.
- Employers must provide spectacles where needed for screen-viewing distance if employees request.

Legislation

- Health and Safety at Work etc. Act 1974.
- Management of Health and Safety at Work Regulations 1999.
- Health and Safety (Display Screen Equipment) Regulations 1992 as amended by the Health and Safety (Miscellaneous Amendments) Regulations 2002.

Statutory requirements

It is a requirement of Regulation 6 of the Management of Health and Safety at Work Regulations that consideration must be given to carry out health surveillance of employees where there is a disease or adverse health condition identified in the risk assessments.

It has been identified that use of DSE by someone deemed to be a 'user' or 'operator' does constitute an adverse health condition.

The Regulations state that it will be generally appropriate to classify people as a user or operator if they:

- normally use DSE for continuous or near-continuous spells of an hour or more at a time; and
- use DSE in this way more or less daily; and
- have to transfer information quickly to or from the DSE; and
- need to apply high levels of attention and concentration; or
- are highly dependent on DSE or have little choice about using it; or
- need special training or skills to use DSE.

The purpose of the eye test is to improve

the comfort and efficiency of the user by identifying and correcting any vision defects specific to DSE use. There is no evidence that DSE usage causes permanent damage to eyesight; what will occur is that pre-existing eye conditions will be accentuated, which can lead to temporary visual fatigue or headaches.

The Regulations require employers to provide users or operators with an appropriate eye and eyesight test if they request it. The employer has a liability to pay for these tests. Note that DSE users are not obliged to have the test.

The employer has a duty to provide tests to employees already designated as a user or operator and to employees who are being recruited or transferred to be users or operators.

The test should include the test of vision and examination of the eye, otherwise known as a sight test in the Opticians Act legislation. The test should take into account the nature of the DSE work carried out. A registered ophthalmic optician or medical practitioner should carry out the tests.

If an employee requests a test for the first time, it must be carried out as soon as practicable. If an employee is to be transferred to a user or operator post, then the test must be carried out before commencement in that post. For people being recruited, once they are definitely going to be an employee, then the test should be carried out before they commence any work that meets the user/operator criteria.

After the first test, the employer must be guided by the optician or doctor as to the frequency of subsequent tests.

If the tests show that the employee requires special corrective appliances (normally spectacles) specifically for distances when using DSE, then the employer has the liability to provide a basic special corrective appliance. Normal corrective appliances are those spectacles prescribed for any other purpose, but the employer has no liability for these.

See also: Display screen equipment (page 202).

Sources of further information

The main source of further information is L26 'Work with Display Screen Equipment: Health and Safety (Display Screen Equipment) Regulations 1992 as amended by the Health and Safety (Miscellaneous Amendments) Regulations 2002 – Guidance on Regulations' (HSE Books, 2003): ISBN 0 7176 2582 6. The document provides all the guidance needed by employers and identifies any further documentation that is relevant.

Facilities management contracts: essential elements

Marc Hanson, CMS Cameron McKenna

What is a contract?

Like all other forms of contract, a facilities management contract is essentially a legally binding and enforceable bargain between two parties. Each party contributes something to the bargain: the facilities management contractor the provision of certain services, and the client payment for those services.

Negotiation

For a contract to be legally binding, there must be an offer from one party, an unconditional acceptance of that offer by the other party, and consideration provided by each party for the promise made by the other party. A client's invitation to tender is not usually an 'offer': it is usually no more than an offer to negotiate.

A facilities management contractor's tender to carry out the services will, usually, amount to the initial 'offer'.

When the client accepts the facilities management contractor's tender and each party gives consideration, then, provided both parties have an intention to be legally bound, a legally enforceable contract will come into place. Offers and acceptance can be made in writing, orally or by conduct.

It is of course unusual for facilities management contractors' tenders to be accepted without qualification by a client. There may be areas of extensive negotiation, e.g. in relation to scope of services and fees. Every time each party provides any revised proposals, then each revised proposal will take effect as a 'counter-offer'.

When eventually all outstanding points have been agreed, one party will invariably 'accept' the other party's final 'offer'.

When does the contract start?

The process of negotiating a facilities management contract can be protracted. In many cases, services may be provided to the client and payment may be made without any form of contract having been signed. Where relationships subsequently deteriorate, it can be extremely difficult to establish whether there was ever a binding contract in place and, if there was, on what terms it was made.

Whether a binding contract exists in such circumstances will depend on whether the parties managed to agree all the key terms of the contract and whether the terms of the alleged contract included all terms that would be essential for a contract to exist. It would be unlikely that there was a contract agreed if key elements of the contract were still outstanding, e.g. if the exact scope of the services was undecided or if

a price had not been agreed. However, a contract can still come into effect where certain points in the contract terms are still to be agreed, provided that the key elements have been finalised and agreed.

Scope of contracts

When drafting facilities management contracts, it is important to ensure that they cover the complete understanding and agreement between the parties. As such, it is necessary to include not only a list of the services to be provided by the supplier but also a mechanism for dealing with changes to the services and also any details as to what equipment or facilities are to be provided to the supplier by the client in relation to the services.

Payment

Careful thought needs to be given as to how payment to the facilities management contractor will be structured. Will it be on the basis of a lump-sum price, by prime cost or by reference to a schedule of rates? If the price is to adjust, then a mechanism needs to be set out allowing for this, detailing the circumstances in which adjustments will be made. Careful consideration also needs to be given to any mechanism to be included in the contract that would allow the contract price to be adjusted to reflect perform-

ance or non-performance by the supplier of the services.

Service levels

Service levels should be included in the contract against which the performance by the supplier can be assessed. Consideration needs to be given as to how poor performance is dealt with and whether the liability of the supplier under the contract is to be limited in any way.

Duration

The duration of a facilities management contract is of critical importance, and this should be clearly stated in the contract together with the circumstances in which it can be extended or terminated by either party.

Facilities management contracts should also address other key areas such as compliance with statutory requirements, transfer of undertakings provisions, insurance requirements and provisions dealing with dispute resolution.

See also: Contract disputes (page 148).

Sources of further information

Guide to Facilities Management Contracts, 2nd edition, written by Marc Hanson (ISBN 1 900648 19 9, £49.50) is available from Workplace Law Publishing. Call 0870 777 8881, or visit www.workplace.law.net.

Family-friendly rights

Pinsent Masons Employment Group

Key points

- Pregnant employees, regardless of their length of service, are entitled to 26 weeks' ordinary maternity leave.
- Pregnant employees with at least 26 weeks' continuous service at the fourteenth week before the expected week of childbirth are entitled to 26 weeks' unpaid additional maternity leave to follow straight on from ordinary maternity leave.
- An employee who is the father of the child or the mother's husband or partner is entitled to take one or two weeks' paid paternity leave on the birth or adoption of a child.
- Eligible employees are now entitled to take 26 weeks' paid adoption leave and 26 weeks' unpaid adoption leave.
- Employees (both male and female) with one year's continuous service are entitled to take up to 13 weeks' unpaid parental leave, or 18 weeks in the case of a disabled child, to care for each of their children.
- Employees who have responsibility for looking after a child can request a variation in their contractual hours.

Legislation

- Employment Rights Act 1996.
- Employment Relations Act 1999.
- Maternity and Parental Leave etc. Regulations 1999.
- Employment Act 2002.
- Maternity and Parental Leave (Amendment) Regulations 2002.
- Paternity and Adoption Leave Regulations 2002.
- Flexible Working (Eligibility, Complaints and Remedies) Regulations 2002.

Employment Act 2002

The Employment Act 2002 contains a number of family-friendly provisions relating to maternity rights, paternity leave and adoption leave. Four new sets of Regulations implement changes to the previous law and create new rights for pregnant women and parents.

Maternity rights

The Maternity and Parental Leave (Amendment) Regulations 2002 provide for ordinary maternity leave (OML) to be extended from 18 to 26 weeks and for additional maternity leave (AML) to be extended so as to end 26 weeks from the end of OML. Further, qualification for AML is reduced to 26 weeks' service at the beginning of the fourteenth week before the expected week of childbirth (EWC).

The employee is now required to inform her employer before the end of the fifteenth week before EWC or the date on which she intends to start her OML. There are also changes to notification requirements.

Employees are entitled not to be unreasonably refused time off with pay to attend antenatal care appointments subject to providing their employer with details about the appointment. Thereafter, women are protected from suffering treatment to their detriment by employers (including dismissal) because they are pregnant. Pregnancy-related dismissals can be automatically unfair, and one year's continuous service is not needed to claim unfair dismissal. There is also a crossover with sex discrimination laws which prevent dismissals in the 'protected period' between conception and the end of a maternity leave period.

Women entitled to OML have a statutory right to return to their job without giving notice. During OML employment terms continue to apply to the employee except for the right to pay.

The new provisions clarify the previously difficult position as to whether the woman's contract continues in the AML period. They confirm that in that period only certain terms and conditions of employment continue in force. Care should be taken to ensure that during the woman's absence she is kept informed of any new vacancies or promoted positions which become available

to avoid any claims that she is being discriminated against.

Employers must not allow women who qualify for maternity leave to work at all in the two weeks immediately following childbirth.

Maternity pay is often covered in the contract of employment, but must be no less than the statutory maternity pay (SMP) equivalent. The maternity pay period is currently 26 weeks. SMP is £102.80 per week (or 90% of the employee's average weekly earnings if less).

Paternity leave

The Paternity and Adoption Leave Regulations 2002 came into force on 8 December 2002 and provide rights for employees who qualify to take adoption and paternity leave.

An employee is entitled to take paternity leave when the purpose of the absence is to care for a newborn child or to support the child's mother.

To qualify for paid paternity leave, employees must:

- be the father of the child or the mother's husband or partner (partner is a person of the same or different sex who lives with the mother and the child and is in an enduring family relationship but who is not a relative of the mother);
- have or expect to have responsibilities for the upbringing of the child; and
- have 26 weeks' service

Statutory paternity pay is paid for two weeks and is £102.80 (or 90% of the employee's average weekly earnings if less).

Employees cannot lawfully be treated less favourably or dismissed due to taking or requesting paternity leave. Any such dismissal will be automatically unfair.

Adoption leave

The Paternity and Adoption Leave Regulations 2002 provide that eligible employees now have the statutory right to 26 weeks' ordinary adoption leave paid at £102.80 per week (or 90% of average weekly earnings if less) and 26 weeks' unpaid additional adoption leave.

To be eligible for adoption leave, employees need to be an individual who has been newly matched with a child for adoption by an adoption agency, or be one member of a couple where the couple has jointly been newly matched with a child for adoption by an adoption agency (the couple must choose which partner takes adoption leave) and have completed at least 26 weeks' continuous service with the employer ending with the week (beginning with the Sunday and ending with the Saturday) in which the employee is notified of being matched with the child for adoption.

The partner of an individual who adopts or the other member of a couple who are adopting jointly may be entitled to paternity leave pay.

Adoption leave will not be available in circumstances where a child is not newly matched for adoption (e.g. when a step-parent is adopting a partner's child).

Parental leave

Employees, both mothers and fathers, who have completed one year's service with their current employer are entitled to take 13 weeks' (18 where the child is disabled) unpaid parental leave to care for their child.

Parental leave can usually be taken up to five years from the date of birth or in the case of adoption five years from the date of placement (or up to the child's eighteenth birthday if that is sooner) where the child was born or adopted on or after 15 December 1999. In the case of children born or adopted between 15 December 1994 and 14 December 1999, the employee's right lasts until 31 March 2005 (or in the case of adoption until the child's eighteenth birthday if that is sooner) and in this case one year's service with a previous employer between 15 December 1998 and 9 January 2002 gives entitlement.

At the end of parental leave an employee is guaranteed the right to return to the same job as before, or, if that is not practicable, a similar job which has the same or better status, terms and conditions as the old job. If, however, the period of parental leave is for a period of four weeks or less, the employee is entitled to go back to the same job.

Wherever possible, employers and employees should make their own arrangements about how parental leave will work, how much notice should be given, arrangements for postponing the leave when the business cannot cope and how it should be taken.

Where employers and employees have not entered into an agreement about these matters, or until they have done so, the fallback scheme set out in the Regulations applies. The fallback scheme provides for employees to take parental leave in blocks or multiples of one week, after giving 21 days' notice, up to a maximum of four weeks' leave in a year and subject to postponement by the employer for up to six months where the business cannot cope. Leave cannot be postponed when the employee gives notice to take it immediately after the time the child is born or is placed with the family for adoption.

Flexible working

Parents and others (these are listed in the Flexible Working Regulations) who have responsibility for looking after a child can request a variation in their contract of employment to have a more flexible working pattern. If an employee makes such a request and the employer does not agree to the change, the employer must follow a set procedure for meeting the employee to discuss the request, making a decision and issuing a decision with reasons. If the employer fails to follow the procedure, the employee may make an application to the employment tribunal.

See also: Flexible working (page 280); New and expectant mothers (page 398).

Sources of further information

Department of Trade and Industry (DTI): www.dti.gov.uk.

Department for Work and Pensions (DWP): www.dwp.gov.uk.

Advisory, Conciliation and Arbitration Service (ACAS): www.acas.org.

'Maternity Policy and Management Guide, version 1.0 (ISBN 1 900648 46 6, £34.99), 'Paternity Policy and Management Guide, version 1.0' (ISBN 1 900648 66 0, £34.99) and 'Flexible Working Policy and Management Guide, version 1.0' (ISBN 1 900648 62 8, £34.99) are available as electronic downloads from the Workplace Law Network.

Call 0870 777 8881 for details, or visit www.workplacelaw.net.

Fire extinguishers

Andrew Richardson, Scott Wilson

Key points

The legislation covering fire extinguishers is the Fire Precautions (Workplace) Regulations 1997. These Regulations require employers to:

- assess the fire risk in the workplace;
- provide reasonable firefighting equipment;
- check that people know what to do in the event of fire; and
- ensure that fire safety equipment is maintained and monitored.

Legislation

- Health and Safety at Work etc. Act 1974.
- Management of Health and Safety at Work Regulations 1999.
- Fire Precautions (Workplace) Regulations 1997.

Risk assessments

The employer has a duty to assess the fire risk in its premises. There are five steps to a fire risk assessment:

- Identify the potential fire hazards.
- Decide who may be in danger and their locations.
- Evaluate the risks and decide if existing control measures are adequate.
- Record findings and actions.
- Review and revise those assessments periodically.

Classes of fire

In order to fight a fire, you need to determine the following:

- Is the firefighting equipment suitable for the fire risk?
- Is the equipment located correctly?
- Has the equipment got the correct signage?
- Have personnel been trained to use the equipment provided?

In order to determine what firefighting equipment is suitable, you have to identify the classes of fire that may occur in your workplace. There are six classes into which all fires will fall:

- Class A: fires involving solids (wood, paper, plastics, etc., usually organic in nature).
- Class B: fires involving liquids or liquefiable solids (petrol, oil, paint, wax, etc.).
- Class C: fires involving gases (LPG, natural gas, acetylene, etc.).
- Class D: fires involving metals (sodium, magnesium, any metal powders, etc.).

- Electrical fires: although not deemed as a class, electrical equipment fires need categorising.
- Class F: fires involving cooking fats/oils.

Once you have determined the class of fire, you can then select the appropriate firefighting equipment. This can include portable extinguishers, hosereels, sprinkler systems, hydrant systems or fixed firefighting systems.

Portable firefighting equipment

Portable fire extinguishers come in a variety of types as shown in the table below. All are coloured red, but each may have a colour H coded panel to aid in identifying the type.

Fire extinguishers have limitations: they can be used only on the appropriate class of fire, they are of limited duration, and they have a limited range.

The fire extinguishers should be sited:

- conspicuously and readily visible;
- on all escape routes;
- close to specifically identified danger areas;
- close to room exits, inside or outside dependent on risk;
- at the same location on each floor;
- grouped together to form a fire point;
- no further than 30 metres from any person;
- with handle 1.1 metre from floor level; and
- away from extreme heat or cold.

Fire extinguishers should be maintained in accordance with BS 5306-3:2003 'Fire extinguishing installations and equipment on premises. Part 3'. This details monthly inspections, annual inspections, and maintenance and discharge test requirements.

Hosereels

Hosereels are primarily utilised on Class A fires. An adjustable nozzle allows the

---

Types of portable fire extinguisher

Type	Colour code	Suitable for
Water	Red	Class A fires only
Foam	Cream	Class B fires, but can also be used on Class A
Dry powder	Blue	Class B fires, but can also be used on Class A and electrical
Halon	Green	Do not use*
Carbon dioxide	Black	Electrical fires and small Class B fires
Special powder	Blue	Class D fires
Wet chemical	Canary yellow	Class F fires

* Effectively banned after 31 December 2003 under the Montreal Protocol because of their ozone-depleting properties. If you have any of these in your workplace, you should arrange to have a replacement system installed as soon as possible.

---

water to be in a jet or spray form: a jet can be used at the base of a fire and a spray allows a larger area of coverage and can be used for protection of personnel. Hosereels obviously have a continuous supply of water, which is provided in greater quantity than from an extinguisher, and hence they have a greater range.

Their limitations are that greater physical effort is required to operate them, they wedge open fire doors allowing possible smoke spread, they should be used only on Class A fires, they are a trip hazard and there is a tendency to remain fighting the fire for longer periods.

Hosereels should be provided for every 800 square metres of floor area or part thereof and should be in prominent and accessible locations at exits so that they can extend to all parts in all rooms. Hosereels should be inspected monthly and an annual test carried out to check their full functional capability.

Training

The Health and Safety at Work etc. Act 1974 requires employers to provide information, instruction, training and supervision to ensure the health, safety and welfare of employees. The Management of Health and Safety at Work Regulations 1999 state that employers need to take into account the capabilities of their employees before entrusting tasks and that they should have adequate health and safety training and be capable enough at their jobs to avoid risk.

Firefighting is a high-risk activity. If you as an employer have a fire procedure that instructs your employees to tackle the fire, then you have a legal obligation to ensure they are adequately trained. Most instructions to tackle fire usually end with 'if it is safe to do so': unless you are trained, how will you know whether it is safe? Your local fire brigade will be

---

Sources of further information

L21 'Management of Health and Safety at Work Regulations 1999. Approved Code of Practice and Guidance', 2nd edition (HSE Books, 2000): ISBN 0 7176 2488 9

'Fire Safety: An Employer's Guide' (Home Office, Scottish Executive, Department of Environment (Northern Ireland) for HSE: HMSO, 1999): ISBN 0 11 341229 0.

The above documents provide all the guidance needed by employers and identify any further documentation that is relevant.

Where your workplace includes dangerous substances such as those with the potential to create risk of fire or explosion including petrol, liquefied petroleum gas (LPG), paints, varnishes, solvents and certain types of dust that are explosive (e.g. wood dust), you may have duties under the Dangerous Substances and Explosive Atmospheres Regulations 2002.

---

able to guide you on the training available, and advise you about local variations to emergency procedures, if any, in your area.

See also: Fire risk assessments (page 271); Means of fighting fire (page 267).

Fire legislation

Kevin Bridges, Osborne Clarke

Key points

Existing fire safety legislation has developed in piecemeal fashion, often as a response to particular tragic fires in which large numbers of lives have been lost. As a result, fire safety provision is scattered over some 100 pieces of legislation. As the law currently stands, there are two main overlapping fire regimes in place, the Fire Precautions Act 1971 and the Fire Precautions (Workplace) Regulations 1997 (as amended).

The Fire Precautions Act 1971 establishes a regime based around certification of general fire precautions by local fire authorities.

The Fire Precautions (Workplace) Regulations 1997 impose a regime which is typical of other health and safety obligations based on risk assessments.

Legislation

- Fire Precautions Act 1971.
- Fire Precautions (Workplace) Regulations 1997.
- Fire Precautions (Workplace) (Amendment) Regulations 1999.
- Building Regulations.
- Management of Health and Safety at Work Regulations 1999.
- Fire Certificates (Special Premises) Regulations 1976

Fire Precautions Act 1971

The types of premises designated as requiring fire certificates are:

- hotels and boarding houses; and

- factories, offices, shops and railway premises.

The owner or occupier must apply for a fire certificate to the relevant fire authority, who will then undertake an inspection.

Questions to be asked are as follows:

1. Do people work at the premises?
2. Do the premises provide sleeping accommodation?
3. Are the premises a factory, office, shop or railway?

If the answer to all these questions is 'no', then the premises will not require a fire certificate. However, a duty to consult with the local fire authority arises under separate legislation for certain types of premises, e.g. children's homes,

homes for the elderly or disabled, licensed premises and schools.

If the answer to any of these questions is 'yes', then the following questions need to be asked:

4. Is sleeping accommodation provided for more than six people?
5. Is sleeping accommodation provided on any floor above the first floor?
6. Is sleeping accommodation provided below the ground floor?

If the answer to any of the above is 'yes', a fire certificate will be required.

If the building is a factory, office, shop or railway premises, then if there are more than 20 persons in aggregate or more than 10 people working other than on the ground floor a fire certificate is required, unless the fire authority has granted an exemption for low-risk premises.

Fire Precautions (Workplace) (Amendment) Regulations 1999

These Regulations came into force on 1 December 1999 and amend the Fire Precautions (Workplace) Regulations 1997 (FPWR 1997). The FPWR 1997 came into force on 1 December 1997 and imposed requirements on every employer and occupier in respect of every workplace (other than an excepted workplace) which is to any extent under his control so far as the requirements relate to matters within his control.

The FPWR 1997 now apply to most workplaces including those for which a fire certificate is in force or for which an application for a fire certificate is pending under the Fire Precautions Act 1971 (FPA 1971). However, the following workplaces are still exempt from the requirements of the Regulations:

- Workplaces used only by the self-employed.
- Private dwellings.
- Construction sites or any workplace to which the Construction (Health, Safety and Welfare Regulations) 1996 apply.
- Any aircraft, locomotive or rolling stock which is in use as a means of transport.
- Mines, other than any building on the surface of a mine.
- Agricultural or forestry land situated away from the undertaking's main buildings.
- Offshore installations (workplaces to which the Offshore Installations and Pipelines Work (Management and Administration) Regulations 1995 apply).

The Regulations require that a suitable and sufficient fire risk assessment must be made under Regulation 3 of the Management of Health and Safety at Work Regulations 1999, which came into force on 29 December 1999. Employers with five or more employees must record the significant findings of the risk assessment in writing. It must be kept for inspection, reviewed and revised as and when necessary.

The purpose of a fire risk assessment is to identify those measures which need to be taken to comply with Part 2 of the FPWR 1997, which contains three main provisions. Regulation 4 makes provision for firefighting and fire detection, Regulation 5 covers emergency routes and exits in the case of fire, and Regulation 6 deals with the maintenance of workplaces and safety devices.

The responsibility of the employer under the FPWR 1997 is unconditional in that he must ensure that the requirements of Part 2 are complied with to safeguard the safety of his employees notwithstanding the acts or omissions of others upon whom requirements are also imposed in respect of the same workplace (e.g. the owner, landlord or managing agents).

Building Regulations

These Regulations cover the structural safety requirements of new buildings and significant alterations to existing buildings. The detail is found in Approved Document B, the latest edition of which came into force on 1 July 2000.

Buildings are required to be designed and constructed so that there are appropriate provisions for the early warning of fire and appropriate means of escape to a place of safety outside the building capable of being safely and effectively used at all material times.

Management of Health and Safety at Work Regulations 1999

These Regulations make explicit the requirement for a risk assessment relating to fire safety and for the assessment to take account of general fire precaution requirements for firefighting, fire detection, and emergency routes and their maintenance.

Fire Certificates (Special Premises) Regulations 1976

These Regulations deal with those premises where the nature or scale of processes or storage of substances are hazardous and have a direct bearing on fire safety. The Regulations require certification along the lines of the FPA 1971, but certificates are issued and enforced by the HSE rather than local fire authorities.

Future developments

Plans to reform the law relating to general fire safety in non-domestic premises were laid before Parliament on 10 May 2004 by the Office of the Deputy Prime Minister (ODPM). The aim of the reforms is to simplify, rationalise and consolidate existing fire safety legislation. The proposal is to remove the overlap by introducing a Regulatory Reform (Fire Safety) Order to be enforced by local fire authorities. The Order would replace the FPA 1971 and the FPWR 1997 and a duty will

---

Sources of further information

Office of the Deputy Prime Minister (ODPM): www.odpm.gov.uk. Work carried out by the ODPM on fire issues includes fire safety and prevention, national policy, developing legislation and guidance, advice and support to fire authorities and brigades, arson reduction, research and statistics.

The employer's guide to fire safety issued by the Home Office, the HSE, the Department of the Environment (Northern Ireland) and the Scottish Executive can be accessed at
www.archive.official-documents.co.uk/document/fire/index.htm.

Information on the HSE's role in workplace fire safety can be found at www.hse.gov.uk/spd/spdfire.htm.

---

be created for fire authorities to promote community safety. Clarity and rationalisation of existing fire law is the main objective of the reform and there will no longer be a requirement to apply for a fire certificate, as the FPA 1971 will be revoked.

The Order is to be based around the same risk assessment principles as the FPWR 1997, but the protection will extend to all occupants, not just employees.

The responsible person in relation to each building will be the employer or, if there is no employer, the occupier. If there is no occupier and no employer present in the building, then the owner will be responsible. The new regime will cover all workplaces and places which have public access, although not domestic dwellings.

The date for the implementation of the proposed changes is eagerly awaited and until then the current law remains in force.

See also: Building Regulations (page 92); Fire: means of escape (page 263); Fire risk assessments (page 271).

Fire: means of escape

David Sinclair, Rollits

Key points

Employers and those who have control of premises have a statutory duty under fire, health and safety legislation to ensure that people can be safely evacuated in the event of a fire.

The requirement to provide and maintain means of escape in the event of fire applies equally to premises which require a fire certificate under section 1 of the Fire Precautions Act 1971 and those which fall within the requirements of the Fire Precautions (Workplace) Regulations 1997 (as amended).

The Building Regulations 2000 require means of escape to be incorporated into any new and most refurbished buildings.

In providing means of escape, an employer or the controller of premises is required to provide a sufficient number of safe routes which protect those evacuating from the effects of fire and from the ingress of smoke into the route. Means of escape should also be adequately lit and the exits must be suitably signed.

Legislation

- Fire Precautions Act 1971.
- Fire Safety and Safety in Places of Sport Act 1987.
- Health and Safety (Safety Signs and Signals) Regulations 1996.
- Fire Precautions (Workplace) Regulations 1997 (as amended).
- Building Regulations 2000.

Fire Precautions Act 1971

Section 1 of the Fire Precautions Act 1971 (FPA) requires that means of escape be provided in the following premises for which a fire certificate is mandatory, unless premises are exempt under section 5 of the FPA:

- Premises providing sleeping accommodation.
- Institutions providing treatment or care.
- Places of entertainment, recreation or instruction, as well as those housing a club, society or association.
- Premises used for the purposes of teaching, training or research.
- Premises which are accessed by members of the public, whether for payment or not.
- Places of work (except construction sites).

Where premises have a fire certificate, the certificate will stipulate the minimum means of escape to be provided in that premises.

Employers and controllers of premises will still have to give due regard to the findings of their risk assessments, required under the Fire Precautions (Workplace) Regulations 1997 (as amended) (FPWR), which may identify additional requirements.

Employers and controllers of premises whose premises are exempt from the requirement to have a fire certificate under the provisions of section 5A of the FPA, must under section 9A of the FPA still provide a means of escape.

Fire Safety and Safety in Places of Sport Act 1987

Part I of the Fire Safety and Safety in Places of Sport Act 1987 amends the FPA allowing local fire authorities to exempt certain categories of designated premises from the requirement to have a fire certificate.

Employers and controllers of premises should note, however, that the fire authority has the power to withdraw its exemption at any time if it believes that there is a serious risk to persons in the premises from fire, provided it has given notice to the occupier.

Premises for which an exemption to the requirement to have a fire certificate is in place will fall within the requirements of the FPWR.

Fire Precautions (Workplace) Regulations 1997

Regulation 5 of the FPWR places a duty on employers and controllers of premises or buildings which do not require a fire certificate to provide routes of escape and emergency exits, which must be kept clear at all times.

Emergency routes and exits

The basic principles with regard to the design of means of escape are that, wherever possible, there should be at least one alternative means of escape and, where direct escape from a building is not possible, people should be able to reach a place of relative safety.

A place of safety is an area of the building which provides people with a means of escape, or a place of refuge, which is free from smoke and fire for a specified minimum period of time.

Speed of evacuation

The size and number of escape routes in a building will depend on the number of people normally in the building, the activities undertaken there and the speed at which people can be evacuated.

In deciding how quickly people can be evacuated, employers and controllers of premises need to consider:

* how much time people will have available in the event of a fire;
* the distance to a place of safety;
* whether people have to travel down stairs;
* the number of people to be evacuated;
* the time of day and how alert people are likely to be; and
* their ability to escape without assistance.

Dimensions of emergency routes

The requirements for the minimum dimensions and means of construction of protected routes are set out in Schedule 1 of the Building Regulations

2000 and Approved Document B (Fire Safety).

The number, size and construction of protected routes will depend on the number of people using the route, as well as the distance they have to travel and time they will need to reach an external place of safety or be rescued.

Fire routes and exits must be kept clear at all times and employers and controllers of premises need to ensure that nothing is done to reduce or negate the integrity of protected routes and fire exits.

Compartments

The Building Regulations 2000 require buildings to be designed and constructed in compartments, so as to contain any fire.

Breaches in fire compartments to allow the transfer of cables and the like should be sealed with fire-resistant materials or surrounded with intumescent materials, which will expand and seal the gap in the event of a fire.

Emergency doors

The minimum standards for doors (fire doors) in fire compartment walls are set out in Approved Document B.

Fire doors through which people need to pass to reach a fire exit should be fitted with an effective self-closing device and labelled 'Fire Door Keep Shut'.

Doors to cupboards and other openings do not need to be fitted with a self-closing device, but they should be labelled 'Fire Door Keep Locked'.

Emergency lighting

All means of escape should be adequately lit and, where this cannot be guaranteed by natural light, emergency lighting will have to be provided.

Emergency lighting systems must be able to function in the event of any failure of the main lighting system which would present a hazard.

Emergency lighting should:

- clearly indicate the escape route;
- provide sufficient light along escape routes to allow people to move to final exits safely; and
- ensure fire equipment and alarm points are easily located.

BS 5266:1999 'Emergency lighting' sets out at Part 1 a code of practice for the emergency lighting of premises.

Fire signs

Regulation 4 of the Health and Safety (Signs and Signals) Regulations 1996 requires employers to provide and maintain fire safety signs in means of escape.

BS 5499:1990 'Fire safety signs, notices and graphic symbols' sets out the standard for fire safety signs.

Disabled people

Section 19 of the Disability Discrimination Act 1995 requires employers and controllers of premises to make reasonable physical adjustments to the fabric of the building or provide auxiliary aids to ensure that disabled employees or disabled people who are accessing their goods, services or facilities can escape safely in the event of a fire.

In buildings constructed or altered since May 2000, means of escape for disabled people is incorporated into the Building Regulations, supported by BS 5588: Part 8.

In other buildings, or in new buildings where there is a conflict between legislation and Approved Document B,

employers are required to assess the risks
to disabled people and make reasonable
adjustments.

See also: Emergency procedures (page
218); Fire risk assessments (page 271);
Lighting (page 367); Safety signage
(page 483).

Means of fighting fire

David Sinclair and Chris Platts, Rollits

Key points

Employers and those who have control of premises have a statutory duty under fire safety and health and safety legislation to ensure the provision of appropriate means of fighting fires.

Where there are premises for which a fire certificate under the Fire Precautions Act 1971 applies, the certificate will specify the minimum firefighting requirements for the building, but additional firefighting provision may be required as a result of risk assessments.

The firefighting requirements of other buildings need to be assessed under the requirements of Regulation 2 of the Fire Precautions (Workplace) Regulations 1997 (as amended).

Legislation

- Fire Precautions Act 1971.
- Fire Precautions (Workplace) Regulations 1997 (as amended).
- Provision and Use of Work Equipment Regulations 1998.

Firefighting systems

Firefighting equipment can be either active or passive and it is designed to extinguish fires by:

- starving the fire of fuel;
- smothering the fire to remove or reduce the concentration of oxygen; or
- cooling the fire to the extent that it cannot support combustion.

Active systems

Active systems, such as sprinklers, gas floods and portable fire extinguishers, become active only when a fire occurs, or with human intervention.

Passive systems

Passive systems form part of the structure of the building and involve the division of the building into fire-resisting compartments.

Where compartments are breached to allow movement through the building or the provision of services, 'fire stops' need to be installed to maintain the integrity of the fire resistance of the compartment in the event of a fire.

Breaches in compartment walls for services, etc., should be kept to a minimum and all openings should be protected with intumescent materials (i.e. pipe wraps, seals, etc.) or fire dampers. These should comply with BS 5588:1999 'Fire precautions in the design, construction and use of buildings: code of practice for ventilation and air conditioning ductwork'.

Firefighting equipment: statutory requirements

Firefighting equipment in workplaces falls within the requirements of the Provision and Use of Work Equipment Regulations 1998 (PUWER), which prescribe the following:

- Equipment should be suitable for the purpose for which it is provided, bearing in mind the risks posed by the activities and people in that work area. The equipment provided should take account of the activities and people working in or using an area, as well as the environmental conditions (e.g. adverse weather conditions or the presence of corrosive chemicals).
- Equipment should be capable of being used only for the purpose for which it is provided. It is essential that the correct type of firefighting equipment is provided (e.g. no water-based extinguishers where there is electrical equipment) and if equipment is used correctly it must not increase the risks to the user or others.
- Equipment should be regularly inspected and maintained in an effective state (see 'Maintenance' below). Inspection procedures should take account of the likelihood of equipment being damaged, moved or abused and the need for

more frequent maintenance than that specified by the manufacturer should be considered as part of risk assessment.
- People who may have to use the equipment should receive adequate information and instructions in its use (see 'Training' below). This is particularly important as, unless they are confident in the equipment's capabilities and limitations, people may fail to use it or use it incorrectly in a fire situation.

Maintenance

Regulation 6 of the Fire Precautions (Workplace) Regulations 1997 (as amended) (FPWR) requires that all firefighting equipment provided in a workplace must be maintained in an efficient state, in good working order and in good repair. As a minimum, maintenance of firefighting equipment should be undertaken in accordance with the manufacturers' instructions.

Regulations 4 and 5 of the FPWR require employers to develop and maintain a suitable system of maintenance for any firefighting equipment or devices provided in the workplace.

Training

Regulation 13 of the Management of Health and Safety at Work Regulations 1999, Regulation 9 of the PUWER and Regulation 4 of the FPWR require employees (and others) to be provided with adequate training prior to being entrusted to undertake the use of firefighting equipment.

Disability discrimination

Sections 6 and 21 of the Disability Discrimination Act 1995 require employers

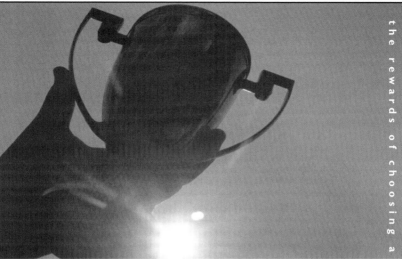

to make reasonable adjustments to the workplace to facilitate the use of work equipment, etc., by disabled people.

As part of their risk assessments, employers will have to consider the needs of disabled employees and others with regard to the type, size, location and siting of firefighting equipment and, where necessary, they will have to make 'reasonable adjustments' to ensure the safety of their employees and visitors.

Considerations may include resiting, or reducing the size of, fire extinguishers so that wheelchair users can easily access them.

> *See also*: Fire extinguishers (page 255); Fire risk assessments (page 271).

Fire risk assessments

Kevin Bridges, Osborne Clarke

Key points

The purpose of a fire risk assessment is to identify those measures that need to be taken to comply with Part 2 of the Fire Precautions (Workplace) Regulations 1997 (as amended). These Regulations contain three main provisions. Regulation 4 makes provision for firefighting and fire detection, Regulation 5 covers emergency routes and exits in the case of fire, and Regulation 6 deals with the maintenance of workplaces and safety devices.

The risk assessment should:

- identify the hazards by looking systematically at sources of ignition, fuel and work processes;
- identify those at significant risk in case of fire;
- assess the risks, considering the adequacy of existing fire safety measures, including:
  - control of ignition sources and sources of fuel
  - fire detection and warning systems
  - means of escape
  - means for fighting fire
  - maintenance and testing of fire precautions
  - emergency plans in the event of fire
  - fire safety information and training of employees
- record the findings and prepare an action plan for improvements; and
- be reviewed and revised periodically and when new risks are introduced to the business.

Legislation

- Fire Precautions (Workplace) Regulations 1997.
- Fire Precautions (Workplace) (Amendment) Regulations 1999.
- Management of Health and Safety at Work Regulations 1999.

Fire Precautions (Workplace) (Amendment) Regulations 1999

These Regulations came into force on 1 December 1999. They amend the Fire Precautions (Workplace) Regulations 1997 (FPWR 1997), which came into force on 1 December 1997.

The effect of the amending Regula-

---

tions was to apply the FPWR 1997 to most workplaces including those for which a fire certificate is in force or where an application for a fire certificate is pending. The main exceptions are construction sites, ships, mines, quarries and agricultural or forestry land.

The Regulations require employers to carry out a fire risk assessment and to provide and maintain such fire precautions as are necessary to safeguard those who use the workplace. They also require the provision of relevant information, instruction and training to employees about fire precautions.

The FPWR 1997 require that a suitable and sufficient fire risk assessment must be made under Regulation 3 of the Management of Health and Safety at Work Regulations 1999. Employers with five or more employees must record the significant findings of the risk assessment in writing. It must be kept for inspection, reviewed and revised as and when necessary.

For fire risk assessments there are five steps that an employer will need to take.

1. Identify potential fire hazards in the workplace

This involves identifying potential sources of ignition such as smokers' materials, naked flames, electrical, gas- or oil-fired appliances, machinery, faulty electrical equipment, static electricity, potential arson, etc. You should then identify sources of fuel (combustible materials) including flammable substances, wood, paper and card, plastics, rubber, foam and flammable gases (such as liquefied petroleum gas). The assessment must consider the workplace as a whole, including all work processes, outdoor locations and areas that are rarely used or visited.

2. Decide who might be in danger (e.g. employees, visitors, disabled persons)

The assessment must identify who is at risk in the event of fire, how they will be warned and how they will escape. Locate where people may be working (whether at permanent or occasional workstations) and consider who else is at risk such as customers, visiting contractors or disabled people. These individuals may be unfamiliar with your fire precautions and will be at higher risk.

3. Evaluate the risks

Evaluate the risks arising from the hazards and decide whether you have done enough to reduce the risk or need to do more. You should consider:

- the likelihood of fire occurring and whether it is possible to reduce the sources of ignition or minimise the potential fuel for a fire;
- the fire precautions you have in place and whether they are sufficient for the remaining risk and will ensure everyone is warned in case of fire (i.e. fire resistance and structural separation, fire detection and warning systems);
- the means by which people can make their escape safely or put the fire out if it is safe to do so (i.e. means of escape and means of fighting fire); and
- maintenance and testing of fire precautions to ensure they remain effective.

4. Record the findings

Where you employ five or more employees, you must record the significant findings of your assessment, together

---

Fire risk assessment checklist

The following table is a summary of the factors that ought to be considered as part of any fire risk assessment.

Stage of assessment	Considerations
Sources of ignition	Heaters, boilers, smokers' materials, electrical appliances, risk of arson, hot processes or surfaces, etc.
	Remove or replace *Maintain plant and equipment* *Improved security*
Combustible materials	Solids, liquids, gases, finished goods, waste materials, furniture, building construction, etc.
	Keep to a minimum *Store away from sources of ignition* *Good housekeeping*
Sources of oxygen	Natural air flow, ventilation and air-conditioning systems. Oxidising materials and piped/cylinder supplies.
	Keep doors and windows closed *Shut down unnecessary ventilation systems* *Control the storage and use of materials and sources of oxygen*

with details of any people you identify as being at particular risk. If you employ more than five people, you must also produce a written emergency plan the purpose of which is to ensure that the people in your workplace know what to do if there is a fire and to ensure that the workplace can be evacuated safely. All employees should receive information, instruction and training in fire precautions and your emergency plan. In particular they should know how to prevent fires and what action to take in the event of fire.

5. Keep the assessment under review and revise it when necessary

Changes to the workplace which have an effect on either fire risks or precautions should trigger a review of your risk assessment. Examples that may lead to increased risks or new hazards include changes to work processes, furniture, plant, machinery, substances, building layout or the numbers likely to be present in the building.

See also: Emergency procedures (page 218); Fire: means of escape (page 263); Means of fighting fire (page 267).

Sources of further information

The employer's guide to fire safety issued by the Home Office, the HSE, the Department of the Environment (Northern Ireland) and the Scottish Executive can be accessed at
www.archive.official-documents.co.uk/document/fire/index.htm.

First aid

Andrew Richardson, Scott Wilson

Key points

- The Health and Safety (First-Aid) Regulations 1981 require employers to provide adequate and appropriate equipment, facilities and personnel so that first aid can be given to their employees if they are injured or become ill at work.
- When people at work are injured or fall ill, they must receive immediate attention.
- An ambulance must be called in serious cases.
- Employees need to assess what their first-aid needs are.
- The minimum first-aid provision on any worksite is:
  - a suitably stocked first-aid box; and
  - an appointed person to take charge of first-aid arrangements.
- First-aid provision needs to be available at all times people are at work.

Legislation

- Health and Safety at Work etc. Act 1974.
- Management of Health and Safety at Work Regulations 1999.
- Health and Safety (First-Aid) Regulations 1981.

Requirements and guidance

The aim of first aid is to reduce the effects of injury or illness suffered at work. The Regulations place a duty upon all employers to assess the first-aid requirements within their workplace, to appoint competent personnel, and to provide equipment and facilities to enable first aid to be given to their employees if they are injured or become ill at work.

To assess the first-aid requirements within each workplace, the employer should consider:

- the hazards and risks in the workplace;
- how many people are located in their premises;
- previous accident/incident history;
- the nature and distribution of the workforce;
- the remoteness of the workplace in relation to emergency medical services;
- the needs of travelling, remote and lone workers;
- employees working on shared or multi-occupancy sites; and
- annual leave and other absences of first-aiders and appointed persons.

It should be noted that the first-aid provision for anyone other than employees, including the public, cannot be made under the Health and Safety at Work etc. Act 1974. Employers can consider it but should be aware that employer's liability insurance will not cover litigation as a result of first aid to non-employees; however, public liability insurance may.

The Regulations stipulate that first-aid equipment must be provided. The minimum requirement is a first-aid container, the contents of which will depend on the risks identified in the risk assessment. The HSE publishes guidance on suitable contents of first-aid boxes (see 'Sources of further information' below).

First-aid rooms must be provided where the risk assessment has identified they are necessary, usually in high-risk working environments. The guidance notes detail what is reasonably expected to be provided in such a room.

When the employer assesses the risk and identifies the need for personnel to give first aid, then sufficient numbers of people of the appropriate competency, in the appropriate locations, need to be arranged. The guidance offers suggestions as to the competency and numbers of personnel required based on whether the workplace is a low, medium or high risk and how many people are employed at the site.

The competency of personnel falls into two categories: first-aiders and appointed persons. The Regulations detail the criteria which each of these positions must meet, including qualifications and training.

The Regulations place a duty upon the employer to inform all its employees of the arrangements made in connection with first aid. The guidance suggests the setting-up of a procedure for informing staff that would include the details of the first-aid provision and how employees are told of the location, equipment, facilities and personnel. It also suggests the provision of notices that are clear and easily understood to relay all or some of the information. Finally it suggests that first-aid information is included in induction training to ensure all new employees are aware.

> *See also:* Accidents (page 69); Risk assessments (page 469).

Sources of further information

'First aid at work: The Health and Safety (First-Aid) Regulations 1981 – Approved Code of Practice and Guidance' (HSE Books, 1997): ISBN 0 7176 1050 0. This document assists employers in understanding the Regulations and provides practical and realistic advice on how you can ensure compliance.

HSE leaflet INDG214 'First aid at work – your questions answered' is also available as a download and gives basic information: www.hse.gov.uk/pubns/indg214.pdf.

Fixed-term workers

Pinsent Masons Employment Group

Key points

- Legislation introduced in 2002 provides statutory protection for fixed-term employees.
- The Regulations state that fixed-term employees have the right not to be treated less favourably than comparable permanent employees because they are employed on a fixed-term basis, unless the different treatment can be objectively justified.
- Employees cannot agree to waive their right to bring a claim for unfair dismissal as part of a fixed-term contract.
- After four years on successive fixed-term contracts, employees will be regarded as permanent.
- Workplace managers should take care in using fixed-term contracts, and should not now assume that they provide employers with any greater protection than they would have in relation to employees on other forms of contracts.

Legislation

- Employment Rights Act 1999.
- Fixed-term Employees (Prevention of Less Favourable Treatment) Regulations 2002.

Who has fixed-term contracts?

At present it is estimated that between 1.1 million and 1.3 million workers in the UK are employed on fixed-term contracts. Approximately half of all fixed-term employees are public sector employees mainly working in education, healthcare and public administration, while the remainder are employed predominantly by larger businesses.

The Regulations apply only to 'employees' rather than a wider category of workers.

What is a fixed-term contract?

The Regulations define a fixed-term contract as a contract of employment that will terminate:

- on the expiry of a specific term; or
- on the completion of a particular task; or
- on the occurrence or non-occurrence of any other specific event other than the attainment by the employee of any normal and bona-fide retiring age in the establishment for an employee holding the position held by him.

Scope of the Regulations

The Regulations came into force on 1 October 2002. They transposed the EC Directive on Fixed-term Work into UK law.

There are a number of categories of employees that are specifically excluded from the scope of the Regulations, namely: employees working under contracts of apprenticeship; agency workers; people employed on training schemes supported by the Government or an EU institution; people employed on work experience placements of one year or less that they are required to attend as part of a higher-education course; and serving members of the armed forces.

The main provisions of the Regulations can be summarised as follows:

- Fixed-term employees have the right not to be treated less favourably than comparable permanent employees because they are employed on a fixed-term basis, unless the different treatment can be objectively justified.
- Fixed-term employees are not treated less favourably than similar permanent employees as regards the terms of their contract, or by being subjected to any other detriment by an act, or deliberate failure to act, of the employer.
- The right not to be treated less favourably includes a right not to be treated less favourably in relation to the opportunity to secure any permanent position in an organisation. An employer will be required to objectively justify any difference in the availability of internal permanent vacancies between fixed-term and permanent employees.

- An employee who considers that he has been treated by an employer in a manner which infringes a right conferred by the Regulations may submit a request in writing to the employer for a written statement of the reasons for the treatment. Under the Regulations the employer must provide a written statement within 21 days of the request.
- After four years on successive fixed-term contracts (discounting any period before 10 July 2002) an employee shall be regarded as a permanent employee.
- A waiver of redundancy rights in fixed-term contracts is unlawful.
- An employee shall not be subjected to a detriment for relying upon his rights under the Regulations.

Termination of employment

Failure to renew a fixed-term contract on its expiry constitutes a dismissal for the purposes of employment legislation. In such circumstances, workplace managers should take care to avoid the possibility of a claim for unfair dismissal being brought by a fixed-term worker (see 'Dismissal', page 197), remembering the statutory process and steps required to be taken for compliance.

Whether the dismissal was fair or unfair will be determined by whether or not the employer can show that it acted reasonably in not renewing the contract.

Previously, employers have tried to get around this problem by including clauses in the fixed-term contract under which the employee in question agreed to waive his right to bring a claim for unfair dismissal due to the expiry and non-renewal of the contract if it was for one year or longer. Further, employers often engaged in the practice of renewing a fixed-term contract for a further fixed-term period, and still including such an unfair dismissal waiver relating to the end of that further term. However, section 18 (1) of the Employment Rights Act 1999 provided that these waivers of unfair dismissal rights would no longer be effective. The waiver of redundancy rights in fixed-term contracts was made unlawful as from 1 October 2002.

By virtue of the Regulations a dismissal will be automatically unfair if the reason for the dismissal is that the employee has brought proceedings against the employer under the Regulations, or requested from the employer a written statement of reasons for less favourable treatment or otherwise done anything under the Regulations in relation to the employer or any other person. No qualifying period of employment is required for such a claim.

Enforcement

Under the Regulations a fixed-term employee may bring a complaint to an employment tribunal that he has suffered less favourable treatment, not been informed of available vacancies or suffered a detriment. The complaint will require to be brought within three months of the date of the act complained of.

See also: Dismissal (page 197); Redundancy (page 455).

Sources of further information

The DTI page on fixed-term employees can be viewed at www.dti.gov.uk/er/fixed/fixed-pl512.htm.

Flexible working

Mark Kaye, Berwin Leighton Paisner

Key points

From 6 April 2003 employers have been under a legal obligation to consider applications for flexible working.

Legislation

- Employment Act 2002.

The law

Parents of young children will have the right to submit a request to their employer to allow them to work 'flexibly', by changing hours, changing days or working from home. The change, if agreed, will be a permanent change to the employee's terms and conditions. The right applies to parents of children under 6 (or under the age of 18 if disabled) with more than 26 weeks' service who have responsibility for the child's upbringing and make the request to enable them to care for the child.

The procedure is as follows:

- The employee makes a written, signed and dated request, specifying the change requested and proposed date from which it should apply. The request should also state what effect (if any) the employee thinks the change will have on the employer and how any such effect may be dealt with.
- The employer must either agree or hold a meeting to discuss the application with the employee within 28 days of the application being made.
- The employer must notify the employee of its decision within 14 days of the meeting (which may include detailing any compromise agreed in the meeting).
- Any refusal must specify the grounds (see below) with a sufficient explanation for the refusal.
- The employee has the right of appeal against any refusal within 14 days of receiving the employer's notification.
- The employer must hold a meeting with the employee within 14 days of receiving the notice of appeal in order to discuss the appeal.
- The employer must give the employee notice of its decision within 14 days of the appeal meeting. If the appeal is dismissed, grounds of the dismissal must be provided by the employer.

The following are permitted reasons for refusing a request:

- Burden of additional costs.

- Detrimental effect on ability to meet customer demand.
- Inability to reorganise work among existing staff.
- Inability to recruit additional staff.
- Detrimental impact on quality.
- Detrimental impact on performance.
- Insufficiency of work during the period the employee proposes to work.
- Planned structural changes.

These allow an employer to refuse a request, for example, where the employee wishes to change his days or hours from peak periods to quiet times or where the operational needs of the business require staff at a particular time. For example, a bartender who asked to change his hours to work from 11 a.m. to 5 p.m. could have his request turned down on the grounds that customer demand is highest in the evening.

An employee can complain to a tribunal that the ground given did not fall within one of the permitted reasons or that the employer's decision was based on incorrect facts. However, the tribunal cannot question the commercial validity of the employer's decision or substitute its own view on the employer's business reason. The tribunal's role is to determine whether the employer has given

serious consideration to a request to work flexibly and whether the employer has complied with the statutory procedure.

If the employee's complaint is successful, the tribunal can either order that the employee's request is reconsidered or award up to eight weeks' pay, subject to the statutory cap, currently £270, making the maximum award £2,160. It is worth noting, however, that these rights exist independently of other employment rights and that therefore an employee can bring a sex discrimination claim, for example, arising out of the same facts as a claim under the flexible working provisions and could potentially be successful in one claim and fail in the other.

Practical guidance for employers

- Treat requests for flexible working seriously.
- Follow the statutory procedure.
- If the request cannot be accommodated, identify the reason and provide an explanation.
- Allow the employee to appeal.

See also: Family-friendly rights (page 251); Homeworking (page 324).

Sources of further information

The DTI's page on flexible working can be viewed at www.dti.gov.uk/er/flexible.htm.

'Flexible Working Policy and Management Guide', version 1.0 (ISBN 1 900648 62 8, £34.99) is available as an electronic download from the Workplace Law Network. Call 0870 777 8881 for details, or visit www.workplacelaw.net.

Fuel storage

David Symons, Atkins Environment

Above-ground storage

The Control of Pollution (Oil Storage) (England) Regulations 2001 control the storage of bulk oil in England. Similar requirements apply in Scotland and Wales. The Regulations apply now for all new tanks and for any existing tank close to a watercourse or borehole. For all other tanks the Regulations will apply from 1 September 2005.

Containers controlled by the Regulations

The Regulations apply to all external above-ground containers of more than 200 litres capacity used for the storage of fresh oil and petrol. The Regulations do not apply to most private dwellings, petrol stations or farms.

Requirements of the Regulations

These include the following:

- The tank must be of adequate strength.
- The tank must be surrounded by an impermeable bund of not less than 110% of the tank capacity.
- There must be no drain point.
- Fill points must have at least a drip tray.

Permanent tanks

- Underground fill pipes must have a range of control measures. If not, they must be tested for leaks every ten years (every five if they have mechanical joints).
- An automatic overfill prevention device must be present if the filling operation is controlled from a place where it is not reasonably practicable to see the tank and any vent pipe.

Mobile bowsers

- Filling points must be fitted with a lock.
- There must be controls for flexible pipes.

Underground tanks

Defra has published a code of practice for the good design, operation and man-

---

Sources of further information

Full copies of the code of practice on underground storage tanks can be downloaded from Defra's website: www.defra.gov.uk.

The Environment Agency (www.environment-agency.gov.uk) has published a series of Pollution Prevention Guides for the safe storage and handling of fuels.

agement of underground storage tanks (USTs).

Operators of USTs are not legally required to follow the code, but in the event of a release from the tank then whether the operator has followed the code will be a material fact in any prosecution.

Under the code, the operators of USTs should conduct a risk assessment. In this process they will need to identify high-risk situations (such as old plant or inadequate operating procedures) and develop and implement a plan addressing these matters. Measures to control releases from USTs may include ground-water-monitoring wells, leak detection, new tanks, training of operators and emergency procedures.

> *See also*: COSHH/hazardous substances (page 153); Emergency procedures (page 218); Risk assessments (page 469).

Furniture

Phil Reynolds, Furniture Industry Research Association

Key points

Furniture is an unexpectedly complex commodity to specify because it encompasses many different requirements and crosses many different areas. There is more to getting it right than glancing through the pages of a glossy catalogue and basing choice on appearance and price.

First of all, employers have a responsibility to provide a safe working environment with regard to structural stability, fire safety, cabling and increasingly the science of ergonomics. Personnel need to know how to adjust furniture to their physique and the tasks they perform. Company image and regulatory compliance apart, a workforce operating in a comfortable environment is likely to be better motivated and less prone to absenteeism than one that has 'to make do and mend'.

So how does the facilities manager or specifier decide which products to choose? The first, and most fundamental, requirement is a test certificate. Has the product been tested to the relevant standards – British, European or international – by an accredited test laboratory?

Legislation

- Health and Safety at Work etc. Act 1974.
- Management of Health and Safety at Work Regulations 1999.
- Workplace (Health, Safety and Welfare) Regulations 1992.
- Provision and Use of Work Equipment Regulations 1998.
- Health and Safety (Display Screen Equipment) Regulations 1992 as amended by the Health and Safety (Miscellaneous Amendments) Regulations 2002.
- Electricity at Work Regulations 1989.
- Furniture and Furnishings (Fire) (Safety) Regulations 1988, amended 1989 and 1993.
- Disability Discrimination Act 1995.

Structural stability

Check that all tables, chairs and storage furniture have been tested to the appropriate standards. This should prove that the item is suitably strong, durable and stable in use to minimise the risk of any accident.

Fire safety

There is no legislation regarding flammability for office and contract furniture; this is different from the domestic market, where there are strict requirements designed to protect people in their homes. Instead, it is the responsibility of the local fire officer to decide the fire hazard rate of the building based on location and use. Once a rating has been set (usually 'low' for offices, rising to 'high' in institutions such as prisons and student accommodation), the furniture must meet these requirements. The relevant British Standard is BS 7176:1995 'Specification for resistance to ignition of upholstered furniture for non-domestic seating by testing composites'. In a new or refurbished building it is wise to consult with the fire officer prior to specification.

Cabling with desks

If a desk is provided with cabling (power or data) or provision for it to be fitted, the item should conform to specification BS 6396:2002 'Electrical systems in office furniture and office screens'. This covers the basic requirements for electrical cabling and should ensure an appropriate degree of safety. It may also fall under the Electricity at Work Regulations.

Ergonomics

The science of ergonomics is fitting equipment and tasks to people, and not the other way around.

The whole installation – desks and chairs used in conjunction with computer equipment – should conform with the Health and Safety (Display Screen Equipment) Regulations 1992. So look for compliance with BS EN ISO 9241:1999 Part 5.

Incorrect posture can cause a multitude of long-term health problems including back pain and repetitive strain injury. Personnel should be instructed in how to adjust their furniture correctly so that it meets their specific needs – it is a waste of money to buy expensive, adjustable furniture and then not train people how to operate the controls, but it often happens.

Some forward-looking employers are specifying sit/stand desks that enable the user to alternate between sitting and standing – an approach advocated by many ergonomists including Levent Caglar, senior ergonomist at the Furniture Industry Research Association (FIRA).

The marketplace is flooded with products claiming to be 'ergonomic', many of which fall far short of any decent ergonomic criteria. To give specifiers a reliable measure of true ergonomic performance, FIRA has instigated an Ergonomics Excellence Award. Items must meet, or in some instances exceed, the relevant British and European standards together with ergonomic criteria set by FIRA.

In addition the Disability Discrimination Act 1995 imposes extra requirements on employers to provide suitable furniture for both disabled visitors and employees. This includes not only work desks and chairs, but also reception counters and visitor areas.

Current standards

Desking : strength, stability and safety requirements

BS 4875:2001 Part 5 'Strength and stability of furniture. Requirements for strength, durability and stability of tables and trolleys for domestic and contract use'

BS EN 527:2000 Part 1 'Office furniture. Work tables and desks. Dimensions'

BS EN 527:2002 Part 2 'Office furniture. Work tables and desks. Mechanical'

BS EN 527:2003 Part 3 'Office furniture. Work tables and desks. Methods of test for the determination of the stability of the mechanical strength of the structure'

Seating: strength, stability and safety requirements

BS 5459:2000 Part 2 'Office pedestal seating for use by persons weighing up to 150kg and for use up to 24 hours a day including type-approval tests for individual components'

BS EN 1335:2000 Part 1 'Office furniture. Office work chair. Dimensions'

BS EN 1335:2000 Part 2 'Office furniture. Office work chair. Safety requirements'

BS EN 1335:2000 Part 3 'Office furniture. Office work chair. Safety test methods'

BS EN 13761:2002 'Office furniture. Visitors' chairs'

BS 7945:1999 'Non-domestic furniture. Seating. Determination of stability'

Storage: strength, stability and safety requirements

BS 4875:1998 Part 7 'Strength and stability of furniture. Methods for determination of strength and durability of storage furniture'

BS 4875:1998 Part 8 'Strength and stability of furniture. Methods for determination of stability of non-domestic storage furniture'

BS 5459:1983 Part 3 'Specification for performance requirements and test for office furniture. Storage furniture'

Screens: strength, stability and safety requirements

BS EN 1023:1997 Part 1 'Office furniture. Screens. Dimensions'

BS EN 1023:2000 Part 2 'Office furniture. Screens. Mechanical safety requirements'

BS EN 1023:2000 Part 3 'Office furniture. Screens. Test methods'

Cable management

BS 6396:2002 'Electrical systems in office furniture and office screens. Specification'

Flammability

BS 7176:1995: 'Specification for resistance to ignition of upholstered furniture for non-domestic seating by testing composites'

Sources of further information

For more information on strength, stability, safety, flammability and cable management systems, contact Phil Reynolds: preynolds@fira.co.uk.

For more information on ergonomics and the DDA, contact Levent Caglar: lcaglar@fira.co.uk.

Or visit www.fira.co.uk.

Ergonomics

BS EN ISO 9241:1999 Part 5 'Ergonomic requirements for office work with visual display terminals (VDTs). Workstation layout and postural requirements. Office accessories'

FIRA Standard PP045:2003 'Strength and durability of VDU platforms and support arms'

See also: Disability access (page 179); Display screen equipment (page 202); Electricity and electrical equipment (page 214); Fire risk assessments (page 271); Homeworking (page 367); Lighting (page 000); WRULDs (page 549).

Gas safety

Phil Wright, SafetyCO UK

Key points

- Anyone in control of commercial premises must ensure the safe condition of gas appliances.
- CORGI-registered engineers must be used to carry out works on gas appliances.
- Annual checks are not required on gas appliances and systems used in non-residential properties.

Legislation

- Gas Safety (Installation and Use) Regulations 1998.

The Regulations were introduced because of the increase in the number of deaths (approximately 30 a year) from badly installed and poorly maintained gas appliances and fittings. The Regulations apply to the installation, maintenance and use of gas appliances (both portable and fixed), fittings and flues in domestic and commercial premises.

Compliance

Any person who has control of a premises, either landlord or managing agent, has a duty to make sure that the installation, servicing, repair and maintenance of gas appliances, fittings and flues are carried out to a standard that ensures they operate in a safe condition.

If the equipment is not maintained, this can lead to prosecution of the person responsible for maintenance. If the occupier has either died or suffered ill health due to poorly installed or maintained gas appliances and the case is taken to Crown Court, this could lead to unlimited fines plus potential civil action (should an occupier or their family choose to take such action).

CORGI

CORGI (Council of Registered Gas Installers) is the national watchdog for gas safety in the UK.

Anyone who has the responsibility for gas maintenance must ensure that they appoint a competent person to undertake work on a gas appliance – installation, servicing, maintenance or repair. This restricts work to persons who are CORGI-registered.

Employers should note the following:

- CORGI-registered persons will carry an ID card with their registration number and the type of gas work

---

they can carry out. The registration with CORGI does not necessarily mean that person is competent to inspect, repair or maintain every gas appliance.

- If there is some doubt about a person's competency, then CORGI should be contacted direct for more details: 0870 401 2300.
- For domestic properties, annual safety checks on the appliances, flues and fittings should also be done by a CORGI-registered person. These annual checks should be recorded and held by the landlord or managing agent.
- Any alterations to gas appliances have to be undertaken by a CORGI-registered person.
- If a fault is found on an appliance, fitting or flue, then again the remedial work must be done by a CORGI-registered person.

Other considerations

- Annual checks are not required on gas appliances and systems used in non-residential properties. However, the gas plant and equipment must still be installed and maintained

regularly.
- If a new supply is installed in a premises, it must have emergency controls to isolate the supply.
- A diagram showing the location of meters, valves, risers, gas appliances, isolation valves, etc., should be (as good practice) available for the premises.
- Any uncontrolled gas escapes should be reported to Transco on the emergency number: 0800 111999.
- Since 31 October 1998 it has been illegal to install instantaneous water heaters which are not room-sealed or not fitted with a safety device that isolates the gas supply to that appliance before dangerous fumes can build up.

Record keeping

- Records of safety checks should be held by the landlord or managing agent for at least two years.
- These written checks must be given to a tenant within 28 days of the check.
- Records must be kept to demonstrate that the systems have been installed and regularly maintained to a suitable standard.

Sources of further information

L56 'Safety in the installation and use of gas systems and appliances. Gas Safety (Installation and Use) Regulations 1998. Approved Code of Practice and guidance' (HSE Books, 1998): 0 7176 0797 6.

HSE Gas Health and Safety web page: www.hse.gov.uk/gas.

HSE gas safety advice line: 0800 300 363.

HSE local authority circular summarising the Gas Safety (Installation and Use) Regulations 1998: www.hse.gov.uk/lau/lacs/33-6.htm.

CORGI: www.corgi-gas-safety.com.

Glass and glazing

Catherine Hogan, Glass and Glazing Federation

Key points

There are a number of regulations that impact on glazing and glass safety. The Workplace (Health, Safety and Welfare) Regulations 1992 address the issue of glazing in Regulation 14 and window design in Regulations 15 and 16.

Glazing requirements

Regulation 14 requires that, where necessary for reasons of health or safety, doors and low-level glazing in a workplace shall be glazed in a safety or robust material, or shall be protected against breakage. This does not mean that all glass in existing workplaces must be replaced with safety glass. A risk analysis must be carried out to see where there is danger – and that danger must be eliminated.

The HSE's revised Code of Practice, paragraph 147, says that particular attention should be paid to doors, and door side panels, where any part of the glazing is at shoulder height or below, and to windows where any part of the glazing is at waist height or below.

These cases are the same as those referred to in Approved Document N of the Building Regulations as 'critical locations'. Therefore glazing which meets the requirements of Document N (or BS 6262 Part 4) for these critical locations should meet the requirements of Regulation 14.

Regulation 14 also says that glazing in critical locations must be marked, or incorporate appropriate design features, to make its presence apparent – the objective being to avoid breaking the noses of people who might otherwise walk slap into the glazing, not realising it was there.

Reducing the risks

Various options are given in the Approved Code of Practice (ACoP) to Regulation 14 on how to reduce the risk of accidents at critical locations.

They include:

- the use of glazing that is inherently robust, such as polycarbonate or glass blocks;
- the use of glass which, if it breaks, breaks safely – e.g. glass which meets BS 6206, the UK standard test for soft body impact; and
- the use of thick ordinary glass which meets certain thickness criteria.

Window design requirements

Regulation 15 focuses on window design.

It requires that the operation of opening, closing or adjusting a window must not expose the operator to any risk. According to the Glass and Glazing Federation (GGF), this means that 'appropriate controls', such as window poles, must be provided where necessary; opening restrictors must be provided if there is a danger of falling out of the window; and the bottom edge of an opening window must be at least 800mm above floor level.

A further refinement is that opening windows must not project into an area where passers-by are likely to collide with them.

Regulation 16 requires that all windows and skylights shall be designed so they can be cleaned in safety. Essentially, this means that, if they cannot be cleaned from floor level or other suitable surfaces, windows must be designed to be cleanable from the inside.

The ACoP to Regulation 16 makes a variety of recommendations about the safe use of ladders, cradles and safety harnesses. It also cross-refers to BS 8213: Part 1 1991 'Windows, doors and rooflights: code of practice for safety in the use and during the cleaning of windows'.

Glazing options

So what are your options when it comes to ensuring that the regulatory requirements are fulfilled in the most cost-effective way?

Choices include toughened or laminated glass, or the use of safety film.

Toughened glass is a glass that has been modified by thermal treatment to give strength, safety up to BS 6206 Class A, and improved resistance to heat. Its light transmission is equal to ordinary glass.

Laminated glass consists of two or more sheets of ordinary or heat-treated glass bonded together under heat and pressure by interlayers of transparent polymer. There are various types of laminated glass, including laminated safety glass, laminated security glass and bullet-resistant glass. Its most significant feature is that, if the glass fractures on impact, fragments will remain bonded to the plastic interlayer. This minimises the risk of serious cuts from flying glass and maintains a protective barrier.

Film is a tough sheet of micro-thin high-clarity polyester that can be applied easily in situ to the interior or exterior of existing windows, glass doors and partitions. It is available in single-ply and multi-ply formats. The correct application of film on glass can upgrade the original glazing to meet the requirements of Government regulations on health and safety and British Standards.

Energy efficiency requirements under the Building Regulations

Amendments to Part L of the Building Regulations came into force on 1 April 2002, bringing new requirements for energy efficiency in buildings. The Building Regulations Part L were amended in October 2001, and new approved Documents L1 and L2 – giving approved guidance on how the new Part L can be complied with – were published at the same time. The main changes affect glazing (see below) and some installations of oil-storage tanks, combustion devices and some plumbing.

The new regulations will apply to new buildings, and to extensions and alterations to existing ones. Local authority building control departments are a traditional source of help on how organisations can meet the regulations (see also 'Sources of further information' below).

Fenestration Self-Assessment Scheme (FENSA)

To assist the effective implementation of the requirements of Part L, a scheme for the self-certification of replacement glazing has been set up by the GGF. This scheme is known as the Fenestration Self-Assessment Scheme (FENSA).

Since 1 April 2002 all replacement glazing has come within the scope of the Building Regulations, so that anyone who installs replacement windows or doors has to comply with strict thermal performance standards. The Building Regulations have controlled glazing in new buildings for many years, but this represents only a very small percentage of the total building stock.

When the time comes to sell property – says the GGF – the purchaser's solicitors will ask for evidence that any replacement glazing installed after April 2002 complies with the new Building Regulations. There will be two ways to prove compliance:

- a certificate showing that the work has been done by an installer who is registered under the FENSA Scheme; or

- a certificate from the local authority saying that the installation has approval under the Building Regulations.

See also: Building Regulations (page 92).

Sources of further information

Contact the GGF (tel. 0870 042 4255; fax 0870 042 4266; email info@ggf.org.uk) or visit www.ggf.org.uk.

The BRE has put together a useful selection of common questions and answers about Part L of the Building Regulations and the Approved Documents online at www.projects.bre.co.uk/partlfaq/default.htm.

Head protection

Phil Wright, SafetyCO UK

Key points

The Construction (Head Protection) Regulations 1989 require suitable head protection to be provided and worn when there is a risk of head injury. Unless there is no foreseeable risk of injury, employees must be provided with head protection and a decision must be made as to when, where and how it should be worn.

You are allowed to make rules governing when and where head protection should be worn. These rules must be in writing and brought to the attention of all those who may be affected by them.

Legislation

- Construction (Head Protection) Regulations 1989.
- Personal Protective Equipment Regulations 1992.
- Management of Health and Safety at Work Regulations 1999.

Compliance advice

Helmets are available in a variety of designs and it is important that the right type is provided for the work to be done. Properly fitting head protection is of utmost importance and therefore it must be adjustable. However, it must also be compatible with the type of work to be done. For example, an industrial safety helmet with little or no peak is suitable for a surveyor taking measurements, or to allow unrestricted upwards vision for a scaffolder.

Helmets must also be compatible with any other personal protective equipment (e.g. ear defenders or eye protectors).

Maintenance

It is the employer's responsibility to maintain the head protection, and to ensure its serviceability it should be inspected before use by the wearer. It is worth noting that the self-employed must maintain their own.

Dos and don'ts

Do:

- wear the helmet the right way round;
- wear a chinstrap where necessary;
- wear the helmet so that the brim is level when the head is upright; and
- keep a supply of helmets for visitors.

Don't:

- use your helmet for carrying materials;

- paint it or use solvents for cleaning;
- store it in direct sunlight;
- modify, cut or drill it; or
- share your head protection.

Risk assessment

Where there is significant risk, the legislation sets out a hierarchy of control measures. The provision of head protection should always be regarded as a last resort. It may be possible to:

- stop access to areas where head injuries could be caused;
- provide protected routes;
- avoid the movement of loads overhead;

- fit some form of protection (e.g. guardrails, toe-boards) to prevent falling objects; or
- mark and cushion fixed hazards such as pipes and low access points.

Exception

Sikhs at work while wearing their turbans are exempt from the wearing of head protection.

See also: Construction site health and safety (page 145); Personal protective equipment (page 425).

Sources of further information

BS EN 397:1995 'Specification for industrial safety helmets'.

INDG262 'Head protection for Sikhs wearing turbans' (HSE Books, 1998).

Health and safety at work

Stuart Armstrong, Pinsent Masons

Key points

- The Health and Safety at Work etc. Act 1974 (HSWA) imposes general duties on employers, the self-employed, controllers of premises and all employees to ensure health, safety and welfare.
- Legislation is supported by Approved Codes of Practice (ACoPs) and guidance notes.
- Occupiers of premises also owe a duty of care to both lawful visitors and trespassers.
- Employers may be liable for acts committed by employees during the course of their employment.

Legislation

- Health and Safety at Work etc. Act 1974.
- Management of Health and Safety at Work Regulations 1999.
- Workplace (Health, Safety and Welfare) Regulations 1992.
- Occupiers' Liability Acts 1957 and 1984.
- Employers' Liability (Compulsory Insurance) Act 1969.
- Employers' Liability (Compulsory Insurance) Regulations 1998.

Overview

The HSWA imposes general duties on all employers and the self-employed to ensure the safety of all those affected by their business activities, and on employees to look after their own safety. It also allows outdated, prescriptive legislation to be replaced by objective-setting Regulations, supported by ACoPs and guidance notes.

The European Union has instigated the majority of recent changes in UK health and safety legislation by issuing EU directives which require Member States to pass their own legislation. The HSWA allows such requirements to be implemented as additional Regulations.

Case law has developed alongside legislation, imposing civil duties of care on employers and the self-employed to look after the health, safety and welfare of their employees and the health and safety of others affected by their operations.

Health and safety in the workplace is governed by both criminal and civil law.

Health and Safety at Work etc. Act 1974

Before the introduction of the HSWA, health and safety legislation had developed in a piecemeal fashion, providing specified industries and hazardous activities with a set of prescriptive rules to follow. In 1974 this haphazard approach was replaced by the HSWA, which is now the cornerstone of modern health and safety legislation.

The HSWA imposes duties on everyone at work: employers, the self-employed, and employees. The principal duties it imposes are as follows.

Section 2: Duties of employers to employees

Employers must ensure, so far as is reasonably practicable, the health, safety and welfare of their employees. To do this they must provide:

- safe plant and safe systems of work;
- arrangements for the safe use, handling, storage and transport of articles and substances;
- adequate information, instruction, training and supervision;
- safe places of work, including safe access and egress; and
- a safe working environment with adequate welfare facilities.

All employers must make and review a suitable and sufficient assessment of the risks of their activities to employees or persons not in their employment who may be affected.

An employer with five or more employees must prepare and regularly review a written health and safety policy statement, detailing the organisational arrangements for health, safety and welfare, and bring it to employees' attention.

Employers must make such arrangements as are necessary to effectively plan, organise, control, monitor and review any protective measures. Employers of five or more employees must record the arrangements.

Employers must appoint competent persons to assist with the measures necessary for ensuring health and safety and must also consult with employee representatives (including trade unions) when making health and safety arrangements.

Section 3: Duties of employers to others

An employer must, so far as is reasonably practicable, conduct his business so as to ensure that non-employees are not exposed to health and safety risks. If the employer is a self-employed person, then he must also, so far as is reasonably practicable, conduct his business to ensure that he is not exposed to such risks. This duty extends to contractors, visitors and members of the public.

Section 4: Duties relating to premises

Those individuals or organisations with total or partial control of work premises must, so far as is reasonably practicable, ensure the health and safety of all non-employees who work there, to the extent of their control.

Landlords and managing agents may therefore be responsible for the safety of those working in the common parts of buildings (e.g. cleaners, maintenance staff, etc.). Non-domestic tenants are responsible for the health and safety of any person in the areas covered by their lease.

Section 6: Duty of manufacturers

Anyone who designs, manufactures, imports or supplies articles or substances for use at work must ensure, so far as is reasonably practicable, that those articles are safe for their intended use and during cleaning and maintenance. In the UK this duty is supplemented by the EU CE marking regime requirements.

Section 7: Duties of employees

While at work, employees have a duty:

- not to endanger themselves or others through their acts or omissions; and
- to co-operate with their employer, e.g. by wearing protective equipment.

Section 8

No person shall misuse anything provided in the interests of health, safety or welfare.

Section 36

Where any offence was committed due to an act or default of some other person, that person shall be guilty of the offence whether or not the person committing the offence is charged.

Section 37

Where an offence by the company or organisation is proved to have been committed with the consent, with the connivance or by the neglect on the part of any director, manager or secretary (or similar person), then he will also be guilty of the offence and may be punished accordingly.

Section 40

This section of HSWA was recently examined by the courts in the light of human rights legislation. It allows the normal standard of proof in criminal prosecutions (for the prosecution to prove beyond reasonable doubt that the offence occurred) to be reversed. As a

consequence, defendants in health and safety prosecutions are required to prove that they have done everything reasonably practicable (or everything practicable for some offences) to safeguard the health and safety of employees, non-employees or members of the public.

'Reasonably practicable'

Many health and safety duties require the duty holder to do everything 'so far as is reasonably practicable'. This phrase means doing less than everything physically possible (i.e. everything 'practicable') and involves a balance to be struck between, on the one hand, the cost of preventing the risk to health and safety and, on the other hand, the inconvenience and cost in terms of money and other resources of overcoming that risk. If it proves disproportionate for the company to take an additional step, then the test is satisfied.

Assistance on what is reasonably practicable comes from ACoPs and guidance documents issued by the HSE, plus relevant British Standards and industry guidance.

However, in practice this test is very difficult to satisfy as it is frequently the case that when an incident is viewed with hindsight an additional measure with a small resource implication may have been taken in relation to that incident. The courts frequently err on the side of caution, which makes this a very difficult test to satisfy. In addition, the courts have also determined that the standard of care is the same regardless of the size of the company.

Employers should record their risk assessments and the decisions to implement or reject certain safety measures. Since safety measures must be proportionate to the risk they are averting, the first step is to identify and assess the risk, after which the available control measures should be identified and assessed. If the time and cost involved in the control measure are disproportionately high in comparison with the risk involved, then in theory the duty to do everything reasonably practicable will be satisfied even though the measure is not implemented. In practice considerable evidence of the reasons for this decision will be required if this defence is to be used in relation to a health and safety incident.

The difficulty for many employers in making this judgement is that the question of whether the correct balance is reached is one that only a court can definitely decide after looking at all the evidence in each case.

Regulations

Parliament has passed numerous Regulations made under the provisions of section 15 of the HSWA that impose detailed obligations on employers and those controlling work activities. The most important of these are covered in other articles.

Approved Codes of Practice

ACoPs have a 'quasi-legislative' status.

Although they do not provide definitive interpretation of legislation (only the courts can do that), compliance with the relevant ACoP does provide good evidence of compliance with the relevant statutory duty, and crucially evidence of doing everything 'reasonably practicable'.

Prosecution

Health and safety prosecutions take place in the criminal courts, starting formally with the receipt of a summons to appear at the magistrates' court. This is usually issued in a court near where the accident occurred. Generally, the case may be heard in the magistrates' court, where the maximum penalty is a £20,000 fine and/or (for a small number of charges) six months' imprisonment for each charge. Cases that are complex, or result from a more serious outcome, will be committed (referred) by the magistrates to the Crown Court, where the maximum penalty rises to an unlimited fine and/or two years' imprisonment (again for specific charges only).

Maximum penalties under the HSWA and the various Regulations it allows to be introduced follow the table below.

Mitigation and aggravation

Frequently in health and safety investigations the measures which an employer

Maximum penalties available under HSWA and associated Regulations		
Breach of	Magistrates' court	Crown Court
HSWA	£20,000 fine and/or up to six months' imprisonment	Unlimited fine and/or up to two years' imprisonment
Regulations	£5,000 fine and/or up to six months' imprisonment	Unlimited fine and/or up to two years' imprisonment

takes may amount to either a complete or partial defence to the charges. In addition, the same information may also amount to mitigation of the offence committed. The courts have given guidance on the particular factors which amount to mitigating or aggravating features of an offence. These include the following:

Mitigating features

- A prompt admission of guilt.
- The defendant fell only a little way short of meeting the test of reasonable practicability.
- Previous safety record.
- The extent of risk/danger created by the offence.
- The steps taken by the company to remedy deficiencies.

Aggravating features

- Failure to heed warnings.
- Whether death or a serious injury resulted from the breach.
- Whether cost cutting contributed to the incident.
- A deliberate breach will seriously aggravate the offence and will probably elevate any fine imposed.

Civil action

Anyone who suffers injury or ill health as a result of work activities can bring a personal injury claim against those responsible. To be successful, the claimant must prove that:

- the defendant owed him a duty of care;
- that duty was breached; and
- the injury or injuries was or were a foreseeable result of the breach.

The existence of a duty of care is easy to prove in an employer–employee relationship, since, under common law, the employer has a duty to provide:

- safe plant and equipment;
- safe systems of work; and
- competent fellow workers.

These civil common law duties mirror the duties under section 2 of the HSWA. Most health and safety provisions do not give an automatic right of civil action when breached (an action for breach of statutory duty). However, a breach of the HSWA, or its subordinate Regulations, does provide good evidence of a breach of the equivalent common law obligation.

Occupiers' Liability Acts

Occupiers of premises are under statutory duties contained in the Occupiers' Liability Acts 1957 and 1984:

- The 1957 Act imposes a duty to take reasonable steps to ensure that lawful visitors to the premises are safe.
- The 1984 Act imposes a duty to take reasonable steps to ensure that trespassers are not injured. This is a slightly lower standard of care than that for lawful visitors.

A breach of these Acts is not a criminal offence but will support a civil case for negligence or for a breach of statutory duty.

Vicarious liability

An employer may be responsible for the wrongful acts of employees carried out during their ordinary duties in the course of their employment. If the act results in an injury, then a claimant can sue the employer under normal negligence principles on the basis of vicarious liability.

Personal injury claims

Personal injury claims must commence within three years from the date of knowledge that a claim could be brought. In an action for negligence, this will be the date when the claimant knew, or should have known, that there was a significant injury and that it was caused by the defendant's negligence.

For some claims (e.g. for occupational hearing loss or asbestosis), the date of knowledge may be several years after the exposure to harm. To ensure such claimants are not prejudiced, the courts have held that the three-year time limit only runs from the date of diagnosis by a medical consultant.

Damages

Successful claimants receive monetary damages, which are assessed under a number of headings:

- loss of earnings (both before and after trial);
- damage to clothing, property, etc.;
- pain and suffering;
- medical or nursing expenses; and
- inability to pursue personal/social/ sports interests or activities.

Most personal injury claims are paid for out of insurance (employers' liability or public liability), subject to exclusions and excesses. The Employers' Liability (Compulsory Insurance) Act 1969 and 1998 Regulations require employers to hold a minimum of £5m insurance cover for such actions.

See also: Health and safety enforcement (page 306); Health and safety management (page 311); Health and safety policies (page 316); Occupier's liability (page 409).

Sources of further information

Copies of legislation, ACoPs and guidance documents are available via the HSE information line (tel. 07801 545 500) or from your local HSE office or local authority environmental health department.

'Health and Safety Policy and Management Guide, version 1.0' (ISBN 1 900648 35 0, £59.99) is available as an electronic download from the Workplace Law Network. Call 0870 777 8881 for details, or visit www.workplacelaw.net.

Health and safety consultation

Sean Elson, Kennedys Health and Safety Team

Key points

There is a general duty on every employer imposed by section 2(6) of the Health and Safety at Work etc. Act 1974 (HSWA) to consult with safety representatives of trade unions.

For the purposes of discharging that duty, the Safety Representatives and Safety Committees Regulations 1977 (the 1977 Regulations) set out details as to the appointment of safety representatives together with their functions and the employer's duty to consult.

The Health and Safety (Consultation with Employees) Regulations 1996 (the 1996 Regulations) subsequently extended this duty to cover those employees whose union is not recognised or who do not have a union.

As a consequence an employer might have to consult employees under both sets of Regulations where employees have a different status as to representation in the workplace.

Legislation

- Health and Safety at Work etc. Act 1974.
- Safety Representatives and Safety Committees Regulations 1977.
- Health and Safety (Consultation with Employees) Regulations 1996.

Safety representatives and committees

For the purposes of the appointment of safety representatives or committees and the duty to consult, a recognised trade union is one where the employer, or two associated employers, recognises the union for the purpose of collective bargaining.

The recognised trade union may appoint safety representatives from among the employees in all cases where an employer by whom it is recognised employs one or more employees.

A person ceases to be a safety representative for the purposes of these Regulations when:

- the trade union which appointed him notifies the employer in writing that his appointment has been terminated; or
- he ceases to be employed at the workplace; or
- he resigns.

An employer has a duty under section 2(7) of HSWA to establish a safety committee with a function of keeping under review the measures taken to ensure the health and safety at work of its employees where requested in writing by at least two safety representatives. The committee should be established not later than three months after the request is made.

Functions of safety representatives

As well as having a function in relation to the employer's duty to consult in accordance with section 6(2) of HSWA, safety representatives also have other functions set out in the 1977 Regulations. The most important of these are to investigate potential hazards and dangerous occurrences or the causes of any accidents in the workplace. Others include investigating complaints by any employee they represent relating to that employee's health, safety or welfare at work and to make representations to the employer arising out of their investigations or from complaints received or on general matters affecting health and safety at the workplace

Additional functions are to carry out inspections of the workplace and to receive information from HSE inspectors and consult with those inspectors as the representative of the employees.

Employer's duty to consult safety representatives

In addition to the general duty to consult safety representatives for the purposes of effectively promoting and developing measures to ensure the health and safety at work of employees, the 1977 Regulations state that every employer shall consult safety representa-

tives in 'good time' regarding a number of specified matters. These are as follows:

- The introduction of any measure at the workplace which may substantially affect the health and safety of the employees whom the safety representatives concerned represent.
- Arrangements for appointing or, as the case may be, nominating persons in accordance with the Management of Health and Safety at Work Regulations 1999 or the Fire Precautions (Workplace) Regulations 1997.
- Any health and safety information that the employer is required to provide.
- The planning and organising of any health and safety training that the employer is required to provide
- The health and safety consequences for the employees of new technologies into the workplace.

The 1977 Regulations also provide for inspection of the premises and of certain documents by safety representatives on reasonable notice.

Employer's duty to consult employees

The 1977 Regulations apply where there is a recognised trade union. The 1996 Regulations created a duty to consult those employees who did not have the benefit of safety representatives.

The matters on which the employer has to consult are effectively identical to those on which he must consult safety representatives where he recognises a union, and which are set out above.

The persons to be consulted are:

- the employees directly; or
- in respect of any group of em-

ployees, one or more persons in that group who were elected, by the employees in that group at the time of the election, to represent the group for the purposes of such consultation (these are referred to as 'representatives of employee safety').

When the employer consults these representatives, he should inform the employees of the names of the representatives and the group of employees represented by them.

An employer shall not consult a person as a representative if:

- that person has notified the employer that he does not intend to represent the group of employees for the purposes of consultation; or
- that person has ceased to be employed in the group of employees which he represents; or
- the period of his election has expired and that person has not been re-elected; or
- the person has become incapacitated from carrying out his functions under the 1996 Regulations.

If an employer has been consulting representatives and then decides to consult the employees directly, he shall inform the representatives and the employees of this.

The 1996 Regulations also impose a duty on the employer to provide employees and representatives with such information as is necessary to enable them to participate fully and effectively in the consultation. Where the employer consults representatives, he shall also make available information contained with records for the purposes of RIDDOR.

Functions of representatives of employee safety

These are very similar to those of appointed safety representatives. They are:

- to make representations to the employer on potential hazards and dangerous occurrences at the workplace which either affect, or could affect, the group of employees they represent;
- to make representations to the employer on general matters affecting the health and safety at work of the group of employees they represent and in particular in relation to those matters on which the employer has a duty to consult; and
- to represent the employees they represent in consultations at the workplace with inspectors of the HSE.

Payment for time off and training

Both the 1977 and the 1996 Regulations provide that the employer shall permit safety representatives or representatives of employee safety to take such time off with pay during working hours as is necessary for performing their functions.

In relation to training, the 1977 Regulations provide that the employer will permit safety representatives paid time off to undergo training. The situation is more onerous for employers in relation to representatives under the 1996 Regulations. In those circumstances the employer shall ensure that representatives are provided with such training in respect of their functions as is reasonable in all the circumstances and it will be the employer who has to bear the cost connected with that training including travel and subsistence.

Employer's liability for breaches

A breach of the general duty under section 2(6) of HSWA is a criminal offence punishable by a maximum fine of £20,000 in a magistrates' court or an unlimited fine in the Crown Court.

A breach of the Regulations is punishable by a £5,000 fine in a magistrates' court or an unlimited fine in the Crown Court.

A breach of the general duty under section 2(6) or of the 1996 Regulations does not result in civil liability for a breach. Civil liability does exist for a breach of the 1977 Regulations and both sets of Regulations provide for an employee to take action in an employment tribunal in relation to an employer's failure concerning paid time off for the purposes of the provisions within the Regulations.

See also: Health and safety at work (page 295); Health and safety management (page 311); Trade unions (page 499).

Sources of further information

INDG232 'Consulting employees on health and safety – a guide to the law' (HSE Books, 1999): ISBN 0 7176 1615 0.

Health and safety enforcement

Stuart Armstrong, Pinsent Masons

Key points

- Inspectors have wide powers of investigation.
- Enforcement notices are an easy way for inspectors to order improvements.
- Prohibition notices can require work to stop immediately, and continue to have effect during an appeal (unless the tribunal hearing the appeal directs otherwise). Improvement notices are suspended pending the outcome of any appeal which has been lodged.
- Criminal prosecutions can be brought for breaches of health and safety legislation.
- Conviction usually results in a fine (which can be substantial) and an order to pay prosecution costs – neither of which are recoverable from insurance.

Legislation

- Health and Safety at Work etc. Act 1974.
- Health and Safety (Enforcing Authority) Regulations 1998.
- Police and Criminal Evidence Act 1984.

Overview

The Health and Safety at Work etc. Act 1974 (HSWA) set up the Health and Safety Executive (HSE) as the body responsible for promoting and enforcing health and safety legislation.

The HSE and local authorities together represent the enforcing authorities for all health and safety legislation (including pre-1974 provisions).

The HSWA provides powers of investi-gation, which are in some respects more rigorous than those of the police, since no separate warrant is required to enter premises and persons can be compelled to answer relevant questions and to sign a declaration as to the truth of those answers.

Enforcing authorities regularly serve improvement and prohibition notices to compel employers to take remedial action. Contravention of such notices is a criminal offence.

The ultimate sanction for breaching health and safety legislation is criminal prosecution of the individual or organi-sation responsible.

Although the principal penalty is a fine (which regularly exceeds £150,000 for serious offences), individuals can be (but rarely are) sent to prison for up to two years for committing certain offences.

Enforcing authorities

The enforcing authority for different workplaces is specified in the Health and Safety (Enforcing Authority) Regulations 1998. The general rule is that the HSE is the enforcing authority. However, health and safety is enforced by the relevant local authority in certain workplaces, including:

- offices;
- retail outlets;
- catering services;
- exhibitions; and
- sports grounds and theatres.

In this article, an 'inspector' means an officer of the relevant enforcing authority.

Powers of investigation

Section 20 of the HSWA gives inspectors wide powers to investigate suspected health and safety offences. These include the power to:

- enter and search premises without a warrant;
- direct that the whole premises, or any part of them, be left undisturbed;
- take measurements, photographs, recordings or samples;
- take possession of items for testing or use as evidence;
- interview any person; and
- demand copies of documents as evidence.

Interviews

Section 20

Under section 20, inspectors can require interviewees to answer questions and sign a declaration that those answers are true. Although there is no right to remain silent, the evidence obtained cannot be used to prosecute interviewees or their spouse. It can, however, be used against any other individual, or company including the interviewee's employer.

PACE

Where an inspector suspects that a particular individual or a company may have committed an offence, he will usually offer to interview the individual suspect or a person with authority to speak on behalf of the company (as relevant) under the Police and Criminal Evidence Act 1984 (PACE), sometimes in addition to conducting an interview under section 20. Interviewees must be cautioned before the interview, which is generally tape-recorded.

Unlike interviews conducted under section 20, answers to questions in PACE interviews may be used to prosecute the interviewee or the company that the interviewee represents.

Individuals have the right to refuse a PACE interview or to remain silent at any point during such interviews, but an adverse inference may be drawn where an interviewee fails to answer when questioned about some issue which he later uses as part of his defence.

Where an individual would prefer not to attend a PACE interview, he may instead offer to answer any written questions in writing.

Voluntary statements

Inspectors often ask individuals with relevant information to provide a voluntary written statement (which is admissible in court under section 9 of the Criminal Justice Act 1967).

Voluntary statements offer no protection to their makers and can be used against the individual concerned and others. They are frequently compiled after a 'quick chat' or a 'quiet word' with an inspector. The maker of the statement is then asked to sign the statement (under some pressure) and he is not encouraged to make any changes to it before it has been written down.

Changes to the statement after it has been written down and read by the maker are cumbersome and time-consuming. Few interviewees have the patience and nerve to demand that statements are altered to reflect accurately what they actually say, rather than what the inspector thinks he heard.

Enforcement notices

Inspectors can serve improvement and prohibition notices upon certain persons carrying out certain activities. In practice, improvement and prohibition notices are most often served on employers.

An improvement notice is a notice requiring a person to remedy a breach of health and safety law within a specified period. A prohibition notice is a notice prohibiting a person from carrying on certain activities which in the inspector's opinion involve or will involve a risk of serious personal injury.

For inspectors, the main advantages of a prohibition notice over an improvement notice are that it can have immediate effect, and there is no need to specify any particular breach of legislation. One important difference between these types of notice is that on appeal a prohibition notice is stayed until the appeal is determined, while an improvement notice remains in force until the appeal is heard.

Failure to comply with an improvement or prohibition notice is a criminal offence, punishable by a fine of up to £20,000 and/or up to six months' imprisonment (if the matter is heard in a magistrates' court) or an unlimited fine and/or up to two years' imprisonment (if the matter is heard in the Crown Court)

Criminal prosecution

There are two main types of health and safety offence:

- summary offences which are tried only in the magistrates' court;
- offences which can be tried in either the magistrates' court or the Crown Court ('either way' offences) depending on their seriousness.

Burden of proof

In criminal law, the burden of proof generally falls on the prosecution, which must prove beyond all reasonable doubt that the defendant committed the particular offence.

However, where a health and safety duty requires something to be ensured 'so far as is reasonably practicable', then it is the defendant who must prove, on the balance of probabilities, that it was not reasonably practicable to do more in the circumstances. This makes the prosecution's task easier (particularly following an accident), since, with the benefit of hindsight, it is often possible to identify additional safety measures which could have been implemented.

Many other health and safety duties are absolute duties to do everything 'practicable' to ensure that the duty has been carried out. For these duties, it is irrelevant whether the duty holder can show that it did all that was 'reasonably practicable'. The prosecution does not need to prove that the defendant intended to commit these offences, merely that it contravened the statutory duty. Again, this can be relatively easy for the prosecution to prove as the accident will frequently be enough to demonstrate that the duty has been breached.

Level of penalty

Until recently, the average fines for health and safety offences were comparatively low. The Court of Appeal criticised this in November 1998 when providing sentencing guidelines. Since then, fines for serious offences (particularly following fatalities and high-profile disasters) have risen sharply.

The current largest fine against a single company is £2m (Thames Trains on 5 April 2004).

However, fines are steadily increasing for all health and safety offences, and there is a tendency for fines to exceed £150,000 in most high-profile cases.

A convicted organisation or individual will generally also be ordered to pay part, or all, of the prosecution's costs, which can exceed the amount of the fine.

Although insurance policies will sometimes cover legal fees in defending a prosecution, they cannot cover the payment of fines or costs orders as a matter of public policy.

In some instances it is also possible for a court to order the disqualification of directors or senior managers from acting as a director or taking part in the promotion, formation or management of a company for up to 15 years.

Recent developments

In July 2003 the Health and Safety Commission (HSC) updated the HSE and Local Authority Enforcement Policy which inspectors refer to when deciding what health and safety enforcement action to take. The Enforcement Policy provides inspectors with guidance about the principles to follow and the factors they must take into account when considering prosecutions.

One of the aims of the Enforcement Policy is to hold duty holders, including directors and managers, to account where they have failed in carrying out their responsibilities. The policy now states that inspectors should identify and prosecute individuals if a prosecution is warranted.

At the same time the HSC also published a circular regarding its policy on prosecuting individuals. The circular states that, where a body corporate has committed an offence, then there is likely to be some personal failure by directors, managers or employees. In deciding whether to prosecute individuals, enforcing authorities must consider whether there is sufficient evidence to provide 'a realistic prospect of conviction' and whether a prosecution is in the public interest.

In general, prosecuting individuals is stated to be warranted where there have been substantial failings by them, such as where they have shown wilful or reckless disregard for health and safety requirements, or there has been a deliberate act or omission that seriously imperilled their own health or safety or that of others.

In July 2004 the HSE issued a new guidance document entitled 'Investigating Accidents and Incidents'. The guidance suggests that health and safety investigations form an essential part of compliance with obligations under the

Management of Health and Safety at Work Regulations 1999. It also emphasises the importance of identifying 'root causes' of past failures (of which a written record should be kept) and suggests that they are almost always failings at managerial level. However, in practice it is likely that organisations will no doubt be reluctant to produce a document which can later be used as evidence against the organisation or its directors or managers in a health and safety prosecution.

In producing an accident or incident report it is possible to do so in contemplation of legal proceedings or simply to address the root causes of an incident. Legal advice should be sought in these circumstances in order to minimise the likelihood that any report commissioned can be used against the company involved.

See also: Health and safety at work (page 295); Health and safety management (page 311).

Sources of further information

The HSE website – www.hse.gov.uk – has information on recent prosecutions.

The HSE publishes details of convictions at www.hse.gov.uk/prosecutions.

The TUC's website for health and safety information on prosecutions and safety campaigns is www.tuc.org.uk/h_and_s/index.cfm.

Health and safety management

Stuart Armstrong, Pinsent Masons

Key points

The Management of Health and Safety at Work Regulations 1999 require employers to manage health and safety by:

- identifying the hazards associated with work activities and workplaces;
- assessing the risks from hazardous work activities and workplaces;
- implementing risk avoidance and risk control measures using standard principles of prevention;
- providing effective systems to plan, organise, control, monitor and review preventive and protective measures in place;
- providing health surveillance where required by specific Regulations or by risk assessment;
- appointing competent health and safety advisor(s);
- implementing emergency procedures where appropriate;
- consulting, informing and training employees;
- co-operating with other employers and their employees where appropriate; and
- ensuring the health and safety of young persons and new and expectant mothers.

Legislation

- Health and Safety at Work etc. Act 1974.
- Management of Health and Safety atWork Regulations 1999.

Overview

Historically, legislation provided prescriptive rules to try to prevent injuries and ill health. The Health and Safety at Work etc. Act 1974 (HSWA) imposes a framework of objective-setting legislation on employers, the self-employed and others controlling workplaces or work activities.

This means that employers must manage health and safety in the same way that they manage any other commercial activity (e.g. finance).

The general duties imposed by the HSWA are supported by more detailed provisions in the Management of Health and Safety at Work Regulations 1999 (MHSWR).

Many of the general obligations under the MHSWR overlap with other more specific health and safety legislation. Compliance with such specific obligations will usually be sufficient to comply with the MHSWR.

Risk assessments

The MHSWR require employers to make a suitable and sufficient assessment of the risks to the health and safety of their employees and others affected by their activities. As circumstances change, these risk assessments need regular review and revision.

Preventive measures

Schedule 1 of the MHSWR sets out the general principles of prevention which should be used when considering measures to prevent or control exposure to health and safety risks:

- avoid risks;
- evaluate risks which cannot be avoided;
- combat risks at source;
- adapt work to the individual, by reviewing the design of workplaces, choice of work equipment and working methods;
- adapt to technical progress (through regular reviews of risk assessments);
- replace the dangerous with non-dangerous or less dangerous (e.g. equipment or substances);
- develop a coherent overall prevention policy;
- give priority to collective measures (which protect all those exposed to the risk) over individual protection;

and
- give appropriate instructions to employees.

Health and safety systems

Models of health and safety management systems have existed for a number of years, including BS 8800:1996, HS(G)65 (now HSG 65) and OHSAS 18001:1999. HSG 65 recommends and Regulation 5 of the MHSWR requires every employer to make and give effect to appropriate arrangements for the effective planning, organisation, control, monitoring and review of preventive and protective measures. The HSE's new guidance entitled 'Investigating Accidents and Incidents', released in July 2004, suggests that effective accident and incident investigation forms an essential part of this process. More advanced health and safety systems may be capable of accreditation to OHSAS 18001. Guidance on how to implement OHSAS 18001 is given in OHSAS 18002:1999.

Health surveillance

Employers must ensure that their employees are provided with such health surveillance as is appropriate having regard to the risks to their health and safety identified by risk assessments. The level, frequency and procedure of the health surveillance should be determined by a competent person acting within the limits of his training and experience. Health surveillance records should be kept, frequently even after the employee has left the employer's service, and in some instances for up to 40 years.

Appointing competent advisors

Every employer must appoint one or more competent persons to assist it in relation to compliance with statutory health and safety requirements. A person is competent if he has sufficient training and experience, or knowledge and other qualities, to enable him to be practical and reasonable and to know what to look for and how to recognise it (*Gibson -v- Skibs A/S Marina and Orkla A/B and Smith Coggins Ltd* [1966] 2 All ER 476). There is no requirement for formal qualifications. However, the Institution of Occupational Safety and Health (IOSH) recommends a diploma-level qualification associated with full membership of the professional institutions, as does the International Institute of Risk and Safety Management (IIRSM).

The HSE's preference as expressed in the Approved Code of Practice to the MHSWR is for the appointment of a competent person from within the employer's organisation wherever possible, rather than relying solely on external consultants.

Emergency plan

Employers must establish procedures to deal with serious and imminent danger, and appoint competent persons to implement those procedures in so far as they relate to evacuation. Employers must consider all potential dangers, e.g. fire, bomb threats, terrorism and public disorder.

Employers must also arrange contacts with the necessary emergency services (police, fire and ambulance services) as appropriate.

Information and training

Every employer should provide its employees and others working on its premises with comprehensible information on the risks to their health and safety (identified by risk assessments) together with details of the relevant preventive or protective measures.

Employees should be trained upon their induction and whenever working arrangements or conditions change (e.g. following the introduction of new machinery or following a revised risk assessment). In some instances there should also be regular refresher training.

Co-operation and co-ordination

Where two or more employers share work premises (e.g. contractors working in the client's premises) they must co-operate with each other to ensure the health and safety (including fire safety) of all persons working on the premises. This may include the appointment of and co-operation with a nominated person appointed to co-ordinate joint health and safety arrangements.

Employees' duties

Employees must:

- comply with any requirements or prohibitions imposed by their employer;
- use machinery, equipment, dangerous substances and safety devices provided in accordance with any training they have received; and
- inform their employer of serious and imminent danger or shortcomings in health or safety arrangements.

New or expectant mothers

Where the employer's activities could pose a risk to pregnant employees (or their babies), the employer must carry out a specific risk assessment, then take preventive or protective action to minimise that risk. If such action would not avoid the risk, then the employer must:

- alter the employee's working conditions or hours of work if it is reasonable to do so to avoid the risk;
- if this is not possible, then offer her alternative work in accordance with section 67 of the Employment Rights Act 1996; or
- if this is not possible, then suspend the employee from work for as long as necessary to avoid the risk.

The employer must go through the above process if the employee has a certificate from her doctor or midwife indicating that she should not work at night. An employer is not under any duty to alter a woman's working conditions until informed in writing that she is a new or expectant mother.

Young persons (under 18)

Before employing any young person, every employer must carry out a risk assessment which takes into account:

- the inexperience, lack of awareness of risks and immaturity of young persons;
- the layout of the workplace or workstation;
- the nature, degree and duration of exposure to physical, biological and chemical agents;
- the form, range and use of work equipment and the way in which it is handled;
- the organisation of processes and activities; and
- the extent of health and safety training provided.

In particular, no young person should do work:

- beyond his physical or psychological capacity;
- involving harmful exposure to toxic, carcinogenic or mutagenic substances, or to radiation;
- involving a risk of accidents which young persons may not recognise or avoid, owing to their lack of attention, experience or training; or
- where there is a risk to health from extreme cold or heat, noise or vibration.

Before employing a child (anyone under 16), the employer must provide a parent of the child with information on the health and safety risks identified by a risk assessment, details of the preventive and protective measures in place, and any information on shared workplaces and measures required for co-ordinating between two or more employers.

A young person who is over 16 may be employed to carry out work in a hazardous environment where the work is necessary for his training, provided that he is properly supervised and any risk is reduced to the lowest level reasonably practicable.

See also: Children at work (page 139); Emergency procedures (page 218); Health and safety at work (page 295); Health and safety enforcement (page 306); Health and safety policies (page 316); Health surveillance (page 318); New and expectant mothers (page 398); Risk assessments (page 469); Young persons (page 561).

Sources of further information

The Stationery Office website: www.legislation.hmso.gov.uk/si/si1999/19993242.htm for a copy of the MHSWR, SI 1999/3242.

L21 'Approved Code of Practice: Management of health and safety at work' (HSE Books, 2000): 0 7176 2488 9.

HSG65 'Successful health and safety management' (HSE Books, 1997): 0 7176 1276 7.

INDG322 'Need help on health and safety? Guidance for employers on when and how to get advice on health and safety' (HSE Books, 2000): 0 7176 1790 4.

BS 8800:1996 'Guide to occupational health and safety management systems'.

OHSAS 18001:1999 'Occupational health and safety management systems – specification'.

OHSAS 18002:1999 'Guidelines for the implementation of OHSAS 18001'.

'Health and Safety Policy and Management Guide, version 1.0' (ISBN 1 900648 35 0, £59.99) is available as an electronic download from the Workplace Law Network. Call 0870 777 8881 for details, or visit www.workplacelaw.net.

Health and safety policies

Sean Elson, Kennedys Health and Safety Team

Key points

There is a requirement for every employer, regardless of size, to have a health and safety policy. It is important to note that it is not just a case of producing one and never looking at it again: it must be put into effect to enable the business to manage its health and safety duties and responsibilities.

This requirement is contained in the Management of Health and Safety at Work Regulations 1999, which say that:

- every employer shall make and give effect to such arrangements as are appropriate, having regard to the nature of his activities and the size of his undertaking, for the effective planning, organisation, control, monitoring and review of the preventive and protective measures; and
- where the employer employs five or more employees, he shall record the arrangements.

Legislation

- Management of Health and Safety at Work Regulations 1999.
- Health and Safety at Work etc. Act 1974.
- Management of Health and Safety at Work Directive (89/391/EEC).

Duties of the employer

Every employer must have a health and safety policy and, if he has more than five people working for him, this should be in writing.

An employer is unlikely to fulfil his duty by the use of a generic non-specific policy: it should relate to that particular business and the health and safety issues that are relevant to it.

This is especially true because the Regulations also require every employer to carry out a 'suitable and sufficient' assessment of the risks to the health and safety of his employees to which they are exposed while they are at work; and the risks to the health and safety of persons not in his employment arising out of, or in connection with, the conduct by him of his undertaking.

The carrying-out of a risk assessment and the creation of a policy can be seen as supplementing one another.

Scope of the policy

The Regulations clearly accept that this is not a process where 'one size fits all'. They refer to 'the nature of [the employer's] activities and the size of his undertaking'.

316

If the business is small, perhaps operating in a benign office environment, then the drafting of the policy should be relatively straightforward. This is as compared to a much larger enterprise that uses potentially dangerous machinery or industrial processes, perhaps including chemicals. There the policy would be expected to be far more wide-reaching and detailed to reflect the increased level of risk.

In its publication 'An introduction to health and safety: health and safety in small businesses', the HSE provides a specimen health and safety policy, together with a risk assessment, that would be suitable for adoption by a small business. It should be noted that these still require actual input regarding the risks, etc., facing the particular business.

The Regulations were intended to give effect to the EU Management of Health and Safety at Work Directive (89/391/EEC). It is useful to look at that Directive to understand what was intended in relation to the management of health and safety at work.

The Directive sets out a number of general principles of prevention. One of these was that the employer develop a coherent overall prevention policy which covers:

- technology;
- organisation of work;
- working conditions;
- social relationships; and
- the influence of factors related to the working environment.

Where the Regulations refer to 'preventive and protective measures' that is defined as 'the measures which have been identified by the employer or by the self-employed person in consequence of the assessment as the measures he needs to take to comply with the requirements and prohibitions imposed upon him by or under the relevant statutory provisions'.

Employer's liability for breaches

A breach of the Regulations is a criminal offence punishable by a £5,000 fine in the magistrates' court or an unlimited fine in the Crown Court.

A breach of the Regulations does not result in civil liability.

> *See also*: Health and safety at work (page 295); Health and safety enforcement (page 306); Health and safety management (page 311).

Sources of further information

INDG259REV1 'An introduction to health and safety: health and safety in small businesses' (HSE Books, 2003): ISBN 0 7176 2685 7.

'Health and Safety Policy and Management Guide, version 1.0' (ISBN 1 900648 35 0, £59.99) is available as an electronic download from the Workplace Law Network. Call 0870 777 8881 for details, or visit www.workplacelaw.net.

Health surveillance

David Sinclair, Rollits

Key points

Employers who expose their employees to certain chemicals, physical agents, materials or ergonomic risks may be required to undertake systematic, regular and appropriate health surveillance on those employees.

Health surveillance may be either specified in regulations or covered by the umbrella provisions of health and safety legislation.

Where health surveillance is required, it should only be undertaken by competent people, who in many cases must be medically qualified.

Employers are required to provide adequate information to employees on health surveillance provisions, results and the records they keep. Records may have to be kept for up to 50 years.

Legislation

- Data Protection Act 1998.
- Health and Safety (Display Screen Equipment) Regulations 1992.
- Manual Handling Operations Regulations 1992
- Noise at Work Regulations 1989
- Management of Health and Safety at Work Regulations 1999
- Control of Asbestos at Work Regulations 2002.
- Control of Substances Hazardous to Health Regulations 2002.

Specific and non-specific duties

Health and safety regulations can specify mandatory health surveillance – i.e. the Control of Substances Hazardous to Health Regulations 2002 and the Control of Asbestos at Work Regulations 2002 – where employers expose their employees to certain biological hazards, chemicals or physical agents (e.g. asbestos, lead, noise, radiation and vibration).

In such circumstances, the relevant regulations will specify the type, level and frequency of the surveillance to be undertaken, along with details on what records are to be kept by the employer and for how long.

In circumstances where there is no specific duty on the employer to carry out health surveillance, the employer has general duties under section 2 of the Health and Safety at Work etc. Act 1974 and Regulation 6 of the Management of Health and Safety at Work Regulations 1999 to carry out appropriate health surveillance.

This general duty applies where the employer's risk assessments identify that:

- there is an identifiable disease or adverse health condition related to the work; and
- there is a valid technique available to detect indications of the disease or condition; and
- there is a reasonable likelihood that the disease or condition may occur under the particular conditions of the work; and
- health surveillance is likely to further the protection of the health and safety of the employees concerned.

Health surveillance can only be carried out in the above circumstances where the techniques used to undertake the surveillance pose a low risk to the employee.

Employers may need to carry out health surveillance in situations such as the following:

- pre-employment, to confirm an individual's suitability for the job;
- post-accident (or during long-term illness);
- on fork-lift truck and other machinery operators; and
- on drivers to test for colour blindness tests.

In these circumstances, employers should seek expert assistance in deciding what surveillance to undertake.

Objectives

The objectives of health surveillance are to:

- protect the health of individual employees by detecting, as early as possible, adverse changes which may be caused by exposure to hazardous substances;
- help to evaluate the measures taken to control exposure; and
- collect, keep, update and use data and information for determining and evaluating hazards to health.

Procedures

There are a number of health surveillance procedures which can be used by employers, including:

- biological monitoring, i.e. taking samples of blood, urine, breath, etc. to detect the presence of hazardous substances;
- biological effect monitoring, i.e. assessing the early biological effects in exposed workers;
- clinical examinations by occupational doctors or nurses to measure physiological changes in the body of exposed people, e.g. reduced lung function; and
- medical enquiries (often accompanied by medical examination) by a suitably qualified occupational health practitioner to detect symptoms in people.

Competent people acting within the limits of their training and experience should determine the appropriate level, frequency and procedure to be followed.

For most types of health surveillance the appropriate competent person will be a suitably qualified occupational medical practitioner, occupational health nurse or occupational hygienist.

Once health surveillance has been started, it must be maintained throughout the remainder of the employee's period of employment, unless the risks to which the employee is exposed and the associated health effects are rare and short term.

Display screen equipment

Regulation 5 of the Health and Safety (Display Screen Equipment) Regulations 1992 (DSE Regulations) places a duty on employers to provide, when requested to do so, an eye or eyesight test to employees who are about to become (or who are already) display screen 'users'.

Eye and eyesight tests are defined in section 36(2) of the Opticians Act 1989 and the Sight Testing Examination and Prescription (No. 2) Regulations 1989, which specify what examinations the doctor or optician should perform as part of the test.

Although the employer only needs to provide the eye or eyesight test when requested to do so, he is under a duty by Regulation 7(3) of the DSE Regulations to provide employees with adequate information about the risks to their health and their entitlement under Regulation 5.

Records

Where health surveillance is undertaken in compliance with particular regulations, those regulations will state what data is to be collected and the minimum period for which information is to be stored.

Other health surveillance records should be kept for:

- the period specified in the regulations, or
- three years after the end of the last date of the individual's employment (the date after which the employee cannot normally bring a claim against the employer),

whichever is the longer.

Data gathered during health surveillance is regarded as 'sensitive data' within the meaning of section 2 of the Data Protection Act 1998.

As such, all health surveillance data must be processed in accordance with the requirements of that Act. Detailed advice should be sought as to these requirements.

To comply with the employer's duty to provide information to employees (and others that might be affected), employers should provide the appropriate people with the general results of health surveillance, but keep confidential individuals' surveillance data.

See also: COSHH/hazardous substances (page 153); Data protection (page 163); Display screen equipment (page 202); Eye and eyesight tests (page 246); Furniture (page 284).

Sources of further information

INDG304 'Understanding health surveillance at work: an introduction for employers' (HSE Books, 1999): ISBN 0 7176 1712 2.

HSG61 'Health surveillance at work' (HSE Books, 1999): ISBN 0 7176 1705 X.

Working at height

Phil Wright, SafetyCO UK

Key points

- It is important to understand what is actually meant by the term 'working at height'. The relevant legislation has always required that, so far as is reasonably practicable, suitable and sufficient steps must be taken to prevent a person falling a distance of 2 metres or more or any distance likely to cause injury.
- The so-called '2 metre rule' is set to change following the introduction of the Work at Height Regulations, which are expected to come into force in 2005. The effect of these Regulations is to remove any reference to a 'safe' height at which work can be conducted, meaning that a situation such as using a footstool or small stepladder could be classed as work at height.

Legislation

- Construction (Health, Safety and Welfare) Regulations 1996.
- Workplace (Health, Safety and Welfare) Regulations 1992.
- Work at Height Regulations (due for implementation in 2005).

Proposals are currently in place to introduce new, tighter Regulations for work at height, in line with European legislation under the Temporary Work at Height Directive (1001/45/EC). The Work at Height Regulations were due to be implemented by 19 July 2004 in this respect. However, following a long consultation period, at time of going to press the date for implementation of the new Regulations has not been agreed.

Ladders

Year after year a considerable number of workers suffer fatal falls from ladders and many more suffer less serious injuries. Despite this, many still treat ladders as harmless items of work equipment.

There are two main causes of ladder accidents:

- Those in which something was wrong with the ladder.
- Those in which there was something wrong with the way in which it was used.

Inspection, maintenance and training in the safe use of ladders must be addressed by employers.

Scaffolding

Injuries are not limited to those who erect, alter and dismantle scaffolds, but are also suffered by those who work on or near them and can on many occasions involve members of the general public.

The accidents involve not only people falling but also materials falling or part of the scaffold collapsing.

Scaffolds may only be erected, altered and dismantled by competent persons.

It is also a requirement of the Regulations for scaffolds to be inspected:

* upon completion;
* at intervals not exceeding seven days;
* after alteration;
* after adverse weather; and
* after anything likely to have affected their safety.

Once a scaffold has been inspected, a record of the findings must be kept and sent to the person in control within 24 hours of the inspection.

Scaffolds may only be inspected by a competent person.

Roof work

Accident statistics show that a considerable number of workers fall from roofs and through roofs during both construction and maintenance works.

Nearly all roof-work fatalities could be prevented by the provision and correct use of readily available equipment.

To prevent operatives falling from sloping roofs, four basic systems have been devised:

* roof edge barriers;
* special working platforms – below eaves level;
* normal scaffold working platforms; and
* use of roof ladders.

Fragile roofs

All fragile roofs – except those constructed of glass – should carry a large warning notice (in yellow and black). However, because of the UK's multinational workforce, a sign worded in English will not necessarily meet the requirements of the Health and Safety (Safety Signs and Signals) Regulations 1996.

When working on a fragile roof, the hazardous area must be adequately guarded or covered to prevent a risk of falling.

Harnesses

The use of fall-arrest systems are becoming ever more popular, especially as every year an average of 13,900 operatives in the UK are reported as receiving injuries or having been killed as a result of falling from height while at work.

The National Access and Scaffolding Confederation (NASC) has introduced guidance on the wearing of fall-arrest systems for scaffolders. The use and maintenance of this type of equipment are of utmost importance.

New Regulations

The proposed new Work at Height Regulations remove the '2 metre rule', to classify as work at height any activities taking place at heights which present a risk. The new Regulations also require a risk assessment to be carried out prior to commencement of any work at height. The scope of the Regulations applies to all workplaces, and not just those in the construction sector.

See also: Safety signage (page 483).

Sources of further information

HSG33 'Health and safety in roof work' (HSE Books, 1998): ISBN 0 7176 1425 5.

'A head for heights: guidance for working at height in construction' (HSE Books, 2003: VHS PAL video): ISBN 0 7176 2217 7.

CIS10REV3 'Tower scaffolds' (HSE Books, 1997).

National Access and Scaffolding Confederation (NASC): www.nasc.org.uk.

Homeworking

Alan Denbigh, Telework Association

Health and safety

Health and safety authorities have wide powers of inspection and enforcement, and all HSE legislation includes workplaces in the home. For employees, common practice is that all equipment should be supplied by, and remain the property of, the employer, largely for reasons of data security and responsibility for health and safety. In some situations it may be appropriate for employees to use their own equipment, but, if this occurs, the equipment must be assessed from a health and safety viewpoint as well as for its suitability.

Furniture needs to be adjustable to provide correct working heights – a good-quality, comfortable, adjustable chair is especially important. In order to reduce risk of RSI or other injuries due to poor work furniture, the employer is advised to supply all working furniture. Lighting should be reviewed as home lighting is unlikely on its own to be adequate for office work. As a general guide, employers should treat the work area and equipment used as though they were in the main office.

Legislation

The main legislation relevant to homeworkers (or teleworkers) is the Display Screen Equipment Directive (90/270/EEC) which requires:

- a clear and stable screen, bright and free from glare, which should swivel and tilt easily;
- adequate arrangement of keyboard characters, adjustable keyboard with sufficient space to support the hands and arms of the user;
- sufficient user space to change positions and vary movements, a sufficiently large work desk, a document holder that is adjustable and stable;
- satisfactory lighting conditions;
- minimised glare and reflection at the workstation, and minimisation of radiation levels;
- a work chair that is adjustable in height, including the backrest;
- a footrest available if required; and
- that environmental factors should be minimised including effects of reflection or glare, noise, heat and humidity.

Working environment

Employers should put in place a system for their homeworkers to report accidents or hazards, as there would be in a conventional workplace. Practical experience within the Telework Association suggests that the following areas also often need attention:

- There should be a sufficient number of power sockets, avoiding overuse of extension leads, trailing cables and adaptors. Home offices may need rewiring for more sockets: have the homeworker's installation checked by an electrician.

- The use of IT equipment usually requires an additional two power outlets, and one or two telecoms sockets. Safely stowing cabling is important.

- Electrical equipment needs to be checked for safety (e.g. all cable grips in place, no burn marks on plugs or cracked sockets).

- Shelves should be conveniently situated so that when heavy files are placed and replaced there is no risk of stress on the spine or overbalancing.

- Office chairs and tables should all be of the appropriate height and adjustability for long periods of work.

- If the homeworker wears reading glasses, the prescription should be correct for close work. Anyone working with computers should have their eyes tested, and the optician should be informed of the computer work.

- Spotlights and anglepoises are generally less tiring than fluorescents in small spaces. Light levels should be about 350 lux.

- Computer screens should be positioned at right angles to windows. Blinds to prevent sunlight making screens hard to read should be installed where needed.

- Temperatures should be as near as possible to 18.5°C. Small home offices can easily overheat because IT equipment generates heat: temperatures may become uncomfortably hot in summer unless adequate ventilation can be provided.

- Adequate ventilation is also important where equipment such as laser printers may give off ozone or other fumes.

- Psychologically, most homeworkers prefer to be situated so that they can see out of a window if possible, although, as noted above, it is important to avoid problems with glare and reflection on computer screens.

- Rest breaks are vital. There are now a number of software packages which can be set up to remind homeworkers to take frequent breaks and so interrupt their more concentrated work environment.

Risk assessments

Employers with more than five workers have a legal requirement to carry out a conventional health and safety workplace risk assessment on a homeworker's home offices. This can be done either by the company or by the homeworker himself (e.g. using a checklist) if he is suitably trained. This assessment involves the following:

1. Identifying hazards that may cause harm, however small (such as keeping potentially harmful substances out of children's reach).

2. Deciding who might be harmed and how (e.g. the homeworker, members of the household, visitors).

3. Assessing the risks and taking appropriate action (e.g. deciding what steps must be taken to eliminate or reduce the identified risks).

4. Recording the findings – what steps have been taken to reduce or eliminate risks? Inform the homeworker, or anyone else affected by the work, of the findings.

5. Check the risks from time to time and take steps if needed, especially if there is a change in working procedures.

The HSE produces a booklet on safety for homeworkers and the Institute of Occupational Safety and Health has an excellent datasheet on its website including a homework premises assessment form stressing the importance of adequate training and of regular reassessment of the risks. For details, see 'Sources of further information' on page 328.

Planning and Building Regulations

Planning permission

Setting up a home office constitutes a 'change of use' in strict planning terms. However, so far as planning departments are concerned, the average homeworker is unlikely to require planning permission, particularly if he is not creating a nuisance to neighbours.

Surrey County Council provided the following advice to its own homeworking staff:

'Teleworking at or from home does not represent a significant change of use of a building likely to cause a nuisance or hazard to your neighbours. Unless you intend to make structural alterations to accommodate your working area, or extra noise, pollution etc. is generated because you are working at/from home, there is no requirement for planning permission.'

Some other councils differ on whether home offices constitute a 'material' or 'ancillary' change of use (turning an outhouse into a garage and car repair workshop is rather more material than putting a computer into a spare bedroom).

Material changes of use require permission; ancillary changes or temporary changes probably do not. Decisions on whether the change of use is 'material' are based on whether it will cause increased traffic, changes to the visible appearance of the property, nuisance such as noise or smells, or unsocial working hours.

While unfortunately some local authorities have not yet taken into account that homeworking reduces traffic and generally involves no alterations other than provision of electrical sockets and telephone lines, other authorities adopt a sensible approach.

Oldham Borough Council, for example, recognises homeworking formally in its planning guidelines, and regards home offices as ancillary changes of use. The Oldham document is available to other planning authorities, which can use it as a blueprint for their own guidelines if they wish.

Babergh District Council in Suffolk prepared its own leaflet 'Working from Home – balancing the issues' because 'we often get asked questions about homeworking and we are aware that there are people who don't really want to ask the question'.

The document 'Planning Policy Guidance 13' (PPG13), originally issued in 1994 by the Department of Transport and since revised, contains recommendations for local authorities to 'take a flexible approach to the use of residential properties for homeworking, consistent with the need to protect the residential environment for neighbouring development'.

So far as the associated matter of rating is concerned, the precise situation had always been a little ambiguous before a Lands Tribunal appeal judgment (*Tully -v- Jorgensen* (2003)) found in favour of a full-time homeworker who used one room entirely as an office. The impact of this judgment is that if one works from home, uses office equipment, has not made structural alterations and does not employ people from the premises, then business rates will not be levied.

A practical piece of advice for homeworkers is to ensure that their activities do not cause annoyance to neighbours – and hence visits from council officials are much less likely to occur.

Building a workspace

If the establishment of the home office involves any building work, such as conversion of a loft space, there are strict building regulations which must be adhered to, mainly relating to means of escape in case of fire. Loft ladders and space-saver stairs are not favoured, according to Paul Kalbskopf, building control officer at Stroud District Council, because they require familiarity of use for safe passage.

Rooflights should also act as a means of escape, so that the homeworker could get out or a fire officer could get in if necessary.

The homeworker may need to upgrade the floor between the loft and the rest of the house to give half an hour of fire resistance. Kalbskopf recommends contacting an architect, and then approaching building control and planning departments for advice before starting work.

Another alternative to loft conversion which has been successfully used by a number of homeworkers is a personal office which, depending on specifica-

tion, can cost around £5,000 and may not need planning permission.

Tax implications for homeworkers

If you claim tax relief on mortgage payments for the work part of the house, that part of the house is potentially liable for capital gains tax. The precise implications of this will vary from year to year, and so, particularly if the homeworker is self-employed, it is advisable for him to discuss these with an accountant who will also advise on the proportions of household expenses attributable to home-office use that can be legitimately claimed.

'Business' charges by public utilities

There have been rare instances of power utility companies charging a non-domestic rate. The practical situation is that they would have to know that someone is working from home before any change could be made, and that the exact conditions vary from company to company.

For telephone service, BT does not compel people to use the business rate, but points out that the business service has the advantage of Yellow Pages and Business Pages entries.

BT also puts business users on a higher priority for fault correction than residential users. In both cases compensation is paid if the fault is not repaired within 24 hours.

Insurance

The insurance market has pretty much caught up with the shift to homeworking. It is still the case that a standard home contents policy is unlikely to cover home-office equipment, but specific policies targeted at home offices have been produced to replace the plethora of computer, office and home policies pre-viously designed to confuse the home-worker. These new policies also cover important business issues that can affect homeworkers such as public liability, employee liability and loss of earnings.

Areas particularly to consider are the following:

- Insurance against loss of data (e.g. through virus or malicious attack). Employers should clarify the pos-ition on home-stored data with their insurers.

- Public liability or employer's liab-ility insurance if other people work at or visit the homeworker's home office (this is mandatory in the Republic of Ireland). It is also impor-tant for employers to ensure that employees other than the home-worker visiting the home office are covered (e.g. managers or those involved in health and safety checks).

- Business interruption insurance, which, in the case of the self-employed or small home-based busi-nesses, would provide compensation for the costs of putting a business back together and other expenditure incurred after an incident.

- Computer breakdown insurance – in some situations this can be cheaper than holding a maintenance con-tract and ensures that expensive part replacements are covered. Employers need to check rather than assume that this insurance applies to computers off site.

- Cover off the premises (e.g. for portable computers at the home-worker's home or in transit).

See also: Display screen equipment (page 202); Eye and eyesight tests (page 246); Fire: means of escape (page 263); Furniture (page 284); Insurance (page 332); Working time (page 253).

Sources of further information

The Teleworking Handbook: www.telework.org.uk.

INDG226 'Homeworking: guidance for employers and employees on health and safety' (HSE Books, 1996): ISBN 0 7176 1204 X.

The excellent datasheet 'Teleworking' can be downloaded from the Institute of Occupational Health and Safety's website: www.iosh.co.uk. The datasheet includes a homework premises assessment form and stresses the importance of adequate training and regular reassessment of the risks.

Human rights

Susan Thomas and Gabriella Wright, Charles Russell
Employment and Pensions Service Group

Key points

- An employee of a public authority can bring a claim directly under the Human Rights Act based solely on a breach of a right provided by that Act.
- An employee of a semi-public authority or private employer can *only* bring a claim under the Human Rights Act which is attached to an existing employment claim.
- Disciplinary procedures, dismissal procedures, codes of conduct and other employee policies should be reviewed to ensure that any interference with human rights is justifiable.

Legislation

- Human Rights Act 1998.
- European Convention on Human Rights and Fundamental Freedoms.

Application of the Human Rights Act

The Human Rights Act 1998 (HRA) adopted the European Convention for the Protection of Human Rights and Fundamental Freedoms into UK law on 2 October 2000. The rights and freedoms set out in the Convention which are relevant to the workplace are:

- prohibition of slavery and forced labour (Article 4);
- right to a fair trial (Article 6);
- right to respect for private and family life (Article 8);
- freedom of expression (Article 10); and
- freedom of assembly and association (Article 11).

The HRA requires public authorities to act in compliance with the Convention. Public authorities include all courts and tribunals, and any person exercising functions of a public nature.

This means that the HRA affects different types of employers differently, as outlined below.

Public authorities

Employees can bring a claim against a public authority employer *directly* for a breach of a right set out in the HRA.

Public authority employers include the Government, local authorities, the police, the Advertising Standards Authority and so on.

Semi-public authorities

Private bodies which carry out public functions are also defined as public authorities, but only in so far as they are carrying out their *public function*. The relationship between employer and employee would normally be considered to be private, and any related acts to be outside the public function scope. This means that semi-public authority employers are affected by the HRA in the same way as private employers.

Semi-public authorities include privatised utility companies, or a private security company exercising public functions in relation to the management of a prison.

Private employers

These are organisations which carry out no public function. The HRA is only indirectly enforceable against such employers, in that an employment tribunal's decision about workplace conduct and workplace decisions must be compatible with the HRA. Therefore, if an employer were to have disregarded an employee's human rights in its treatment of the employee in a dismissal situation, for example, a tribunal might find that the employer's actions make the dismissal unfair.

An employee cannot directly bring a claim for breach of the HRA, but may 'attach' a claim that the employer has breached the HRA to an existing employment claim, such as unfair dismissal.

The Act sets out some 'justifications' which an employer may be able to rely on, such as the prevention of crime, or the prevention of infringement of rights of others.

Example

P was employed by the Probation Service, and worked mainly with sex offenders. His employer discovered that he sold bondage and sado-masochism products on the Internet, and dismissed him. P brought a claim for unfair dismissal and breach of his rights under Articles 8 and 10 of the Convention (the right to respect for private life and the right to freedom of expression respectively). The Employment Appeal Tribunal decided that a probation officer, as a professional, had a reputation to maintain; and that P's activities were publicised on a website and in the public domain, and were therefore not part of his private life. This meant that Article 8 was not engaged. There was an interference with P's right to freedom of expression, but this was justified due to the potential damage to the Service's reputation.

Issues for employers

Disciplinary procedures

Any disciplinary procedure should be fair in setting out allegations and evidence relied on accurately, in allowing an opportunity to hear and consider the employee's case, and in allowing a mechanism for appeal, so that the employee's right to a fair trial is respected.

Dismissal

Any dismissal procedure must also be fair, and any reason given for dismissal must not represent an unreasonable breach of a Convention right. For example, dismissing an employee on the grounds of membership of a political party may lead a tribunal to find that the dismissal was not fair, since to uphold such a reason for dismissal would represent an unreasonable breach of the employee's freedom of expression.

Investigating a complaint

The investigation of an employee's complaint should not involve breach of a Convention right. For example, one individual was awarded £10,000 compensation when her employer tapped her phone without warning during its investigation of her sex discrimination complaint.

Codes of conduct

Codes of conduct should be reviewed to ensure that they do not unnecessarily restrict an employee's Convention rights. For example, provisions on how an employee wears their hair, or whether they wear a nose ring, could raise issues about the way an individual expresses his or her personality in the workplace.

Employee checks

The right to respect for private life may include matters such as moral or physical integrity, so that 'private' in this context means 'personal'. This means that a security check which collects wide-ranging information about a person's personal affairs may go too far. Also potentially challengeable would be a practice of carrying out drug tests on workers without a policy in place making it clear to those workers that they can be drug tested and also making clear why it is necessary for the employer to have this power (an example of where drug testing might be justifiable would include where workers are in high-risk situations such as pilots or train drivers).

Employers should also ensure that any procedures such as security checks comply with the requirements of UK data protection legislation.

See also: Data protection (page 163); Disciplinary and grievance proceedings (page 184); Discrimination (page 189); Dismissal (page 197); Monitoring employees (page 392); Private life (page 439).

Sources of further information

Information Commissioner's Office: www.informationcommissioner.gov.uk.

Advisory, Conciliation and Arbitration Service (ACAS): www.acas.org.uk.

'Data Protection Policy and Management Guide, version 1.0' (ISBN 1 900648 33 4, £34.99) is available as an electronic download from the Workplace Law Network. Call 0870 777 8881 for details, or visit www.workplacelaw.net.

Insurance

Ciaron Dunne, Workplace Law Group

Key points

- Employers are required by law to insure motor vehicles and their own liability to employees.
- There is a raft of other policies available to insure against the unexpected in the workplace: this article summarises some of the most common options.

Legislation

- Employers' Liability (Compulsory Insurance) Act 1969.
- Insurance Mediation Directive.
- Motor Vehicles (Compulsory Insurance) (Information Centre and Compensation Body) Regulations 2003.
- Road Traffic Acts 1988 and 1991.

Compulsory insurances

Employer's liability

With some exceptions, the Employers' Liability (Compulsory Insurance) Act 1969 requires employers to insure their liability to their employees for personal injury, disease or death sustained in the course of their employment in Great Britain. There is currently a penalty of up to £2,500 for failure to insure on any day.

Employers are also required to display a certificate of employer's liability insurance at each place of work, and must also retain expired certificates in case of future claims. Employers are legally required to insure for at least £5 million. The Association of British Insurers (ABI)

advises that, in practice, most policies offer £10 million minimum cover.

The Department for Work and Pensions has consulted on removing the requirement for compulsory employer's liability insurance for incorporated owners/sole employees. Such a change seems likely, although no timetable is in place at time of writing.

Motor

Third-party motor insurance (as a bare minimum) is compulsory. Employers should also take steps to make sure that employees using private cars for work-related activities are insured to do so. The EU Motor Insurance Directive requires fleet policyholders to register their vehicles with the Motor Insurance Database. For more information visit www.miic.org.uk.

Other workplace insurances

Buildings and contents

The ABI advises that:

- business premises should be insured for the full rebuilding cost (including professional fees and the cost of site clearance) and not just for the market value;

- stock should be insured for its cost price without any addition for profit;
- plant and business equipment can also be insured, on either an 'as-new' or a wear-and-tear basis; and
- contents are usually covered against theft provided there has been forcible and violent entry to or exit from the premises. Damage to the building resulting from theft or attempted theft will also normally be covered.

Business interruption

Business interruption insurance should be enough to cover any shortfall in gross profit caused by damage to your property (e.g. fire). It should also cover any increase in working costs, and restart costs.

Directors' and officers' liability

Directors' and officers' liability insurance would reimburse the individual director or company officer for personal liability. Alternatively, it can compensate the company itself where it has reimbursed a director or officer for a personal liability.

Employees

- Employers can take out key-person insurance which would compensate the company in the event of an injury or death preventing a key member of staff from working.
- Fidelity insurance would cover you for the costs of employee dishonesty (e.g. theft). This would not normally be covered under buildings and contents insurance.
- Make sure that personal assault is covered in your contents insurance. This will provide compensation for you or your employees following injury during theft or attempted theft of money.
- Some employers provide income protection insurance, private medical insurance, life insurance, or personal accident and sickness insurance as an employee benefit.

Legal expenses

Legal expenses insurance would meet the cost of bringing or defending legal action. Most notably, legal expenses insurance is useful in insuring against tribunal claims, or court action taken by, for example, the Inland Revenue.

Professional indemnity

Professional indemnity insurance protects advisors who give professional advice – e.g. solicitors, accountants, architects and building surveyors.

Public liability

Public liability insurance would pay damages to members of the public for death, personal injury or damage to their property that occurs as a result of your business. It also covers associated legal fees, costs and expenses. Minimum cover offered is usually £1 million.

Important considerations

- Insurance is subject to insurance premium tax. Life insurance, pensions and income protection insurances are exempt.
- It is important for employers to bear in mind that fines as a result of prosecution (e.g. by the HSE for a health

and safety offence) cannot be insured against.

Selling insurance: new regulations

New wide-ranging regulations (under the EU Insurance Mediation Directive) governing the selling and administering of insurance policies by intermediaries will have a considerable effect on a number of industries, including the construction and engineering and property sectors, when they come into force on 14 January 2005.

The new regulations look set to apply to any company which purchases or arranges insurance for a third party or assists a third party in the preparation of an insurance claim. It is likely that the regulations will apply only where remuneration is received by the company for the provision of such services, though the application of the regulations will depend upon the particular circumstances of the parties and the nature of the transaction.

The following are examples of activities which will technically fall within the ambit of the regulations:

- contractors who obtain insurance on behalf of, or handle claims for, third parties, e.g. developers or funders;
- employers who obtain project insurance on behalf of the other parties involved with the project;
- insurance arrangements for joint venture companies;
- landlords who take out insurance in joint names with tenants; and
- property management service companies which arrange insurance on behalf of clients.

Any businesses carrying out such activities, unless otherwise exempt, will be required to obtain authorisation from the Financial Services Authority (FSA) or become an appointed representative of a firm authorised by the FSA. It will be a criminal offence to carry out any of the regulated activities without obtaining authorisation or becoming an appointed representative, even if the business is already contractually obliged to provide these services.

The FSA has indicated that it could take up to six months to process an application for authorisation. Therefore businesses will need to act immediately to ensure that they will be able to comply with the regulations when they come into force early in 2005.

The FSA is likely to provide further guidance on the extent and application of the regulations in the coming months.

> *See also*: Directors' responsibilities (page 175); Driving at work (page 208); Health and safety at work (page 295); Occupier's liability (page 409).

Sources of further information

Association of British Insurers: www.abi.org.uk.

Motor Insurers' Information Centre: www.miic.org.uk.

Financial Services Authority: www.fsa.gov.uk.

Intellectual property

Stephen Harte, MacRoberts

Key points

- Every business uses and creates intellectual property, and, as with any other business asset, steps must be taken to manage and protect this valuable resource.
- Copyright, database right and design right arise automatically, but steps may have to be taken to make sure the correct party owns them.
- Patents, registered trade marks and registered designs are granted on application to the Patent Office in Newport, Wales.
- Internet domain names are administered by a network of domain name registries.
- Intellectual property is territorial and an international protection strategy may be needed.
- Intellectual property infringement can be extremely expensive.

Legislation

- Copyright, Designs and Patents Act 1988.
- Patents Act 1977.
- Trade Marks Act 1994.
- Registered Designs Act 1949.

Copyright

This protects the expression of an idea – not an idea itself – and covers:

- original literary, dramatic, musical or artistic works;
- sound recordings, films or broadcasts; and
- the typographical arrangements of published editions.

Computer software is protected by the law of copyright as a literary work.

Copyright arises automatically when a work is created – there is no need to do anything such as register the work to create copyright – and lasts for the life of the author plus 70 years.

Copyright is infringed by someone copying a whole or a substantial part of a copyright work without the permission of the copyright owner. There is no infringement where identical work was separately developed without copying.

The author of a copyright work is the first owner of the copyright unless the author was an employee acting within the course of his employment, in which case the employer is first owner.

The only way of transferring ownership of copyright is by written assignation.

Where a self-employed contractor creates a copyright work, it does not belong to the person paying for the services unless the contractor assigns the copyright in writing. It is important to address this issue on commissioning the work and, in any event, before the contractor is paid.

Patents

Patents protect inventions. To be patentable, a patent must:

- be novel;
- involve an inventive step; and
- be capable of industrial application.

An invention is not novel where anyone else knows about it and so a business must make sure that its employees and anyone to whom the invention is disclosed are bound by confidentiality obligations.

Patent protection is obtained by making an application to the Patent Office in Newport, Wales. A UK patent is only effective in the UK and thought must be given to international patent protection in key markets. This can be expensive.

Once a patent is granted, full details of the invention are published. Some businesses prefer to keep their technology confidential and so forgo patent protection to avoid publishing.

A patent owner can stop anyone from using the technology for 20 years and a patent is infringed even if the infringer can show that his invention was independently developed without copying.

As with copyright, it is the inventor who has the right to apply for the patent unless the inventor was an employee acting within the course of his employment, when the employer can apply. In such cases, the law can require the employer to make a compensatory payment to the employee if the patent is particularly valuable.

Trade marks

A trade mark is any sign which a business uses to distinguish its goods and services from those of others in the marketplace. A business's good name and reputation is embodied in its trade marks and this can be a very valuable asset. Trade marks are commonly works or signs but also can be sounds, shapes, smells and anything else capable of distinguishing goods and services.

Trade marks can be registered in the UK through the Patent Office and many businesses will also seek to implement an international protection strategy.

A registered trade mark is infringed by someone

- using an identical trade mark in respect of identical goods or services; or
- where there is a likelihood of confusion by the public, using a similar trade mark for similar goods or services.

Even where a trade mark has not been registered, it may be possible to enforce rights in an unregistered trade mark which represents significant business goodwill through taking a passing-off action.

Before choosing a trade name, care should be taken to make sure that it does not infringe any other trade mark. It is possible to search the Trade Marks Register and it can be useful to check other sources of market information to confirm that no similar marks are being used.

Database right

A database can be an important business asset. Some sophisticated databases are protected by the law of copyright, but any database is protected by database right which stops someone else from using the database without permission. Unauthorised use of a database may also give rise to issues under the Data Protection Act 1998.

Designs

The shape or decoration of a product can be protected by registering a design with the Patent Office. As with patents, the design must be novel and protection lasts for 25 years, stopping anyone else using a similar design even if they can show they did not copy the registered design.

The shape or configuration of three-dimensional objects can also be protected by design right – a right which lasts for ten years for creation of the design and which, like copyright, arises automatically and stops others from copying the design.

Internet domain names

These are granted by various domain name registries and are subject to the terms and conditions of that registry. A business should register domain names for its common brands and may wish to think about registering misspellings too. A common mistake is for the registration to be made accidentally in the name of the individual staff member rather than the business itself, which can cause problems when trying to sell the business and its assets later.

Infringement

Court orders can be obtained to stop infringement, and infringers can be liable in damages or to account for any profits made by them. Serious cases of infringement can amount to piracy and involve criminal penalties.

See also: Data protection (page 163); IT security (page 338).

IT security

Elizabeth Brownsdon and Emilia Linde, Bird & Bird

How would you feel if, one morning, you came into the office to find that your strategic operating system was suddenly unavailable due to attack or misuse and would remain so for a prolonged period? What if highly confidential information such as customer credit card or account details or employee records had been stolen? What damage would this do to the operation and reputation of your business?

Most workplace managers do not need to be convinced of the devastating effect on business of such attacks. A common initial reaction might be to ask how this could happen. No doubt the board/stakeholders/financiers of the business would be asking themselves the same question. This would be a real moment of truth for the management of the business, and one when those businesses which had the foresight to prepare for and manage system security risk would reap the dividends. However, if managing a business is seen to be all about managing risk while achieving the highest return on investment (ROI), is IT system vulnerability really a very serious risk?

The threats

There are a number of possible threats to system integrity and/or availability.

Malicious viruses

It is a certainty that a virus will attempt to attack your network. Indeed, more than 40% of UK small businesses have been affected by viruses during the past 12 months at an average cost of £2,500 a time. Most people are familiar with the most well-known and widespread viruses, such as Melissa or Code Red, or worms such as 'I love you'. However, there are estimated to be many more virus threats on the loose at present. New viruses, worms, Trojan horses and zombies are being created all the time (along with some new and even stranger names for them, no doubt). For instance, the novelty of 2004 has been the 'Slammer worm'. It has so far primarily hit the e-commerce industry, but has also targeted small businesses. Therefore no firewall or scanning of viruses is capable of eliminating all risk from intrusion by malicious viruses.

Hacking

Again, no system is foolproof. Any network which has an external connectivity – which must surely include most businesses of any size these days – is open to the risk of hacking. Hacking may involve a variety of unacceptable activities, e.g. malicious file destruction, theft of money or intellectual property or a catastrophic denial of service attack.

Hacking is definitely on the increase, but it is difficult to find accurate figures because, like corporate fraud, most activity is not reported due to the embarrassment and damage to business reputation. The Computer Misuse Act, for example, has been in force for ten years, but, as there have ever only been a handful of successful prosecutions under this Act, it is clearly not providing a deterrent. The IT industry has been lobbying for changes to the law and this subject is currently being reviewed by the Home Office.

The biggest threat of hacking, however, is from inside a large organisation, and businesses should be particularly wary in times of economic slowdown. Unfortunately, staff who are laid off may become disgruntled and present a real security risk.

Equally, businesses may be looking to terminate costly relationships with technology suppliers. Difficulties may arise where the supplier has control of the source code, passwords and so on.

ROI and risk management

Businesses take on financial risk with a view to making a return on their investment. How does investing in security fit this model? The answer seems to be that security risk is not a risk which in itself provides a direct return on investment. It is more about loss avoidance. Reducing the risk of a disastrous system failure will contribute to the bottom line because in the current climate doing nothing or nothing much will ensure that the risk is realised.

It would be naive to suggest that the risk of system intrusion or failure could be eliminated, but it can be properly managed. Indeed, it is worth bearing in mind that every director has a duty to manage serious corporate risk. As with most business risks, a judgement has to be made on:

- which risks can be reduced by using security products or services?
- which risks can be covered by insurance?
- which risks are to be borne by the organisation?

The proportion of risk in the first and last categories is to a large extent determined by the steps an organisation takes to protect its systems and equipment. In any event, it will need to keep its house in order if it is to avoid invalidating its insurance.

What do you need to do to protect your systems and equipment?

There are many measures which are common sense and which should form part of your general security policy. Costs range from the minimal, where it is simply a case of more vigorously applying existing procedures, to the highly expensive, where the latest technology is implemented.

Physical security

Some physical measures that should be adopted are as follows:

- Control and monitor access to your building properly using a record of visitors and badging. Also consider installing CCTV systems. Note, however, that CCTV must be used in a proportionate way.
- Require all staff to take responsibility for security by, for example, challenging 'strangers' out of hours and/or who appear in restricted or non-public areas.
- Keep an inventory of computer equipment and carry out periodical stock checks.
- Make sure that the most important

servers are situated in a secure and non-visible part of the premises.

- If appropriate, use biometrics (e.g. retina/iris scans, finger/handprint or facial feature scans, voice pattern scans, keystroke analysis) to identify those authorised to access the most sensitive equipment.
- Staff using laptops and other portable computer equipment should be reminded to ensure that they keep the equipment secure at all times.

Basic system administration

Basic system administration measures include the following:

- Write a system security policy and require staff to apply it and police it. Employee contracts should oblige staff to avoid opening emails and attachments when they do not know their origin. Restrict staff use of hotmail and similar email services as these could increase the risk of virus attacks. Also consider blocking access to certain sites whose content may be of an illegal or pornographic nature.
- Oblige staff to follow instructions from their IT managers, such as warnings about current virus attacks.
- Segment the network with appropriate authorisation procedures to limit the number of IT support staff who have entire system access.
- Limit system privileges as much as possible and develop a hierarchy of access.
- Implement an effective password policy and require regular password changes.

- Restrict staff use of wireless access to the company network and monitor use of dial-up networking.

Protective software and audit activity

These are some of the software protection and audit measures that can be employed:

- Ensure that virus-sweeping software is regularly updated across the network.
- Carry out regular monitoring of the firewall and general network integrity.
- Use code review software and consider penetration testing.

What can you do to limit the damage if an incident does occur?

The following procedures and precautions are recommended:

- Implement an effective backup policy with secure off-site storage.
- Have a contingency plan in place for restoring/recovering/recreating important data in the event of a natural disaster as well as malicious or negligent damage.
- Ensure that forensic evidence is not destroyed in the course of the disaster response as this may deny recourse against the perpetrators or, more importantly, prevent discovery of what went wrong.
- Document IP rights and, where relevant, secure software source code (both sensible business practice) to assist fast remedies in preventing unauthorised use by hackers.
- Ensure that system security obligations are written into staff employment contracts to avoid arguments over what staff were required to do or not do.

Importance of security

Security is not just flavour of the month in the IT world. As the use of technology becomes an increasingly integral and crucial part of the operation and delivery of business, the stability and security of data will be a business priority and an important part of workplace management. As a final thought, how many directors of large corporates know who has administrator/controlling access to the systems on which their business depends?

See also: Crisis management and business continuity (page 158); Emergency procedures (page 218).

Sources of further information

'IT and E-mail Policy and Management Guide, version 1.0' (ISBN 1 900648 37 7, £34.99) is available as an electronic download from the Workplace Law Network. Call 0870 777 8881 for details, or visit www.workplacelaw.net.

Jury service

Helen Abbott, Workplace Law Group

Key points

- Ensure that you cover jury service and related salary payments in your staff handbook or contract of employment.
- Instruct your employees to claim compensation for loss of earnings from the court.
- Deduct compensation for loss of earnings from salary payments.
- Plan ahead to cover absences caused by jury service.
- Consider requesting your employee to ask for a deferment if jury service would cause hardship.

Legislation

- Juries Act 1974.

Jury selection

All jurors are selected at random by computer from the electoral register. Everyone on the electoral register between the ages of 18 and 70 may be selected even if they are not eligible to serve on a jury. Some people never get called; others get called more than once. Jurors usually try the more serious criminal cases such as murder, rape and assault and are asked to decide on guilt or innocence.

Eligibility

Jury service is a public duty and four weeks' notice is usually given. Unless someone is disqualified, has the right to be excused or has a valid reason for discretionary excusal, then they must serve. The main categories of people who are disqualified from jury service are:

- members of the legal profession;
- prison officers and governors;
- probation officers;
- police officers; and
- ministers of religion.

Those on bail or those who have been on probation within the last five years or sentenced to prison or community service within the last ten years are not eligible.

Jury service is an average of ten working days but may be longer or shorter than this depending on which case the juror is put onto when they attend court.

Deferral and excusal

Anyone may apply for discretionary deferment or excusal. Jury service can only be deferred once up to a maximum of 12 months from the original date. The normal expectation is that *everyone* summoned for jury service will serve at the time for which they are summoned.

Only in extreme circumstances will a person be excused. The normal procedure is to defer the individual to a more appropriate time, e.g. if a holiday is booked or to avoid a shift or night worker attending on a rest day.

Application for excusal could be given on the following grounds:

- insufficient understanding of English;
- membership of religious orders whose ideology or beliefs are incompatible with jury service;
- valid business reason (e.g. if a small business would suffer unusual hardship) – however, application for deferral or excusal cannot be accepted from third parties such as employers;
- conflict with other important public duties; and
- illness or a physical disability.

Loss of earnings

With regard to loss of earnings, courts can pay for these together with travel costs and a subsistence rate. Currently, losses of earnings are paid up to a maximum of £52.63 a day for the first ten days and a maximum of £105.28 for subsequent days. Public transport costs will be paid although jurors must obtain permission from the court before using taxis. The subsistence rate for meals is currently £4.51 a day. Payment is made directly to the juror and courts cannot pay third parties such as employers.

As soon as a summons has been received, the employee should forward the juror's loss of earnings certificate provided by the court (Form 5223) to their employer. Employers should note the dates and organise a deduction from salary of the amount representing the value of the allowance for days attended at court. However, unless specified in the contract of employment or staff handbook, there is no legal right to receive regular salary payments while undertaking jury service.

In circumstances where deduction of the jury service allowance results in a nil salary payment, any additional superannuation contributions can be deducted from the next available salary payment to provide continuity of pensionable service.

Employment rights

Jury service will constitute continuity of employment. This means that an employee will continue to accumulate or keep existing employment rights gained through length of service.

It is not advisable to refuse permission to release your employee for jury service. This could result in contempt of court issues with penalties such as a fine or even imprisonment for the employer. Dismissing your employee may result in a claim against your business for compensation for the loss of employment.

Good planning ahead will help to minimise the impact on the business. Encourage employees to inform you immediately when summoned because this will give you approximately four weeks to make the necessary plans. Alternatively, if you work in a small business, you may consider requesting your employee to apply for a deferment.

See also: Absence management (page 65).

Sources of further information

Court Service www.courtservice.gov.uk.

Jury Central Summoning Bureau: 0845 3555 567 (local rate) 9 a.m. to 5 p.m. Monday to Friday.

Landlord and tenant: lease issues

Edited by Hugh Bruce-Watt, Pinsent Masons

Key points

- Leases are documents which pass exclusive legal possession/control or exclusive occupation of land or premises for an agreed period in return for rent, usually paid monthly or quarterly.
- The landlord (who is not necessarily the freeholder) retains his title and receives the rent.
- The tenant pays the rent and enters into covenants (obligations) restricting and regulating his use of the premises, and other aspects as well as positive obligations such as repairs and decoration.
- A lease may be transferred to a new tenant subject to restrictions within the lease. Usually, the landlord's consent is required but is not to be unreasonably withheld.

Legislation

- Law of Property Act 1925.
- Landlord and Tenant Act 1927.
- Leasehold Property (Repairs) Act 1938.
- Landlord and Tenant Act 1954.
- Landlord and Tenant Act 1985.
- Landlord and Tenant Act 1988.
- Landlord and Tenant (Licensed Premises) Act 1990.
- Landlord and Tenant (Covenants) Act 1995.
- Land Registration Act 2002.
- Commonhold and Leasehold Reform Act 2002.
- Land Registration Rules 2003.

Advantages of leases

The granting or taking of a lease is an alternative to holding a freehold interest in property. There may be the following advantages to both parties:

- The landlord retains an interest in the property.
- The landlord can enforce both positive and negative obligations against the tenant.
- The lease may have investment value to the landlord, with the payment of rent creating an income stream.
- Payment of rent at regular intervals may be a more manageable cost to the tenant than raising finance to acquire the freehold.
- The tenant can have flexibility as to the duration of his interest in the property.
- Leases are an effective means of splitting up the disposal of a multi-occupied building.

Heads of terms

- Heads of terms may be agreed by the parties before a lease or agreement for lease is entered into.
- Heads of terms represent agreement in principle as to the basic matters to be contained within the lease and any other related documents. The more detailed the heads of terms, the less argument there will be in agreeing the terms of the lease.
- Heads of terms will generally not be legally binding between the parties, although, at a practical level, they may be difficult to renegotiate once specific principles have been agreed. It is therefore important for a landlord or tenant to involve surveyors and lawyers at an early stage.

The surveyor

Commercial property surveyors will generally represent each party's interest, and each party will usually pay his own surveyor's fees on the grant of a lease.

The surveyors will advise their clients on and negotiate such matters as:

- the premises to be let;
- amount of the rent;
- length of the lease;
- options to break the lease early;
- whether the tenant has statutory security of tenure;
- rent reviews;
- rights over common parts;
- management of the building;
- parking;
- use of the premises;
- restrictions on assignment;
- who is responsible for repairs;
- insurance responsibilities; and
- tenant's guarantee.

These should all be covered in the heads of terms.

Agreement for lease

The parties may enter into an agreement for lease in advance of the lease itself being granted. An agreement for lease is simply a contract between the parties for the landlord to grant and the tenant to accept a lease at a future date or following certain agreed conditions being satisfied within a set period.

The form of the lease has to be agreed and attached to the agreement for lease. Once an agreement for lease has been exchanged, neither party may unilaterally withdraw from the transaction without being in breach of contract (see page 113 in 'Buying and selling property').

Leases for three years or less taking immediate effect do not have to be in writing. However, oral leases are highly undesirable.

An agreement for lease can have advantages to both parties:

- It creates certainty that the lease will be granted, on the given date or on satisfaction of any relevant conditions. This assists both parties in forward planning.
- The agreement for lease represents a tangible asset for the landlord from an investment perspective, and the tenant will be able to prepare for his future occupation of the property.
- A landlord may wish to be sure he has a tenant for his premises before acquiring them or carrying out works to them.

Conditional agreement

An agreement for lease may be made conditional on any matters which either party requires to be satisfied before being obliged to complete the lease. Examples include:

* obtaining planning permission;
* the carrying out of works by one of the parties;
* obtaining consents needed under a superior lease; and
* obtaining a licence to carry out the tenant's business (e.g. sale of alcohol).

Where an agreement for lease is conditional, the terms of the conditions are of fundamental importance.

It is important that surveyors' and legal advice is obtained.

Principal issues in the lease

Parties

The lease will be granted by the landlord (or lessor) to the tenant (or lessee). The landlord will want to be satisfied that the proposed tenant has the financial status to pay the rent and other sums due under the lease and to perform the various tenant's covenants.

Generally speaking, from an investment standpoint, the stronger the tenant, the more valuable the lease will be to the landlord.

The landlord will usually want to see evidence of the tenant's financial status. This may include, for instance, providing copies of accounts and references. If the tenant is a new company without a proven track record, or is not perceived to be financially strong, the landlord may require additional security, such as third-party guarantees or a rent deposit.

Property to be leased

The lease will need to clearly define the extent of the premises. This is particularly the case where the letting is only part of a building. Relevant issues include the extent to which parts of the exterior, roof, foundations and other structural parts are to be included or excluded. This will also affect the tenant's repairing obligations, which will generally be by reference to the extent of the premises that are leased. Access and parking must also be agreed.

Term

The length of the term is a basic issue which is likely to affect the other terms of the lease. From the tenant's standpoint, the length of term will be influenced by the tenant's need for the premises in question, and any plans which the tenant may have for the future. New lease accounting standards may have an impact on the length of the term and the tenant's obligation to pay stamp duty land tax, which can be considerable in the case of longer leases (e.g. SDLT for commercial premises with a rent of £100,000 a year will cost the tenant over £15,000 for a 20-year lease, under £4,000 for a five-year lease and zero for a one-year lease). Break rights do not reduce the tax.

From the landlord's perspective, a longer lease, with regular upwards-only rent reviews, will be more valuable from an investment standpoint, creating greater certainty as to the landlord's future income stream and an enhanced capital value.

Security of tenure

Subject to specific exclusions, business leases granted for more than six months benefit from security of tenure under the Landlord and Tenant Act 1954. This entitles the tenant to the grant of a new lease at the end of the original agreed term, unless the landlord has specific grounds to resist this right. The landlord can, subject to restrictions, override the tenant's rights on various grounds including showing an intention to demolish or reconstruct the property and requiring possession for its own business.

Subject to these and other exceptions and to the tenant complying with various procedural requirements, the courts have power to intervene if the parties cannot agree on a new lease.

As the procedures for invoking these rights are both complex and prescriptive, it is important that you seek legal advice on any proposed renewal at the relevant time.

Contracting out

It is possible for the parties to contract out of the security of tenure provisions in the lease. To do so, the landlord must send a notice to the tenant which is in a prescribed form. The notice explains the effect of contracting out of the security of tenure provisions. Two weeks later the tenant must sign a declaration to the effect that he has understood the terms of the notice and has agreed to contract out of security of tenure. The two-week period can be waived if the tenant signs a statutory declaration before an independent solicitor.

Contracting out of security of tenure is an important issue in negotiating a new lease and obtaining legal advice is recommended.

Licences

It is sometimes suggested that the landlord can prevent the Landlord and Tenant Act from applying by granting an occupation licence instead of a lease, so that the tenant does not have exclusive possession of the property which he occupies. Licences are to be treated with caution as such arrangements cannot be guaranteed to be legally effective. They are often used for short-term arrangements in business centres.

Break options

Either the landlord or the tenant may be granted a right to terminate the lease before the expiry of the agreed term. From a landlord's standpoint, break options granted to a tenant may reduce the investment value of the lease. A tenant may, nevertheless, want the flexibility to terminate the lease early, either at a fixed date or dates, or possibly through a rolling break on or after a given period during the term.

The landlord may expect some incentive to agree to this, in the form of a higher rent or a compensation payment if the tenant subsequently exercises the break right.

Many landlords seek to impose conditions on the exercise of tenants' break rights, e.g. performance of tenant's covenants. These are strictly construed and constitute a trap for the unwary tenant as they can render the break right illusory

Superior leases

If the landlord does not own the freehold to the property, but instead occupies the premises under an existing lease, then it will be necessary for a tenant to take account of the terms of any superior leases. This will be important for the following reasons:

- He must ensure that the superior lease lasts longer than the new underlease.
- The superior lease(s) may require that consents are obtained from the superior landlord(s), in order to permit the underlease to the undertenant, or to permit other matters such as changing the use or carrying out alterations.
- The landlord may want to pass on obligations under the superior lease by requiring the undertenant to perform these. From an undertenant's standpoint this may be not be acceptable or reasonable. For example, repairing or service charge obligations in a superior lease may be geared to a much longer term than the sublease.
- Where the superior lease contains restrictions affecting the use or occupation of the premises, the undertenant will generally be subject to these same restrictions. It is important, therefore, that an undertenant knows what these are and that it is able to comply with them.
- An undertenant will want to ensure that its intermediate landlord does not breach its obligations to its superior landlord(s), as this could give rise to a potential forfeiture action by the superior landlord, which in turn could prejudice the undertenant's position.

Rent

Rent is important for both the landlord and the tenant. It affects the affordability of the premises to the tenant, and the income stream received by the landlord.

It is common for rents of commercial properties to be calculated by reference to a rate per square foot. In addition to the rate itself, the basis of measurement will need to be agreed. Surveyors commonly measure a premises on either a net or gross basis. Your surveyor or solicitor will be able to advise you further on these issues. Other issues to consider include the following:

- Is the tenant to receive an initial rent-free period? This is particularly common where the tenant needs to carry out fitting-out works.
- Is the rent exclusive or inclusive of other payments, such as insurance premiums or service charges? Exclusive rents are most common in commercial leases, but a rent that is inclusive of insurance premiums and service charges may be appropriate for both parties on a short-term letting or where the premises are a small part of a much larger building.
- Will value added tax be payable on the rent?

Rent reviews

If the lease is for more than five years, it is common for the landlord to require the rent to be reviewed at periodic intervals. The most common review cycle in today's market is for five-yearly reviews, although other cycles as frequent as three-yearly are sometimes agreed. It should be noted, however, that cycles more frequently than every five years can increase the tenant's stamp duty land tax costs.

Rents can be reviewed by reference to a fixed percentage increase or to an index such as the Retail Price Index.

The most common system, however,

remains upward-only review to the open market rent at the relevant review date. On each review date the rent becomes the rent which a new tenant would pay for those premises.

'Upward only' means that the rent will be increased to the open market rent, but, if rental values stay the same or fall during the review period, the rent will remain the same and will not fall. This means that the landlord's income stream is protected against falls in rental value in the future. Although the Government is keen to promote flexibility in the letting market, including 'upward or downward' reviews, this has yet to receive general acceptance and legislation has been threatened.

Tenant's covenants

The issues of most frequent concern are as follows:

Permitted use

The landlord will generally want to restrict the use of the premises to a given category of use or uses (such as retail or office), so he retains some control. If the permitted use is too restrictive, then this could have adverse rent review consequences for the landlord. The tenant needs to check that the permitted use gives sufficient flexibility for its present purposes and for any changes which might be needed in the future or for an assignee.

Alterations

The degree of control over alterations required by the landlord is likely to be influenced by the nature of the building and the length of the term. A landlord will not want the tenant to have the ability to carry out alterations which may adversely affect the future letting of the premises, and may also require the tenant to reinstate any alterations at the end of the term.

The tenant will, again, need to ensure there is sufficient flexibility for any changes which may be needed, either now or in the future.

A distinction may be drawn, for instance, between alterations affecting either the structure or the exterior (which are generally barred) and those, such as the erection of internal partitioning, that affect only the interior and are non-structural (which are generally permitted with the landlord's consent).

Repairs

The lease will govern the extent to which the parties are liable for repairs. An institutional landlord will frequently want the lease to be on a full repairing and insuring basis (known as an FRI lease). The tenant would be responsible for any repairs which arise during the term, and the landlord would be entitled to the premises back at the end of the term: sometimes these would be in a better state of repair and condition than they were at the start. Conversely, a tenant may look to limit his repairing obligations, particularly if the lease is for a relatively short term and the tenant's interest is therefore limited.

Other issues to consider include the following:

* Should there be a schedule of condition attached to the lease, providing evidence of the premises' condition at the start of the lease, and for the tenant's obligations to be limited accordingly?
* With new or recently constructed

premises, will the tenant have the benefit of warranties from the building contractor, services subcontractor and professionals responsible for the design of the premises and supervision of the work?

• The tenant may seek to avoid liability for inherent defects, covering defects arising from deficiencies in the building's initial design or construction.

When considering repairing obligations, it is important to bear in mind not only the tenant's obligations to repair the premises themselves, but also its liability to contribute to the cost of repairs to other parts of the building through the service charge.

Assignment and subletting

Unless there are special circumstances, such as a very short term or very generous break rights, a tenant will generally want the ability to assign the remaining period of the lease to a third party, or possibly to underlet either the whole or part.

When the lease is assigned, the assignee becomes the landlord's tenant. A landlord will wish to keep control over who can occupy the premises in the future and to know that any substituted tenant will be able to pay the rent. The landlord will always require the right to approve any new tenant or undertenant, but most leases stipulate that such approval cannot be unreasonably withheld provided the assignment or sublease affects the whole of the premises.

Insurance

The lease should state who is responsible for insuring the premises and who pays the premiums. The landlord will frequently want to retain control for insuring the building but to pass on the premium, or an appropriate proportion of it, to the tenant. This is particularly the case in a multi-occupied building or where the landlord has a portfolio of properties which are insured on a block policy. If there is a superior lease, this may also specify insurance requirements.

A landlord will also want there to be loss-of-rent insurance so that the landlord's income stream is maintained if the premises are damaged or destroyed so as to be unfit for occupation. The tenant normally pays the cost of this.

Since 9/11 there has been a debate with regard to uninsurable risks, possibly terrorism or flooding in a flood plain area. Currently most leases do not permit suspension of rent or termination by the tenant in such circumstances. Unless leases are amended, there is considerable risk to the tenant.

Position following destruction or damage

The parties need to consider whether either the landlord or the tenant (or both) should have any rights to terminate the lease if the premises are destroyed by an insured risk. If the lease is not terminated, the tenant will want to ensure that due rent is suspended and that the landlord has an obligation to reinstate the premises as quickly as possible so that the tenant can resume occupation.

Service charge

The lease may require the tenant to pay a 'service charge'. This is particularly common in the case of a multi-occupied building, which may include common parts, or where there are services such as security, reception facilities or cleaning. The service charge may also cover repairs and maintenance to the building as a whole, so that each of the tenants contributes an appropriate proportion of these costs.

Service charge provisions are also common where premises are part of a larger estate, such as a retail or industrial park. In those instances, where there are other services such as car parking facilities, additional security and landscaped areas, the service charge payable by each tenant can be a considerable sum.

Particular issues include:

- the services which the landlord is required to provide;
- the basis of calculation of the cost and the likely amount of each payment;
- the method of payment;
- the ability of the landlord to vary, add to or suspend services;
- the tenant's right to check the landlord's expenditure; and
- any cap on the level of the service charge.

With commercial property, there are no statutory restrictions limiting the level of service charge which can be imposed, or requiring the landlord to undertake services at the most competitive cost. Issues such as these need to be dealt with in the drafting of the lease. The landlord's ability to pass on particular costs needs to be examined carefully against the length of the lease and the condition of the building (and sometimes the estate) of which it forms part.

Assignment of an existing lease

The lease may be sold or transferred, possibly at a price according to its value, to a new tenant (known as the 'assignee').

It is likely that consents will be needed from the landlord, in relation both to the assignment itself and to any changes which the new tenant wants to make, such as changing the use, or making alterations. The landlord will usually want his fees paid by the tenant, who may try to pass the cost on to the assignee.

The terms of the assignment need to be agreed between the assignor and the assignee – this is similar to the arrangements outlined in 'Buying and selling property' (page 111).

The tenant will usually have no right to renegotiate the terms of the lease itself at this stage to accommodate the assignee.

In leases granted before 1996 the tenant will remain liable to the landlord for performance of the covenants in the lease even after the lease is assigned. Generally this is not the case for leases granted after 1995, but the tenant may still have to guarantee the immediate assignee's performance of the covenants in the lease. This is a complex area of law on which legal advice should be taken.

Land registration

Leases of seven or more years must be registered at the Land Registry. Exceptionally shorter leases must also be registered where there are express rights within them over other property (e.g. common parts or services) as otherwise these rights are not enforceable.

Key questions

1. Preliminary issues

- Is a new lease to be granted or will the tenant acquire an existing one? If it is an existing lease:
    - is there a superior lease?
    - are any consents required from the freeholder or from superior landlords?
    - what professional advice will be needed to assist in the negotiation of the heads of terms and the lease documentation?
- Generally, has the proposed landlord or assignor a proper title?

2. Is an agreement for lease necessary or desirable?

- When does the tenant want to occupy?
- Are there any conditions which need to be satisfied before the lease can be granted or assigned?
- Are any works required prior to the grant or assignment of the lease?
- If works are required, who will carry them out, and at whose cost?

3. What are the costs?

- Surveyor's fees.
- Legal costs.
- Search fees.
- Survey/valuation fees.
- Stamp duty land tax.

4. Rent and other payments

- What is the initial rent?

- Are there to be rent reviews? If so, at what intervals and on what basis?
- Are there any other expenses such as service charges and insurance premiums?
- Is there a premium?
- Is VAT payable? Can the tenant recover this?

5. Terms of the lease

- Who will be the landlord and the tenant?
- Does the landlord require guarantors or other security?
- What will be the contractual term?
- Will the tenant have security of tenure?
- Will either party get break rights?
- What is the extent of the property to be let?
- Does the lease provide sufficient control for the landlord, and sufficient flexibility to the tenant, as to issues such as permitted use, alterations and alienation?
- What are the arrangements concerning insurance and following events of damage or destruction?
- What services will the landlord be responsible for carrying out?
- What will the tenant have to contribute by way of service charge?

See also: Buying and selling property (page 111); Landlord and tenant: possession issues (page 354).

Landlord and tenant: possession issues

Edited by Nicola Seager, Pinsent Masons

Key points

- The Landlord and Tenant Act 1954 gives certain tenants of business premises the right to remain in occupation when their lease term comes to an end.
- This right continues until the landlord or the tenant serves a notice under the Act to bring the lease to an end.
- The landlord or the tenant can apply to the court to order a new lease. The tenant will be entitled to a new lease unless the landlord is able successfully to apply to terminate the lease or to oppose an application by the tenant on one or more grounds set out in the Act (see below). The Act does not, however, usually protect a tenant who fails to observe the covenants in the lease or who does not continue to occupy the premises for business purposes.

Legislation

- Landlord and Tenant Act 1954.

Landlord's notice (section 25)

A landlord of business premises can terminate a business tenancy by serving a notice pursuant to section 25 of the Landlord and Tenant Act. The landlord must give between six and 12 months' notice to the tenant expiring not earlier than the date of termination of the lease.

A landlord must use the appropriate form of notice or a 'form substantially to the same effect'. The two main forms which a landlord may want to use cover the situations where a landlord does and does not oppose the grant of a new tenancy.

If the landlord does not oppose the grant of a new tenancy, he must set out his proposals for the new tenancy including the property to be demised, the new rent, and other terms. If the landlord opposes the tenant's right to a new lease, the ground(s) of opposition must be stated (see below).

Tenant's notice (section 26)

It is also possible for a tenant to start the lease renewal process by serving a notice under section 26 of the Act.

The notice must be for a period of between six and 12 months and cannot expire earlier than the date of expiry of the lease. If the landlord wishes to oppose the tenant's right to a new lease, he must serve a counter-notice within

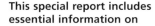

two months, stating the ground(s) of opposition.

Application to the court

Where there has been no application to renew the lease and the landlord has given a section 25 notice saying that he is opposed to the grant of a new tenancy or has served a counter-notice to a tenant's section 26 request to that effect, the landlord may apply to terminate the lease. The Act specifies certain deadlines for making applications which can be extended by written agreement before the deadline expires.

Alternatively, if the landlord does not oppose the grant of a new tenancy, he could apply for an order that the tenant has a new lease. Similarly, if the tenant wants a new tenancy he could make an application. Again, there are time limits for bringing applications, but these can be extended by written agreement before the deadline expires.

Grounds of opposition

The seven grounds of opposition, which entitle the landlord to refuse a new lease if he can prove one or more of them, are:

(a) disrepair caused by tenant;

(b) tenant's delay in paying rent;

(c) other substantial breaches of covenant by tenant;

(d) landlord is willing to supply alternative accommodation;

(e) the tenancy is of part only and the landlord wishes to let property as a whole;

(f) landlord intends to demolish or reconstruct the premises; and

(g) landlord intends to occupy for his own business.

If the landlord successfully opposes the grant of a new lease on grounds (a), (f) or (g), he will have to pay compensation to the tenant of once or twice the rateable value of the premises.

Excluding security of tenure

It is possible for a landlord and tenant of business premises contractually to exclude security of tenure in respect of a business lease by following the notice procedure laid down in the Act.

Briefly the landlord must serve a notice on the tenant not less than 14 days before the tenant enters into the tenancy, or becomes contractually bound to enter into the tenancy. Then the tenant (or a person authorised by him) must make a declaration in prescribed form or substantially in that form before he enters into the tenancy or becomes contractually obliged to do so. If the landlord's notice is given within 14 days of the tenant entering into the tenancy or becoming contractually obliged to do so, the tenant (or a person authorised on his behalf) must make a statutory declaration in prescribed form, or substantially that form, before the tenant enters into the lease or becomes contractually obliged to do so.

The exclusion must be reflected in the tenancy or instrument creating the tenancy in a manner prescribed by the Act.

Where a business lease has been excluded in this way, the procedures described above do not apply. The tenant must leave the premises when the lease term has ended.

Forfeiture

The security of tenure provided by the Act will not assist a tenant who commits breaches of the lease. Leases invariably contain a forfeiture clause which allows the landlord to terminate the lease in the event of default by the tenant. When the breach involves failure to pay rent, the landlord has the right to forfeit after a period of usually seven, 14 or 21 days from when the rent fell due. Where the breach involves something other than non-payment of rent, the landlord has to serve a notice under section 146 of the Law of Property Act 1925, which notifies the tenant of the breach, requires it to be remedied, if that is possible, and gives the tenant a reasonable time within which to remedy the breach. If the tenant fails to remedy the breach within a reasonable time, the landlord can go on to forfeit.

Following forfeiture, the tenant then has the right to apply to court to ask for 'relief' from forfeiture, which will normally be granted provided that the breaches are remedied and the landlord's costs are paid.

Forfeiting a lease

There are two ways in which a landlord can forfeit a lease:

- by issuing and serving court proceedings; and

- by 'peaceable re-entry' which involves the landlord breaking into the premises and changing the locks.

Peaceable re-entry

Peaceable re-entry is a risky step for a landlord to take. It is possible for a landlord to 'waive' the right to forfeit a lease by, for instance, demanding rent after a breach.

If a landlord attempts to re-enter premises in such circumstances, the re-entry will be unlawful and the landlord can be sued. A landlord also has a duty of care in respect of any items belonging to the tenant which remain in the premises after a re-entry. It is a criminal offence for a landlord to re-enter if he is aware that someone is in the premises who is resisting the landlord's re-entry. The landlord cannot peaceably re-enter if someone is living in the premises.

See also: Landlord and tenant: lease issues (page 345).

Legionella

Phil Wright, SafetyCO UK

Key points

- The Control of Substances Hazardous to Health Regulations 2002 (COSHH Regulations) relate to the risk from hazardous micro-organisms such as legionella bacteria (the cause of legionnaires' disease) and the chemicals used to dose water systems such as bromine/chlorine biocides.
- The Regulations require anyone who is in charge of premises to undertake a risk assessment of such systems and to put in place the necessary precautionary measures to prevent the occurrence of legionella and control the health risk from the use and handling of treatment chemicals.
- The Notification of Cooling Towers and Evaporative Condensers Regulations 1992 require those having control of premises to notify the local authority of certain equipment that could pose a risk of legionella, such as cooling towers and evaporative condensers where the water is exposed to air.
- No new device should be installed without first notifying the local authority.

Legislation

- Control of Substances Hazardous to Health Regulations 2002.
- Notification of Cooling Towers and Evaporative Condensers Regulations 1992.

Compliance

In order to control the risk of legionella, an understanding of how the bacteria grow and affect the human body is necessary:

- Legionella bacteria are found in natural water sources and water systems. They grow in temperatures of between 20°C and 45°C and are destroyed in temperatures above 60°C.
- The bacteria require nutrients in order to grow and survive. Sludge, sediment and scale provide this.
- Legionnaires' disease is spread by inhalation of water droplets containing legionella bacteria.
- Symptoms of legionnaires' disease are flu-like, with high fever and headache. The disease can be fatal and generally affect vulnerable people such as the elderly, children and the infirm.
- There is no risk of infection from one person to another.

Persons in charge of premises must identify all plant equipment that could encourage the growth of legionella.

Plant equipment that could pose this risk is:

- cooling towers;
- evaporative condensers;
- hot water systems with volumes greater than 300 litres;
- hot and cold water systems in buildings such as hospitals, nursing homes, etc., where there are vulnerable people;
- humidifiers and air washers which create water sprays at temperatures above 20°C; and
- spa baths and pools where the warm water is agitated and recirculated.

Risk assessment

Where it is not practicable to avoid using the above-mentioned types of plant, then a responsible person (e.g. the facilities manager) must draw up a written scheme to control and reduce the risk.

The scheme should include:

- current plans of the systems;
- details of the safe operation of the plant; and
- the necessary precautions to prevent the bacteria growing.

The precautions should include:

- water treatment;
- temperature control;
- routine maintenance schedules;
- sampling regime to ensure the precautions are working; and
- details of the person undertaking the sampling and subsequent analysis with a record of the results kept.

Any sampling and analysis should be done by someone who is capable of sampling and interpreting the results.

Record keeping

Records should be kept by the person who produced the written schemes in order to monitor and manage the precautionary measures.

The records that should be kept are:

- the written scheme;
- maintenance records, e.g. dates of drain, downs, remedial works carried out;
- details of the competency of the persons carrying out the maintenance; and
- water treatment records.

All these records must be kept for a minimum of two years

Water treatment

Any water treatment must be carried out by a person who has knowledge of the systems and the chemicals he is using. He must also be aware of the legionella health risks arising from working with this plant.

Management of the risk

Legionella bacteria cannot be prevented from entering any water as they are so widespread. Therefore a controller of premises can only reduce the risk of outbreaks.

This can be achieved as follows:

- Locate cooling towers away from any of a building's air intakes.
- Avoid stagnant water and 'dead-legs'. Cover tanks to prevent the entry of dirt and debris. Tanks should be regularly inspected and tested.
- Avoid water temperatures between

20°C and 45°C, but be aware of the risk of scalding if the water temperature is too high.

- Clean and disinfect cooling tower systems every six months. Descaling all the components should also be undertaken. Try to avoid using high-pressure jet washers to clean the systems as aerosol can be created.

See also: Water quality (page 534).

Sources of further information

L8 'Legionnaire's disease: the control of legionella bacteria in water systems' (HSE Books, 2000): ISBN 0 7176 1772 6.

'An introduction to the control of legionella bacteria in water systems' (HSE Books, 2003: VHS PAL video): ISBN 0 7176 2580 X.

TM13 'Minimising the risk of Legionnaires' disease, (Chartered Institution of Building Services Engineers, 2000): ISBN 1 90328 723 5.

The Control of Legionellae by the Safe and Effective Operation of Cooling Systems (British Association for Chemical Specialities, 1989 (plus 1995 update)): ISBN 0 95149 500 3.

'Legionella Policy and Management Guide, version 1.0' (ISBN 1 900648 74 1, £74.99) is available as an electronic download from the Workplace Law Network. Call 0870 777 8881 for details, or visit www.workplacelaw.net.

Lift safety

David Sharp, Workplace Law Group

Key points

- All passenger lifts supplied after 30 June 1999 should be fitted with safety features to assist trapped occupants in the event of a mechanical breakdown.
- Building managers have a responsibility under the Lifts Regulations 1997 to keep records relating to the operation, maintenance and repair of passenger lifts in premises under their control.
- The safety of lifting equipment in general (including machinery for lifting loads, as well as people) is covered under the Lifting Operations and Lifting Equipment Regulations 1998.
- The greatest risk relates to the maintenance – rather than use – of lifts. According to the Lift and Escalator Industry Association, in the last decade inadequate controls on the top of lift cars have resulted in four fatal accidents, four potentially fatal accidents, four amputations, and 19 other serious accidents.

Legislation

- Health and Safety at Work etc. Act 1974.
- Lifts Regulations 1997.
- Lifting Operations and Lifting Equipment Regulations 1998.
- Management of Health and Safety at Work Regulations 1999.
- Provision and Use of Work Equipment Regulations 1998.

Statutory requirements

While the Lifts Regulations 1997 mainly govern the manufacture of passenger lifts and lift components, they are of interest to building managers who are responsible for the safe use of lifts and lift maintenance. The Regulations were introduced to ensure manufacturers designed enhanced safety features into lifts, including:

- a means of two-way communication in the event of a breakdown;
- adequate ventilation during a prolonged stoppage; and
- the operation of emergency lighting systems during a power failure.

The Regulations apply to all lifts, safety components and component parts where lifts are permanently service buildings or constructions, with one or two minor exceptions (such as mountain trains, mine winding gear and theatre elevators). They do not apply to lifts and safety components already in service before 1 July 1997. Manufacturers were given a

---

two-year grace period to comply with the requirements of the Regulations, so that all lifts supplied after 30 June 1999 must be compliant.

The Regulations require building managers to keep documentation such as:

- an instruction manual containing the plans and diagrams necessary for use;
- a set of guidelines relating to maintenance, inspection, repair, periodic checks and rescue operations; and
- a log book in which repairs can be recorded.

Apart from the safety and health of people using the lifts, it is the ongoing maintenance of lifts which poses potentially the greatest hazard. Regulation 5 of the Lifting Operations and Lifting Equipment Regulations 1998 (LOLER) covers the safety of people working on lifting equipment, including provisions to prevent falling.

Employers should ensure that passenger lifts have been properly examined after installation before commissioning their first use. They will also need to be tested by a competent person and inspected prior to use, and at regular intervals during use. A regular examination should take into account the condition and operation of:

- landing and car doors and their interlocks;
- worm and other gearing;
- main drive system components;
- governors;
- safety gear;
- suspension ropes;
- suspension chains;
- overload detection devices;

- electrical devices (including earthing, earth bonding, safety devices, selection of fuses, etc.);
- braking systems (including buffers and overspeed devices); and
- hydraulics.

Risk assessment

A risk assessment should be undertaken before maintenance work on lifts is carried out, and the maintenance instructions provided by the manufacturers and installers should be given careful consideration. Only competent persons should be employed to maintain lifts. The person responsible for the building should ensure that a permit to work system is in place to control access to the lift shaft and to dictate a safe system of work.

A note on signage

Lifts should not be used in the event of a fire unless they have been specifically designed to do so, and signs should be displayed to this effect. Many lifts are only supported by two-way communication in the event of breakdown during normal office hours. In order to control the risk of people becoming trapped in lifts outside these times, signage to this effect can also be displayed. However, you should be aware that since 1 October 2004 under Part III of the Disability Discrimination Act 1995 it is unlawful to discriminate against disabled people without reasonable grounds to do so.

See also: Lifting equipment (page 364); Permits to work (page 422); Safety signage (page 483).

Sources of further information

INDG339 'Thorough examination and testing of lifts: simple guidance for lift owners' (HSE Books, 2001): ISBN 0 7176 2030 1.

BS 7255:2001 'Code of practice for safe working on lifts'.

Safety Assessment Federation (SAFed): *Lifts Guidelines on the Thorough Examination and Testing of Lifts* (SAFed, 1998): ISBN 1 901212 35 1 (Ref. LG1). Available from SAFed, Nutmeg House, 60 Gainsford Street, Butler's Wharf, London SE1 2NY (tel. 020 7403 0987; email info@safed.co.uk).

Lift and Escalator Industry Association, 33/34 Devonshire Street, London W1G 6PY (tel. 020 7935 3013; fax 020 7935 3321; email enquiries@leia.co.uk; website www.leia.co.uk).

Lifting equipment

David Menzies, SafetyCO UK

Key points

- The introduction of the Lifting Operations and Lifting Equipment Regulations 1998 (LOLER) widened the scope of legislation on lifting equipment to all sections of industry, not just construction. They apply to any equipment used at work for lifting or lowering loads.
- All lifting equipment and accessories are deemed work equipment under the Provision and Use of Work Equipment Regulations 1998 (PUWER), which require the employer to supply and maintain equipment that is correct and suitable for the specific task.
- The Reporting of Injuries, Diseases and Dangerous Occurrences Regulations 1995 (RIDDOR) classify the collapse, overturning or failure of any lift, hoist, crane or derrick to be a notifiable dangerous occurrence, even if no one is injured.

Legislation

- Lifting Operations and Lifting Equipment Regulations 1998.
- Provision and Use of Work Equipment Regulations 1998.
- Health and Safety (Safety Signs and Signals) Regulations 1996.

Compliance advice

Lifting equipment includes the following:

- Crabs.
- Winches.
- Pulley blocks or gin wheels.
- Hoists.
- Cranes.
- Excavator drag lines.
- Piling frames.
- Overhead runways.
- Goods hoists.
- Mobile elevated work platforms (MEWPs).
- Scissor lifts.
- Vehicle hoists.
- Forklift trucks.
- Lorry loaders (hiabs).
- Passenger lifts.

Accessories such as chains, slings and eyebolts are also covered by the Regulations.

LOLER additionally applies to employees' own equipment if used at work, but does not apply to escalators or lifts in shopping centres.

Before any lifting operation is undertaken, a suitable and sufficient risk assessment needs to be carried out by a competent person to establish a safe system of work.

This should take account of the following issues, where relevant:

- Comprehensive planning of the operation.
- Testing and examination of all equipment, with the provision of all test certificates.
- Supervision by trained and competent persons who have the authority to curtail operations if necessary.
- The prevention of unauthorised use of the equipment, by both operatives and trespassers.
- The safety of all persons involved in the lifting operation together with others, such as the general public.

Hired lifting equipment

Both the hirer and the hire company have responsibilities when lifting equipment is brought onto premises:

- The hire company must ensure that the equipment is maintained, inspected and tested as appropriate and provide all necessary information to the hirer.
- The responsible person hiring the equipment must ensure that he has selected suitable equipment and that it complies with all relevant legislation.

Basic requirements for lifting equipment

- It must be strong and stable enough for the particular use.
- It must be marked to indicate safe working load.
- It must be positioned and installed to minimise risks.
- The work should be planned, organised and carried out by competent persons.

- It must be subject to ongoing and thorough examination.
- Inspections must be made by competent persons where appropriate.

Specific requirements for lifting persons

- Employers should ensure that any person in or on the equipment will not be crushed, trapped, struck by or fall from the carrier.
- Suitable devices must be provided to prevent the equipment falling.
- There must be suitable arrangements for freeing any person trapped in a carrier.
- If the risk of the carrier falling cannot be overcome, the suspension rope or chain must be enhanced (significantly over-specified and therefore under-loaded).

Specific requirements for thorough examination and inspections

- A competent person must examine all lifting equipment and accessories thoroughly before they are put into service for the first time.
- Where the safety of lifting equipment depends upon the installation conditions, the equipment must be examined to ensure it was correctly installed and is safe to operate.
- Lifting equipment exposed to conditions causing deterioration must be examined thoroughly at least every 12 months (six months for equipment used for lifting people).

Specific requirements for reports, defects and information

- The competent person carrying out the examination must make a report to the employer containing specific details of any defects.

- If the competent person considers that a defect presents an existing or imminent risk of serious personal injury, he must send a copy of the report to the enforcing authority.

- An employer notified of any defect must ensure that the equipment is not used until it has been rectified.

- Reports must be kept for inspection until the next report or for two years, whichever is the later.

- Reports on equipment being put into service for the first time must be retained until the lifting equipment ceases to be used.

See also: Construction site health and safety (page 145); Health and safety enforcement (page 306); Working at height (page 321).

Sources of further information

INDG290 'Simple guide to the Lifting Operations and Lifting Equipment Regulations 1998' (HSE, 1999): ISBN 0 7176 2430 7.

HSG6 'Safety in working with lift trucks' (HSE Books, 2000): ISBN 0 7176 1781 5.

GS6 'Avoidance of danger from overhead electrical power lines' (HSE Books, 1997): ISBN 0 7176 1348 8.

PM28 'Working platforms on fork-lift trucks' (HSE Books, 2000): ISBN 0 7176 0935 9.

GA700/04/D3 'Lifting equipment and accessories for lifting' (Construction Industries Training Board, 2004).

Lighting

Jonathan David, Society of Light and Lighting

Legislation

In general there is little in the legislation governing lighting in the workplace, and what the law does require is mostly qualitative (sufficient and suitable) rather than quantitative. The major provisions are found in the Health and Safety at Work etc. Act 1974 and the Health and Safety (Display Screen Equipment) Regulations 1992, but other legislation such as the Disability Discrimination Act 1995 also has to be complied with.

Health and Safety at Work etc. Act 1974

The primary requirement in the Act is that lighting should be 'sufficient and suitable'; only the courts can define what that is, and there are very few reported cases. The HSE publishes the guide 'Lighting at work' (HSG38, ISBN 0 7176 1232 5) which indicates what it believes to be the minimum acceptable standards. However, these cover only very general work types, defined in terms of the visual difficulty of the task. Note that these levels are for safety, not effective or efficient performance of the task.

Emergency lighting is now required by various provisions of the Act and it should be assumed that it is required in all workplaces and most other buildings used by the public. The detailed requirements are in British Standards (see 'Best practice guidance' below).

Health and Safety (Display Screen Equipment) Regulations 1992

These Regulations include provisions for lighting of workplaces where display screen equipment (DSE) is used. Note that this covers far more than just offices. DSE is found in many environments including factory equipment controls and on forklift trucks in warehouses. Again, the requirements of the Regulations are general, but are supplemented by an HSE guidance document 'Display screen equipment work. Guidance on regulations' (L26, ISBN 0 7176 0410 1). This covers far more than just lighting, but provides useful practical guidance on issues which the HSE expects to see addressed.

Disability Discrimination Act 1995

Lighting is one of the areas to which 'reasonable adjustments' need to be made if otherwise disabled people are likely to be disadvantaged (see also 'Building Regulations' below).

Other legislative provisions

There are many small references to lighting in legislation covering specific industries, especially foodstuffs and catering, and heavy industry involving hazardous processes. These are too numerous to discuss in this article.

Lighting

Building Regulations

Lighting is covered in the Building Regulations, Part L, at present under revision (for up-to-date information on the situation, go to www.odpm.gov.uk and follow the links). This currently prescribes minimum efficiencies for lighting equipment for various building types, as well as minimum control requirements, though this is likely to be replaced for new buildings by a requirement that the whole building meets specific carbon emission targets. The revised Building Regulations will also provide the means for implementing the EU Energy Performance of Buildings Directive which will require energy labelling of buildings.

Part L also now requires proper commissioning of new lighting installations and their controls, and this requirement is likely to be strengthened when the new Approved Document is issued. At the request of the Office of the Deputy Prime Minister (ODPM), the Society of Light and Lighting and the Chartered Institution of Building Services Engineers (of which the SLL is part) published 'Commissioning Code L: Lighting in 2003' (ISBN 1 903287 32 4) to give guidance on acceptable procedures.

Part M of the Building Regulations and the Disability Discrimination Act 1995 are also relevant although neither says a great deal specifically about lighting. However, lighting should be suitable for the visually impaired and where appropriate the hearing impaired. This normally means careful control of glare, adequate illuminances, good colour rendering and good modelling (e.g. to enable the deaf to lip-read). It is not recommended that lighting levels be increased above those in published guidance, except where a building is being specifically designed for the use of the partially sighted and the type of vision problem is known. It is normally appropriate instead to provide supplementary local lighting to meet the needs of the individual.

Two frequently asked questions

1. *Is it mandatory to provide daylight in offices?* The answer is yes, if it is reasonably practicable – unlike the situation in countries such as Germany where it is mandatory. However, the interpretation of 'reasonably practicable' is open to wide variation, and in practice the provision has no force.

2. *Do employers have to provide the recommended illuminance if the employee requests a lower level?* There is no authoritative answer to this question as it has not been tested in court, but it would be unwise to let the illuminance in the space drop below 200 lux since this is the minimum in the European Standard for continuously occupied spaces and is also the level recommended for office tasks in the HSE's guide 'Lighting at work'.

Note, however, that the recommendations in the Schedule of the SLL's Code for Lighting are for the task area, and that lower levels of lighting are suggested for surrounding areas. In offices, the task area will normally be only the area of the desk.

Environmental issues

The Waste Electrical and Electronic Equipment Directive applies to lighting, uniquely of all the fixed parts of buildings. There are specific requirements for recycling lamps and luminaires, and restrictions on dumping lamps containing mercury or sodium in the Landfill Regulations. The lighting industry has developed a recycling scheme to deal with the specific issues raised for discharge lamps (including fluorescent and compact fluorescent) called Sustainalite (www.sustainalite.co.uk).

It is worth noting that it has been suggested that current UK office specification practice may have to change as a result of the WEEE Directive. It will no longer be acceptable for almost unused luminaires installed as part of the landlord's scheme to be replaced when a tenant arrives. This may drive developers towards a shell and core approach, with no lighting installed until the tenant's needs are known. Developers wishing to promote themselves as having environmentally conscious credentials will particularly have to take this into account.

Best practice guidance

Since the only British Standard covering lighting of buildings (BS 8206-1) is very out of date and likely to be withdrawn shortly, the only relevant standard is BS EN 12464-1 'Light and lighting. Lighting of workplaces. Part 1: Indoor workplaces' (2002). However, the general reference document, which incorporates the relevant information from BS EN 12464-1, is the SLL's Code for Lighting 2004 available as a CD-ROM (ISBN 1 903287 47 2) or as printed extracts (ISBN 7506 5637 9).

This provides extensive guidance on the lighting of all types of building and associated spaces. Note that Part 2 of the European Standard covering exterior workplaces is currently in draft and may be published during 2005. When it is issued, the Code for Lighting will be updated to take account of its recommendations.

Neither British Standards nor the recommendations of professional bodies such as the SLL have any legal status except as best current practice.

The SLL also publishes a series of Lighting Guides covering specific building types. The Lighting Guide which is relevant to the greatest proportion of buildings is 'Lighting Guide 3: The visual environment for display screen use'. There has been considerable controversy in this area, because the Lighting Guide was published in 1996 and display screen technology and software have advanced greatly since then. In addition, BS EN 12464-1 contains guidance on lighting for DSE which is felt to be out of date. An addendum was published in 2001 to address these issues and the SLL is currently revising its guidance: an interim stage is included in the 2003 version of 'Lighting Guide 7: Office lighting', which is available only on the CD-ROM version of the Code for Lighting 2004 (a new printed edition should be available shortly). The essential change is relaxation of the luminaire luminance limits when modern screens and software are in use, and a recommendation for ensuring that there is adequate light on the walls and ceiling. The addendum formally withdrew the Luminaire Category Rating system as no longer relevant; not that this has never had any kind of legal status.

The current guidance on emergency lighting is in BS 5266 'Emergency lighting'. Part 1 of this standard is the code of practice and Part 7 is the UK implementation of the European Standard EN 1838. Other parts of the standard cover specific issues such as wayfinding. The draft European Standard prEN 50172 'Emergency escape lighting systems' is likely to replace the existing BS 5266-1. Especially important is regular planned maintenance and testing of emergency lighting, and this is provided for in the standards.

Note that emergency lighting should include luminaires outside the final exit to the building to assist adaptation to outside night-time lighting levels. This is particularly important for the elderly and the visually impaired.

The SLL will shortly publish 'Lighting Guide 12: Emergency lighting design guide' (ISBN 1 903287 51 0) which covers all aspects of emergency lighting from design to maintenance.

Exterior lighting of areas such as public car parks and access roads, including those in shopping centres, is covered by BS 5489-1 'Code of practice for the design of road lighting. Lighting of roads and public amenity areas' (2003).

See also: Building Regulations (page 92); Disability access (page 179); Display screen equipment (page 202); Electrical waste (page 522).

Lightning conductors

Edited by Nicola Seager, Pinsent Masons

Key points

- A lightning protector system protects buildings by providing a low-resistance alternative between the highest point of the building and the earth.
- Various consents may be needed for the installation of a lightning conductor. Planning consent will probably not be required, but listed building consent, conservation area consent or scheduled monument consent may be required.

Purpose of lightning conductors

In certain atmospheric conditions a build-up of static electricity results in a discharge between the sky and the earth and the 'strike' may hit the earth at its highest point. A lightning conductor channels the electric current generated from storm clouds and directed towards buildings or structures along the path of least resistance to earth.

A lightning protection system can reduce the amount of damage which may be caused to buildings by providing a low-resistance alternative between the highest point of the building and the earth. In its basic form, it usually takes the form of a metal rod installed at the pinnacle of the building and a connection of the rod to the earth.

Standards and specifications

Benjamin Franklin invented lightning rods in 1747 when he realised that attaching a conductor to a rod could divert the 'strike' of lightning harmlessly to earth. His concept remains the basis of lightning-rod designs today. Evidently, the lightning protection system has been improved and modified since Franklin's time and the relevant specifications are found in BS 6651:1999 'Code of practice for the protection of structures against lightning'.

BS 6651 clearly advises strict adherence to the provision of a conventional lightning protection system – to the total exclusion of any other device or system for which claims of enhanced protection are made.

The principal components of a conventional structural lightning protection system, in accordance with BS 6651, are as follows:

- *Air termination network*. This network is the point of connection for a lightning strike. It typically consists of a meshed conductor arrangement of copper or aluminium tapes covering the roof of the structure, designed to intercept the lightning.

- *Down conductors.* These are the means of carrying the current of a lightning strike safely to the earth termination network. The rods are attached to the external facade of the structure.
- *Earth termination network.* This is the means of dissipating the current to the general mass of earth. They can take the form of earth electrodes in the form of rods and plates or earth rod clamps, all of which serve the purpose of establishing a low-resistance contact with the earth.

There are, however, other lightning protection systems available, including the 'early streamer emission' device. This is a modern alternative to the rod. The device emits a stream of charged particles vertically upwards which helps attract the 'strike'. The lightning is then safely passed to the earth through the rest of the system. However, not everyone in the industry supports the application of this method.

The effect of a lightning conductor had been improved by using an isotope named americium-241 (a sealed source of ionising radiation) attached to the spike. However, all radioactive material is subject to control by the Environment Agency and its use on lightning conductors has not been permitted since February 2000. Therefore any remaining sealed sources should be removed with expert advice and guidance. Great care must be taken in particular in handling the sealed sources and ensuring appropriate disposal.

The British Standards Institution (BSI) provides advice on other British Standards relating to electrical installations and good earthing practice. There are also various international standards which provide useful guidance. The European International Electrotechnical Commission (IEC) prepares standards that serve as a basis for national standardisation. The UK is a member of the IEC through the BSI and BS 6651 reflects the standards of the IEC. The IEC standard 61024 'Protection of structures against lightning' is an internationally recognised standard, as is IEC 61312 'Protection against lightning electromagnetic impulse'.

Planning consents

Planning permission is not normally required to erect a conductor on most buildings since it is not 'development' for the purposes of the Town and Country Planning Act 1990. However, if a lightning protection system is sufficiently complex, has a degree of permanence and affects the external appearance of a building, it may require planning permission.

If the building concerned is listed, a scheduled ancient monument or within a conservation area, care needs to be taken as it will be subject to special controls.

If a building is listed, listed building consent from the appropriate local planning authority is required. Any works which affect the character of a building of special architectural or historic interest must be authorised. It would depend on each individual case whether the erection of a lightning conductor would have this effect as location and materials are relevant factors. While compliance with BS 6651 ensures that technical issues are adequately addressed, it does not necessarily ensure that aesthetic criteria are met. Therefore placing the conductor behind a buttress or otherwise out of sight could avoid affecting the character of the building.

If the building is an ancient monument, it could be damaged by the attachment of a conductor or a lightning protection scheme. Any addition to a scheduled monument needs prior consent and this includes any machinery attached to a monument (if it cannot be detached without being dismantled). In all the above cases reference should be made to English Heritage or Cadw (as appropriate) or the local planning authority before erecting a conductor on an ancient monument or a listed building since unauthorised works to either are a criminal offence.

If the building is in a conservation area, there may also be controls affecting the erection of a lightning conductor and a preliminary check should be made with the conservation officer of the relevant planning authority before proceeding with any work.

Lone working

David Sharp, Workplace Law Group

Key points

'Lone working' is the term used to cover situations where work is being undertaken by people working in isolation. In such cases, the risks to the safety and health of such people might be increased for the very reason that they are alone, and hence this type of situation needs careful consideration.

- Lone working is more common than many people think. Lone workers include cleaners, IT personnel, mobile maintenance staff, sales reps and security guards – in fact, anyone working alone.
- The risks from lone working can be increased where the job involves work with electrical equipment, out of hours, off site or with the public.
- Employers are responsible for the health, safety and welfare at work of their employees and the health and safety of those affected by the work. These responsibilities cannot be transferred to employees who work alone or without close supervision. It is the duty of employers to organise and control solitary workers. Employers have responsibilities to take reasonable care of themselves and other people affected by their work and co-operate with their employees in the discharge of their legal obligations.
- Risk assessments should be undertaken for all lone working situations, and control measures put in place. Special thought needs to be given to communication with people working alone and the provision of first aid in the event of an accident.

Legislation

- Health and Safety at Work etc. Act 1974.
- Management of Health and Safety at Work Regulations 1999.

What is lone working?

Lone working is a very common scen-ario, and for many organisations on financial grounds a necessary part of the way their business operates.

Activities such as cleaning are usually required to be undertaken out of work-ing hours, for the very reason that they cannot be carried out effectively while other work (e.g. in shops or offices) is going on. For this reason, cleaners will

---

often carry out their work in the morning, before normal office hours, or after the staff have left for the evening. On grounds of cost, cleaners often work unsupervised and alone. They might be arriving or leaving the workplace during the twilight hours of the morning or evening, and they might be the first people to discover any signs of a break-in or disturbance. Cleaners will generally be working with chemicals, liquids and electrical equipment, and are just as prone to slipping on wet floors as anyone else.

Security guarding is another example of lone working, where duties are frequently carried out by single workers in unsociable hours at isolated locations.

Other occupations such as consultants, estate agents and social services require a high proportion of lone working, where it is necessary to travel to a variety of locations, often to meet people in order to carry out their work.

Remember that lone working is not a formal categorisation of work: anyone who stays late at the office to finish off a report, or who pops in at the weekend to prepare for the coming week, is a lone worker.

Risk assessment

As an employer, you need to make sure that you are fully aware of all lone working that is going on in your organisation, whether it is undertaken by people who are employed by you directly (such as your sales force) or by people who work on your premises (such as your cleaners). You will need to carry out a risk assessment for lone working, and then put in place any control measures to make sure you are doing all that is reasonably practicable to ensure the safety and health of

the people who are working alone.

A risk assessment should be carried out for lone working as with other areas of risk in the workplace. A risk assessment for lone working needs to take particular account of the specific hazards associated with the work task, and of the people who are carrying it out. Every lone working situation will be different, but some common issues to consider are as follows:

- *Access to and egress from the place of work.* Can the lone worker get to and from the workplace safely? Is the work being carried out in a confined space?
- *Nature of the work.* What sort of work is being undertaken? Are lone workers dealing with the public, where they might face aggressive or violent behaviour? Do they have to carry heavy items, or work in outdoor weather conditions?
- *Location of work.* Where does the work take place? Where work is carried out by mobile workers or off site, the employer will have little control over first-aid provision and emergency procedures. Does work take place at height?
- *Time of work.* When does the work take place? We are all naturally tired first thing in the morning and last thing at night. Are there any increased risks related to the time of day, such as pub closing time or rush hour? According to research conducted in 2004, tired drivers are the cause of one in ten accidents.
- *Use of work equipment.* What, if any, work equipment do they need to use? Use of electrical equipment or machinery will increase the risk.

Don't forget that drivers will be using a very complex piece of work equipment – a car, van or truck – to carry out their work. Check that they have been trained how to use it.

• *People.* Who are the people who are working alone? You will need to consider their age, maturity, experience, health and fitness, and general state of mind. Where young people or new and expectant mothers are concerned, the risks will be increased.

An evaluation of the risks should highlight the control measures which are required to ensure work is carried out in a suitably safe manner. Some common control measures for lone workers are the following:

• *Redesign of the task to eliminate the need for lone working.* For example, by changing shift patterns to implement a buddy system where two people work together at all times.

• *Provision of information, instruction and training.* This might include training in the safe use of work equipment, or how to handle aggressive behaviour when dealing with the public.

• *Establishment of communication and supervision procedures.* To ensure that a manager is able to contact the worker at regular intervals; to make sure that arrangements in the case of an emergency have been put in place; and to check that a lone worker has arrived back safely once work has been completed.

• *Provision of mobile first-aid facilities.* To ensure that lone workers can deal with minor injuries themselves.

• *Health surveillance of lone workers.* At regular intervals, to ensure that workers are fit and healthy to carry out the tasks required of them.

See also: Confined spaces (page 142); Health surveillance (page 318).

Sources of further information

The HSE website contains a number of case studies of work-related violence which provide valuable insight into lone working situations, with real examples of occupations such as bus drivers, electrical engineers, estate agents, security guards, taxi drivers and window cleaners.

See www.hse.gov.uk/violence/loneworkers.htm.

INDG73REV 'Working alone in safety: controlling the risks of solitary work' (HSE Books, 1998): ISBN 0 7176 1507 3.

Machine guards and safety devices

David Sharp, Workplace Law Group

Key points

- Operation of dangerous work equipment requires the use of machine guards and other safety devices, as specified under the Provision and Use of Work Equipment Regulations 1998.
- According to HSE accident statistics there were 38 fatalities as a result of contact with moving machinery during 2002/3.
- Failure to ensure that machine guards are used properly is harder for employers to defend under health and safety legislation because the duty to comply is more stringent and does not allow them to take into account mitigating factors such as time, cost and inconvenience.

Legislation

- Health and Safety (Miscellaneous Amendments) Regulations 2002.
- Provision and Use of Work Equipment Regulations 1998.

Statutory requirements

Guards are fitted on machinery as a control measure to prevent the risk of accident or injury caused by contact with moving parts. Machine guarding is covered by the Provision and Use of Work Equipment Regulations 1998 (PUWER). Regulation 11 states that measures must be taken which:

- 'prevent access to any dangerous part of machinery or to any rotating stock-bar'; or

- 'stop the movement of any dangerous part of machinery or rotating stock-bar before any part of a person enters a danger zone'.

It is worth noting that this requirement under health and safety law is to do what is 'practicable' – not 'reasonably practicable' – to comply. What this means is that, unlike many of the employer's duties under health and safety law, there can be no argument about the time, cost or inconvenience it takes to make sure guards are used. The only justification can be whether there is no technical solution to protect workers from the dangerous machinery in question – an unlikely argument to win in the event of an accident.

Types of guard and safety device

There are a number of types of guard and control device to protect from dangerous machine parts, including the following:

- *Fixed guards*. These are always in position, and difficult to tamper with, but can restrict access and make cleaning difficult.
- *Adjustable guards*. These can be adjusted by the user, or automatically by the machine as work is passed through them. They allow better access, but increase accidental risk of contact with dangerous parts.
- *Interlocking guards*. These ensure that equipment can only be operated when a moveable part connects to the power source, so that they default to safe. A good example here is the door of a photocopier machine, which disconnects the power when opened.
- *Trip devices*. These detect the presence of an operator within a danger zone to shut off power, using trip switches, pressure pads or laser sensors.
- *Other measures*. These include two-handed control devices and hold-to-run controls, which default to safe if the operator releases them.

Risk control measures

One of the most common areas of risk with the use of machine guards is human intervention by the operator. This can be as a result of human error, in that guards have not been properly reinstated following cleaning or maintenance; or it can be as a result of overconfidence or negligence, where an operator thinks he can work faster or better without the guard in place. For these reasons, it is imperative that employers monitor work with dangerous machine parts closely and at regular intervals, carry out regular inspections to ensure the safe operation of guards and safety devices, and ensure that operators are provided with all the information, instruction, training and supervision that is necessary.

Recent and proposed changes

While PUWER remains substantially in force, some amendments were introduced under the Health and Safety (Miscellaneous Amendments) Regulations 2002 which affect the employer's approach to work with dangerous machine parts. The HSE had been concerned under the original regulations that there was too much leeway for employers to simply provide training and instruction to workers as a control measure when using dangerous machinery, instead of starting with the safest option of fitting fixed guards. Under the 2002 amending regulations, 'information, instruction, training and supervision' are now seen as an additional requirement, but not as one of the principal control measures to manage risk when working with dangerous machine parts.

The UK is required by the European Commission to report on the introduction of national legislation brought in to comply with European Directives. In autumn 2004 the UK Government reviewed the effectiveness of PUWER, and the report suggests that some minor changes might be in the pipeline during 2005.

Sources of further information

L22 'Safe use of work equipment. Provision and Use of Work Equipment Regulations as applied to woodworking. Approved Code of Practice and guidance' (HSE Books, 1998): ISBN 0 7176 1630 4.

INDG291 'Simple guide to the Provision and Use of Work Equipment Regulations 1998 (HSE Books, 1999): ISBN 0 7176 2429 3.

L112 'Safe use of power presses. Provision and Use of Work Equipment Regulations 1998 as applied to power presses. Approved Code of Practice and guidance' (HSE Books, 1998): ISBN 0 7176 1627 4.

L114 'Safe use of woodworking machinery. Provision and Use of Work Equipment Regulations 1998 as applied to woodworking. Approved Code of Practice and guidance' (HSE Books, 1998): ISBN 0 7176 1630 4.

Manual handling

Edited by Phil Wright, SafetyCO UK

Key points

The employer shall:

- so far as is reasonably practicable to do so, avoid the need for its employees to undertake any manual handling operations at work which involve a risk of their being injured;
- where it is not reasonably practicable to avoid the need for manual handling which involves the risk of injury:
  - assess the risk of all such manual handling operations, considering the factors set out in the table on page 381;
  - take appropriate steps to reduce the risk of injury to the lowest level reasonably practicable;
- take appropriate steps to provide its employees with general indications of the weight of each load and, so far as is reasonably practicable, precise information on the weight of each load and the heaviest side of any load; and
- ensure that any risk assessment made shall be reviewed if:
  - there is reason to suspect it is no longer valid; or
  - there has been a significant change in the manual handling operations to which it relates.

If, as a result of such review, changes are necessary, the employer should make them. Therefore, the employer's obligations under the Regulations are ongoing.

Legislation

- Manual Handling Operations Regulations 1992.

Employees' duties

Each employee, while at work, shall make full and proper use of any system of work provided for his use by his employer in accordance with the employer's duties.

Factors to which the employer must have regard and questions he must consider when making an assessment of manual handling operations are in the table on page 381.

Case law

In the case of *Hawkes -v- London Borough of Southwark* (1998), a carpenter, Mr Hawkes, employed by Southwark Council was asked by a supervisor to install some doors on each floor of a block of flats. The doors were heavier and more awk-

---

Factors to be considered in risk assessments of manual handling operations

Factors	Questions
1. The tasks	Do they involve: holding or manipulating loads at distance from trunk? unsatisfactory bodily movement or posture, especially: – twisting the trunk? – stooping? – reaching upwards? excessive movement of loads, especially: – excessive lifting or lowering distances? – excessive carrying distances? – excessive pushing or pulling of loads? risk of sudden movement of loads? frequent or prolonged physical effort? insufficient rest or recovery periods? a rate of work imposed by a process?
2. The loads	Are they: heavy? bulky or unwieldy? difficult to grasp? unstable, or with contents likely to shift? sharp, hot or otherwise potentially damaging?
3. The working environment	Are there: space constraints preventing good posture? uneven, slippery or unstable floors? variations in level of floors or work surfaces?
4. Individual capability	Does the job: require unusual strength or height? create a hazard to those who might reasonably be considered to be pregnant or to have a health problem? require special information or training for its safe performance?
5. Other factors	Is movement or posture hindered by personal protective equipment or by clothing?

ward to lift than ordinary internal doors and, as the flats had no lifts, they had to be carried up the stairs. When Mr Hawkes reached one of the landings and attempted to turn the door he was carrying, he lost his balance and fell down the stairs, injuring his foot. He claimed compensation on the grounds that there had been a breach of the Regulations. In particular, it was argued that there had been no risk assessment by his employer which would have identified the risk of any injury in carrying the doors.

The Court of Appeal commented that 'a proper risk assessment would have concluded that the task of moving the doors to where they would hang was a two-man job, so that the defendants [Southwark Council] would have been obliged to provide Mr Hawkes with some-

one who could help'.

The decision in Hawkes makes it clear that the onus is on the employer to demonstrate that appropriate steps have been taken.

See also: Construction site health and safety (page 145); Risk assessments (page 469).

Sources of further information

CRR346 'Second evaluation of the Manual Handling Operations Regulations 1992 and guidance' (HSE Books, 2001): ISBN 0 7176 2041 7.

INDG143REV2 'Getting to grips with manual handling: a short guide' (HSE Books, 2004): ISBN 0 7176 2828 0.

HSG15 'Manual handling: solutions you can handle' (HSE Books, 1994): ISBN 0 7176 0693 7.

HSG149 'Backs for the future: safe manual handling in construction' (HSE Books, 2000): ISBN 0 7176 1122 1.

Minimum wage

Pinsent Masons Employment Group

Key points

- The National Minimum Wage Act 1998 came into force on 1 April 1999. It provides for a single national minimum wage with no variations by region, occupation or size of company. It covers all relevant workers employed under a contract of employment or any other contract.
- The detailed rules of the national minimum wage (NMW) are contained in the National Minimum Wage Regulations 1999. These are updated annually with new minimum rates.
- All relevant workers must be paid the minimum hourly wage averaged across a 'relevant pay period'. The hourly rate was increased for workers aged 22 and over to £4.85 from October 2004.
- Rules exist to say what is relevant pay, and how relevant hours are calculated for different types of workers.
- The NMW applies to gross earnings and is calculated before tax, National Insurance contributions and any other deductions.
- Employers must keep records.
- Employment tribunals and Inland Revenue inspectors can enforce the duties of employers.

Legislation

Both the Act and the Regulations came into force on 1 April 1999.

Together, they introduced the concept of a national minimum wage together with employers' obligations and the mechanisms by which workers can enforce these obligations.

Hourly rates and other rules

The present hourly rate (which has been effective since October 2004) is £4.85 per hour for workers aged 22 and over. How-ever, there are four main exceptions to this:

- In October 2004 a new minimum rate of £3.00 per hour was introduced for those under 18 but above the school minimum leaving age.
- There is no minimum wage for apprentices under the age of 26 and in the first 12 months of an apprenticeship contract.
- The minimum wage for workers between the ages of 18 and 22 inclusive is currently £4.10 per hour.
- The minimum wage for workers

aged 22 or more who have agreed to undergo at least 26 days of 'accredited training' (which has a particular definition) within the first six months of their employment is currently £4.10 per hour.

According to the Act, the term 'worker' has a specific meaning. It is wider than the term 'employee' and covers a contractor carrying out services personally, unless the employer is the client or customer of the person involved. Truly self-employed people are not 'workers'.

Whether a worker has been paid the requisite minimum wage is determined by reference to his total pay over a relevant period. It is necessary to determine a worker's average minimum pay over a 'pay reference period'. This period is specified in the Act as one month unless the worker is specifically paid by reference to a shorter period (e.g. weekly or fortnightly).

In basic terms the calculation to determine if the minimum wage has been paid is the total relevant remuneration divided by hours worked in the pay reference period.

The Regulations contain detailed and complicated rules relating to pay reference periods, as well as how to calculate what remuneration actually counts towards assessing whether a worker is being paid the required amount. Further, only certain time will count in the calculation of hours worked – only 'working time' counts.

For example:

- travelling to and from home is not working time, but travelling for the purposes of duties during work is;
- time spent training at a different location from a worker's normal

place of work is working time; and

- deductions from wages due to an advance or overpayment of wages are not subtracted from the total remuneration.

Generally commission, bonuses and tips paid through payroll systems are included in relevant pay to calculate the hourly pay. Benefits in kind such as uniforms, meals and private health insurance do not count. The only benefit in kind which counts is accommodation. Gross pay figures should be used. Also, different types of workers will demand different consideration, particularly where hours vary from week to week. Those types of workers are:

- time workers (paid by hours worked in any event);
- salaried hours (an annual salary with set hours – e.g. 9 a.m. to 5 p.m.);
- output workers (e.g. piece workers, who should be paid for each hour or a 'fair estimate'); and
- unmeasured work (no specified hours – all hours worked should be paid for, but the employer and worker can enter into a 'daily average agreement' to clarify the position, although sometimes as with agricultural workers there are specific legal requirements as to what must be included).

Records

Employers are obliged to keep records which are sufficient to show that they have paid their workers the appropriate minimum wage. It is important that employers maintain sufficient records as they may be asked to prove that they are paying the NMW. A worker has the right to inspect these records if he believes he is being paid less than the required amount. An employer must respond to this request within 14 days (or a later date if one has been agreed between the employer and the worker).

Enforcement

If the employer fails to produce the relevant records, the worker is entitled to complain to an employment tribunal, which can impose a fine on the employer up to 80 times the relevant hourly minimum wage.

The Act implies a right to the NMW into contracts of employment, so a worker who has been underpaid can commence proceedings in an employment tribunal to recover the difference between the wages paid and the NMW. It is presumed that the worker has been underpaid unless the employer can prove otherwise.

The Home Secretary can appoint public officers, who have a variety of enforcement powers. These include powers to require employers to produce records to evidence compliance with the NMW, to require any relevant person to furnish them with additional information, and to gain access to premises for the carrying out of these powers.

Inspections and enforcement can be carried out by Inland Revenue inspectors.

The Act also creates a number of criminal offences, based on obligations under the Act. These include:

- refusing to pay the required minimum wage;
- failing to keep records proving that the minimum wage has been paid for three years;
- entering false information into these records; and
- obstructing a public officer.

See also: Working time (page 552); Young persons (page 561).

Sources of further information

The DTI page on the national minimum wage can be viewed at www.dti.gov.uk/er/nmw.

National Minimum Wage Helpline: 0845 6000 678.

Low Pay Commission: www.lowpay.gov.uk.

Mobile phone masts

Edited by Siobhan Cross, Pinsent Masons

Key points

- There are many opportunities for property owners to obtain revenue from the siting of mobile phone masts on buildings, and joint ventures between building owners and mobile network operators are becoming more common.
- There are also other opportunities for building owners to work with telecommunications companies to increase the services that are offered both to tenants of their buildings and to visitors, often sharing the resulting income with the operator.
- Ensure that the documentation is suitable for your needs. Operators will proffer a standard document, but you should take professional advice to ensure that the document represents the terms that have been agreed, is suitable for your needs and does not prejudice your property interests.

Mobile phone masts

All commercial property owners will have received requests from time to time from the four GSM mobile network operators – O2, Orange, T-Mobile and Vodafone – to permit installations of mobile network apparatus forming part of their networks on rooftops or other structures. The apparatus typically consists of a base transceiver station (BTS), normally housed in a small cabin or equipment room, together with an array of antennae used for receiving and transmitting signals both from subscribers and between cells forming the operator's network.

The arrangements in each case will also include a power supply for the BTS, and an arrangement for the connection of the BTS to the fixed-wire network. This is usually achieved by way of a fibre-optic connection from the BTS direct to a fixed-wire network (usually BT), or by use of a microwave dish which sends the signal to the nearest convenient point where it can be connected to the fixed network.

Third-generation networks

Another opportunity available for property owners is to work with the five third-generation (3G) licensees (the four GSM licensees plus Hutchison 3G) in connection with the construction of their 3G networks. The technology involves cells of a very much smaller size than is the case with GSM traffic. It follows that there will be a need for many more base stations, and these are required in a hurry as the operators are keen to re-cover the substantial sums that they have already paid to the Government for the spectrum licences.

Tower companies

A third opportunity for property owners is to deal with a set of new intermediary players, known as 'tower companies', which instead of building one base station tower for one operator are now building larger towers and renting the antenna space out to multiple operators. The property owner can either enter into a partnership agreement with a tower company in respect of the rights to site towers on its buildings or other property, or appoint the tower company as a managing agent.

Other opportunities

Other opportunities for joint ventures between property owners and telecoms companies include the following:

- Installation of in-building systems. These will permit users within a limited area – shopping centres, airports, holiday camps – to receive services without interference. The necessary infrastructure is expensive to install (e.g. the equipment for a regional shopping centre might cost £500,000) and therefore tends to be shared between operators. The landowner benefits from receiving a share of the revenue and making the property more attractive to visitors, tenants and other users of the property.
- Installation of high-speed connections, to allow organisations to have permanent connections to the Internet. Larger organisations can afford their own connections, but it is also

possible for smaller organisations to obtain such facilities by joining forces. Landlords of office buildings are in an ideal position to provide such services to their tenants, in partnership with so-called building local exchange carriers (BLECs). Once again, the landlord can expect to share the revenues while the BLEC bears the installation costs. Such a system can be expected to make a building more attractive to potential tenants.

Typical contents of a telecommunications agreement

The contents of telecoms agreements vary according to the circumstances, but typically will include provisions regulating:

- the type of arrangement to be created (lease, licence and so on) and how long it is to last for;
- the exact location of the site;
- the amount of the rent, whether it is subject to review and, if so, on what basis;
- any rights of way (or other rights – e.g. power or fibre) that the operator will need;
- the obligations to be undertaken by each party;
- whose responsibility it is to obtain planning permission if this is required;
- the type and amount of equipment to be installed;
- whether subletting or sharing is to be permitted and, if so, on what terms; and,
- if the arrangement is by lease, whether it should be excluded from the security-of-tenure provisions of the Landlord and Tenant Act 1954.

Operators have standard agreements that they will proffer, but they may not be suitable for every transaction and will need to be checked carefully with the help of professional advice.

Electronic Communications Code

Telecoms operators may enjoy various rights under the Electronic Communications Code, which is part of the Telecommunications Act 1984 (as amended by the Communications Act 2003). Those rights can make it difficult to remove them from property at the end of an agreement with them. Professional advice will be needed on the implications of these rights in the light of any particular building, as well as on the terms of the agreement itself.

Health concerns

There have been some well-publicised health and safety issues recently in relation to mobile phones network equipment. Research is continuing, but for the present the perceived risks arising from these will need to be managed and apportioned between the parties within the agreement between them.

See also: Landlord and tenant: lease issues (page 345).

Money laundering

Elizabeth Robertson, Fraud Regulatory Department, Peters & Peters

Key points

- Anti-money laundering law has never been a more prominent subject.
- The impetus behind the drive of governments worldwide to implement legislation to combat money laundering was given extra force by the events of 11 September 2001.
- Attention has increasingly focused on 'gatekeepers', the professionals such as lawyers, tax advisors and accountants who have become an essential resource to the criminals who need to 'clean' huge sums of money made from the proceeds of crime.
- Businesses and professionals need to consider the new substantive money laundering and tipping-off offences that apply to everyone. In addition, the widened regulated sector is obliged to appoint money laundering reporting officers (MLROs) and implement training and record-keeping regimes.

Legislation

- Part 7, Proceeds of Crime Act 2002.
- Money Laundering Regulations 2003.
- Terrorism Act 2000.
- Anti-terrorism, Crime and Security Act 2001.

Main cases

- *P -v- P* [2003] EWHC Fam 2260.

Proceeds of Crime Act 2002

The Proceeds of Crime Act (POCA) consolidates and amends earlier anti-money laundering legislation. Separate offences for terrorist financing are now covered by the Terrorism Act 2000.

Prior to February 2003 the money laundering offence was limited to the proceeds of indictable crime, drugs and terrorism. POCA has now extended that definition to the proceeds of *any* criminal conduct. The definition in section 340(2) of the Act also means that a prosecution can be made for conduct committed outside the UK which would be an offence if it were carried out in the UK. It is not necessary to prove that it would also be an offence in the foreign jurisdiction.

- Sections 327, 328 and 329 define the substantive money laundering offences and apply to everyone.
- Section 327: concealing, disguising, converting, transferring or removing criminal property.

- Section 328: entering into or becoming concerned with an arrangement which one knows or suspects facilitates the acquisition, retention, use or control of criminal property.
- Section 329: acquisition, use and having possession of criminal property.

The maximum punishment for the above offences is 14 years' imprisonment.

There are several defences to sections 327 to 329. Section 338 provides that an authorised disclosure can be made before a 'prohibited act' occurs, i.e. before any concealing, arranging or acquiring takes place. It will be necessary to receive the appropriate consent before completing any transaction which would amount to a 'prohibited act'. If a voluntary report is made to the National Criminal Intelligence Service (NCIS) and the appropriate consent is given, there should be a defence to a charge under sections 327 to 329. Professionals and banks may find it difficult to provide a client with a credible reason for the delay while waiting for permission to transact from NCIS.

Section 335 provides time limits for the delay between the authorised disclosure being made and the appropriate consent being given or presumed.

Section 330 sets out the offence of failure to report, which is limited to the regulated sector. The new offence of failure to report will apply not only where a person has knowledge or suspicion but also where a person should have reasonable grounds for knowledge or suspicion (the 'objective' test). It provides a defence for a legal advisor receiving information in 'privileged circumstances' and a 'reasonable excuse' defence. An employee will also have a defence if he has not received appropriate training from his employer (section 330(7)).

Sections 333 and 342 set out the tipping-off offences and, again, apply to everyone. Tipping off occurs when someone who knows or suspects that disclosure to NCIS has been made then makes a disclosure which is likely to prejudice a subsequent investigation. If a person does not know or suspect that a disclosure is likely to prejudice any investigation which might be conducted as a result of that disclosure he will not commit the offence of tipping off.

Money Laundering Regulations 2003

The Money Laundering Regulations (the Regulations) have implemented the Second EU Money Laundering Directive. The Directive, passed in December 2001, progresses the EU gatekeepers' initiative to impose anti-money laundering procedural and reporting obligations on lawyers, accountants and other 'gatekeepers'.

The Regulations came into force on 1 March 2004 and create an extended regulated sector.

The Regulations are directed at all those whose activities comprise 'relevant business' including accountants, tax advisors, estate agents, independent financial advisors, antique dealers and other high value dealers (HVDs) (see Regulation 2(2)). A variety of new businesses will therefore be caught by the Regulations.

Practical implications of the legislation

Everyone must be aware of the law under POCA, which governs everyone and imposes new stricter duties on the regulated sector.

The main impact in the UK has been the extension of the regulated sector to include gatekeepers who will now have to set up anti-money laundering procedures in their businesses in order to comply with the Regulations.

Many firms and individuals will have been subject to money laundering legislation/regulations for some years and will therefore have had to put into place certain anti-money laundering systems and controls. Under the Regulations every person who carries out relevant business in the UK must:

- comply with the requirements of Regulations 4 (identification procedures), 6 (record-keeping procedures) and 7 (internal reporting procedures);
- establish such other procedures of internal control and communications as may be appropriate for the purposes forestalling and preventing money laundering; and
- take appropriate measures so that employees are:
  – made aware of the provisions of the Regulations and of section 340(11); and
  – given training in how to recognise and deal with transactions which may be related to money laundering.

The four key elements are as follows:

- Knowing your customer (identification procedures).
- Record-keeping procedures.
- Internal reporting procedures

including designating someone as the MLRO.
- Training for all staff.

Within each firm, the MLRO has the greatest responsibility for ensuring compliance with the Regulations. The post carries with it the additional potential liability to commit a criminal offence under sections 331, 332 and 336 of POCA.

Regulation 7(1)(a) refers to a person being 'designated as the MLRO'. Whether it is a partner who is designated or someone else suitably qualified, the MLRO must have the full backing of those who control the organisation.

In order to ensure compliance, businesses must implement and maintain systems and procedures in accordance with Regulations 4 to 7 inclusive. They must also ensure that all staff are given training as required by Regulation 3(1)(c), especially training 'in how to recognise and deal with transactions which may be related to money laundering'. Ensuring that staff are properly trained is imperative. As mentioned above, this is underlined by section 330(7) of POCA, which provides a defence for an employee who has not been trained to recognise and deal with transactions involving money laundering.

The cost of training and complying with the new law is sure to have a big impact, but the consequences of non-compliance in terms of loss of reputation and possible criminal penalty are extremely serious.

Monitoring employees

Paula Hargaden, Bird & Bird

The monitoring of emails, Internet use and telephone calls by both public and private organisations has become a highly discussed topic. Many organisations have a legitimate need to record commercial transactions, to monitor the quality of service being provided and in some circumstances to monitor their employees' activities. Organisations which undertake such monitoring should be aware of the rights of monitored employees and of any third party (e.g. customers) who might be caught by such monitoring. Organisations should also be aware of their obligations under the law and any best practice guidance available. The consequences of implementing monitoring incorrectly include:

- damage to employment and public relations;
- complaints to the Information Commissioner's Office; and
- use in employment tribunal proceedings.

This article should be read in conjunction with those on 'CCTV monitoring' (page 127) and 'Data protection' (page 163).

Human Rights Act 1998

The Human Rights Act 1998 (HRA) came into force on 2 October 2000 and requires the UK courts and tribunals to give effect to the rights under the European Convention for the Protection of Human Rights and Fundamental Freedoms. Under the HRA, it is unlawful for a public authority to act in a way which is incompatible with a Convention right, and therefore actions can certainly be brought against public authorities for Convention violations. However, it is less clear whether the HRA can be applied in private law actions, e.g. by one company against another. There are those that argue that the courts themselves are public authorities and therefore have a duty to apply Convention principles when they are adjudicating any dispute, not just proceedings against another public authority.

Even if the Convention is not directly applicable to private parties, it seems that the courts will be influenced by and will gradually apply Convention principles in all forms of litigation. For example, Oftel, the former telecommunications industry regulator, in its guidance on the recording of employees' private telephone calls (Oftel press release, 19 August 1999), simply assumed that the HRA would apply to all companies and not just to public authorities. It is likely, therefore, that the HRA will have an indirect but powerful influence on private law rights and obligations.

Therefore, when considering any monitoring activity, organisations should be aware of and understand the impact of Article 8 of the HRA, which provides that: 'Everyone has the right to respect for his private and family life, his home and correspondence.'

Regulation of Investigatory Powers Act 2000

The introduction of the Regulation of Investigatory Powers Act 2000 (RIPA) in October 2000 laid down the legal basis for monitoring. RIPA, which replaced the earlier Interception of Communications Act, sets out provisions for authorising surveillance and specifically addressing the legality of surveillance over some private networks.

Like the earlier legislation, RIPA makes it an offence to intercept a communication in the course of its transmission by means of a public telecommunications system or postal service.

RIPA also makes it a criminal offence to intercept a communication made over certain private telecommunications systems which are attached to a public telecommunications system. For the interception to be caught by this provision, it must be intentional, made without lawful authority and made without the authority of the person who controls the operation or use of the system. As an organisation will have the right to control the use of its own private telecommunications system, its subsequent decisions to intercept communications would clearly not amount to a criminal offence. This provision will not therefore restrict organisations from carrying out monitoring over their own networks.

Section 1(3) of RIPA will, however, restrict monitoring by organisations. This provides that anyone who intercepts a communication over a private network may be liable to the sender or the recipient, or intended recipient, of the communication that is intercepted. However,

as there are many legitimate occasions on which an organisation would wish to monitor communications, RIPA sets out some broad exceptions to this principle.

Section 4(2) of RIPA also gives the Secretary of State the power to implement Regulations to authorise conduct which appears to him to constitute a legitimate practice required by a business in order to monitor or keep a record of business communications. It is under this authority that the Telecommunications (Lawful Business Practice) (Interception of Communication) Regulations 2000 were introduced.

The Regulations only authorise the interception of communications wholly or partly in connection with an organisation's business and only if such interception is effected solely for the purpose of monitoring or keeping a record of communications relevant to the organisation's business. This would mean, for example, that if an organisation makes available an Internet terminal or a telephone in the staff canteen solely for the employees' private use and not in connection with the employer's business, then the organisation would not be entitled to intercept any such communications under the Regulations.

The Regulations do authorise employers to intercept communication without consent in order to:

- establish the existence of facts relevant to the business;
- ascertain compliance with relevant regulatory or self-regulatory practices and procedures;
- ascertain the standards achieved by employees (i.e. quality checking);
- prevent or detect crime;
- investigate or detect unauthorised

use of the telecommunications system; and

• ensure the system's security and effective operation.

In order to obtain the benefit of the Regulations, the organisation must also make all reasonable efforts to inform users of the system that communications may be intercepted. 'Users' has been interpreted by the DTI to mean employees and others using the organisation's system for the purposes of receiving and making outbound calls (but not people calling into the system).

For employers who are public authorities, RIPA also imposes supplemental restrictions on their ability to carry out covert monitoring. Surveillance is covert if it is carried out in a manner that is calculated to ensure that persons who are subject to the surveillance are unaware that it is or may be taking place.

Data Protection Act 1998

Where monitoring of employees involves the processing of personal data, the Data Protection Act 1998 (DPA) will apply (see 'Data protection' (page 163)) and employers will need to comply with any relevant obligations under the DPA. This will be the case particularly where monitoring is automatic (e.g. the automatic recording and monitoring of telephone calls, emails and Internet access). Monitoring which is not done automatically but which creates paper records that are then entered into a computer system or are filed in a structured filing system will also be covered. However, if an organisation arranges for a supervisor to listen into a call but no record of the call is made, then the DPA is not relevant – although other legislation such as RIPA

may still need to be considered.

There are two key provisions in the DPA that affect monitoring:

• transparency; and
• proportionality/necessity.

In order to establish transparency, the fair processing code in the DPA obliges organisations to inform individuals about whom they collect personal data as to the purpose of the processing – including, in this case, monitoring. The individuals should not be misled as to the purposes for which the information was obtained and are also entitled to know the identity of the party controlling the information.

The data protection principles further provide that personal data may only be collected where it is necessary for one of the lawful bases for processing, and where it is relevant and not excessive for the purpose for which it is collected. It must not be retained longer than is necessary.

These tests of transparency, necessity and proportionality are, in broad terms, consistent with the principle stated at a high level in Article 8(2) of the European Convention of Human Rights.

It is important to remember that the Information Commissioner, as a public authority, is bound to act in a way which is consistent with Convention rights. This will extend to interpreting the DPA so as to promote these principles.

Organisations should be particularly careful if it is possible that sensitive personal data, such as information about an individual's health, could be captured by monitoring as there are stricter requirements for the processing of such data.

The DPA grants the individuals' rights to compensation and rectification, blocking, erasure and destruction of personal data. A monitored individual will also have the right to be provided with copies of all information held about him. The Information Commissioner may also be able to take action against organisations which do not comply with their obligations under the DPA.

Employment Practices Code

The Information Commissioner has issued an Employment Practices Code for the use of personal data in employer–employee relationships. The Code has no specific legal status and there are no specific sanctions for failing to comply with this Code. However, it provides an indication as to how the Commissioner will apply the DPA and it is possible that employment tribunals may have regard to the Code.

Part 3 of the Code is concerned with processing, which the Information Commissioner classifies as 'monitoring'. The Code suggests that this means: 'Activities that set out to collect information about workers by keeping them under some form of observation, normally with a view to checking their performance or conduct. This could be done either directly, indirectly, perhaps by examining their work output, or by electronic means.'

Some of the examples of monitoring are exactly the kinds of activity that one would expect to be covered. For example:

- using automated software to check whether a worker is sending or receiving inappropriate emails;
- randomly checking emails to detect evidence of malpractice;
- examining logs of websites or telephone numbers to check for inap-

propriate use; and
- use of CCTV cameras – e.g. to ensure compliance with health and safety rules.

The Code also covers some activities that one may not have expected to be covered. So, for example, it would also apply to electronic point of sale information gathered through checkout terminals used to monitor the efficiency of checkout operators and videoing workers to collect evidence of malingering. The Code is also intended to cover information obtained through credit reference agencies to check that workers are not in financial difficulty.

The key message in the Code is that monitoring must be proportionate. In the Commissioner's view monitoring is an interference with workers' privacy which is permissible only where 'any adverse impact of monitoring on workers [can] be justified by its benefit to the employer and/or others'.

The Code provides employers with detailed guidance to help organisations ensure that monitoring is proportionate. Recommendations cover:

- carrying out impact assessments;
- notifying employees with a sufficient level of detail that monitoring is being carried out;
- ensuring that information collected through monitoring is only used for the purpose for which it was collected;
- ensuring that information collected through monitoring is stored in a secure way and access is limited;
- ensuring that individuals can gain access to monitoring information if requested in a subject access request;
- providing monitored individuals

with an opportunity to make representations; and

- ensuring that the organisation can meet any necessary condition in the DPA if it is collecting sensitive personal data.

There is also guidance concerning specific types of monitoring, such as the monitoring of electronic communications, video and audio monitoring, and covert monitoring.

The Code suggests that organisations should adopt a policy on the monitoring of electronic communications which states that video and audio monitoring is intrusive and justifiable only in restricted circumstances and that covert monitoring is rarely acceptable.

Regulation of Investigatory Powers Orders

The Enterprise Act 2002 gave new powers of surveillance to the Office of Fair Trading (OFT) for the purposes of investigating cartel activities. Sections 199 and 200 of the Enterprise Act 2002 amended the Regulation of Investigatory Powers Act 2000 to grant the OFT the powers of intrusive surveillance and property interference.

In addition to the Enterprise Act powers, the Regulation of Investigatory Powers (Directed Surveillance and Covert Human Intelligence Sources) Order 2003 has added the OFT to a list of bodies given certain powers under RIPA.

The legislation allows:

- authorised OFT officers access to communications data such as telephone records;
- authorised OFT officers to conduct directed surveillance (e.g. watching a person's office); and
- the use of covert human intelligence sources (i.e. the use of informants).

The OFT can only exercise these powers after authorisation by a senior OFT official and following the Home Office Codes of Practice. The OFT is subject to regular inspection by the Interception Commissioner and the Surveillance Commissioners to ensure the powers are used appropriately.

The power of access to communications data is only available to the OFT in the investigation of criminal cartel cases under the Enterprise Act 2002. The

---

Sources of further information

The Employment Practices Code can be found at the Information Commissioner's website: www.informationcommissioner.gov.uk.

Information about the OFT's powers can be found on its website: www.oft.gov.uk.

Information about RIPA can be found on the Home Office site: www.homeoffice.gov.uk.

'Data Protection Policy and Management Guide, version 1.0' (ISBN 1 900648 33 4, £34.99) is available as an electronic download from the Workplace Law Network. Call 0870 777 8881 for details, or visit www.workplacelaw.net.

---

powers do not enable the OFT to obtain details about the content of the calls or other communications, but only details of the times, duration and recipients of communications.

Authorisations to use the power can only be given when they are necessary and proportionate in order to investigate a cartel.

The OFT officers can also carry out directed surveillance, i.e to observe a person with the objective of gathering private information to obtain a detailed picture of the person's life, activities and associations.

Summary

The recording and monitoring of phone calls, emails and Internet access is legally and politically sensitive. If organisations intend to record or monitor communications, they should first establish a coherent policy that meets all relevant legislative requirements. Part 3 of the Employment Practices Code should be a help to organisations in adopting monitoring policies that are likely to be successful and that avoid the legal pitfalls outlined above.

> *See also*: CCTV monitoring (page 127); Data protection (page 163).

New and expectant mothers

Ciaron Dunne, Workplace Law Group

Key points

- Employers must carry out risk assessments for new and expectant mothers.
- If the risks cannot be controlled, the employer may need to change the working conditions, offer alternative employment, or suspend the employee on full pay.
- New and expectant mothers have special protection under employment law, including the protection from being dismissed for any reason connected with the pregnancy.

Legislation

- Workplace (Health, Safety and Welfare) Regulations 1992.
- Management of Health and Safety at Work Regulations 1999.
- Maternity and Parental Leave etc. Regulations 1999.
- Maternity and Parental Leave (Amendment) Regulations 2002.

Health and safety

By 'new and expectant mothers', the Management of Health and Safety at Work Regulations 1999 specifically mean women who are pregnant, have given birth within the previous six months (including still-born births and miscarriages), or are breastfeeding. The Regulations set out what measures employers must take in relation to the health and safety of new and expectant mothers, as follows.

Risk assessments

The Regulations require employers to carry out specific risk assessments for new or expectant mothers (Regulation 16).

The employer must make sure that the employee's (and the baby's) health is not put at risk by the kind of work undertaken, the working conditions, and any chemical or biological agents used. This is the procedure to be followed:

- The employer must carry out a workplace risk assessment and do all that is reasonable to remove or reduce the risks found.
- If there are still risks, the employer must change working conditions or hours of work to remove the risk;
- if this is not possible or would not avoid the risk, the employer must offer a suitable alternative job (at the same rate of pay);
- if this is not possible, the employer

Risk assessment checklist

The HSE provides the following checklist for identifying hazards which could affect new and expectant mothers:

Physical hazards
Awkward spaces and workstations
Vibration
Noise
Radiation

Biological agents
Infections

Chemical hazards
For example, chemical handling (handling drugs or specific chemicals such as pesticides, lead, etc.)

Working conditions
Inadequate facilities (including restrooms)
Excessive working hours (e.g. night work)
Unusually stressful work
Exposure to cigarette smoke
High or low temperatures
Lone working
Work at heights
Travelling
Exposure to violence

can suspend the employee on full pay for as long as necessary.

Notification

The employer is not required to take any action in relation to an employee until she has notified the employer in writing of the pregnancy (Regulation 18).

Night work

New and expectant mothers can be exempted from night work by a medical certificate from a doctor or midwife (Regulation 17). The employer should either find suitable alternative employment for the employee (at the same rate

of pay) or – if that is not possible – suspend the employee on full pay for as long as necessary.

Rest facilities

Furthermore, the Workplace (Health, Safety and Welfare) Regulations 1992 require employers to provide suitable rest facilities for pregnant or nursing employees.

Employment

New and expectant mothers are also entitled to special protection by employment law. Maternity leave, maternity pay, time off for antenatal care, detrimental treatment, return to work, and pregnancy-related dismissals are covered in 'Family-friendly rights', page 251. The rights can be summarised as follows:

- Pregnant employees are entitled to time off for antenatal care (when recommended by a doctor or midwife). The employee is entitled to be paid at her normal rate during such time off.
- Employees are protected from any unfair treatment related to pregnancy.
- Employers cannot dismiss (or select for redundancy) employees for any reason connected with the pregnancy.
- If an employee is dismissed during pregnancy or maternity leave, she is entitled to a written statement of the reasons.
- All pregnant employees are entitled to 26 weeks' ordinary maternity leave. Pregnant employees who have completed 26 weeks' continuous employment by the beginning of the fourteenth week before the expected week of childbirth are entitled to 26 weeks' additional maternity leave.
- An employee is not allowed to return to work within two weeks of childbirth (or four weeks if she works in a factory).
- Normally, an employee who resumes work after ordinary maternity leave is entitled to return to the same job on the same terms and conditions as if she had not been absent, or a suitable alternative.
- Parents with children under 6 years old are entitled to request flexible working arrangements.

See also: Discrimination (page 189); Family-friendly rights (page 251); Flexible working (page 280); Health and safety management (page 311); Risk assessments (page 469).

Sources of further information

HSE website on health and safety for new and expectant mothers: www.hse.gov.uk/mothers/index.htm.

HSG122 'New and expectant mothers at work: a guide for employers' (HSE Books, 2002): ISBN 0 7176 2583 4.

'Maternity rights – A guide for employers and employees' (DTI): www.dti.gov.uk/er/individual/matrights-pl958.pdf.

Night working

Pinsent Masons Employment Group

Key points

Employers should ascertain whether they employ workers who would be classified as night workers. If so, they should check:

- how much working time night workers normally work;
- if night workers work more than eight hours per day on average, whether the amount of hours can be reduced and if any exceptions apply;
- how to conduct a health assessment and how often health checks should be carried out;
- that proper records of night workers are maintained, including details of health assessments; and
- that night workers are not involved in work which is particularly hazardous.

Legislation

- Working Time Regulations 1998.

The Working Time Regulations provide basic rights for workers in terms of maximum hours of work, rest periods and holidays. Night workers are afforded special protection by the Regulations. Depending on when they work, workers can be labelled 'night workers'.

Once that label is applied, an employer must take all reasonable steps to ensure that the normal hours of a night worker do not exceed an average of eight hours for each 24 hours over a 17-week reference period (which can be extended in certain circumstances). In addition, an employer must offer night workers a free health assessment before they start working nights and on a regular basis

thereafter. The other provisions in the Regulations relating to rest breaks and holidays apply equally to night workers.

What is night-time?

Night-time is a period of at least seven hours which includes the hours of midnight to 5 a.m. These hours can be varied through particular forms of agreement, but in the absence of such an agreement night-time is usually 11 p.m. until 6 a.m. A 'night worker' is any worker whose daily working time includes at least three hours of night-time:

- on the majority of days he works;
- on such a proportion of days he works as is agreed between employers and workers in a collective or workforce agreement; or
- sufficiently often that he may be

said to work such hours as a normal course, i.e. on a regular basis.

If workers work less than 48 hours on average per week, they will not exceed the night work limits.

Special hazards

Where a night worker's work involves special hazards or heavy physical or mental strain, there is an absolute limit of eight hours on any of the worker's working days. No average is allowed. Work involves a 'special hazard' if either:

- it is identified as such between an employer and workers in a collective agreement or workforce agreement; or
- it poses a significant risk as identified by a risk assessment which an employer has conducted under the Management of Health and Safety at Work Regulations 1999.

Health assessment

All employers must offer night workers a free health assessment before they begin working nights and thereafter on a regular basis. Workers do not have to undergo a health assessment, but they must be offered one.

All employers should maintain up-to-date records of health assessments. A health assessment can comprise two parts: a medical questionnaire and a medical examination. It should take into account the type of work that the worker will do and any restrictions on the worker's working time under the Working Time Regulations. Employers are advised to take medical advice on the contents of a medical questionnaire.

New and expectant mothers

New and expectant mothers have certain special rights in relation to night work (see 'New and expectant mothers', page 398).

See also: Health surveillance (page 318); Lone working (page 374); New and expectant mothers (page 398); Working time (page 552).

Sources of further information

DTI guidance on night working is available online at www.dti.gov.uk/er/work_time_regs/wtr3.htm.

Noise at work

Andrew Richardson, Scott Wilson

Key points

- Employers have a legal duty to safeguard their employees' hearing.
- Employers must assess the risks of hearing loss and implement risk control measures.
- There are three action levels of daily personal noise exposure.
- Employers must take at least the stated measures to reduce noise exposure, from providing ear protection or installing soundproof enclosures to using quieter processes or equipment.
- Control measures may include health surveillance, where noise exposure levels are significant.

Legislation

- Health and Safety at Work etc. Act 1974.
- Management of Health and Safety at Work Regulations 1999.
- Noise at Work Regulations 1989.

Statutory requirements

Hearing loss can be greatly reduced if machinery manufactured is quieter, if employers introduce policies and risk control measures to reduce exposure to noise, and if the employees utilise the risk control measures.

Under the Health and Safety at Work etc. Act 1974 an employer has a legal duty to safeguard its employees. Under the Management of Health and Safety at Work Regulations 1999 there is a duty to carry out risk assessments, implement risk control measures and where necessary carry out health surveillance.

The Noise at Work Regulations 1989 require the employer to carry out noise assessments using the following five basic steps:

1. Identify where there is likely to be a noise hazard.
2. Identify all workers likely to be exposed to the hazard.
3. Evaluate the risks arising from the hazard and establish the noise exposure.
4. Record the findings.
5. Review the assessments and revise as necessary.

Employers have an overriding duty to reduce the risk of damage to their employees' hearing from exposure to the noise to the lowest level reasonably practicable.

However, the Regulations identify

---

various action levels at which various actions need to be taken by the employer. These levels include reference to daily personal noise exposure, which is defined as the personal exposure to noise at work (over an eight-hour day), taking account of the average levels of noise in working areas and the time spent in them but not including the wearing of any ear defenders or protectors.

The action levels are as follows:

- First action level: a daily personal noise exposure of 85dB(A).
- Second action level: a daily personal noise exposure of 90dB(A).
- Peak action level: a peak sound pressure of 200 pascals (140dB(C)).

If an employee is exposed to the first action level or above, but below the second action level, then the employer must provide suitable and sufficient personal ear protection. However, it is not compulsory for workers to use it.

If an employee is exposed to the second action level or above or to the peak action level or above, then the exposure to the noise must be reduced so far as is reasonably practicable (excluding the provision of ear protection). An example would be the provision of a soundproof enclosure.

If it is not reasonably practicable to reduce the noise, then an ear protection zone must be demarcated and identified, ear protection must be provided to all workers likely to be exposed, the employer must ensure it is being worn and the employer must provide information on how to obtain that protection.

With the exception of ear defenders issued because of exposure between the first and second action levels, the employer has to ensure that all other equipment and ear protection is utilised and maintained in a suitable manner. This will mean regular checks on the use and condition.

Employees have a duty to comply with and use the measures the employer introduces and to report any defects or difficulties in complying with the Regulations. Information, instruction and training have to be provided for all employees likely to be exposed to the first action level or above.

Future changes

A European Directive, the Physical Agents (Noise) Directive (2003/10/EC), was adopted by the UK in 2002 and came into effect in February 2003. This Directive tightens the legal requirements in relation to noise by lowering the exposure action values to 80db(A) and 85dB(A). The

---

Sources of further information

The HSE has published L108 'Reducing noise at work – guidance on the Noise at Work Regulations' (HSE Books, 2000): ISBN 0 7176 1511 1. The document provides all the guidance needed by employers and identifies any further documentation that is relevant.

Basic HSE advice 'Noise at work – advice for employers' can be downloaded at www.hse.gov.uk/pubns/indg362.pdf.

Noise at Work Regulations must be replaced with new Regulations within three years.

The HSC published a consultation doc-ument in April 2004, and consultation closed in June 2004. The new Regulations are expected early in 2006.

Nuisance

Edited by Michael Brandman, Tarlo Lyons

Key points

- A nuisance may arise by reason of unjustified acts or omissions in the occupation or use of land or property.
- Some nuisances can be the subject of private civil law claims whereas others constitute criminal offences or are enforced by local authorities.

Private nuisance

A private nuisance is an unjustified act or omission connected with the use or occupation of property which causes damage to neighbouring property or its use or enjoyment.

You may encounter a nuisance either when you are adversely affected by a situation or when another party claims that a nuisance has been committed by you. Generally only a person or organisation which is in occupation or legal control of the affected land may take legal action concerning a private nuisance.

Private nuisance problems may lead to litigation or be settled by some form of mediation. Specialist legal advice is usually necessary. Evidence for or against the nuisance is always crucial, so formal records and other evidence should be kept. Certain defences are allowable to specific nuisances.

In most cases a claimant must prove a legal right of occupation of his land (e.g. as a leaseholder). However, departing from the previously accepted law, in a recent case a 'tolerated trespasser' with exclusive possession was allowed to sue a local authority.

There must be provable damage, whether direct damage to land, interference or encroachment.

Normally the damage caused must have been reasonably foreseeable by the person who caused the damage.

Liability may lie with more than one party at the same time.

A number of specialist defences can be raised by a defendant.

Certain types of 'damage' may not be claimed. For example, personal injury claims cannot be made in private nuisance.

Examples of private nuisance

- Structural damage as a result of piledriving.
- Resurfacing of a driveway so that water flows onto a neighbour's land causing damage.
- Allowing a building to become so dilapidated or infested that the building, or part of it, falls onto

---

neighbouring land or the claimant's property is affected by vermin or damp.

- Encroachments, e.g. tree branches overgrowing neighbouring property or tree roots growing into neighbouring land. Tree problems are very often the cause of private nuisance actions. They are also often encountered in boundary disputes.

- Noise nuisance, e.g. from persistent loud music. This is a very commonly encountered nuisance and one where the local authority can be involved (see 'Statutory nuisance' below).

- Loss of amenity caused by smoke, fumes, vibration, smells or dust. In regard to this type of private nuisance and noise nuisance, the locality must be considered as well as the conduct. While conduct may be a nuisance in one area, it may be tolerated in another. Compare (a) a residential estate with (b) an industrial estate.

Adopted nuisance

A nuisance need not have been originally created by a defendant if, with knowledge, he has adopted or acquiesced in it – e.g. a new occupier does nothing to prevent damage caused by encroaching tree roots.

Rylands -v- Fletcher

The rule in *Rylands -v- Fletcher* arises from a 1865 court case. This established a tort (civil wrong) whereby a defendant would be strictly liable for all foreseeable consequences where damage was caused by the escape of something dangerous which had accumulated on the land for some 'non-natural' purpose. The original

case concerned a leak of water from a reservoir.

- The absence of wilful default or negligence by the defendant is irrelevant.

- The substance that 'escapes' must as a result be likely to do mischief.

- The substance must have accumulated on the land and escaped from the land.

- Damages can only be claimed in respect of damage to the land or to objects on the land.

- The damage must have been foreseeable by the defendant as a result of the escape.

- Certain defences to strict liability are recognised – e.g. Act of God or acts by trespassers or strangers which result in the damage.

Examples of the application of Rylands -v-Fletcher

- An electric current discharging into the ground.
- Explosives.

However, the escape of water from a sewer serving a block of flats was recently held to be non-actionable on the basis that the sewer was an ordinary incident of domestic activity.

Public nuisance

A public nuisance is a criminal offence.

An individual claimant who wishes to pursue a civil claim in public nuisance must prove that the nuisance affects a widespread class of people as opposed to an individual alone.

The class of people affected can be broad, e.g. all the staff of a building or a group of neighbours.

A civil claimant must prove special

damage, which goes beyond damage suffered by others affected by the same circumstances. For that reason private claims in public nuisance areas are rare. Any sort of damage can be the subject of compensation.

Examples of public nuisance

- Highway nuisance such as obstructions on the highway.
- Dangerous premises abutting the highway.
- Impeding rights of access to and from property adjoining the highway.

Statutory nuisance

Certain types of nuisance are also subject to statutory control. The Environmental Protection Act 1990 (EPA) covers many statutory nuisances and provides a procedure for enforcement. Almost all statutory nuisances are enforced by local authorities. They do not depend on a complainant having occupation rights (although usually he will).

The EPA covers a wide range of nuisances such as condition of premises, smoke emissions, emissions of fumes, gases, dust, steam and smells, problems due to the keeping of animals, and noise problems, both from premises and from vehicles and equipment.

If a nuisance falls under the provisions of a statute, enforcement by a local authority is likely to be more efficient and certainly less costly than pursuing a claim in private nuisance.

The local authority will require good evidence of the nuisance. It will usually inspect and, in cases of noise, will employ decibel meters.

Enforcement is by way of abatement notices. You may encounter these either by asking the local authority to take action to serve one or by having one served on you. There are specific procedures for service of notices, appealing against notices and offences in connection with them. Specialist advice will be needed. Failure to comply with an abatement notice (which is not successfully appealed) will constitute a criminal offence.

Examples of statutory nuisance

- Emission of smoke, fumes or gases to residential premises.
- Premises which are so dilapidated or neglected as to be prejudicial to health or a nuisance.
- Loud music being played several nights each week after 11 p.m.
- Nuisance from animals.

See also: Property disputes (page 443).

Occupier's liability

Chris Platts, Rollits

Key points

The concept of an occupier of property or premises having a responsibility towards those who visit or use such premises is nothing new. This has existed for many years. The converse applied in relation to trespassers and other unlawful visitors who were owed no duty at all apart from where they were the victims of intentional or reckless injury. Times change and the law has moved on. The purpose of this article is to consider the responsibilities occupiers have – or, put another way, what liability potential can arise for them – and to discuss some common situations.

Legislation

- Occupiers' Liability Act 1957.
- Occupiers' Liability Act 1984.
- Defective Premises Act 1972.
- Health and Safety at Work etc. Act 1974.

Occupiers' Liability Act 1957

Broadly, this Act requires all occupiers of premises to take such care as is in all the particular circumstances reasonable to ensure that a visitor would be safe in using the premises for the purposes for which he is invited or permitted to be there.

Accidents will always occur to a lesser or greater degree. In considering a claim by a claimant against an occupier, and in deciding whether the circumstances show the occupier has kept his visitor reasonably safe, a court is free to consider all relevant circumstances. These might be:

- lighting;
- any warnings given;
- the purpose of the visit;
- the conduct of the visitor;
- the knowledge of the occupier of any hazard including any warning of that hazard given about it – in practice a whole host of circumstances or considerations might arise; or
- the state of the premises.

Who is responsible?

It is not the purpose of this article to define every situation where an individual or business may be an occupier. Suffice to say both landlord and tenant can be an occupier for the purposes of these duties. A landlord may be responsible for common areas, whereas a tenant would be treated as an occupier for the premises which are let to him. A good (but not necessarily the only) test to apply is whether there is a sufficient degree of control over the premises to constitute occupation. This is illustrated in the decided cases.

In one case a child, who had fallen from the roof of living accommodation, could not succeed in his claim because the roof was not occupied by the owner. The occupier did not know the child had been on the roof, nor did they have effective control over the roof. The extent of control over the roof was a question of fact and degree and the court decided it was not fair to impose an additional duty on the defendant in that claim.

Is there a danger?

Where an accident occurs, the court has to consider whether the cause of the accident was a source of real danger. A danger to a visitor is likely to produce liability unless an occupier can demonstrate taking reasonable care to avoid the danger. The history of the location may well in those circumstances be a material factor. However, the courts will not take a step too far and will not find that there is a duty for an occupier to warn visitors of obvious matters; nor will the courts look at matters with the benefit of hindsight. This duty under the Occupiers' Liability Act is not absolute and is subject to reasonable limits.

Organised events

Organisers of events are of course wanting to attract visitors. Duties are owed by the occupier to such visitors but also others who may help organise events or indeed in some way participate by organising 'sideshows'. It is important to consider the insurance arrangements for those organisers and any participants. Otherwise there may be unlikely and unforeseen consequences.

A most recent example of this involved a claimant who sustained injuries while using a 'splat wall'. This activity involved participants bouncing from a trampoline and sticking to a wall by means of Velcro material. The claimant was injured because the apparatus had been negligently set up by a contractor company whose insurance had expired. The court held that, as part of the organiser's (for organiser read occupier) general duty to take reasonable care in these circumstances, they should have been satisfied that the contractor was sufficiently experienced and competent. Having insurance or otherwise was part of competence. Therefore, it was held that the organiser should have enquired into the insurance position. Their failure to do so meant they were liable. This duty did not, however, extend to seeing the policy.

Another particularly unusual case involved a claimant who was injured while he assisted a two-man stunt team who were conducting a pyrotechnic display. Unfortunately, he was injured when gunpowder exploded in his face. The stunt team did not possess any insurance cover. The claimant pursued the club that organised the display on the basis it had failed to take reasonable care to select a reasonably competent stunt team. The court concluded that the club had allowed a dangerous event to take place with no public liability insurance and no written safety plan on the part of the stunt team. It had, therefore, as occupier of the premises where the event took place, failed to take ordinary precautions. Liability therefore attached to the club.

Trespassers

The Occupiers' Liability Act 1984 imposes a duty on an occupier even in relation to those who trespass onto his property. If an occupier is aware of a danger or has reasonable grounds to believe that a danger exists, and he knows or has reasonable grounds to believe that a trespasser is in the vicinity of such danger, then he may be found liable to the trespasser for injuries caused. The risk has to be one against which in all the circumstances of the case the occupier may reasonably be expected to offer some protection.

To balance the situation, there will be no liability on an occupier if he is unaware of the existence of any hazard or had no reasonable grounds for suspecting that such hazard could exist. Nor will there be liability if there is no reason to assume that a trespasser would be in the vicinity of a hazard at a particular time of night.

Not all visitors, however, are invited or welcome or do what was perhaps intended. As one judge said in a case in 1927, 'when you invite a person into your house to use the staircase you do not invite him to slide down the banisters'. That may not stop an occupier being liable in such circumstances.

Health and Safety at Work etc. Act 1974

General duties, of course, exist under the Health and Safety at Work etc. Act for an employer to look after both his employees and visitors. An employer clearly can be an occupier. The duty, effectively, extends to keeping all affected by a business safe, subject to limits of reasonable practicability. A breach of this Act does not of itself form the basis for a claim for damages, but it could form a basis for a prosecution by an enforcing authority.

The ambit of this Act can be far more wide-ranging than might appear to be the case at first sight, but it is not the purpose of this article to do other than simply alert an occupier to the possibility of a prosecution in the event of such a breach.

Conclusion

Potentially an occupier cannot win. A claim or a prosecution are both unwelcome prospects. Taking all possible precautions, and taking steps to ensure safety of all visitors is a matter of common sense. Trespassers, you might be tempted to think, are another matter, but this may not be the case. Generally, a sensible approach to safety on your premises will stand you in good stead.

See also: Health and safety at work (page 295); Insurance (page 332); Trespassers and squatters (page 503); Visitor safety (page 518).

Parking

David Lentz, Parkserve Management

With increasing concern for traffic congestion and pollution, the Government has introduced a number of initiatives to constrain the use of the motor car, especially where those drivers contribute to the daily rush hour. In Central London, exceptional circumstances have attracted the introduction of road charges, with a significant and positive impact upon the reduction of, principally, private motor car traffic. A similar solution could not be justified in all towns and cities.

Workplace parking levy

Highway authorities have an alternative recourse to introduce a workplace parking levy to combat rush-hour congestion subject to improved local public transport and enhanced on-street parking controls. Certain organisations and businesses out of town, or whose staff and customers do not contribute to the rush hour, are at present exempt.

The levy is charged as a supplement to the standard annual business rates and based upon an application for a licence for a declared number of parking spaces. Enforcement is carried out by the random visits of authority inspectors. Financial penalties will apply where it can be shown that the licensed number of parking spaces has been exceeded.

It can be assumed that some employers will prefer to give up spaces to gain relief from the levy. In such cases, it may also be assumed that, with increased on-street parking controls, those displaced employees who cannot be persuaded to use public transport will seek alternative off-street parking places, especially where there may be no parking charges. It is recommended that employers and their associations involve themselves from the outset in any public consultation process.

If the levy becomes inevitable, it should be a priority to protect against unauthorised use of private parking places, if necessary, by barriers that can be controlled by pass-card or similar systems. Visitors' and delivery vehicles cannot always be anticipated, but simple add-on systems and voice communications exist to enable barriers to be safely opened from a remote reception or office to allow authorised access and egress.

Protect your parking rights and resources

As an additional means of safeguarding the use of spaces, it is recommended that the rights of entry to and use of the property by car drivers be governed by a 'contract to enter/wait/park'. This should be displayed as a conspicuous sign at the entrance to the property. In this way, the contract is an offer that may be refused and so drivers can turn away before entering. However, if drivers pass the contract – the sign – by entering, it may be deemed that they have given their consent to the posted terms and conditions of entry and will be bound by any sanction for non-compliance that has been published thereon. The wording of these signs should be periodically reviewed, as usually, once written, they are rarely revisited, even if circumstances change.

For the avoidance of doubt, your contract signs should ideally include a factor for every conceivable contingency and be repeated in conspicuous positions where drivers can see them after leaving their vehicles. Similarly, while a property owner cannot be held responsible for the autonomous criminal actions of third parties, it is common to display a disclaimer notice to that effect. With 'autocrime' ever on the increase, it is appropriate to remind drivers to remove all valuables and securely lock their vehicles.

Safer Parking Scheme

Although the perception of autocrime far exceeds the facts, large or long-term car parks used by employers, staff, customers and others could benefit from the principles of the Safer Parking Scheme (formerly the Secured Car Parks Scheme). This is the initiative of the Association of Chief Police Officers and is administered by the British Parking Association, which would be pleased to provide further information

Requirement to meet the needs of the disabled driver

By 1 October 2004 owners or operators should have taken all 'reasonable' steps to comply with the Disability Discrimination Act 1995 (DDA) including any changes to their car parks to ensure that there is no disadvantage to disabled people when using that service. As the Act covers the widest spectrum, employers should positively give consideration and take action to meet the varying needs of disabled people (not always visually apparent) wherever change may be necessary, through consultation, education and constant review at every level.

When assessing the area needed for staff and customer parking, it should be noted that the current UK standard for parking spaces is 2.4 metres wide by 4.8 metres long. The standard for manoeuvring (roadways) between bays is 6 metres. These dimensions are neither minimum nor written in tablets of stone and may be revised to suit your particular needs.

Approximately 6% of parking should be allocated to disabled drivers unless otherwise restricted and dedicated. Employers should, however, adhere to

---

Sources of further information

No two car parks are the same. Much 'best practice' is the consequence of personal experience or Codes of Practice rather than direct legislation.

The British Parking Association is probably best placed to locate specialist consultants or members who can tailor their advice to your specific and individual environmental, liability or health and safety issues. The Association's website is www.parking.org.uk.

---

the standard for parking spaces for disabled people (3.6 metres width), where the difference (1.2 metres) is yellow hatched to enable sufficient access for wheelchair users. These spaces should carry the 'wheelchair' logo on the surface of the bay and display the appropriate sign at a driver's eye level. Your duty to avoid discrimination by hindrance and disadvantage to disabled people does not end here. Elsewhere in the car park, or on your property, impediments or obstructions, however apparently minor, should be removed or changed. If such action is not reasonably possible, then an alternative facility should be provided to avoid the obstacle to person or service.

See also: Disability access (page 179); Discrimination (page 189); Wheelclamping (page 537).

Part-time workers

Pinsent Masons Employment Group

Key points

- It has always been risky to treat part-time workers less favourably than comparable full-time workers, owing to the potential for a claim of sex discrimination.
- Regulations introduced in 2000 now provide protection for part-time 'workers' (wider than the term 'employees') irrespective of sex discrimination.
- Part-time workers can request a written statement from their employers if they suspect discrimination.
- Employers should review their practices and procedures to ensure that they are compliant with current legislation.

Legislation

- Part-time Workers (Prevention of Less Favourable Treatment) Regulations 2000.
- Amendment to Part-time Workers (Prevention of Less Favourable Treatment) Regulations 2001.
- Part-time Workers (Prevention of Less Favourable Treatment) Regulations 2000 (Amendment) Regulations 2002.

Overview

The Part-time Workers (Prevention of Less Favourable Treatment) Regulations 2000 (the Regulations) came into force on 1 July 2000 to provide a basic right for part-time workers not to be treated less favourably on the grounds of their part-time status than comparable full-time workers unless this can be justified on objective grounds. This means part-time workers are entitled, for example, to:

- the same hourly rate of pay;
- the same access to company pension schemes;
- the same entitlements to annual leave and to maternity and parental leave on a pro-rata basis;
- the same entitlement to contractual sick pay; and
- no less favourable treatment in access to training.

Definitions

The Regulations apply to 'workers' and not just to 'employees'. The wider definition will include part-time workers who may not be employees, such as home workers and agency workers.

A part-time worker is someone who is 'paid wholly or partly by reference to the time he works and, having regard to the custom and practice of the employer in relation to workers employed by the worker's employer under the same type of contract, is not identifiable as a full-timer'.

A part-time worker must therefore be identified by reference to the particular circumstances of each employer.

'Less favourable treatment'

To assert less favourable treatment, a comparison must be made with a particular full-time worker. However, the Regulations only allow part-time workers to compare themselves with full-time workers working for the same employer on a similar contract.

By virtue of the Amendment Regulations which came into force on 1 October 2002, a part-time worker can compare himself to a full-time worker regardless of whether either of the contracts is permanent or for a fixed term.

Where they believe they are being treated less favourably than comparable full-timers, part-time workers may request a written statement of the reasons for their treatment from an employer, to be provided within 21 days.

Discrimination at all stages of employment – recruitment, promotion, terms of employment and dismissal – is potentially unlawful. Promotion is an area where employers have often in the past favoured full-time staff over part-timers. Previous or current part-time status should now not form a barrier to promotion to a post, whether the post itself is full-time or part-time.

Part-time employees must not receive a lower basic rate of pay than comparable full-time employees, unless this can be 'objectively justified' (e.g. by a performance-related pay scheme).

The same hourly rate of overtime pay should be paid to part-timers as to comparable full-time employees, once they have worked more than the normal full-time hours. Currently, the law does not provide part-time workers with an automatic right to overtime payments once they work beyond their normal hours.

The Regulations will allow part-time workers to participate in the full range of benefits available to full-timers such as profit-sharing schemes, unless there are objective grounds for excluding them. Any benefits should be pro rata to those received by comparable full-time workers.

Employers will be obliged not to exclude part-time workers from training schemes as a matter of principle. They should take great care to ensure that part-timers get the same access to training as full-time workers.

Part-time workers must be given the same treatment in relation to maternity leave, parental leave and time off for dependants as their full-time colleagues, on a pro-rata basis where this is appropriate. Similarly, career break schemes should be made available to part-time workers in the same way, unless their exclusion is objectively justified.

Less favourable treatment will only be justified on objective grounds if it can be shown that the less favourable treatment is to achieve a legitimate objective (e.g. a genuine business objective), that it is necessary to achieve that objective and that it is an appropriate way to achieve the objective.

Dismissal

There are certain situations in which a dismissal by an employer for a specific reason will be treated as being automatically unfair. Where someone is dismissed for holding the status of a part-time worker, this will be deemed automatically unfair. No qualifying period of employment is required for such a claim.

If there is a redundancy situation, then part-time workers should be treated just as favourably as full-timers, unless this difference in treatment can be objectively justified. Part-time status should not be a criterion for selection for redundancy.

Practical points

Government guidance has been published with the Regulations and may be accessed at www.dti.gov.uk/er/pt_detail.htm.

Employers will find it useful to take note of the following points:

- They should review periodically when they can offer posts on a part-time basis. If an applicant wishes to work part-time, the employer should ascertain whether a part-time worker could fulfil the requirements of the job.
- Employers should look seriously at requests to change to part-time working and, where possible, explore how this can be carried out.
- They should review how individuals are provided with information on the availability of part-time and full-time positions.

- Employers are encouraged to keep representative bodies informed about certain aspects of the business's use of part-time workers.
- Managers should amend their handbooks to include a section on part-time workers and the consequences of breaching the Regulations.
- Disciplinary procedures should be amended to make it a disciplinary offence to discriminate against part-time workers.
- Awareness of the rights of part-time workers may need to be raised and training provided on the subject.

Enforcement

Employees are able to present a claim to an employment tribunal within three months seeking compensation if they believe that their rights have been infringed.

See also: Dismissal (page 197);
Family-friendly rights (page 251);
Redundancy (page 455).

Sources of further information

Department of Trade and Industry (DTI): www.dti.gov.uk.

Advisory, Conciliation and Arbitration Service (ACAS): www.acas.org.uk.

Pensions

Andy Williams and Kris Weber, Charles Russell Employment and Pensions Service Group

---

Key points

- There are two types of pension provision in the UK: state benefits and private arrangements.
- State benefits comprise the basic state pension and S2P. Employees who have paid sufficient National Insurance contributions automatically qualify for both types of benefit.
- Private pension arrangements can take the form of either occupational schemes or personal pensions. Different rules and regulatory requirements apply to each type of arrangement.
- Every employer with five or more staff must offer them access to a stakeholder pension scheme (which is a type of personal pension) unless it is exempt because it offers them another type of pension.

Legislation

- Social Security Contributions and Benefits Act 1992.
- Part XIV, Income and Corporation Taxes Act 1988 (as amended by the Income Tax (Earnings and Pensions) Act 2003).
- Pension Schemes Act 1993.
- Pensions Act 1995.
- Welfare Reform and Pensions Act 1999.
- Child Support, Pensions and Social Security Act 2000.
- Occupational Pension Schemes Practice Notes, IR12, published by the Inland Revenue.
- Personal Pension Schemes Guidance Notes, IR76, published by the Inland Revenue.

Overview

This article covers the two types of pension provision in the UK: state benefits and private pension arrangements.

State benefits

State benefits can be divided into two tiers of benefit: the basic state pension and the state second pension. Both are compulsory, in that employees must pay National Insurance contributions (NICs) and therefore build up rights to a state pension.

Basic state pension

All employees with a sufficient working history receive a flat-rate basic state pension (2004–5: £79.60 per week for a single person) from the Government at their state pension age, currently 60 for women and 65 for men.

State second pension

Employees may also become entitled to the state second pension (known as S2P and formerly known as SERPS or the state earnings-related pension scheme) from the Government. This is also financed by employees' NIC payments and is payable from state pension age; again the amount of this pension depends upon the amount earned during the employee's working lifetime. Employees may choose to 'contract out' of S2P and divert their NIC payments to a private pension scheme.

Private pension arrangements

Private pension provision in the UK is highly regulated, by both the Government and various regulatory bodies. Other than in respect of stakeholder pensions (see below) there is no element of compulsion. Nonetheless, many employers do still voluntarily make private pension provision for their staff.

There are two types of private pension arrangement: occupational pension schemes, which an employer establishes and operates for its staff; or employees' own personal pensions, which are individual investment contracts marketed and sold by insurance companies.

Most private schemes benefit from tax approval by the Inland Revenue. In return for complying with certain requirements laid down by the tax authorities, these schemes enjoy generous tax reliefs.

One of the most important Revenue requirements is the maximum (or 'capped') salary that may be taken into account when calculating the benefits of most members (2004–5: £102,000). As a result, some employers also establish unapproved top-up schemes for high-earning senior staff.

Occupational pension schemes

Traditionally most occupational pension schemes were established on a defined benefit (DB) basis, meaning that the pension payable at retirement was calculated by reference to a salary-related formula in the scheme's rules. After employees have made their contributions, it becomes the employer's obligation to inject as much additional funding as necessary to provide the promised level of benefits.

For a number of reasons, DB schemes are no longer as popular. Many are being replaced by defined contribution (DC) schemes. The risk of investment returns and annuity rates in DC schemes is borne by the scheme's members, as the only promise from the employer is to pay a predefined amount into the scheme.

When an employee leaves the company that operates any kind of occupational pension scheme, his benefits will normally remain in that scheme until he reaches retirement age, when they will become payable to him. Alternatively, at any time until one year prior to this date, he may instead choose to transfer these benefits to a pension scheme operated by his new employer or to his own personal pension.

Personal pension schemes

Insurance companies operate (and look after the assets of) personal pension schemes. All personal pensions operate on a DC basis. Employees and employers can make contributions to a personal pension.

Employers frequently offer staff membership of their 'group personal pension' scheme (GPP). Each employee in such a scheme has his own personal pension, underneath an umbrella agreement between his employer and the insurance company. If the employee leaves the company's employment, his pension will automatically follow him to his new employer and he will usually be able to continue contributing to it until his retirement.

Contributions to personal pension schemes are limited to between 17.5% and 40% of capped salary, depending on age.

Life assurance

Both occupational schemes and GPPs are often linked to a life assurance scheme providing a tax-free lump sum defined as a multiple of salary (up to the maximum 4 × capped salary permitted by the Inland Revenue) in respect of employees who die while in the company's service.

Stakeholder pensions

Private pension provision has been compulsory since October 2001, as a result of the Government's introduction of stakeholder pensions. A stakeholder pension is simply a personal pension that meets certain requirements, relating to the maximum level of charges it may make, and the minimum level of contributions

it must permit to be made to it.

Employers' obligations are:

- to designate a stakeholder pension for their staff (having first consulted with employees about the introduction of the stakeholder); and
- to allow employees to have their contributions to the stakeholder deducted from their salaries and passed directly to the insurance company operating the stakeholder.

There is no obligation upon employers to actually contribute anything towards employees' stakeholder pensions, although they may choose to do so. Consequently the consultation exercise is often the costliest (and most time-consuming) part of the exercise. Employers who fail to comply with the law relating to stakeholder pensions risk civil penalties of up to £50,000 from Opra, the pensions regulator.

However, some employers are exempt from the obligations laid down by the stakeholder pensions legislation. In particular, it does not apply to:

- employers with fewer than five employees;
- employers who operate an occupational or personal pension scheme for their employees which meets certain criteria.

There are also various other exceptions in relation to short-term and low-earning employees.

See also: Retirement (page 463).

Sources of further information

Inland Revenue Pension Schemes Area:
www.inlandrevenue.gov.uk/pensionschemes.

Inland Revenue Stakeholder Pensions web page: www.inlandrevenue.gov.uk/
stakepension.

Occupational Pensions Regulatory Authority (Opra): www.opra.gov.uk.

Permits to work

Phil Wright, SafetyCO UK

Key points

- Any person who may control a premises could be required to enforce the use of a permit to work.
- Permits should be issued only by someone who understands the risks and the control measures that it is necessary to put in place (authorising person).
- A permit has to be task specific and the necessary risk assessments and method statements still need to be prepared. A permit is not a replacement for these.
- A permit should be used only for a limited duration, be clearly dated and have specific conditions attached to it.
- Permits should not be transferred to other people or companies.
- Any safety precautions required should be done before work starts. The permit should state these requirements (e.g. electrical isolation or discharge of pressuring systems).
- The authorising person should sign and date the permit only when he is satisfied that all the precautionary measures have been taken.
- If the risks are too high (e.g. because of bad weather conditions or dangerous structure), then a permit should not be issued.
- When operating several permits at once, a permit register should be used to prevent conflicts in work activities. Each permit should have a unique number for easy reference.
- All permits should be retained for at least three years by the authorising person.

Legislation

- Health and Safety at Work etc. Act 1974.
- Management of Health and Safety at Work Regulations 1999.
- Confined Spaces Regulations 1997.
- Electricity at Work Regulations 1989.
- Construction (Health, Safety and Welfare) Regulations 1996.

Where permits apply

Permits are used to control high-risk activities and areas where specific hazards could be present, such as the following:

- Hot works.
- Roof works.
- Confined spaces.
- HV electrical work.

- Asbestos.
- Excavation works.
- Lift works.
- Pressure systems.
- Demolition works.
- Work on scaffold towers and mobile elevated working platforms (MEWPs).
- Work which can be carried out only by removing normal control measures (e.g. live working on a supply to a critical piece of equipment).

Permitting conditions

Listed below are some examples of control measures that should be considered when issuing a permit.

Roof works

- Adequate means of access either temporary or permanent (e.g. roof ladders, crawling boards).
- Testing of the roof's fragility.
- Provision of edge protection.
- Prevention of falls of materials or objects.
- Personal protective equipment.

Confined spaces

- Atmospheric monitoring.
- Isolation of any fluid or energy.
- Emergency rescue procedures.

- Consideration of type and use of personal protective equipment – particularly breathing apparatus.

Hot works

- Ensuring that sprinklers (if installed) are isolated and reactivated after the works.
- Good housekeeping: combustible materials such as flammable liquids or gases, paper or cardboard should be removed from the area.
- Using protective non-combustible curtains to protect property and persons.
- Regular maintenance and inspection of all 'hot works' equipment.
- Ensuring that a fire-trained person visits the area 30 to 60 minutes after the hot works have finished to make sure that no smouldering embers or hot surfaces remain.
- Provision of suitable fire extinguishers.

See also: Asbestos (page 79); Confined spaces (page 142); Construction site health and safety (page 145); Electricity and electrical equipment (page 214); Lift safety (page 361); Working at height (page 321).

Sources of further information

'Guidance on permit-to-work systems in the petroleum industry' (HSE Books, 1997): ISBN 0 7176 1281 3.

Personal protective equipment

Andrew Richardson, Scott Wilson

Key points

- Personal protective equipment (PPE) is worn or held by a person at work to protect him from risks to his health and safety.
- Waterproof and weatherproof clothing only falls within the Regulations if it is necessary to protect the wearer from health and safety risks due to adverse climatic conditions.
- The Personal Protective Equipment at Work Regulations 1992 apply in most instances; there are six other sets of Regulations which include their own particular PPE requirements.
- PPE is at the bottom of the hierarchy of risk control measures; PPE should be used only as a last resort.
- Employers must decide if PPE is necessary and, if so, must select suitable PPE, provide it free of charge, and maintain it and replace it as necessary.
- In addition, employers must provide: accommodation for PPE; information, instruction and training about it and how to use it; and a system for employees to report defects and losses.

Legislation

- Health and Safety at Work etc. Act 1974.
- Management of Health and Safety at Work Regulations 1999.
- Personal Protective Equipment at Work Regulations 1992.
- Personal Protective Equipment Regulations 2002.

Personal Protective Equipment Regulations 2002

The PPE Regulations came into force on 15 May 2002 and deal with the suitability of PPE brought to market. The Regula-tions place a duty on responsible persons who put PPE on the market to ensure that the PPE satisfies the basic health and safety requirements that are applicable to that type or class of PPE, and that the appropriate conformity assessment procedure is carried out. Since 1 July 1995 all new PPE should have the CE mark identifying that the equipment satisfies certain safety requirements and has been tested and certified by an independent organisation.

Personal Protective Equipment at Work Regulations 1992

The PPEW Regulations form part of a

number of health and safety regulations which implement EC directives. The Regulations exist to ensure that certain fundamental duties covering the provision and use of PPE are applied whenever PPE is required.

The Regulations define PPE as 'all equipment (including clothing affording protection against the weather) which is intended to be worn or held by a person at work which protects him against one or more risks to his health and safety'.

Protective clothing includes aprons, clothing for adverse weather conditions, gloves, safety footwear, safety helmets, high-visibility waistcoats, etc. Protective equipment includes eye protectors, life jackets, respirators, underwater breathing apparatus and safety harnesses.

The guidance notes identify items including uniforms, food hygiene protective clothing, cycle helmets, motorcycle leathers, shin guards, etc., which are not covered. Waterproof, weatherproof or insulated clothing improves the comfort of the wearer, but is only subject to the Regulations if employees must wear it to protect them against adverse climatic conditions that would affect their health and safety.

The Regulations do not apply to PPE

provided under the following Regulations, which have their own specific requirements:

- Control of Lead at Work Regulations 2002.
- Ionising Radiations Regulations 1999.
- Control of Asbestos at Work Regulations 2002.
- Control of Substances Hazardous to Health Regulations 2002.
- Construction (Head Protection) Regulations 1989.
- Noise at Work Regulations 1989.

The Management of Health and Safety at Work Regulations 1999 require employers to carry out a suitable and sufficient risk assessment to enable the most appropriate means of reducing the risks to acceptable levels. When determining the most suitable risk-control measures, there is a risk-control hierarchy. PPE is the final category, and, in effect, PPE should not be used unless the risks to health and safety cannot be adequately controlled in any other way.

The Regulations place the following responsibilities on the employer, who must:

Sources of further information

The primary source of further information is L25 'Personal protective equipment at work – Personal Protective Equipment at Work Regulations 1992 – Guidance on Regulations' (HSE Books, 1992): ISBN 0 7176 0415 2. The document provides all the guidance needed by employers and identifies any further documentation that is relevant.

Basic HSE guidance, 'A short guide to the Personal Protective Equipment at Work Regulations 1992', can be downloaded at www.hse.gov.uk/pubns/indg174.pdf.

- assess the risk and determine if PPE is needed;
- select suitable PPE;
- provide the PPE;
- maintain all PPE and replace as necessary;
- provide accommodation for the PPE;
- provide information, instruction and training on the PPE provided; and
- provide a system to allow employees to report defects or loss of PPE.

Employers are not allowed to charge for PPE.

The Regulations require the employee to take reasonable care of the PPE provided, and, under the Health and Safety at Work etc. Act, the employee has a duty to use the PPE.

See also: COSHH/hazardous substances (page 153); Head protection (page 293); Noise at work (page 403); Risk assessments (page 469).

Pest control

Tony Wuidart and David Cross, Igrox Limited

Key points

Put simply, pest management or control is the destruction or prevention of unwanted pests.

Many differing techniques are used, but the basic principles are common to most situations. These involve environmental management to exclude pests from sites, restrict access to food, water and harbourage, and, as a last resort, physical or chemical control.

Legislation

- Protection of Animals Act 1911.
- Wildlife and Countryside Act 1981.
- Wild Mammals Protection Act 1996.
- Prevention of Damage by Pests Act 1949.
- Food Safety Act 1990.
- Food Safety (General Food Hygiene) Regulations 1995.
- Food and Environmental Protection Act 1985.
- Control of Pesticide Regulations 1986.
- Health and Safety at Work etc. Act 1974.
- Biocidal Products Directive (98/8/EC).
- Control of Substances Hazardous to Health (COSHH) Regulations 1999.

What is a pest?

A pest is any animal that is found in the wrong place at the wrong time and whose presence could result in damage, contamination and/or spread of disease.

The most common pest species include those shown in the table on page 429.

Types of service available

- Contracted pest control services monitoring entire sites on a regular basis against specific pests, to ensure that the site remains pest free.
- Employment of a pest control company to eradicate a localised pest problem such as a wasps' nest or mouse infestation.
- Preventive proofing to buildings to deter pests from entering or roosting on sites.
- Supply of insect control devices such as fly killers.
- Supply of insect-monitoring devices, such as moth pheromone pots and flea traps, which are used to establish the presence and scale of an infestation.
- Fumigation of containers, commodities and entire buildings to eradicate deep-seated infestations.

Common pest species

Commensal	
Rodents	Brown rat, black rat, house mouse
Birds	Feral pigeon, woodpigeon, Collard dove, starling, house sparrow, jackdaw, jay, magpie, carrion/hooded crow, rook, herring gull, lesser black-backed gull, great black-backed gull
Textile pests	Including: varied carpet beetle, fur beetle, common clothes moth, case-bearing clothes moth and many more
Stored product	
Insects	Grain weevil and beetle, flour beetle, book lice, warehouse moth, Mediterranean mill moth
Public health	
Insects	Flies, fleas, cockroaches, bed bugs, wasps, ants
Vertebrate pests	Rabbit, grey squirrel, mole, feral cat, Canada goose

---

• Localised heat treatments for the control of insects such as bed bugs in bedroom furniture.

Categories of legislation

Legislation covering pest control can be split into three categories.

1. Species protection legislation

Protection of Animals Act 1911

This Act provides general protection for domestic and captive animals and makes it an offence to do or omit to do anything likely to cause unnecessary suffering. This would include not providing food and water to animals confined in a cage or live capture traps.

Amendments to this Act include the prohibition of the use of poisons on any land or building except for the purpose of destroying insects, rats, mice and other small ground vermin.

Wildlife and Countryside Act 1981

This Act provides protection for certain animals and the environment. From a pest control point of view, the Act covers most of the legislation affecting birds and lists birds that may be taken by authorised persons. (Refer to the list of pest birds in the table at the top of the page.) An authorised person is the owner or occupier of the land on which the birds are to be controlled, or any person authorised by the owner or occupier.

Birds from this list may be controlled using live capture traps or by shooting (excluding weapons with a muzzle diameter greater than 1.25 inches) under a general licence which is updated and issued by the Department for Environment, Food and Rural Affairs (Defra). Certain species of bird from this list may also be controlled using mist nets (for house sparrows in doors only) or stupefying baits under a specific, one-off licence which is applied for and issued under the discretion of Defra Wildlife Administration Unit.

Birds can only be controlled in order to:

- prevent spread of disease;
- protect public health and safety; and
- protect crops, livestock, forestry, fisheries and water.

Wild Mammals Protection Act 1996

This Act is designed to protect wild mammals against abuse and cruel treatment.

It makes it an offence to mutilate, kick, beat, impale, stab, burn, stone, crush, drown, drag or asphyxiate any wild mammal with intent to inflict unnecessary suffering.

2. Environmental health legislation

Prevention of Damage by Pests Act 1949

This Act requires, as far as is practicable, that districts are kept free from rats and mice.

It requires local authorities to carry out periodic inspections, to destroy rats and mice on their land, and to enforce the same duties onto owners and occupiers.

Food Safety Act 1990

This Act makes it an offence to sell food for human consumption that fails to comply with food safety requirements.

This would be the case if the food was contaminated with droppings or pest bodies.

The defence under the Food Safety Act is due diligence, which means that everything reasonably practicable must have been done to avoid contamination.

Food Safety (General Food Hygiene) Regulations 1995

These Regulations made under the Food Safety Act 1990 require food businesses

to practise a high standard of food safety in a wide range of areas. Those relating to pest control are as follows:

- Food premises must be constructed in such a way that there is no cross-contamination by pests.
- Windows opening to the outside from areas where food is prepared, treated or processed must be fitted with insect-proof screens which can be easily removed for cleaning.
- Refuse stores must be designed and managed in such a way that they are protected against access by pests.
- Adequate procedures must be in place to ensure pests are controlled.

3. Legislation on pesticide use

The following legislation covers the duties placed on pesticide users and their employers.

Food and Environment Protection Act 1985

Part III of this Act is of direct concern to pest control as it provides for the making of Regulations concerned with the control of pesticides with a view to protecting the health of human beings, creatures and plants, safeguarding the environment and securing safe, efficient and humane methods of controlling pests.

Control of Pesticide Regulations 1986

These Regulations were introduced under the Food and Environmental Protection Act 1985 and stipulate that only approved pesticides may be advertised, supplied, stored or used in the UK and that only those with provisional or full approval may be sold.

Health and Safety at Work etc. Act 1974

This Act provides a comprehensive

system of law covering the health and safety of people at work and members of the public who may be affected by activity at work.

Biocidal Products Directive (98/8/EC)

The Directive is intended to harmonise arrangements for the authorisation of pesticides used in public health pest control, wood preservatives, industrial preservatives, disinfectants and certain germicidal chemicals.

The Directive was implemented in March 2000, but full harmonisation could take as long as ten years to complete.

Control of Substances Hazardous to Health (COSHH) Regulations 1999

These Regulations were introduced under the Health and Safety at Work etc. Act 1974 and make it necessary to assess the risk to health arising from work involving a hazardous substance and, if a risk is identified, to determine what precautions are required either to eliminate or to reduce the risk. This may involve the use of personal protective equipment for people working with the substance, or the exclusion of personnel from an area while a substance is being applied.

Forthcoming developments

There are some major developments that

Pest control checklist

Taking account of the following recommendations will help ensure that you comply with legislation at your site:

- When pest activity is identified, prompt action should be taken to eradicate it and to prevent re-infestation.
- All staff should be aware of the problems caused by pests, should take relevant action to prevent pests entering buildings, and should maintain high standards of hygiene and housekeeping to deny pests access to food and/or harbourage.
- If you employ external contractors, they should be members of the British Pest Control Association (BPCA) or the National Pest Technicians Association (NPTA).
- Documented evidence of monitoring and treatments, including types, quantity and location of any pesticides used, should be kept and maintained.
- Pest control contractors should hold sufficient public liability insurance to cover your needs.
- Pest control contractors should be able to demonstrate that their staff have received sufficient training to enable them to be competent to do the job.
- If you wish to carry out your own in-house pest control, the person responsible for doing the work should have received suitable training and preferably hold a Level 2 certificate in pest control. This is a nationally recognised RSH qualification which has recently superseded the RSH certificate in pest control and the BPCA diploma part 1.

---

will affect, or will be likely to affect, the pest control industry:

- Methyl bromide gas is being phased out and no more production will take place in 2005. Residual stocks will be used in 2005 and only companies that have successfully applied for a critical-use exemption will be able to use it in 2006.
- It will no longer be legal to use the gassing compound Cymag to control rabbits and rats from January 2005.
- It is expected that changes to waste disposal regulations will affect the way in which pesticides can be safely disposed of.

See also: Biological hazards (page 84); COSHH/hazardous substances (page 153).

Sources of further information

British Pest Control Association, 1 Gleneagles House, Vernon Gate, South Street, Derby DE1 1UP (tel. 01332 294288; fax 01332 295904; email enquiry@BPCA.org.uk).

National Pest Technicians Association, NPTA House, Kinoulton, Nottingham NG12 3EF (tel. 01949 81133; fax 01949 823905; email officenpta@aol.com).

ADAS Environment, Gleadthorpe Research Centre, Meden Vale, Mansfield, Nottinghamshire NG20 9PF (tel. 01632 844331; fax 01632 844472; email adasenvironment@adas.co.uk).

Details of the *ADAS Pest Manual*, a reference manual for the management of pests, can be found at www.adas.co.uk/environment.

Central Science Laboratory, Sand Hutton, York, North Yorkshire YO4 1LZ (tel. 01904 462000; fax 01904 462111).

Defra, Wildlife Section, Tollgate House, Houlton Street, Bristol BS2 9DJ (tel. 0117 987 8000; fax 0117 987 8182).

Planning procedures

Edited by Bonnie Martin, Pinsent Masons

Key points

- Planning permission (subject to a number of exceptions) is required for material changes of use of land and operational development.
- An application for planning permission will be made to the local planning authority (LPA).
- Failure to secure planning permission, or comply with planning conditions, may entitle the LPA to take enforcement action.
- There is a right of appeal to the Planning Inspectorate.

When is planning permission required?

Planning permission is required for development, which means:

- operational development (which includes building, engineering or mining operations); or
- material changes in the use of any buildings or other land.

Operational development

Building operations include the demolition of buildings, the rebuilding of buildings, structural alterations of, or additions to, buildings and any other operations normally undertaken by a person carrying on business as a builder.

A building includes any structure or erection, and any part of the building, structure or erection, but does not include plant or machinery.

Not all structures are considered by the law to be buildings. The three primary factors are size, degree of permanence and physical attachment.

Material changes of use

In order to assess whether planning permission is required for a material change of use, it is necessary to look at the primary use of a piece of land or building and the extent of any ancillary uses. Ancillary uses do not require planning permission. For example, the primary use of a building may be for office purposes, but there may be ancillary storage uses within that building.

In addition, a slight or trivial change of use will not require planning permission. For example, a small amount of storage use in an office building would not require planning permission.

Demolition

Although demolition constitutes development, currently planning permission is only required for demolition of dwelling houses and adjoining buildings. No planning permission is required for demolition of other buildings, provided they are not in a conservation area, are not listed buildings and are not scheduled ancient monuments.

Exceptions

Legislation provides that certain operations or material changes of use are exempted from the need for planning permission. For example, internal or external improvements, alterations or maintenance work, none of which materially affect the external appearance of buildings, may not require planning permission. Some of these concessions are removed in respect of certain sensitive areas, such as conservation areas or national parks.

The Town and Country Planning (General Permitted Development) Order 1995 grants an automatic planning permission for certain operational development and material changes of use including certain industrial and warehouse developments subject to a series of complicated conditions and restrictions. Government directions and planning conditions can withdraw these rights.

Securing a grant of planning permission

If a particular proposal requires planning permission, a formal planning application needs to be made to the relevant LPA. If the proposal is acceptable in planning terms, planning permission should be granted either conditionally or unconditionally.

Usually the permission will automatically run with the land. A person who buys a piece of land which has the bene-fit of a planning permission can implement that planning permission and build in accordance with any approved plans. It may be necessary to secure the copyright in any approved plans.

Only two types of planning permission can be obtained:

- detailed planning permission; and
- outline planning permission, which establishes the principle of development. Any such permission would include a condition requiring reserved matters (e.g. design, means of access, external appearance) to be submitted to the LPA within three years of the date of the outline permission.

Environmental impact assessment

In respect of certain types of development or activity, an environmental impact assessment will need to be submitted. The assessment is required to ensure that the effect of development on the environment, in particular of certain specified public and private projects, is taken into account as part of the decision-making process and before consent is granted. It is the initial outline planning permission rather than any subsequent reserved matters application to which the assessment regulations apply.

Keeping permissions alive

All permissions are subject to strict time limits. If development is not begun within those time limits, the permission will lapse. In the case of a detailed permission, the usual time limit condition requires development to be started within five years from the date of the detailed permission.

In the case of an outline planning permission, the usual time limit condition requires development to start no later than five years from the date of the outline planning permission or, if later, two years from the final approval of reserved matters. To keep the permission alive, work must commence within the time limits. Alternatively an application for the renewal of any permission can be made, but success cannot be assumed.

Breach of planning control

A breach of planning control can take one of three forms:

- the carrying out of operational development without the benefit of planning permission;
- the carrying out of a material change of use of any building or land without the benefit of planning permission; or
- the breach of a condition attached to a permission.

LPAs have wide powers of enforcement (including criminal sanctions) should development be carried out without any necessary planning permission or failing to comply with planning conditions.

Listed buildings and conservation areas

Buildings may be 'listed' as being of special historic or architectural interest. Any works which affect the character of a listed building require a listed building consent. Non-compliance with the listed building legislation can lead to enforcement action and criminal sanctions.

LPAs must determine, after consultation, whether any part of their area should be designated as a conservation area. Such designation has the following consequences:

- building design has to be of a high quality;
- restrictions are placed on demolition; and
- trees are protected.

Planning appeals

If the LPA refuses to grant planning permission, listed building consent or the modification of a planning condition, the applicant has the right to appeal to the Planning Inspectorate. An appeal can be pursued through written representations, a hearing or a public inquiry.

The appeal is determined by a planning inspector appointed by the Secretary of State for the Office of the Deputy Prime Minister. He will be independent from the local planning authority. The process may take many months or even years. In respect of certain more complex sites, the decision is made by the Secretary of State following receipt of a report by an appointed planning inspector.

Power lines

Edited by Hugh Bruce-Watt, Pinsent Masons

Key points

- Power companies can negotiate rights to install power lines and equipment with landowners, or may use compulsory powers. In either case compensation will be payable to the landowner.
- Power companies have the right to fell or lop trees if they present a danger to the power lines.

Legislation

- Electricity Act 1989.

Overview

This article concentrates on who can install power lines, what agreements they enter into and how they can compulsorily acquire rights where landowners refuse to grant them voluntarily

Who can install power lines?

The generation, supply and transmission of electricity are activities regulated by section 6 of the Electricity Act 1989 (the Act). No person (which includes companies) may carry out these activities without a licence issued by the Secretary of State. It is only such licence holders that are permitted to install electricity lines on or above land.

However, before installing any power lines, licence holders must also obtain the Secretary of State's consent pursuant to section 37 of the Act and this consent may be subject to any conditions

the Secretary of State considers appropriate.

The most common licence holders are the regional electricity companies which took over the supply of electricity from the area boards following the changes introduced by the Act. These include, for example, London Electricity plc, Powergen plc, National Power plc and other such well-known companies.

Agreements relating to power lines

Before a licence holder can install a power line it also needs the consent of all landowners whose land will be subject to the installation of the power line. The most common forms of agreement giving effect to the licence holder's right to install a power line are as follows.

Easements

Easements are rights in land which can be granted permanently or for a set number of years. An easement is a legal right attached to the land. Therefore it binds any future owner of the land upon which the power line has been installed and will benefit any successor to the licence holder who has installed the power line. Where an easement is granted it will give the licence holder the right to install the line and to retain it permanently and will generally include such ancillary rights as are reasonably necessary for the exercise or enjoyment of the rights granted.

Wayleaves

Wayleaves are access to property granted by a landowner for payment. They are very common, especially where licence holders require rights over residential properties. They are of a less permanent nature than easements and are personal to the parties to the agreement. It is important to note, however, that wayleaves can only be terminated in one of three ways, namely when the period of the wayleave expires, or if the landowner gives notice under the termination provisions of the wayleave, or if the ownership of the land changes and the wayleave ceases to be binding on the new landowner. Even in these circumstances notice must be properly served on the licence holder and the right to keep the power lines on the land can be obtained compulsorily (see below).

Following the proper service of a notice, if the licence holder does not make an application to compulsorily acquire the right or does not negotiate a new wayleave, it must remove the power lines within three months of the service of the notice.

Compulsory powers

Where a licence holder requires power lines and the consent of the landowner cannot be obtained, the Act provides a mechanism for the compulsory acquisi-tion, on payment of compensation, of the necessary rights.

The Act provides two routes for the acquisition of such rights.

Compulsory purchase

Schedule 3 to the Act permits the Secretary of State to authorise the compulsory acquisition of land by a licence holder where that land is required for any purpose connected with the activities it is authorised to carry out. This extends to both the transfer of any existing right or the creation of any new right in the land, as well as the compulsory purchase of the land itself. This would include, for example, an easement. Before making an order for compulsory purchase, any interested party is afforded the opportunity to make objections. This can result in an inquiry being held to determine whether the order will be beneficial.

Necessary wayleaves

Paragraph 6 of Schedule 4 to the Act allows a licence holder to apply to the Secretary of State for a necessary wayleave where:

- the licence holder has given the landowner 21 days' notice to grant the wayleave and the landowner has failed to do so;
- the licence holder has given the landowner 21 days' notice to grant the wayleave and the landowner has made it subject to conditions to which the licence holder objects; or
- the landowner has given notice to the licence holder requiring the licence holder to remove an existing power line in place under a wayleave.

Before making any order in relation to a necessary wayleave, the Secretary of State must give both parties the opportunity of stating their case.

Compensation

Whether land is acquired compulsorily or by agreement, the licence holder must pay compensation to the land-owner for the rights it has acquired in the land. The compensation, based on the provisions of the Land Compensation Act 1961, should take into account:

- the value of land taken, applying normal market rules;
- injurious effect on land such as dangers associated with electromagnetic fields;
- the visual impact of the power lines;
- loss of development value;
- loss of use of the land and the effect on quiet enjoyment of it; and
- the landowner's legal and surveyor's costs.

The rule-of-thumb guide is that the landowner should be in no worse a position than before the acquisition of the right. The compensation may be payable as a lump sum or as a periodic payment.

Other rights for licence holders

The Act provides other rights for licence holders including the right to fell or lop trees causing or likely to cause an unreasonable source of danger due to their proximity to the power lines and the right to enter property to carry out such felling or lopping. Licence holders also have the right to disconnect other services to property if required to allow maintenance works, together with the right to break up streets (private or public) in order to repair and maintain electricity cables and power lines.

Practical issues

Unless the grounds for objection are very strong, it is sensible to deal with the licence holder's request by way of agreement. This also enables the landowner to negotiate on a level playing field, although the compulsory powers will always be in the background should negotiations break down.

Aside from the property issues, appropriate indemnities should be sought from licence holders to cover eventualities such as the death or injury caused to any person on the land and any potential nuisance caused by the existence of the power lines. Landowners should also ensure that the licence holder makes good any damage caused to the land in the process of installing or maintaining the power lines.

Finally, landowners should be aware of Schedule 6 (as amended by the Utilities Act 2000) to the Act, which contains the Public Electricity Supply Code. This provides that any person intentionally or by culpable negligence damaging or allowing any power line to be damaged is liable on summary conviction to a fine.

Private life

Gabriella Wright, Charles Russell Employment and Pensions Service Group

Key points

- It is reasonable for workers to have a legitimate expectation that they can keep their personal lives private and workers are entitled to a degree of privacy in the workplace.
- Interference in a worker's private life is justifiable in certain circumstances. However, disciplining or dismissing without proper justification could give rise to an unfair dismissal claim and special protections are in place to ensure that workers are not discriminated against because of issues in their home life.
- Employers have an obligation to take into account a worker's human rights. The use of personal data by an employer, in particular 'sensitive data', is strictly regulated in the UK, principally under the Data Protection Act 1998.

Legislation

- Human Rights Act 1998, Schedule 1.
- Employment Rights Act 1996.
- Employment Equality (Sexual Orientation) Regulations 2003.
- Employment Equality (Religion or Belief) Regulations 2003.
- Data Protection Act 1998.
- Access to Medical Reports Act 1988.

General rules

Most employees would have an expectation that what they do in private or in their own time is their own affair. It is reasonable for workers to assume that they can keep their personal lives private, and workers are entitled to a degree of privacy in the workplace. However, the right to respect for privacy is not absolute. Sometimes it is fair and reasonable, because of the impact that the individual's private activities have on either his work or the workplace, for the employer to interfere.

Generally, to be actionable, outside conduct must be relevant to the individual's job. If an employer is wanting to dismiss for conduct outside work, generally the conduct must make the individual unsuitable for the job. Before dismissal, alternative positions might have to be considered (e.g. an employee-driver facing a temporary driving ban might be able to undertake alternative work in the short term or perform his driving duties by alternative means).

Where an employer is, in principle, justified in probing into an employee's private life, the law protects an employee in a number of respects. The employer must ensure that it is not contravening these protections if any disciplinary action or dismissal is going to be fair.

Where disciplinary action or dismissal for outside conduct is contemplated, general principles of fairness require an investigation, and a proper disciplinary process to be followed.

Relying on a criminal conviction to justify dismissal will not necessarily be fair. The employer must generally conduct its own investigation and satisfy itself that dismissal is reasonable and appropriate.

Principal protections for workers are given in the legislation discussed in the following paragraphs.

Human Rights Act 1998

The relevant parts of the Human Rights Act 1998 (HRA) for these purposes are the right to respect for private and family life and the right to freedom of expression. It is possible to interfere with a worker's human rights where this can be justified in a work context.

While the rights of employees under the HRA are only directly enforceable against a public sector employer, all employers must be aware of these rights to ensure that their treatment of employees is fair. As tribunals have to take account of the HRA, if an employee's human rights have been disregarded in a disciplinary investigation leading to dismissal, for example, it could result in the tribunal finding the dismissal unfair. See the separate article on 'Human rights' (page 329) for further details on how the HRA impacts in the workplace.

Data Protection Act 1998

Information about a worker's private life

will involve personal data and, in many cases, sensitive personal data. The Data Protection Act (DPA) regulates the use of personal data by an employer and covers data contained in some manual records as well as all computerised records.

The Employment Practices Code issued by the regulatory body, the Information Commissioner, assists employers in complying with the DPA. It emphasises the need, when intruding into a worker's privacy, to carry out an impact assessment, which balances the employer's objectives against any adverse impact of the intrusion for the employee. An area where impact assessments are especially relevant is workplace monitoring (see 'Monitoring employees', page 392).

Sensitive personal data includes information about a person's ethnic or racial origins, political opinions, religious or other beliefs, trade union membership, health and criminal record. Before using 'sensitive personal data', it may be necessary to obtain explicit consent from the employee. Consent is not necessary where the data is to be used for, among other things:

- ensuring a safe system at work or otherwise to comply with health and safety rules; or
- preventing or detecting crime.

Therefore, where an employer suspects that an employee has been involved in a criminal offence outside work which is relevant to the job that he performs, or within the workplace, intrusion into the employee's privacy may well be justified under the DPA.

Discrimination legislation

The rules governing discrimination most

likely to be relevant to a worker's private life are the Employment Equality (Sexual Orientation) Regulations 2003 and the Employment Equality (Religion or Belief) Regulations 2003. They make it unlawful for employers to discriminate on grounds of actual or perceived sexual orientation, religion or belief. Full details of the scope of the protection are provided in the article on 'Discrimination' (page 189).

Sexual orientation covers orientation towards persons of the same sex, of the opposite sex, and of the same sex and the opposite sex. Religion or belief covers religion, religious belief or similar philosophical belief.

The Regulations prohibit:

- direct discrimination – e.g. dismissing someone because he frequents gay clubs or bars;
- indirect discrimination – e.g. inviting only spouses of employees to a work social event, or holding all social events on a Friday, or catering only for employees of a Christian belief;
- victimisation – e.g. not promoting someone because he has made (or intends to make) a complaint about being discriminated against on orientation or religious grounds;
- harassment – being unwanted conduct that has the purpose or effect of violating a person's dignity or creating an intimidating, hostile, degrading or offensive environment.

Tribunal cases

As noted above, the general rule is that off-duty conduct can be a valid reason for dismissal if it is relevant to the person's employment and makes that employee unsuitable for the job.

Examples of past tribunal cases include the following:

- A teacher of teenage pupils fairly dismissed after having allowed others to grow cannabis in his garden, in view of the position of responsibility and influence that he held.
- A manager fairly dismissed after having smoked cannabis in front of subordinates at a work party, because the employer decided that her conduct had undermined her authority at work.
- A teacher fairly dismissed after his conviction for an offence of gross indecency with a man.
- An air traffic controller fairly dismissed for use of drugs outside work, because of a need to maintain public confidence in the safety of the air traffic control system. While there were no signs of the employee being anything other than fully capable at work, dismissal was a proportionate response in the circumstances.
- A probation officer fairly dismissed for participation outside work in activities involving bondage and sado-masochism. The court decided that the individual's human right to respect for his private life had not been infringed because his activities were public knowledge, and although his right to freedom of expression was infringed the employer was entitled to protect its reputation and maintain public confidence in the probation service.
- An employee unfairly dismissed when banned from driving, because he had offered to perform his duties

using public transport, at his own expense, which was, in the circumstances, a workable alternative

- A postman unfairly dismissed after a conviction for football hooliganism, because the Post Office could not show that its reputation had been damaged by the conduct.

Practical steps for employers

Have clear rules on what amounts to acceptable conduct both in and outside work.

- Communicate the rules to employees.
- Ensure that the rules are followed, consistently, in practice.
- Ensure that any allegations of inappropriate off-duty conduct are properly investigated and that, where relevant, the requirements of the HRA and the DPA are taken into account.
- Be satisfied that the off-duty conduct makes the employee unsuitable for the job.
- Check whether there is any alternative to dismissal.
- Do not automatically assume that a criminal conviction will justify an employee being dismissed.

See also: Data protection (page 163); Disciplinary and grievance procedures (page 184); Discrimination (page 189); Dismissal (page 197); Human rights (page 329); Monitoring employees (page 392).

Sources of further information

The Employment Practices Data Protection Code may be found at www.informationcommissioner.gov.uk.

Guidance for employers on sexual orientation and religious discrimination may be found at www.acas.org.uk.

'Data Protection Policy and Management Guide, version 1.0' (ISBN 1 900648 33 4, £34.99) is available as an electronic download from the Workplace Law Network. Call 0870 777 8881 for details, or visit www.workplacelaw.net.

Property disputes

Edited by Michael Brandman, Tarlo Lyons

Key points

- Keep copies of documents and records of telephone calls and other conversations.
- Act quickly. Some remedies are available only if you act without delay.
- Take professional advice at an early stage.
- Consider mediation as a means of resolving disputes. It is often quicker and cheaper than litigation. The courts encourage mediation, and successful litigants have in some cases been refused costs against their opponents in circumstances where mediation has been offered and rejected. However, the Court of Appeal recently ruled that litigants cannot be forced into mediation against their will.

Strategy

Always verify your rights before tackling the problem. Start by assembling and checking the relevant documents. They will often tell you what your position is.

In a landlord and tenant dispute, consider:

- the lease;
- rent review documents;
- licences for alterations;
- licences for change of use; and
- guarantees.

In a neighbour dispute, consider:

- title deeds; and
- planning documents.

In disputes with the previous owner, consider:

- the contract;
- pre-contract enquiries and replies;
- the transfer or conveyance; and
- relevant correspondence.

Gather your evidence

You may need to be able to prove your case in court or in some other kind of dispute resolution process. Good-quality evidence will help you.

It is important that you always do the following:

- Keep a written record of relevant events. Keep a log setting out times, dates and people involved as events unfold. This is essential where the events complained of are changing. Where there are, for example, building works, or where conduct of individuals is the problem, make a careful note of things that happen from day to day.

- Take photographs before and after any alterations are made.
- Keep an accurate written record of telephone calls and other conversations.

Act quickly

Remember that property disputes rarely just go away. The property does not move and the value of property makes it likely that disputes will continue until they are resolved by some sort of process.

Delay in reacting to circumstances may result in some emergency remedies being unavailable. Injunctions or restraining orders preventing further building works or demolition works, for example, can be obtained only where prompt action is taken.

Delay may result in a change in the balance of power. It is almost always easier to prevent a building from being constructed, or from being demolished, than it is to obtain an order for the removal or reconstruction of such a building.

Take professional advice

The value of the property as an asset usually warrants good professional involvement. Surveyors are necessary in many disputes (e.g. repair and boundaries). A planning expert will help to win arguments about the right to construct or alter a building, even before an application for planning permission is determined.

Expert evidence will often be necessary if a dispute goes to court. Early involvement of expert professionals ensures that case preparation is carried out along the right lines from the beginning.

Solicitors should be asked to provide an early assessment of the strengths and weaknesses of any case as soon as a problem arises. Weaknesses can then be addressed and strengths shown to the opponent in the best possible light. The aim is always to find an early resolution.

Resolving disputes

Always choose the best strategy for the particular dispute when you have gathered together your documents, evidence and expert advice.

If an injunction or restraining order is necessary to prevent a problem from becoming entrenched or to avoid a major change in the position on the ground, then court action will be necessary.

Lawyers will assist in the preparation of witness statements and expert evidence. Restraining orders can be obtained on the same day where the matter is extremely urgent, or more usually within three to seven days from the commencement of action.

Many disputes are settled by mediation, rather than through the courts. This allows the parties to remain in control of the procedure and to create a solution that may be more flexible than possibilities available through the courts. Mediation is a form of facilitated negotiation and is voluntary – in a mediation, no one can be forced into a solution against their will. It is almost always quicker and cheaper than litigation.

Statutory time limits

In some cases (e.g. applications for renewal of business leases and applications for judicial review of planning decisions) there are strict and very short time limits within which to bring proceedings. In such cases obtaining prompt legal advice can be crucial. Mediation must not be allowed to delay the issue of proceedings when time is critical.

See also: Dilapidations (page 171); Landlord and tenant: lease issues (page 345); Landlord and tenant: possession issues (page 354); Planning procedures (page 428).

Sources of further information

The leading independent organiser of the mediation process is the Centre for Effective Dispute Resolution (CEDR): tel. 020 7536 6000; www.cedr.co.uk.

Radiation

Ciaron Dunne, Workplace Law Group

Key points

- Specific regulations require employers to protect employees from the adverse affects of ionising radiation (e.g. X-rays).
- Employers also have a general duty to protect employees from non-ionising radiation (e.g. over-exposure to the sun).

Legislation

- Ionising Radiations Regulations 1999.
- Management of Health and Safety at Work Regulations 1999.
- Radioactive Substances Act 1993.

Types of radiation

There are two types of radiation, which have quite different effects:

- Non-ionising electromagnetic radiation (e.g. ultraviolet and radio waves) does not change the structure of atoms.
- Ionising electromagnetic radiation has enough energy to ionise or change atoms.

Non-ionising radiation

Non-ionising radiation includes the following bands of the electromagnetic spectrum:

- Ultraviolet (e.g. sunshine, welding). Possible effects include skin cancer, blindness, arc eye, blisters and burns.

- Infrared (e.g. from fire). Effects include blistering, burns and blindness.
- Microwaves (e.g. in a commercial kitchen), which can damage internal organs.
- Radio waves (e.g. in the telecommunications industry).
- Lasers, which can cause blindness or burns.

Employers should conduct a risk assessment, as required by the Management of Health and Safety at Work Regulations 1999. The effects from these electromagnetic frequencies can be controlled by compliance with guidelines published by the National Radiological Protection Board (NRPB).

Ionising radiation

Ionising radiation is hazardous because it can change the structure of atoms in the human body. It occurs in the following forms:

- *Particles*. Alpha particles (e.g. found in smoke detectors) can cause

---

Checklist of radiation control measures

Ultraviolet
- Keep skin covered (long sleeves, gloves, high collars, welding mask).
- Used screened areas.
- Interlocking guards fitted to lamp housings.
- Dull or matt surfaces to reduce reflection.
- Avoid working outdoors between 11 a.m. and 3 p.m.

Infrared
- Keep your distance.
- Use protective filters in eye protection (e.g. sunglasses).
- Use reflective clothing and cover skin.

Microwaves
- System should be enclosed to prevent exposure.
- Interlocking guards should be fitted to doors.
- Keep metals and explosive or flammable materials well away.

Radio waves
- Keep your distance from the source.
- Avoid touching metal surfaces that have been exposed to radio frequencies.

Lasers
- Install fixed shielding
- Dull or matt surfaces to reduce reflection.
- Use eye protection.
- Use remote interlocks and control access.

damage if inhaled. Beta particles can penetrate up to 5mm into the human body.
- *Rays.* These can be natural (e.g. gamma rays) or man-made (e.g. X-rays). These can pass right through a human body, but can be stopped by substances such as lead.

The Ionising Radiations Regulations 1999 apply to a large range of workplaces where radioactive substances and electrical equipment emitting ionising radiation are used. They require employers to keep exposure to ionising radiation as low as reasonably practicable. Employers should bear in mind the following types of control:

- Engineering controls, including shielding and ventilation.
- Procedural controls, e.g. restricted access and safe systems of work.
- Personal protective equipment – this should be used as a last resort.

The Regulations contain specific requirements which may apply depending on the nature of the work. They include the following:

- Employers should notify enforcing authorities before starting work.

- Employers should appoint a radiation protection advisor.
- A licence is required from the Environment Agency to store radioactive material.
- Authorisation is required to dispose of radioactive waste.

See also: Risk assessments (page 469).

Sources of further information

HSE radiation web page: www.hse.gov.uk/radiation.

INDG337 'Sun protection: advice for employers of outdoor workers' (HSE Books, 2001): ISBN 0 7176 1982 6.

L121 'Work with ionising radiation. Approved Code of Practice and guidance' (HSE Books, 2000): ISBN 0 7176 1746 7.

National Radiological Protection Board: www.nrpb.org.

Rates and revaluation

David Webb, Paddison & Partners

Current rateable values, which came into force in April 2000, are to be replaced on 1 April 2005 following the fourth revaluation in 15 years. The valuations are carried out by the Valuation Office Agency, an executive agency of the Inland Revenue, undertaking almost 2 million valuations across England and Wales. The law is different in Scotland, where valuations are carried out by assessors attached to local authorities.

Why have revaluations?

Revaluations have always been carried out periodically but have been on a five-year cycle since 1990. The idea is to reflect changes in values in the property market, so that, for instance, a shopping parade that becomes unpopular over time has this decline reflected in rates paid.

What is rateable value?

Rateable values are intended to reflect annual rental values, essentially on full repairing and insuring terms. The date these values are taken is fixed as being two years before the revaluation to allow time for the Valuation Office Agency to gather and analyse evidence. It follows that any rent reviews or new lettings agreed around April 2003 should produce rateable values that correspond closely. The set valuation date also means that all properties are valued by reference to the same fixed point, even if they did not exist at the time, to ensure fairness.

How are rate bills calculated?

A business's rate bill, notionally, is the rateable value multiplied by the rate in the pound, fixed nationally (although there is now a body of opinion pressing for a return to locally fixed poundages). The rate in the pound in England for 2004/5 is £0.456, so a rateable value of £20,000 produces a bill of £9,120.

Transitional arrangements

On revaluation, movements in value can be so marked that a rate bill could, in theory, rise dramatically from one year to the next. To cushion the impact, any large increases are phased in, but, to pay for this, those whose bills should reduce considerably are penalised by having the decrease introduced gradually. Consequently, in the first years following a revaluation, many occupiers do not pay the 'correct' amount, but rather their bills are based on those for the previous year, adjusted up or down a little. In the past, this has meant that many never pay the 'correct' amount, so for the next revaluation it is envisaged that the transitional arrangements will be amended to work their way out of the system in the first four years.

New initiatives for 2005

The Valuation Office Agency is keen to

get things right more often and provide more transparency in its dealings with ratepayers. It is also under political pressure to reduce to a minimum the number of appeals it receives. As a step towards this goal, most occupiers will have received a copy of their proposed new valuation in October 2004. It is believed that there will then be time before April 2005 for any queries to be answered, and factual errors corrected, so that appeals will not be necessary. As with all new initiatives, only time will tell if this will cause more problems than it is intended to solve.

How will values change in 2005?

On figures available to date, the 2005 revaluation will see an overall increase in value of 17.9% across England and Wales. Of course, this disguises wide variations, regionally and between classes of property. In general, the largest increases will be in the South and East, with shops suffering most.

Legislation provides that the overall 'take' from business rates should only rise in line with inflation, so there will be a corresponding decrease in the rate in the pound, and many occupiers will pay less for a while.

How to mitigate liability

Unless there is a good reason not to do so, and here advice may be needed, the rateable value should be appealed. April 2000 figures can still be appealed until March 2005, and any success will have the dual effect of reducing existing liability and providing a lower base for subsequent years if transition is involved.

Councils have been known to send out incorrect bills – check the calculations.

Seek specialist advice

Rating can often be a complicated business, and occupiers should consider taking advice. Even the checking of a rate demand can necessitate a detailed knowledge of the process, and challenging the value takes time and research. There are also several ways to save rates other than by reducing the rateable value.

When looking for help, seek out a chartered surveyor experienced in the field, and take no notice of glossy brochures or a smooth sales pitch.

Sources of further information

Valuation Office Agency: www.voa.gov.uk.

Recruitment and selection

Helen Abbott, Workplace Law Group

Key points

- Make an accurate assessment of the requirements of a vacancy.
- Produce a constructive job description, person specification and recruitment advertisement.
- Prepare a shortlist and interview questions using the job description/person specification to identify key skills and competencies.
- Undertake training to develop effective interviewing skills.
- Keep within legal and policy requirements throughout the process.
- Make use of your personnel/HR department for advice.

Legislation

- Data Protection Act 1998.
- Disability Discrimination Act 1995.
- Employment Act 2002.
- Employment Equality (Religion or Belief) Regulations 2003.
- Employment Equality (Sexual Orientation) Regulations 2003.
- Employment Relations Act 1999.
- Equal Pay Act 1970.
- Race Relations Act 1976.
- Rehabilitation of Offenders Act 1974.
- Religious Belief Discrimination Act 2003.
- Sex Discrimination Act 1975.

Importance of effective recruitment

Effective recruitment is central and crucial to the successful day-to-day functioning of any organisation. Successful recruitment depends upon finding people with the necessary skills, expertise and qualifications to deliver organisational objectives and the ability to make a positive contribution to the value and aims of the organisation.

Do you really need to recruit?

Recruitment is not only carried out to fulfil current needs. Those responsible for recruiting should always be aware of future plans which have implications for recruitment. When an employee leaves, think carefully about whether you need to recruit a direct replacement. Could the workload and responsibilities be shared among other staff, or would it be more cost-effective to consider contractors or agency staff?

Job descriptions

If you have decided to recruit, does the job description or person specification need to be updated? Have the tasks, responsibilities or skills altered? If an

---

employee has left, this is a good time to make changes.

Job descriptions and person specifications are very useful tools. They will provide guidance, consistency and objectivity throughout the recruitment process. Briefly, the aim of a job description is to give a reasonable idea of what a particular job might involve. It should not attempt to list every possible task or be a set of work instructions. It is important to retain some flexibility for both employee and employer. With regard to content, it should outline the main duties and responsibilities. Other details such as reporting structure, objective(s), and where the job is located can be added. However, you should not include salary details and hours of work because these are contractual matters which belong in the contract of employment.

A person specification gives further detail and describes the type of person and competencies needed to perform the job. It can be divided into categories such as qualifications (necessary to do the job), training, experience, knowledge, skills and personal qualities relevant to the job, such as ability to work in a team. All of these can be further divided into essential or desirable criteria.

Recruitment advertising

Having a job description and person specification will make drafting the recruitment advertisement much easier. You will be able to clearly outline the experience, key skills and competencies required. To attract better-quality applicants, ensure that you devote more words to describing the job rather than the organisation. Consider including your website address for further informa-

tion. Advertisements should be clear and state briefly:

- the requirements of the job;
- the necessary and the desirable criteria for job applicants;
- the activities and working practices of the organisation;
- the job location;
- the reward package;
- job tenure (e.g. contract length); and
- the application procedure.

Shortlisting

Use the job description/person specification to match potential applicants to the skills and experience required. Try not to make assumptions and be as objective as possible. When rejecting candidates, it is useful to record your reason(s). This will enable you to give accurate feedback or to justify your decision if asked for feedback at a later stage.

Throughout the recruitment process, bear in mind the legal requirement not to discriminate, either directly or indirectly. This includes the criteria within the job description, the language in the recruitment advertisement, the questions asked at interview and the subsequent selection decision. Penalties for discrimination are currently uncapped and recent cases have resulted in large compensation awards against employers, running into hundreds of thousands of pounds.

Training

There is a large amount of employment legislation which relates to recruitment and selection, so training is highly recommended in order to avoid costly and embarrassing mistakes. Unfortunately, untrained interviewers can make subjective judgements based on non-job-related criteria. Selection processes should be based only on:

- ability to do the job;
- ability to make a contribution to the organisation's effectiveness; and
- potential for development.

Selection interview checklist

Do:
- undertake training to ensure that you are aware of equal opportunities legislation and understand how discrimination can occur;
- interview in a quiet place away from interruptions such as visitors or the telephone (including your mobile phone) ringing;
- help the candidate to relax and put them at ease: understand their fears, respect their self-esteem, offer a drink, use humour if appropriate;
- place chairs at right angles at the same height as yours;
- ensure you are well briefed about the job and your organisation: this will provide a good introduction to the interview;
- prepare your interview questions in advance: ensure that you use competency-based questions and ask all candidates the same questions;
- ask probing or building questions for more information;
- ask a number of 'open-ended' questions (including some 'reflecting back' questions);
- speak clearly;
- listen attentively;
- make a note of responses to your questions while they are fresh in your mind;
- ensure that conversation is shared

with the candidate;
- ask about general health, medical conditions, medication, etc.;
- ask about disabilities and what reasonable adjustments could be made to enable the candidate and your business to work together;
- confirm notice periods, dates of any booked holidays, current salary, name and contact details of referees, etc.; and
- encourage the candidate to ask questions.

Don't:
- keep the candidate waiting for a long period;
- place a physical barrier, such as a desk, between you;
- interrupt;
- stick to questions which require a yes or no answer;
- ask 'leading questions' to prompt for desired responses;
- launch straight into questions without putting the candidate at ease;
- appear disorganised or disjointed;
- appear uninterested or inattentive;
- use jargon or emotive language;
- undermine the candidate's confidence;
- make judgements too early; or
- break the law.

After the interview

Follow up interviews promptly by sending out regret letters to unsuccessful candidates and making a written offer of employment to the successful candidate. Briefly, this should include:

- details of the terms and conditions that will apply;

- any conditions to which the offer is subject;
- timescale to notify acceptance or rejection of the offer; and
- start date.

See also: Discrimination (page 189).

Sources of further information

Leighton, Patricia and Proctor, Giles: *Recruiting Within the Law*, 3rd edition (Chartered Institute of Personnel and Development, 2003): ISBN 1 84398 005 3.

Fox, Glen and Taylor, Dean: *The Complete Recruitment and Selection Toolkit* (Chartered Institute of Personnel and Development, 2000): ISBN 0 852928 69 6.

Evans, M.: 'How to recruit people with disabilities', *People Management*, Vol. 7, No. 18, 13 September 2001, pp. 50–51.

Grout, Jeff: 'How to recruit excellent people', *People Management*, Vol. 8, No. 9, 2 May 2002, pp. 44–45.

'Labour saving devices', *IRS Employment Review*, No. 774, 18 April 2003, pp. 34–40.

Redundancy

Alan Masson and Jill Sutherland, MacRoberts

Key points

Redundancy has a particular meaning in the employment context. It is a fair reason for dismissal provided that legal requirements are met in relation to consultation, selection for redundancy, notice period and redundancy payments. Failure to meet any of these requirements may lead to compensation claims.

Most compensation claims arise because employers have not planned the implementation of redundancies appropriately. Dealing with redundancies is unpleasant, but ignoring or rushing the process often makes matters worse.

Legislation

- Trade Union and Labour Relations (Consolidation) Act 1992.
- Employment Rights Act 1996.
- Employment Act 2002.
- Employment Act 2002 (Dispute Resolution) Regulations 2004.

Definition

Redundancy is defined in section 139 of the Employment Rights Act 1996 as where an employee is dismissed from employment, wholly or mainly, because:

- his employer has ceased or intends to cease carrying on business for the purposes for which the employee was employed either completely or in the place the employee was employed; or
- the requirements of the employer's business for employees to carry out work of a particular kind have ceased or diminished or are expected to cease or diminish, whether that is across the business or simply at the particular place the employee is employed.

Redundancy payments

By statute, a redundancy payment should be paid to each employee who has at least two years' continuous employment and is not over 65 years old. Payments are based on age and length of service. Statutory redundancy payments are calculated by reference to the rate of the employee's weekly pay (currently capped at £270 per week, likely to increase from 1 February 2005), which is multiplied:

- by 1.5 for every year in which the employee was 41 years old or more;
- by 1 for every year in which the

employee was between 22 and 40; and

- by 0.5 for every year in which the employee was between 18 and 21.

The maximum payment is 30 weeks.

A redundancy ready reckoner is available to identify the statutory redundancy payment due.

Getting it wrong

If you get collective consultation wrong, you may face claims from employee representatives or employees for protective awards. These are to be calculated to penalise the employer, not compensate the employee, and can amount to 90 days' pay per employee.

You can also face claims of unfair dismissal from individuals if you get any aspect of the redundancy process wrong. Normally employees will need one year's continuous employment to make such a claim. The current statutory maximum compensatory award for unfair dismissal is £55,000 (likely to increase from 1 February 2005). This is in addition to a basic award calculated on the same basis as a statutory redundancy payment. If the latter has been paid, only a compensatory award can be made. The statutory dispute resolution measures empower employment tribunals to increase compensatory awards by between 10% and 50% depending on the circumstances (but not beyond the statutory maximum).

Redundancy process checklist

The following is a checklist of the most important issues involved in a redundancy process. It is not a comprehensive guide, nor is it intended to be a substitute for legal advice in relation to individual circumstances.

Step 1

Think about the planning process as soon as the possibility of redundancy has been identified.

Step 2

Is there a redundancy policy that you need to apply? Don't forget that policies can be created by custom and practice if they are consistently applied over a period of time. These policies may require you to deal with certain issues in a particular manner. What follows is a simple summary of the statutory requirements where there is no such policy.

Step 3

Consider the number of individuals that may be made redundant at the end of the process. If it is greater than 19, from one establishment, over a 90-day period, there is an obligation to enter into collective consultation with appropriate representatives. Individual consultation will be required irrespective of the numbers of redundancies. Where collective consultation is required, individual consultation follows immediately afterwards.

How will you select individuals to be made redundant? Identify clear, lawful and objectively justifiable criteria. Identify to whom they are to be applied (the pool for selection).

Step 4

If collective consultation is required, the first issue is how soon to begin it. Consultation must take place in 'good time' and at least:

- 90 days before the first of the dismissals is due to take effect where the employer is proposing to dismiss

macROBERTS

Glasgow: 152 Bath Street, G2 4TB
Tel 0141 332 9988

Edinburgh: Excel House, 30 Semple Street, EH3 8BL
Tel 0131 229 5046

www.macroberts.com

100 or more employees at one establishment within a period of 90 days or less; and

- 30 days before the first dismissal takes effect where the employer proposes to dismiss at least 20 but less than 100 employees at one establishment within 90 days or less.

Collective consultation should start once a proposal has been formulated, even although that proposal is still at a formative stage.

Next, do you have appropriate representatives to collectively consult with (e.g. a recognised trade union)? If you do not, carry out elections, in accordance with the statutory requirements set out in the Trade Union and Labour Relations (Consolidation) Act 1992 (TULRA), section 188A.

Intimation of the proposed redundancies should be given to the Secretary of State for Trade and Industry using Form HR1 prior to commencing collective consultation. Send a copy of the HR1 to the representatives.

Call for volunteers for redundancy.

Collective consultation, like individual consultation, needs to include consultation about ways of:

- avoiding dismissals;
- reducing the numbers of employees to be dismissed; and
- mitigating the consequences of dismissals.

Consultation needs to be undertaken with a view to reaching agreement. Listen to the issues raised by the representatives and deal with each constructively. Ultimately you will either reach agreement or you will not. Either way, the next step is individual consultation.

Step 5

The statutory dispute resolution provisions, in force from 1 October 2004, apply to redundancy dismissals unless there is a sudden closure of the business in unforeseen circumstances. This requires the reasons for the provisional selection for redundancy to be set out in writing, a meeting to be held with each employee to discuss the issues, a written decision and a right to an appeal meeting. The employee has a statutory right to be accompanied at each meeting.

Discuss the implications for each employee provisionally selected at the meeting. Consider what alternative employment you have to offer in advance of the first meeting. Review it before the second meeting.

Do not dismiss at the first meeting. Explain why the employee has been selected provisionally by reference to the selection criteria and selection pools. Seek the employee's views and take time to consider them and respond constructively.

Any alternative employment should be discussed with the employee. Does it constitute suitable alternative employment? Is the employee willing to accept it? What trial period will be given?

Have a second meeting with the employee. Review the issues. If there is no suitable alternative employment and the employee does not raise any new issue, you can confirm selection for redundancy. Write to the employee confirming the decision. Remind him of his right to appeal it. Pay any notice and redundancy payments due.

See also: Dismissal (page 197); Trade unions (page 458).

Sources of further information

General information on redundancy processes is available from ACAS (www.acas.org.uk) and the DTI (www.dti.gov.uk).

A redundancy ready reckoner is available at www.dti.gov.uk/er/redundancy/ready.htm.

'Redundancy Policy and Management Guide, version 1.0' (ISBN 1 900648 43 1, £34.99) is available as an electronic download from the Workplace Law Network. Call 0870 777 8881 for details, or visit www.workplacelaw.net.

References

Pinsent Masons Employment Group

Key points

- The subject of employee references will usually arise when offering a prospective employee a contract of employment or when providing a reference for a current or former employee.
- An employer is under no statutory obligation to provide a reference for a current or former employee, unless a term in the contract of employment compels it, or, as in some regulated industries such as financial services, it is obliged to provide a reference under the regulations of a relevant body.
- If a reference is given, the referee must take great care in compiling it and must use all reasonable skill and care to ensure the accuracy of the facts contained in the reference and the reasonableness of the opinions contained within the reference as the referee may be liable as a consequence of a defective reference.
- Employers should be aware that if the reference results in the former employee suffering a loss or failing to be employed by the new employer then the content of the reference will be made known to the individual.

Offering a prospective employee a contract of employment

When recruiting new staff it is common for a prospective employer to make a job offer expressly conditional on receiving satisfactory references from the prospective employee's previous employer.

If the prospective employer's decision to employ is conditional upon receipt of a satisfactory reference, this must be made clear in the offer letter. To avoid dispute, it should be made clear that it is for the employer to determine what is satisfactory.

Providing a reference for a current or former employee

An employer is under no statutory obligation to provide a reference for a current or former employee, unless a term in the contract of employment compels it, or, as in some regulated industries such as financial services, it is obliged to provide a reference under the regulations of a relevant body.

However, if a reference is given, the referee must take great care in compiling it, for he may be liable as a consequence of a defective reference.

Duties are owed by the employer to recipients of references and to the subject of those references.

When giving a reference about an exiting employee who is seeking employment with another employer, there are a number of points that an employer must consider:

- An employer must use all reasonable skill and care to ensure the accuracy of the facts contained in the reference and the reasonableness of the opinions contained within the reference. Failure to do so may amount to a breach of the implied term of trust and confidence, entitling the employee to resign and claim constructive dismissal.
- Even if the reference is factually accurate, the employer must be careful not to give an unfair impression of the employee concerned. Therefore the employer should not include a disproportionate amount of negative facts and exclude those that are to the credit of the employee (e.g. stating that he always took long lunches, but not stating that he always worked late in the evening).
- Where an employee has been the subject of disciplinary action, this should only be referred to in the reference being provided where the employer:
  – genuinely believes the statement being made to be true;
  – has reasonable grounds for believing that the statement is true; and
  – has carried out as much investigation into the matters referred to in the statement as is reasonable in the circumstances.
  It would accordingly not be appropriate for an employer to refer to a disciplinary incident where the

employment is terminated before a full investigation was conducted.
- Other than in certain circumstances (e.g. where industry rules or practice require full and frank references), references do not have to be full and comprehensive. The employer's obligation is to provide a true, accurate and fair reference that does not give a misleading impression overall. Some employers will limit the reference to basic facts such as the dates of employment and the position held. Employers are entitled to set parameters within which the reference is given, e.g. by stressing their limited knowledge of the individual employee.

A practical danger

References could be used in evidence where the dismissal of an employee is the subject of litigation, so employers should take care in giving a reference in such circumstances. It is not unusual for employers to give positive references to employees who have been sacked for poor performance, as part of a negotiated settlement in such circumstances. Should they choose to do so in terms which are misleadingly favourable to the employee, the referee may find himself liable to a subsequent employer who relies on the references.

Employees' claims

The most common action for an employee who is the subject of an inaccurate reference is a damages action in respect of any economic loss which may flow from a carelessly or negligently prepared reference.

In order to establish that an employer is in breach of its duty to take reasonable care in the preparation of a reference, the employee must show that:

- the information contained in the reference was misleading;
- by virtue of the misleading information, the reference was likely to have a material effect upon the mind of a reasonable recipient of the reference to the detriment of the employee;

- the employee suffered loss as a result; and
- the employer was negligent in providing such a reference.

See also: Dismissal (page 197).

Sources of further information

Advisory, Conciliation and Arbitration Service (ACAS): www.acas.org.uk.

Chartered Institute of Personnel and Development (CIPD): www.cipd.co.uk.

Retirement

Andy Williams and Kris Weber, Charles Russell Employment and Pensions Service Group

---

Key points

- Parties in an employment relationship are currently free to choose whatever contractual retirement age they wish.
- This is due to change from 2006, with the introduction of age discrimination, when it is expected that any contractual retirement age below 70 will be outlawed.
- When choosing a contractual retirement age, careful consideration should be given to the age(s) at which state and private pension benefits may be drawn.

Legislation

- Social Security Contributions and Benefits Act 1992.
- Part XIV, Income and Corporation Taxes Act 1988 (as amended by the Income Tax (Earnings and Pensions) Act 2003).
- Pension Schemes Act 1993.
- Pensions Act 1995.
- Welfare Reform and Pensions Act 1999.
- Child Support, Pensions and Social Security Act 2000.
- Occupational Pension Schemes Practice Notes, IR12, published by the Inland Revenue.
- Personal Pension Schemes Guidance Notes, IR76, published by the Inland Revenue.

Introduction

'Retirement' in an employment situation embraces two distinct concepts: contractual retirement and retirement for pension purposes. The former relates to the point at which an employee ceases to work; the latter relates to when he or she is able to draw pension benefits. The two are frequently not the same.

Contractual retirement

An employer is able to set whatever contractual retirement age (CRA) it wishes in relation to its employees. The most common CRA is now either 60 or 65 for both sexes, although historically men tended to have a higher CRA than women (as this mirrored the difference in the state pension age between men and women). For a number of reasons, there has been a recent upward trend in CRAs generally.

The effect of a CRA is that the employment relationship will automatically terminate when the employee reaches that

---

age, without the need for either party to serve notice on the other.

The CRA should be specified in the written terms and conditions of employment at the outset of the employment relationship. However, there is no legal requirement to specify a CRA. If no CRA is set, one may arise by virtue of the employer's custom and practice. Failing that, the only way for the employment relationship to end is for one party to serve notice in the usual way.

The employer and employee are free to agree to change the CRA during the course of the employment relationship, but the employer should ensure that staff are treated consistently and fairly.

Retirement for pension purposes

There are two types of arrangement: pension benefits payable by the state and those arising out of private arrangements.

State pension benefits

State pension benefits consist of a basic state pension and a state second pension (or S2P). Both types of pension are payable from the state pension age (SPA). This is currently 65 for men and 60 for women.

The SPA is in the process of being equalised, by raising the SPA for women to 65. This will affect women born between 1950 and 1955, with those born before 1950 retaining an SPA of 60, those born after 1955 having an SPA of 65 and those born in between those dates having a staggered SPA of between 60 and 65.

There is no requirement for CRAs to dovetail with the SPA. (Indeed, having a different CRA for men and women, to dovetail with the current SPA, would be

unlawful.) This can lead to financial difficulties for employees who have a CRA lower than their SPA, as their employment is automatically terminated but they are not entitled to receive any state pension benefits.

Private pension benefits

Private pension benefits can take two forms: occupational pension schemes and personal pensions. Employers establish and operate occupational schemes for their staff, whereas personal pensions are individual investment contracts marketed and sold by insurance companies to employees, to which the employer may (but need not) contribute.

Occupational schemes will specify a normal retirement age (NRA). This is the age at which employees who are members of the scheme are able to draw their benefits from the scheme. The NRA must be the same for men and women who carry out equal work, but it is possible to have different NRAs for different categories of employee (such as administrative staff and directors).

The scheme will normally set out the basis on which early and/or late retirement can be taken before and after the NRA.

Personal pensions are more flexible – anyone with their own personal pension has the right to draw their benefits from it at any time they choose over the age of 50.

The earlier the benefits are taken, the less time there will be to allow the funds to build up, so generally the less money there will be with which to purchase an annuity. In addition, drawing benefits earlier means that the scheme will need to pay out an annual pension for a longer period of time. Therefore the pension will be of a lower amount.

Consequently many individuals find themselves unable in practice to draw their personal pension benefits as early as they might wish.

Phased retirement

Employees are able to continue to work while drawing their personal pension benefits. However, generally speaking, it is not possible to draw pension benefits from an occupational scheme and continue to work in that job.

As part of the Government's reforms to simplify the pension taxation system, phased retirement is being introduced with effect from 2006. This will allow any private pension benefits (occupational or personal) to be drawn at any age from age 50 onwards, regardless of any employment the individual starts or continues to carry out. This minimum age of 50 is due to be raised to 55 from 2010 for those drawing benefits from an

occupational scheme.

Age discrimination

Laws prohibiting discrimination in the workplace on the grounds of age are due to come into force in 2006. While the details of these new laws are some way from being finalised, it is expected that CRAs of under 70 will be outlawed. It is currently uncertain as to how this new law will affect certain types of occupational scheme (those providing defined benefits), which need to specify an NRA as the basis for calculating benefits payable from the scheme.

See also: Discrimination (page 189); Pensions (page 418).

Sources of further information

Inland Revenue Pension Schemes Area: www.inlandrevenue.gov.uk/pensionschemes/index.htm.

Inland Revenue Stakeholder Pensions web page: www.inlandrevenue.gov.uk/stakepension.

Occupational Pensions Regulatory Authority (Opra): www.opra.gov.uk.

RIDDOR

Bob Suttle, SafetyCO UK

Key points

- Reporting of accidents and ill health in the workplace is a legal requirement.
- The HSE and local authorities use the information to identify trends and how risks arise and to investigate serious accidents.
- Every week, two construction industry workers are killed at work.
- According to HSE statistics for the period 2002/3, there were 226 fatal injuries among employees and the self-employed, and 156,423 non-fatal major injuries and 'over-three-day injuries' reportable under RIDDOR. The number of fatalities among workers in 2003/4 was 235.

Legislation

- Reporting of Injuries, Diseases and Dangerous Occurrences Regulations 1995.

Reporting procedure

Before 1 April 2001 all reports were required to be sent via form F2508 or F2508A to, in most cases, the local enforcing authority or in some instances direct to the HSE. Now reporting is simplified. You do not need to keep forms F2508 and F2508A or identify which is the relevant reporting office. There is a central reporting facility in Caerphilly: the Incident Contact Centre (ICC).

Reports can be made to the ICC over the telephone (8.30 a.m. to 5.00 p.m.), by fax, on the Internet, by post or via email (see 'How to report incidents to the ICC' on page 467). The information will be processed by the ICC and forwarded to the relevant enforcing authority. You

may, if you wish, continue to contact your local enforcing authority direct to report an incident – e.g. in an out-of-hours emergency situation (such as a fatality) when the ICC helpline is closed. However, in non-emergency cases the authority will usually pass the information to the ICC for processing before it is returned to them for any potential follow-up action. You should remember that fatalities should be reported under RIDDOR by the fastest means.

When you have provided information to the ICC, you will be sent a copy of the incident report, giving you the chance to amend any errors. You must then keep a record of that report for inspection by visiting officers if an investigation ensues.

What must be reported

- A death or major injury.
- An over-three-day injury (an injury

How to report incidents to the ICC

Telephone: 0845 300 9923.

Fax: 0845 300 9924.

Internet: www.riddor.gov.uk. Or alternatively link from HSE website: www.hse.gov.uk.

Post: Incident Contact Centre, Caerphilly Business Park, Caerphilly CF83 3GG.

Email: riddor@natbrit.com.

which is not major but which results in an employee or self-employed person being unable to work for more than three days).

- A work-related disease.
- A dangerous occurrence (when something happens which had the potential to result in a reportable incident but, this time, did not).

Important points about each of these are as follows.

Death

- If death results from an accident at work, the HSE must be notified by the quickest method.
- If death results from an accident within one year of that accident, notification must be sent whether the accident was previously reported or not.

Major injury

- Fracture of the skull, spine or pelvis.
- Fracture of any bone in the arm or wrist (but not the hand) and in the leg or ankle (but not the foot).
- Amputation of the hand or foot, finger, thumb or toe or any part of these if the joint or bone is completely severed.

- Loss of sight through a penetrating injury, chemical or hot burn to the eye.
- Injury requiring immediate medical attention including burns from electrical shock.
- Loss of consciousness due to lack of oxygen.
- Injury resulting from absorption, inhalation or ingestion of a substance.
- Acute illness resulting from exposure to pathogens or infected material.
- An injury requiring resuscitation or admittance to hospital for more than 24 hours.

Over-three-day injury

Where an employee has three consecutive days off, excluding the day of the accident but including days designated as non-working (e.g. weekends).

Work-related disease

- Certain poisonings.
- Skin cancer.
- Lung disease including occupational asthma, farmer's lung, asbestosis and mesothelioma.
- Infections such as leptospirosis, hepatitis, tuberculosis and anthrax.

Dangerous occurrence

Dangerous occurrences specified in the Regulations including the following:

- The collapse, overturning or failure of lifting equipment (crane, forklift truck).
- The collapse or partial collapse of a scaffold over 5 metres high or erected near water where there would be a risk of drowning.
- Any unintended collapse of any building or structure under construction, alteration or demolition involving a fall of 5 tonnes or more of walling or flooring.
- The sudden uncontrolled release of 1 tonne or more of a highly flammable liquid.

Record keeping

Records may be kept in any form, but details kept must include the following:

- Date and method of reporting.
- Date, time and place of event.
- Personal details of those involved.
- A brief description of the nature of the event or disease.
- All workplace accidents should be recorded in an accident book. This would be the first recording stage. The second stage would normally be to keep a copy of the incident report to the ICC (as amended if necessary).

See also: Accidents (page 69); Workplace deaths (page 167).

Sources of further information

L73 'A guide to the Reporting of Injuries, Diseases and Dangerous Occurrences Regulations 1995' (HSE Books, 1999): ISBN 0 7176 2431 5.

HSE31REV1 'RIDDOR explained. Reporting of Injuries, Diseases and Dangerous Occurrences Regulations' (HSE Books, 1999): ISBN 0 7176 2441 2.

Risk assessments

David Menzies, SafetyCO UK

Key points

A risk assessment is a common-sense check of what could harm persons at work or others affected by that work. For the vast majority of employers and controllers of premises, it is certainly not rocket science: it should provide current legislation and best practice standards to formulate a safe system of work.

Legislation

- Health and Safety at Work etc. Act 1974.
- Management of Health and Safety at Work Regulations 1999.

Management of Health and Safety at Work Regulations 1999

The Management of Health and Safety at Work Regulations came into force in 1999 and supersede the original 1992 Regulations.

These earlier Regulations introduced the need for employers to make a suitable and sufficient assessment of health and safety risks to employees and other persons affected by the work activities.

Regulation 3 of the 1999 Regulations includes the requirements of the Fire Precautions (Workplace) (Amendment) Regulations 1999, and the need for employers to carry out specific risk assessments when employing young persons (i.e. 16- and 17-year-olds).

Risk assessments, as with other duties in health and safety legislation, are required to be carried out by competent persons.

Purpose of risk assessments

The purpose of a risk assessment is to enable a safe system of work to be established covering:

- people;
- premises;
- plant; and
- procedures.

A proper assessment of risk is fundamental to the good management of any business.

When enforcing authorities carry out inspections or investigations, risk assessments are usually the first port of call. If there has been no recorded assessment of risk, and something serious has occurred, the employer may be exposed to further action by the enforcing authorities.

Various recent successful HSE prosecutions have confirmed that persons carry-

---

ing out risk assessments should recognise their own level of competency and not stray into areas outside their knowledge and understanding.

Five steps

It is generally accepted that a risk assessment should involve five steps:

1. Assess the actual work task/location.
2. Identify the potential hazards involved.
3. Evaluate the likelihood and severity of these hazards occurring.
4. Decide upon the control measures necessary to eliminate or minimise the risk of harm being caused.
5. Record, implement, monitor and review the assessment.

Hierarchy of risk control

The competent person carrying out the assessment should consider measures to reduce the risk taking due account of the 'hierarchy':

- Do not do the task – design improvements or change the process.
- Substitute – use less hazardous materials.
- Minimise – limit exposure to individuals by job rotation.
- General control measures – barriers or warning systems.
- PPE – the last resort because it protects only the individual.

Types of risk assessment

Generic and site-specific assessments

Generic risk assessments are general assessments covering repetitive work tasks. The intention is that with the necessary control measures in place the residual risk rating should be considered low.

Site-specific assessments are specific to the premises and would take into account any additional hazards that could be present due to:

- work conditions;
- work location; or
- time constraints.

The problem with always using generic assessments is that the compiler and user can become complacent.

The ability to incorporate enhanced control measures considered necessary by the persons involved in the task should therefore be included in a generic assessment.

Terms used in risk assessment

Harm: death, bodily injury, damage to physical or mental health.
Hazard: the potential for anything to cause harm (machinery/substances/noise).
Likelihood: the likelihood of the harm actually occurring.
Severity: the consequences of that harm occurring.
Risk rating: Likelihood x Severity = Risk rating.
Control measures: the actions to be taken to remove or minimise the risk.

Qualitative and quantitative assessments

- Risk assessments can be qualitative (with words) or quantitative (with numbers).
- For a quantitative assessment, a matrix could be used with different ratings to cover the likelihood of an accident occurring, and the severity.
- The danger with this type of assessment, particularly for commonplace hazards, is that undue emphasis can be placed on the rating given rather than the control measures necessary to reduce the risk.
- Whatever type and system used it is important that the risk assessment is clear and concise. This increases the likelihood that it will be understood and used.

Carrying out risk assessments

Just as there is no actual definition of risk assessment in the Management of Health and Safety at Work Regulations, there is no definitive method of setting out a risk assessment. The minimum standard that the law will accept in creating and maintaining a safe and healthy workplace is where all reasonably practicable measures are taken. This allows the competent person carrying out the assessment to balance the cost, time and effort in devising a safe system of work against the consequences of an accident.

The information available to the competent person could include:

- the actual regulations covering the specific work task – e.g. the requirements for the use of ladders can be found in the Workplace (Health, Safety and Welfare) Regulations 1992 and the Construction (Health, Safety and Welfare) Regulations 1996;
- good practice guidance notes from the HSE, special interest groups and trade associations;
- the employer's own health and safety policy and arrangements document (which may be even more stringent than the actual regulations);
- the employees involved in the task, who can bring practical experience to the process; and
- external consultants.

With regard to the cost of the control measures deemed necessary, no allowance would be made by the enforcing authorities for the size, nature or profitability of the business.

Should an accident occur, the problem for the assessor is that he would need to prove that it was not reasonably practicable to have done more. With

---

Sources of further information

INDG163REV1 'Five steps to risk assessment' (HSE Books, 1998): ISBN 0 7176 1565 0.

'Risk Assessment Policy and Management Guide, version 1.0' (ISBN 1 900648 33 4, £74.99) is available as an electronic download from the Workplace Law Network. Call 0870 777 8881 for details, or visit www.workplacelaw.net.

---

hindsight it is very often the case that further control measures could have been brought into use.

For that reason those carrying out assessments often err on the side of caution – and that is no bad principle.

What to do with the completed risk assessment

Record in writing, and then review and change when necessary (this could be due to changes in legislation or, for example, as a result of an accident).

Ensure all persons involved in the work activities are made aware of and understand the assessment.

Ensure that the control measures in the assessment are being complied with when the task is actually being carried out.

See also: Fire risk assessments (page 271).

Security licensing

Robert Buxton, Security Industry Authority

The Security Industry Authority

It is estimated that there are 500,000 individuals working in the private security industry in England and Wales. Variation in the quality of training, regulation and licensing has led to low levels of professionalism within the industry and small pockets of criminal elements operating in some sectors. Consequently the public's perception of the industry as a whole has been damaged. To address this and to raise standards of professionalism, training and probity, the Security Industry Authority (SIA) was created.

The SIA is a non-departmental public body formed under the Private Security Industry Act 2001 (PSIA) with the remit to regulate and license the private security industry in England and Wales. The Scottish Executive has expressed a readiness to extend the SIA's remit to Scotland and the legislative process is under way.

The SIA licenses individuals working in private security, starting with an estimated 85,000 people working as door supervisors, then moving on to license vehicle immobilisers (wheelclampers), security guards, key holders, security consultants and private investigators. By April 2005, when the 13-month process of introducing door supervisor licences across England and Wales will have been completed, all local authority and police door supervisor schemes will cease to be valid and it will be illegal to work as a door supervisor or to provide door supervisors in England and Wales without an SIA licence.

Everyone working as a door supervisor operative, manager, employer or director in the door supervision sector will require an SIA licence. The licence is *personal* to the individual: it is his responsibility to obtain it and to see that it is kept up to date. Licensees will be responsible for ensuring that they only employ, or use companies or agencies that supply, SIA-licensed door supervisors.

Why regulation is needed

Variation in the quality of training, regulation and licensing of the door supervision sector has led, not only to a restrictive and complicated system operating within local authority boundaries, but to small criminal and violent elements operating in the sector. These people have damaged the public's perception of the security industry and their bad press could have a detrimental effect on the reputation of town centres. A report in the *Sheffield Star* highlighted the problem: 'A doorman was jailed after causing grievous bodily harm to a reveller at a city nightclub. The doorman "launched" the customer down a flight of stairs while escorting him off the premises. The doorman had been allowed to work despite having a criminal record dating back 27 years including assaults, wounding, kidnap, possession of an offensive weapon and making threats to kill.'

This is the sort of incident the SIA is planning to eradicate from door supervision by introducing a system of robust checks and training for the industry. The SIA consulted widely with trade associations, the police and local government to establish criteria for training and licensing; it believes that they are reasonable and attainable, but will deter the undesirable element from involvement in the private security industry. In setting those standards, the SIA took into account the changing role of those already employed in the industry and the requirements for new skills and knowledge, particularly conflict management and communication – basic skills needed by the modern-day door supervisor.

As with any professional qualification, there is a robust process to go through before achieving recognition. The SIA's criteria are as follows:

- Individuals have to provide proof of identity and age.
- A criminal record check is carried out.
- The training standards that the SIA has set must be met and a national qualification attained.
- Individuals must have the right to work in the UK.
- Individuals must not have been sectioned under the Mental Health Act in the last five years.

Not everyone with a criminal record will automatically be refused a licence as the SIA recognises employment plays an important part in rehabilitation. It will take into account the seriousness and relevance of any offences and how long ago they occurred. The SIA website has an 'indicator' where applicants with a criminal history can obtain an early indi-cation whether or not they meet the criteria to obtain a licence.

The new SIA training package is designed to meet the needs of the modern door supervisor working at a busy pub and club at any city centre. The new training is in two parts, with two assessments, and will normally be delivered over four days. The programme covers the roles and responsibilities of a door supervisor: appropriate behaviour, civil and criminal law, search and arrest procedures, recording incidents and crime scene prevention, emergency procedures, and communication and conflict management.

The training package can be delivered by training providers and further education colleges approved and overseen by the qualifications-awarding bodies. The cost of the training varies. Some far-sighted local authorities offer the training for free, but the usual cost is around £200, although subsidies are often available. Some past training may be taken into consideration and could partly or fully exempt a door supervisor from taking the full SIA training package.

Applying for a licence

Applying for a licence is simple. The SIA call centre takes calls and issues individual part-completed application packs. Once the applicant has returned the completed forms to the SIA with necessary supporting documents, the Authority carries out a criminal records check, verifies the qualifications and assesses the application. If all is in order, then a licence will be issued. The application process usually takes between four and six weeks. Applicants can also use the SIA website to apply.

The fee for a three-year door supervisor national licence is £190. The licence fee covers the costs for the service of processing applications and issuing a licence, identity and criminality checking, publicity, enforcement of SIA licensing and the call centre.

Enforcement

A national network of SIA investigators works closely with the Authority's partner organisations such as the police, local authorities and the industry itself to ensure strict compliance with the regulations and licensing. Like the SIA, they want to see only professional, trained and qualified security staff working to protect the public.

There are substantial penalties for anyone guilty of an offence under the Private Security Industry Act 2001 – i.e. using or supplying unlicensed security staff or working without an SIA licence:

- On summary conviction at a magistrates' court the maximum penalty is six months' imprisonment and/or a fine of up to £5,000.
- On conviction at Crown Court the maximum penalty is five years' imprisonment and/or an unlimited fine.

Current developments

The SIA is on course for the full introduction of SIA door supervisor licences on 11 April 2005.

Since 1 November 2004 vehicle immobilisers (wheelclampers) have been able to apply for their licence application packs. As with door supervisors, vehicle immobilisers (those that operate on private land and charge a fee for release of a vehicle) will undergo an identity and criminal record check and will need to take and pass a set training course. From 28 February 2005 it will be illegal to operate as a front-line vehicle immobiliser (operative) or a non-front-line immobiliser (supervisor, manager or director) without an SIA licence. The vehicle immobiliser licence application fee will be £190 for a one-year front-line licence and £190 for a three-year non-front-line licence.

SIA licences for the private security guarding sector will be introduced during 2005. The Authority has announced the competencies and training required for security guards and details of the licensing timetable will be announced shortly.

> *See also*: Criminal records (page 156); Wheelclamping (page 537).

Sources of further information

The SIA's website (www.the-sia.org.uk) gives more detail about the Authority, the licensing scheme, and the training and awarding bodies and also has up-to-date information on the latest developments.

The door supervisor 'Get Licensed' information booklet can be obtained by telephoning the SIA's call centre on 08702 430 100.

Shared premises/common parts

Edited by Hugh Bruce-Watt, Pinsent Masons

Key points

- Tenants in occupation of shared premises are usually subject to a service charge imposed by the landlord for the provision of services. The services include repair and maintenance for which the landlord is responsible, and insurance for the building as a whole. The landlord will seek to recoup the cost of all services by the service charge.
- Tenants should carefully negotiate the provisions requiring them to pay for maintenance and repair so as to avoid incurring costs which may benefit the landlord's premises long after the expiry of their lease.

Service charge

The main issue for a tenant in shared premises is the payment of service charge – what benefits it provides and obligations it imposes. The parties' interests will of course be contradictory. The landlord will want to try to recover all costs incurred in connection with the building and will want a free rein to decide what work is needed and who to charge it to. The tenant ideally will want to limit liability to basic services provided and for these to be reasonable amounts known in advance for budgeting purposes. A happy medium is found only by careful wording of the relevant provisions in the lease and a pragmatic working relationship between the landlord (or his managing agents) and the tenants.

Repair and maintenance

The lease will contain a clause requiring the landlord to maintain and repair the main structure and exterior of the building and the common parts.

The tenant will usually be responsible for internal repair and may be required to decorate the interior, usually every five years, leaving it in the same condition as when taking on the lease. Anything more onerous than this is an unnecessary burden on the tenant.

The tenant should ensure that the precise areas of the building contained in the common parts, for which the landlord has responsibility, are clearly identified in the lease to avoid later dispute and are sufficient for their use of the building. Such items as windows and doors could be either an integral part of the structure of the building or an internal fixture. The tenant should not wait for any dispute to arise before trying to decide who is responsible.

Any major repair works carried out will be reflected in an increased service charge. Tenants of new buildings should be vigilant that they are not asked to contribute towards the cost of the original construction of the building.

Repair or improvement?

A tenant does not have any input as to the cost of whether repairs are done on a cheaper or more expensive basis unless there is a specific reference in the lease for the landlord to obtain approved estimates. The landlord therefore could seek to add some expensive long-term structural repairs to the service charge which could be seen as an improvement rather than a necessary repair.

Tenants under a short-term lease should not be responsible for extensive long-term repairs and should ensure that the wording of the lease makes it clear that they are not required to contribute.

Insurance

It is usually the landlord's responsibility to provide adequate insurance cover for the building. The cost of this is recouped via the service charge. With shared premises this will invariably be by way of a block policy.

The tenant should ensure that the lease contains a clause providing that:

• in the event of the building (or the means of access) being damaged or destroyed, the landlord is obliged to use the insurance monies to reinstate the building and make up the shortfall;

• the rent be suspended until the building is reinstated; and

• the tenant has an option to determine the lease if the building is not reinstated within a specified period.

Calculation of service charge

The lease will specify the proportion of the costs of the service charge. This may simply be by reference to a fair proportion, by reference to the relative floor size occupied by each tenant, or by some other method.

Tenants should ensure they are aware of exactly what services are included in the service charge (which should be scheduled in the lease), as, for example, a tenant on the ground floor does not want to pay a proportion of maintenance towards the lift (although in practice the landlord is unlikely to accept such a restriction).

The landlord can be required to certify, by way of a certificate issued by an accountant or surveyor, that the service charge is properly calculated in accordance with the lease.

See also: Insurance (page 332); Landlord and tenant: lease issues (page 345).

Sickness leave

Nicole Hallegua, Berwin Leighton Paisner

Key points

- Contracts of employment and statements of terms must state whether or not the employer makes payments for periods of absence due to sickness and, if so, upon what terms.
- Certain qualifying employees are entitled to statutory sick pay (SSP), in respect of which, for a specified period, employers are responsible.
- When terminating the employment of those who are absent due to sickness (whether for conduct, capability or some other substantial reason), consideration must be given to (a) the fairness of the decision and procedure followed, (b) the existence of permanent health insurance schemes and (c) the question of disability discrimination.

Legislation

- Employment Rights Act 1996.
- Social Security Contributions and Benefits Act 1992 (as amended).
- Disability Discrimination Act 1995.
- ACAS Code of Practice on Disciplinary and Grievance Procedures (April 2003).

Sickness leave: entitlement to sick pay

Most employees have an entitlement (either contractual or statutory) to be paid sick pay from their employer while absent from work due to ill health.

Contractual sick pay

In practice, most employers operate company sick pay schemes that expressly outline each employee's contractual entitlement. Provided the employer pays to the employee the minimum level of remuneration he would be entitled to under the Social Security Contributions and Benefits Act 1992 (as amended) (SSCBA), the employer can opt out of the SSP scheme.

Statutory sick pay (SSP)

The legislative provisions dealing with payment of SSP are lengthy and technical. Broadly speaking, the SSCBA provides that all employees, subject to certain specified exceptions, are entitled to receive SSP from their employers. This entitlement is limited to 28 weeks in a three-year period.

To qualify for SSP, certain prerequisite conditions must be satisfied. Essentially these are as follows:

- The individual must be an 'employee', not a worker, during 'the period of incapacity for work' (PIW).
- The employee must have four or more consecutive days of sickness (including weekends and holidays) during which he is too ill to be capable of doing his work.
- The employee must notify his employer of his sickness leave (subject to certain statutory requirements and any agreement between them).
- The employee must provide evidence of his inability to do his normal job. This is usually done by self-certification (days 1 to 7 inclusive) and a doctor's certificate (day 8 onwards).

Those who do not or no longer qualify for SSP may be entitled to other social security benefits, e.g. incapacity benefit, statutory (and/or contractual) maternity pay, etc.

All employers have a statutory obligation to keep (and retain for at least three years) records for SSP purposes. As a minimum, for each employee, an employer must record PIWs and details of payments made (or not made) in respect of PIWs.

Sickness leave: dismissals

When dealing with sickness leave, a distinction should always be made between absences on grounds of longer periods of medically certificated illness (capability issue) and those bouts of persistent short absences caused by unconnected minor illnesses that may call for disciplinary action (conduct issue). In both dismissal scenarios, a potentially fair reason must exist and the employer must act reasonably in all the circumstances in dismiss-ing the employee as a consequence of the reason (see 'Dismissal', page 197). Further, what may be considered fair and reasonable will vary according to the particular circumstances of each individual case.

Conduct

A dismissal on the grounds of conduct owing to persistent periods of absences from work should be fair provided the employer:

- has reasonable grounds to believe the employee is guilty of misconduct;
- before any disciplinary meeting, investigates the extent of and reasons for the employee's absences (thereby allowing the employee an opportunity to explain);
- informs the employee of the level of attendance he is expected to attain, of the time within which he should achieve it, and that he may be dismissed if there is insufficient improvement; and
- thereafter monitors the situation, and offers support or assistance if appropriate, for a reasonable period prior to dismissal.

Capability

A dismissal on the grounds of incapability due to ill health should be fair where the employer:

- investigates the employee's true medical position and prognosis for recovery (e.g. by obtaining a medical report with the employee's consent);
- after considering the requirements of the business, the possibility of alternative employment and the likelihood of the employee return-

ing to work in the foreseeable future, concludes there is no alternative but to dismiss; and

- consults with the employee about the possibility of his employment being terminated prior to dismissal.

Only when an employer obtains a clear prognosis of the employee's state of health will it be able to adequately assess the requirements of the business and what other alternative positions may be offered to the particular employee.

Sickness leave: dismissals and permanent health insurance (PHI) schemes

Where an employee has a right to receive permanent health benefits, the grounds on which an employer can dismiss are considerably restricted. In short, an employer will act unlawfully when it dismisses an employee who is in receipt of benefit under a PHI scheme. This is because there is an overriding implied term that an employer should not dismiss the employee while he is incapacitated and thereby deprive him of the very disability benefit that it is the primary purpose of PHI schemes to provide.

However, in such circumstances employers may be able to dismiss for good cause such as gross misconduct or for some other form of fundamental breach by the employee. Potentially, dismissal for capability or a genuine redundancy situation could also be a good cause for dismissal in these circumstances. What is crucial is that the 'good cause' must be something other than the ill health.

Sickness leave: dismissals and disability discrimination

Any worker who is dismissed in the light of his illness could potentially bring a claim under the Disability Discrimination Act 1995. To do this he would need to show that, by reason of the dismissal, the employer treated him less favourably because of his illness and that the illness constitutes a disability as defined by the legislation, i.e. 'a physical or mental impairment which has a substantial and long-term adverse effect upon a person's ability to carry out normal day-to-day activities'. If proven, the ultimate question then becomes whether the employer can be expected to wait any longer for the employee. To avoid a finding of discrimination and unfair dismissal, the employer will need to justify the reason for dismissing the employee and show that it made all 'reasonable adjustments' as are practicable in the circumstances (see 'Discrimination', page 189).

Sickness leave: notice rights

Where an employee who is incapable of work because of sickness or injury has his employment terminated with the statutory minimum period of notice and his contract of employment or statement of terms specifies normal working hours, he is entitled to receive a minimum hourly rate of pay during that notice period for any period during normal working hours in which he is too ill to be capable of doing his work.

Where an employee who is incapable of work because of sickness or injury has his employment terminated with the statutory minimum period of notice and his contract of employment or statement of terms does not specify normal working hours, he is entitled to a week's pay for each week during that notice period when he is too ill to be capable of doing his work.

See also: Absence management (page 65); Dismissal (page 197); Discrimination (page 189); Employment contracts (page 225).

Sources of further information

ACAS: www.acas.org.uk.

DTI: www.dti.gov.uk.

Information from the Department for Work and Pensions on statutory sick pay: www.dwp.gov.uk/lifeevent/benefits/statutory_sick_pay.asp.

Safety signage

Andrew Richardson, Scott Wilson

Key points

- A safety sign provides information or instruction about health or safety at work.
- Employers must provide safety signage where there is a risk that it is not possible to avoid or control by other means.
- Safety signs are not a substitute for other methods of controlling risks, such as engineering controls and safe systems of work.
- The Workplace (Health, Safety and Welfare) Regulations 1992 require traffic routes and some dangerous locations to be marked.

Legislation

- Health and Safety at Work etc. Act 1974.
- Management of Health and Safety at Work Regulations 1999.
- Health and Safety (Safety Signs and Signals) Regulations 1996.
- Workplace (Health, Safety and Welfare) Regulations 1992.

Statutory requirements

The Management of Health and Safety at Work Regulations 1999 require employers to carry out a suitable and sufficient risk assessment to identify the hazards, assess the risk and identify means of reducing the risks to acceptable levels.

The Health and Safety (Safety Signs and Signals) Regulations 1996 implement the EC Safety Signs Directive (92/58/EEC), the purpose of which is to encourage the consistency of safety signage throughout the EU. The Regulations require employers to provide safety signage where there is a residual risk, and to inform and warn employees following implementation of risk control measures.

A safety sign is defined in the Regulations as 'a sign referring to a specific object, activity or situation and providing information or instruction about health or safety at work by means of a signboard, a safety colour, an illuminated sign, an acoustic signal, a verbal communication or a hand signal'.

The Regulations prescribe that signage should be coded by colour and shape, with pictograms to illustrate the message. The types of signs to be used are indicated in the table on page 000.

The Regulations state that traffic signage must be provided to ensure the safe movement of vehicles around the employer's premises.

The Regulations require marking of

Sign types specified in the Safety Signs and Signals Regulations

Colour	Sign type	Information/examples
Red	Prohibition/danger	Round shape – black pictogram on white background, red edging with diagonal line Examples: No smoking; No access
Yellow	Warning	Triangular shape: black pictogram on yellow background with black edging Examples: Danger – Electricity; Biological risk
Blue	Mandatory	Round shape: white pictogram on blue background Examples: Safety helmet must be worn; Ear protection must be worn
Green	Emergency escape/First aid	Rectangular or square in shape: white pictogram on green background Examples: Emergency exit running man sign; First-aid post
Red	Firefighting	Rectangular or square shape: white pictogram on red background Examples: Fire hosereel; Fire extinguisher

pipework in the workplace that contains a dangerous substance. The employer should mark the pipework at appropriate points (e.g. sampling and discharge points) with a triangular warning sign as described in the table, the pictogram being based on the dangerous substance symbol (e.g. toxic, corrosive, flammable) that is appropriate.

These Regulations are retrospective. Therefore all signage currently utilised in workplaces must be compliant. Fire safety signage compliant with BS 5499: Part 1 is deemed to meet these Regulations although their detail is different from above.

Sources of further information

The principal source of information is L64 'Safety Signs and Signals – Guidance on Regulations – The Health and Safety (Safety Signs and Signals) Regulations 1996' (HSE Books, 1997): ISBN 0 7176 0870 6. This document provides all the guidance needed by employers and identifies any further documentation that is relevant.

BS 5378:1980 Parts 1 and 3 'Safety signs and colours'.

BS 5499:1990 Part 1 'Fire safety signs, notices and graphic symbols'.

The signage must be sufficiently large and clear for it to be seen and understood. However, employers must not have too many signboards in close proximity as this may cause confusion or lead to information being overlooked.

The employer must maintain the signage in a condition that ensures it can continue to be used for the purpose that it was intended. This would involve routine inspection and cleaning.

The employer also has a duty to ensure his employees are familiar with all of the signage and know what each sign means. Therefore all employees need to be informed and trained as appropriate.

These Regulations do not cover the supply of articles and dangerous substances which are covered by their own legislation such as the Chemicals (Hazard Information and Packaging for Supply) Regulations 2002 and the Supply of Machinery (Safety) Regulations 1992.

See also: Fire: means of escape (page 263).

Smoking

Stuart Armstrong, Pinsent Masons

Key points

- Employers should seek to protect employees from the inherent risks of passive smoking.
- To avoid claims for unfair dismissal from smokers, any smoking policy must be reasonable.
- The reasonableness of a policy will depend on both its form and the manner of its introduction.

Legislation

The Health and Safety at Work etc. Act 1974 (HSWA) places duties on employers and the controllers of premises to safeguard the health and safety of employees, non-employees and members of the public visiting premises.

The Management of Health and Safety at Work Regulations 1999 (MHSWR) require employers to assess the risks to employees from hazards which they may be exposed to at work. While the Approved Code of Practice (ACoP) to the MHSWR allows employers to ignore trivial risks or those from life in general, this exemption will not apply to passive smoking where the risks are considered to be significant.

The Workplace (Health, Safety and Welfare) Regulations 1992 and the ACoP accompanying them require employers to provide effective and suitable ventilation (Regulation 6) and to protect non-smokers from the effects of tobacco smoke in restrooms and rest areas. However, it should be noted that improved ventilation alone may not provide an adequate safeguard against exposure. Regulation 25(3) requires employers to protect non-smokers from discomfort caused by tobacco smoke in restrooms and rest areas. The ACoP suggests that methods of achieving this include the prohibition of smoking in those places or the provision of separate areas for smokers and non-smokers.

The Code of Practice 'Smoking in public places: guidance for owners and managers of places visited by the public' and the HSE booklet 'Passive smoking at work' give guidance to employers and have been revised to:

- set out the benefits of a smoking policy;
- recommend that employers give priority to non-smokers; and
- suggest ways in which employers can achieve a smoke-free environment.

486

More details of the guidance provided in the HSE booklet on the last point are given in the section 'Health and Safety Commission guidance' below.

Employer's obligations

The courts have tended to imply a right to protection for employees in the workplace, stating that there is a term implied into employment contracts that 'the employer will provide and monitor for his employees, so far as is reasonably practicable, a working environment which is reasonably suitable for the performance by them of their contractual duties.'

Applying this formula, it has been held that a non-smoker was constructively dismissed (i.e. there was a serious breach of her employment contract) as a result of being required to work in a smoke-affected atmosphere, despite her protests.

The HSWA also imposes on employers a general duty to protect people who are not employees themselves but may be affected by an employer's activities. Therefore workplace managers must take care to consider the effect of employees smoking when they come into contact with members of the public or other organisations during their working day.

Employers who choose to introduce anti-smoking measures must take care that by doing so they are not seen to be victimising smokers – who may previously have enjoyed an unfettered right to smoke in the workplace – in order to avoid the possibility of their claiming constructive unfair dismissal. The best way to avoid this problem is to introduce a reasonable and carefully considered smoking policy and to consult employees on its introduction.

International examples

The introduction of bans on smoking in bars in New York has allegedly seen a reduction in pollution levels following the ban but a decrease of $28.5m in wage and salary payments. In Dublin, there have been a reported 2,000 job losses following the implementing of a ban on smoking in bars there in March 2004, but the Irish Revenue Commissioner has reported a 16% decrease in tobacco sales.

In Norway, rather than implementing a complete ban, non-smoking areas and requirements for better ventilation are part of a 15-year staged process for the introduction of a ban. Norway has banned smoking in bars following the initiative in Ireland and bar owners face the prospect of losing their licences if smokers are not persuaded to stop lighting up.

Other countries that have introduced bans or restrictions include the Netherlands, South Africa and Tanzania.

UK proposals

On 10 November 2004 the Scottish First Minister, Jack McConnell, announced that the Scottish Executive had decided to ban smoking in all enclosed public places in Scotland from spring 2006. The announcement followed a record public consultation exercise in which 53,948 Scottish people took part.

In the following week, on 16 November, the UK Government published a White Paper in which, among other public health proposals, plans were announced to make most enclosed public areas in England, including smoking rooms in offices and factories, smoke-free by 2008. Health Secretary John Reid announced that smoking restrictions were to be phased in with a ban on smoking in NHS and Government buildings in 2006, in enclosed public spaces in 2007 and in licensed premises by 2008. Only public houses not preparing and serving food and private clubs whose members voted to allow smoking would be exempt from the ban.

Health Minister Jane Hutt told the Welsh Assembly that it was to receive full powers over the future of smoking in public places in Wales. In 2003 the Assembly voted for a total ban, even though it did not have the power to implement it. Any Bill prepared by the UK Parliament would contain clauses that applied in Wales. These clauses would have to be agreed in Westminster before the UK Government could change the law.

While the UK Government proposals did not go as far as those of the Scottish Executive, they went much further than many commentators had expected. Wide consultation with interested parties including the catering industry and pro-smoking pressure groups was promised.

It is uncertain at present how these proposals will affect previous rulings of the Employment Appeals Tribunal, which in 1997 held that the employer was in breach of an implied term for the provision of a reasonably suitable working environment following its failure to deal adequately with the employee's complaint about a smoky atmosphere at work.

What seems to be clearer is that a 1992 decision that there was neither an express nor an implied term in an employee's contract entitling the employee to smoke at work will be affected by the decision to introduce a statutory ban on smoking in public areas.

Introducing a smoking policy

An employer should consider both the form of the policy and the manner of its introduction. Whether a policy is reasonable or not will be a question of fact. However, a prudent employer should take account of:

- the practicalities of the workplace (e.g. can a segregated smoking room be allocated to smokers?);
- the nature of the business, including whether clients will be regularly visiting the building;
- workplace opinion;
- assistance to smokers in adapting to the new policy;
- consultation with individuals and/or their representatives;
- staging the introduction of the policy over a reasonable period; and
- ensuring that employees are fully aware of the possible sanctions for breach of the policy, including cross-references to the disciplinary procedure.

Once a policy is in place it must be consistently enforced. It would, however, be sensible to support smokers during the early period of the policy and to avoid overly harsh sanctions during those early stages.

Health and Safety Commission guidance

A lengthy consultation process has taken place on whether the Health and Safety Commission (HSC) should publish an ACoP to deal with the problem of passive smoking in the workplace. However, owing to perceived difficulties with the enforcement of such a code of practice, this idea has been scrapped and instead the general guidance booklet 'Passive smoking at work' has been issued.

The guidance suggests a number of ways in which an employer may reasonably and practically control environmental tobacco smoke including:

- a total or partial ban on smoking in the workplace;
- the physical segregation of non-smokers from tobacco smoke;
- providing adequate ventilation; and
- implementing a system of work that reduces the time an employee is exposed to environmental tobacco smoke.

When choosing to adopt these measures, an employer should continue to take account of the considerations set out above in order to ensure that the new smoking policy is deemed to be a reasonable one.

It is interesting to note that enforcement officers are encouraged to take a proactive role and draw employers' attention to HSC guidance and put a smoking policy in place. Where they consider that smoking creates a significant risk they may seek compliance with the MHSWR.

The Health Education Authority has produced guidance on the introduction of workplace smoking policies and the Department of Health has reached an agreement with the British Beer and Pub Association (formerly the Brewers and Licensed Retailers Association) and other trade organisations over a set of principles known as the Charter. This represents an industry standard and may be viewed by the courts as having a similar standing to ACoPs.

HSE solicitors have advised local authorities (in HELA guidance document 91/1) that the Control of Substances Hazardous to Health Regulations 1994 (COSHH) do not apply to smoking at work because the hazard does not arise out of or in connection with the work activity.

See also: Health and safety at work (page 295); Health and safety management (page 311); Health and safety policies (page 316); Ventilation and temperature (page 513).

Sources of further information

INDG63REV1 'Passive smoking at work' (HSE Books, 1997): ISBN 0 7176 0882 4.

HSE page on passive smoking at work: www.hse.gov.uk/hthdir/noframes/smoking.htm.

'Smoking at Work Policy and Management Guide, version 1.0' (ISBN 1 900648 65 2, £34.99) is available as an electronic download from the Workplace Law Network. Call 0870 777 8881 for details, or visit www.workplacelaw.net.

Staff handbooks

Helen Abbott, Workplace Law Group

Key points

- Ensure that staff handbooks are easy to read.
- Use a format that is easy to update.
- Reduce printing costs by publishing on your company intranet site.
- Ensure that all staff have access to the staff handbook.
- Ask new starters to sign to confirm they have read and understood the contents of the staff handbook.
- Build time into induction training to read the staff handbook.

Legislation

- Equal Pay Act 1970.
- Sex Discrimination Act 1975.
- Race Relations Act 1976.
- Employment Act 1989.
- Trade Union and Labour Relations (Consolidation) Act 1992.
- Disability Discrimination Act 1995.
- Employment Rights Act 1996.
- National Minimum Wage Act 1998.
- Working Time Regulations 1998.
- Employment Relations Act 1999.
- Part-time Workers (Prevention of Less Favourable Treatment) Regulations 2000.
- Fixed-term Employees (Prevention of Less Favourable Treatment) Regulations 2002.
- Employment Rights Act 2002.
- Information and Consultation of Employees Regulations 2004.

Drafting a staff handbook

An increasing number of companies issue their new staff with staff handbooks. These will incorporate some of the features of a contract of employment (see 'Employment contracts', page 225). They should aim to satisfy the legal obligations of the employer to issue the terms and conditions of employment specified in the statement of particulars.

Additionally, staff handbooks are a very convenient way of giving new employees as much information as practicable about the structure and culture of an organisation. This will include details of the organisation's personnel and employment procedures such as salaries and pensions, holiday and sick pay, and disciplinary and grievance procedures.

Because of the wide range of subjects that can be addressed in staff handbooks, they are a very useful source of information for management and staff, as well as being an excellent induction tool.

Great care needs to be exercised when writing staff handbooks, in order that policies and procedures that are non-contractual remain so. In addition, an awareness and understanding of current employment legislation will be needed to ensure that policies and procedures comply with the law. At present, employment legislation is updated twice a year (April and October), so you need to be prepared to update policies on a regular basis. Think ahead and read about changes proposed by the Government and how they are likely to affect your policies and procedures, e.g. the age discrimination legislation proposed for 2006.

To keep printing costs to a minimum, choose a format that is easy to update and limit the use of colour, perhaps to just one or two. One option is to use your intranet site to publish your handbook in a PDF format so that existing staff can download and read a copy. However, this will depend on the nature of your organisation, the types of jobs and skills within it, and whether staff have ready access to computers. You need to ensure that all employees have access to a copy of the handbook.

The staff handbook will be a crucial document in any dispute between parties that reach an employment tribunal. Be clear and specific about important issues such as disciplinary and grievance procedures, pay structure and reviews, holidays, sick pay and other areas where there is scope for dispute. Draw on your previous experience and consult senior managers about areas which have been problematic or unclear in the past and decide where your organisation stands on them. Think about frequently asked employment questions from staff and try to cover those areas.

Finally, set aside 20 to 30 minutes of induction time to enable new starters to read the handbook and ask any questions. Require new staff to sign to say they have read, have understood and accept the terms and conditions outlined in the handbook.

Content checklist

Essential:

- Disciplinary and grievance procedure.
- Family-friendly policies including maternity, paternity and adoption leave, emergency time off for dependants, and parental leave.
- Holiday leave and pay.
- Sick leave and pay.
- Equal opportunities
- Pay and benefits (including overtime pay).
- Deductions from wages (including recovery of overpayments).
- Hours of work.
- Notice periods.
- Health and safety policy (this could be published as a separate document or handbook).
- Information and consultation arrangements (if any).
- Collective agreements (if any).

Optional:

- Introduction to the organisation.
- Organisation chart.
- Internet and email policy.
- Bullying and harassment.
- Incapacity and capability.
- Absence policy.
- Performance management/appraisals.
- Drugs and alcohol.
- Smoking.
- Training.

- Dress code.
- Gifts and hospitality.
- Expenses procedure.
- DSE eyesight policy (could be included in health and safety handbook).
- Company equipment (mobile phones, laptops, tools, etc.).
- Forms for in-house use.
- Housekeeping.
- Flexible working arrangements.
- Reference policy.
- Redundancy.
- Bereavement/compassionate leave.
- Jury service.
- Bank holiday working.
- Time off for trade union representatives (if applicable).
- Whistleblowing.
- Stress.

Checklist of dos and don'ts

Dos:

- Ensure that you are familiar with current employment legislation and how this affects your policies and procedures.
- Use bullet points, short sentences and paragraph subheadings.
- Write confidently, concisely and directly.

- Write formally.
- Choose a format that is easy to update – loose-leaf or ring binders are helpful.
- Try to make your handbook attractive to encourage staff to read it.
- Think about a frequently asked questions (FAQs) section.
- Consult senior managers and staff representatives (if applicable) when drafting new policies and procedures.
- Get the contents checked from a legal perspective before publishing.
- Get it proofread to reduce errors or typing mistakes.

Don'ts:

- Use scene-setting, padding or long lead-ins.
- Use long paragraphs.
- Use foreign phrases or Latin.
- Use jargon, clichés or humour.
- Be vague – this can lead to misinterpretation resulting in disputes with your employees.
- Ignore current employment legislation or best management practice.

See also: Employment contracts (page 225).

Sources of further information

Evans, Alastair and Walters, Mike: *From Absence to Attendance*, 2nd edition (CIPD, 2002): ISBN 0 85292 935 8.

Evans, Michael: *Employing People with Disabilities* (CIPD, 2001): ISBN 0 85292 900 5.

Jackson, Tricia: *Drugs and Alcohol Policies* (CIPD, 1999): ISBN 0 85292 811 4.

Stredwick, John and Ellis, Steve: *Flexible Working Practices* (CIPD, 1998): ISBN 0 85292 744 4.

Stress

Jessica Burt, CMS Cameron McKenna

Key points

- All employers owe a legal duty of care to their employees. Injury to mental health is treated in the same way as injury to physical health.
- Sixteen general propositions for bringing any civil claim for compensation for stress have been provided and are listed below (see 'Criteria for civil cases').
- A successful claim must show that, on the balance of probabilities, an employer had knowledge or deemed knowledge of the foreseeability of harm to a particular employee, so that the lack of his taking reasonable steps to, as far as is reasonably practicable, alleviate the risk of or prevent that harm occurring constituted a breach of duty of care to the employee, and that this caused the injury or loss.
- The HSE has urged employers to carry out risk assessment and implement measures to eliminate or control workplace stress or risk criminal prosecution. The HSE's Management Standards on stress (a web-based toolkit to help businesses comply with their duties) were published on 3 November 2004. Employers will need to take on board this HSE guidance in order to provide best practice in health and safety.

Legislation

- Health and Safety at Work etc. Act 1974.
- Management of Health and Safety at Work Regulations 1999.

Main cases

- *Walker -v- Northumberland County Council* [1995] 1 All ER. 737.
- *Sutherland -v- Hatton* [2002] EWCA Civ 76, CA 05/02/02.
- *Barber -v- Somerset County Council* [2004] UKHL13.

Legal aspects of stress claims

All employers owe a legal duty of care to their employees. Injury to mental health is treated in the same way as injury to physical health.

Criteria for civil cases

These criteria set out by the Court of Appeal in *Sutherland -v- Hatton* received virtually unqualified support from the House of Lords in *Barber -v- Somerset County Council*:

1. The ordinary principles of employers' liability apply.

2. There are no occupations that should be regarded as intrinsically dangerous to mental health.

3. The threshold question to be answered in any workplace stress case was stated as: 'whether this kind of harm to this particular employee was reasonably foreseeable'. This has two components: (a) an injury (as distinct from occupational stress) that (b) is attributable to stress at work (as distinct from other factors).

4. Foreseeability depends upon what the employer knows (or ought reasonably to know) about the individual employees.

5. Factors likely to be relevant in answering the threshold question include:
   (a) the nature and extent of the work done; and
   (b) signs from the employee of impending harm to health.

6. The employer is generally entitled to take what he is told by his employee at face value, unless he has good reason to think to the contrary.

7. To trigger a duty to take steps, the indications of impending harm to health arising from stress at work must be plain enough for any reasonable employer to realise that he should do something about it.

   This area was reviewed by the House of Lords in *Barber -v- Somerset*. While the employer may be entitled to assume that his employee is up to the normal pressures of the job and accept what he has been told by the employee, there is also an expectation that the employer keeps abreast of developing knowledge and practice and applies best practice according to his knowledge of the risks as a positive duty. Additionally, all factors should be taken into account, such as time off sick, as well as specific indications of stress from employees.

8. The employer is in breach of duty only if he has failed to take steps that are reasonable in the circumstances.

9. The size and scope of the employer's operation, its resources and the demands it faces are relevant in deciding what is reasonable; these include the interests of other employees and the need to treat them fairly (e.g. in any redistribution of duties).

10. An employer can only be expected to take steps that are reasonable.

    The employer is in breach of duty only if he has failed to take steps that are reasonable in the circumstances, bearing in mind the magnitude of the risk of harm occurring, the gravity of the harm that may occur, the costs and practicability of preventing it, and the justifications for running the risk. An employer can only reasonably be expected to take steps that are likely to do some good. However, it is possible that if such a defence is run the court is likely to require expert evidence, and it is advised that employers have a policy on what to do in certain circumstances that may reinforce any action taken.

Guidelines for employers

11. An employer who offers a confiden-

tial advice service, with referral to appropriate counselling or treatment services, is unlikely to be found in breach of duty.

12. If the only reasonable and effective step would have been to dismiss or demote the employee, the employer will not have been in breach of duty in allowing a willing employee to continue in the job.

However, in light of the lead judgment of Lord Walker in *Barber* that there is a requirement for 'drastic action' if an employee's health is in danger, it may be said that in the absence of alternative work, where an employee was at risk, ultimately the employer's duty of care would not preclude dismissing or demoting the employee at risk.

13. In all cases, it is necessary to identify the steps that the employer both could and should have taken before finding him in breach of his duty of care.

14. The claimant must show that the breach of duty has caused or materially contributed to the harm suffered. It is not enough to show that occupational stress alone has caused the harm; it must be attributable to a breach of an employer's duty.

Apportionment

15. Where the harm suffered has more than one cause, the employer should pay only for that proportion of the harm suffered that is attributable to his wrongdoing, unless the harm is truly indivisible. It is for the defendant to raise the question of apportionment.

16. The assessment of damages will take account of pre-existing disorder or vulnerability and of the chance that the claimant would have succumbed to a stress-related disorder in any event.

It is not the case that one or other of the tests is more important; all 16 have to be looked at in respect of each individual case.

Additionally, stress now raises its head more often in claims involving bullying and harassment, disability, discrimination and constructive dismissal. Failure to recognise and address stress issues in the context of these types of claim could result in significant liability for an employer. For instance, where an employee may establish that he falls within the definition of a disabled person under the Disability Discrimination Act 1995 and an employer fails to make reasonable adjustments to the workplace for this disability, compensation would also be payable for the psychiatric or physical injuries occurring from stress suffered as a result of this.

Criteria for criminal liability

Where no action is taken by an employer on stress, he may be deemed to have fallen short of his duty to take all reasonably practicable measures to ensure the health, safety and welfare of employees and others sharing the workplace and to create safe and healthy working systems (HSWA).

Equally, there is the requirement to undertake risk assessments of stress and put in place appropriate preventive and protective measures to keep the employees safe from harm (MHSWR). West Dorset Hospitals NHS Trust was the first organisation to have an improvement notice issued against it with the require-

---

Combating stress: an employer's checklist

- No employer has an absolute duty to prevent all stress, which can be as a result of interests outside work. However, once an employee has raised the issue of stress, an employer is under a duty to investigate properly and protect the employee as far as is reasonably practicable.
- Health monitoring: both through a confidential advice line and/or regular company medicals.
- Counselling: an employer who offers a confidential advice service, with referral to appropriate counselling or treatment services, is unlikely to be found in breach of duty. This is of course relative to the problem and the service provided but is a good indication that a proactive approach by an employer can protect him from stress claims and enforcement action.
- Pre-employment health check: this may allow vulnerable potential employees to be excluded from stressful roles. At a pre-employment health assessment the primary responsibility of the occupational physician is to the employer (*Katfunde -v- Abbey National and Dr Daniel* (1998) IRLR 583).
- Regular medicals: these are a useful tool in alerting employers of any risks. However, medical confidentiality has to be observed and express consent given by employees for their clinical information to be shared with employers.
- Dismissal: in the absence of alternative work, the employee deemed at risk should be dismissed or demoted.
- Written health and safety policy: clear guidance in a company's health and safety policy on how stress should be dealt with shows that the company is complying with the health and safety regulations to provide a safe working environment for employees and enables staff to follow a set procedure. It would also stand as a defence where an employee fails to disclose that he is suffering from stress because of ignorance of a company's procedures.
- Equally, a bullying and harassment code should be in force and there should be a clear complaints-handling procedure.
- Risk assessments/implementation of the Management Standards: risk assessments should cover all workplace risks and should therefore include stress; HSE guidance can be found at www.hse.gov.uk/pubns/indg281.pdf. Additionally, implementation of the steps set out in the HSE's Management Standards will also protect employers so long as action is taken to reduce the risks when problems are found.
- Working time: employers can combat stress by monitoring and recording employees' working time with action being taken if the benchmark set out in the Working Time Regulations 1998 is breached.
- Compliance with the new HSE Management Standards will assist in showing that an employer has met the reasonable standard of duty of care required.

ment it assess and reduce the stress levels of its doctors or other employees or face court action and a potentially unlimited fine. The HSE has urged employers to carry out risk assessments and implement measures to eliminate or control workplace stress or risk criminal prosecution.

Unlike civil litigation, any criminal prosecution carries with it the threat of an unlimited fine and/or imprisonment.

As part of the general duty to keep

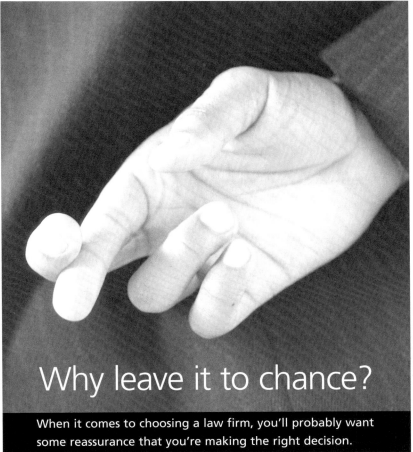

Why leave it to chance?

When it comes to choosing a law firm, you'll probably want some reassurance that you're making the right decision.

Often there can be no greater reassurance than the testimony of existing clients.

Our clients tell us consistently that we're good at building strong relationships, founded on a thorough understanding of their business; that we respond quickly to their requests; and that we're good problem solvers.

But don't just take our word for it. We'd be happy to put you in contact with some of our clients.

Contact Marc Hanson (marc.hanson@cmck.com) for further information.

C/M/S/ Cameron McKenna

abreast of developing knowledge and practice, employers should be aware of the HSE's Management Standards for workplace stress (www.hse.gov.uk/stress/standards/index.htm).

The Management Standards look at six key areas (or 'risk factors') that can be causes of work-related stress: 'demands', 'control', 'support', 'relationships', 'role' and 'change'.

The standard for each area contains simple statements about good management practice that can be applied by employers.

The targets imposed by the HSE in its consultation process have been removed in the published guidance, but the toolkit does allow for measurement against an aspirational target where companies may aim to be in the top 20% of organisations.

In order to comply with the Management Standards employers will need to:

- assess the risk and potential causes of stress within the organisation, e.g. reviewing sickness absence records or conducting specific stress-related surveys;
- consider this information in relation to the six risk factors; and
- decide on improvement targets and action plans, in consultation with staff or their representatives. (Care should be taken that action plans, if any, are realistic and are actually implemented, but in such a way that more stress is not caused to employees.)

HSE guidelines such as these have evidential value. They assist in the interpretation of legislation and the reasonable standard of duty of care owed to employees by employers as, although they are not legally binding, courts have regard to HSE standards in interpreting legislation. Therefore compliance with these Management Standards will assist in showing that an employer has met the reasonable standard of duty of care required.

Any breach of an employer's statutory or regulatory duties under health and safety legislation towards his employees giving rise to criminal liability may also be relied upon by a civil claimant as evidence of the employer's breach of duty in a negligence action and, indeed, in support of a claim for constructive dismissal.

Conclusion

In order to protect themselves against enforcement action as well as employee claims, employers are advised to organise risk assessments of potential stressors, to make facilities such as counselling and grievance procedures available to employees, and to show a receptive and flexible response to complaints. In addition, compliance with the new HSE Management Standards will assist in showing that an employer has met the reasonable standard of duty of care required.

See also: Bullying and harassment (page 108); Discrimination (page 189); Dismissal (page 197); Health and safety enforcement (page 306); Health and safety policies (page 316); Health surveillance (page 318); Risk assessments (page 469); Working time (page 552).

Trade unions

Pinsent Masons Employment Group

Legislation

- Trade Union and Labour Relations (Consolidation) Act 1992.
- Employment Relations Act 1999.
- Employment Relations Act 2004.

Trade unions and collective agreements

A trade union is an organisation consisting of workers whose main purpose is the regulation of relations between the workers and their employers.

In some industries negotiated collective agreements exist relating to pay and terms of employment, and in some circumstances those agreements can also form part of the workers' contracts of employment.

A collective agreement may not always be enforceable between the union and the employer. However, the terms of a collective agreement may become incorporated into an individual employee's contract of employment, and so themselves become terms and conditions of employment.

Collective agreements can be incorporated if the employment contract expressly says so, or if the custom and practice in the industry is that the collective agreements are implied to be incorporated. However, some parts of collective agreements are not appropriate for incorporation.

Generally, once the terms of a collective agreement are incorporated into a contract of employment, they become terms of the contract and in some cases can remain in force even if the original collective agreement terminates.

The Employment Relations Act 2004, although receiving Royal Assent on 16 September 2004, is not yet fully in force and the sections dealing with trade union recognition are not due to be implemented until April 2005. This article deals with the law in its current state.

Membership

Employers are prevented from offering inducements to their employees not to be a member of a trade union, not to take part in the activities of a trade union, not to make use of the services of a trade union and not to give up the right to have their terms and conditions of employment determined by a collective agreement. Further protection is provided to ensure that employees should not suffer detrimental actions for being a union member or using a union's services.

Trade union recognition

The Employment Relations Act 1999 (ERA) created rules for trade unions to be recognised by employers on a statutory basis as long as certain conditions are fulfilled (see 'Statutory recognition' below).

In general terms, however, 'recognition' of a trade union is important in a number of ways. If a union is recognised, employers will have certain duties – e.g.:

- to consult with the union and its representatives on collective redundancy situations;
- to disclose information for collective bargaining purposes; and
- to allow time off to employees engaged in trade union activities or duties.

In addition, in certain circumstances, employers are under a duty to consult with recognised trade unions concerning TUPE transfers.

Statutory recognition

In certain circumstances, even outside the provision of the ERA, trade union recognition can take place voluntarily.

An employer can voluntarily recognise a trade union, either expressly by stating so or by clear conduct which shows an implied agreement to recognise that union.

Accordingly, an employer that actually enters into negotiation with a trade union about terms and conditions of employment, conditions of work, employee discipline, trade union membership, etc., may be deemed to recognise the union voluntarily.

However, the statutory procedure also allows the trade union to apply for recognition. The procedures are complex and are set out in Schedule 1 to the Trade Union and Labour Relations (Consolidation) Act 1992 (TULRA), the legislation containing the new recognition machinery introduced by Schedule 1 to ERA. The following paragraphs provide a summary of the principal provisions in force

as at December 2004. The Employment Act 2004 has introduced a number of changes to the process for the determination of a bargaining unit. It has also sought to clarify the extent of the topics for collective bargaining and made changes to the conduct of ballots including making specific provision for workforce consultation and meetings. It is likely that these changes will be introduced in April 2005.

To trigger the statutory procedure, the trade union must apply to the employer in respect of the workers who wish to constitute a bargaining unit (BU). A BU is determined by a number of factors which may result in a sector of the workforce being identified as a BU even though they may not have been the subject of separate negotiations in the past or the wish of the employer to negotiate with the whole workforce.

The request to the employer must:

- be in writing;
- identify the relevant trade union and the BU; and
- state that the request is made under paragraph 8 of Schedule A1 to TULRA.

Further, the trade union must be independent and the employer must employ at least 21 workers.

The employer should, within ten working days of receiving the written request from the trade union, accept the request, reject it or offer to negotiate.

If the parties agree on the BU and that the trade union should be the recognised BU, that is the end of the statutory procedure.

However, if the employer rejects the trade union's request outright or fails to respond, the union can apply to the

Central Arbitration Committee (CAC). Finally, if the employer offers to negotiate, the parties have at least six weeks from the initial claim to try to reach agreement.

The employer and the trade union may request the Arbitration, Advisory and Conciliation Service (ACAS) to assist in conducting negotiations. In these cases and if the employer has shown his willingness to negotiate within ten working days from the date of request, the CAC cannot be involved.

The trade union may approach the CAC if no agreement is reached between the parties, and if the employer fails to respond to the request within the 10-working-day period. In addition, if no agreement is reached before the end of a 20-working-day period, or if the parties agree a BU, but do not agree that the trade union is to be recognised, the trade union may apply to the CAC. On a practical note, if the employer reaches an agreement with the trade union that a ballot on recognition can take place, it may wish to include an undertaking by the trade union that the latter will not make another request for recognition for a period of time.

The CAC may accept the request if the initial request for recognition was valid and is on the face of it 'admissible'. The CAC will normally decide within ten working days of it receiving the request whether it may accept the claim. The CAC decides if the application is admissible by asking whether the trade union has 10% membership and whether the majority is likely to be in favour of recognition.

The CAC will try to help the parties to agree a BU within 20 working days of it receiving the request. If an agreement is reached between the parties, or if the CAC determines the BU and this BU is different from the one originally proposed, then the admissibility test must be applied again.

If the CAC is satisfied that more than 50% of the workers constituting the BU are members of the trade union, it must issue a declaration that 'the trade union is recognised as entitled to conduct collective bargaining on behalf of the workers constituting the BU'.

If :

- the majority of the workers are not members of the trade union; or
- if in the interests of good industrial relations; or
- if a significant number of the trade union members within the BU informs the CAC that they do not wish the trade union to conduct collective bargaining on their behalf; or
- if evidence leads the CAC to doubt whether a significant number of trade union members really want the trade union to be recognised,

then the CAC can arrange to hold a secret recognition ballot in which the workers constituting the BU are asked whether they want the trade union to conduct collective bargaining on their behalf.

Within ten working days of receiving the CAC notice, the trade union and the employer may notify the CAC that they do not want a ballot to be held. If a ballot is held in any event or if no objection is made, the ballot will be conducted by a 'qualified independent person' (QIP), who is appointed by the CAC. A QIP can, for example, be a practising solicitor.

The ballot must take place within 20 working days from the day the QIP is appointed, or such longer period as the CAC may decide. It may be conducted at a workplace, by post or by a combination of these two.

The CAC must inform the employer and the trade union of the result of the ballot as soon as it is reasonably practicable after it has itself been so informed by the QIP.

If 'a majority of the workers voting in the ballot, and at least 40% of the workers constituting the BU, vote in favour of recognition, the CAC must issue a declaration that the trade union is recognised as entitled to conduct collective bargaining on behalf of the BU'.

The parties will then have a 30-working-day negotiation period in which they may negotiate with a view to agree-ing a method by which they will conduct collective bargaining. If no agreement is reached, the employer or the trade union may apply to the CAC for assistance.

If an agreement still cannot be reached, the CAC must take a decision.

The employer must every six months invite the trade union representatives to a meeting for the purpose of consulting on the employer's training of workers within the BU. The first meeting must be held within six months of when the bargaining method was first specified.

See also: Employment disputes (page 228).

Sources of further information

ACAS: www.acas.org.uk.

DTI web page on trade unions and collective rights: www.dti.gov.uk/er/union.htm.

Trespassers and squatters

Edited by Bonnie Martin, Pinsent Masons

Key points

- A trespasser or squatter is a person who occupies land without the owner's consent.
- The recommended remedy is for the landowner to obtain a court order to require the trespasser to leave. Self-help is not advisable as it is easy to commit an offence under the Criminal Law Act 1977. The police have rights to arrest trespassers in some cases but rarely use them.
- Trespassers have certain rights even though they are occupying land without the owner's permission.

Steps available to a landowner

Police

The police have powers to arrest and remove trespassers or squatters in certain circumstances:

- If there is evidence that a squatter has used force to break into a building – e.g. a witness has seen the squatter breaking a lock or window – then the police can arrest the squatter on suspicion of causing criminal damage. Once the squatters have been removed, the landowner can re-secure the premises.
- The police have powers to arrest a person for a breach of the peace and/or for the offence of aggravated trespass under sections 68 and 69 of the Criminal Justice and Public Order Act 1994. However, while the police may be prepared to use their powers in the case of disruptive trespassers who are seeking to prevent a lawful activity, they are less likely to do so in the more usual situation where land is occupied by passive squatters.

In practice the police tend not to get involved until a court order has been obtained from the civil courts.

Self-help

A landowner is entitled to use reasonable force to prevent a person from committing an act of trespass on his land. However, the use of reasonable force is not usually appropriate because of the following factors:

- It is a criminal offence under section 6(1) of the Criminal Law Act 1977 for a person to use or threaten violence to secure entry if there is someone present on the property who is opposed to entry. Violence includes violence to property as well as to persons and so an owner who smashes a window or a lock to gain access where there are trespassers in the building can commit a criminal offence even if he is the owner of the building.

- What constitutes reasonable force is a question of fact and degree and gives rise to considerable uncertainty.
- The use of any force can cause a situation to degenerate into violence.

Court order

There is a special procedure to obtain a possession order against trespassers or squatters. Generally a claim must be started in the County Court for the District in which the land is situated although in exceptional circumstances the claim can be brought in the High Court. Generally a hearing date will be given when the original application is issued by the court.

The trespassers must be served, in the case of residential property, not less than five days before the hearing date and in the case of all other land not less than two days before the hearing date.

Where the names of the trespassers are not known, service can be effected by attaching the claim form and any witness statements to the main door or some other part of the building where it is clearly visible and by placing it through the letter box in a sealed transparent envelope addressed to the occupiers. Where the premises are not residential, service may be effected by placing stakes (to which the relevant document are attached) on the land at prominent positions.

There is also a procedure to obtain interim possession orders. The court issues the claim form and the application for the interim possession order, setting a date for the hearing not less than three days after the date of issue. All documents have to be served within 24 hours of the issue of the application.

If an interim possession order is granted, the defendant will be required to vacate the premises within 24 hours, and it is a criminal offence if he does not. There are two potential difficulties with the interim possession proceedings. First, having made an interim possession order, the court sets a date for a hearing; hence there is a need for a second attendance at court. Second, it is not possible to get a court bailiff to enforce an interim possession order; hence, if the trespassers do not vacate the premises and the police cannot be persuaded to assist, it will be necessary to wait until after the second court hearing to obtain a warrant of possession such that the court bailiff will assist.

Squatters' rights

Surprising though it may seem, a person who is trespassing on another person's land does have certain limited rights. These rights have changed following the coming into force of the Land Registration Act 2002 on 13 October 2003:

- A person who has occupied another person's land without permission and has excluded the landowner from that land (e.g. by enclosing the land with a fence) for a period of 12 years prior to 13 October 2003 can become the legal landowner of the land he has unlawfully occupied.
- If the landowner sells that land in the next three years up to 13 October 2006, the new owner will still be

bound by the claim of the squatter. After that date, the squatter's claim will only survive a sale of the land if he is in actual occupation of the land in question.

- Following 13 October 2003, the squatter only needs to prove possession of the land for ten years. However, the Land Registration Act 2002 has introduced a new three-part test that the squatter must pass to claim legal ownership of the land. It is expected that this will make it easier for the landowner to prevent the squatter from replacing him as the legal owner of the land even though the squatter has been in possession for the required ten years.

- Adverse possession most frequently happens when an adjoining landowner extends his garden. However, it does occasionally occur with much bigger parcels of land and buildings. Consequently, once evidence of an encroachment or squatter comes to light, a landowner should take prompt action.

- It is a criminal offence for a person to use or threaten violence to secure entry to a property occupied by a squatter if the squatter is opposed to that entry (Criminal Law Act 1977, section 6(1)). In practice this means that a landowner cannot force entry to a building unless he is satisfied that the squatter is not actually in the building at that time.

- A landowner owes a limited duty of care to a trespasser and may be liable in damages for a trespasser injured as a result of a hazard on the land. This is particularly the case in respect of children.

See also: Occupier's liability (page 409); Visitor safety (page 518).

TUPE

Pinsent Masons Employment Group

Key points

One of the biggest employment law issues for workplace managers is the impact of the Transfer of Undertakings (Protection of Employment) Regulations 1981 (TUPE) on a change of service provider. Where TUPE applies, it provides that contracts of employment and associated liabilities transfer by operation of law from the outgoing service provider to the incoming service provider.

Legislation

- Transfer of Undertakings (Protection of Employment) Regulations 1981.
- Acquired Rights Directive 2001 (2001/23/EC).

There is currently amending legislation pending, but at the time of going to press the date on which it will become law is still uncertain.

Does TUPE apply?

TUPE applies if there is a 'relevant transfer' of an 'undertaking'. The 'undertaking' can include the provision of a service. Hence, the transfer of responsibility for providing facilities management services on a retainer can amount to a TUPE transfer.

Whether there has been a 'relevant transfer' is not always straightforward. The key questions are:

- is there any undertaking or entity?
- does the undertaking retain its iden-

tity after the transfer?
- has there been a change in employer?

The law in this area is notoriously uncertain, but there will ordinarily be a 'relevant transfer' if there is a transfer of significant assets from the old employer to the new employer, or where a substantial proportion of the workforce transfers in terms of skill and number. In some types of service provision, such as cleaning or security, the transfer of assets will be less important. Recent case law suggests that the incoming employer or service provider cannot simply refuse to take on staff to avoid the application of TUPE.

In each case a general review of a number of key indicators is necessary to determine whether there has been a 'relevant transfer'. These include:

- the type of undertaking being transferred;
- whether tangible assets (such as build-

---

ings, property, etc.) are transferred;

- whether intangible assets (such as goodwill) are transferred;
- whether the majority of employees are taken on by the new employer;
- whether customers are transferred;
- the degree of similarity between the activities carried on before and after the transfer; and
- the period for which activities cease (if at all).

The original employer is known as the 'transferor' whereas the new employer to whom the business is transferred is known as the 'transferee'.

Implications of TUPE

If TUPE applies, a summary of the principal implications is as follows:

- Employees who were working immediately before the transfer in the relevant business become employees of the transferee.
- The terms and conditions of their employment transfer to the transferee. All contractual terms transfer except occupational pension schemes.
- In broad terms, liabilities in relation to the transferring employees transfer to the transferee.
- Changes to terms and conditions of the transferring employees will be void if made in connection with the transfer.
- Employee dismissals which are for a reason connected to the transfer will be automatically unfair.
- Collective agreements and trade union recognition in respect of transferring employees usually transfer to the transferee.
- Obligations exist for both parties to

inform and (in certain circumstances) to consult with employee representatives.

Which employees transfer?

Even if TUPE does apply, only those employed 'in the undertaking or part transferred' will transfer. As such, they must be 'assigned' to the undertaking.

The key questions will be the amount of time they spend working for the business, whether they are part of the organisational framework, the nature of their responsibilities and reporting lines.

Also, only those employed 'immediately before the transfer' will transfer, or those who would have been employed immediately before the transfer if they had not been otherwise unfairly dismissed for a reason connected to the transfer.

There is nothing to prevent the transferor from inserting employees into the business just before the undertaking is transferred. Only proper investigation and due diligence on the part of the transferee can sort out whether such potentially undesirable employees have been 'dumped' into the business.

Employees have the right to object to transferring to a new employer. However, if they exercise this right, their employment terminates immediately and they have no right to claim compensation as a result. An exception is that the employee would still have the right to claim constructive dismissal if the reason for the resignation was because of actual or planned detrimental changes to his terms and conditions.

The worker must be an employee (not a self-employed contractor) of the transferor.

Changing terms and conditions

It is not possible to change terms and conditions of employment for a reason connected to the transfer, even if the employee agrees to the changes. Any such change is void. Changes can only be made if they are unconnected to the transfer. There is no particular time period stated by TUPE following which a change will no longer be connected to the transaction. That will simply be a matter of fact as to whether the link has been broken.

One way of circumventing this difficulty is to terminate employment and to re-engage on revised terms. If an employee is dismissed for a reason connected to the transfer, that dismissal is automatically unfair.

The employee would then have the right to claim unfair dismissal. So this route is only viable with the consent of the employee.

Legal advice should be sought to manage any change to terms and conditions the reason for which could be considered to relate to the transfer.

Information and consultation

Both the transferor and the transferee must provide information and, if necessary, consult with 'appropriate representatives' (i.e. trade unions if they exist, or elected employee representatives) of any employees affected by the transfer.

The transferor must provide the following information:

- confirmation that the transfer is to take place;
- when it will take place;
- the reasons for it;
- the 'legal, economic and social implications' of the transfer; and
- any 'measures' which the transferor envisages taking towards the affected employees (if there are no such measures, that should be made clear).

The transferee is under a duty to give information to the transferor as to the measures it intends to take in relation to the affected employees.

If there are no 'measures' then there is no need to consult. However, the information must be given sufficiently in advance of the transfer to enable proper consultation to take place if necessary. The consultation must be with a view to seeking agreement.

The company must then provide information to and consult with the 'appropriate representatives' on:

- matters relating to the development of the undertaking;
- changes in employment patterns; and
- decisions likely to lead to substantial changes in work organisation or contractual relations, such as changes to terms and conditions, TUPE transfers and collective redundancies.

Legislative developments

The UK Government is required to amend the TUPE Regulations to comply with the revised Acquired Rights Directive (2001/23/EC). While the Government has consulted on proposals to implement the revised EC Directive, new regulations are still awaited. The expected amendments to the TUPE Regulations include:

- the adoption of a more specific definition of a transfer of an undertaking;

- the potential application of TUPE to most transactions relating to outsourcing and changes of service provider;
- allowing greater flow of information between parties to transactions;
- potential duties to replicate pensions or to provide compensation for loss;
- provisions to allow terms and conditions to be changed by the transferee if done for an 'economic, technical or organisational reason'; and
- specific provisions to assist in insolvency situations.

The Government has recently issued its consultation document on the draft regulations implementing the EC Information and Consultation Directive. The regulations will eventually apply to all businesses with more than 50 employees.

This EC Directive gives employees a right to be informed and consulted about the company's economic situation, employment prospects, and developments likely to lead to substantial changes in work organisation including transfers and redundancies. The UK has until 23 March 2005 to implement the Directive into UK law.

See also: Employee consultation (page 221).

Sources of further information

Department of Trade and Industry: www.dti.gov.uk.

Vehicles at work

Andrew Richardson, Scott Wilson

Key points

- There are many specific industries where vehicles are designed and used for specific workplace tasks. These are beyond the scope of this article, which only covers general issues.
- Employers who need to provide vehicles as part of their safe systems of work must ensure that they put appropriate control measures in place.
- The issues which frequently need to be covered by the safe system of work include:
  – the workplace (vehicle routes, provision for pedestrians, signage)
  – vehicles (safety features, good maintenance)
  – employees (driver training, traffic hazard briefing)
  – vehicle activities (loading and unloading, refuelling or recharging, reversing, tipping, sheeting and unsheeting).

Legislation

- Health and Safety at Work etc. Act 1974.
- Management of Health and Safety at Work Regulations 1999.
- Workplace (Health, Safety and Welfare) Regulations 1992.
- Provision and Use of Work Equipment Regulations 1998.
- Traffic Signs Regulations and General Directions 1994.

Statutory requirements

From the employer's perspective the principal legal duty is, so far as reasonably practicable, to provide and maintain a safe system of work and to take all reasonably practicable precautions to ensure the health and safety of all the workers in the workplace.

The Management of Health and Safety at Work Regulations 1999 require that all employers assess the risks to the health and safety of their employees and of anyone who may be affected by their work activity. The risk assessment process should cover the following:

- Identification of all the hazards involving vehicles – moving vehicles, causing injury or damage by driving, loading and unloading or refuelling or recharging vehicles, maintenance.
- Consideration of the risks involved.
- Identifying the people involved.
- Evaluating the existing control measures.

The 4 C's system

In order to provide and maintain a safe system of work and so on, you need an effective management system. The HSE advocates the 4 C's system:

- *Control.* By taking responsibility for safety, showing commitment, clearly allocating responsibility and ensuring employees are held accountable for their responsibilities.
- *Communication.* Strong lines of communication informing on the safety policy, allocation of responsibilities, details of the safe working practices, details of where employees can obtain information, instruction and training, and feedback to employees as to how well they have complied.
- *Co-operation.* Co-operation is important because it confirms that all employees, visitors and contractors have accepted their responsibility and are going to implement the safe working practices.
- *Competence.* Employers need to ensure that all employees are capable of carrying out the tasks they are allocated safely in relation to vehicles; this can include medical examinations, aptitude tests and recognised qualifications/certificates/licences.

- Recommending new control measures.
- Recording the assessment.

It is important that all of the risks are addressed: eliminate them if possible and, if not, put into place risk control measures that will reduce the risks to acceptable levels. In relation to vehicles, the risk control measures will include safe systems of work (see panel above).

The Management of Health and Safety at Work Regulations also require that employers shall:

- in entrusting tasks to employees, take into account their capabilities as regards health and safety; and
- ensure that employees are provided with adequate health and safety training on being recruited into the employer's undertaking and on being exposed to new or increased risks at the workplace.

The Workplace (Health, Safety and Welfare) Regulations place the following duties, in relation to vehicles, upon employers:

- The workplace shall be organised in such a way that vehicles can circulate in a safe manner.
- Traffic routes must be suitable for the vehicles using them.
- All routes must be suitably indicated.
- The workplace shall be maintained in an efficient state, in efficient working order and in good repair.
- Every floor in a workplace and the surface of every traffic route shall be kept free of obstruction.

The Provision and Use of Work Equipment Regulations 1998 place the following duties, in relation to vehicles, upon employers:

- To ensure that work equipment (which includes vehicles) is so constructed or adapted as to be suitable for the purpose for which it is used or provided.
- In selecting the work equipment, every employer shall have regard to the working conditions and to the risks to the health and safety of persons which exist in the premises or undertaking in which that work equipment is to be used, and any additional risk posed by the use of that work equipment.
- To ensure the work equipment is maintained in an efficient working order and in good repair.

Common factors that will need consideration by employers in the majority of workplace situations are the following:

- Vehicle routes laid out to meet the needs of pedestrians and vehicles.
- Traffic routes appropriate to the types and quantities of vehicles.
- Safety features in place, e.g. signs and markings, barriers and humps.

- Reversing manoeuvres minimised.
- Safe parking for all drivers.
- Loading and unloading procedures arranged for safety.
- Vehicles fitted with all necessary safety equipment and features.
- Vehicles maintained in good working order.
- Driver selection and training procedures sufficient to ensure that employees asked to drive at work are suitably experienced and competent, and remain so.
- Adequate briefing on workplace driving hazards.
- Adequate supervision and inspection of workplace driving activities to ensure safe systems of work are being followed.

See also: Driving at work (page 208); Risk assessments (page 469); Work equipment (page 545).

Sources of further information

HSG136 'Workplace transport safety – guidance for employers' (HSE Books, 1995; reprinted with amendments 2000): ISBN 0 7176 0935 9. Provides a good level of general information for employers.

HSG6 'Safety in working with lift trucks ' (HSE Books, 2000): ISBN 0 7176 1781 5.

INDG199 'Managing vehicle safety at the workplace', which provides useful basic information, can be downloaded at www.hse.gov.uk/pubns/indg199.pdf.

'Driving at Work Policy and Management Guide, version 2.0' (ISBN 1 900648 41, 5, £74.99) is available as an electronic download from the Workplace Law Network. Call 0870 777 8881 for details, or visit www.workplacelaw.net.

Ventilation and temperature

Bob Towse, Heating and Ventilating Contractors' Association

Key points

- Requirements for the provision of ventilation to buildings are set out in the Workplace (Health, Safety and Welfare) Regulations 1992.
- These Regulations came into force on 1 January 1993 for new buildings and on 1 January 1996 for existing buildings.

The Regulations apply to a wide range of workplaces, not only factories, shops and offices but also, for example, schools, hospitals, hotels and places of entertainment. The Regulations replaced several pieces of older law, including parts of the Factories Act 1961 and the Offices, Shops and Railways Premises Act 1963.

General requirements

The Regulations require the workplace and the equipment devices and systems to be maintained (including cleaned as appropriate) in an efficient state, in efficient working order and in good repair. This requirement specifically includes ventilation provided under Regulation 6 and requires that 'effective and suitable provision shall be made to ensure that every enclosed workplace is ventilated by a sufficient quantity of fresh or purified air'.

Regulation 6 covers general workplace ventilation, not local exhaust ventilation for controlling specific hazardous materials or substances hazardous to health.

The Regulations do not define a level of adequate ventilation, but the Workplace Health, Safety and Welfare

Approved Code of Practice (ACoP) gives some basic guidance. It states, for example, that workplaces should be sufficiently well ventilated so that stale air, and air which is hot or humid because of the processes or equipment in the workplace, is replaced at a reasonable rate. In many cases natural ventilation through windows or other openings is sufficient, but mechanical ventilation or air-conditioning may be required to meet certain circumstances.

Temperature in indoor workplaces

Regulation 7 requires that 'during working hours, the temperature in all workplaces inside buildings shall be reasonable'.

The ACoP suggests that, in the typical workplace, the temperature should be at least 16°C unless much of the work involves severe physical effort, in which case the temperature should be at least 13°C.

These temperatures would be considered by most building occupants to be below comfort levels. However, the ACoP defines a reasonable temperature as one which should secure the thermal comfort of people at work, allowing for clothing, activity level, radiant heat, air movement and humidity.

For air-conditioned buildings in the UK, the Chartered Institution of Building Services Engineers (CIBSE) recommends a dry resultant temperature of between 21°C and 23°C during winter and between 22°C and 24°C in summer for continuous sedentary occupancy.

It is recognised that room temperatures in buildings without artificial cooling will exceed the summer values for some of the time but should not exceed 25°C for more than 5% of the annual occupied period (typically 125 hours).

Ventilation

The ACoP requires that mechanical ventilation systems should never operate at 100% recirculation (no fresh air), which is considered unhealthy.

All spaces which rely on mechanical means of ventilation must be supplied with outdoor air at a rate sufficient to dilute internally generated pollutants.

Ventilation should also remove and dilute warm, humid air and provide air movement which gives a sense of freshness without causing a draught. If the workplace contains process or heating equipment or other sources of dust, fumes or vapours, more fresh air will be needed to provide adequate ventilation.

The HSE guide 'General Ventilation in the Workplace' confirms that a fresh air supply rate of 8 litres per second per person should provide a clean and hygienic workplace in open-plan offices, shops and some factories. Higher fresh air supply rates of up to 32 litres per second per person are recommended for heavily contaminated buildings.

The CIBSE Guide A: 'Environmental Design' recommends the following outdoor air supply rates for sedentary occupants:

- 8 litres per second per person – no smoking.
- 16 litres per second per person – 25% smoking.
- 24 litres per second per person – 45% smoking.
- 36 litres per second per person – 75% smoking.

Supply air quality

Air introduced from outside a building should be free from any impurities likely to be offensive or cause ill health. Outdoor air is generally considered acceptable provided that the air intake is not sited so that excessively contaminated air (such as might be found near flues, extract outlets or car parks) is drawn into the building.

The level of air pollution in some locations may mean that outdoor air is not suitable to introduce into a building unless it has first undergone adequate particle filtration.

Air that is recirculated should be adequately filtered before being redistributed within the building.

Maintenance

The ACoP requires that 'any device or system used to provide fresh air to a building or space should be maintained in an efficient state so as to ensure that the air produced or delivered is both suitable and sufficient for use within the workplace'.

The term 'efficient state' relates to good working order and not productivity or economy. In particular, the plant should be kept clean and free from any substance or organism which may contaminate the air passing through it.

The ACoP refers to the need to 'regularly and properly clean, test and maintain mechanical ventilation and air-conditioning systems to ensure that they are kept clean and free from anything which may contaminate the air'.

Depending on use, compliance with this duty is likely to require a suitable system of maintenance, inspection, adjustment, lubrication and cleaning, as well as the keeping of accurate records.

CIBSE and the Heating and Ventilating Contractors' Association (HVCA) each publishes a number of guides intended to assist in this purpose.

See also: Smoking (page 486).

Vibration

Ciaron Dunne, Workplace Law Group

Key points

- Employers are required to protect employees from the harmful effects of vibration at work.
- Employees particularly at risk from vibration include operators of pneumatic drills and hand-held power tools.
- New regulations are due to come into effect in 2005 which would impose specific requirements on employers.

Legislation

- Management of Health and Safety at Work Regulations 1999.
- Provision and Use of Work Equipment Regulations 1998.

Vibration-related disorders

Vibration is a major cause of occupational ill health. Around 3,000 new claims for industrial injury disability benefit are made each year in relation to vibration white finger (VWF) alone. The courts have also awarded large sums of compensation in recent years including an estimated £3bn for 165,000 ex-miners, and most recently £212,000 for a railway employee.

Hand-arm vibration syndrome (HAVS) is a group of diseases caused when the hand and arm are exposed to vibration – e.g. VWF. VWF occurs when excessive vibration affects the blood flow in the hands, causing a loss of dexterity. Construction workers, miners, workers who use hand-held or hand-guided power tools, and workers who hold materials that vibrate when fed into machines are particularly exposed to VWF. Other effects of HAVS include damage to sensory nerves, muscles and joints in the hands and arms.

There is also increasing concern over whole body vibration (WBV), which can cause adverse effects when vibrations pass through the body of the operator. Pneumatic drills and mobile work equipment could cause exposure to WBV.

Work-related upper limb disorders (WRULDs) comprise a group of diseases which affect the upper body, including repetitive strain injury (RSI). WRULDs can also be caused by exposure to vibration.

Changes in the pipeline

Proposals for new Control of Vibration at Work Regulations – which would implement the EU Physical Agents (Vibration) Directive (2002/44/EC) – would require employers to take action to prevent their employees from developing diseases caused by exposure to vibration at work from equipment, vehicles and machines.

The Regulations must come into force by July 2005 to implement the European Directive on time. The UK negotiated a transitional period for the exposure limit values up to 2010 (with a further four years to 2014 for the agriculture and forestry sectors) in the case of work activities where older machinery may be an obstacle to compliance. The UK also insisted on an option for averaging exposure over a week to allow high exposure on one or two days to be offset by low exposure on others.

Control measures

- Try to find an alternative way of working that does not involve the use of vibrating equipment.
- Check the vibration data for equipment before purchase – choose equipment with the lowest vibration rating.
- Conduct a risk assessment in line with the Management of Health and Safety at Work Regulations 1999.

- Maintain and inspect equipment in line with the Provision and Use of Work Equipment Regulations 1998.
- Design jobs to minimise the time spent on vibrating machinery (e.g. by job rotation).
- Provide operators with sufficient information, instruction, training and supervision.
- Avoid using vibrating equipment in damp, cold conditions, when blood circulation is less good.
- Use personal protective equipment (e.g. protective gloves) as a last resort.

The HSE provides a considerable amount of free information on what the risks are and how to control exposure to vibration at work (see below).

See also: Personal protective equipment (page 425); WRULDs (page 545); Work equipment (page 549).

Sources of further information

HSE vibration web page: www.hse.gov.uk/vibration.

INDG175REV1 'Health risks from hand-arm vibration: advice for employers' (HSE Books, 1998): ISBN 0 7176 1553 7.

INDG338 'Power tools: how to reduce vibration health risks' (HSE Books, 2001): ISBN 0 7176 2008 5.

Visitor safety

Andrew Richardson, Scott Wilson

Key points

- Employers have a duty to provide a safe environment for visitors to their premises.
- Children are less careful than adults and need more controls.
- The duty extends to uninvited visitors such as trespassers, and to tenants.
- Employers are liable for the actions of their employees which injure visitors.
- Employees must help their employer to ensure a safe and healthy workplace.

Legislation

- Occupiers' Liability Acts 1957 and 1984.
- Health and Safety at Work etc. Act 1974.
- Management of Health and Safety at Work Regulations 1999.

Occupiers' Liability Acts 1957 and 1984

From the employer's perspective, the Occupiers' Liability Act 1957 places a common law duty of care upon the occupier to all visitors to take such care as is reasonable to see that visitors will be reasonably safe in using the premises for the purposes for which they were invited or permitted to be there. The Act also points out that children will inevitably be less careful than adults.

The Occupiers' Liability Act 1984 amended the 1957 Act slightly to include a duty to unlawful visitors (e.g. trespassers) such that if:

- the occupier is aware of the danger, and
- the occupier knows the person could put himself at risk, and
- the risk is a risk that the occupier could reasonably be expected to do something about,

then the same common law duty of care is owed as is owed to lawful visitors.

Employers are also liable for the actions of their employees and, in relation to visitors, have a vicarious liability for those actions. If an employee injures a visitor during the course of his work, then the employer is liable.

Health and Safety at Work etc. Act 1974

Under section 3 of the Act an employer has a duty to 'conduct his undertaking in such a way as to ensure, so far as is reasonably practicable, that persons not in his employment [e.g. visitors] who may be affected thereby are not thereby exposed to risks to their health and

safety'.

Section 4 requires that anyone in control of the premises or plant used by persons not in their employment should, so far as is reasonably practicable:

- ensure safe access and egress to the premises and plant; and
- ensure that plant or substances in the premises, or provided for their use, are safe and without risk to health.

These obligations are also transferred to any tenants of a building.

Section 7 places a general obligation upon all employees to take reasonable care of their own health and safety and that of others who may be affected by their own acts or omissions. They also have to co-operate with the employer so as to ensure that the employer can comply with all of the above statutory obligations.

Finally, under section 8, no person should intentionally or recklessly misuse or interfere with anything provided under the Act and other legislation in the interests of health and safety.

Management of Health and Safety at Work Regulations 1999

These Regulations identify a number of general duties that, if followed, will allow the employer to meet those obligations detailed in the Acts mentioned

above. These are principally to carry out risk assessments and to set up emergency procedures.

All employers must assess the risks to health and safety of their employees and of anyone who may be affected by their work activity: this will include visitors. The risk assessment process should:

- identify all the hazards;
- consider the risks involved and identify the people involved (employees, visitors, the public);
- evaluate the existing control measures and recommend any new control measures;
- record the assessment; and
- review and revise the assessment as necessary.

It is important to address all of the risks, eliminate them if possible, and, if not, put into place control measures that will reduce the risks to acceptable levels.

The Regulations also require employers to set up emergency procedures for serious and imminent dangers and to appoint competent persons to ensure compliance with those procedures. The procedures should cover all visitors to the premises.

See also: Emergency procedures (page 218); Health and safety at work (page 295); Health and safety management (page 311); Occupier's liability (page 409); Risk assessments (page 469); Trespassers and squatters (page 503).

Sources of further information

A useful source of information is L21 'Management of Health and Safety at Work Regulations 1999 – Approved Code of Practice and guidance' (HSE Books, 2000): ISBN 0 7176 2488 9. The document provides guidance to employers on managing the risk to visitors and identifies any further documentation that is relevant.

Electrical waste

David Symons, Atkins Environment

The Environment Department (Defra) has issued draft Regulations and supporting guidance to implement the EU Directive on Waste Electrical and Electronic Equipment (WEEE). The Directive aims to increase recycling rates for WEEE and will come into force on 15 July 2005. Much of the draft Regulations relates to household waste, but there are also specific requirements for business WEEE.

What is covered?

For businesses, IT equipment, telephones, small hand-held equipment, lights and light bulbs will be covered by the Regulations.

Who is responsible for recycling?

This depends on the time the equipment was bought and how the equipment is replaced. The proposed arrangements are as follows:

- A producer who supplies new equipment to a business user to replace original equipment purchased before 13 August 2005 must finance the costs of recovery and disposal of up to 80% of the weight of the replaced equipment (whether or not he supplied this original equipment). The precise target depends on the category of the electrical equipment.
- If the business user is not making a like-for-like replacement purchase,

then he is responsible for financing recovery and disposal of up to 80% of the weight of any equipment he discards if he bought the equipment before 13 August 2005.

- For waste resulting from new products sold after 13 August 2005, the Regulations provide for there to be an obligation on the producer. However, the producer and the business user can freely negotiate to reach agreement on how to allocate the responsibility for the financing of collection, treatment, recovery and environmentally sound disposal of the 'future' WEEE.

What are the next steps?

The consultation is now closed and Defra is planning the final approach for the regulation. At present it is envisaged that producers of WEEE will have to register (either directly or via a collective scheme) with a national clearing house which will take responsibility for discharging producers' obligations. There is no *de minimis* exemption for small producers at this stage, although this is hinted at in the draft guidance (see 'Sources of further information' below).

What do businesses have to do?

- For waste from equipment purchased before 13 August 2005, businesses will have responsibility for financing its collection and recycling at the end of its life, unless they are purchasing replacement products.

- Purchasing staff should be clear about the financial responsibility for new electrical products bought after 13 August 2005. In legislation, it will be the supplier's responsibility for financing collection and recovery, unless an alternative arrangement is negotiated.
- Where companies use a facilities management contract to carry out actions which generate electrical waste (such as changing light bulbs), the FM contractor may have to register with a compliance scheme.

Other points to remember

In addition to the WEEE Directive, note the following points when you are disposing of equipment:

- Remember that the data on IT equipment may be sensitive. If so, employ an appropriate technique such as shredding the hard drive or placing the equipment near to a strong magnetic field to erase the data on the machine before disposal.
- Old IT equipment may be classified as waste. Make sure you comply with waste legislation).

See also: Waste management (page 526).

Sources of further information

The text of the WEEE Directive: www.dti.gov.uk/sustainability/pdfs/ finalweee.pdf.

The Government's consultation paper on implementing the Directive into UK legislation: www.dti.gov.uk/sustainability/weee.

Hazardous/special waste

David Symons, Atkins Environment

Legislation

- Special Waste Regulations 1996.
- Landfill (England and Wales) Regulations 2002.
- Draft Hazardous Waste Regulations.

At the time of writing (November 2004), the process and arrangements for disposing of hazardous wastes are in a state of flux. The Government introduced legislation governing the final disposal of hazardous wastes in July 2004. Further changes, covering the segregation of these wastes and their management at the place of production, are subject to consultation and are likely to come into force in July 2005.

The current situation

Waste which is toxic or dangerous has historically been classified as 'special waste' in the UK. Around 5 million tonnes are generated each year, 40% of which has been disposed to landfill. Around 200 landfill sites used to accept hazardous wastes, providing a relatively inexpensive and convenient disposal option.

What has changed?

- In addition to special waste, a new term, 'hazardous waste', has been introduced from July 2004. Hazardous waste includes all waste which is special, and also includes additional types of wastes, such as computer monitors and fluorescent tubes.
- Disposal of hazardous with non-hazardous wastes is now banned:
  – Only dedicated hazardous waste landfills are allowed to receive hazardous wastes.
  – Landfills not authorised to receive hazardous wastes will only be able to accept non-hazardous or stable, non-reactive hazardous waste (this may include asbestos) deposited in separate cells.
- Hazardous wastes must be pretreated before being landfilled:
  – Pretreatment must change the characteristics of the waste in order to reduce its volume or hazardous nature, or to allow easier handling and recovery.
  – Examples of pretreatment include stabilisation, solidification, incineration and bioremediation.
  – It is uncertain what, if any, wastes will be exempt from pretreatment.
  – Waste producers will not necessarily have to pretreat their own wastes but may need to liaise with their waste contractors over waste information and characteristics. The responsibility for pretreatment is currently unclear.

What has still to change?

Proposals to do away with the term 'special waste' altogether were issued by

Defra and the Welsh Assembly in September 2004. Under the proposals:

- the current requirement to pre-notify the regulators of special waste movements will be abolished;
- sites producing more than 50kg of hazardous waste per year, and/or more than two consignments per year, will be required to register with the Environment Agency and to keep records of each consignment of hazardous waste for three years; and
- all hazardous wastes must be treated to meet waste acceptance criteria. This is likely to involve additional stages of pretreatment, including restricting organic solvents and measures to reduce the hazards of leachate at the receiving landfill.

Defra has indicated that the Regulations will come into force in July 2005. The requirement for waste producers to register with the Agency will take effect in April 2005.

What should you do now?

Although uncertainty exists, waste producers must take action now to make sure that they minimise the risk of business impact and to avoid breaking the law.

1. Understand the new regime. Understand what wastes are likely to be defined as hazardous under the new regime. Make sure that all hazardous wastes are stored separately.
2. Make sure that you are segregating all hazardous wastes from your general waste, disposing of hazardous waste separately to a licensed contractor.
3. Register with the Environment Agency from April 2005 if you produce more than 50kg of hazardous waste and/or more than two consignments per year. Most small offices are unlikely to exceed the 50kg threshold. Larger sites, however, may come close given the broader definition of hazardous waste which includes fluorescent tubes and much electrical equipment.
4. Keep accurate records. Pay particular attention to keeping accurate duty of care and waste carrier records so you do not inadvertently send waste to an unlicensed carrier.

See also: Waste management (page 526).

Sources of further information

The consultation and the draft Regulations which will replace the Special Waste Regulations can be accessed at www.defra.gov.uk/corporate/consult/wastereg-haz/consult.pdf.

Waste management

David Symons, Atkins Environment

Legislation

- Environmental Protection Act 1990, Part II: Waste on Land.
- Environmental Protection (Duty of Care) Regulations 1991.
- Waste Management Regulations 1996.
- Waste Management Licensing Regulations 1994, plus subsequent amendments (1995).
- Control of Pollution (Amendments) Act 1989.
- Controlled Waste Regulations 1992, plus subsequent amendments (1993).
- Waste Management: The Duty of Care Code of Practice.
- Special Waste Regulations 1996.
- Landfill (England and Wales) Regulations 2002.
- Draft Hazardous Waste Regulations.

There are strict controls on the storage and disposal of wastes in the UK. While many of these Regulations have been in force for several years, important new controls are being introduced for hazardous wastes.

General guidance

Step 1. Identify all types and sources of waste from your business

The best idea is to create a list of all of the various waste streams. So this might include:

- general waste;
- waste packaging materials;
- sanitary waste from toilets;
- medical waste from first-aid or healthcare centres;
- building and other construction wastes; and
- waste oils from maintenance operations.

As a minimum, waste managers need to separate 'hazardous waste' – fluorescent tubes, computer monitors, oils, chemicals, etc. – from general wastes. If you are unsure about whether an item of waste is 'special' or not, you should either speak to your local Environment Agency office or call the DTI-sponsored Envirowise programme (helpline 0800 585 794).

Step 2. Store wastes in a secure manner

Wastes should not be able to blow around or leak. Do not burn, bury or pour away wastes on your site since this is illegal.

Step 3. Identify the best means of disposal

Check whether any of the materials can be recycled, reclaimed or reused. Not only is this friendlier to the environment, but it can have cost benefits too: someone else might be able to use or convert what you throw away. Check with any local waste clubs, communal initiatives or charities.

Ensure that arrangements are cost-effective: in addition to contractors' costs, escalating landfill tax and other measures make waste disposal expensive.

Where applicable, compactors can reduce the waste's volume, which therefore means fewer collections. Similarly, extracting waste oil from cleaning waters can have a huge impact on waste costs.

Step 4. Select authorised contractor(s)

You must only transfer your waste to a contractor that is either authorised (such as a registered carrier or holder of a waste management licence) or exempt (a charity or voluntary organisation). Some forms of waste treatment and disposal are excluded from the licensing system.

Note also that some commercial or trade wastes can be handled by your local authority's collection or disposal schemes, but check with them first.

Ensure that waste contractors' authorisations are current and valid for your waste materials. Check actual copies of contractors' licences and, if unsure on any point, double-check with the Environment Agency.

If you suspect any problems, suspend waste transfers and alert the Environment Agency.

Step 5. Keep a paper trail

All waste transfers must be accompanied by a waste transfer note. This should include a description of the waste and also the name of the person to whom you transfer the waste. A transfer note should be completed for each individual transfer or, alternatively, you can complete a 'season ticket' which covers a sequence of similar waste transfers for 12 months. Waste carriers or contractors will often provide this as part of their overall service, but remember that you still have legal responsibility for ensuring that it is correct.

All waste transfer notes must be kept on file for a minimum of two years. Special waste transfers must be kept on file for three, although note that there are plans to replace the current consignment note system (see 'Hazardous/special waste', page 524).

Additional points for landlords or managing agents

Where landlords or their managing agents arrange for waste to be disposed of on behalf of their tenants, then Environment Agency rules include this as a waste-brokering operation. You may therefore have to register as a waste broker with the Environment Agency. Speak to either the Environment Agency or Envirowise if you are uncertain.

Environmental considerations

It is important to continue to fulfil your duty of care with respect to waste management as described above. In particular, you need to update information and systems when changes occur and regularly audit compliance.

See also: Electrical waste (page 522); Hazardous/special waste (page 524).

Sources of further information

A considerable amount of information on waste management can be found on the Environment Agency's website: www.environment-agency.gov.uk.

The DTI's Envirowise programme can supply information and assistance via its helpline: 0800 585 794.

Water fittings

Dr Steve Tuckwell, Water Regulations Advisory Scheme

Key points

- National regulations or byelaws apply to all plumbing systems in premises that have a connection to the public water supply.
- The regulations' purpose is to prevent waste, misuse, undue consumption, contamination and erroneous measurement of water supplied by a public water supplier.
- The installers and users of plumbing systems have a legal duty to comply with the regulations or byelaws.
- All plumbing fittings and water-using appliances must be designed, constructed, installed and maintained to meet the requirements of the regulations.
- In most circumstances, it is a criminal offence to begin the installation of water fittings or appliances, or to use them, without the consent of the water supplier.
- Consent is gained by notifying the water supplier in advance of installation work.

Legislation

- Water Supply (Water Fittings) Regulations 1999.
- Scottish Water Byelaws 2003.
- Northern Ireland Water Regulations.

The Water Supply (Water Fittings) Regulations came into force in England and Wales on 1 July 1999 to replace the suppliers' Water Byelaws which had applied since 1989. The byelaws in Scotland were replaced on 4 April 2000, with technically identical requirements which have been updated as the Scottish Water Byelaws 2003. Within the next two years Northern Ireland will update its regulations so that there will be uniformity throughout the UK. In this article,

'regulations' refers to the legislation covering Scotland, England and Wales.

In all premises that have a public water supply connection, these regulations control the design and installation of water systems, their maintenance and their disconnection, together with the use of the water that is supplied. They apply to pipework, including the underground supply pipe connecting premises to the water main, to all fittings such as pipes, valves, pumps and storage cisterns, and to all appliances, machines, sanitaryware and hosepipes that are connected to the plumbing system or receive water from it. The regulations do not apply to premises that have no public water supply, e.g. those with only a privately owned borehole or well supply. However, the regulations do provide a code of practice for plumbing systems used with private supplies, where prevention of contamination and waste of water are equally important.

Implications

What are the implications for workplace managers? It is important that the regulations are complied with in order to protect all those people using your premises against contamination of the drinking water, to ensure reliable and robust plumbing systems, to obtain efficient use of water and to avoid criminal prosecution. Although these are broadly the same purposes as served by the former water supply byelaws, the introduction of the regulations has brought about some changes.

The main changes are in the areas of backflow protection, requirements for WCs and urinals, water conservation and the notifications that premises owners or occupiers have to give when certain types of alterations or additions to the water supply are made. A new concept, that of approved contractors, has also been introduced. Approved contractors are permitted to do certain types of work without the prior consent of the water supplier, so providing more flexibility in carrying out work. They also provide their clients with the reassurance of a certificate guaranteeing compliance of their work with the regulations. These aspects are described more fully below.

Notification

The regulations require prior notification to the water supplier of the intention to install any water fittings. The only exception is the extension of the water system of an existing house, which does not have to be notified unless there are certain specific items to be installed (see below). A table included in the regulations lists certain types of fittings that need specific approval. Many of these relate to water conservation requirements such as: the need to notify the installation of a bath having a capacity of more than 230 litres, a pump drawing more than 12 litres per minute, a water treatment unit incorporating reverse osmosis, producing a waste water discharge or requiring the use of water for regeneration or cleaning, an automatic garden watering system, the laying of underground pipes outside the minimum depth of 750mm or the maximum of 1,350mm, and the construction of a swimming pool with a capacity greater than 10,000 litres being replenished automatically and from the water supplier's mains.

The remaining items requiring notification relate to contamination hazards such as the installation of a bidet with an ascending spray or flexible hose, and backflow protection devices designed to protect against the highest two categories of risk.

The written notification must include plans of the relevant parts of the premises, plans of the plumbing layout and fittings to be installed, and details of the person making the notification and that to whom a consent should be sent. The water supplier must either grant consent, with conditions if necessary, or refuse consent, within ten working days of receipt of the notification; otherwise consent is deemed to have been given and installation can start. A leaflet summarising notification requirements is available on the WRAS website.

Suitability of fittings

There is no need to remove, replace, alter, disconnect or stop using any fittings that were lawfully installed under the byelaws before the regulations came into force. However, in all new installations or modifications or extensions of existing systems, water fittings must comply – by being of an appropriate quality and standard and suitable for their intended purpose. To demonstrate that they are compliant, fittings must:

- carry an appropriate CE mark;
- conform with an appropriate European harmonised standard or European Technical Approval (ETA);
- be manufactured in accordance with an appropriate British Standard or an equivalent standard of a state that is a member of the European Economic Area; or
- comply with the performance specification approved by the 'regulator' (e.g. the Secretary of State).

Currently there are no relevant CE marks or harmonised standards available. Some water fittings with 'Kitemarks' are manufactured to relevant British Standards. The easiest way to demonstrate compliance of water fittings is to choose those that manufacturers have voluntarily submitted for checking by WRAS. These fittings and materials are assessed by the water suppliers' representatives themselves and are listed as WRAS Approved Products in the *Water Fittings and Materials Directory*.

The owner or occupier of the property is liable if installed fittings do not comply with the regulations and if the installation has not been carried out 'in a workmanlike manner' – e.g. in accordance with an appropriate standard such as BS 6700 for the design of plumbing installations in buildings.

Preventing contamination by backflow

If the usual direction of flow of water in pipes is reversed, there is a risk of contamination being drawn into the pipework and affecting drinking water supplies, either in the premises themselves or in adjacent premises. Under the byelaws, there were three classes of risk of backflow, with appropriate methods of protection. The regulations have defined five 'fluid categories' for these risks and permitted some new devices for preventing backflow. When designing new plumbing systems or making changes to existing ones, a risk assessment is required to determine the level of risk and suitable protective devices must then be installed. More information is given about this in the WRAS *Water Regulations Guide*.

Requirements for WCs and urinals

From 1 January 2001, the maximum flush volume for new WCs is 6 litres and European-style drop valves, flap valves, flushing valves and flushing cisterns are permitted, provided they have undergone testing in accordance with a performance specification approved by the regulator. It is an offence to use valves and WCs that do not comply. Like-for-like replacements of already installed WCs exceeding 6 litres flush will still be permitted. WC cisterns no longer have to have an external warning pipe to indicate if the inlet valve is leaking. Instead an internal arrangement is permitted allowing water to run into the back of the WC pan via the flush pipe. Dual-flush WCs are reintroduced, but the smaller flush must not be greater than two-thirds of the larger flush.

Water saving

In June 2003 the regulator approved the retro-fitting of devices into existing 7.5- or 9-litre 'byelaws' WC cisterns, which were installed before July 1999, to modify them to provide dual-flush or interruptible flush. This offers significant water savings for older premises.

Under byelaws, cisterns were required for flushing urinals, but in non-domestic premises the regulations permit automatic urinal control with water direct from the mains supply, via suitable backflow protection. This is a major water conservation initiative and workplace managers should now give consideration to taking advantage of it.

In addition to water conservation arising from the use of new types of WCs and urinals, the legislation makes reference to recycled or 'grey' water and the need to mark pipes carrying such water to reduce the risk of dangerous cross-connection with wholesome water.

Approved contractors

The regulations define 'approved contractors' and give them certain benefits and responsibilities. They can be accredited by the water suppliers or other organisations authorised by the Secretary of State. Among the water suppliers in England and Wales, Anglian, Severn Trent, Thames and Yorkshire Water operate their own schemes; the remainder support the Water Industry Approved Plumbers Scheme (WIAPS) administered

by WRAS. Members of WIAPS have demonstrated their experience in plumbing and knowledge of the regulations. Names and addresses of WIAPS members are given on the WRAS website. Other schemes are operated by the Institute of Plumbing and Heating Engineering (formerly the Institute of Plumbing), the Association of Plumbing and Heating Contractors, and the Scottish and Northern Ireland Plumbing Employers' Federation.

Approved plumbers must give their customers a certificate of compliance for their work which the customers can use as a defence in the event of any prosecution for non-compliance associated with the installation work. Approved plumbers can also undertake some types of work without the need for prior consent, which can provide flexibility for the timing of projects.

Practical conclusions

Workplace managers need to be fully aware of the legal requirements that the regulations place upon the owners and occupiers of premises. Not only does this make sense to avoid possible prosecution and remedial costs if contraventions are found by the water suppliers that enforce the regulations, but it will prevent contamination of drinking water in the premises and ensure efficient use of water.

See also: Legionella (page 358); Water quality (page 534).

Sources of further information

The Water Regulations Advisory Scheme (WRAS) can be contacted at Unit 30, Fern Close, Pen-y-Fan Industrial Estate, Oakdale, Gwent NP11 3EH (tel. 01495 248454; fax 01495 249234; email info@wras.co.uk). The WRAS website (www.wras.co.uk) provides downloads of advice leaflets and guidance notes, details of other publications, recent interpretations of the regulations, and lists of WIAPS-approved contractors.

WRAS publishes *The Water Regulations Guide* (£18.45), which gives the text of the regulations and Scottish byelaws, the Government's guidance to the regulations and the water supply industry's advice on how to comply.

The Water Fittings and Materials Directory, published twice per year by WRAS in hard-copy and CD versions, includes lists of the materials and fittings which have been approved by the water industry as complying with the regulations. It also includes lists of BS Kitemarked fittings and other approved materials and fittings. For prices and further details, see the WRAS website.

Defra web page on the Water Supply (Water Fittings Regulations) 1999: www.defra.gov.uk/environment/water/industry/wsregs99/index.htm.

BS 6700:1997 'Specification for the design, installation, testing and maintenance of services supplying water for domestic use within buildings and their curtilages'.

'Legionella Policy and Management Guide, version 1.0 (ISBN 1 900648 74 1, £74.99) is available as an electronic download from the Workplace Law Network. Call 0870 777 8881 for details, or visit www.workplacelaw.net.

Water quality

Edited by David Symons, Atkins Environment

Legislation

- Environmental Protection Act 1990.
- Water Resources Act 1991.
- Water Industry Acts 1991 and 1999.
- Groundwater Regulations 1998.
- Anti-Pollution Works Regulations 1999.

Most commercial premises generate some form of liquid waste such as sewage, waste chemicals, cleaning effluents and contaminated surface run-off. There are three ways of disposing of these:

- into foul drains and sewers;
- into controlled waters, such as rivers or canals with or without treatment; or
- through licensed waste management contractors.

Discharges to foul drains and sewers

Most sites have two drainage systems – surface water drains that remove storm run-off, and foul sewers that channel effluents towards sewage works. It is essential that you have a good understanding of the layout of the drains under your site so that discharges are made to the correct system.

If you discharge just domestic effluent to the foul drain, then you generally do not need a discharge consent. Discharge of anything else to these drains, such as process wastewaters, potentially contam-inated surface run-off, condensate from compressors, cooling waters or detergents, is more likely to require a consent. Consents are usually issued by your local water company, such as Thames Water or United Utilities. Consents stipulate the volume and the strength of the effluent which you can discharge. If you are unsure whether you need a consent, it is best to write to the water company to check.

Do not pour anything apart from domestic effluent into the foul drains. Foul drains flow to a sewage treatment works and, from there, into a watercourse. Oils or other chemicals poured into the drains cannot be treated by the sewage treatment works and so will contaminate the watercourse.

Discharges to storm drains

Storm drainage networks generally discharge directly to a local watercourse without treatment. Because there is no treatment, you must not discharge anything other than clean water to this system unless you have a discharge consent from the Environment Agency. Storm drains should only take rainwater from roofs, yards and roads. You should not wash spilled materials into the drains or wash vehicles in areas where the run-off will discharge into the storm system.

Oil water interceptors are often required in car-park areas and capture spilled oils and fuel before they enter the storm drain. If interceptors are installed on your system, you should make sure that these are checked and emptied on a regular basis.

If you have any uncertainties about the need for a consent or if circumstances have changed since an original consent was approved or deemed unnecessary, stop the discharges and check with the Environment Agency as soon as possible.

In the event of any pollution incident involving contamination of controlled waters or land, notify the Environment Agency immediately (incident hotline 0800 80 70 60).

Waste disposal

Where there is no connection to mains sewers or where your effluent is too strong to be disposed directly to a sewer, then you will need to dispose of the liquid as waste. See 'Waste management' (page 526) and 'Hazardous/special waste' (page 524) for full information on this topic.

Pollution prevention

Major prosecutions are often the consequence of a pollution incident that can be prevented or mitigated by careful design and planning. A comprehensive range of pollution prevention measures is essential to minimise the effects of incidents and limit potential liabilities:

- Make sure you know the types of environmental hazard that are present: what quantities there are, how they behave if released – physically, chemically and biologically – and what they could affect.
- Install portable or fixed pipe/pump

systems to move liquids around site.
- Use suitable means of storage with adequate containment for all tanks, barrels and holding areas, including any pipes, valves and gauges. Closed loop systems are often an effective solution (e.g. for vehicle washing facilities). Containment structures need to be regularly inspected and maintained. Applying sealants to bund walls and floors protects against cracks, fissures and minor leaks. Ensure that all connections are in good working order, and that any tanks or pipework that are being replaced are completely empty before dismantling.
- Where surface run-off may be contaminated with silts, heavy metals, chemicals or oils (e.g. car parks, access roads, yards, refuse compactors), potential pollutants should be controlled at source or before discharge by oil separators, gullies, raised kerbing, etc.
- Where significant construction work is undertaken, use a combination of alternative drainage techniques such as SUDS (sustainable urban drainage systems): see 'Sources of further information'.
- Avoid underground storage and pipe systems wherever feasible. Where these are already installed, you may need to check for leaks. Pressure tests and sending cameras down the pipes can be very expensive but are cheaper than remediation.
- Protect facilities against accidental misuse, vandalism or other interference. Supervise deliveries; install alarm systems, lockable gates, doors and valves, etc.
- In the event of spillage, every effort

should be made to contain the liquid – it must not be flushed away or allowed to spread except when there is a danger to life or health. Block off drain entry points or divert spills into holding tanks or 'sacrificial' areas.

- Provide 'spill kits' or sufficient absorbents as well as drain covers, seals and/or booms. Ensure that these materials are replenished regularly. Contaminated absorbent materials may require disposal by special waste contractors. Consider the health and safety implications of pollution incidents (risk assessment, provision of safety information, training and protective equipment).
- Train staff and contractors in correct disposal routines and emergency drills.
- Identify potential risks (e.g. risk of flooding if your site is on a floodplain) and maintain suitable contingency plans. As necessary, advise the relevant authorities, post key information (internal/external contacts, COSHH information, site plans, etc.) and provide equipment to deal with emergencies. Carry out regular drills.

Conclusion

Make sure you have all necessary consents and that you comply with their requirements, including pollution prevention measures.

Reduce or eliminate liquid wastes wherever possible.

A good environmental management system will help ensure compliance and avoid increasing liabilities.

See also: Biological hazards (page 84); COSHH/hazardous substances (page 153); Environmental management systems (page 240); Risk assessments (page 469); Hazardous/special waste (page 524); Waste management (page 526).

Sources of further information

The Environment Agency has a number of useful Pollution Prevention Guidelines (on containment structures, SUDS, etc.) available to print or download on www.environment-agency.gov.uk.

Wheelclamping

Dale Collins, Osborne Clarke

Key points

- Land owners and occupiers who allow their land to be used as a car park have the right to restrict that right to specified persons, e.g. those who have purchased and are using a valid ticket. Running with that right is the right to demand a payment for unlawful use and the ability to prevent the removal of unauthorised vehicles until such time as a payment is made.
- Where such a system is in place, however, the land owner or occupier must ensure that the person using the car park is aware of that fact to prevent actions for trespass and criminal damage being pursued.
- In addition, with the coming into force of the Private Security Industry Act 2001, the wheelclamper must be licensed with the local authority, failing which criminal offences are committed with, potentially, large fines being imposed.

Legislation

- Private Security Industry Act 2001.

Cases

- *Arthur -v- Anker* (1996) 3 All ER 783.
- *Vine -v- Waltham Forest London Borough Council* (2000) *The Times* 12 April 2000.

The law

A private landowner has a right to take reasonable steps to protect his land, and any interest in that land, from harm. Anything placed on that land without his consent is a trespass. A trespass is an actionable tort (civil wrong) which gives rise to a claim in damages for compensation. It also gives rise to the right of 'self-help': in other words, the ability to take action oneself to remove the trespassing article.

Clearly, vehicles parked unlawfully on private land are trespassing, and, although there may be no physical damage being caused by their being parked on the land, a claim can arise as damage does not need to be physical: it can arise from the landowner being unable to use that space. The car-park owner or manager will want the car removed and the ability to claim immediate damages to represent the loss. He does not want to have to issue proceedings in court. The only way to do this is to ensure that the car is not removed without such payment being made.

The way to do this is through the use of wheelclamps.

However, the placing of a wheelclamp on another person's vehicle is itself a trespass, allowing the car owner to bring a claim for damages. In addition, should the installation of the clamp (or its removal) cause damage, the clamper could be liable for that damage and face a charge of criminal damage in the criminal courts.

Also, the wheelclamping itself does not remove the problem, i.e. the loss of car-parking space. In fact, it exacerbates the problem by potentially keeping the vehicle in situ.

Thus, in addition to the clamping, which is essentially a detention to secure payment of the fee, it is also necessary to have the ability to remove the obstructing vehicle. This removal can again cause damage.

So, from where do wheelclampers derive their authority preventing them being pursued or prosecuted?

It is all a question of consent.

Where it can be proved that the driver either saw or should have seen a sign prohibiting parking and warning that a wheelclamping regime was in place, the wheelclamping is lawful as the driver is said to accept, either explicitly or by implication, the consequences of his action.

This is best seen in the cases of *Arthur - v- Anker* (1996) and *Vine -v- Waltham Forest London Borough Council* (2000). In the former, the wheelclamper's actions were held to be lawful as the driver had seen the sign but decided to ignore it. In the latter, as the driver had not seen the sign prohibiting parking, she was found not to have consented to the wheelclamping and thus could recover damages.

In the Vine case, Lord Justice May stated: '... a motorist who appreciates that there are warning signs obviously intended to affect the use of private property for parking vehicles, but who does not read the detailed warning, might, depending on the facts, be held to have consented to, or willingly assumed, the risk of a vehicle being clamped, if the unread warning sign in fact gives sufficient warning that trespassing vehicles would be clamped.'

In other words, if the notices are such that it could not reasonably be argued that they were not seen, and if they were signs which made it abundantly clear what would happen if unauthorised parking occurred, the court would infer consent.

Fee

What is a reasonable fee?

In the Arthur case, Master of the Rolls Bingham in his judgment stated: 'I would not accept that the clamper could exact any unreasonable or exorbitant charge for releasing the car, and the court would be very slow to find implied acceptance of such a charge.'

In the Vine case the fee was £105, and in the Arthur case it was £40 to release the clamp and £90 plus storage to return the car. In both of those cases these fees were considered reasonable.

It is clear that the recovery of the costs associated with the wheelclamping scheme is acceptable, but if an attempt was made to make a large profit that would not be acceptable.

Removal

The problem with simply wheelclamping a vehicle which is illegally parked is that it does not free up the space: in other words, it does not solve the problem. The owners of a private car park are entitled, therefore, to reduce their losses by removing the vehicle, provided that removal is specified on the notice.

The additional difficulty with removal, however, is that there is an increased danger of damage being caused during the removal process. However, whether the trespassing owner will be entitled to claim for such damage will again be down to a question of consent. By parking unlawfully in the full knowledge that removal is a possibility, the driver is accepting that there may be some damage incurred, and provided that damage is not unreasonable or unexpected there should be no claim.

Practical guidance

Signage is vitally important in this area. Signs must be prominently displayed where they can be read and where they will be visible to anyone using that car park, and must include, as a minimum, the following information:

- The notice must specify that wheel-clamping is in operation, the consequences of parking unlawfully and the cost of removal. (It may be worth considering that as well as written warnings there should be some type of pictogram making it clear that there is no parking except by permit).
- The notice must contain the contact details for the removal of the wheel-clamp (and that removal must be able to take place within a reasonable time).
- If the vehicle is to be removed that fact must be stated.

A very useful document for use is that issued by the British Parking Association entitled 'Code of Practice for Clamping Vehicles on Private Land and in Private Car Parks Accessible to the Public'

(issued July 2000).

The document provides what is effectively good practice, including information on the types of vehicle that should not be clamped, expected release times to be achieved (usually no more than two hours and certainly never beyond four) and the types of sign to be used in car parks and to be placed on a vehicle following the clamping.

Other practical issues to be considered include the following:

- Photographing the car in relation to the sign (useful evidence).
- Checking the insurance position with regard to public liability.
- Training for those carrying out the wheelclamping and risk-assessing their tasks.

Recent developments

The Private Security Industry Act 2001 has been effective from 1 April 2003. The Act created the Security Industry Authority (SIA), whose job it is to regulate and oversee the private security industry, which includes those undertaking wheelclamping.

The 'regulation' is by way of a licensing regime for those involved and the development of criteria for their professional training.

Not only do those working for wheel-clamping firms have to be licensed; so, too, do in-house clampers.

The licence costs £190 and is valid for one year for operatives and for three years for supervisors and managers. Before such a licence is issued, the individual will be checked out by the SIA (criminal record checks and so on) to ensure he is fit to hold a licence.

Undertaking clamping without a

licence is a criminal offence for the individual, giving rise to a fine of £5,000 and/or six months' imprisonment.

In addition, the occupier of the land on which the wheelclamping takes place also commits an offence if an unlicensed clamper is working on his site. The only defence is that either he did not know that the person did not hold a licence or he took all reasonable steps to prevent such an unlicensed person from clamping on the land.

In the magistrates' court the penalty is the same as it is for the unlicensed clamper, but the matter may be heard in the Crown Court, where there is an unlimited fine and up to five years' imprisonment.

Where the occupier is a company, not only can the company be held liable, but, where it can be shown that a director, manager or similar officer consented to, connived in or was negligent as to the offence, then that individual can also be personally prosecuted.

There is little doubt that the regulation of those who undertake wheelclamping (or more strictly vehicle immobilisation) on private land is needed. Examples of the boorish behaviour of some 'clampers' are many and varied:

- A man who broke down on a busy road pulled into the car park at a local pub. He went to find a phone box so that he could call out the RAC, leaving his 82-year-old disabled wife in the vehicle. Clampers appeared immediately and demanded that the woman move the car. Her disability prevented her from doing this, so they clamped the vehicle and demanded £80 for its removal.
- A clamper in London impounded a

car without notifying the owner and then gave it to his daughter to drive.
- A hearse was clamped with a dead body in the back.
- Some clampers have demanded wedding rings, gold teeth or even sexual favours in lieu of payment.
- Clampers in Doncaster threatened to hold a mother's 3-year-old daughter ransom.
- Pending the introduction of the licensing regime, some local authorities took their own measures to curb bad practice.

In May 2004, Portsmouth City Council and the local police sought and obtained an interim anti-social behaviour order against a wheelclamper who was responsible for the following incidents:

- Cars in a particular car park were all clamped on the blind side with no warning signs on the windscreens, resulting in their being damaged when the unwitting owners returned and drove them away unaware that they had been clamped. One owner, who did £300 of damage to his vehicle, was laughed at and told to 'get more glasses' when he challenged the clamper.
- A taxi driver taking money to his son to pay a clamping charge was also clamped and blocked in when he drove into the same car park.
- A man was clamped for the second time when he returned to the car park where he had previously been clamped. He returned because he had appealed the first fine, received no reply and went back to get the clamper's telephone number to follow up. His engine was running

and he had pulled only slightly off the road.

- A woman who went to pick up her son took a short cut across a private car park in order to reach a side road. Her exit from the car park was blocked by the clamper demanding money even though her engine was running and her handbrake was not on.

- Clampers attempted to clamp two drivers who had executed three point turns in the road – even though only their rear wheels came in contact with the private car park.

- A woman with her children turned her car in the forecourt of a garage with no intention of stopping. A tow truck pulled in front of her and her car was clamped.

The order prohibits the clamper from:

- clamping without adhering to the British Parking Association codes of practice;
- clamping on land without the written authority of the legal occupier;
- clamping without signs clearly displayed warning of the use of wheelclamps;
- clamping or demanding money without producing the written authority of the legal occupier of the

land and proof of identification;

- clamping or attempting to clamp a vehicle while the engine is running and occupied;
- blocking or attempting to block the pathway of a vehicle on the road or private land should the vehicle be occupied and the engine running;
- threatening, abusing or intimidating motorists where a wheelclamp has or is being applied; and
- inciting, encouraging, aiding or abetting any other person to undertake any of the above.

See also: Parking (page 412); Security licensing (page 473).

Whistleblowers

Pinsent Masons Employment Group

Key points

- The Public Interest Disclosure Act 1998 protects workers from detriment as a consequence of disclosing wrongdoings on the part of their employer.
- To fall within the protection, the employee's disclosure must have been made in a certain way, about certain matters, to certain people.
- The definition of those protected under the Act goes beyond employees and includes contractors.

Legislation

- Employment Rights Act 1996.
- Public Interest Disclosure Act 1998.
- Public Interest Disclosure (Prescribed Persons) Order 1999.
- Public Interest Disclosure (Prescribed Persons) (Amendment) Order 2003.

Protection

The Public Interest Disclosure Act 1998 has become known as the 'Whistleblowers' Act' because it protects workers who suffer detriment as a result of 'blowing the whistle' – disclosing wrongdoing – on their employers, provided that the informer goes through the correct channels.

To be protected, the worker must be able to show that:

- in his reasonable belief the disclosure relates to one of a list of specified wrongdoings; and
- the disclosure is made by one of six

specified procedures to specified people.

List of wrongdoings

A protected disclosure is a disclosure made by a worker which tends to show that:

- a criminal offence has been, is being or is likely to be committed;
- a person has breached, is breaching or is likely to breach a legal obligation;
- a miscarriage of justice has occurred, is occurring or is likely to occur;
- the health and safety of an individual has been, is being or is likely to be endangered;
- the environment has been, is being or is likely to be endangered; or
- there is an attempt to cover up one of the above.

Procedures for disclosure

In order to be protected, the disclosure

---

must be made only to the category of persons set out in the Act, not any person.

Any one of six methods of disclosing will be protected so long as the worker can show that he was justified in choosing that method.

1. Disclosure to employer

The disclosure must be in 'good faith' (i.e. honestly, even if it is careless or negligent) and can be to the employer (e.g. telling the chairman that a director is fiddling expenses) or to a third party if one is involved (e.g. a supplier). A policy may also exist allowing workers to complain to a particular person (e.g. an external accountant).

2. Disclosure to legal advisor

A disclosure made 'in the course of obtaining legal advice' will be protected even if it is not made in good faith.

3. Disclosure to Ministers

A disclosure can be made 'in good faith to a Minister of the Crown' if the employer is one appointed by an Act of Parliament (e.g. an NHS trust).

4. Disclosure to prescribed persons

The current list of 'prescribed persons' (see Employment Rights Act 1996, section 43F) is given in the Public Interest Disclosure (Prescribed Persons) (Amendment) Order 1999.

Specific persons are listed for particular purposes or industries including the HSE, Financial Services Authority, Inland Revenue and Serious Fraud Office. The worker must reasonably believe that the information disclosed is substantially true and that it falls within the remit of the prescribed person.

5. Other external disclosure

Wider disclosures are possible to persons such as the media, police and MPs but to remain protected the worker must pass a number of tests.

The worker must:

- make the disclosure in good faith and not for personal gain;
- reasonably believe that the information disclosed and allegations are substantially true;
- show it is reasonable to make the disclosure, and that one of the following reasons is true:

  – the worker reasonably believes at the time of making the disclosure that he will be subjected to a detriment by the employer if disclosure is made to the employer or to a prescribed person; or

  – evidence will be concealed or destroyed if disclosure is made to the employer; or

  – the worker has previously made disclosure of the same information to the employer or to certain prescribed persons.

There is a list of considerations governing whether the disclosure is 'reasonable' or not. These are:

- the identity of the person to whom the disclosure is made;
- the seriousness of the wrongdoing;
- whether the wrongdoing will or is likely to continue or recur;
- whether the disclosure is made in breach of a duty of confidentiality which the employer owes to any other person;
- whether the employee has previously disclosed substantially the

same information to the employer, or to a prescribed person;

- whether they have taken action and what action they have taken or might have taken; and
- if a previous disclosure is made to the worker's employer, whether the worker complied with any whistle-blowing procedure authorised by the employer.

6. Exceptionally serious failures

Where the wrongdoing is 'exceptionally serious', the other methods of disclosure can be overridden. However, the employee takes clear risks. He must:

- make the disclosure in good faith and not for personal gain;
- reasonably believe that information and allegations are substantially true;
- show that the wrongdoing is of an 'exceptionally serious nature': this is a matter of fact (the worker could be mistaken, even if he *believes* it is serious – if wrong, he loses protection); and
- show it is reasonable for the worker to make the disclosure bearing in mind the identity of the person to whom the disclosure is made.

What can the worker claim?

Legal protection is given to workers who make a protected disclosure in certain specified circumstances (see above). They will have the right not to be subjected to any detriment by their employer on the ground that they have made a protected disclosure, and not to be dismissed and not to be selected for redundancy for this reason.

'Detriment' does not technically include dismissal. However, a dismissal will be regarded as automatically unfair if it is due to the worker making a disclosure, and no qualifying period of service is needed for a worker to bring such a claim of unfair dismissal. There is no limit on the amount of compensation which can be awarded.

Practical issues

Employers should consider introducing a whistleblowing policy, separate from disciplinary and grievance procedures, in order to encourage such matters to be resolved within the organisation and in a regulated manner. Further, any provision in a contract of employment purporting to prevent a worker from making a protected disclosure will be void.

See also: Discrimination (page 189).

Sources of further information

Arbitration, Conciliation and Advisory Service (ACAS): www.acas.org.uk.

Financial Services Authority (FSA): www.fsa.gov.uk.

Public Concern at Work: www.pcaw.co.uk.

Work equipment

Ciaron Dunne, Workplace Law Group

Key points

- The Provision and Use of Work Equipment Regulations 1998 (PUWER) came into effect on 5 December 1998, replacing the previous 1992 Regulations.
- PUWER applies to all new and second-hand work equipment, from scissors to scaffolding and power presses.
- PUWER sets out specific requirements for managing the health and safety aspects of work equipment, from inspection and maintenance regime to machine guarding.

Legislation

- Provision and Use of Work Equipment Regulations 1998.

Scope

'Work equipment' is defined as 'any machinery, appliance, apparatus, tool or installation for use at work (whether exclusively or not)'. The Regulations therefore apply to all types of work equipment, including scissors and mobile phones, but are particularly important in relation to dangerous machinery such as abrasive wheels, cars, forklift trucks and power presses.

Suitability

One of the key provisions of PUWER is that all work equipment must be suitable – i.e. employers must reasonably foresee how work equipment will affect the health or safety of any person, and take that into account when choosing and using the equipment.

Employers must make sure that work equipment is used only for operations for which it is suitable, and under suitable conditions. Risk assessments must take into account:

- the initial integrity of the equipment;
- the place where it will be used; and
- the purpose for which it will be used.

Specific requirements

PUWER contains a raft of specific requirements in relation to work equipment. These are summarised as follows.

Regulation 5. Maintenance

Employers must make sure that work equipment is maintained properly, and that – where a maintenance log is kept for machinery – it is always up to date. The three most common maintenance regimes are planned preventive (e.g. servicing), condition-based (monitoring) and breakdown repairs.

Regulation 6. Inspection

Employers must inspect work equipment after assembly and before it is used for the first time (or for the first time in a new location), and it must be inspected regularly where conditions are likely to cause deterioration (e.g. scaffolding). Employers must record inspections, and must hand over evidence of inspection if the work equipment is sold, leased or hired out to another organisation.

Regulation 7. Specific risks

Where the work equipment presents a specific risk (e.g. a chainsaw), employers must restrict use (or maintenance/inspection) of that equipment to designated people.

Regulation 8. Information and instructions

Employers must provide people who will use the equipment with adequate health and safety information and, if necessary, written instructions.

Regulation 9. Training

Employers must make sure that all people who will use the equipment are adequately trained in that use, and in the health and safety issues relating to the work equipment. Refresher training should also be provided, particularly where circumstances change (e.g. changes to working conditions or systems of work).

Regulation 10. Conformity with EU requirements

All products must be supplied with adequate operating instructions and specific health and safety information, and must carry a CE mark and an EU declaration of conformity.

Regulation 11. Guarding

Employers must take measures to:

- prevent access to dangerous parts of machinery; and
- stop the movement of a dangerous part before any part of a person enters a danger zone.

PUWER states that the preferable type of guarding is a fixed guard (i.e. a guard which is screwed or bolted on, which encloses all of the dangerous parts, and which is removed only for maintenance/inspection). If fixed guards are not possible, employers should consider (in the following order):

- interlocking guards (if the guard is not in place, then the equipment will not operate – e.g. a washing-machine door);
- automatic guards (which physically move the operator away from danger); and
- trip devices (which would stop the machinery).

Regulation 12. Protection against specified hazards

Employers are required to put in place measures to minimise the effects of certain specified hazards, and to reduce the likelihood of the hazard occurring. The hazards specified are:

- any article or substance falling or being ejected from work equipment;
- rupture or disintegration of parts of work equipment;
- work equipment catching fire or overheating;
- the unintended or premature discharge of any article or of any gas,

dust, liquid, vapour or any other substance; and

- the unintended or premature explosion of the work equipment or any article or substance produced, used or stored in it.

The Regulation specifies that any measures put in place must be over and above the use of personal protective equipment.

Regulation 13. Extreme temperatures

Employers must make sure that operators are protected from equipment that utilises very high or low temperatures – e.g. flat irons and snow machines.

Regulations 14–18. Controls

Controls (e.g. start and stop buttons) are subject to strict requirements under PUWER. For example, controls must be clearly visible and identifiable.

Regulation 19. Sources of energy

Employers must make sure that there is a suitable (clearly identifiable and readily accessible) way to isolate the work equipment from its energy source. If the power is disconnected, then the equipment should not automatically start again when the power is switched back on.

Regulation 20. Stability

Machinery must be clamped down, if necessary, to control any risks to health and safety,

Regulation 21. Lighting

Employers must make sure that suitable lighting is provided for the safe operation of machinery.

Regulation 22. Maintenance operations

Equipment must be set up so that maintenance operations can be carried out safely. Preferably, it should be possible to turn the power off before carrying out any maintenance operations.

Regulations 23 and 24. Markings and warnings

Employers must make sure that equipment is suitably marked with health and safety information.

Sources of further information

INDG291 'Simple guide to the Provision and Use of Work Equipment Regulations 1998' (HSE Books, 1999): ISBN 0 7176 2429 3.

L22 'Safe use of work equipment. Approved Code of Practice and guidance' (HSE Books, 1998): ISBN 0 7176 1626 6.

L112 'Safe use of power presses. Approved Code of Practice and guidance' (HSE Books, 1998): ISBN 0 7176 1627 4.

L113 'Safe use of lifting equipment. Approved Code of Practice and guidance' (HSE Books, 1998): ISBN 0 7176 1628 2.

L114 'Safe use of woodworking machinery. Approved Code of Practice and guidance' (HSE Books, 1998): ISBN 0 7176 1630 4.

Regulations 25–30. Mobile work equipment

PUWER contains special requirements for mobile work equipment (e.g. forklift trucks). For example:

- employees can only be carried on mobile work equipment that is suitable for carrying persons;
- where employees are carried on such equipment, employers must minimise the risks to health and safety, e.g. by providing restraining systems (seatbelts); and
- employers must minimise the risks of overturning.

Regulations 31–35. Power presses

PUWER also contains specific require-

ments relating to the use of power presses. In particular, the requirements relate to examination, inspection, reporting and recording information.

See also: Electricity and electrical equipment (page 214); Lifting equipment (page 364); Lighting (page 367); Machine guards and safety devices (page 377); Personal protective equipment (page 425); Vehicles at work (page 510).

Work-related upper limb disorders (WRULDs)

Andrew Richardson, Scott Wilson

Key points

- Musculo-skeletal problems of the arm, hand, shoulder and neck can be found across a broad range of work activities. These are properly referred to as work-related upper limb disorders (WRULDs). Often, especially where pain in the arm occurs among computer users, some forms of WRULD are referred to as repetitive strain injury (RSI). This can be confusing because RSI is not a medical diagnosis. For clarity and to avoid confusion, only WRULDs will be referred to in this article.

- WRULDs is a generic term for a group of musculo-skeletal injuries that affect the muscles, tendons, joints and bones, usually in the hand, arm or shoulder, and generally caused by frequent or repetitive movement of the arms, wrists and fingers.

- ULDs can be caused by non-work activities. Employers need to ensure that the tasks they allocate to workers do not make the injury any worse.

- WRULDs can be avoided by ergonomic improvements in the workplace, i.e. improving the interface between man and machine. The job must be matched to the person.

- Employers need to make adjustments to the task, workstation, work environment and/or work organisation.

Legislation

- Health and Safety at Work etc. Act 1974.
- Management of Health and Safety at Work Regulations 1999.
- Health and Safety (Display Screen Equipment) Regulations 1992 (as amended by the Health and Safety (Miscellaneous Amendments) Regulations 2002).
- Provision and Use of Work Equipment Regulations 1998.
- Personal Protective Equipment at Work Regulations 1992.
- Manual Handling Operations Regulations 1992.
- Reporting of Injuries, Diseases and Dangerous Occurrences Regulations 1995.

Dealing with WRULDs

WRULDs are musculo-skeletal disorders of the arm, hand, shoulder and neck. They can range from temporary fatigue or soreness of the limbs through to chronic soft tissue disorders such as tendonitis and carpal tunnel syndrome. Personnel can also suffer from occupational cramp. Symptoms of WRULDs include tenderness, aches, pains, stiffness, weakness, tingling, numbness, cramp and swelling.

WRULDs can be caused by forceful or repetitive activities or poor posture. They are widespread across a range of industries and jobs, but are particularly associated with the work of computer users and assembly workers.

The way that the workplace is arranged and managed can cause WRULDs or make existing medical conditions worse.

Employers have a legal duty under the Health and Safety at Work etc. Act 1974 and the Management of Health and Safety at Work Regulations 1999 to carry out risk assessments and put into place measures to prevent WRULDs and/or stop any existing medical conditions becoming worse.

The HSE advocates the following management framework to all employers for dealing with WRULDs:

- *Understand the issues and commit to action.* Both the employer and employee should have an understanding of WRULDs and should be committed to carrying out actions to prevent them. Positive leadership, with a policy on WRULDs and the necessary systems in place, will help promote a positive safety culture.

- *Create the right organisational environment.* This should foster active employee participation and involvement, establish clear lines of communication and encourage employer–employee partnerships in carrying out the following framework steps.

- *Assess the risk of WRULDs in your workplace.* Managers and workers should carry out assessments in a systematic way to identify the risks and prioritise them for action.

- *Reduce the risks of WRULDs.* A process of risk reduction should be undertaken using an ergonomic approach. Where possible, risks should be eliminated or reduced at source. Implementation should include the workforce, as this makes it more effective.

- *Educate and inform your workforce.* The provision of education and information is vital. Training will support all aspects of this framework and should be an ongoing activity, not a one-off task.

- *Manage any incidence of WRULDs.* Employees should be encouraged to identify symptoms and to report them as soon as possible before they become persistent. Employers should respond quickly by reviewing the risks and introducing more effective controls. Employers must reassure employees that reporting symptoms will not prejudice their job or position. Early medical detection can stop further deterioration and help aid return to work.

- *Carry out regular checks on programme effectiveness.* This will ensure the framework remains effective and will improve its effectiveness.

Where workers use computer equipment, employers must comply with the requirements of the Display Screen Equipment Regulations.

See also: Display screen equipment (page 202); Furniture (page 284).

Sources of further information

The main document which sets out how employers, together with their employees, can manage the risk of WRULDs is HSG60 'Upper limb disorders in the workplace' (HSE Books, 2002): ISBN 0 7176 1978 8. The book details the management framework outlined above and also covers case studies for WRULDs, a detailed risk assessment process including a checklist, medical aspects of WRULDs and legal requirements.

The HSE information and guidance leaflets 'Working with VDUs' and 'Aching arms (or RSI) in small businesses' can be downloaded at www.hse.gov.uk/pubns/indg36.pdf and www.hse.gov.uk/pubns/indg171.pdf respectively.

Working time

Pinsent Masons Employment Group

Key points

- The Working Time Regulations 1998 (which implement the EC Working Time Directive into UK law) regulate hours worked, rest breaks and holidays.
- The DTI guidance notes should be read with the Regulations.
- Employees can opt out of the 48-hour week, and other rights can be softened or extended in 'special cases' or by agreement. (However, on 22 September 2004 the EC published proposals for restricting the opt-out provision of the Working Time Directive together with some other measures.)
- The Regulations do not apply to some sectors, or to time which is not 'working time'.

Legislation

The Working Time Regulations 1998 came into force on 1 October 1998. They have been amended by the Working Time (Amendment) Regulations 2001 and the Working Time (Amendment) Regulations 2003.

Two versions of DTI guidance have been published to assist companies to comply with the Regulations. The Regulations protect workers against working too many hours and not receiving proper rest, and allow them minimum paid holiday rights. Night workers have special rights (see 'Night working', page 401).

Workers

The Regulations apply to 'workers' – i.e. not only to employees, but also to agency workers, freelance workers and those performing a contract for services. The Regulations do not apply to individuals who are genuinely self-employed. Young workers have special rights (see 'Young persons', page 561).

The Regulations do not apply to workers employed in some industry sectors including workers in the transport sector and sea fishing, other workers at sea, and certain activities of the armed forces, police or other civil protection services. The Regulations were amended from 1 August 2003 to extend working-time measures in full to all non-mobile workers in road, sea, inland waterways or lake transport, to workers in the railway and offshore sectors and to all workers in aviation who are not covered by the Aviation Directive.

Since 1 August 2004 the Regulations have also applied to junior doctors, with some exceptions and special rules.

48-hour week

An employer is expected to take all reasonable steps in keeping with the need to protect health and safety, to ensure that in principle each worker works no more than 48 hours on average in each working week. Young workers may not ordinarily work more than eight hours a day or 40 hours a week.

The average is calculated across a 17-week rolling reference period (which in certain circumstances can be extended).

Work for any employer is included, so care is needed if an employer knows or should know that an employee has more than one job. A worker cannot be forced to work more than these hours if the hours constitute 'working time'.

'Working time' is defined as 'the time when a worker is working, at his employer's disposal and carrying out his activity or duties'. This leads to uncertainty, but working time will therefore not usually include, for example, a worker's time spent travelling to and from work, during rest breaks where no work is done, or attending evening classes or day-release courses. Recent cases and guidance suggest that employees who are 'on call' are 'working' if on site, but not if otherwise free to pursue leisure activities until called to work.

The Regulations allow a worker to opt out of the 48-hour-week restriction by written agreement in a number of ways, including by way of an amendment to the individual's contract of employment, but it must be in writing and terminable by the worker on a minimum of seven days' (but not more than three months') notice.

Where a worker has contracted out of the 48-hour week, the employer no longer needs to keep records showing the number of hours actually worked by the opted-out individual.

In these circumstances only a list of those who have opted out is necessary.

See 'EC proposals for change' on page 555 for amendments to 'on-call' time and the opt-out provision proposed by the EC in September 2004.

Rest periods

The Regulations provide for rest periods to be given to workers.

Employers must provide that rest periods can be taken, but there is no need to ensure they are actually taken. The rest period is in addition to annual leave and can be paid or unpaid.

The provisions can be summarised as follows:

- There should be a minimum rest period of 11 uninterrupted hours between each working day.
- Young workers are entitled to 12 hours' uninterrupted rest in each 24-hour period.
- Days off can be averaged over a two-week period.
- Workers who work for six hours are entitled to a 20-minute break.
- There should be adequate rest breaks where monotonous work places the worker at risk.

Special cases

Workers can be asked to work without breaks in a number of 'special cases'.

Also, where special cases exist, the 17-week average period for the 48-hour week can be extended to 26 weeks. These include:

- where there is a 'foreseeable surge of activity';

- where 'unusual and unforeseeable circumstances beyond the control of the worker's employer' exist;
- where continuity of service or production is needed (e.g. hospital care, prisons, media, refuse and where a need exists to keep machines running);
- where permanent presence is needed (e.g. security and surveillance); and
- where there is great distance between the workplace and an employee's home, or between different places of work.

The basis of the special cases is that, if they exist, there is a reasonable need for work to be carried out quickly in a confined period. If because of one of the 'special cases' a worker is not able to take a rest break when he would ordinarily be entitled to do so, he should be allowed to take an equivalent rest break as soon as reasonably practicable thereafter.

Unmeasured working time

The provisions relating to the 48-hour week, night work and minimum rest periods will not apply where a worker's work is not measured or predetermined or can otherwise be determined by the worker himself.

Examples are managing executives or other persons who have a discretion over whether to work or not on a given day without needing to consult the employer.

The Working Time Regulations 1999 extend the scope of the unmeasured working-time exemption to include the concept of 'partially unmeasured working time', so that where a worker 'voluntarily' chooses to work outside the scope

of the hours predetermined by his employer (more likely than not his contractual hours and any contractual overtime), only those hours which were predetermined by his employer will count for the purposes of calculating his working time.

The extra hours will not count so long as they are worked by the worker's choice and not under any compulsion.

Annual leave

Every worker whether full- or part-time is entitled to four weeks' annual leave (pro rata) in each leave year. However, where a worker begins employment part way through a leave year, he is entitled in that leave year to the proportion of the four-week annual leave which is equal to the proportion of the leave year for which he is employed.

There is no statutory right to take bank holidays.

It is not possible to pay a worker instead of allowing annual leave to be made available.

Contractual holiday provisions should be checked to ensure enough holiday is given, but can also be used to fill in gaps in the Regulations, including, for example, in relation to the clawback of overpaid holiday pay when an employee leaves.

For the purposes of the statutory leave entitlement, workers are entitled to be paid a 'week's pay' for each week of annual leave. This is calculated in a particular manner. Effectively, where a worker is paid an annual, monthly or weekly amount to which he is contractually entitled, his holiday pay will be the weekly equivalent of that amount. However, where a worker receives a varying amount of pay each week which is not contractually provided for or agreed, a 'week's pay' must be calculated in accordance with the average amount of pay the worker received in the 12-week period prior to the date of payment. Specific pro-rata rules apply to untaken holiday when an employee leaves.

The Regulations provide a right to stipulate when a worker can take his leave entitlement, including notice provisions for the employer and the employee.

Agreements

Various parts of the Regulations can be disapplied or softened by specific agreements.

A 'relevant agreement' is usually a contract between an employer and a worker.

A 'workforce agreement' means an agreement between an employer and its workers or their elected representatives.

Records

Employers must keep adequate records to show in particular whether the limits in the Regulations dealing with the 48-hour week and night work are being complied with.

The courts will expect employers to be able to show they are complying with the Regulations and policing working time.

Officers of the HSE are entitled to investigate an employer's working-time practices and can demand to see copies of its records.

Enforcement

The method of enforcing the Regulations depends upon whether the provision relied upon is a limit or an entitlement. The HSE and local authorities are respon-

sible for enforcing the limits set out in the Regulations.

Workers may present a complaint to an employment tribunal in connection with any failure by their employer to provide them with the relevant protections afforded by the Regulations. Where a worker is also an employee, and is dismissed as a result of exercising a right under the Regulations, his dismissal will be deemed to be automatically unfair (see 'Dismissal', page 197).

It is automatically unfair to dismiss an employee for reasons connected with rights and entitlements under the Regulations. Employees may present a claim to an employment tribunal regardless of age or length of service.

EC proposals for change

On 22 September 2004 the EC proposed restrictions to the opt-out provision of the Working Time Directive, frequently used by UK employers and employees to keep working hours above the maximum 48 hours per week permitted under the Directive.

According to the Commission, the proposed measures will allow Member States to retain the right to opt out of the 48-hour limit provided:

- it is expressly allowed under a collective agreement in organisations where trade unions are recognised; and
- the individual worker involved consents.

An individual can agree to opt out with his employer directly when, under national legislation or practice, collective bargaining cannot be used to negotiate agreements on working time.

This is particularly the case, says the

EC, where no collective agreement is in force and there is no staff representation at company level that is empowered to conclude such an agreement.

The proposed measures then place restrictions on the use of the opt-out. These state that:

- a worker's individual consent cannot be given at the same time as the contract of employment is signed or during any probation period;
- it has to be given in writing;
- it is valid for a maximum of one year (renewable);
- no worker can work more than 65 hours a week unless provided for in a collective agreement; and
- employers are obliged to keep records of the number of hours actually worked and make these records available to the responsible authorities, if required.

In a related move, Member States will be able to extend the standard reference period for calculating the average working week of 48 hours from four months to up to one year, provided they consult the two sides of industry. This will give companies greater flexibility and adaptability for the demands of their business, says the EC.

The proposals also create a new category of on-call time – the 'inactive' part of on-call time. This is the time in which the worker, although available for work at his place of employment, does not carry out his duties. This will not be counted as working time, unless otherwise stipulated by national law or collective agreement.

Finally, the proposal also specifies that compensatory rest has to be granted within a reasonable time and in all cases within 72 hours.

See also: Dismissal (page 197); Night working (page 401); Young persons (page 561).

Sources of further information

DTI Working Time Regulations web page: www.dti.gov.uk/er/work_time_regs.

Workplace health, safety and welfare

Ciaron Dunne, Workplace Law Group

The Workplace (Health, Safety and Welfare) Regulations 1992 came into effect on 1 January 1993. These Regulations apply to a wide range of workplaces, including factories, shops, offices, schools, hospitals, hotels and places of entertainment. They do not apply to construction sites.

Below is a summary of the main requirements.

Regulation 6. Ventilation

Effective and suitable provision shall be made to ensure that every enclosed workplace is ventilated by a sufficient quantity of fresh or purified air. (See also 'Ventilation and temperature', page 513.)

Regulation 7. Temperature in indoor workplaces

Regulation 7 requires that 'During working hours, the temperature in all workplaces inside buildings shall be reasonable.' The Approved Code of Practice (ACoP) that accompanies the Regulations suggests that in a typical workplace (shops, offices, factories, etc.) the temperature should be at least 16°C. If much of the work requires severe physical effort, the temperature should be at least 13°C. (See also 'Ventilation and temperature', page 513.)

Regulation 8. Lighting

Lighting should be sufficient to enable people to work and move about safely. Natural light is preferred by the Regulations. Furthermore, automatic emergency lighting should be provided where failure of artificial lighting could create a risk. (See also 'Lighting', page 367.)

Regulation 9. Cleanliness and waste materials

Employers have a duty to keep the workplace (including furniture, fittings, floors, walls and ceilings) clean, and a further duty not to let waste accumulate.

Regulation 10. Room dimensions and space

Regulation 10 requires that 'Every room where persons work shall have sufficient floor area, height and unoccupied space.' This requirement is expanded in the ACoP, which states that workrooms should have enough 'free space' to allow people to get to and from workstations and to move within the room with ease.

The ACoP states that each person should have a total minimum of 11 cubic metres of space (when the room is empty), where the maximum height used is 3 metres. Therefore, in a room with a ceiling that is 3 metres or higher, the minimum 'free' floor area should be 3.7 square metres. However, depending on the type of furniture in the room, 3.7 square metres may be insufficient to comply with the requirement for sufficient free space.

Regulation 11. Workstations and seating

Workstations must be arranged so that they are suitable for any person who is likely to work at the station and any work that is likely to be done there. The workstation must also be arranged so that it enables that person to leave it swiftly or to be assisted in an emergency.

A suitable seat must be provided for each person at work whose work (or a substantial part of it) can or must be done seated. The seat should be suitable for the person doing the work and the work that needs to be done. When necessary, a suitable footrest should be provided.

For workstations with visual display units (VDUs), the employer should also refer to the Health and Safety (Display Screen Equipment) Regulations 1992. (See 'Display screen equipment', page 202.)

Regulation 12. Condition of floors and traffic routes

Floors and traffic routes (e.g. corridors) should not have holes and slopes or be uneven or slippery. Traffic routes should be kept free from obstructions and from any article or substance which may cause a person to slip, trip or fall.

Handrails should be provided on all staircases, except where they would cause an obstruction. The HSE recommends that open sides of staircases should be fenced with an upper rail at 900mm or higher and a lower rail.

Regulation 13. Falls or falling objects

Where there is a risk of a person falling a distance likely to cause personal injury, secure coverings or fencing should be provided. The HSE recommends that if a person might fall 2 metres or more, or might fall less than 2 metres and risk serious injury, fencing should be at least 1,100mm high and have two guardrails. (See also 'Working at height', page 321.)

Objects need to be stored in such a way that they are not likely to fall and cause injury.

Regulations 14, 15 and 16. Windows

Transparent or translucent surfaces (e.g. windows) shall be made of safety material, i.e. be protecting against breakage. Where there is a danger that someone might walk into them (e.g. a glass door), then they should be marked (e.g. using stickers) to make them obvious.

If a window, skylight or ventilator can be opened, then it must be possible to do it in a safe manner. When open, the window should not create a hazard.

All windows and skylights in a workplace must be able to be cleaned safely, and consideration must also be given to any equipment that needs to be used when cleaning. (See also 'Glass and glazing', page 290.)

Regulation 17. Traffic routes

Where vehicle traffic occurs in a workplace (e.g. a loading dock), the employer must take steps to manage the risks to drivers and pedestrians – e.g. speed limits, clear signage, segregation of traffic and people, marked routes. Protection from exhaust fumes also needs to be considered. (See also 'Vehicles at work', page 510.)

Regulation 18. Doors and gates

Sliding doors or gates must be fitted with protection against coming off the track during use. Powered doors or gates (e.g. lift doors) must have effective features to prevent them trapping people and they must be able to be operated manually if the power fails.

With doors or gates which open both ways, it must be possible to view the other side of the door (e.g. through a vision panel).

Regulation 19. Escalators and moving walkways

Escalators and moving walkways should work safely and be fitted with one or more emergency stop controls which are easily identifiable and readily accessible. (See also 'Lift safety', page 361.)

Regulations 20 and 21. Sanitary conveniences and washing facilities

Suitable and sufficient sanitary conveniences and washing facilities should be provided at readily accessible places, and should be kept clean and well lit. Washing facilities should have running hot and cold or warm water, soap and a means of drying.

The minimum number of facilities is:

- up to five people – one toilet and washstation;

- six to 25 people – two toilets and washstations; and

- one extra toilet and washstation for each subsequent 25 people.

For men a mixture of toilets and urinals can be provided.

Regulation 22. Drinking water

Employers must provide an adequate supply of fresh drinking water. This must be clearly marked (for health and safety reasons), and cups or glasses must be provided (unless a water fountain is used).

Regulations 23 and 24. Clothing

Employers should provide facilities for employees to change clothing. Employers should also provide a facility to store clothes not worn at work, as well as special clothing which is worn at work but is not taken home. The accommodation should be secure and, where possible, should allow clothing to dry.

Regulation 25. Facilities for rest and to eat meals

Eating facilities should enable hot drinks to be obtained or prepared. Restrooms and areas should protect non-smokers from discomfort caused by tobacco smoke. The HSE recommends that work areas (e.g. desks) can be counted as rest areas and as eating facili-

---

Sources of further information

L24 'Workplace health, safety and welfare. Workplace (Health, Safety and Welfare) Regulations 1992. Approved Code of Practice and guidance' (HSE Books, 1996): ISBN 0 7176 0413 6.

INDG244 'Workplace health, safety and welfare: a short guide for managers' (HSE Books, 1997): ISBN 0 7176 1328 3.

---

ties, provided they are adequately clean and there is a suitable surface on which to place food. Canteens or restaurants may be used as rest facilities provided there is no obligation to purchase food. Suitable rest facilities must be provided for new and expectant mothers.

Young persons

Pinsent Masons Employment Group

Key points

- A young person is a person who has ceased to be a child and who is under the age of 18 years. A child (see page 139) is a person not over compulsory school age, currently 16 years.
- Young workers have particular rights under the Working Time Regulations 1998, particularly relating to rest breaks and night work assessments.
- Particular hourly rates apply to young workers for national minimum wage purposes. General health and safety duties prevent young workers being used for work beyond their capabilities.

Legislation

- Children and Young Persons Act 1933 (as amended).
- Employment Rights Act 1996 (as amended).
- National Minimum Wage Act 1998.
- Management of Health and Safety at Work Regulations 1999 (replacing the Health and Safety (Young Persons) Regulations 1997).
- Working Time Regulations 1998.
- Working Time (Amendment) Regulations 2002.

General health and safety issues

Every employer should ensure that young persons employed by him are protected at work from any risks to their health or safety which are a consequence of:

- their lack of experience;
- their absence of awareness of exist-

ing or potential risk; or
- the fact that young persons have not yet fully matured.

Failure to do so may result in civil liability for a breach of statutory duty on the part of the employer.

Risk assessments

An employer should not employ a young person unless he has carried out a risk assessment to ensure that all relevant hazards and consequent risks have been identified.

In particular, an employer should consider:

- if the work is beyond the young person's physical or psychological capacity;
- if there is harmful exposure to radiation or agents which could be toxic or carcinogenic; or
- if there is a risk to health from

---

extreme cold or heat, noise or vibration.

This risk assessment must take into account various issues such as the inexperience and immaturity of the young person, the nature of the workstation, the risks in the workplace including the equipment which the young person will use, and the extent of the health and safety training provided. An employer cannot rely on a risk assessment which had been previously carried out for a mature adult. Employers should consider how these risks may be greater in respect of young persons than for other workers, and if he is at significant risk from carrying out any task a young person should be prohibited from undertaking it.

Daily rest

Young workers are entitled to a break of at least 12 consecutive hours in any 24-hour period.

Weekly rest

Young workers are entitled to a weekly rest period of at least 48 hours in each period of seven days (i.e. two days off each week). In addition, if owing to the nature of the work and because of technical or organisational reasons a young worker cannot take two days off per week, then the rest can be spread across 36 hours in a week.

Rest breaks while at work

If a young worker is required to work for more than four and a half hours at a stretch, he is entitled to a rest break of at least 30 minutes. A young worker's entitlement to rest breaks can be changed or excluded only in exceptional circum-

stances. If a young worker is working for more than one employer, the time he is working for each one should be added together to see if he is entitled to a rest break in a total four and a half hour period of work.

A young person's entitlement to breaks can be changed or not taken in exceptional circumstances only. The circumstances and 'special cases' are narrower than those for older workers (see 'Working time', page 552) and include the situation where no adult is available to do the work. Where this occurs, the worker should receive compensatory rest within three weeks.

Compensatory rest is a period of rest of the same length as the period of rest that a worker has missed.

Annual leave

Young workers have the same entitlements as adult workers in respect of annual leave. (Under the Working Time Regulations 1998, all adult employees are entitled to at least four weeks' paid annual leave.)

Time off for study and training

Young persons who are not in full-time secondary or further education are entitled to take time off during working hours for the purposes of study or training leading to an external qualification (academic or vocational) which 'enhances the young person's employment prospects'. The length of time that can be taken is that which is reasonable in the circumstances, and the young person should be paid for the time taken off at his normal hourly rate.

Night work and health assessment

Young workers are given special protection as regards night work. Ordinarily they may not work at night between 11 p.m. and 7 a.m. if the contract of employment provides for work after 10 p.m. However, exceptions apply in particular circumstances in the case of certain kinds of employment.

Young workers require a health and capabilities assessment. Special consideration should be given to young workers' suitability for night work, taking account of their physique, maturity and experience.

In addition, all employers must offer young night workers a free health assessment before they begin working nights and thereafter on a regular basis. Young workers do not have to undergo a health assessment, but they must be offered one. All employers should maintain up-to-date records of health assessments.

National minimum wage

The National Minimum Wage Act 1998 came into force on 1 April 1999 and provides for the minimum level of pay to which almost all workers in the UK are entitled. Since 1 October 2004 most workers over 16 years of age have been covered by the Act.

Practical points to remember

Workplace managers should check:

- whether they employ young workers; and
- if they do, how many rest periods and breaks young workers are receiving.

If young workers are not receiving the correct rest periods, managers should consider:

- how these can be given; and
- whether the amount of hours worked can be reduced.

Managers should always ensure that:

- proper records of young workers are maintained, including details of health assessments;
- young workers are not involved in work which is particularly hazardous; and
- young workers are receiving the national minimum wage.

See also: Children at work (page 139); Minimum wage (page 383); Night working (page 401); Risk assessments (page 469); Working time (page 552).

Directory of information sources

Access Association
01909 533196
www.accessassociation.co.uk

Acoustic Shock Programme
020 8776 8690
www.acousticshock.org

Action on Smoking and Health (ASH)
020 7739 5902
www.ash.org.uk

Advisory, Conciliation and Arbitration
Service (ACAS)
08457 474 747
www.acas.org.uk

Age Concern
020 8765 7200
www.ageconcern.org.uk

Age Positive
08457 330 360
www.agepositive.gov.uk

Alcohol Concern
020 7928 7377
www.alcoholconcern.org.uk

Asbestos Removal Contractors
Association (ARCA)
01283 531126
www.arca.org.uk

Association for Project Safety (APS)
0131 221 9959
www.aps.org.uk

Association for Specialist Fire
Protection (ASFP)
01252 739142
www.asfp.org.uk

Association of British Insurers (ABI)
020 7696 8999
www.abi.org.uk

Association of Building Engineers (ABE)
01694 404121
www.abe.org.uk

Association of Chief Police Officers
(ACPO)
020 7227 3434
www.acpo.police.uk

Association of Consultant Approved
Inspectors (ACAI)
020 7491 1914 (Hon. Secretary)
www.acai.org.uk

Association of Consultant Architects
(ACA)
020 8325 1402
www.acarchitects.co.uk

Association of Consulting Engineers
(ACE)
020 7222 6557
www.acenet.co.uk

Directory of information sources

Association of Industrial Road Safety
Officers (AIRSO)
01903 506095
www.airso.org.uk

Association of Plumbing and Heating
Contractors (APHC)
024 7647 0626
www.aphc.co.uk

Association of Security Consultants (ASC)
07071 224865
www.securityconsultants.org.uk

Automobile Association (AA)
0870 600 0371
www.theaa.com

Bathroom Manufacturers Association
(BMA)
01782 747123
www.bathroom-association.org

Better Regulation Task Force (BRTF)
020 7276 2142
www.brtf.gov.uk

BioIndustry Association (BIA)
020 7565 7190
www.bioindustry.org

Blind in Business
020 7588 1885
www.blindinbusiness.org.uk

BRE Certification Ltd
01923 664100
www.brecertification.co.uk

British Approvals for Fire Equipment
(BAFE)
020 8541 1950
www.bafe.org.uk

British Association for Chemical
Specialities (BACS)
01524 849606
www.bacsnet.org

British Association of Occupational
Therapists (BAOT)/College of
Occupational Therapists (COT)
020 7357 6480
www.cot.co.uk

British Association of Removers (BAR)
020 8861 3331
www.bar.co.uk

British Automatic Sprinkler Association
(BASA)
01353 659187
www.basa.org.uk

British Cement Association (BCA)
01276 608700
www.bca.org.uk

British Chambers of Commerce (BCC)
020 7654 5800
www.britishchambers.org.uk

British Cleaning Council (BCC)
01562 851129
www.britishcleaningcouncil.org

British Fire Consortium (BFC)
01273 297274
www.britishfireconsortium.co.uk

British Fire Protection Systems
Association (BFPSA)
020 8549 5855
www.bfpsa.org.uk

British Institute of Architectural
Technologists (BIAT)
020 7278 2206
www.biat.org.uk

British Institute of Cleaning Science
(BICSc)
01604 678710
www.bics.org.uk

British Institute of Facilities
Management (BIFM)
01799 508606
www.bifm.org.uk

British Occupational Health
Research Foundation (BOHRF)
020 7317 5898
www.bohrf.org.uk

British Occupational Hygiene
Society (BOHS)
01332 298101
www.bohs.org

British Parking Association (BPA)
01444 447300
www.britishparking.co.uk

British Pest Control Association (BPCA)
01332 294288
www.bpca.org.uk

British Plastics Federation (BPF)
020 7457 5000
www.bpf.co.uk

British Property Federation (BPF)
020 7828 0111
www.bpf.org.uk

British Red Cross Society
020 7235 5454
www.redcross.org.uk

British Retail Consortium (BRC)
020 7854 8900
www.brc.org.uk

British Safety Council
020 8741 1231
www.britishsafetycouncil.co.uk

British Security Industry Association
(BSIA)
01905 21464
www.bsia.co.uk

British Standards Institution (BSI)
020 8996 7000
www.bsi-global.com

British Woodworking Federation (BWF)
0870 458 6939
www.bwf.org.uk

Building Cost Information Service Ltd
(BCIS)
020 7695 1500
www.bcis.co.uk

Building Research Establishment Ltd
(BRE)
01923 664000
www.bre.co.uk

Building Services Research and
Information Association (BSRIA)
01344 426511
www.bsria.co.uk

Business Continuity Institute (BCI)
0870 603 8783
www.thebci.org

Business in the Community
0870 600 2482
www.bitc.org.uk

Cadw
020 2050 0200
www.cadw.wales.gov.uk

Call Centre Association (CCA)
0141 564 9010
www.cca.org.uk

Carbon Trust
0800 585 794
www.thecarbontrust.co.uk

Central Arbitration Committee (CAC)
020 7251 9747
www.cac.gov.uk

Centre for Accessible Environments
(CAE)
020 7840 0125
www.cae.org.uk

Centre for Corporate Accountability
(CCA)
020 7490 4494
www.corporateaccountability.org

Centre for Effective Dispute
Resolution (CEDR)
020 7536 6000
www.cedr.co.uk

Centre for Facilities Management
(Salford University) (CFM)
0161 295 5357
www.cfm.salford.ac.uk

Chartered Institute of Arbitrators
020 7421 7444
www.arbitrators.org

Chartered Institute of Building (CIOB)
01344 630700
www.ciob.org.uk

Chartered Institute of Environmental
Health (CIEH)
020 7928 6006
www.cieh.org.uk

Chartered Institute of Personnel
and Development (CIPD)
020 8971 9000
www.cipd.co.uk

Chartered Institute of Purchasing
and Supply (CIPS)
01780 756777
www.cips.org

Chartered Institute of Wastes
Management (CIWM)
01604 620426
www.ciwm.co.uk

Chartered Institution of Building
Services Engineers (CIBSE)
020 8675 5211
www.cibse.org

Chartered Management Institute
01536 204222
www.managers.org.uk

Chartered Society of Physiotherapy (CSP)
020 7306 6666
www.csp.org.uk

Chemical Hazards Communication
Society (CHCS)
0700 790337
www.chcs.org.uk

Chemical Industries Association (CIA)
020 7834 3399
www.cia.org.uk

Chief and Assistant Chief Fire
Officers' Association (CACFOA)
01827 61516
www.fire-uk.org

Chubb UK
01932 785588 (Chubb Fire)
01932 738600 (Chubb Electronic Security)
www.chubb.co.uk

CIFAS (the UK's Fraud Prevention Service)
www.cifas.org.uk

CIRIA (formerly Construction Industry
Research and Information Association)
020 7549 3300
www.ciria.org.uk

Civil Contingencies Secretariat
(Cabinet Office)
www.ukresilience.info

Clay Pipe Development
Association (CPDA)
01494 791456
www.cpda.co.uk

Commercial Occupational Health
Providers Association (COHPA)
01933 227788
www.cohpa.co.uk

Commission for Architecture
and the Built Environment (CABE)
020 7960 2400
www.cabe.org.uk

Commission for Racial Equality (CRE)
020 79390000
www.cre.gov.uk

Concrete Society
01276 607140
www.concrete.org.uk

Confederation of British Industry (CBI)
020 7379 7400
www.cbi.org.uk

Confederation of Paper Industries (CPI)
01793 889600
www.paper.org.uk

Consortium of European Building
Control (CEBC)
01473 748182
www.cebc.co.uk

Constructing Excellence
020 7592 1101
www.constructingexcellence.org.uk

Construction Confederation
020 7608 5000
www.thecc.org.uk

Construction Health and Safety
Group (CHSG)
01932 561871
www.chsg.co.uk

Construction Industry Council (CIC)
020 7399 7400
www.cic.org.uk

Construction Industry Training
Board (CITB)
01485 577577
www.citb.co.uk

Contract Flooring Association (CFA)
0115 941 1126
www.cfa.org.uk

Contractors Health and
Safety Assessment Scheme (CHAS)
020 8545 4858
www.chas.gov.uk

Corporate Social Responsibility website
www.csr.gov.uk

Council of Registered Gas Installers
(CORGI)
0870 401 2200
www.corgi-gas-safety.co.uk

Countryside Agency
01242 533222
www.countryside.gov.uk

Cranfield Institute for Safety, Risk
and Reliability
01234 755001
www.cranfield.ac.uk/safety

Creating More Balance
0114 249 4923
www.cmb.org.uk

Criminal Records Bureau (CRB)
0870 9090811
www.crb.gov.uk

Crown Prosecution Service (CPS)
020 7796 8000
www.cps.gov.uk

CSR Academy
020 7215 4174
www.csracademy.org.uk

Department for Education and Skills
(DfES)
0870 000 2288
www.dfes.gov.uk

Department for Environment, Food and
Rural Affairs (Defra)
0845 933 5577
www.defra.gov.uk

Department for Transport (DfT)
020 7944 8300
www.dft.gov.uk

Department for Work and Pensions
(DWP)
020 7712 2171
www.dwp.gov.uk

Department of Health (DH)
020 7210 4850
www.dh.gov.uk

Department of Trade and Industry (DTI)
020 7215 5000
www.dti.gov.uk

Design Council
020 7420 5200
www.design-council.org.uk

Disability Matters
01264 811120
disabilitymatters.com

Disability Rights Commission (DRC)
08457 622 633
www.drc-gb.org

ELECSA Ltd
0870 749 0080
www.elecsa.org.uk

Electrical Contractors' Association (ECA)
020 7313 4800
www.eca.co.uk

Emergency Planning Society
0845 600 9587
www.emergplansoc.org.uk

Employee Assistance Professionals
Association (EAPA)
0800 783 7616
www.eapa.org.uk

Employers for Work-Life Balance
0870 165 6700
www.employersforwork-
lifebalance.org.uk

Employers' Forum on Age (EFA)
0845 456 2495
www.efa.org.uk

Employers' Forum on Disability
020 7403 3020
www.employers-forum.co.uk

Energy Institute
020 7467 7100
www.energyinst.org.uk

Engineering and Construction Industry
Association (ECIA)
020 7799 2000
www.ecia.co.uk

Engineering Council UK (ECUK)
020 7415 6000
www.engc.org.uk

Engineering Employers Federation (EEF)
020 7222 7777
www.eef.org.uk

English Heritage
020 7973 3000
www.english-heritage.org.uk

ENTO (formerly Employment NTO)
0116 251 7979
www.ento.co.uk

Environment Agency
08708 506 506
www.environment-agency.gov.uk

Environment Council
020 7836 2626
www.the-environmentcouncil.org.uk

Environment and Heritage Service
(Northern Ireland) (EHSNI)
028 9054 6514
www.ehsni.gov.uk

Environmental Services Association
(ESA)
020 7824 8882
www.esauk.org

Envirowise
0800 585 794
www.envirowise.gov.uk

Equal Opportunities Commission (EOC)
0845 601 5901
www.eoc.org.uk

Ergonomics Society
01509 234904
www.ergonomics.org.uk

European Agency for Safety and Health
at Work
 +34 944 794 360
www.agency.osha.eu.int

Facilities Management Association (FMA)
020 8897 8521
www.fmassociation.org.uk

Fall Arrest Safety Equipment Training
(FASET)
020 7397 8128
www.faset.org.uk

Federation of Environmental Trade
Associations (FETA)
0118 940 3416
www.feta.co.uk

Federation of Master Builders (FMB)
020 7242 7583
www.fmb.org.uk

Federation of Small Businesses (FSB)
01253 336000
www.fsb.org.uk

Financial Services Authority (FSA)
020 7066 1000
www.fsa.gov.uk

Fire Extinguishing Trades Association
(FETA)
020 8549 8839
www.feta.org.uk

Fire Industry Confederation (FIC)
020 8549 8839
www.the-fic.co.uk

FireNet International
www.fire.org.uk

Fire Protection Association (FPA)
01608 812500
www.thefpa.co.uk

Fire Service College
01608 652154
www.fireservicecollege.ac.uk

Food Standards Agency (FSA)
020 7276 8000
www.food.gov.uk

Fork Lift Truck Association (FLTA)
01256 381441
www.fork-truck.org.uk

Forum of Private Business (FPB)
01565 634467
www.fpb.co.uk

Friends of the Earth
020 7490 1555
www.foe.co.uk

Furniture Industry Research Association
(FIRA)
01438 777700
www.fira.co.uk

Glass and Glazing Federation (GGF)
0870 042 4255
www.ggf.org.uk

Greenpeace
020 7865 8100
www.greenpeace.org.uk

Groundwork UK
0121 236 8585
www.groundwork.org.uk

Hazards Forum
020 7665 2230
www.hazardsforum.co.uk

Health and Safety Commission (HSC)
020 7717 6000
www.hse.gov.uk

Health and Safety Executive (HSE)
08701 545 500
www.hse.gov.uk

Health and Safety Executive for
Northern Ireland (HSENI)
028 9024 3249
www.hseni.gov.uk

Health and Safety Laboratory (HSL)
0114 289 2920
www.hsl.gov.uk

Health Development Agency (HAD)
020 7430 0850
www.had.nhs.uk

Health Facilities Management
Association (Hefma)
0113 392 6846 (Hon. Secretary)
www.hefma.org.uk

Health Protection Agency (HPA)
020 7339 1300
www.hpa.org.uk

Healthy Workplace Initiative (HWI)
www.signupweb.net

Heating and Ventilating
Contractors' Association (HVCA)
020 7313 4900
www.hvca.org.uk

Her Majesty's Stationery
Office (HMSO)/The Stationery Office
0870 600 5522
www.hmso.gov.uk; www.tso.co.uk

Her Majesty's Treasury
020 7270 4558
www.hm-treasury.gov.uk

Historic Scotland
0131 668 8600
www.historic-scotland.gov.uk

Home Office
0870 000 1585
www.homeoffice.gov.uk

Hotel and Catering International
Management Association (HCIMA)
020 8661 4900
www.hcima.org.uk

HSE Books
01787 881165
www.hsebooks.com

Incident Contact Centre Website
www.riddor.gov.uk

Independent Safety Consultants
Association (ISCA)
01621 874938
www.isca.org.uk

Industrial Rope Access Trade
Association (IRATA)
01252 739150
www.irata.org

Industry Committee for
Emergency Lighting (ICEL)
020 8675 5432
www.icel.co.uk

Information Commissioner's Office
01625 545700
www.informationcommissioner.gov.uk

Inland Revenue
08457 143 143
www.inlandrevenue.gov.uk

Institute of Acoustics (IOA)
01727 848195
www.ioa.org.uk

Institute of Alcohol Studies (IAS)
020 7222 4001
www.ias.org.uk

Directory of information sources

Institute of Customer Service (ICS)
01206 571716
www.instituteofcustomer.service.com

Institute of Directors (IoD)
020 7839 1233
www.iod.com

Institute of Environmental Management
and Assessment (IEMA)
01522 540069
www.iema.net

Institute of Food Research (IFR)
01603 255000
www.ifr.bbsrc.ac.uk

Institute of Maintenance and Building
Management (IMBM)
01252 710994
www.imbm.org.uk

Institute of Plumbing and Heating
Engineers (IPHE)
01708 472791
www.iphe.org.uk

Institute of Risk Management (IRM)
020 7709 9808
www.theirm.org

Institution of Civil Engineers (ICE)
020 7222 7722
www.ice.org.uk

Institution of Electrical Engineers (IEE)
020 7240 1871
www.iee.org

Institution of Fire Engineers (IFE)
01608 812580
www.ife.org.uk

Institution of Gas Engineers
and Managers (IGEM)
01509 282728
www.igaseng.com

Institution of Lighting Engineers (ILE)
01788 576492
www.ile.org.uk

Institution of Mechanical
Engineers (IMechE)
020 7222 7899
www.imeche.org.uk

Institution of Occupational
Safety and Health (IOSH)
0116 257 3100
www.iosh.co.uk

Institution of Structural
Engineers (IStructE)
020 7235 4535
www.istructe.org.uk

International Facilities
Management Association [USA]
+1 713 623 4362
www.ifma.org

International Institute for
Environment and Development (IIED)
020 7388 2117
www.iied.org

International Institute of Risk
and Safety Management (IIRSM)
020 8600 5538
www.iirsm.org

International Stress Management
Association UK (ISMA UK)
0700 780430
www.isma.org.uk

Joint Industry Board for the
Electrical Contracting Industry (JIB)
020 8302 0031
www.jib.org.uk

Knowledge-Counsel
01344 779438
www.knowledge-counsel.com

Land Registry
020 7917 8888
www.landreg.gov.uk

Lead Development Association
International (LDAI)
020 7499 8422
www.ldaint.org

Lift and Escalator Industry
Association (LEIA)
020 7935 3013
www.leia.co.uk

Local Authority Building Control (LABC)
020 7641 8737
www.labc.co.uk

London Fire Brigade
020 7587 2000
www.london-fire.gov.uk

Low Pay Commission
020 7215 5773
www.lowpay.gov.uk

Mastic Asphalt Council (MAC)
01424 814400
www.masticasphaltcouncil.co.uk

Mind
0845 7660163
www.mind.org.uk

Mobile Operators Association (MOA)
020 7331 2015
www.ukmoa.org

Motability
0845 456 4566
www.motability.co.uk

Motor Insurers' Information Centre
(MIIC)
08702 416 732
www.miic.org.uk

National Access and Scaffolding
Confederation (NASC)
020 7397 8120
www.nasc.org.uk

National Association for the Care
and Resettlement of Offenders (Nacro)
020 7582 6500
www.nacro.org.uk

National Association of Pension
Funds (NAPF)
020 7808 1300
www.napf.co.uk

National Examination Board in
Occupational Safety and Health
(NEBOSH)
0116 263 4700
www.nebosh.org.uk

National Federation of Builders (NFB)
020 7608 5150
www.builders.org.uk

National Federation of Master
Steeplejacks and Lightning
Conductor Engineers (NFMSLCE)
0115 955 8818
www.nfmslce.co.uk

National Federation of Master Window
and General Cleaners (NFMW&GC)
0161 432 8754
www.nfmwgc.com

National Federation of Demolition
Contractors (NFDC)
01784 456799
www.demolition-nfdc.com

National Group on Homeworking (NGH)
0113 245 4273
www.homeworking.gn.apc.org

National Inspection Council for
Electrical Installation Contracting
(NICEIC)
020 7564 2323
www.niceic.org.uk

National Pest Technicians Association
(NPTA)
01949 81133
www.npta.org.uk

National Quality Assurance (NQA)
01582 539000
www.nqa.com

National Radiological Protection Board
(NRPB)
01235 831600
www.nrpb.org

National Register of Access Consultants
(NRAC)
020 7735 7845
www.nrac.org.uk

National Security Inspectorate (NSI)
0870 2050000
www.nsi.org.uk

National Trust
0870 609 5380
www.nationaltrust.org.uk

NHS Plus
0800 092 0062
www.nhsplus.nhs.uk

Noise Abatement Society (NAS)
01273 682223
www.noiseabatementsociety.com

Northern Ireland Committee of the Irish
Congress of Trade Unions (NIC.ICTU)
028 9024 7940
www.ictuni.org

Occupational Pensions Regulatory
Authority (Opra)
01273 627600
www.opra.gov.uk

Occupational Road Safety Alliance
(ORSA)
www.orsa.org.uk

Office Furniture Advisory Service (OFAS)
01344 779438
www.ofas.org.uk

Office of Communications (Ofcom)
020 7981 3040
www.ofcom.org.uk

Office of the Deputy Prime Minister
(ODPM)
020 7709 9808
www.odpm.gov.uk

Office of Gas and Electricity Markets
(Ofgem)
020 7901 7066
www.ofgem.gov.uk

Office of Government Commerce (OGC)
0845 000 4999
www.ogc.gov.uk

Office of Water Services (Ofwat)
0121 625 1300
www.ofwat.gov.uk

Painting and Decorating Association
(PDA)
024 7635 3776
www.paintingdecoratingassociation.co.uk

Patent Office
08459 500 505
www.patent.gov.uk

Planning Inspectorate
0117 372 8000 (England)/
029 2082 5670 (Wales)
www.planning-inspectorate.gov.uk

Public Concern at Work
020 7404 6609
www.pcaw.co.uk

Race Relations Employment Advisory
Service (RREAS)
0121 452 54548

Recruitment and Employment
Confederation (REC)
020 7462 3260
www.rec.uk.com

Repetitive Strain Injuries
Association (RSIA)
023 8058 4314
www.rsi.org.uk

RIBA Bookshops
020 7496 8390
www.ribabookshops.com

RICS Books
0870 333 1600
www.ricsbooks.com

Robust Details Ltd
0870 240 8210
www.robustdetails.com

Royal Association for Disability
and Rehabilitation (RADAR)
020 7250 3222
www.radar.org.uk

Royal Automobile Club (RAC)
020 8917 2500
www.rac.co.uk

Royal Environmental Health
Institute of Scotland (REHIS)
0131 225 6999
www.royal-environmental-health.org.uk

Royal Incorporation of
Architects in Scotland (RIAS)
0131 229 7545
www.rias.org.uk

Royal Institute of British
Architects (RIBA)
020 7580 5533
www.riba.org

Royal Institution of Chartered
Surveyors (RICS)
0870 333 1600
www.rics.org

Royal National Institute of the
Blind (RNIB)
020 7388 1266
www.rnib.org.uk

Royal National Institute for Deaf People (RNID)
020 7296 8000
www.rnid.org.uk

Royal Society for the Prevention of Accidents (RoSPA)
0121 248 2000
www.rospa.org.uk

Royal Society for the Promotion of Health (RSPH)
020 7630 0121
www.rsph.org

Safety and Reliability Society (SaRS)
0161 228 7824
www.sars.org.uk

Safety Assessment Federation (SAFed)
020 7403 0987
www.safed.co.uk

St John Ambulance
0870 104 950
www.sja.org.uk

Scottish and Northern Ireland Plumbing Employers' Federation (SNIPEF)
0131 225 2255
www.snipef.org

Scottish Association of Building Standards Managers (SABSM)
www.sabsm.co.uk

Scottish Building Standards Agency
0131 244 7442
www.sbsa.gov.uk

Scottish Centre for Facilities Management (Napier University) (SCFM)
0131 455 2642
http://sbe.napier.ac.uk/scfm

Scottish Environment Protection Agency (SEPA)
01786 457700
www.sepa.org.uk

Scottish Trades Union Congress (STUC)
0141 337 8100
www.stuc.org.uk

Security Industry Authority (SIA)
08702 430 100
www.the-sia.org.uk

Security Industry Training Organisation (SITO)
01905 20004
www.sito.co.uk

Security Institute
01353 741099
www.security-institute.org

Sign Design Society
01582 13556
www.signdesignsociety.co.uk

Society of Light and Lighting (SLL)
020 8675 5211
www.cibse.org

Society of Occupational Medicine (SOM)
020 7486 2641
www.som.org.uk

Specialist Access Engineering and Maintenance Association (SAEMA)
020 7397 8122
www.seama.net

Stress Management Society
0870 199 3260
www.stress.org.uk

Suzy Lamplugh Trust
020 8876 0305
www.suzylamplugh.org

Tailored Interactive Guidance on
Employment Rights (TIGER)
www.tiger.gov.uk

Telework Association (TCA)
0800 616008
www.telework.org.uk

Think! Road Safety Website
www.thinkroadsafety.gov.uk

Trades Union Congress (TUC)
020 7636 4030
www.tuc.org.uk

Transco
01926 653000
www.transco.uk.com

United Kingdom Accreditation Service
(UKAS)
020 8917 8555
www.ukas.com

Valuation Office Agency (VOA)
020 7506 1700
www.voa.gov.uk

Wales Trades Union Congress
(TUC Cymru)
029 2034 7010
www.wtuc.org.uk

Water Regulations Advisory Scheme
(WRAS)
01495 248454
www.wras.co.uk

Water Research Centre (WRc plc)
01793 865000
www.wrcplc.co.uk

Water UK
020 7344 1844
www.water.org.uk

Welding Institute (TWI)
01223 891162
www.twi.co.uk

Work Foundation
0870 165 6700
www.theworkfoundation.com

Working Balance
0161 975 6292
www.workingbalance.co.uk

Working Families
020 7253 7243
www.workingfamilies.org.uk

Working Well Together (WWT)
020 7556 2244
www.wwt.uk.com

Workplace Law Group
0870 777 8881
www.workplacelaw.net

Index

absence
  alcohol and, 75
  long-term, 67
  lost working time and, 66
  management of, 65–7
  measuring and monitoring, 66
  problems caused by, 65
  reducing, 66–7
  short-term, 67
  unauthorised, 67
access, disability, 105, 179–82
Access to Neighbouring Land Act, 90
accidents
  electrical, 214–15
  investigation of, 69–71
  reporting, 125, 466–8
  to visitors, 409–10
  working at height and, 321–2
Addison -v- Ashby (2003), 140
adoption leave, 253
advisors, appointment of, 312–13
age discrimination, 195–6
agency workers, 72–3, 235
air quality, 514
alcohol, 75–7
  absence and, 75
  consumption guidelines, 76
  effects of, 76–7
  problems caused by, 75
  strength of, 76
alternative dispute resolution, 230–1
Anti-social Behaviour Act 2003, 90
Approved Codes of Practice, status of, 298
approved inspector's building control, 93
Approved Inspectors Regulations, 104
Arthur -v- Anker (1996), 538
asbestos, 79–83
  -containing materials, management
    of, 79–83
  deaths and diseases due to, 79

duty to manage, 80
  management plan, 80, 83
  risk assessments and, 80
  surveys, 80–2
Asbestos (Prohibition) Regulations 1992, 83
attendance records, 66

bacteria, as biological hazard, 84
Bairstow -v- Queens Moat Houses Plc, 176
Barber -v- Somerset County Council (2004), 494
belief, discrimination on grounds of, 198, 441
Biocidal Products Directive, 431
biological hazards, 84–5
  risk assessments and, 85
bomb alerts, 86–7
boundaries, 88–91
  adjacent to highways, 89
  disputes and, 91–2
  hedges and trees as, 90
  height of, 89
  insurance and, 90
  maintenance of, 89–90
  ownership of, 89
break options (in leases), 348
Building Act 1984, 92
building control, systems of, 93
Building (Inner London) Regulations 1987, 95
Building Regulations
  access to and use of buildings (Part M), 105, 182, 368
  Approved Documents, 94
  combustion appliances and fuel
    storage systems (Part J), 103
  conservation of fuel and power (Part L), 104–5, 236, 291–2, 368
  contraventions of, 93–4
  definition of building work, 92–3

Index